Introduction to SPORT MANAGEMENT

THEORY AND PRACTICE

Kendall Hunt
publishing company

Mark **Nagel** | Richard **Southall**

University of South Carolina, Columbia | University of South Carolina, Columbia

Book Team

Chairman and Chief Executive Officer	Mark C. Falb
President and Chief Operating Officer	Chad M. Chandlee
Vice President, Higher Education	David L. Tart
Director of Publishing Partnerships	Paul B. Carty
Product/Development Supervisor	Lynnette M. Rogers
Vice President, Operations	Timothy J. Beitzel
Project Coordinator	Sara McGovern
Permissions Editor	Caroline Kieler
Cover Designer	Heather Richman

Cover images © Shutterstock, Inc.

www.kendallhunt.com
Send all inquiries to:
4050 Westmark Drive
Dubuque, IA 52004-1840

ISBN 978-1-5249-9987-2

Printed in the United States of America

brief table of contents

table of contents

CHAPTER 14: Interviews ... 411

CHAPTER 15: Sport-Management Resources

GLOSSARY ... 525

INDEX ... 537

preface

The initial inspiration to write this book occurred in 1999. While at the North American Society for Sport Management Conference (NASSM) in Vancouver, BC, this text's coeditors attended an academic presentation that detailed the need for and importance of theory in published sport-management research. The presenter, as well as many in the audience, made repeated comments denigrating "practical" research, devoid of any theoretical foundation. Later that day, the authors attended a different academic presentation, in which the presenter and members of the audience decried the lack of practical application in many of the articles currently being published in scholarly sport-management journals. A scan of each room revealed we were the only people who had attended both presentations. This simple observation confirmed the "chasm" we had sensed had developed between two academic sport-management "camps."

At the conclusion of that day's academic program, we continued discussing the relative importance of both theory and practice in the field of sport management and the distinct philosophical differences apparent in the sport-management academic community. It seemed then—and still appears now—that far too often neither "side" is able to acknowledge the other's contribution to sport management. One of our professional goals (established during those Vancouver conversations) was to constantly work to meld theory and practice in our future teaching and research activities. As doctoral students in 1999, neither of us contemplated eventually writing an Introduction to Sport Management textbook, but during our numerous conversations over the years, a discussion of integrating theory and practice was a constant theme. When we were approached about developing the first edition of this text, one of the first things we discussed was the serendipity of this project based upon our "Vancouver" conversations. The first edition was received favorably by a variety of academics, practitioners, and students and we are honored to have been asked to write a second edition. We have added a new chapter about the role of Congress in the sport industry and have incorporated a variety of updates in each of the other chapters.

Though the divide between theory and practice in sport-management research and curricula is less than it was in 1999, it is certainly greater than it could or should be in the future. There are still far too many research papers and presentations that leave people asking one of two questions: "How can this be applied to the real world?" or "Is there a theoretical foundation that underpins this research?" We hope this book is well received by both sport-management academics and practitioners, who recognize we have attempted to provide students with theoretical foundations from which to view current sport-industry issues.

The authors and interviewees are reflective of sport management's diversity. In addition, though each has a unique background and may be more or less theoretical in their perspective, they all hope sport-management students will enter the industry with the tools to succeed. Many of the chapters are designed to provide not only an introduction to a sport-management subtopic, but also a useful foundation from which a student will be well-prepared for specific sport-management courses as they progress in their academic program. In addition, there are specific chapters designed to help students better understand the many opportunities available in sport management and how to begin their career.

We also recognize this text may not satisfy every student's or faculty member's needs and that some readers may disagree with the order in which we present the material. However, we do hope each chapter provides sufficient detail, that upon completion students better understand the main activities a professional working in this "area" regularly undertakes and the major issues facing that functional area now and in the future. In addition, we are confident the end-of-chapter interviews reinforce the principles introduced and provide sound career advice.

To the students who we are privileged to have utilize this text, we want to welcome you to our field. Sport management is a wonderful discipline in which to work and conduct research. We hope your future career in sport management provides you with as much enjoyment as it has us.

Mark Nagel
Richard Southall

features of the text

Student-Oriented Pedagogy

Because we recognize the importance of assessing student comprehension, we have included the following features in the chapters to facilitate student learning and to help instructors measure learning outcomes.

- **Chapter Objectives** help students focus on the overall concepts, theories, and skills discussed in the chapter.
- **Glossary of Key Terms** defines all the terms in the text; key terms are identified at the beginning and throughout each chapter.
- **Study Questions** located at the end of each chapter challenge and test the students' knowledge of the chapter content.
- **Learning Activities** are provided to help stimulate discussion and increase understanding of chapter concepts by turning knowledge into action.

The book contains 28 interviews with sport-management practitioners. The interviews come from a wide variety of practitioners and are provided to give the student a glimpse of real-world experience and detail specific strategies to begin and sustain a successful career in sport management.

The final chapter of the book is devoted to external resources from books to websites to provide the student a wealth of additional information on a wide range of sport-management topics.

Instructor Resources

The following resources are designed to aid instructors and were developed by the text's authors and contributors. The resources are available upon adoption of the text.

- **Test Bank.** The test bank offers several different types of questions to better assess student comprehension.
- **PowerPoint Slides.** Chapter content is provided in a PowerPoint format. Instructors may choose to use the presentations as they are provided or to add their own content and enrichment features.

acknowledgments

I am indebted to numerous people who helped make this book a reality. Without the support of my family this project would not have been possible. My wife Leslie helped create a schedule that enabled me to work on this while my children, parents, siblings, and close friends showed patience when I was working to keep things moving toward completion. Leslie and my children, Annie and Canton, always provide inspiration to be the best that I can be as a professor and as a husband and father. As my kids grow older, I hope that someday they can find joy and inspiration in their interests the same way I have found mine in the playing and business of sport.

My coauthor Richard Southall provided ideas, insights, edits, and encouragement while we worked from initial idea to completed manuscript. It is always a pleasure to work with him on our numerous projects. Richard definitely makes me a better scholar and for this I am always grateful.

I must also thank the contributors who graciously provided their chapters and interviews for this book. The chapter authors remained patient and focused even when it seemed like we kept asking them to add content or make changes, while the interviewees were willing to provide their time and expertise so that readers would better understand the industry.

The faculty and staff in the Department of Sport and Entertainment Management at the University of South Carolina have consistently helped me to achieve my professional goals. Their ideas and encouragement were invaluable, especially when they provided insights about what updates should be provided for the second edition.

Finally, I have had the pleasure of teaching wonderful sport-management students during my career. They have provided inspiration to search for new knowledge. While writing this book, I thought often of various conversations I have had with students inside and outside of the classroom. I hope that I have been able to teach them as much as they have taught me.

Mark Nagel

There are numerous people I need to thank for their help and support. First and foremost, I want to thank my family.

My life-partner, wife, best friend, and colleague Deb has been—and always will be—my glue. She makes everything "work." My children—Jason, Crystal, and Elizabeth—are my heroes. They provide me with wisdom and perspective if and when I forget to notice the joys of life. To my stepchildren—Sally and Joe—thanks for allowing me to share your mom!

While both my parents are now deceased and cannot read my "thank you," I want anyone reading this to know how blessed I was to have two phenomenal parents, who were not only wonderful role models, but supportive of me through my ups and downs. To my three "brothers" —Steve, Tom, and Robert—thank you for being there when I need you. To my sisters—Velma, Mary, Sandy, Carol, and Rose—thank you for being unique, yet all accepting me for who I am. To my stepfather, Elmer, thanks for taking care of my mom after my dad passed away and being another father to me.

And finally, I want to thank my grandchildren—Jack, Abbie, Siena, Evey, and Sara—for helping me see beyond today and envision a tomorrow, after I'm gone, that will be as good, or better, than today.

I want to thank my family for making my life so worth living. I hope they know a simple "Thank you" does not convey the depth of my feelings.

To my close friends, including Drake, Cam, Dusty, Jimmy & Rachel, Fritz, Billy, Sonny & Pam, Ellen, Allen, Linda, Ron & Natalie, John, and Sal & Jessie. Thank you for being part of my life and for all the wonderful times over the years.

My coeditor Mark Nagel was the driving force behind this project, keeping things moving forward from conception to completion, by providing leadership and inspiration. During the past decade-plus he has become not only a valued collaborator on numerous research activities, but a trusted friend and advisor. I appreciate him more than I can ever express. It's wonderful to be in offices next door to each other.

I know I speak for Mark in thanking the book's chapter authors and interviewees, whose contributions make this a unique blend of sport-management theory and practice. Each chapter author willingly made suggested changes and edits, and gave us outstanding content for this book.

The interviewed sport practitioners openly shared their experiences and provided readers with an invaluable window on the sport industry. Without their willingness to share their expertise and knowledge this book would not have been possible.

Also, thanks to my colleagues at the University of South Carolina. I cannot express my gratitude for welcoming me to the Sport and Entertainment Department. It's what I was hoping for when I made the move!

Finally, I want to thank the many sport-management students and faculty I have had the honor of working with throughout my career. To the sport-management alumni of the University of West Georgia, who truly believed "close to home, close to each other, and close to perfection" was possible, thank you for setting the bar so incredibly high. Also, thanks to the students at The University of Memphis, who showed me what was possible when a dedicated group of students worked together for a common goal. Thank you for being the incubator. To the students and faculty at UNC, as well as past and current CSRI interns and staff, thank you for being wonderfully critical thinkers, challenging me as well as the status quo, and providing an opportunity to integrate theory and practice.

Richard Southall

We would both like to thank the people at Kendall Hunt, specifically Paul Carty, Lynne Rogers, and Sara McGovern, for their support and patience throughout the writing and publishing process.

We gratefully acknowledge the constructive comments of the colleagues who provided content reviews. They include:

Suzannah Armentrout
Minnesota State University
Scott Armstrong
Olivet Nazarene University
Christina Belisle
Lesley University
Curtis Bickham
University of Wisconsin, Parkside
Robert Boland
New York University
Scott Bradshaw
Bucks County Community College
Martin Brett
DeSales University
Jennifer Breuer
Trinity University
Robert Brown
Daniel Webster College
Michael Burch
Virginia Commonwealth University
Steve Chen
Moorehead State University
Beth Cianfrone
Georgia State University
Dexter Davis
Niagara University
Paul Davis
Nebraska Wesleyan University
Larry Degaris
University of Indianapolis
Linda Draft
University of Wisconsin, Parkside
George Drops
National University
Chad Fagan
Northwood University
Annemarie Farrell
Ithaca College
Nicole Fennern
St. Mary's University
Michael Fetchko
La Roche College
Bob Foley
College of St. Joseph
Jaehyun Ha
College of St. Rose
Curt Hamakawa
Western New England College
Clark Haptonstall
Rice University
Brian Hofman
Ohio Northern University
Dee Jacobsen
Louisiana State University
Liz Jorn
Truman State University
DaeHyun Kim
University of Florida
Yongseek Kim
New Mexico Highlands University
Michael Klecan
Ocean County College
David Klenosky
Purdue University
Jordan Kobritz
Eastern New Mexico University
Myroslaw Kyj
Widener University
Robert Lade
Northwest Missouri State University
Seungeun Lee
York College
Mary Beth Leibold
Siena Heights University
Don Luy
Millikin University

Maria Macarle
Dowling College
Daniel Montgomery
Delta State University
Joy Moyer
Bucks County Community College
Steven Murray
Mesa State College of Colorado
Eric Newman
California State University, San Bernardino
John Pagliasotti
Southwestern Oklahoma State University
Stephen Peck, Jr.
Jefferson College
Raymond Phillips
Wesley College
Alan Platt
Florida Golf Coast University
Julie Powell
Union University
Brenda Riemer
Eastern Michigan University
Marshall Robb
William Woods University
Maura Rosenthal
Bridgewater State College
Gary Sailes
Indiana University
Scott Thorne
Southeast Missouri State University
Sam Todd
Georgia Southern University
Tyrone E. Tubbs, Sr.
University of Louisville
Diane Tunnell
Gonzaga University
Barbara Vano
St. Thomas Aquinas College
Dr. James Velasquez
D'Youville College
Abby Weber
Lindenwood University
Thomas Werner
Southern Illinois University
Brian Wood
California University of Pennsylvania
Scott D. Yakola
Duke University

about the authors

Dr. Mark S. Nagel is presently a professor of Sport and Entertainment Management at the University of South Carolina. He is also the Associate Director of the College Sport Research Institute (CSRI) at The University of South Carolina. He also serves as an adjunct faculty member at the University of San Francisco (USF), St. Mary's College of California, and the IE Business School in Madrid, Spain. He is a former treasurer of the Sport and Recreation Law Association and the North American Society for Sport Management. Prior to working in academe, Dr. Nagel held numerous positions in sport management including campus recreation and athletic coaching. He was an assistant coach with the USF women's basketball team that advanced to the NCAA Tournament Sweet 16 in 1996.

Dr. Nagel has previously coauthored two other widely utilized textbooks, *Financial Management in the Sport Industry* and *Sport Facility Management: Organizing Events and Mitigating Risks.* He has authored/coauthored over 40 peer-reviewed articles, 10 academic book chapters, and 20 articles in professional journals. In addition, he has contributed to multiple technical/research reports and wrote the Legal Guidelines and Professional Responsibilities chapter in the American Council on Exercise (ACE) Personal Trainer Manual, ACE Health Coach Manual, and the ACE Group Fitness Instructor Manual.

Dr. Richard M. Southall is an associate professor of Sport and Entertainment Management at the University of South Carolina. He is also the Director of the College Sport Research Institute (CSRI) at The University of South Carolina, He is a former president of the Sport and Recreation Law Association (2004–2005) and a coauthor of another widely utilized textbook, *Sport Facility Management: Organizing Events and Mitigating Risks.* He has authored/coauthored over 35 peer-reviewed articles, 15 academic book chapters, and over 50 research reports, commentaries, and professional journal publications.

He received his doctorate in Sport Administration from The University of Northern Colorado in 2001. His undergraduate degree (B.A.—summa cum laude) from Western State College of Colorado included concentrated coursework in English, history, and philosophy. Dr. Southall's areas of professional expertise include legal, political, marketing, sociocultural, and ethical issues in college sport. He is a nationally recognized expert on the partners, products, structure, associations, and processes of big-time NCAA college sport.

about the contributors

Matthew Bernthal received his Ph.D. in marketing from The University of South Carolina, where he is an associate professor in the Sport and Entertainment Management Department. Bernthal teaches various courses in sport and entertainment marketing, and has consulted with numerous firms in the sport and entertainment industry. His research has appeared in the *Journal of Consumer Research, Sport Marketing Quarterly, Journal of Nonprofit and Public Sector Marketing, School Psychology International, Journal of Sport Behavior,* and other journals. His research primarily involves sport and entertainment consumer motivation and marketing ethics.

Dr. William Bowden is president of Strategic Management Consultants. He holds degrees from Southern College, Southern Nazarene University, the University of Tulsa, and the University of Edinburgh. A well-known athletic administration consultant, he specializes in working with business and educational institutions in developing leadership enhancement, continuous quality improvement programs and internal assessment programs. He is a former college professor and college administrator.

Dr. Matthew Brown has been at the University of South Carolina since 2005 where he teaches and researches in the areas of sport business and finance. His research has led to publications in journals like the *Journal of Sport Management, Sport Marketing Quarterly, Entertainment and Sport Law Journal,* the *International Journal of Sport Finance,* and *Sport Management Review.* In addition, Dr. Brown has made more than 40 national and international research presentations. Dr. Brown currently serves as the graduate director for the Department of Sport and Entertainment Management. Previously, he has served as the chief financial officer of the Southern Ohio Copperheads and treasurer of the Board of Directors of the Southern Ohio Collegiate Baseball Club.

Dr. Ronald Dick is an Associate Professor of Sport Marketing in the School of Business at Duquesne University. He previously was an Assistant Professor in Sport Management at James Madison University and an Associate Professor at the University of New Haven. He has 15 years experience in the NBA with the Philadelphia 76ers and New Jersey Nets. Dr. Dick has also served as the Assistant Dean for Sport Athletic Programs at Marian College (WI) and Assistant Athletic Director for Ticket Operations at the University of Houston. He has an Ed.D. from Temple University, an MBA from St. Joseph's University, and a B.S. from St. Joseph's University.

Martin B. Gold is a prominent Washington, D.C., attorney. He is the author of *Senate Procedure and Practice*, a leading primer on the rules and process of the United States Senate, and was counsel for two Senate Majority Leaders of the United States Senate. Mr. Gold has presented hundreds of seminars worldwide on congressional procedures and policies. He founded two leading lobbying firms that engaged in lobbying issues for sport entities. Mr. Gold has a B.A., M.P.A, and J.D. from The American University.

Howard C. Liebengood has a M.S. in Sport and Leisure Commerce from the University of Memphis and a B.A. in History from Purdue University. He was a motorsports professional and captured an endurance racing championship. He works in Washington, D.C., as a federal law enforcement officer.

Dr. Ronald Mower is Assistant Professor in the Department of Kinesiology, Sport Studies, and Physical Education at The College at Brockport, State University of New York (SUNY) in Brockport, New York. With interests in the globalization of sport, physical culture and social justice, urban health & sport ethnography, and critical pedagogy, Ron has the good fortune to integrate these scholarly pursuits with his teaching of graduate and undergraduate courses in sport sociology, sport history, and qualitative research methods. Ron is also a Faculty-in-Residence mentor at SUNY Brockport, supporting the academic and personal success of on-campus undergraduates in the Living & Learning Communities with enriching extracurricular activities, advisement, and mentoring.

Brad Schultz, Ph.D., an Associate Professor in the School of Journalism and New Media at the University of Mississippi, is the editor and creator of the *Journal of Sports Media,* a scholarly journal that publishes twice yearly. His research focuses on the effects of new media on sports journalism, and he has published nearly two dozen scholarly articles in various journals as well as three books. Before entering academia, Schultz spent 15 years in local sports television as an anchor, producer, news director, writer, videographer, and reporter. Schultz lives in Oxford, Mississippi, with his wife and two children.

Linda A. Sharp is a Professor in the Sport Administration program at the University of Northern Colorado. She received her J.D. from Cleveland-Marshall College of Law and practiced corporate law before entering academe. Her research interests are the legal, ethical, and policy aspects of education, particularly higher education and sport. She is the lead author of the textbook *Sport Law: A Managerial Approach,* Third Edition. Professor Sharp is also a consultant on sport and higher education issues.

Dr. Jason Simmons is an Assistant Professor of Sport Administration at the University of Cincinnati. He holds a doctoral degree in educational leadership and organizational development with a concentration in sport administration from the University of Louisville, as well as a master's degree in sport administration from the University of Louisville. He teaches undergraduate courses in sport public relations, sport marketing, and sport facility management. His research interests focus on sport consumer behavior, specifically fan-family conflict and sport communication.

Crystal Southall, Ph.D., is a faculty member in the Department of Recreation, Exercise and Sport Science at Western State Colorado University, in Gunnison, Colorado. Her dissertation, entitled "Professional Basketball Consumer Behavior: An Analysis of the NBA Servicescape and Attendee Attitudes," examined the influence of involvement, loyalty, and sport servicescape in the creation of sport consumer attitudes and behaviors. Dr. Southall earned her M.S. in Sport and Leisure Commerce from the University of Memphis and her B.A. in History from the University of Colorado at Boulder. Her research focuses on college sport's institutional logics, as well as the NBA servicescape.

Dr. Deborah Yow is the highly effective director of athletics at North Carolina State University. Prior to arriving at NCSU, she served 16 outstanding years as the director of athletics at the University of Maryland, where her teams won a remarkable 20 National Championships during her tenure. She has served as the President of the national Division-IA Athletic Directors Association and the National Association of Collegiate Directors of Athletics (NACDA) and is a member of the Board of Directors of the National Football Foundation. She has been honored by Street and Smith's *SportsBusiness Journal* as one of the 20 most influential people in intercollegiate athletics, was cited in *The Chronicle of Higher Education* in October 2007 as one of the "Ten Most Powerful People in College Athletics/The Builder," and she has received the Carl Maddox Sport Management Award presented by the United States Sports Academy for excellence in athletics administration. She has authored and coauthored over 30 books and articles on leadership, management, and intercollegiate athletics and has lectured in prestigious academic and business settings across the United States and abroad.

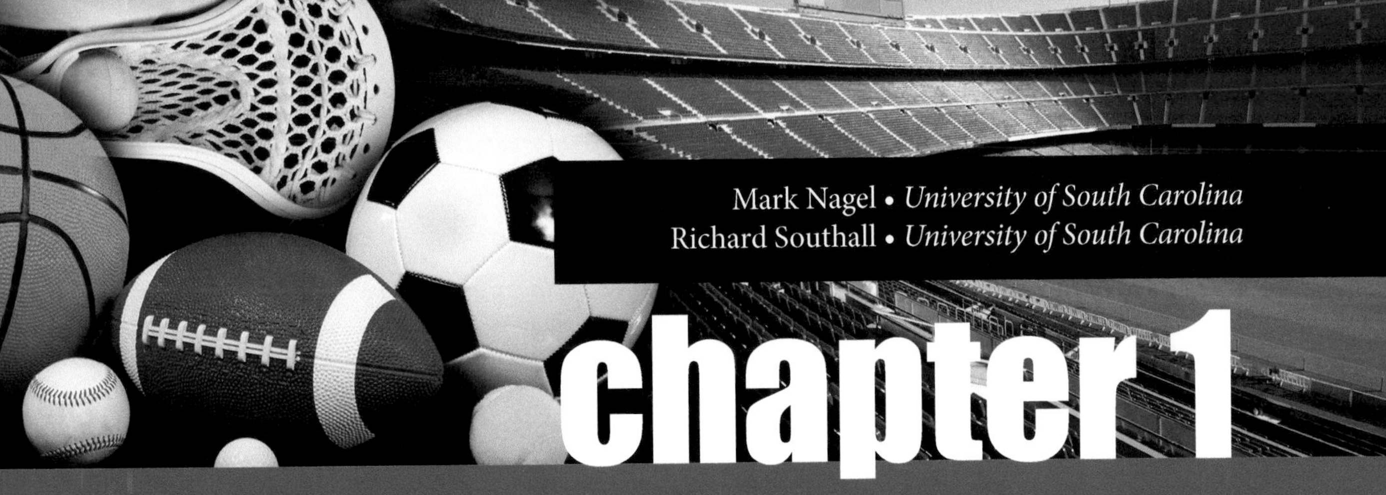

Mark Nagel • *University of South Carolina*
Richard Southall • *University of South Carolina*

chapter 1

Do You Really Want to Work in the Sport Industry?

CHAPTER OBJECTIVES

After reading this chapter, you will be able to:

- Understand the difference between being a sport fan and a sport manager.
- Discuss the competitive nature of the sport-management field.
- Understand the importance of theory and practice as it applies to sport-management education, research, and employment.
- Explain how various sport-management functional areas are applicable to a sporting event.

KEY TERMS

Metadiscrete experiential learning

SWOT Analysis

I have been in both the college and professional sports ranks for 40 years. Having served as General Manager of the Philadelphia 76ers, Washington Wizards, New Jersey Nets, Portland Trail Blazers, and also as Executive Director of Philadelphia's Big 5: St. Joseph's University, Temple University, Villanova University, University of Pennsylvania, and LaSalle University; I have seen first-hand the explosion of sport and the importance of sales revenue.

There doesn't seem to be a day that goes by where I am not approached by an enthusiastic young person, or a concerned parent, and asked, "What is the best way to get a job working in sport?"

My reply to the question is always the same three-pronged answer: "Can you play? Can you coach? Can you sell?" Now, if your answers to the first two parts of my question are "no," then I would suggest you better be able to sell. Players and coaches are responsible for putting the "best product" on the floor or field. It's the front office staff's job to ensure that all of the duties leading up to and throughout each and every game are handled smoothly and efficiently. And with the economic demands facing franchises today, every person within the sound of your voice must be viewed as a potential customer.

The world of Sport Management has changed dramatically in my 40 years in the business, and the days of pledging to simply "work hard" and "learn on the job" are over. In today's market, the competition for front-office positions is as fierce as the battles being waged for a team roster spot or a coaching slot. If you are successful in selling yourself to a potential sports employer, you will be expected to arrive with the necessary tools to make an immediate contribution in the front office department to which you are assigned.

—John Nash

Introduction

Each year, throughout the United States and around the world, thousands of students enroll in sport-management classes. Since 1990, the number of sport-management academic programs has increased from a few dozen to over 250. This growth reflects students' escalating interest in sport and this academic major. However, though thousands of students annually enroll in sport-management courses, for the vast majority, their initial attraction to sport management arises out of their previous experiences as an athlete or fan.

A typical initial exchange between a sport-management professor and a student enrolled in an introduction to sport-management class may involve the professor asking, "Why do you want to major in sport management?" and the student responding, "I love SPORTS. I really enjoyed playing SPORTS in high school and want SPORTS to stay a part of my life" or "I have been a SPORTS fan my entire life and I want to be close to what I love." In some cases, a student might think that, since "SPORTS are fun to play and watch, a sport-management major will probably be enjoyable and easy."

These student responses reflect the perceptions of many non-sport-management faculty and administrators. As many people involved in sport know, sport management is often viewed—by students, faculty, and the general public—as an "easy major," designed to keep college athletes eligible. As any sport marketer will attest, overcoming a negative product image is difficult, but can be accomplished through educating all relevant stakeholders (see Chapters 3 and 11). While there is certainly nothing wrong with having an interest in SPORTS, merely being a former athlete or a fan is not enough to succeed. Simply put, SPORT MANAGEMENT is the process of satisfying sports consumers' wants, needs, and desires. While many of this book's authors were fans first, they are now sport managers; they work in the SPORT INDUSTRY. This change involves a fundamental shift in perspective. SPORTS CONSUMERS experience or "consume" the sport product. A SPORT MANAGER is usually "behind the curtain" or "backstage," and does not get to simply enjoy the game. A sport manager is involved in the sport-production process. FANS consume; MANAGERS direct the process.

When working in the sport industry, managers must always remember what it means to be a SPORTS FAN, as this memory assists them in selling the sport product. However, a sport manager CANNOT BE A FAN. If your goal is to someday regularly attend games, meet and interact with famous athletes and coaches, and spend your time being entertained in a luxury suite, a sport-management career should not be your goal.

Going Pro in Something Other Than Sport

For years, one of the marketing campaigns of the National Collegiate Athletic Association (NCAA) has included the tagline, "There are more than 400,000 'student athletes' and most of them will go pro in something other than sports" (Brown, 2009, para. 4). This marketing slogan is consistent with Oriard's (2009) discussion of the difficult and unlikely path for college football players who aspire to a professional football career, since of the approximately 54,000 college football players each year, roughly 1,000 will sign a National Football League (NFL) contract, only about 330 will actually make an NFL roster, and only approximately 165 will have a four-year (or longer) NFL career.

Just as few college athletes will become professionals, not all sport-management students will become sport managers. However, even though it may be difficult to land a sport-industry job, and even more challenging to carve out a career in sport, majoring in sport management can result in profound

How Do Sport Managers Create Opportunities for Marketing and Financial Success?

Many people do not immediately recognize what sport management is or what sport managers often do to create, market, sell, supervise, and successfully execute a sporting event. This story from Sundeep Kapur, expert in OMNI-channel marketing strategies (see page 477), may shed some light not only on this industry but on how students should think about executing marketing plans that raise revenue and provide both excitement and fulfillment for sport consumers.

I want to share a story about an online Chuck-a-Puck Contest that will get all of the students reading this to better understand what I do and what every sport marketer should be doing:

In 2009, I was working with the digital marketing manager for a regional hockey team; the team was a startup in an area not very familiar with the sport so ticket sales were low. We managed to sell 4,000 of their 12,500 seats in season tickets, another 2,000 would typically sell on their own and our sales team was able to move an additional 1,000 through corporate sales/event nights. This left us with 5,000 empty seats every game night.

Disappointed with the empty seats, the owners tasked us with boosting ticket sales—the digital marketing manager tried everything, promoting to his email list (approximately 7,000 names), working closely with the advertising group for television, print, and outdoor ads. He tried PR initiatives and even dressed up in a sandwich board to hand out tickets. Nothing really worked.

So one afternoon, while stuffing envelopes, we decided to promote a contest. We put out an email to his entire list (7,000 names), asking recipients to print out the email and bring it to the game. Those who did would receive a puck to chuck into the goal during intermission. Only 700 opened the email and 200 brought in the email as instructed and had their chance to chuck-a-puck. There were five winners, who received merchandise, free tickets, or photos with the players. Despite this seemingly small response, we created a buzz!

After the contest, the announcer told everyone where to sign up for the next game and their chance to play. By the next week we had 1,400 new subscribers, the email went out and had 3,600 opens—2000+ people printed to play at the next game (we still had five winners). By the third game we had even more subscribers, an open rate above 60%, and a huge conversion. Response was so overwhelming that we pressed further by giving the non-winners an opportunity to fill out an online preference survey with the chance to win box seats for the next game.

Five years later the digital marketing manager promotes his events on social media. He uses intrigue to engage his fans. He uses online contests to grow his reach. He leverages social media and mobile to survey his recipients. He even gets his fans to predict plays. He was a one-man band, but sales are so good he now has a marketing team—a very productive one, too.

So the moral of this story is that a little interaction with your customers goes a long way. This one contest helped the manager (1) grow his contact list, (2) get more "cheeks in seats," and (3) actually CONNECT with customers (he collected personalized information that could be leveraged for future campaigns).

As a sport manager where increasing sales and generating revenue is critical, think of ways to solicit interaction; it could revitalize your email campaigns, reduce direct mail cost, and give you access to the personal information you need to attract advertisers. Who knows, you may even unload some of those expensive "Jack Nicholson" seats.

This one project was one of my big wins with a sport team. It got me to the big leagues in the sport industry!

positive effects for the vast majority of students, many of whom go ". . . pro in something other than sports. The knowledge, skills, and attitudes students can develop by majoring in sport management can stay with them their entire working career, whether in the sport industry or another field.

Although there may not be hundreds of thousands of sport-management majors who graduate each year, with hundreds of sport-management programs in North America alone, there is a great deal of competition for any sport-industry job. In addition, just like you, students from other majors, including business, journalism, liberal arts, and so on are also attracted to SPORTS. The competition for internships, as well as part-time or full-time entry-level positions, is fierce. It is not uncommon for people wanting to break into the sport industry to "settle for" performing multiple internships before landing a full-time sport-industry job.

In addition to fierce competition, entry-level sport-industry jobs are usually low-paying positions, with the expectation of long days and numerous responsibilities. The excitement fans associate with attending a sport event is the result of many sport managers doing their job. The sport-entertainment product does not magically appear; it is planned, developed, and managed by and through a host of trained professionals. Simply stated, working in the sport industry is hard work, with long hours, and (at least initially) low pay. If your primary motivation is potential initial salary, the sport industry is probably not the place for you. While working for low pay is not an ideal situation, it allows new sport managers to discover if they truly have a passion for a sport-industry career. Those who are able to "work through" the initial few years of low pay and long working hours usually find a sport-management career is more enjoyable and fulfilling than many other career options. Many established sport managers remark they have friends who wish they would have pursued a career based upon a love for the industry rather than the size of the initial paycheck.

Speaking openly and honestly about the state of the sport industry today is not meant to discourage students from pursuing a sport-business career. Part of becoming a sport-business professional is identifying and understanding the sport-industry's pros and cons. The importance of performing a **SWOT** (Strengths, Weaknesses, Opportunities, and Threats) **analysis** will be discussed in several chapters in this text. Being honest about the sport-industry's job prospects is part of performing a career SWOT analysis. In this context you should perform a SWOT analysis on yourself as well as the sport industry.

SWOT analysis
An investigation that determines an organization's strengths, weaknesses, opportunities, and threats.

Where Theory and Practice Lead to Action

Just as there is a difference between being a sports consumer and being a sport manager, there is sometimes a "disconnect" among sport-management faculty. This disconnect is often the result of faculty who see themselves as either

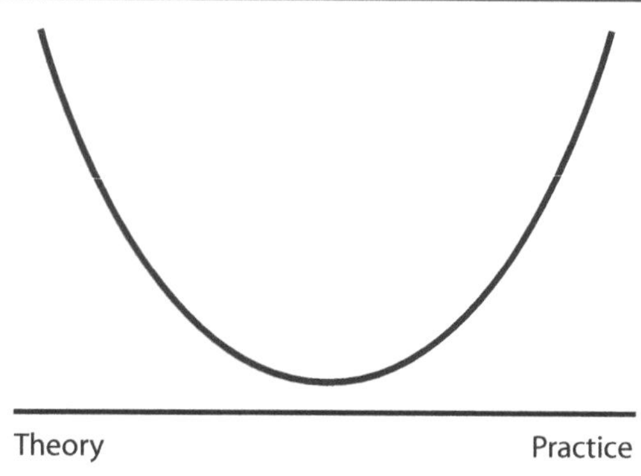

FIGURE 1.1 Current Sport Management Faculty Focus

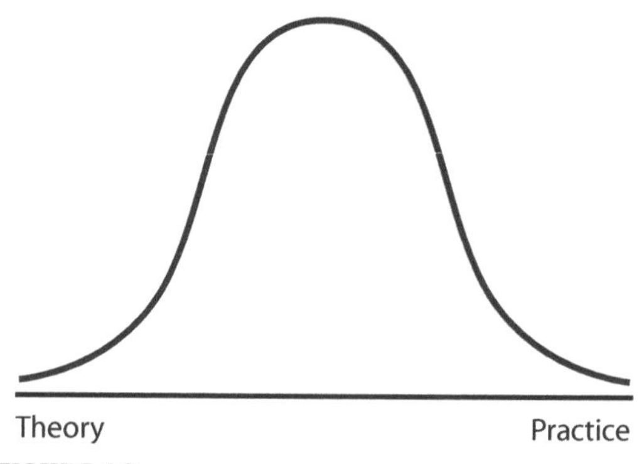

FIGURE 1.2 Ideal Sport Management Faculty Focus

"theoreticians" or "practitioners." This chasm can be graphically represented as a bimodal distribution (see Fig. 1.1) in which faculty members seemingly feel they must choose between either a "theory" or "practice" perspective. This text's design, format, and content proposes abandoning this polarizing, either-or worldview and adopting a more "normal" distribution (see Fig. 1.2) in which sport-management faculty and students, as well as sport-industry practitioners, recognize that theory informs practice, and theory must be validated in the "real" world.

If sport management, as an academic discipline, wants to serve the needs of students and the sport industry, it seems logical it can no longer be fragmented into two camps whose members seldom talk to each other. Sport-industry practitioners need to be aware of and utilize solid research, based upon sound theoretical frameworks, and sport-management researchers need to reach out to offer practical solutions to sport-industry needs. In addition, this new "normal" should become sport-management's organizational culture, or "how we do things in sport-management education." Fundamentally, sport-management education should be theoretically grounded, but practically oriented. Figure 1.3 illustrates the interlocking relationship between theory and practice that should occur.

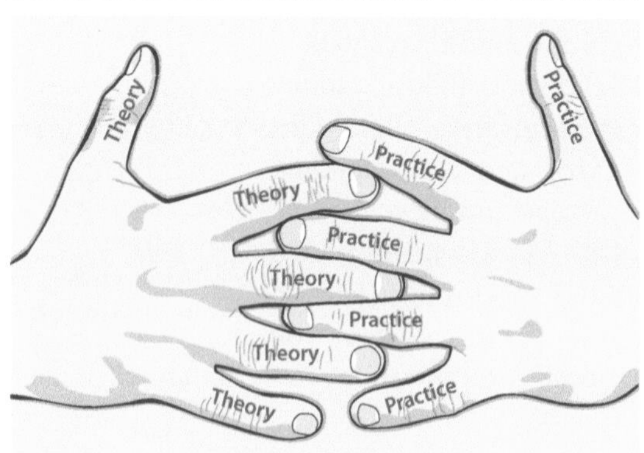

FIGURE 1.3 Molding Theory and Practice Creates Stronger Research and More Effective Practitioners

Just as researchers must reach out to the sport industry, basing and testing practical decisions against existing theories would fundamentally improve the sport industry. Such an approach would free sport managers from having to reinvent the proverbial wheel or make the same mistakes over and over again in order to learn how to effectively manage. Such an integrated, new-normal approach to sport-management education ultimately results in stronger internship experiences and a greater likelihood of career success, and has become an accepted theoretical sport-management educational model, called **metadiscrete experiential learning** (Southall, Nagel, LeGrande, & Han, 2003; Irwin, Southall, & Sutton, 2007; Southall & Dick, 2010).

Metadiscrete experiential learning
A learning model in which staff from partnering sport businesses serve as instructional leaders and facilitators alongside sport-management faculty, that "... enhances student understanding of entrepreneurship, sales, sponsorship, event management, and marketing research within the context of the university's sport management program" (Southall et al., 2003, p. 23). Greater knowledge gain is possible because in a metadiscrete experience, the roles of teacher and practitioner are not separate and distinct, but are dual aspects of the same function.

Integration of Sport-Management Functional Areas

Just as a sport organization's "organizational chart" identifies specific functional areas, this text is divided into identifiable chapters that represent facets of the sport industry. However, just as functional areas—and the duties and responsibilities of employees within these functional areas—do not exist in a vacuum, this text's chapters are not discrete silos of information. Sport management involves integrating theory and practice in order to manage (i.e., plan, organize, supervise, develop, control, implement, and evaluate) across functional areas (see Figure 1.4). As you continue your sport-management education, do not myopically focus on a functional area in which you think you want to work.

As many of the interviews throughout this text highlight, it is crucial to "SEE THE BIG PICTURE." In the sport industry every functional area is part of the sport product. Too many students say, "I only want to work in______________. I don't need to know anything about ______________." Top-level sport managers synthesize information related to many functional areas in order to make informed decisions.

As you continue your sport-management education, you will undoubtedly develop an area of interest and a desire to work or become an expert in a specific functional area. That is to be expected; however, it is important to always remember how you and your area of expertise fit into the sport product. Dissecting a hypothetical college-sport event can help identify the interconnections.

FIGURE 1.4 The Interlocking Components of Sport-Management Decision Making

Fundamentally, the decision to sponsor a college athletic program and at what level to compete is based on beliefs within society about whether or not sport is or is not consistent with a university's mission. For many, college sport is the tie that binds the institution's various communities (faculty, staff, students, alumni, local residents, etc.) together. On many campuses, particularly those that compete at the NCAA Division-I level, athletics is a dominant subculture, with large financial outlays for scholarships, facilities, coaches and administrators, and travel. For other schools, such as those that compete in the NCAA Division-III level, intercollegiate athletic opportunities are offered, but there are no athletic scholarships, coaches typically also work as faculty members, and minimal travel budgets are provided. Some other campuses do not offer intercollegiate athletics at all, preferring to offer only intramural opportunities for students. The institution's view of athletics' importance can change. In the last 10 years, numerous NCAA Division-II institutions have enhanced their commitment to athletics and have sought membership in the more "prestigious"—and more expensive—NCAA Division-I level. Some Division-III members have also developed their programs to compete at the Division-II level.

Though many of these moves have been to "higher" levels, there have been some institutions that have deemphasized "big-time" athletics on their campuses. The University of Chicago once competed at the highest level of athletics. (Jay Berwanger won the first Heisman Trophy in 1935.) The University of Chicago later left the Big Ten Conference and decreased its financial commitment to its intercollegiate athletic program. More recently, Birmingham-Southern College moved from NCAA Division I to Division III. Ironically, though Birmingham Southern College eliminated their athletic scholarships as a condition of Division III membership, they were able to increase overall academic and need-based scholarships to students on campus while also increasing the total number of intercollegiate athletic opportunities.

Sport managers must incorporate a variety of knowledge in various areas and skill sets to successfully execute sporting events. They also must often work nights and weekends to make events successful for fans.

Harrelson Photography for Darlington Raceway.

If a school commits to sponsoring an athletic department (at whatever level), then it must prepare to manage the various sporting events that will occur on its campus. An event cannot occur without a facility. Even outdoor sports such as cross-country require some sort of a venue, as well as facilities for spectators, race officials, and members of the media. In addition to the "playing field" and areas for spectators and the working press during the competition, facility managers are responsible for event elements, such as parking, concessions, and restrooms. Fundamentally, a facility must provide a safe environment. In addition, it should be designed and operated in a manner that either maximizes potential revenue streams, or minimizes operational expenses.

Once an event has been scheduled in an identified facility, various athletic-department functional areas must execute their roles to ensure the event's success. If one of the goals is to have spectators at the event, the sales staff must work to sell tickets, sponsorships, and, in some cases, media rights. These can be done locally, regionally, nationally, or, in some cases, globally. In their initial representation, sport events have a short shelf life; once the event is completed there is not an additional opportunity to sell any unused tickets. The sales staff has to work to identify potential customers and to attempt to tie the potential customers' wants, needs, and desires to the benefits the event offers.

Typically, a sales staff works closely with a marketing department. It is much easier to sell tickets and sponsorships to events that are well known among various consumer groups and across various business sectors. An efficient marketing department can generate revenue well in excess of the salaries and overhead necessary for its operation. Though the sales department and marketing department will typically work to identify potential customers and media rights holders, the public-relations department will also interact with various potential customers and the media.

Public-relations departments typically focus upon two main areas: community relations and media relations. While the marketing and sales departments typically focus on sales for specific events, the community-relations component of a public-relations department will focus upon generating goodwill among various constituent groups. In some cases, such groups may not want to or be able to attend an event, but are still potentially important. Reading to kids in schools, visiting hospitals, and interacting with senior citizen groups are typical community-relation-building activities. Though these constituent groups may not immediately buy tickets to events, generating goodwill by interacting with them can help build overall athletic-department support in the community.

Separate from such community relations, the public-relations department's media-relation component typically involves attracting members of the press to events and then working to enhance their experience so members of the media will produce positive accounts of the event. In addition, media-relations departments also work with non-attending media outlets to help promote event or department activities and accomplishments, through press releases and media guides.

As various departments prepare for the event, all personnel must adhere to various legal requirements. Facility operations, marketing and sales activities, and public-relations initiatives must adhere to local, state, and national laws. Sport events often involve activities that may be inherently dangerous for participants and spectators. Ensuring the safety of participants and attendees is an important legal requirement. In addition, laws governing employee behavior must be followed. With an eye toward minimizing litigation, aspects of scheduling and event operations are detailed in contracts and other important legal documents. An athletic department will typically employ at least one person specifically responsible for legal affairs, but the more knowledge all departmental staff members have about the law and its application to operating an event, the more likely the sport event will be successfully managed.

Though laws establish required behaviors, ethical standards are also an important consideration when conducting an event. Everyone must establish their own ethical standards, but it is important that such individual standards are consistent with organizational policies and procedures, and the organization's culture. A difference in opinion regarding what is ethical can lead to conflicts within an organization. In 1990, the National Basketball Association (NBA) banned the use of courtside advertising for "liquor" company sponsorships. In 2009, the NBA rescinded the rule, resulting in extensive discussion among a variety of individuals and organizations (Hollencamp, 2009). Though it was certainly "legal" for the NBA to allow its teams to sell liquor advertisements, some believed it had declined to do so until the economic downturn resulted in a heightened need for revenues. Numerous critics noted the league regularly conducts public-relations campaigns aimed at helping children and other constituents and that increased advertising for liquor companies contradicted those other messages (Hollencamp). In addition, the fact that not every NBA franchise elected to sell liquor advertising once the ban was lifted, reflected the different ethical standards of NBA owners and franchises related to this potential revenue stream.

A similar situation has recently arisen in the NCAA. Though the NCAA bans alcohol sales at its championship events, individual schools can sell alcohol if they want in their own facilities. In 2012, only 21 FBS schools sold alcohol at their sporting events. In 2014, a number of schools changed their policies to increase revenue. Among them was the University of Texas, the athletic department that generates by far the largest amount of money in all of college sports (Nagel, 2014). Though many of these schools had long claimed selling alcohol at sporting events was inconsistent with their "educational" mission, the desire for increased revenue appeared to trump that ethical position (see Chapter 5).

Organizing an event involves a variety of financial decisions. To remain financially viable, any organization must generate revenues that exceed expenses. A college sport event will have a variety of revenue sources and potential expense areas. It is ultimately an athletic director's responsibility to ensure the athletic department is not operating in a financial deficit and therefore is a drain on the university. Over the past 10 years, there have been numerous examples where athletic departments have lost money. In some cases money from the institution's general fund has been utilized to cover these losses. On other campuses, student fees have been raised to ostensibly balance the books. In some cases, since generating additional revenue (whether by utilizing institutional resources, selling more tickets or increasing media rights, or raising student fees) is not an option, some athletic departments have had to cut costs, either by reducing team budgets, or, in some cases, by eliminating teams from their athletic programs.

Event management requires the analysis of a variety of factors across the various functional areas. The need to undertake strategic management actions to predict, identify, and solve problems is critical to an organization's success. Though most organizations typically do not have a position titled "strategic manager," the ability to analyze available resources, identify potential opportunities, and take actions necessary to benefit the entire organization is needed in every functional area.

Conclusion

Sport management is a popular area of academic study. Though having an interest in SPORTS is certainly helpful, a career in sport management is not just becoming an adult fan. For many graduating students, working in the sport industry is an attractive career choice. It is important for sport-management students to recognize that each year there are many more applicants for sport-management positions than there are job openings, so throughout their undergraduate education, students should prepare themselves to be a competitive candidate for a variety of sport-industry positions. Since there is so much interest in sport management, employers typically can offer low-paying jobs that require long hours to entry-level employees. Though this reality may be initially discouraging, if new sport managers can maintain their focus during the early phase of their career, higher pay in an enjoyable job will likely result.

A final word of unsolicited advice: During this course, and throughout your sport-management career, remember the importance of integrating theory and practice. A strong theoretical foundation can be immensely valuable for making informed practical decisions. Remember, each sport-management subarea covered in this text does not exist in a silo. Decisions made in one area typically impact many other, if not all, areas of a sport organization. Highly successful sport managers learn to recognize the importance of every facet of the organization, and remember to always SEE THE BIG PICTURE!

Good luck on your sport-management journey!

chapter 1

Interviews

Interview 1.1

Todd Koesters
Assistant Professor,
University of South Carolina
Former Churchill Downs
Entertainment Group
Former Vice President,
Sports Group GMR Marketing

Q: Can you briefly describe your career path?

A: I completed my undergraduate studies at The Ohio State University (OSU) with a BA in English and then graduated from Capital University Law School and Ohio University (OU) in a joint degree program in law and sports administration and facility management. My paid and unpaid internships while in school included working at OSU in the Athletic Compliance Office, serving as a legal intern for the Ohio Civil Rights Commission, and working as the External Operations Director for the Mid-American Conference's Men's and Women's Swimming and Diving Championships hosted by OU.

After graduate school, I completed an internship with a small NASCAR-specific marketing agency called Agency Won and then accepted my first full-time job in sport management with the same company. During my time there I worked on several NASCAR marketing programs and was then exposed to the world of agency acquisitions and holding companies when Agency Won merged with a holding company called Disson, Furst and Partners (DF&P). DF&P was a collection of niche sports and event agencies that offered expertise in multiple disciplines. The business experiences learned during that merger proved invaluable to my career in sport management.

Following my time with DF&P, I accepted an Account Executive position with GMR Marketing, a leader in event, lifestyle, and sport marketing. My job with GMR was in their newly formed Sports Division and included opening their Charlotte Office in my house. As we grew the business—and following an 18-wheeled truck unloading its cargo onto my driveway—my wife was able to convince my bosses that GMR needed a real office that did not include our garage as the fulfillment center. My 10-year stay at GMR shaped the foundation of my development as a marketer in the sport management industry and taught many invaluable lessons for business and life.

After leaving GMR in the fall of 2009, I joined Churchill Downs Entertainment Group, a wholly owned subsidiary of Churchill Downs Incorporated, that was formed in 2009. I served as Vice President, Marketing and Sales. Though the Kentucky Derby is certainly the signature event, the company owns multiple racetracks and the newly formed subsidiary was tasked with expanding the company's entertainment offerings. Our first event in July 2010 was a three-day music festival at the iconic track. The festival was named HullabaLOU and included more than 65 performances from acts such as Bob Jovi, Kenny Chesney, and the Dave Matthews Band.

After leaving Churchill Downs Entertainment Group, I accepted my current position as an Assistant Professor in the Sport and Entertainment Department at the University of South Carolina. In my role, I teach sales and contracts/negotiations classes as well as conduct research and complete consulting projects.

Q: What have been some of the biggest challenges you have faced during your career?

A: Determining a career path is always a challenge, particularly when the industry is continually changing. I am constantly setting new goals for myself. From the time I decided to work in sports, I had to figure out what specific subarea I would devote my concentration. Once I decided to work for an agency, there were multiple opportunities, some of which were presented to me, and others that I created. I have constantly had to determine how short-term career decisions can build toward a longer-term set of goals. Oddly enough, one primary long-term goal I set for myself after making the agency decision was achieved by the time I was 31 years old. I realized what I thought would be a "final" destination point was really just the starting point of a new phase in my career. When I was in school, my vision and understanding of job titles and responsibilities was naive. Early in my career I thought the end destination involved having a fancy job title, good salary, and extensive professional responsibilities. I realize now those things are certainly nice to have, but they are not really part of the big picture in my overall setting of career goals. I think a lot of people in sport management realize after a few years in their career that finding a place where you are challenged and fulfilled is much more important than the short-term needs that most of us concentrate on when we are in school. There is always much more that can be done in this industry as new challenges regularly present themselves.

Q: Now that you are a full-time professor, how do you help people conceptualize the sport-management industry?

A: I have found a model that helps students better understand how the sport industry functions and what potential opportunities may exist. The first portion of the model involves determining how an organization should be categorized. Sport organizations will typically operate as one of the following:

1. Property—Teams, athletic departments, venues, and leagues and their employees (athletes, coaches, front office staff, etc.) typically operate as a property. When many students initially think of sport management, they often narrowly define the industry as only involving the property. One of the reason entry-level pay is often low in this sector is because most sport management students narrow their focus to working for a team, college athletic department, league, etc., and many of these entities may only have a few dozen full-time employees and turnover occurs less often than in other industries or sport-management sectors.
2. Sponsor—Companies who pay to be associated with the property. For many students, the countless number of companies that sponsor various sporting events are too often not seen as part of the sport industry or as potential employers. Companies such as Coca-Cola or MillerCoors have dozens or even hundreds of employees who work to identify and evaluate sport properties for potential sponsorship investments. In many cases career opportunities with sponsors may not appear as "glamorous" as working for a team. However, since most sponsors operate more like a "normal" business, salaries for employees tend to be higher and there is more room for potential advancement because the company does a variety of things inside and outside of sport.
3. Broadcast Rights Holders and Media Companies—Television, radio, Internet, and other telecommunications companies are an integral component of the sport industry. Though some may view these entities as sponsors, they fulfill a different role. Technological advances are certainly changing the entire sport industry and broadcast rights holders are no exception.
4. Agencies and Service Providers—Any company who represents the interest of others in the buying and selling of sports. Most students know that players and coaches typically retain agents. Few students know that companies such as IMG, CBS Collegiate Sports Properties, and Learfield Communications, Inc. often represent colleges in their negotiations with sponsors and broadcast rights holders. Fewer students are aware of companies such as GMR Marketing that help sponsors enhance the value of their relationships with properties. Ticketing companies such as Ticketmaster or Stubhub are agencies that provide a service specific to a particular facet of the sport industry.

Once the organization can be categorized, the "space" in which it operates must be determined. Organizations can operate and wield influence in four ways:

1. Locally
2. Regionally
3. Nationally
4. Globally

Understanding the extent to which a sport organization operates is important. In some cases, certain aspects of an organization may operate in different areas. For instance, the Pittsburgh Steelers of the National Football League sell tickets and sponsorships primarily in their local and regional market. In this case, their local market is the Pittsburgh metropolitan area and their region is most of Pennsylvania, excluding the Philadelphia metropolitan market. However, due to the NFL's national media agreements, the Steelers have been able to build their brand identity throughout the United States. Though this brand-building may occur nationwide, the Steelers are unlikely to sell many tickets or sponsorships outside of their region. However, they do sell licensed merchandise throughout various areas of the United States.

Though the NFL is the most popular and powerful sport league brand in the United States, the limited American football participation in most of the world is somewhat limiting the NFL's international initiatives (compared to other leagues such as the National Basketball Association and Major League Baseball). The NFL has been playing and broadcasting games in various international markets, but their marketing efforts in many countries focus on explaining what American football is and why it is exciting. NFL franchises like the Steelers would certainly like to expand their international presence, but doing so takes time, effort, and a financial commitment. Currently, most NFL teams focus a large percentage of attention on their local and regional initiatives.

Analyzing an organization's characteristics and geographic areas of influence is important, as it will help an organization better understand where to allocate resources and when to potentially alter their current practices. Students can utilize this model to better understand the industry and better prepare for interviews with potential employers.

Q: As you teach students to better understand and apply this model, what specific skills do you emphasize?

A: One of the things that irritates me is the term "sports marketing." It is amazing the number of students I speak with who say they want a career in sports marketing but they do not know the first thing about marketing. In all of my previous industry positions, I considered myself a marketer who leverages sports to achieve sales and marketing goals. The way I explain it to students is there are two ways to look at it depending upon word placement. There is the "SPORTS business" with the first word being more important than the second. People who work in the SPORTS business are typically involved with "talent." Players, coaches, general managers, scouts, etc. would fall into this category. Most of the students in sport management programs will work in the BUSINESS of sport. This world involves sales, marketing, sponsorship evaluation, accounting, administration, and various other functional areas. General business principles are critical, though they must be applied differently in sport than in some other industries. If students want to work in the BUSINESS of sports, classes taken and skills developed should reflect an understanding of business and how various principles apply to the subareas discussed earlier.

Q: What publications do you regularly read?

A: I have referred to my copy of *Kellogg on Marketing* by the Kellogg Marketing Faculty at Northwestern University so often that the binding is becoming worn! I also regularly read *Harvard Business Review, USA Today, The Wall Street Journal,* and of course the *SportsBusiness Journal* and *SportsBusiness Daily*. I also try to regularly read *Advertising Age, Brand Week,* and *Event Marketer Magazine* as time permits.

I think it is important to stay on the cutting edge in the industry so I typically buy 15+ new books a year from the business section of the local bookstore. I also regularly buy books that cover the BUSINESS of sports but rarely buy books covering the SPORTS business.

Q: As you work and study the industry, what trends do you see emerging?

A: Three areas of importance in the BUSINESS of sport industry include: (1) globalization (Thomas Friedman's book *The World is Flat* has accurately discussed many of the major issues in the world), (2) technology trends that enable active engagement with customers, and (3) the importance of employees developing sales skills as revenue generation continues to be the primary focus of any entity involved in sport.

Q: Do you advise students to potentially pursue a graduate degree?

A: Absolutely. Graduate school is an investment in your future that will pay dividends in the short and long run. I chose a joint masters degree and JD because there were not as many options in sport management as there are now. Law school was beneficial for me in a variety of ways. One only needs to look at a history of league commissioners and other prominent BUSINESS of sport leaders to see how attorneys have impacted the industry. Pursuing a law degree is certainly not a requirement for success. There are now many good MBA and MSA programs around the country. There are also some that focus too much on the "fan" side of sports and not enough on the BUSINESS of sport. My advice to students who have a sport management undergraduate degree from a top program would be to pursue either law school or an MBA program. For students with undergraduate degrees in business, I would push them towards a MSA program.

Q: Is there any additional advice you would like to provide?

A: In this industry, as well as life in general, nothing replaces hard work and dedication. Everyone, even people with industry "connections," are going to have to undertake tasks that are not glamorous or exciting early in their career (and often even later in their career). The more you can do now while you are students, the better you will be prepared to seize opportunities as they are presented. Do not ever feel you are entitled to anything. This has been one of the biggest downfalls for many graduate students. Earning an MBA or MSA is certainly important, but it does not make one immune to needing to prove yourself in an organization.

Interview 1.2

Steve Williams
Manager, Marketing Partnerships
Verizon Wireless

Q: Could you briefly describe your career path from undergraduate student to your current position?

A: As an undergraduate at Bowling Green State University, I was a volunteer intern in the Athletic Department in the marketing and promotions department. I then went to Miami University to attain my MBA. While there I also worked in the marketing and promotions office as a Graduate Assistant to the Athletic Department. After receiving my MBA, I taught in the business school for three years while my wife finished her studies. With the dream of working in Sport Marketing still alive, we decided to move to Charlotte, North Carolina for opportunities in the motorsports industry. I took a job as Marketing Director of a local YMCA while I continued to search for a job in motorsports. I volunteered at the North Carolina Speedway, as well as with other smaller companies in NASCAR and began to build a strong network within the sport. Within 11 months I had received two job offers that launched my career in the world of motorsports. I have since developed a diverse background in motorsports working for a licensee, a team, an agency, and of course for the past eight years as a sponsor.

Q: What have been the biggest challenges you have encountered during your career?

A: No matter how well you plan for a single event or even a season-long activation, there will always be unexpected occurrences. The ability to handle those wrinkles shows how well you have truly prepared. My biggest challenge came in 2008. As we were about a month from starting our season-long NASCAR activation, I was told my budget was cut by 20%. This was after we had purchased or been in contract with most of our elements for the season, so I needed to find that money back that was already spent. I was able to put together a package of assets from our activation that we were able to sell to one of our partners with little-to-no sacrifice of our actual activation plan.

Q: Can you discuss how VerizonWireless is involved in the sport industry?

A: No surprise that Verizon is a large national advertiser and sponsor within the industry and in general. We have become much more strategic in the past few years of the properties in which we align ourselves, as we look to become a more iconic technology brand. Our primary properties are the NFL and the Verizon IndyCar Series. Both of these provide the opportunity to offer technology solutions that enhance the sport for the fan.

Q: How has that involvement enhanced VerizonWireless' business and their reputation?

A: Through these partnerships, we are able to bring forth case studies and test cases for technology. We have strategically aligned ourselves with the NFL and the Verizon IndyCar Series as they both give us the opportunity to provide technology solutions that not only enhance the experience of the sport for the fan, but also provide innovations that improve lifestyles away from the track or stadium.

Q: Given the size and impact of VerizonWireless, how do you interact with the various other areas of the company in your role? Is it difficult to keep all of the marketing activities in synergy?

A: Negotiating the waters at a company our size is a big challenge; we are continually working cross-functionally with PR, Legal, Brand Marketing, Network, and Product Development. In addition, we have up to seven agency partners working on our business at any given time. Continual status checks and follow-up is key in making sure projects keep moving and nothing is dropped in the handoff.

Q: Many "new" sport management students to do recognize or understand how important sponsors are to the industry or see the potential employment opportunities. Can you discuss how students can get involved with internships and what types of career opportunities those internships can develop?

A: Network, Network, and then Network again. I am a believer in getting as much experience while you are a student as you can. Each student needs to stand out amongst the thousands of resumes that are sent from people who "want to work in sports." So with that said, you do whatever it takes and seek out every opportunity to gain experience. Volunteer at local events, take leadership roles, and make yourself invaluable. All along you need to continually be building your personal network. Every student should have their own personal brand and be able to tell their brand story at all times; you never know who you may meet or what capacity of the industry you might work.

Q: What are the biggest concerns you have regarding the sport management industry in the future?

A: Fans consume sports in more and more ways every day. At Verizon we are trying to make sure we are on the cutting edge of the technology to provide fans with what they want, when they want it. At the same time, the relevancy of the live event needs to evolve as well. It is concerning that attendance of live events, regardless of sport, is slowing.

Q: What are some things that contribute to the decrease of live attendance? What do you do given this environment?

A: Several factors contribute: time, expense, attention span, and other ways to consume sports, to name a few. When we evaluate properties we are not as concerned with branding or signage. We look at ways we can integrate technology into the lifeblood of the sport and in ways that enhance the fan experience, be that in-venue or as a second screen experience on mobile.

Q: Are there specific skills sport-management students should look to develop while still in school?

A: Start building your personal brand. Meaning, start building experience, growing your network, and setting yourself apart from all of the other candidates in an extremely competitive environment.

Q: What specific classes would you recommend students take to best position themselves for a sport-industry job?

A: Outside of the sport-management curriculum, an Operations Management course is extremely helpful.

Q: What publications do you regularly read to stay apprised of sport-business events?

A: I have a subscription to *SportsBusiness Journal (SBJ).* As it is a weekly publication it is the most up-to-date with helpful information. I also get the *SportsBusiness Daily* email service from *SBJ.* In addition, I regularly attend partnership summits and forums throughout the country to see what others are doing and to continue to grow my network.

Q: Would you recommend students pursue graduate school? If so, when should they pursue a graduate degree and what area of study would you recommend?

A: I have my MBA. I thought that having this would provide a better general business acumen that would only enhance my endeavors in Sport Marketing.

Interview 1.3

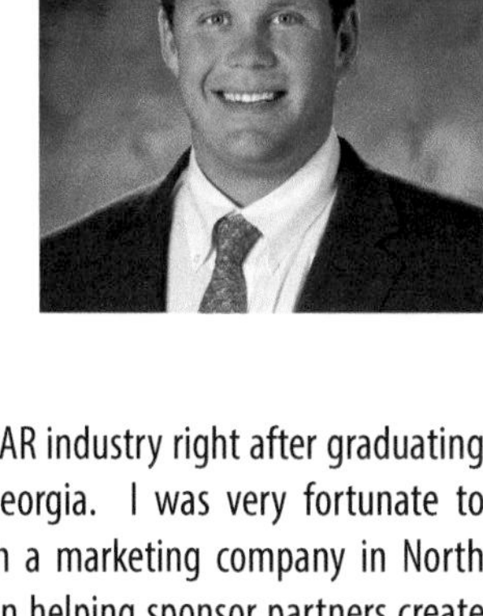

Chip Wile
President
Darlington Raceway

Q: Can you briefly describe your career path?

A: I started in the NASCAR industry right after graduating from the University of Georgia. I was very fortunate to have an opportunity with a marketing company in North Carolina who specialized in helping sponsor partners create and execute programs utilizing the NASCAR machine. After two full NASCAR seasons, I had the chance to work for NASCAR Sprint Cup Series team Bill Davis Racing (BDR) doing public-relations work. I spent the next decade working for BDR, Team Penske, and most recently with Turner Scott Motorsports doing everything from public relations to team and sponsor management. In 2012, I received a job offer with International Speedway Corporation working at Motor Racing Network (MRN) as the director of business development. I managed the relationship with our sister properties as well as acted as the bridge between the industry and MRN. After working in this post for nine months I was promoted to President of Darlington Raceway. I have a fabulous team who are all passionate about this facility. Everyone comes to work every day with a common goal and it shows.

Q: What have been some of the biggest challenges you have faced during your career?

A: One of the biggest challenges I have faced is how to create a return on investment for all of our partners. NASCAR, unlike other major sporting organizations, is dependent on sponsor partners to fund the sport. During the economic downturn in 2008, partners started to expect more and more return for less investment which has required the industry to become more nimble as well as innovative. Each person within an organization had to be willing to go above and beyond in order to make the industry stronger. Long term, this was a blessing as we developed a number of new programs, but it was a shift in the culture which takes time. We are just now seeing the hard work pay dividends.

Q: What are the biggest challenges facing NASCAR and/or the racing industry?

A: Obviously, the on-track product has to continue to be strong. NASCAR has a number of very smart people who spend all of their time figuring out ways to make the on-track product better. As an industry, we must capture the new, younger fan to continue to grow the sport. In order to do this, we have to continue to provide experiences that keep them coming back and keep us relevant within their lives. Everyone in the industry is putting effort and focus to capture these new demographics.

Q: What are the biggest challenges facing Darlington Raceway?

A: Being the oldest speedway on the circuit, Darlington Raceway has to continue to be relevant. Darlington Raceway has grown with the sport. It has hosted NASCAR races for 65 years and is rich in history. It is often compared to the NFL's Lambeau Field. This is something we must embrace. It sets our property apart from the rest of the stops on the circuit. It certainly doesn't have the "new track" feel but is one of the events both fans and competitors circle on their calendars as a "can't miss" event. The facility must continue to enhance the event weekend experience making people want to return year after year. Another challenge the property faces is staying relevant within the community. We are an integral cog within the state of South Carolina that provides a significant economic impact to our community. We must continue to embrace this position and understand we have an obligation to lead by example.

Q: How do you measure customer feedback to ensure that Darlington Raceway is providing the optimal event experience?

A: As a company, International Speedway Corporation uses a service that selects a random group of fans and asks them to complete a survey. The survey consists of a wide range of questions about their experience at the track. We ask them everything from how they would rank our parking to concession items. We then analyze the data and compare it to previous years as well as other facilities to see if we have made improvements to their experience. We also use the data when deciding what capital and event experience improvements to make to the facility.

Q: What are the most important skills you think students should work to develop while still in school?

A: School is a vital tool to success in life. It is not what you learn but how you learn. College provides an opportunity to interact with countless kinds of people. It is important to try to connect with each person individually and learn how to communicate effectively with that person. In our business, there are a number of different kinds of people. There are drivers, mechanics, owners, and business leaders who all have a common goal. And of course there are the many fans who consume our product that must be understood and appreciated. The goal is to succeed but each person's definition of success is a little different. Someone who succeeds in any business learns how to effectively communicate with each group and help them all reach their individual goals which in turn helps the entire organization flourish.

Q: What publications do you regularly read?

A: The *SportsBusiness Journal* is a great publication that gives our senior leadership a pulse on different sports properties and the trends within each. We all have a common goal of staying relevant within our fan base and it is important to understand what other leagues are doing to take their individual discipline to the next level. It is also important to stay current with business trends and economies. *The Wall Street Journal* is a great way to get an overarching perspective on both our national and international economy.

Q: As you work and study the industry, what trends do you see emerging?

A: Fans are expecting more out of experience than ever before. Technology is becoming more and more important to enhancing the guest experience. The power of digital assets is becoming one of the leading measures of success by sponsor partners. It used to be an added value and very little resource was being put against it. Now, one of the first questions you get when you sit in a boardroom is about digital assets and strategy. International Speedway Corporation is investing over $400 million in Daytona International Speedway in order to create an experience unlike any other in sports which shows as a company we are committed to taking our properties to the next level. With the emergence of social interactions with the starts of the sports via digital assets, content is becoming more and more interactive. Asking fans what they want and delivering a compelling product are key to creating a successful experience.

Q: Do you advise students to potentially pursue a graduate degree?

A: The sports business is becoming more scientific each and every day. With the importance of different segmented media and the value that sponsor partners are putting on these assets, a graduate degree seems more important than ever. It certainly isn't a necessity but is something people are continuing to pursue to be more attractive in the marketplace.

Q: Is there any additional advice you would like to provide?

A: Never give up on your dreams. Set goals and put your head down and work hard to achieve them. The business of sports isn't for everyone but for people who have a passion and desire, it is the most rewarding job in the world. I didn't get this opportunity because of something I have accomplished but it is all about the great people who spent the time and helped me along the way. Make sure you help people succeed and it is always repaid tenfold.

References

Brown, G. (2009, January 8). Women's lacrosse. *The NCAA News.* Retrieved March 13, 2010 from http:// www. ncaa.com/sports/w-lacros/spec-rel/010809aaa.html

Hollencamp, K. (2009, February 10). Anti-alcohol organizations blast NBA's ad policies. Retrieved March 14, 2010 from http://news.medill.northwestern.edu/chicago/ news.aspx?id=115141

Irwin, R.L., Southall, R.M., & Sutton, W.A. (2007). Pentagon of sport sales training: A 21st century sport sales training model. *Sport Management Education Journal*, 1(1), 18–39.

Nagel, M.S. (2014, June/July). College sports and alcohol: An evolving future. *Facility Manager*, 30(3), 30-31.

Oriard, M. (2009). *Bowled over.* Chapel Hill, NC: University of North Carolina Press.

Southall, R.M., & Dick, R.J. (2010, March). Assessing sport-sales training effectiveness: Development of a baseline sample. Paper presented at the Association of Marketing Theory and Practice, Hilton Head, SC.

Southall, R.M., Nagel, M.S., LeGrande, D., & Han, M.Y. (2003). Sport management practica: A metadiscrete experiential learning model. *Sport Marketing Quarterly*, 12(1), 27–36.

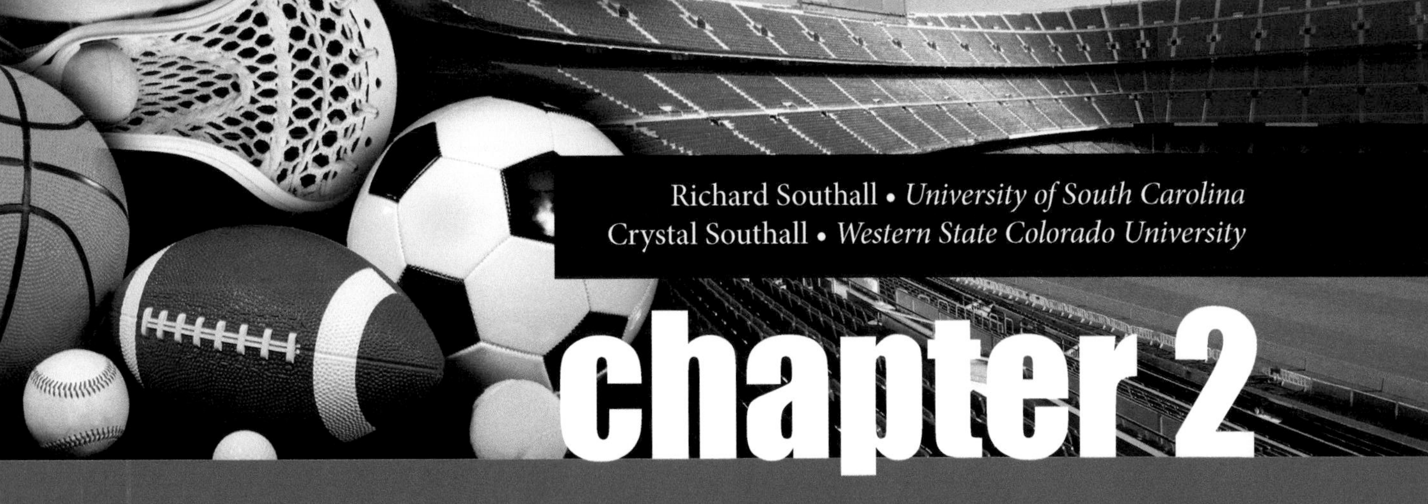

Richard Southall • *University of South Carolina*
Crystal Southall • *Western State Colorado University*

chapter 2

Sociocultural Aspects of Sport

CHAPTER OBJECTIVES

After reading this chapter, you will be able to:

- Critically examine the social and cultural contexts in which sport occurs.
- Identify sociological theories often used to examine sport.
- Detail elements of organizational culture theory.
- Define institutional logics theory and discuss various sports as institutions.
- Utilize presented sociological, cultural, or institutional theories to analyze a given sport-industry issue.

KEY TERMS

Conflict theory

Critical theory

Cultural hegemony

Functionalist theory, or functionalism

Institutional logics

Organizational culture

Sports is human life in microcosm.

—Howard Cosell

Introduction

When students are asked what they like about sports, one of the most-often listed and enduring appeals is the "love of competition" and the fact that athletes win or lose on the basis of their athletic talent. Inherent in this meritocracy is the notion of a "level playing field," on which athletes compete based on a consistently enforced set of rules. As most every American sport fan of your professor's age is aware, this democratic notion of competition was personified in Jesse Owens's display of athletic prowess at the 1936 Berlin Olympics. The functionalist perspective on his multiple gold-medal performances is that they were the result of his strength, power, and skill, not his race, class, or politics.

Suppose you were asked a simple question: "Should sports rules always be enforced?" How would you answer? Most every student would answer, "Of course." But, the answer may not be so simple. This is the essence of this chapter's focus: examining sport from a sociocultural perspective. As we continue through this chapter, we hope to provide you with an opportunity to see how a simple question may have more than one possible answer and that the experiences of individuals and the influence of others within society are critical to understanding differences that exist.

Sports rules are intended to ensure one team or competitor does not gain an unfair advantage over another. The coveted "home-court" advantage does not extend to flaunting a game's fundamental rules by "cheating" or "fixing" a game's outcome. Fundamental rule violations in baseball (committing a balk), football (pass interference), basketball (traveling or fouling), and skiing (missing a gate) must be penalized, since to not do so would violate the fairness of athletic competition, which is one of the fundamental tenets of sport and competition (i.e., even-playing field). That is, all things being equal, the winner of a sporting competition should be determined based on whom, or which team, has competed at the highest level, while ascribing to ALL the rules governing competition.

But what about in-game behaviors that have no direct effect on the outcome of the competition or result in an uneven-playing field, but are still often penalized (sometimes harshly). Further, such penalties themselves often directly influence the outcome of competitions. Examples of such penalized actions include taking off one's helmet after scoring a touchdown or engaging in excessive end-zone celebrations in American football; "trash-talking" or taunting after a spectacular dunk in basketball; or arguing a call with an umpire in baseball or tennis.

A simple answer to our initial question would be, "All sports require rules. Just as in society, a sport's rules should be enforced."

But as you will find as you continue studying the sport industry, thoughtful examination of sport-related issues requires sport managers to have at least a rudimentary understanding of some fundamental sociological and cultural theories and how sport influences and is influenced by these theories. In order for sport-management students to be better informed, they should be willing and able to use theories to critically examine the sport industry and discuss political, social, and cultural sport-related issues.

Many students are interested in a sport-industry career because they "love" sports. Many of you may be current or former athletes. In addition, many students in an introduction to sport-management course are also currently sports fans. For many students, to hear or see the "business of sport" described as a capitalist economy predicated on controlling labor costs and maximizing consumption in order to increase revenue production is a foreign concept. Brohm's (1978) contention that the commodified sport industry's global development paralleled the rise of colonial imperialism also threatens many students' long-held belief that sport involvement is based on athletes, fans, and coaches' "Love of the Game." Initially, it might seem disheartening to discuss sport in the context of modes of production, an accumulation ethic, and a social structure designed to support the recurring production of athletes, sport events, and stadia.

Many sport-management students have not been exposed to some of the sociological or cultural concepts in this chapter. Perhaps some of you will find these theoretical discussions obtuse and overly abstract. In addition, since some of the theories and perspectives presented in this chapter question accepted view of sports, students who are also sports fans may either ignore or denigrate them. We recognize this is not a sport-sociology course, but an introduction to sport-management courses. However, this chapter's purpose is to stimulate discussion and allow faculty and students to openly and critically examine the sport industry. Because sport-management students must undergo a transformation from being simply sport consumers (i.e., fans) to sport managers, this chapter is designed to provide students some theoretical tools, which they may utilize during this transition. As students may discover, becoming a sport manager is a journey that will affect the way in which they view sport.

A Sociocultural Examination of Sport

Sociology is the study of the organization of people within a society and their social relationships. Sociology also extends to the investigation of constructed organizations and institutions, and the processes through which people are linked. These social processes reflect repetitive and recurring organizational and institutional patterns characterizing individual and group choices. Culture refers to the ways in which life is created and organized by people within a particular society. As we will discuss later in this chapter, we construct organizational,

Shutterstock, Inc.

We construct meaning through and within organizational, institutional, and societal settings.

institutional and social "meaning" within organizational, institutional, and societal settings. Consequently, a *sociocultural* investigation of sport involves examining sport within organizational, institutional, and societal settings.

Cultural Hegemony

Some sport sociologists contend 21st-century spectator and participatory sport industries reflect the dominance of what Southall and Nagel (2009) described as "jock capitalism." Jock capitalism encapsulates the **cultural hegemony** of corporatized, commercial sport (Donnelly, 1996; Sack, 1987). Cultural hegemony is the domination of one social, political, or economic group over a culturally diverse society, or another group within society (Southall & Staurowsky, 2013). In today's sport-industry settings, the *hegemon* (those who have societal power) utilizes the sport industry to reproduce this privilege by promoting "entertaining and fun" sport forms that reinforce the values and orientations that encourage capitalist business expansion and profit maximization.

This corporate cultural hegemony is succinctly expressed in the sport-industry maxim, "Nothing happens until we sell something." The focus of Chapter 10 is the importance of sales and revenue generation in the sport industry; however, it should be noted the commercialized sport-industry is neither monolithic nor completely unified. Rather, it is a complex of layered sociocultural structures (classes), each of which may have its own "mission," culture, or dominant institutional logic. In addition, dominant class members may often coexist with those from other classes. For students considering a sport-industry career, it is appropriate to use sociocultural theories to examine the industry in which they want to work. Later in this chapter you will be introduced to some well-known sociological theories from which the sport industry may be viewed (functionalist, conflict, and critical theories). In addition, stakeholder theory will be utilized to examine sport organizations' internal and external relationships. Finally, a more recent theoretical perspective—the theory of institutional logics—will be presented as a means to investigate various sport-industry institutions.

Throughout this chapter, we will return to our initial scenario involving the need for rules in sport, and our discussion of sportspersonship, in order to dissect our initial answer and investigate how and why different people within the sport landscape may adopt different points-of-view on a given issue. In addition, the presented theories will be used to provide context for our discussions.

Study Questions

1. What are the elements of negligence? Define and discuss each.
2. What is the difference between primary assumption of the risk and secondary assumption of the risk?
3. Discuss a number of aspects of competent instruction or training. Give examples of poor instruction in a sport or physical activity of your choice.
4. Explain the concepts of agreement, consideration, capacity, and legality in the formation of contracts.
5. What is the usual remedy in breach of contract actions? When can you use the remedy of specific performance?
6. What is the principle of mitigation of damages?
7. What is the concept of state action? Why is it crucial to any constitutional law claim?
8. What three fundamental aspects must a plaintiff establish before a court will hear a due process claim on its merits?

Learning Activities

1. Read *USA Today's* daily sports pages or visit its sport web pages for a week and identify disputes related to sport law. How many different kinds of legal issues can you identify?
2. Read the following scenario and then answer the questions relating to this example of a case based in negligence.

   Robert Smith is the manager of Fitness World, a corporation that owns a small health and fitness facility. The facility has a weight room, a gymnasium, and a running track. Aerobics classes are offered at this facility. Smith has decided to begin a karate program.

   In an effort to more quickly generate and collect class fees, Smith advertises that classes will begin one month from today. He also begins to search for a karate instructor. Unfortunately, qualified karate instructors are in short supply. As the day for the first class approaches, Mr. Smith hires Ron Jones to serve as a karate instructor. Mr. Jones, although an imposing physical specimen and a former weightlifting champion, has virtually no martial arts training. In college, he took one judo class, but has never formally or informally studied karate. Against this backdrop, the karate class begins with Jones as the instructor.

After about 20 hours of instruction (at Mr. Jones's direction) students engaged in a "free fight" situation. In one of the matches Mr. Jones directed John Jackson, a novice whose only experience in karate was the 20 hours of Fitness World class instruction, to spar with Tommy Tough, an advanced student of karate who held a Brown Belt. During the course of this "free fight," Jackson was kicked in the head by Tough and sustained severe injuries. During the course of this "free fight," Jones was talking with another Fitness World employee and was not—in any way—supervising the Jackson-Tough duo.

There are a number of very credible experts in the field of karate who will testify that it is a recognized principle of good practice among karate instructors not to permit a student with minimal training to engage in a "free fight" situation.

Questions

1. Mr. Jackson has indicated he intends to file suit against Jones and Smith in regard to the foregoing incident. Discuss the elements of negligence and then discuss the allegations of negligence that Jackson's attorney would use as the basis of the suit. Based on the given facts, present and explain as many possible bases of negligence as you can identify.
2. What defenses are available to Jones and Smith in regard to each allegation of negligence? Discuss the applicability of each to the facts at hand.

References

Asquith, C. (2002, November 11). Sue the coach! *Sports Illustrated,* 21.

Garberinio, R.P. (1994). So you want to be a sports lawyer, or is it a player agent, player representative, sports agent, contract advisor, or contract representative? *Villanova Sports & Entertainment Law Forum, 1,* 11.

National Collegiate Athletic Ass'n v. Yeo, 171 S.W.3d 863 (Tex. 2005).

Restatement (Second) Contracts (1981).

Restatement (Second) Torts (1965).

Taylor, S., Jr., & Thomas, E. (2003, December 15). Civil wars. *Newsweek, 142,* 42–53.

Vernonia Sch. Dist. 47J v. Acton, 115 S. Ct. 2386 (1995).

Martin B. Gold
Howard C. Liebengood

chapter 7

Congressional Influence in the Sport Industry

CHAPTER OBJECTIVES

After reading this chapter, you will be able to:

- Understand the unique historical relationship Congress has had with the sport industry.
- Describe different ways Congress can influence sport.
- Identify key pieces of congressional legislation impacting sport business.
- Discuss prominent examples where Congress has held hearings regarding sport business activities.

KEY TERMS

Antitrust laws	Players union
Bowl Championship Series (BCS)	Sports Broadcasting Act of 1961
College football playoff	State of the Union Address
Fantasy sports	Tax-exempt bonds
Internet gambling	Tax-exempt status
March Madness	Television carriage disputes

> *"Today's hearing will not be the end of the inquiring. Far from it. Nor will Major League Baseball be our sole or even primary focus. We're in the first inning of what could be an extra inning ball game."*
> —House Oversight and Government Reform Committee Chairman, Representative Tom Davis

In October 2004, the Boston Red Sox baseball team made a remarkable comeback. Down three games to none in the American League Championship Series to the rival New York Yankees, the Red Sox won the next four games to capture the American League Pennant. The team swept the St. Louis Cardinals in the World Series and broke the "Curse of the Bambino." The City of Boston celebrated their first World Series Championship in 86 years. The victory gave hope to all baseball fans for the following season. If the Red Sox could finally win a World Series after decades of disappointment, then hope would be eternal for all baseball fans their team would be the next World Series Champion. In March 2005, baseball viewers should have tuned into Entertainment and Sports Programming Network (ESPN) for coverage of Major League Baseball's (MLB) Spring Training to receive updates about their favorite teams. Instead, what did viewers see dominating the 24-hour sports network? The live coverage of the House Oversight and Government Reform Committee hearing on the need for federal legislation regulating performance-enhancing drug use in professional sport. The House committee hearing is an excellent example of the scope and reach that Congress can impose on the world of sports.

INTRODUCTION

Since the mid-1960s, Congress has viewed sport as an endeavor, which might require some congressional legislation and oversight (Lowe, 1995). Several sports, such as boxing, horse racing, basketball, hockey, baseball, football, collegiate athletics, and Olympic competition, have received significant congressional attention. Although it may now have been somewhat displaced in popularity by the Ultimate Fighting Championship (UFC), boxing is the sport that has consistently received scrutiny for federal regulation (Lowe). In fact, an early major congressional investigation into the sports industry took place when the House Committee on Interstate Foreign Commerce held 1910 hearings on the distribution of boxing match films (Lowe). Congress has scrutinized boxing for ties to illegal gambling, mob involvement, match fixing, and in-ring deaths. Eventually, Congress passed the 1996 Professional Boxing Safety Act which required safety standards for fighters and established state boxing commissions.

Baseball has received extensive attention from Congress. However, Major League Baseball (MLB) has a unique standing. Because of a 1922 Supreme Court unanimous decision in *Federal Baseball Club of Baltimore v. National League*,

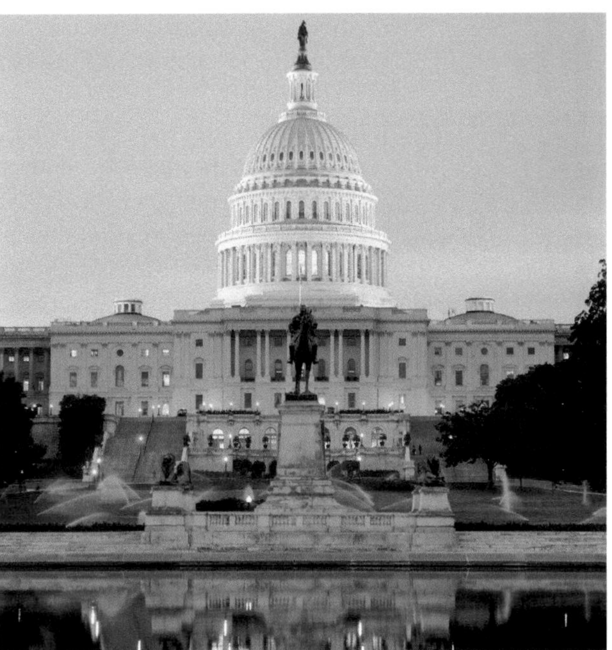
Shutterstock, Inc.

The United States Capitol in Washington, D.C., is where the Senate and House of Representatives pass new laws.

baseball has enjoyed exemption from **antitrust laws**. The Sherman Antitrust Act prevents businesses from illegally forming and engaging in monopolistic practices. In *Federal Baseball Club*, the Court held that baseball was not a business operating in interstate commerce. On that basis, the Court said baseball was subject to state regulation but was not subject to federal antitrust controls. Although it is doubtful that the Court would reach the same conclusion today, the 1922 precedent has been allowed to stand. Neither the Court through litigation nor Congress through legislation has acted to completely reverse it, even though other sports and sport leagues have been denied antitrust immunity since 1922. Nevertheless, baseball has been subject to substantial congressional scrutiny. Not only have there been hearings on whether to permit the antitrust exemption to continue, but Congress has looked at the reserve clause in baseball contracts, work stoppages, steroid use, and other topics (Berenbak, 2011).

Interest from Congress in professional football has grown considerably over the last 50 years. Two legislative actions have contributed to the National Football League (NFL) surpassing baseball to become modern day's national pastime. First, Congress passed the Sports Broadcasting Act of 1961 whereby professional sport leagues were allowed to pool broadcasting rights of games and share revenue from the sale of those rights. Today, the NFL annually collects over $3 billion in broadcast rights (Moran, 2013). Second, Congress approved an antitrust exemption for the merger of the American Football League (AFL) and NFL. If Congress would not have passed such legislation, the landscape of professional football would likely be very different today. Franchise relocation, stadium financing, licensing for cable broadcasts, stadium security, tax-exempt league status, labor unrest, players' pensions, and the Washington Redskins' team name are among other football issues receiving significant congressional attention.

Congress devoted noteworthy antitrust exemption hearings and proposed legislation for the basketball merger of the American Basketball Association (ABA) into the National Basketball Association (NBA) during the 1970s. Instead of granting an antitrust exemption for the leagues to merge, Congress proposed a bill requiring the leagues to engage in new revenue gate sharing, but the bill did not pass (Lowe, 1995). Subsequently, the ABA eventually collapsed and the Nuggets, Pacers, Nets, and Spurs ended up joining the NBA. Recently, members of Congress have taken an interest in the NBA's minimum age rule for entering the top tier of professional basketball.

Historically, congressional interest in hockey has mainly stemmed from inquiries into other sports endeavors (Lowe, 1995). Although concerns about head injuries have mainly focused on football, Congress has also examined it in hockey. Current and former National Hockey League (NHL) players have testified before congressional committees about sports-related concussions.

Congress has increasingly extended its reach into the world of college athletics. Some of this interest stems from the **tax-exempt status** of the National Collegiate Athletic Association (NCAA). Members of Congress have scrutinized the NCAA regarding the commercialization of the **March Madness** Tournament and the substantial revenues generated by big-time basketball and football athletic programs. Other college athletic topics which Congress has considered deal with intellectual property issues regarding the usage of athletes' likenesses, student-athlete payments, and the unionization of college athletes. Congressional pressure also assisted in the new playoff format for crowning a National Champion in Division-I BCS college football.

Other sports-related issues for Congress to address arose after the new millennium. The attacks of September 11, 2001, demonstrated how vulnerable the country can be to acts of terrorism. Because of their high-profile nature and large spectator attendance, sporting events are ideal targets for terrorist activity. Congress and sports leagues have banded together to create legislation to enhance security measures for both professional and collegiate events.

The vast ever-changing technological innovations have caused time and space to compress. Today, parts of the world are now instantaneously connected. Many technological innovations have dramatically improved the lives of consumers. The innovations have also created problematic topics for congressional consideration. Congress has addressed these topics when dealing with Internet gambling and television carriage disputes regarding sports programming.

The list of potential sport-related topics for Congress to consider is long. Critics of congressional involvement claim Congress should concentrate on the economy, unemployment, poverty, health care, foreign affairs, terrorism, and the environment. Furthermore, critics claim members of Congress utilize sport to gain notoriety. But Congress has historically overseen many sport-related matters. Given that sport plays a significant role in the lives of their constituents, it is important to members of Congress.

The purpose of this chapter is to provide sport management students with a basic foundation covering the dynamic relationship existing between Congress and the sport industry. Congress influences sport by passing federal legislation, imposing regulatory authority, impacting the private sector, and affecting state and local issues. Sport-management students need to be cognizant of the scope and reach of Congress, and to a lesser extent, the impact of local and state government action. As a prominent professional-sport lobbyist once stated, "You might not have an interest in Congress, but Congress has an interest in you."

WHAT IS CONGRESS?

Congress is the legislative branch of the federal government. The legislative branch is one of three federal branches along with the judicial branch and the executive branch. Congress is comprised of two chambers: the House of Representatives and the Senate. Currently, 435 members (plus 5 nonvoting delegates) sit in the House of Representatives. Members of the House are referred to as representatives or a congressman/congresswoman. They represent state districts of roughly equal population. For example, the State of California has 53 representatives. The State of Wyoming has only 1 representative for the entire state. All members of the House are up for reelection every two years. The Senate is comprised of 100 senators. Each state elects two senators for a six-year term. Senators' terms are staggered so every two years one-third of the Senate is up for reelection. Each Congress lasts for two years and has two sessions. The first session of the 114th Congress will take place when Congress convenes in January 2015 and the first session of the 115th Congress will take place when Congress convenes in January 2017.

TABLE 7.1 Prominent Sport Figures Who Were Elected to Congress

Athlete	Sport	Member of Congress
Bill Bradley	New York Knicks and Basketball Hall of Fame	Senator
Jim Bunning	Hall of Fame MLB Pitcher -Tigers, Phillies, Pirates, Dodgers	Representative, Senator
Jack Kemp	NFL Quarterback – Buffalo Bills	Representative
Steve Largent	Hall of Fame Wide Receiver - Seattle Seahawks	Representative
Tom Osborne	National Championship Winning Football Coach -University of Nebraska	Representative
Jon Runyan	NFL Offensive Tackle -Titans and Eagles	Representative
Jim Ryun	Track and Field World Record Holder	Representative
Heath Shuler	NFL Quarterback - Washington Redskins, New Orleans Saints	Representative
J.C. Watts	University of Oklahoma -Quarterback	Representative

Members of the Senate and House of Representatives are politicians, policymakers, and parliamentarians (Koempel & Schneider, 2007). As politicians, they represent their constituents. Constituents are the people who reside in a member's state or congressional district. For example, constituents of Utah were upset when the University of Utah's football team did not get an invitation to play in the **Bowl Championship Series (BCS)** National Championship game despite the Utah football team going undefeated in 2008. Subsequently, Utah Senator Orrin Hatch called for Senate committee hearings on the legality of the BCS demonstrating his concern for his constituency. As policymakers, members are expected to offer new legislation when necessary (Koempel & Schneider). California Senators Dianne Feinstein and Barbara Boxer championed legislation waiving certain restrictions on foreign vessels in the waters of the United States, so the city of San Francisco could host the America's Cup sailing competition (Sullivan, 2011). As parliamentarians, members need to have detailed knowledge of the procedural rules for their specific chamber.

UNDERSTANDING THE LEGISLATIVE PROCESS

If an issue attracts the attention of the voting public, then the media, political pundits, congressional staff and politicians, and Congress tend to take notice. Members may introduce legislation, hold congressional committee hearings, and participate in floor debates (Koempel & Schneider, 2007). The legislative process can be difficult and in some cases very time consuming. In order for a measure to become law, the measure must pass both chambers with identical language. Then, the U.S. president decides whether to sign the passed measure into law. If he vetoes it, the legislation will become law anyway only if a two-thirds majority in both chambers votes to override him.

Following is an example of the timeline for passage of very noncontroversial sport-related legislation. During the 106th Congress, Congressman Luis Gutierrez introduced a bill to name a U.S. Post Office in Chicago to honor the late Roberto Clemente. Clemente, the first Latin American player to be enshrined in the Baseball Hall of Fame, was a superstar outfielder for the Pittsburg Pirates during the 1960s and 1970s. He tragically lost his life in an airplane crash during a humanitarian aid trip. Despite the bill having no known congressional opposition, its enactment still took several months.

H.R. 4831 –The facility of the United States Postal Service located at 2339 North California Avenue in Chicago, Illinois, and known as the Logan Square Post Office, shall be known as the Roberto Clemente Post Office.

- Introduced on July 12, 2000

- Referred to Committee on July 12, 2000
- Passed House October 14, 2000
- Passed Senate October 24, 2000
- Signed by President Bill Clinton on November 7, 2000 (Govtrack.US)

Even though legislation can only be introduced by members of Congress, concepts for measures can originate from multiple resources such as campaign promises, media awareness, and special interest groups (Koempel & Schneider, 2007). Congressional staff and members may develop ideas based upon campaign promises. A campaign promise might be to bring a professional sport franchise to the member's state and to support antitrust legislation to facilitate a franchise move by immunizing leagues from lawsuits. The media can spotlight issues that might lead to legislative action. In 2002, *Sports Illustrated* (*SI*) ran a cover story about steroid usage in baseball (Verducci, 2002). In the *SI* story, the 1996 National League Most Valuable Player (MVP), Ken Caminiti, became the first prominent player to publically admit to steroid usage. Caminiti confessed that he used steroids during his 1996 season and described the rampant steroid abuses in Major League Baseball. In the aftermath of the *SI* story, Senator John McCain quickly called for congressional hearings to investigate potential legislation on steroids in sports (Verducci, 2012). Special interest groups and lobbyists also provide members and staff with ideas for legislation. For example, the horse racing industry lobbied members of Congress for exemptions in online gambling legislation to ensure betting on horse races could be conducted on websites such as TwinSpires.com and TVG.com.

The executive branch can be a key igniter for legislative ideas (Koempel & Schneider, 2007). The president uses the **State of the Union Address** to outline legislative agendas and priorities. While giving this address in 2004, President George W. Bush called for the end of performance-enhancing drugs in sport. President Bush stated, "The use of performance-enhancing drugs like steroids in baseball, football and other sports is dangerous. So tonight I call on team owners, union representatives, coaches, and players to take the lead, to send the right signal, to get tough and get rid of steroids now" (Dinan, 2013). Shortly after the president's remarks, congressional committees started to investigate steroid usage in sport.

The legislation process formally begins when a measure, also referred to as a bill, is introduced by members of Congress. Approximately 10,000 bills are introduced in each two-year congressional period (Koempel & Schneider, 2007). When a bill is introduced, the measure is given a prefix and an assigned number. The prefix designates in which chamber the piece of legislation originated. If the bill is introduced in the Senate the prefix is S., and if the bill is introduced in the House of Representative the prefix is H.R. Following is an example of a sport-related bill introduced in the House of Representatives to honor baseball great Hank Aaron:

Hank Aaron Congressional Gold Medal Act: To award a Congressional Gold Medal to Hank Aaron in recognition of his contribution to the national pastime of baseball and his perseverance in overcoming discrimination and adversity to become a role model for all Americans.

The bill's number is usually assigned in the order of introduction from the beginning of each two-year congressional period. Bills remain active for the two-year period of the congressional session. If they are not enacted into law, the bills will die when Congress adjourns.

Once a bill is introduced in either the House of Representatives or Senate, the vast majority are referred to the committee having jurisdiction over the subject covered in the bill (Koempel & Schneider, 2007). A Senate bill requiring the tax code to be amended to exclude professional sport leagues from qualifying as tax-exempt organizations would be referred to the Senate Finance Committee, because this committee has jurisdiction on tax matters. When a bill is referred to committee, the legislation may be scrutinized through committee hearings which are held to shed light on the topic and gauge sentiment for the bill's enactment (Koempel & Schneider). After the hearings have concluded, legislation may move forward to the stage of markup (Gold, 2008). In markup, amendments may be agreed to, as the measure is readied for the House or Senate floor (Gold). Thereafter, the bill is reported out of the committee and placed on the legislative calendar.

The decision whether to hold hearings in the first place and to advance a measure to markup is almost entirely at the discretion of the committee chairman. But even if a bill comes through committee, such does not ensure there will ever be floor consideration. The decision to bring legislation to the chambers' floor for debate resides with the majority party leadership. Depending on the political climate, the Speaker of the House and the Senate Majority Leader can bring bills immediately to their corresponding chamber's floor or keep bills in a form of legislative purgatory by never taking up the measures. If the bills are not considered, or if they fail to pass both chambers, the legislation dies at the adjournment of Congress and the legislative processes starts all over again when a new Congress is sworn into office.

CONGRESS PASSES SPORTS LEGISLATION

Congress influences the world of sports through legislation. For instance, significant revenue is generated through selling broadcast rights; and federal legislation bears significantly on the way those rights are structured and exercised. The Sports Broadcasting Act of 1961 is an excellent example of how Congress passes legislation that affects the sport industry.

Sports Broadcasting Act of 1961

The **Sports Broadcasting Act of 1961** provided an antitrust exemption, whereby professional leagues were allowed to pool their broadcast rights. Prior to 1961, individual teams negotiated broadcast rights with television networks and independent stations (Hylton, 2011). Though the legislation was passed in late 1961, the NFL first spent time lobbying Congress. Then Congress began the formal process of taking an idea and enacting it into law.

During the summer of 1961, Congress conducted committee hearings on a proposed broadcasting bill. The bill would enable professional franchises to pool their individual rights to televise games and share revenues from the sale of those rights without fear of antitrust law violations (Ruane & Yeh, 2013). A provision was added to the bill to prohibit professional football leagues from broadcasting games on Friday evenings to protect high-school football interests and Saturdays until December to protect college football games (Lowe, 1995). The "star" of the hearings was the newly appointed NFL commissioner Pete Rozelle (Lowe).

Rozelle testified that several teams were suffering financially, because they were unable to secure lucrative television deals while teams in strong television markets were able to sign profitable broadcast contracts (Lowe, 1995). The inability for some teams to secure profitable broadcast contracts was creating a negative competitive balance for sport leagues (Lowe; Sampson & Mildner, 2010). Since smaller television market teams were unable to generate the same amount of money as larger market teams, Rozelle advocated that rights be negotiated at the league level. Doing so would ensure league stability, Rozelle said (Lowe).

Pete Rozelle (seen here testifying with Cleveland Browns owner Art Modell) was instrumental in lobbying Congress to pass the Sports Broadcasting Act.

Opponents believed the bill violated the rights of individual teams to negotiate their own contracts which could be more financially beneficial for select teams (Sampson & Mildner, 2010). The United States Justice Department feared the proposed legislation would open the door to further antitrust exemptions for sport leagues in future legislation (Lowe, 1995).

The House Judiciary Committee report on the bill reflected congressional desire to ensure a level of economic parity among professional sports teams (Ruane & Yeh, 2013). The House report contended network contracts would provide professional sport leagues with sufficient resources to sustain such parity (Ruane & Yeh). The report also noted the public interest in watching professional sporting competition justified adjusting antitrust standards for the public's benefit (Ruane & Yeh).

The Sports Broadcasting Act of 1961 passed both the Senate and House of Representatives and President John F. Kennedy signed the bill into law. Congress had acted quickly to grant the antitrust exemption for the professional leagues. Congress passed the legislation in about two months after the bill's formal introduction (Lowe, 1995). This passage ensured all teams could have their games televised and provided an economic floor to sustain competitive balance. Having secured this relief, the NFL divided the broadcast revenues so each of its clubs received an equal share. This five-decade-old policy is still in effect today. In addition, college football was protected as professional football games would not be televised on Saturdays until the college season was completed.

The benefits of the Sports Broadcasting Act provided leagues with substantial financial growth and success. The monies generated from the broadcasting rights have influenced other revenue streams. Game broadcasts have provided additional revenue-generating opportunities, including sponsorships, licensing agreements, merchandising, and tickets sales (Moran, 2013). The Sports Broadcasting Act of 1961 demonstrates how congressional legislation can significantly impact sport.

Unlawful Internet Gambling Enforcement Act

The rapid passage of the Sports Broadcasting Act showcases how Congress can move quickly on issues. However, enactment of the Unlawful Internet Gambling Enforcement Act (UIGEA) serves to demonstrate how difficult it can be for a bill to become law. From the 1990s into the new millennium, the Internet gained mass appeal and usage. During this time, Americans were wagering billions of dollars a year on **Internet gambling** websites (Doyle, 2006). Many of these online gaming endeavors were based in foreign lands and operated beyond the reach of the U.S. law enforcement authorities. Congress was concerned that Internet gambling was unregulated, failed to block access to children, allowed for opportunities for organized crime, and lacked safeguards against fraud. Congress was further worried about the addictive nature of gambling and related social and moral ills.

Starting in 1995 and over four succeeding Congresses, bills were proposed to outlaw Internet gambling. Numerous bills were introduced to expand law enforcement authority, and many measures received bipartisan support. Twice, Internet gambling legislation passed the House but not the Senate. Twice more, it passed the Senate but not the House. Enactment came only in 2006, 10 years after the first of the bills surfaced.

The measures regarding Internet gambling were important to sports entities. Representatives from professional leagues and the NCAA testified during committee hearings that legislation outlawing online wagering was needed to protect the integrity of sporting contests. These witnesses argued gambling on sporting events could create scandals that would harm the integrity of the games.

The legislation was also important to entities that host **fantasy sports** leagues and provide fantasy sports content. They worried Congress would consider fantasy sports to be a form of illegal online gambling.

During this period of Internet gambling growth, fantasy sports were also gaining mass appeal. The economic impact of revenues generated by the fantasy sport industry is extremely important for professional sport leagues and fantasy sports providers. According to a study conducted by the University of Mississippi, the impact of fantasy sports is over $1.5 billion a year (Holleman, 2006). Therefore, it was important for those involved in the fantasy sport industry to ensure the industry was exempt from illegal online gambling legislation. Early in the congressional debate about online gambling, the Major League Baseball Players Association (MLBPA) feared the fantasy sport industry would be criminalized under the original Internet gambling legislation. MLBPA's counsel testified in committee hearings that fantasy sports did not contradict the principles of public policy served by the legislation (McGettigan, 1998). Later versions of Internet gambling bills responded to these concerns with provisions exempting most forms of fantasy sports from the definition of illegal Internet gambling.

Opponents to online gambling bills came from offshore gambling website businesses, the online poker lobby, and members of Congress who believed online gambling should be regulated instead of criminalized. Las Vegas casinos originally opposed Internet gambling but some of them later came to support it as a new revenue source.

In 2006, House bills on Internet gambling emerged from two committees and were merged into one measure. It passed the House 317-93 and was sent to the Senate. Senate Majority Leader Bill Frist tacked the bill onto unrelated legislation, the SAFE Port Act of 2006. That bill, with an Internet gambling section known as the Unlawful Internet Gambling Enforcement Act (UIGEA), passed in late September. President George W. Bush signed the measure into law on October 13, 2006.

UIGEA was an enforcement tool, which blocked processing financial payments for Internet gambling transactions. The passage of illegal online gambling legislation took Congress 10 years, putting on vivid display the uncertainties and pitfalls of the legislative process.

REGULATORY AUTHORITY

The Unlawful Internet Gambling Enforcement Act of 2006 and the Sports Broadcasting Act of 1961 are two measures that illustrate the significant congressional oversight of sport. But passing sport-related legislation is not the only means by which Congress influences the sport industry. Congressional oversight of implementing regulations is also important. Congress sometimes uses the power of oversight to influence the way federal agencies enforce the law (Heniff & Keith, 2007). The relationship between Congress and regulatory authority is evident in stadium overflight restrictions and the tax-exempt status granted to professional leagues.

Stadium Overflights

The attacks of September 11, 2001, were deeply impactful on America, demonstrating vulnerability to acts of terrorism. Strongly associated with American culture, sporting events are targets for terrorists (Baker, 2007; Tolbert, 2003). Popular events such as the Super Bowl, World Series, Kentucky Derby, Daytona 500, and Michigan–Ohio State football games attract large spectator audiences. One can only imagine the terrifying catastrophes which would occur if terrorists attacked these venues. After September 11, sport-event security became the highest priority for those involved in sport (Baker).

After the attacks, the Federal Aviation Agency (FAA) prohibited pilots from flying aircrafts within three nautical miles and 3,000 feet over major professional or college sporting events (Lee, 2002). Six months later, the FAA began to grant waivers, so aircraft could fly within such restricted airspace. These waivers were of particular concern to professional sport executives, university presidents, and college athletic directors. They lobbied Congress in 2002 to create legislation with tighter restrictions on stadium overflights. The Walt Disney Company joined the sport-industry lobby to establish restricted airspace for their theme parks.

The objective of those lobbying Congress was to prevent a real-life *Black Sunday* event from occurring. *Black Sunday* is a novel by Thomas Harris where a terrorist attacks the Super Bowl with an explosive device flown over the stadium during the game. After the September 11, 2001, attacks, NFL Commissioner Paul Tagliabue stated the NFL could survive bad business decisions and mistakes, but the NFL could not survive the publicity and economic liability flowing from terrorist attacks on sporting events (Baker, 2007; George, 2001).

In support of restricted airspace for sporting events, in 2002, Senator John Breaux of Louisiana proposed an amendment to the Aviation Security Improvement Act, to restrict the airspace surrounding sporting events. Opposition to his legislation originated primarily from operators who flew aircraft towing advertising banners and aviation trade associations. Witnessing banner-towing aircraft was rather commonplace at sporting events prior to September 11, 2001. The banner-towing operators believed stadium overflight restrictions would financially harm their industry. Additionally, aviation trade associations were concerned about the effects the legislation would have on airports close to stadiums. The Aviation Security Improvement Act passed the Senate but died in the House of Representatives.

The following year, Congress passed an omnibus appropriations bill to fund the federal government for the fiscal year. Under the leadership of Kentucky Representative Hal Rogers, stadium overflight restrictions were included in the bill. An omnibus bill is a measure which combines several different appropriations bills into one (Koempel & Schneider, 2007). This bill established Temporary Flight Restricted (TFR) airspace for sporting events for one year. The TFR prohibited flights within three miles and 3,000 feet of all NFL, MLB, and NCAA Division-I football games and major motorsport events with seating capacities of 30,000 or more from one hour prior to the sporting event to one hour after the event. In 2004, Congress passed the FAA Reauthorization Act of the Consolidated Appropriations Act, which kept the TFR in place as public law and allowed waivers to the TFR for aircrafts providing safety and security, broadcast coverage, and transportation of team, officials, and equipment.

Tax-Exempt Status

Another example of Congress using its regulatory authority to influence sport is the tax-exempt status Congress has granted to professional sport leagues. During the 1966 congressional debate regarding antitrust exemption for the merger of the AFL into the NFL, Senate Finance Committee Chairman Senator Russell Long of Louisiana tacked the football leagues merger onto a tax bill to ensure passage by both chambers (Blitz, 2014; Lowe 1995). In the tax bill, a special provision was added to the Internal Revenue Code. For two decades, the NFL had operated as a tax-exempt trade association. The new tax provision strengthened the NFL's position by making explicit in law what had been a 20-year-old practice. When Congress passed Public Law 89-800 allowing for the merger, the Internal Revenue Service 501 (c)(6) code for non-profit status included the language "professional football leagues" (Easterbrook, 2013).

Noting this provision, the IRS subsequently ruled that all major professional sport leagues be permitted tax-exempt status. The NHL, Professional Golf Association (PGA), Association of Tennis Professionals (ATP), and others

(Logiuarto, 2014) have taken advantage of these rights. MLB opted out of the tax-exempt status in 2008, and the NBA has never used this status (Dosh, 2013; Weber, 2013).

Critics of the tax-exempt status for major professional sport leagues argue the leagues are taking advantage of provisions in the tax code intended for non-profit business associations. Such associations, they argue, promote industries as a whole rather than the business interests of their individual members (King, 2014). Others believe professional sport leagues that access public financing to build stadiums should not qualify for the tax-exempt status (Weber, 2013).

Professional sport leagues countered these claims by stating only their league offices are tax exempt. The leagues' offices are the administrative and organizational side of sport entities. They write rules, hire referees, coordinate drafts, and negotiate labor disputes (Spector, 2013). For example, in the NFL the monies generated from ticket sales, broadcast fees, merchandise sales, and corporate sponsorships are subject to taxation. The NFL League Office is the only entity of the NFL that is tax exempt, while the income received by the 32 teams from the league is taxable. Proponents of the tax-exempt status claim the league offices act as trade associations, which are non-profit organizations that do not engage in business activities and are used to enhance the industry or professions the associations represent (Blitz, 2014).

Several members of Congress have proposed legislation to end the tax-exempt status for professional sport. In the fall of 2013, Senator Tom Coburn from Oklahoma introduced S.1524-PRO Sports Act, which would amend the tax code to prohibit professional leagues with annual revenues over $10 million from receiving the tax-exempt status granted to trade associations and public interest groups. In January 2014, Representative Jason Chaffetz of Utah introduced a companion bill in the House of Representatives.

CONGRESS INFLUENCES THE PRIVATE SECTOR

Because of congressional involvement, issues impacting the private sector such as steroids use in baseball, a playoff system for crowning the Bowl Championship Series College Football National Champion, and television carriage disputes over sport programming have all received attention from members of Congress. The 1994 MLB season was cut short due to a labor dispute that caused the remainder of the baseball season to be cancelled, including the World Series. After the strike was resolved, many baseball fans demonstrated their displeasure by not attending games. But by the summer of 1998, baseball fans were flocking back to ballparks in large part due to the epic homerun battle between St. Louis Cardinal Mark McGwire and Chicago Cub Sammy Sosa. McGwire and Sosa raced to break Roger Maris's 1961 record of hitting 61 home runs in a season. Both McGwire and Sosa hit over 61 home runs during the 1998 season with

McGwire becoming the first player to break Maris's record. He blasted 70 homeruns for the year. Even though it took 37 years to break Roger Maris's single-season homerun record, it only took three years before Barry Bonds broke McGwire's record with 73 homeruns in 2001. As baseball attendance increased and baseballs skyrocketed out of stadiums on a more regular basis, questions were raised about the use of performance-enhancing drugs by baseball players.

MLB Steroids Congressional Hearings

In June 2002, *Sports Illustrated* ran a cover story detailing the rampant use of performance-enhancing drugs in baseball. In the *SI* expose, former National League MVP, Ken Caminiti, became the first player to publically admit to steroid use, and he claimed half of the MLB players were using steroids (Verducci, 2002).

A few weeks after the cover story was released, Senator John McCain urged Congress to address the issue. The Senate Commerce Committee responded with hearings to investigate steroid use in baseball. Senators John McCain and Bryon Dorgan urged MLB commissioner, Bud Selig, and the head of the MLB **Players Union**, Donald Fehr, that baseball include steroid drug testing in a new collective bargaining agreement (Bloom, 2002). At the time of the committee hearing, MLB did have a very limited testing program in place, monitoring only those substances that were controlled by federal law. Discipline for violations was weak in the eyes of many. Substantially stronger testing regimes existed in the NFL and NBA.

The Senate committee attempted to pressure baseball to clean up its game (Bloom, 2002). Three months after the *SI* story was released, coupled with the national media and congressional attention the story received, MLB instituted a new drug-testing policy; however, the new policy—although somewhat stronger—was unlikely to have much effect on steroid use (Denham, 2010).

During his State of the Union address in January 2004, President George W. Bush urged those involved in sport to adopt strict policies preventing the use of performance-enhancing drugs. In March 2004, the Senate Commerce Committee conducted further hearings on steroid use in sport (Denham, 2010). During the hearing, Senate Commerce Committee Chairman McCain criticized MLB for the league's lax performance-enhancing drug-testing policy (Denham). While serving as the senior senator from Delaware, Joe Biden introduced legislation

NBA Commissioner David Stern served for 30 years and was influential in building the NBA's brand and maintaining a cordial relationship with Congress.

Shutterstock, Inc.

which would become the Anabolic Steroid Control Act of 2004. Senator Biden's measure increased the list of banned anabolic steroids to include steroid precursors such as androstenedione—commonly known as Andro. A bottle of Andro was spotted by reporters in Mark McGwire's locker during his record homerun-hitting season. The measure also provided funds for educational programs for youths regarding steroids and harsher criminal penalties for individuals possessing and distributing steroids.

With the passage of the Anabolic Steroid Control Act of 2004, it appeared that Congress had made progress in ending steroid use in sport. In February 2005, retired baseball player Jose Canseco's tell-all book, *Juiced,* was released. Canseco, a former American League Rookie of the Year and MVP, was a proficient homerun hitter. Canseco admitted to steroid use while playing, but he also detailed the exploits of other steroid users in baseball.

Because of *Juiced*, members of Congress introduced several bills to end the use of performance-enhancing drugs in sport and to encourage MLB to implement stricter drug-testing policies (Denham, 2010). Although none of these measures became law, Congress was seriously considering a federal mandate on drug testing in sport. Pressure on baseball was escalating.

In March 2005, the House Oversight and Government Reform Committee held a hearing entitled, "Restoring Faith in America's Pastime" (Berenbak, 2011). ESPN broadcast live coverage of the hearing. Joining Jose Canseco and MLB Commissioner Bud Selig in testifying were some of MLB's biggest homerun hitters: Mark McGwire, Sammy Sosa, and Rafael Palmeiro. Under oath, McGwire was evasive, and Palmeiro pointed his finger at the House

Mark McGwire and Rafael Palmeiro famously testified before a 2005 House Oversight and Government Reform Committee investigating steroid use in MLB.

committee members to deny adamantly ever using steroids. Palmeiro would later be suspended that same year for violating baseball's steroid policy.

Eventually, MLB and the MLB Players Union capitulated to the threat of legislation, reopened the collective bargaining agreement, and instituted a more rigorous steroid drug-testing policy. If MLB had not taken these steps, Congress would have likely intervened with a federal program for steroid testing. In recent years, MLB has suspended several players for testing positive for banned substances. Congressional intervention through high-profile hearings and the prospect of legislation has a direct effect on private sector behavior.

Bowl Championship Series

Another example of how Congress impacts the private sector is evident by the push from members of Congress for the creation of a **college football playoff** system. From 2003 to 2009, Congress conducted various congressional committee hearings on the Bowl Championship Series (BCS) (Seifried & Smith, 2011). The BCS encompassed the premier college football bowl games (Fiesta, Orange, Rose, and Sugar) and the BCS National Championship Game for schools in the NCAA Division-I Football Bowl Subdivision (FBS). The first congressional hearing on the BCS occurred in 2003 when the Senate Commerce Committee conducted the hearing entitled, "BCS or Bust." The Senate Commerce Committee Chairman, Senator Orrin Hatch of Utah, was concerned about the fairness of the BCS. Senator Hatch took issue with the different payouts from bowl game appearances received by BCS conference schools and non-BCS conference schools in the FBS. Senator Joe Biden believed the BCS created a system of haves and have-nots in college football. Senator Jeff Sessions of Alabama stated he understood there were problems with the BCS, but he was not in favor of a playoff system to decide the college football national champion because it would increase the length of the college football season.

However, public interest and congressional support for a playoff system was gaining momentum. From 2005 to 2009, the House Energy and Commerce subcommittees held hearings on the BCS and the need for playoffs. In 2008, Representative Joe Barton of Texas introduced the College Football Playoff Act of 2008 to prevent the NCAA from calling the final college bowl game the "National Championship" until a playoff system was in place. Barton's measure died in committee, and he subsequently introduced bills with similar language in 2009 and 2011. Neither bills proceeded past the House Energy and Commerce Committee. Several House members voiced their displeasure with the BCS and discussed the need for college football playoffs during hearings and in House resolutions (Seifried & Smith, 2011). Resolutions deal with matters entirely within a specific legislative chamber and do not require the passage from the other chamber of Congress or the signature from the president. However, they do not have the force of the law (Gold, 2008). Many Senate and

House resolutions are used to express the sentiments of the specific legislative chamber (Seifried & Smith). This was the case for the House resolutions calling for a playoff system in college football.

The movement for playoffs was even raised during the presidential campaign of 2008. During the campaign, Senator Barak Obama expressed his desire for a playoff system for college football. After the election, during a *60 Minutes* interview, President-Elect Obama outlined his plan for an eight-team playoff. In July 2009, Senator Orrin Hatch penned a *Sports Illustrated* editorial calling for congressional hearings into the BCS. The editorial piece appeared a day prior to Senator Hatch conducting a Senate Judiciary subcommittee hearing on the matter. Senator Hatch questioned the legality of the BCS under the Sherman Antitrust Act and asked for the Justice Department to investigate. Senator Hatch stated legislation might be needed to ensure that all schools received an equal opportunity to compete in the championship game (Hatch, 2009). He was upset that the University of Utah football team was not invited to play in the BCS National Championship Game. The Utah Utes were one of two teams from non-BCS conferences which had gone undefeated in the regular season of 2008. The other team, Boise State, would be defeated in their bowl game. The Utes were invited to play in the BCS Sugar Bowl, where they defeated the University of Alabama. Even though the University of Utah football team was the only undefeated team in the country at the end of college football play for that year, the University of Florida was crowned the BCS National Champion because Florida won the BCS National Championship Game.

After years of additional complaints by members of Congress, the media, and the general public, in June 2012, the BCS commissioners announced there would be a four-team playoff to decide the college football champion for FBS schools. The College Football Playoff replaced the BCS, and the playoff format started after the 2014 season. The pressure from members of Congress regarding the BCS assisted in the creation of the new College Football Playoff.

Television Carriage Disputes

Congress has also affected the private sector by intervening in television carriage disputes regarding sports programming. **Television carriage disputes** occur when a broadcast or cable network, such as NBC Sports Network, and a satellite or cable provider, such as Time Warner, are unable to agree to contractual terms regarding network programming availability and pricing. This prevents subscribing customers from having access to the network's content (Roe, 2010). The Senate Judiciary Committee held hearings on television carriage issues regarding the NFL Network in 2006. When the NFL started the NFL Network, the programming content consisted of news and archived videos from NFL Films. In 2006, the NFL moved to play select games on Thursday nights, which would be broadcast on the NFL Network (Donohoe, 2013). Some members of the Senate Judiciary Committee expressed concern because the games were moved from free-over-the-air channels to the NFL Network that required payment of additional fees for access on some cable providers.

Although fans in the home and visiting team markets could continue to receive telecasts over-the-air, the move prevented other fans that did not pay for cable or satellite service from watching the Thursday night games. Senate Judiciary Committee Chairman Arlen Specter of Pennsylvania raised issues regarding which tier package the NFL Network would be available. Two cable providers, Comcast and Time Warner, were in disagreement with the NFL regarding distribution and licensing fees. The NFL did not want Comcast and Time Warner to place the NFL Network on special sports-tier packages because it would limit viewers to those who specifically paid for that content. The NFL pushed for the NFL Network to be placed on the expanded basic service tier (Hutson, 2009). The cable companies resisted because they believed the NFL was asking too high of a price for the licensing fees for the content the network provided (Hutson). Because the two sides could not come to an agreement, NFL Network's games were unavailable to Comcast and Time Warner subscribers.

The following NFL season would add further complications to the carriage issue. In 2007, the New England Patriots were one game away from becoming the first team since the 1972 Miami Dolphins to go undefeated in the regular season. For the final game of the regular season, the Patriots played the New York Giants. The game was slated to be aired on the NFL Network. Because of the television carriage disputes between the NFL and Comcast/Time Warner, many football fans would not be able to watch the game. Senator John Kerry of Massachusetts sent a letter to NFL Commissioner Roger Goodell asking the NFL to move the broadcast of the game to free over-the-air channels. Senator Kerry was considering legislative measures if the league and the providers could not resolve their disputes. Senators Patrick Leahy of Vermont and Arlen Specter also sent a letter to Goodell to pressure the NFL to make the game available to more viewers and they threatened to revoke the league's exemption from antitrust laws (Maske, 2007). Three days before the Patriots-Giants game, the NFL announced the game would be aired on free over-the-air channels and the NFL Network (Donohue, 2013). Even though the NFL did not reach an agreement with Comcast until 2009 and Time Warner until 2012 (Donohue), the pressure exerted by Congress precipitated the NFL to show the game on over-the-air channels. Football fans across the country witnessed the Patriots become the first team in 35 years to go undefeated in the regular season. Ironically, the Giants beat the Patriots a few weeks later to win the Super Bowl.

CONGRESS AND THE STATES

Another way that Congress influences the sport industry is by impacting state issues. State issues include new stadium construction financing and state-sanctioned sport betting. State and local governments compete to attract professional sport teams to their areas. They can provide incentives, such as tax subsidies, to attract sport teams and offer to build new stadiums. As will be discussed in the following section, many stadiums have been built, at least in part, through bonds issued by state and local authorities. Such bonds are exempt from federal taxation. Congress intervened with legislation to address the use of **tax-exempt bonds** for new stadium construction financing with the Tax Reform Act of 1986. Several proposals have since been made to deny the use of these bonds for stadiums, but none has been enacted.

Stadium Financing

Throughout the years, state and local governments have used tax-exempt bonds as a mechanism to fund construction of new stadiums. These bonds are a very popular way to finance construction, because the bonds provide that interest payments to bondholders are exempt from federal income tax (Howard & Crompton, 2004). By the 1980s, Congress moved to limit the use of tax-exempt stadium bonds in order to raise federal revenues and to end what some perceived as "corporate welfare" to professional-sport franchises that did not need extensive federal subsidies. One of the harshest critics of the use of tax-exempt bonds for sport facility construction was Senator Patrick Moynihan of New York. Senator Moynihan believed federal subsidies should not be used to fund the private enterprises of sport, and the bonds used to fund stadiums should be subject to taxation (Bhasin, 2000).

When Congress passed the Tax Reform Act of 1986, its intent was to place limitations on the tax-exempt status of bonds used for construction of new sport facilities. The Tax Reform Act of 1986 set up parameters to determine if a bond would be considered exempt. For a bond to qualify as being tax-exempt, the bonds needed to satisfy one of the two provisions in the Tax Reform Act of 1986 (Jensen, 2000). The first provision provided that a bond would qualify as tax-exempt if no more than 10% of the bond proceeds were used by a nongovernment entity (Zimmerman, 1996). Since professional sport teams are nongovernment entities and consume more that 10% of a facility's services during a season, qualifying under this provision would be extremely difficult (Howard & Crompton, 2004; Zimmerman).

The second provision required that a bond would qualify as tax-exempt when no more than 10% of the principal or interest payments originated from revenues generated by the stadium (Howard & Crompton, 2004; Jensen, 2000).

Despite congressional attempts to limit or end tax-exempt bonds dedicated to new stadium construction, proponents for the public financing of stadiums restructured contractual agreements in order to qualify for the tax-exempt status under the 10% revenue test. These agreements have led to favorable lease deals with state and local governments for professional sport teams. For example, a facility can be leased to a professional franchise that contributes less than 10% of the revenues toward the principal and interest payments to the debt of the bonds. In this scenario, a professional-sport team keeps the majority of the revenues a sporting event produces at the stadium thereby ensuring bonds for stadium construction remain tax exempt. The remaining repayment of the bond debt must now come from additional tax sources. These additional tax sources usually originate from dedicated local taxes such as airport taxes, hotel taxes, and rental car taxes.

After the passage of the Tax Reform Act of 1986 and the subsequent alterations of sport facility lease agreements, Senator Moynihan continued to introduce legislation to limit the use of tax-exempt bonds for stadium construction. He believed the original intent of the legislation to limit public financing of stadium construction had not been achieved. During several Senate sessions, Senator Moynihan introduced bills entitled, "Stop Tax Exempt Arena Debt Issue Act (STADIA)". The language of STADIA would reclassify bonds used for stadium financing as private activity bonds which are subject to federal taxation (Bhasin, 2000). However, the measures never passed and Senator Moynihan retired from the Senate in 2000.

Professional and Amateur Sports Protection Act

During the early 1990s, states were moving to pass legislation to authorize state-sponsored gambling in order to generate new tax revenues. In February 1991, Senator Dennis Deconcini of Arizona introduced S.474, the Professional and Amateur Sports Protection Act (PASPA) to restrict the growth of sports gambling. The goals of PASPA were to limit state-sponsored gambling, ensure the integrity of sports competitions, and reduce the promotion of sports gambling to the country's youth (Meer, 2012). Senator Bill Bradley of New Jersey, a former player on the NBA's New York Knicks, was a key proponent of PASPA.

During the debate over PASPA, state legislatures were moving to pass legislation to authorize state-sponsored sports gambling. Without federal action, Congress was concerned that state-sponsored sports betting was likely to spread nationwide (Heitner, 2010). Senator Bradley believed that if one state was to approve state legislation making sports betting legal, the rest of the states would follow suit and Congress would not be able to rescind that right from the states (Heitner, 2010). PASPA was supported by professional-sport leagues, as well as the NCAA. Then NFL commissioner Paul Tagliabue testified in Senate

Committee hearings that sports betting threatened the integrity of sports and, if allowed to spread, would erode the public confidence in amateur and professional sports (Muehle, 2012; Senate Report 102-248, 1991). Primary opposition to PASPA came from Department of Justice (DOJ) officials and Senator Charles Grassley of Iowa. They believed the measure infringed on states' rights. Senator Grassley argued the bill discriminated among states because of a grandfathered exemption in the legislation (Muehle; Senate Report 102-248).

Four states were granted grandfathered exemptions because these states had some form of sports gambling prior to PASPA being enacted. The states that received the exemptions were Nevada, Oregon, Montana, and Delaware. Proponents of PASPA did not want to threaten Nevada's economy, which is supported significantly by the gaming industry (Muehle, 2012). Delaware and Oregon had engaged in previous sport-related state lotteries (Muehle). Despite DOJ and Senator Grassley's opposition to the measure, PASPA passed the Senate in June 1992 and the House in October 1992. President George H.W. Bush signed PASPA into law on October 28, 1992 (Govtrack.us). In 2011, Governor Chris Christie signed legislation that would establish additional gambling options—including betting on sports—in New Jersey. The expansion of gambling contradicts PASPA. New Jersey brought litigation to challenge the law, but on June 23, 2014, the United States Supreme Court refused to hear an appeal from a Third Circuit Court of Appeals upholding PASPA's constitutionality.

The Tax Reform Act of 1986 and PASPA are two examples of how Congress can impact state-related sport issues. The Tax Reform Act of 1986 affects the way sport stadiums and arenas are financed. State and local governments offer favorable lease agreements to professional franchises and issue tax-exempt bonds to finance stadiums. Such governments finance tax-exempt bond debt with revenues generated from sources unrelated to stadium user chargers and rents (Zimmerman, 1996). PASPA prohibited most states from engaging in state-sanctioned sports betting, preventing them from receiving tax revenues from regulating sports gambling (Meer, 2012).

Conclusion

The effect that Congress can have on the sport industry is expansive. Congress influences sport through the passage of federal legislation. The Sports Broadcasting Act of 1961 and the Unlawful Internet Gambling Enforcement Act of 2006 are two examples of the relative ease and difficulty of enacting sport-specific legislation. Through legislation and related regulatory oversight, Congress ensures stadium overflight protections and provides for the tax-exempt status for professional sport leagues. Congress acts with committee hearings and investigations into sport-related issues such as performance-enhancing drug use, college football bowl national championship controversies, and television carriage disputes. State matters including stadium construction financing through tax-exempt bonds and PASPA legislation affecting state-sanctioned sports betting have also received considerable attention from Congress.

It is imperative that future sport managers understand the impact that Congress and other government entities can have upon sport-business practices. By affecting the statutory and regulatory environment, and through its power to command public attention, Congress influences sport organizations. While such engagement is hardly unique to sport, the high public profile and general popularity of the industry especially invites congressional attention. The sport industry exists within this legal and political environment. Those aspiring to leadership in sport management must be aware of it.

Congressional involvement in the sport industry can influence a sport organizations financial status, reputation, and corporate sponsorship opportunities. As future sport-related issues arise, considerable congressional engagement is certain.

chapter 7

Interview

Interview 7.1

Anne Marie Turner
Former lead counsel for the U.S. House Oversight Committee's investigation into professional sports

Q: Can you describe your career path?

A: After graduating law school at Pepperdine University, I moved to Jackson, Mississippi, to pursue a position as a prosecutor. I served as a Special Assistant Attorney General in the Consumer Protection Division of the Mississippi Attorney General's Office. With the Republican success in the 2002 mid-term elections, I decided to move home to Washington, D.C., to work on Capitol Hill. I spent almost four years working as counsel on the House Committee on Oversight and Government Reform for Chairman Tom Davis (R-VA) handling transportation, judiciary/law enforcement, and health issues. During this time, I also served for Chairman Davis on the Select Bipartisan Committee charged with investigating the federal government's preparation for and response to Hurricane Katrina. I then moved to the Senate side to serve as senior counsel to Senator Trent Lott (R-MS) handling his Committee on Commerce, Science, and Transportation portfolio including: transportation, telecommunications, and consumer protection issues. After Senator Lott's retirement, I spent several years consulting. In 2012, I returned to the Hill to serve as senior counsel for the Committee on Financial Services' Subcommittee on Oversight and Investigations for Chairman Spencer Bachus (R-AL) handling oversight of issues within the full Committee's jurisdiction, including the regulatory burden of Dodd-Frank implementation and the efficiency of banking regulators. After Mr. Bachus's chairmanship expired, I joined an international law firm as a partner in the Government Strategies practice group.

Q: Why does Congress have an interest in different aspects of sport?

A: When you provide a platform to politically powerful individuals who already possess a personal interest in professional sport, the members are inclined to use that platform to become engaged. They recognize they are afforded opportunities as members that aren't available in the private sector. Some of them want to capitalize on their chance to be involved in professional-sport issues. Alternatively, if you provide a platform to politically powerful individuals who believe that professional leagues receive special treatment or are not responsive enough to their unions, the members are inclined to use that platform to attempt to equalize the treatment or coerce the leagues into making concessions. Congressional interest is further heightened by the fact that oversight or legislation of high-profile topics—like professional sport—keep the members' names in the press and public consciousness.

Q: What are some of the biggest congressional issues emerging from the sport industry?

A: Over the past decade, Congress has shown interest in the professional sport leagues' drug policy and testing programs, head injuries/player safety, tax-exempt bonds for stadiums and arenas, professional leagues' antitrust exemption, and unionizing college football. Congressional issues can emerge based on news events. For example, members used the situation surrounding the controversial statements made by Los Angeles Clippers owner, Don Sterling, to reignite the call to rename the Washington Redskins.

Q: What advice would you give to sport-management students who are interested in sport public policy issues?

A: If a student is interested in sport public policy issues from a political perspective, I would advise him or her to look for positions with the House and Senate Commerce Committees or with members who serve on those committees. However, it is important to note that given the breadth of public policy issues that arise within the sport industry, one can never properly predict from where the policy issue will arise. I certainly didn't think when I accepted a job at the Oversight Committee that I would be working on sport issues.

If a student is interested in sport public policy issues from a private sector perspective, I would advise him or her to explore opportunities that will provide exposure to the departments within the leagues or associations that handle those policy issues.

Q: How do you feel the MLB Steroids House Government Reform Committee Hearing was perceived?

A: The hearing was perceived in a positive light and considered successful by those who understood that the committee's goal was to address steroid use in Major League Baseball, because the league and the players' union were not taking full responsibility for the problem. The league and its union were seen as turning a blind eye to high-profile players' obvious use of steroids and the two groups appeared to be at an impasse on negotiating a stronger policy with regard to testing and penalties. When Major League Baseball and the players' union said they were unable to move forward with a new steroid policy, the committee felt an obligation to the American people to step in and address an important public policy issue. The committee also has jurisdiction over the Office of National Drug Control Policy, so there was a natural tie-in due to the members' interest in drug-control efforts and education. Before the players and league officials testified at the hearing, the committee welcomed a panel with parents of student-athletes who committed suicide as a result of steroid use and medical experts who explained the dangers of abusing steroids. This panel set the foundation for the committee's goals, which ultimately were achieved when Major League Baseball implemented a more stringent steroid policy.

There were those who did not support the hearing because they felt it was a waste of taxpayer dollars. Those involved would respectfully disagree, as the committee addressed an issue of concern to parents, coaches, and teachers of student-athletes across the country.

Q: What was the biggest surprise from the committee hearings?

A: The biggest surprise stemming from the hearing came afterwards when it was announced that Rafael Palmeiro tested positive for steroid use less than two months after testifying, under oath, that he had never used steroids, "period." Palmeiro responded that he had never knowingly taken steroids and must have received the drug through a contaminated B12 shot. The committee conducted a thorough perjury investigation and because the steroid in question had a detection period of up to four weeks, it was impossible to prove that it was in Palmeiro's blood when he testified. Therefore, there was not enough evidence to determine that he lied under oath at the hearing. It was nevertheless a shocking turn of events.

Study Questions

1. Why will Congress continue to engage in sport-related issues?
2. What are the different ways that Congress can influence the sport industry?
3. What future sport-related issues will Congress consider and why?
4. What congressional committees have directly impacted the sport industry in the past and which ones may investigate various areas of the sport industry in the near future?
5. What members of Congress are actively engaged in sport legislation?
6. What is the most significant impact that Congress has had on the sport industry?

Learning Activities

1. Research a sport-related issue and contact the office of a U.S. representative or U.S. senator regarding the matter. Ask for the member's view on the issue and record the type of official response received.
2. Research a congressional committee hearing involving sport matters. Summarize the hearing to include the name of the congressional committee, the purpose of the hearing, members partaking in the hearing, the testimony of participants, and the short- and long-term outcome of the hearing.

References

Baker, T. (2007). Terrorism: A foreseeable threat to U.S. sport facility owners and operators. In *Issues in Contemporary Athletics* (pp. 101-112). New York: Nova Science Publishers.

Beam, C. (2009, December 09). *Interference!: Why is Congress always meddling with sports?* Retrieved from http://www.slate.com/articles/news_and_politics/explainer/2009/12/interference.html

Berenbak, A. (2011). *Congressional play-by-play on baseball.* Retrieved from www.archives.gov/publications/prologue/2011/summer/baseball.html.

Bhasin, A.K. (2000). Tax-exempt bond financing of sports stadiums: Is the price right? *Jeffery S. Moorad Sports Law Journal*, *7*(2), 181–208

Blitz, M. (2014, January 29). *Why the NFL is tax exempt*? Retrieved from www.todayifoundout.com/index/php/2014/01/nfl-tax-exempt/

Bloom, B. (2002, June 18). *Senate subcommittee investigates steroid use in baseball.* Retrieved from http://mlb.mlb.com/news/article.jsp?ymd=20020618&content_id=55784&vkey=news_mlb&fext=.jsp&c_id=null

Davis, T. (2005, March 17). Retrieved from http://www.foxnews.com/story/2005/03/17/notable-quotes-steroid-hearings/

Denahm, B. (2010). Sport, doping, and public policy. In *Sport and public policy: Social, political, and economic perspectives* (165–180). Champaign, IL: Human Kinetics.

Dinan, S. (2013). *After widely mocked pitch by George W. Bush, steroids knocked out of the ballpark.* Retrieved from http://www.washingtontimes.com/news/2013/aug/6/after-widely-mocked-pitch-by-george-w-bush-steroid/?page=all

Donohue, S. (2013). *NFL Network vs. Comcast and Time Warner Cable – Worst programming dispute of all time.* Retrieved from http://www.fiercecable.com/special-reports/nfl-network-vs-comcast-and-time-warner-cable-worst-programming-disputes-all

Dosh, K. (2013, June 6). *Examining NFL's tax-exempt status.* Retrieved from espn.go.com/nfl/story/_/id/9342479/examining-nfl-tax-exempt-status-challenged-us-senator-tom-coburn.

Doyle, C. (2006, November 15). *Internet gambling: Two approaches in the 109th Congress.* Congressional Research Service Report.

Easterbrook, G. (2013). *The king of sports: Football's impact on America.* New York: Thomas Dunne Books St. Martin's Press.

George, T. (2001, September 18). NFL is tightening security as games resume on Sunday. *New York Times*, C18.

Gold, M. (2008). *Senate procedure and practice.* Lanham, MD: Rowman & Littlefield Publishers, Inc.

Hatch, O. (2009, July 06). *Leveling the playing field: The case for congressional hearings into the BCS.* Retrieved from http://i.cdn.turner.com/sivault/.element/img/1.0/topper_sivault.jpg

Heitner, D. (2010). The plight of PASPA: It's time to pull the plug on the prohibition. *Gaming Law Review and Economics.* Retrieved from works.bepress.com/darren_Heitner/2/

Henniff, B., Jr., & Keith, R. (2007). Legislation in Congress: Federal budget process. In *Congressional deskbook, the practical and comprehensive guide to Congress* (pp. 325–370). Alexandria, VA: The Capitol.Net

Holleman, M.C. (2006, Fall). Fantasy football: Illegal gambling or legal game. *North Carolina Journal of Law & Technology*, *8*(1), 59–80.

Howard, D., & Crompton, J. (2004). *Financing sport.* Morgantown, WV: Fitness Information Technology.

H.R. 4831 (106th). Retrieved from www.govtrack.us/Congress/bills/106/hr4831

Hutson, D. (2009). Paying the price for sports TV: Preventing the strategic misuse of FCC's carriage regulations. *Federal Communications Law Journal*, *61*(2), 407–430.

Hylton, J.G. (2011). *Before the Sports Broadcasting Act: Professional football fifty years ago.* Retrieved from http://law.marquette.edu/facultyblog/2011/12/24/before-the-sports-act-professional-football-fifty-years-ago-2/

Jensen, S. (2000, Spring). Financing professional sports facilities with federal tax subsidies: Is it sound tax policy? *Marquette Sports Law Review*, *10*(2), 25–46.

King, A. (2014, January). *King backs bill to restrict professional sports leagues from qualifying as tax-exempt.* Retrieved from http://www.king.senate.gov/newsroom/press-releases/king-backs-bill-to-restrict-professional-sports-leagues-from-qualifying-as-tax-exempt

Koempel, M.L., & Schneider, J. (2007). *Congressional deskbook, the practical and comprehensive guide to Congress*. Alexandria, VA: The Capitol.Net

Lee, J. (2002, May 27). *Leagues, ads want no fly zone enforced.* Retrieved from m.sportsbusinessdaily.com/Journal/Issues/2002/05/20020527/This-Weeks-Issue/Leagues-Ads-Want-No-Fly-Zone-Enforced.aspx

Logiuarto, B. (2014, February 27). *Sweeping tax reform proposal would end tax-exempt status of pro sports.* Retrieved from www.businessinsider.com/tax-reform-nfl-tax--exempt-pro-sports-leagues-2014-2

Lowe, S.R. (1995). *The kid on the sandlot: Congress and professional sports, 1910-1992*. Bowling Green, OH: Bowling Green State University Popular Press.

Maske, M. (2007, December 20). *League receives more prodding by Congress to settle NFL Network dispute.* Retrieved from http://voices.washingtonpost.com/nflinsider/2007/12/league_receives_more_prodding.html

McGettigan, M. (1998, June 24). Hearing on H.R. 2380, Internet Gambling Prohibition Act of 1997 Before H. Comm. on the Judiciary Subcomm. On Crime, 105th Congress.

Meer, E. (2012). The Professional and Amateur Sports Protection Act (PASPA): A bad bet for the states. *UNLV Gaming Law Journa*l, *2*(2), 281–300.

Moran, T.F. (2013). The Sports Broadcasting Act: Is an update needed? *Student Scholarship.* Paper 273. http://erepository.law.shu.edu/student_scholarship/273

Muehle, M. (2012, October 24). Paving the way for legalized sports gambling. *Rutgers Law Review Commentaries*, *65*(1). Retrieved from http://www.rutgerslawreview.com/wp-content/uploads/archive/commentaries/2012/MuehlePavingTheWayForLegalizedSportsGambling.pdf

Roe, D. (2010, November 13). *What's behind the TV carriage disputes*. Retrieved from www.dailycomet.com/article/20111115/ENTERTAINMENT/10111935

Ruane, K.A., & Yeh, B.T. (2013, August 12). *Selected laws governing the broadcast of professional sporting events*. Congressional Research Service Report.

Sampson, N., & Mildner, G. (2010). Cooperation amidst competition, the nature of sports leagues. In *Sport and public policy: Social, political, and economic perspectives* (pp. 3–21). Champaign, IL: Human Kinetics

Seifried, C., & Smith, T. (2011). Congressional hearings and the Division I (Football Bowl Subdivision) postseason arrangement: A content analysis on letters, testimonies, and symposiums. *Journal of Issues in Intercollegiate Athletics*, *4*, 1–23.

Senate Report 102-248 (1991). S. 474 (102nd) Professional and Amateur Sports Protection Act. Retrieved from https://www.govtrack.us/congress/bills/102/s474

Spector, J. (2013, November 30). Don't strip away the NFL's tax-exempt status. Retrieved from www.usnews.com/opinion/articles/2013/11/30/29twotakesspector

Sullivan, P. (2011). Amid ailing economy, members of Congress delve into sports issues. Retrieved from thehill.com/homenews/house/193231-amid-ailing-economy-members-of-congress-delve-into-sports-issues

Tolbert, B.A. (2003, January 24). Playing it safe: NBA's security chief addresses New York City Law alumni.*UB Law Links*. In *Issues in Contemporary Athletics* (pp. 101-112). New York: Nova Science Publishers.

Verducci, T. (2002, June 3). *Totally juiced.* Retrieved from sportsillustrated.cnn.com/vault/article/magazine/MAG1025902/3/index.htm

Verducci, T. (2012, June 4). *To cheat or not to cheat.* Retrieved from sportsillustrated.cnn.com/vault/article/magazine/MAG 1199041/index.htm

Weber, J. (2013, December 07). *Lucrative NFL's tax-exempt status, demand for state and local money rankles lawmakers.* Retrieved from www.foxnews.com/politics/2013/12/07/lucrative-nfl-tax-exempt-status-demand-for-state-and-local-money-rankles/

Zimmerman, D. (1996, May 29). *Tax-exempt bonds and the economics of professional sports stadiums.* Congressional Research Service Report, 96-460 E.

The next section introduces three commonly utilized sport-sociology theories: functionalism, conflict theory, and critical theory.

Sociological Theories and Practical Applications

Functional Theory/Functionalism

Prior to enrolling in an introduction to sport-management course, most students' sport consumption involves attending sport events, watching or listening to broadcasts, reading a daily newspaper's sport-section or sport magazine—such as *Sports Illustrated* or *ESPN: The Magazine;* and perusing websites, including Yahoo Sports, ESPN.com, SI.com, and Rivals.com. Much of this consumption is mediated reproduction (Southall & Nagel, 2008), which is primarily uncritical and statistically oriented, consisting of game summaries and celebration of athletes, hometown franchises, or mega sport events. Much mainstream sports journalism mythologizes athletes' heroic, almost super-human athletic accomplishments, or sport's redeeming social qualities, including teamwork, discipline, hard work, and courage. Within this context, sport is often described as apolitical and a shining example of a meritocracy, where the participants are judged only on their athletic ability.

© James Rardon/fotolia

Many sport events have political undertones.

The sociological theory encapsulated in such sport consumption is **functionalist theory** or **functionalism** in which organizations, institutions, or society are viewed as rational, organized systems of interrelated parts held together by shared values and social processes that minimize differences and promote consensus among people (Coakley, 2014). Functionalism consistently supports the status quo in which sport teaches participants and spectators societal values by which they should live. In this theory sport unites people, overcoming economic, gender, ethnic, or national barriers. Sport provides a mechanism through which appropriate goals can be set and met. Such goal setting in sport translates to societal cooperation in which members of society fulfill their duties and obligations, allowing for society to provide for the common good.

Consistent with a functionalist perspective, sport is a site that represents and reinforces shared societal values and protects against insidious, radical elements (Oriard, 2009). Functionalists have also credited sports participation (e.g., American football) with imparting valuable life-lessons including loyalty, teamwork, character development, and fundamental societal beliefs in family, friends, and faith (Coakley, 2014). Further, in the United States, since at least the 1950s, in addition to an emphasis on pageantry, many large-scale sport events have also included religious and political undertones, represented by the inclusion of elements such as the national anthem (since World War II), fireworks, giant American flags, patriotic music, and military flyovers.

However, it should be noted a functionalist perspective often exaggerates sports' positive effects. In addition, in many societies there has been a long history of intertwining politics and sport. Consequently, both become entangled in the public's mind with the dominant group's values. Sport, whether in the form of the Olympics or high-school sports, has often been seen as the bastion of the common person. Such a traditional view of sport tends to minimize the possibility that sport is socially constructed and may disproportionately benefit some groups or individuals and exploit others.

Applying Functionalism—Unsporting Behaviors

Going back to our discussion of unsporting behaviors (e.g., verbally taunting or insulting an opponent, making politically or socially "charged" comments to sideline reporters), it is evident that in the United States certain on- and off-the-field or court behaviors by American football and basketball players are routinely penalized, and almost universally criticized by a particular segment of the sport media, as well as sports fans, because they feel they detract from the "spirit or essence of the game." (Note: This "fan segment" will be included in our conflict and critical theory discussions later in the chapter.) Through the years, in college or professional sports, "antics" such as taunting, "trash talking," choreographed or excessive celebrations (e.g., dancing), dunking, uniform dress-code violations, or removing a helmet while on the field have all been identified, at one time, as unsporting and criticized by coaches, media, and fans.

From a functionalist perspective, sport fosters societal values of teamwork, fair play, honesty, and humility. Since in "team" sports the team is inherently paramount, from a functionalist perspective team members should refrain from any actions that focus attention on themselves as individuals. A functionalist would note, trash talking and taunting are fundamentally rude and "thuggish" and often provoke physical violence.

An example of a functionalist reaction to "drawing undue attention" to oneself is the reaction by much of the "mainstream" media and many message-board fans to Richard Sherman's post-game interview after the 2014 National Football Conference (NFC) Championship Game. Late in the game, Sherman (All-Pro cornerback for the Seattle Seahawks) had made a "game saving" deflection of a pass intended for San Francisco 49ers wide receiver Michael Crabtree.

Shutterstock, Inc.

Richard Sherman's stellar play and controversial actions are perceived differently by various followers of the National Football League

The headline of a *NY Daily News* article—"Seahawks' Richard Sherman screams about Michael Crabtree in postgame interview with Erin Andrews"—was indicative of the vitriol directed at Sherman. Rob Raissman, *NY Daily News* columnist sarcastically derided Sherman for showing "…his 'sensitive' side in a postgame rant" (2014, para. 2). Raissman focused on Sherman's remark during the interview, "I'm the best corner in the game! When you try me with a sorry receiver like Crabtree that's the result you are going to get!" (Raissman, 2014, para. 4). While Sherman's statement was clearly boastful, Raissman repeatedly described Sherman as screaming, being "bug-eyed," and selfish. No mention was made that before and during the game numerous players from both teams (as is the norm in the NFL) engaged in trash talking.

Not surprisingly, in today's sport and entertainment industries, Sherman's post-game "trash talking" took on a life of its own on social media. The tweets from Sherman and San Francisco 49ers wide receiver Michael Crabtree (the player for whom the pass Sherman deflected had been intended) also elicited responses from several "functionalist" athletes, including Justin Verlander, 2011 American League Cy Young Award–winning pitcher for Major League Baseball's (MLB) Detroit Tigers, who suggested that if Sherman was an MLB player he would throw at him: "So Russell is a class act! Sherman on the other hand.... If he played baseball would get a high and tight fastball" (Raissman, 2014, para. 14). Interestingly, the mainstream media did not view Verlander's reference to a violent response (e.g., a pitcher throwing at a batter) to Sherman's braggadocio as an unsporting behavior, but simply as an "unwritten rule of baseball."

Functionalists claim prohibitions against unsporting behaviors serve to promote "civil" behavior. In addition, prohibitions are justified for safety reasons (e.g., hanging on the rim after a dunk in a basketball game), or because such behaviors delay or detract from the game action. A functionalist would argue: "Just as 'There's no crying in baseball,' there should not be excessive celebration in sports." Within a functionalist framework, decorum in sport, as in society, allows for cooperation and for everyone to get along. For a functionalist the answer to our question remains: "All sports require rules. Just as in society, a sport's rules should be enforced." (Note: Such a viewpoint is consistent with the deontological ethical framework presented in Chapter 5—Ethics and Ethical Decision Making.)

Conflict Theory

In contrast to functionalism, which emphasizes sport's positive social characteristics, **conflict theory** emphasizes social and political inequalities and the resulting economic and power differentials that occur in the sport context. A conflict-theory analysis of sport focuses on the inherent and endemic conflicts that arise from economic disparities. Rather than occurring as a result of members of society performing their "natural" duties, social order is maintained through a political economy, in which certain groups (e.g., rich and powerful) maintain their economic advantage through coercion and exploitation. The media, business entities, political systems, educational institutions, and sport are examples of institutions that shape society's political economy. In this theory, sport, similar to other societal institutions, is shaped by society's economic structures. Contrary to functionalism, conflict theorists contend societal order results not from consensus, but from economic power and the use of such power to exploit labor.

Conflict theory emphasizes social and political inequalities and the resulting economic and power differentials, and focuses on the inherent and endemic conflicts that arise from economic disparities.

Southall and Nagel's (2009) jock capitalism critique, which epitomizes a conflict-theory perspective, raises the following issues:

- Sport as an "opiate of the masses" or "beer and circus" (See Sperber, 2001.)
- Increased professionalism in college sport
- Exploitation of minority athletes in college sport
- Sport as a tool of militarism/nationalism
- Sport and sexism
- Sex and racism
- Public subsidization of professional sport

Applying Conflict Theory—Unsporting Behaviors

One criticism of the sportspersonship justification for penalizing such behaviors is the inconsistency of such penalties and criticisms. Similar behaviors by athletes of different ethnicities often receive different interpretations and different sanctions by sport leagues, organizations, and fans. Often, it is pointed out, rule-making and enforcing individuals, as well as many of the offended fans, are ethnically different from the "offensive" athletes. In addition, what is acceptable behavior in one sport setting is roundly criticized in another (e.g., in professional football the "Lambeau Leap," in which Packers players jump into the end zone stands after a touchdown is a time-honored tradition [though it is less than 25 years old], but in college football an "excessive celebration" penalty may result from nothing more than too exuberant of a high-five). In addition, fighting is tolerated in hockey, but not in football, basketball, and many other sports.

An example of this double standard was the consistent fines that premier National Football League (NFL) wide receivers Terrell Owens and Chad Johnson (Ochocinco) accrued during their careers. Both players were consistently criticized for their "excessive" and choreographed unsporting behaviors. Similar to the criticism of Richard Sherman that we discussed in the functionalist-theory section, criticism of Owens and Johnson focused on their behaviors being disrespectful to their opponents and to the game of football (as it is "meant to be played"). Meanwhile, college basketball coaches often argue with referees, use foul language in public, and yell at their players in

Fighting may be acceptable in hockey but not in other sports.

front of thousands of spectators. Some sport sociologists suggest that while such actions by coaches may sometimes be criticized, they are more often excused as necessary elements of coaching and often helpful in maintaining player discipline.

While players are consistently criticized for behaviors that draw the spotlight to them as entertainers, historically coaches' unsporting behaviors have been overlooked. While Indiana University President (and later NCAA President) Myles Brand famously fired men's basketball coach Bob Knight for unsporting behaviors, Knight exhibited such behaviors consistently throughout his career. It should be noted that recently (2013-2014) the standard of what is unacceptable behavior by college coaches has seemingly begun to change. In what appears to be a response to increased public scrutiny of big-time college sport, two fairly high profile NCAA Division-I men's basketball coaches—Mike Rice (Rutgers University) and Doug Wojcik (College of Charleston)—were fired for physical, emotional, and/or verbal abuse of their players.

In sports, penalties are designed to compensate for participant actions that result in an unfair competitive advantage. Penalties are necessary to restore and maintain a "level playing field." However, in the case of "unsporting" behaviors, it is hard to see how engaging in them provides much, if any, competitive advantage, since most of them have to do with behavior that takes place outside the real-time competition itself. They have little, if any, influence on the outcome of the contest.

From a conflict-theory perspective, a relevant—and often overlooked—point is that "institutionalized" behavioral penalties in football and basketball (in the United States) are most often assessed to black male athletes. The disproportionate number of such penalties is because they more often engage in such behaviors, which reflect a distinctive black male urban culture (Cunningham, 2009; Simons, 2003). These penalties quite often occur during a "stoppage in play" or after a score. In football, for example, celebrating by taking off one's helmet, taunting, and inciting the crowd occur after play has stopped. In basketball, some of the behaviors such as inciting the crowd, trash talking, and taunting, or hanging on the rim, most often do not take place during play. Interestingly, while one function of trash talking is to intimidate or "get into the head" of an opponent (which may provide some small competitive advantage), most often the overall competitive effect of these unsporting behaviors is minor compared to "competitive advantage" behaviors.

Since the behaviors under discussion do not produce a competitive advantage in the first place, penalizing them places one team at a competitive *disadvantage* and may contribute to an "uneven playing field." The penalties, in fact, contradict the level-playing-field justification for penalizing rule violations. Most penalties attempt to compensate for the competitive advantage gained by the offending team and restore the "level playing field." Interestingly, in U.S. professional football and basketball, the competitive disadvantage of such behaviors is compounded by frequent player suspensions, which preclude the punished athletes from playing in subsequent game(s).

From a conflict-theory perspective, a history of exclusion from "White" society, as well as a historical clustering in certain sports (e.g., football and basketball), American Black male athletes have developed a set of distinctive behavioral cultural patterns (Boyd, 2003; Lane, 2007). These patterns are distinct from jock capitalism's and White middle-class behavioral expectations (Cunningham, 2009; Southall & Nagel, 2009). Many of the behavioral patterns exhibited in these penalized behaviors are usually associated with a subculture with the following social markers: male, African-American, inner city, and/or "hip-hop" sports. "Talking smack" in sports is synonymous with African-American verbal aggressiveness. However, Gates's (1998) theory of African-American literary criticism argues such verbal aggressiveness is part of a long African oral tradition of "signifying" (i.e., saying one thing and meaning something else). Therefore, trash talking, celebration dances, and other expressive behaviors serve multiple functions for the Black athlete; they both heighten competitive motivation and add enjoyment to the game (Andrews, Mower, & Silk, 2010; Boyd, 2003; Eveslage & Delaney, 1998).

Based upon their adoption of a functionalist perspective, many Whites (especially those in positions of authority and power in sport) interpret these behaviors as offensive to White male upper- and middle-class sensibilities and the epitome of poor sportspersonship. Specific to football and basketball, these sports' appropriate or "sporting" behaviors perpetuate the beliefs and attitudes of a predominantly White economic and political system maintained through control of institutions such as schools, media, and sports. To functionalists, these behaviors show a lack of humility, demean and embarrass an opponent, call attention to an individual, and serve to incite a crowd. In addition, these Black males' aggressive behaviors play on White fear of them, leading to physical aggression, which may cause the game to get out of control. As a result these behaviors, which are inconsistent with "accepted" cultural norms, are frequently penalized and labeled "deviant, thuggish, immature, etc." Within the context of sport, this sporting ideology (represented in the institutionalizing of behavioral penalties) supports and maintains the dominant group's cultural hegemony.

Critical Theory

Critical theory is most often credited with having been first developed in 1923 by several scholars at the Institute for Social Research, in Frankfurt, Germany. This theory sought to explain why the socialist revolution prophesied by Marx had failed to materialize. One of the basic elements of critical theory, which focuses on the consequences of socioeconomic class disparities, is that contrary to viewing capitalism as a rational, organized system that minimizes differences and promotes consensus among people, it is a system that promotes and protects the interests of the hegemon (dominant group). According to critical theory many workers "mistakenly" perceive their lives as products of an unchangeable, rational, and inevitable social nature (Agger, 1991; Gramsci, 1971; Horkheimer, 1972). Critical theorists contend capitalists seek to maintain the economic status quo (e.g., capitalism), which serves to protect their interests.

From a critical-theory perspective, capitalists often utilize a view of sport as an apolitical meritocracy to exert their economic and social dominance (hegemony). For example, Southall and Staurowsky (2013) argue exploitation of revenue-sport athletes relies on this false consciousness in order to justify corporate-college-sport hegemony (Sack, 1987; Sack & Staurowsky, 1998):

> After more than five decades, through sophisticated and subtle sociological propaganda, the NCAA national office has achieved spontaneous consent to its collegiate model. This consent has involved almost unanimous approval and support by some (i.e., coaches, conference commissioners, and administrators, corporate partners), and "moral and political passivity" (Gramsci, 1971, p. 333) by others (i.e., presidents, FAR's, and athletes) to the ever-increasing commercial forces and corporate partnerships that place primary importance on big-time football and men's basketball as valued entertainment commodities (p. 421).

Several scholars and media observers (e.g., Hruby, Nagel, Nocera, Rascher, Schwarz, Southall, Staurowsky) have noted recent attempts by U.S. college athletes in the revenue-generating sports of football and men's basketball to assert their workplace, and name, image and likeness rights (e.g., see National Labor Relations Board [NLRB] ruling [2014] and *O'Bannon v. NCAA* [2014]) are primarily intended to address economic inequities within the Collegiate Model of Intercollegiate Athletics. This analysis is consistent with Gramsci's (1971) ideological formulation that workers (e.g., U.S. college and professional team-sport athletes) do have the ability to influence the terms of their consciousness. Consequently, while some college and/or professional players may be trapped within a "false consciousness," critical theorists contend that in the later half of the 20th and the beginning of the 21st century, sport has witnessed an extended ideological struggle between the *domination* of hegemons (i.e., professional-league owners, dictatorial governments, and/or intercollegiate-athletics administrators) and workers' struggle (e.g., U.S. college and professional team-sport players) against such domination.

Domination, in critical theory, is a combination of external exploitation (e.g., the extraction of college profit-athletes' surplus value) and internal self-disciplining that permits unchecked and self-fulfilling external exploitation (Agger, 1991; Horkheimer, 1972; Southall & Staurowsky, 2013). In sport-sociology terms, most sports participants adopt a functionalist perspective and internalize corporate sport's dominant values and norms. This spontaneous consent induces them (e.g., U.S. college profit-athletes) to "willingly" participate in the division of productive and reproductive labor within a corporate-sport setting. Parsons (1991) called this willing participation an example of the "Hobbesian problem of order." Applying this problem to a corporate-sport setting, the question becomes: "Why do people obey sports'—as well as non-sports'—rules within corporate-sport?"

One explanation is that when people are trapped within a contradictory or false consciousness they adopt a mental and emotional state that fluctuates between resistance and conformity, disagreement and apathy (Gramsci, 1971; Southall & Staurowsky, 2013). In sports' settings, just as functionalism contends, participants share certain common values and beliefs that explain their sport-participation to them in a rational way. In particular, participants believe sports are a *meritocracy* in which they can achieve modest personal and social betterment by complying with social norms. But consistent with Gramsci (1971), athletes most often believe (e.g., Michael Jordan, Tiger Woods) that large-scale social changes beyond this are impossible. Consequently—for the most part—modern college and professional athletes abide by sport's rules.

Applying a critical-theory analysis to U.S. college sport, while jock capitalists have never completely achieved unanimous consent to the NCAA Division-I Collegiate Model, exploited profit-athletes are divided and ambiguous in their consciousness, unable to break away from the accepted "folklore" (Gramsci, 1971) that they are "student-athletes." The NCAA-created term (student-athlete) has served for over 50 years as a linguistic and philosophical "armor of coercion" (Adamson, 1980, p. 215) that protects the business interests of corporate stakeholders (i.e., Nike, CBS, adidas, ESPN, Fox Sports, etc.).

Approaches to Sport Socialization

As can be seen, different theoretical perspectives result in distinctively different analyses. The disagreements are based on each theory's inherent fundamental assumptions. These theoretical differences fuel many "heated" sport-issue discussions among fans, students, faculty members, and sport-industry professionals. They form the storylines for many elements of sports-talk radio and TV, sport blogs, websites, and Twitter posts.

Sociological theories help sport-management students investigate how members of society undergo socialization, an active process through which each societal member develops ideas of who they are and what is important to them. This socialization is interactive and ongoing. Each of us affects and influences others, and interprets and accepts/rejects social cues and signals. Various sociological theories provide different socialization perspectives. A functionalist looks at socialization as a process of learning society's rules and roles. A functionalist approach to sport socialization is most interested in studying who and what causes people to participate in sports and the effects (most often assumed to be positive) that sport participation produces. This approach assumes sport participation prepares athletes to assume roles as productive members of society. Most often a functionalist socialization perspective operates from the underlying assumption that sports participation is a "good" thing.

A conflict-theory approach to sport socialization assumes that, while such socialization is an internal and interactive process, its primary purpose in our society is to support capitalism's need to influence societal members in order for them to become sport consumers and sport managers within the existing economic system. This perspective looks at how our existing sport structures replicate and support racist, sexist, militaristic, and apolitical orientations among consumers, participants, and managers. This perspective focuses on how the existing economic system often disproportionately denies sports opportunities to poor and minority athletes, consumers, and sport managers.

A Multiple-Perspective Approach?

After this brief introduction to these sociological perspectives, a sport-management student may have several questions:

- Is there a correct perspective?
- I want to work in the sport industry. How can I adopt a conflict perspective and still work in this field?
- I think sport is a good thing. What purpose does it serve to focus on the negative?
- Instead of adopting a single perspective, is it possible to utilize some elements from more than one theory, while conceding sport may have positive and negative effects?

Adopting a multiple-perspective approach may allow students interested in exploring a sport-management career to concede our modern sport industry may legitimize existing economic and political power structures.

Such a multiple-perspective approach does not depoliticize a sociological examination of the sport industry. It allows that facets of the privatized corporate sport industry, as it is presently constructed, may have negative social implications. In addition, this approach also contends sport does not necessarily have to exclusively exhibit these characteristics, but can also be more egalitarian and inclusive. However, it should be recognized that elements of a more democratic sport culture might not be totally accepted within the modern sport industry in which many sport-management students seek employment. This envisioned "hybrid" sport culture might not be the "idealized" sport culture envisioned by sport-management students or those who presently work in the sport industry. As a result, sport-management students who are sympathetic to such a perspective, but also aspire to be sport managers, may need to reevaluate their career aspirations and make a series of ethical decisions (see Chapter 5) throughout their careers.

Examining Sport Organizations and Sport as an Institution

In addition to investigating sport's place in society, in order to examine where they might fit within the sport industry, sport-management students should be able to examine sport organizations and institutions. Two theoretical frameworks useful in examining individual sport organizations as institutions within society are **organizational culture** and **institutional logics**. In order to use these frameworks, it is necessary to spend some time discussing each theory's elements. We will first define and delineate the fundamentals of organizational culture theory and then do the same for the theory of institutional logics. Finally, using both theories, we will examine specific sport organizations and as well as various institutions within the sport industry.

Organizational culture
Pattern of basic assumptions that a given group has invented, discovered, or developed in learning to cope with its problems of external adaptation and internal integration, and that have worked well enough to be considered valid, and therefore, to be taught to new members as the correct way to perceive, think, and feel in relation to those problems (Schein, 1984).

Institutional logics
A set of material practices and symbolic construction, which constitutes an institution's organizing principles. Such institutional logics (a) determine what are considered acceptable or unacceptable operational means, (b) establish routines, (c) guide the evaluation and implementation of developed strategies, and (d) create precedent for further innovation.

Organizational-Culture Theory

Definitions of Organizational Culture

There have been numerous definitions proposed for organizational culture. The concept of "culture" has its roots in anthropology and sociology, and organizational studies focusing on organizational behavior and psychology. While not the first researcher to define organizational culture, Schein (1984) developed an often-cited definition:

> Organizational culture is the *pattern of basic assumptions* that a *given group* has *invented, discovered, or developed in learning to cope* with its *problems of external adaptation and internal integration,* and that have *worked well enough to be considered valid,* and therefore, to be *taught to new members* as the correct way to *perceive, think, and feel* in relation to those problems (p. 46). (Emphasis in original.)

Schein (1983) also summarized these patterns of basic assumptions as:

1. The organization's relationship to its environment—Is this relationship one of dominance, submission, harmonizing, finding an appropriate niche, or some combination?

2. The nature of reality and truth—This involves linguistic and relational rules that define what is a "fact" and whether truth is "discovered" or "revealed."
3. The nature of human nature—Centered on questions of what it means to be human, is human nature intrinsically "good or evil"?
4. The nature of human activity—What is the right thing to do, based on the above assumptions? What is work and what is play?
5. The nature of human relationships—What is the right way for people to relate to each other, and distribute power and love? (p. 16)

In short, an organization's culture is its organizational "reality."

Consistent with this definition, Peterson, Cameron, Jones, Mets, and Ettington (1986) noted that organizational culture serves to emphasize an organization's unique or distinctive character, which provides a subordinating meaning to members, is deeply embedded and enduring, and is not malleable, changing primarily by cataclysmic events or through slower, intensive, and long-term efforts.

Dominant Culture and Subcultures

Schein's (1984) definition of culture presupposes that an organization must *own* a culture in order for that culture to exist. As a result, an organization's cultural beliefs are its taken-for-granted beliefs. Similar to societal norms, an organization's culture forms the basis of an organization and its members' view of reality. According to this view, such accepted organizational beliefs are not open to interpretation.

However, Martin and Siehl (1983) offered a variation on Schein's single-level "given-group" approach and proposed that an organization's culture often consisted of a dominant culture and at least three subcultures that may exist at any time in an organization. A dominant culture "expresses, through artifacts, core values shared by a majority of the organization's members" (p. 53). According to Koene, Boone, and Soeters (1997) a coherent organizational culture emerges ". . . through the social interaction between organization members" (p. 276). In addition, an organization's dominant culture is strengthened " . . . by weeding out individuals with different opinions and hiring employees with personal views congruent with those of other organization members" (p. 277).

Sport organizations often have strong dominant cultures, and all members of the organization are expected to adhere to the dominant culture. Those members who do not subscribe to this dominant culture will often be asked or forced to leave the organization. Research on college sport reveals that it is quite common for newly hired coaches to "run-off" a former coach's players who do not share his/her organizational culture values (Hill, Mitchell, & Southall, 2010). For example, in 2009 the University of Kentucky's men's basketball program, in the aftermath of hiring John Calipari, had a 60% roster turnover (Hill et al., 2010). The pronouncement that a sport organization is "going in a different direction" may often reflect an attempt to shift a franchise or program's organizational culture. Since sport organizations, like many other entities, expect members to adhere to the organization's culture, prior to seeking employment with a sport organization, sport-management students should attempt to learn as much about "how things are done" within the organization, so they can ascertain the extent to which their personal values are consistent with the organization's cultural values. Sport organizations should also emphasize the organization's culture and norms to interviewees and new employees so they can more seamlessly integrate into the organization.

Types of Subcultures

Even though sport organizations may have a dominant organizational culture, not every organizational member will completely internalize the organization's dominant cultural values. Such members may be part of what have been called organizational subcultures. Martin and Siehl (1983) contend such subcultures exist in all organizations. They identified one type of organizational subculture as an *enhancing* subculture. This subculture reflects O'Reilly and Chatman's (1996) idea of extreme organizational value internalization. An enhancing subculture exists in an " . . . organizational enclave in which adherence to the core values of the dominant culture would be more fervent than in the rest of the organization" (pp. 53–54). The members of an enhancing subculture think of themselves and are viewed by others as "true believers."

In sport, members of an enhancing subculture may engage in what Coakley (2014) refers to as *overconformity,* the unquestioned acceptance of cultural norms. Overtraining, utilizing performance-enhancing drugs (PEDs), working long hours, ignoring family and friends in order to accomplish organizational goals are all examples of overconformity. Such extreme adherence to organizational norms may create conditions that result in blind faith in an ideal, a leader, or belief system.

Another type of organizational subculture is an *orthogonal* subculture. An orthogonal subculture is comprised of members who accept the core values of the dominant culture, but have separate, though not conflicting, assumptions, values, beliefs, and possibly goals that are unique to their particular group. This group's dominant content themes are still congruent with the dominant culture's content themes, but the members also have unique points of emphasis. For example, a sport franchise's coaching staff and its marketing and sales staff may share the core values of the franchise's dominant culture, while still having separate values specific to their roles within the organization. Coaches are focused on winning games, while the marketing and sales staffs are focused on getting fans in the stands! There is no fundamental conflict between these two goals, but most often coaches are not concerned with the marketing mix, and may actually view in-game promotions as intruding upon the game.

A third type of subculture is a *counterculture.* Counterculture members possess core values in direct opposition to the dominant culture and represent a challenge to the dominant culture. Martin and Siehl (1983) proposed that a counterculture's artifacts and practices often "ridicule" elements of the dominant culture's values, and actually support a competing alternate set of values. Members of a counterculture may engage in *underconformity* or deviance based upon ignoring or rejecting organizational norms (Coakley, 2014). Martin and Siehl contend strongly-centralized organizations that permit decentralized diffusions of power are more likely to give rise to nonconforming subcultural enclaves. Such enclaves may include a charismatic challenger who may later be absorbed by the organization in an attempt to deal with the *counterculture.* This absorption is accomplished by giving the challenger " . . . limited power, some formal structural autonomy, and a tacit mandate to gather followers and create a nonconforming enclave" (p. 54) that the organization will seek to control. This absorption of the charismatic leader by the dominant culture actually serves, in many ways, to isolate the countercultural threat. By granting the counterculture some measure of autonomy, innovative ideas and practices may arise. If the results are beneficial to the organization, they can be co-opted by the dominant culture and embraced. On the other hand, if the deviance is not advantageous to the organization, it has been isolated.

In sport the identification of countercultures has often been seen as a direct challenge to an organization's legitimacy. Since many sport organizations are highly structured, with strong "chains of command," countercultures are often not tolerated. College football in the 1960s, including the integration of the Southeastern Conference (SEC) and the changing relationship between coaches and players, has been viewed as an example of societal changes that resulted in the development of subcultures within college football programs that challenged their dominant organizational cultures (Oriard, 2009).

Applying Theory to Practice—Big-Time College Athletic Departments

Intercollegiate athletic departments are increasingly diverse organizations. Not surprisingly, organizational culture research has found members of NCAA Division-I college athletic departments are highly competitive and value having a good reputation. However, it has also been found that since coaches and administrators often have divergent organizational backgrounds, distinct subcultures exist both between and within athletic departments (Putler & Wolfe, 1999; Southall, 2001; Southall, Wells, & Nagel, 2005).

Division-I university athletic departments' subcultures can be broken down into three basic "enclaves." These subcultures are (1) female non-revenue sport coaches, (2) male non-revenue sport coaches, and (3) revenue sport coaches. Not surprisingly, there are significant differences in these coaches' perceptions of departmental expectations regarding winning. As might be expected, the male-revenue-sport coaches' subculture places a higher value on winning and revenue production. They also feel more constrained by departmental and NCAA rules than any other group (Southall, 2001; Southall et al., 2005). Interestingly, research has also revealed NCAA Division-I women's basketball coaches' views are more similar to those held by male revenue-sport coaches than other women's sport coaches. This suggests revenue-production status, not gender of the sport, may be a critical factor. In addition, the fact that the number of women coaching women's college teams is at an all-time low (42.8%) (Metcalfe, 2008) may also be a factor.

Such research is of interest to managers, since they need to be aware of a subculture's values and determine if the subculture is an enhancing, orthogonal, or counter culture. If it is determined that the subculture is, in fact, a counterculture (with values at odds with the stated values of the organization), then the organization should take steps to address this situation. In any sport organization, not everyone is on the same page when it comes to core organizational or cultural values. Like any organization, a college athletic department may often reflect a complex and chaotic clash of organizational values. This is important, since research has found organization members who do not agree with an organization's predominant espoused value system are more likely to engage in organizational deviance (e.g., flout NCAA compliance regulations, not support a marketing campaign, or not pay attention during emergency management planning meetings) (Santomier, Howard, Piltz, & Romance, 1980; Padilla & Baumer, 1994). Athletic directors must work to develop a cohesive workforce, while still equitably managing their department. It should come as no surprise that subcultures exist within professional franchises, parks and recreation departments, or high-school sport teams. Any sport organization is an intricate product of complex, interdependent factors and people, all of whom operate to fulfill their own wants, needs, and desires. In addition, it is important that students who wish to work in the sport industry recognize that since cultural values are creations of people interacting with one another, they cannot be mandated by an outside organization (e.g., the NCAA, National High School Federation, or NFL Commissioner's Office).

Theory of Institutional Logics

A theory useful in examining sport as an institution is the theory of institutional logics. While organizational culture theory focuses on individual organizations, institutional-logics theory is useful in examining the sport industry as a collection of institutions. It has been argued that Western society's major institutions, including Christianity, capitalism, the family, democracy, and the bureaucratic state, have logics that guide action (Friedland & Alford, 1991). In addition to investigations focused on the societal level, there have been field or industry-level examinations in various industries, including financial services

(Lounsbury, 2002), educational publishing (Thornton, 2002), professional sport in the United States (Cousens & Slack, 2005), English rugby union (O'Brien & Slack, 2004), and American college sport (Southall & Nagel, 2008; Southall et al., 2008, Southall, Brown, Nagel, & Southall, 2014).

From this theoretical perspective, each institution within the sport field as Friedland and Alford (1991) noted has " . . . a central logic—a set of material practices and symbolic construction—which constitutes its organizing principles and which is available to organizations and individuals to elaborate" (p. 248). Such institutional logics determine what are considered acceptable or unacceptable operational means, establish routines, guide the evaluation and implementation of developed strategies, and create precedent for further innovation (Duncan & Brummett, 1991; Friedland & Alford; Nelson & Winter, 1982; Washington & Ventresca, 2004). These logics manifest themselves as generalized expectations that allow individuals within sport to engage in coherent, well understood, and acceptable activities. In this sense, then, institutional logics influence how people working within sport communicate, enact power, and determine what behaviors to sanction and reward (Barley & Tolbert, 1997). Eventually, these logics become taken-for-granted "facts" reflected in particular unquestioned courses of action.

Similar to individual organizations, as institutions develop, competing institutional logics may emerge. Such conflict most often results in the emergence of a dominant logic that works to establish local-meaning frameworks that guide strategy and structure by focusing the attention of decision makers towards those issues that are most consistent with the perceived dominant logic and away from those issues that are deemed to be inconsistent (Thornton, 2002).

Applying Theory to Practice— Bowl Championship Series Football Broadcasts

Just as it is important to identify the organizational culture of a sport franchise or athletic department to which they have submitted an application, students should be familiar with a sport institution's overarching material practices and organizing principles. Within big-time NCAA Division-I college sport (e.g., NCAA Football Bowl Subdivision [FBS] and NCAA D-I men's basketball) and two specific sport products (Bowl Championship Series [BCS] and March Madness television broadcasts) there are great opportunities to apply institutional logics theory. As you read the section, pay attention to how the research results are discussed in relation to the theory, and how the theory provides a context for better understanding the sport product.

Big-Time College Sport Telecasts

There is no question NCAA Division-I college sport occupies a central place in American culture. In his 2009 State of the Association address, Dr. Myles

Brand (late president of the NCAA) noted: "[College sport] has become integral to many of our universities and colleges, institutions which are the guardians of our traditions and histories and the harbingers of our futures. College sports generates (sic) a significant economic impact in communities all across the country" (National Collegiate Athletic Association, 2009, para. 14).

University administrators, as well as NCAA National Office executives and network broadcast partners, rarely—if ever—directly address conflicts between educational and commercial logics within the field of college sport. However, they consistently acknowledge the need for increased commercialism in college sport. Since 2003, the NCAA and member D-I universities have consistently embraced increased college-sport commercialization. In fact, the NCAA and university presidents have been applauded by corporate partners for their recognition that " . . . there should be more, not less, [commercialism] as long as it stays within the framework of amateurism and promotes the accomplishments of the athletes and their teams" (Smith, 2009, p. 28). This sense of cooperation is evident in the statement of Tim McGhee, executive director of corporate sponsorship at AT&T, an NCAA corporate champion, " . . . I see an NCAA that is more responsive to corporate partners and how we market our products and services" (Smith, p. 28).

However, Bob Lawless, NCAA Executive Committee Chair, seemed to recognize the possibility of such conflict, noting "There's a realization that when you receive a certain amount of revenue from a network that they're going to generate revenue in order to meet the agreement of the contract" (National Collegiate Athletic Association, 2002, para. 6). However, according to *The NCAA News*, college presidents are unperturbed with " . . . a corporate partner essentially 'sponsor[ing]' the NCAA's educational mission," as long as it is " . . . done well and tastefully" (National Collegiate Athletic Association, para. 2, 6).

Previous research of college-sport broadcasts revealed the apparent existence of two competing institutional logics, (e.g., educational and commercial) within the college-sport field (Southall & Nagel, 2008; Southall et al., 2008). There is evidence to suggest a commercial logic has been dominant for almost as long as the NCAA has been in existence, and college sports have been broadcast. As Oriard (2009) and Washington and Ventresca (2004) have noted, a primary reason why U.S. universities and colleges developed sport programs was to enhance their resources and increase visibility. This is exemplified by the aggressive pursuit of television rights fees by NCAA members since the early 1950s (Dunnavant, 2004), as well as universities' willingness to engage in litigation (e.g., *NCAA v. Board of Regents* and *O'Bannon v. NCAA*) in order to secure and protect commercial-revenue maximization (Oriard, 2009; Washington, 2004).

A primary justification for big-time college sport relates to such athletic contests' potential to communicate (both to fans in stadiums and those watching on television or the Internet) universities' educational stories (Gerdy, 2006). In particular, if college-sport broadcasts are vehicles through which this "educational" purpose is pursued, these portrayed images and conveyed messages should reflect the universities' expressed missions and goals. However, if such messages that reflect commercialized logics are dominant and the NCAA's organizational legitimacy is based upon its market position, then the arrangement's paramount mission—exhibited through telecasts—should be to build and enhance NCAA-member athletic departments' and conferences' competitive market position. The results, in Tables 2.1 and 2.2, summarize the non-football-specific content (e.g., commercials, inserted commercial graphics, public service announcements) from an analysis of telecasts of 2009 BCS Bowl Games (Southall, Southall, & Dwyer, 2009) and 2011 NCAA D-I men's basketball "March Madness" games. This content (i.e., The "stuff" you fast-forward past if you have "Tivoed" the game, and the graphic that always tells you the game action is about ready to resume!) offers evidence a commercial institutional logic now dominates big-time college sport.

TABLE 2.1 NONPROGRAM SUMMARY

2009 BCS Bowl Games

Category	Mean (M) per Broadcast
Advertising Commercials	47 min, 43 sec
NCAA Public Service Announcements	2 min, 13 sec
Corporate Public Service Announcements	60 sec
Graphic Advertisements	25 min, 32 sec
Graphic Advertisements, with verbal commentary	12 min, 48 sec
TOTAL	**89 min, 16 sec**
Academic Graphics (e.g., player majors)	11 sec
Educational Commentary	16 sec
TOTAL	**27 sec**

2011 NCAA March Madness

Category	Mean (M) per Broadcast
Advertising Commercials	39 min, 38 sec
NCAA Public Service Announcements	57 sec
Corporate Public Service Announcements	3 min, 8 sec
Graphic Advertisements	2 min, 4 sec
Graphic Advertisements, with verbal commentary	4 min, 39 sec
TOTAL	**50 min, 26 sec**
Academic Graphics (e.g., player majors)	2 sec
Educational Commentary	9 sec
TOTAL	**11 sec**

TABLE 2.2 EDUCATIONAL MESSAGING SUMMARY

2009 BCS Broadcasts

	Graphic with Academic Information (positive or negative)		Educational Messages by Commentators (positive or negative)	
Game	**Units**	**Time**	**Units**	**Time**
Allstate Sugar Bowl			1 (pos)	15 sec
FedEx National Championship				
FedEx Orange Bowl	9 (pos)	53 sec	5 (1 pos; 4 neg)	60 sec
Rose Bowl presented by CITI				
Tostitos Fiesta Bowl			1 (pos)	7 sec
TOTAL	**9 (pos)**	**53 sec**	**7 (3 pos; 4 neg)**	**82 sec**

(Data excerpted from Southall et al., 2009; Southall, et al., 2014.)

Table 2.1 clearly illustrates how pervasive the selling of non-sport products is during big-time college sport events. In an average 2009 BCS Bowl-game broadcast there were nearly 90 minutes of commercial messages, while in a 2011 March Madness telecast there were just over 50 minutes. Conversely, in events involving teams representing institutions of higher "education," there is less than 30 seconds of educational messages. Citing the increased commercialization and professionalization of college sport apparent in studies such as this one, some critics of college sport have called on the U.S. Congress to rescind college sports' tax-exempt status.

As both tables underscore, corporate college-sport broadcasts provide little evidence of an educational institutional logic. While the primary messages conveyed during any college-sport contest will, of course, be related to the game itself, within these telecasts, discussions of higher education, academics, or broader university missions of teaching, research, or service did not occur. In fact, as Table 2.2 highlights, the 2009 BCS National Championship and Rose Bowl broadcasts contained no educational messaging, while the Tostitos Fiesta Bowl contained only 7 seconds of such messaging. In addition, five of the six ED messages in 2011 March Madness were positive in nature and all occurred during a single broadcast (Marquette vs. Xavier). Two of these comments were part of an NCAA corporate-partner branded "Lowe's Senior Class Award."

Big-time college-sport broadcasts do indeed offer evidence of a "partnership" among stakeholders, but contrary to rhetoric espoused by NCAA and university officials, as well as corporate and broadcast partners, it seems as if this "amateur" sport partnership is built on commercial, not educational, values. While for most American sport fans there is ". . . nothing wrong with money and making it, especially if you can use it to further your mission" (Brown, 2002, p. 4), concerns regarding college sport's lack of academic credibility appear to be accurate. At least one NCAA faculty athletic representative (FAR) has expressed such a concern:

"The problem comes when the money diverts you from what you're supposed to be doing" (Brown, p. 4). During broadcasts, the public is overwhelmingly bombarded with commercial messages. While the NCAA-member schools may promote their athletic "brands," at least during their sport products' telecasts, these universities' educational mission is rarely, if ever, mentioned. Citing this seeming disconnect between higher-education's espoused educational institutional logics (i.e., a commitment to undergraduate and graduate education, research, etc.) and a quasi-professional sport broadcast, in which viewers are inundated with advertisements for non-sport products, some critics have argued the NCAA's Collegiate Model of Athletics has effectively become no more than a point of differentiation to separate NCAA-licensed games and participating teams from other professional televised sport leagues and events.

For our purposes here, it is important sport-management students recognize how a theory, in this case institutional-logics theory, can be used as a lens to interpret data analysis. While a college-sport fan may simply watch a college-sport telecast and sarcastically gripe, "It's too bad this game is interrupting these great commercials!" a researcher views the same game and attempts to understand why there are almost 90 minutes of commercial messaging in a BCS broadcast. Then, perhaps using an ethical framework from Chapter 5, a social critic might make a judgment about whether or not the broadcast is consistent with the sponsoring organization's public mission statement.

Conclusion

This chapter's purpose is to illustrate there is more to studying sport than simply watching *SportsCenter*, reading a box score, or following a fantasy-football player's progress each week. This chapter has focused on a "different" method of viewing sport as a social and organizational institution. Sport is an integral part of many of our lives. Many of you reading this book aspire to a sport-management career. Many sport-management students have been—or still are—athletes. Many have been a "fan" for as long as they can remember, with a favorite player, team, or sport.

Sport is part of many cultures. It is comprised of human beings and constructed and shaped by those same people. Not all sports are the same; they vary just as do the people who compete, view, and manage them. To truly understand and appreciate sport and the sport industry, sport-management students need to be willing and able to use sociocultural theories and apply them to real-world sport situations.

Study Questions

1. Define functionalism, conflict, and critical theories. To which theory are you most sympathetic? Why do you think this is so?

2. Do you think professional or college football and basketball players should be penalized for celebratory or "trash talking" behaviors? If so, why? If not, why not? What elements of the sociological theories presented do you think make the most sense in supporting your position?
3. What is the definition of organizational culture? What types of organizational subcultures do Martin and Siehl identify? Given what you know about college sport on your campus, do you agree with the analysis of the organizational culture of college sport presented in this chapter? Why or why not? What experiences can you draw on to support your position?
4. What do you think is the purpose of big-time college sport? Do you agree with the analysis of college-sport's institutional logics presented in this chapter? If so, why? If not, why not?

Learning Activity

Watch a sport-event broadcast and pay attention to the non-program messages that are represented during the course of the broadcast. What messages are found within the broadcast? What commercials and graphics are displayed? What do the commentators discuss? From this exercise, what conclusions can you draw, if any, regarding the sport's institutional logics?

References

Adamson, W. L. (1980). *Hegemony and revolution: A study of Antonio Gramsci's political and cultural theory*. Berkeley: University of California Press.

Agger, B. (1991). Critical theory, poststructuralism, postmodernism: Their sociological relevance. *Annual Review of Sociology*, 105–131.

Andrews, D. L., Mower, R. L., & Silk, M. L. (2010). Ghettocentrism and the essentialized black male athlete. In D. J. Leonard and C. R. King (eds.), *Commodified and criminalized: New racism and African Americans in contemporary sports*, 69–93.

Andrews, V. (1996). Black bodies white control: The contested terrain of sportsmanlike conduct. *Journal of African American Men, 2*(1), 33–60.

Andrews, V. (1997). African American player codes on celebration, taunting and sportsmanlike conduct. *Journal of African American Men, 2*(2-3), 57–92.

Barley, S.R., & Tolbert, P.S. (1997). Institutionalization and structuration: Studying the links between action and institution. *Organization Studies, 18,* 93–117.

Boyd, T. (2003). *Young, black, rich & famous: The rise of the NBA, the hip hop invasion, and the transformation of American culture.* Lincoln, NE: University of Nebraska Press.

Brand, M. (2009, January 15). The 2009 NCAA State of the Association speech. *The NCAA News Online.* Retrieved September 23, 2009 from http://www.ncaa.org/wps/ncaa?ContentID=43942

Brohm, J. (1978). *Sport: A prison of measured time.* London: Ink Links.

Brown, G.T. (2002, March 18). The $6 billion plan: NCAA wants TV contract to increase revenue, decrease tension between scholarly mission and commercial image. *The NCAA News.* Retrieved May 5, 2006 from http://www. ncaa.org/wps

Coakley, J.J. (2014). *Sport in society* (11th ed.). Boston: McGraw Hill.

Cousens, L., & Slack, T. (2005). Field-level change: The case of North American major league professional sport. *Journal of Sport Management, 19*, 13–42.

Cunningham, P. L. (2009). "Please don't fine me again!!!!!" Black athletic defiance in the NBA and NFL. *Journal of Sport & Social Issues, 33*(1), 39–58.

Donnelly, P. (1996). The local and the global: Globalization in the sociology of sport. *Journal of Sport & Social Issues, 20*(3), 239–257.

Duncan, M.C., & Brummett, B. (1991). The mediation of spectator sport. In L.H. Vande Berg & L.A. Wenner (Eds.), *Television criticism: Approaches and applications* (pp. 367–387). New York: Longman.

Dunnavant, K. (2004). *The fifty-year seduction: How television manipulated college football, from the birth of the modern NCAA to the creation of the BCS.* New York: St. Martin's Press.

Eveslage, S., & Delaney, K. (1998). Talkin' trash at Hardwick High: A case study of insult talk on a boys' basketball team. *International Review for the Sociology of Sport, 33*(3), 239–54.

Friedland, R., & Alford, R.R. (1991). Bringing society back in: Symbols, practices, and institutional contradictions. In W.W. Powell & P.J. DiMaggio (Eds.), *The new institutionalism in organizational analysis* (pp. 232–262). Chicago: University of Chicago Press.

Gates, H. (1998). *The signifying monkey: A theory of African American literary criticism.* New York: Oxford University Press.

Gerdy, J.R. (2006). *Air ball: American education's failed experiment with elite athletics.* Oxford, MS: University Press of Mississippi.

Gramsci, A. (1971). *Selections from the prison notebooks* (Q. Hoare & G. N. Smith, Eds.). New York: International Publishers.

Hill, D., Mitchell, C., & Southall, R.M. (2010, April). *Understanding the commonality of roster turnover on NCAA men's basketball teams.* Paper presented at the annual Scholarly Conference on College Sport, Chapel Hill, NC.

Horkheimer, M. (1972). *Critical theory*. New York: Herder & Herder.

Koene, B. A., Boone, A.J.J., & Soeters, J. L. (1997). Organizational factors influencing homogeneity and heterogeneity of organizational cultures. In S. A. Sackman (Ed.), Cultural complexity in organizations (pp. 273–293). Thousand Oaks, CA: Sage Publications.

Lane, J. (2007). *Under the boards: The cultural revolution of basketball.* Lincoln, NE: University of Nebraska Press.

Lounsbury, M. (2002). Institutional transformation and status mobility: The professionalization of the field of finance. *Academy of Management Journal, 45*, 255–266.

Martin, J., & Siehl, C. (1983). Organizational culture and counterculture: An uneasy symbiosis. *Organizational Dynamics, 12,* 52–64.

Metcalfe, J. (2008, May 18). Women coaches are few in women's sports: In push to win, some wonder if role models lost. *AZcentral.com.* Retrieved April 1, 2010 from http://www.azcentral.com/news/articles/2008/05/18/20080518women coaches0518.html

National Collegiate Athletic Association. (2002, March 18). CEOs don't blink on corporate tag. *NCAA News*. Retrieved October 4, 2009 from https://www.ncaa.org/wps/wcm/connect/ncaa/ncaa/ncaa+news/ncaa+news+online/2002/association-wide/ceos+don_t+blink+on+corporate+tag+-+3-18-02

NCAA v. Board of Regents of the University of Oklahoma, 468 U.S. 85 (1984).

Nelson, R.R., & Winter, S.G. (1982). *An evolutionary theory of economic change.* Cambridge, MA: The Belknap Press of Harvard University Press.

O'Bannon v. NCAA, No. CV 09-3329 (N.D. Cal. July 21, 2009).

O'Brien, D., & Slack, T. (2004). The emergence of a professional logic in English rugby union: The role of isomorphic and diffusion processes. *Journal of Sport Management*, *18*, 13–39.

O'Reilly III, C.A., & Chatman, J.A. (1996). Cultures as social control: Corporations, cults, and commitment. *Research in Organizational Behavior, 18,* 157–200.

Oriard, M. (2009). *Bowled over: Big-time college football from the sixties to the BCS era.* Chapel Hill, NC: The University of North Carolina Press.

Padilla, A., & Baumer, D. (1994). Big-time college sports: Management and economic issues. *Journal of Sport and Social Issues, 18,* 123–143.

Parsons, T. (1991). *The social system*. London: Routledge.

Peterson, M.W., Cameron, K.S., Jones, P., Mets, L.A., & Ettington, D. (1986). *The organizational context for teaching and learning: A review of the research literature.* Ann Arbor, MI: National Center for Research to Improve Postsecondary Teaching and Learning, University of Michigan.

Putler, D.S., & Wolfe, R.A. (1999). Perceptions of intercollegiate athletic programs: Priorities and tradeoffs. *Sociology of Sport Journal, 16,* 301–325.

Raissman, B. (2014, January 20). Seahawks' Richard Sherman screams about Michael Crabtree in postgame interview with Erin Andrews. *New York Daily News.* Retrieved from http://www.nydailynews.com/sports/football/seahawks-sherman-flips-post-game-interview-article-1.1584972#ixzz3BhCZ8PMu

Santomier, J.P., Howard, W.G., Piltz, W.L., & Romance, T.J. (1980). White sock crime: Organizational deviance in intercollegiate athletics. *Journal of Sport and Social Issues, 4*(2), 26–32.

Sack, A. (2009). Clashing models of commercial sport in higher education: Implications for reform and scholarly research. *Journal of Issues in Intercollegiate Athletics,* 76–92. Retrieved from http://csri-jiia.org/documents/ publications/research_articles/2009/JIIA_2009

Sack, A.L. (1987). College sport and the student-athlete. *Journal of Sport and Social Issues, 11*(1/2), 31–48.

Sack, A.L., & Staurowsky, E.J. (1998). *College athletes for hire: The evolution and legacy of the NCAA amateur myth.* Westport, CT: Praeger Press.

Schein, E.H. (1983, Summer). The role of the founder in creating organizational culture. *Organizational Dynamics,* 13–28.

Schein, E.H. (1984). Coming to a new awareness of organizational culture. *Sloan Management Review, 25*(2), 3–16.

Simons, H.D. (2003). Race and penalized sports behaviors. *International Review for the Sociology of Sport, 38*(1), 5–22.

Smith, M. (2009, September 21-27). 'The right man at the right time': NCAA's Brand brought academic reform, a respect for need to generate revenue. *Street & Smith's SportsBusiness Journal, 12*(21), 1, 28–29.

Southall, R. M. (2001). *A study of organizational culture of Mountain West Conference intercollegiate athletic departments.* (Doctoral dissertation, University of Northern Colorado). Dissertation Abstracts International, *61*(12), 470.

Southall, R.M., & Nagel, M.S. (2008). A case-study analysis of NCAA Division I women's basketball tournament broadcasts: Educational or commercial activity? *International Journal of Sport Communication, 1*(4), 516–533.

Southall, R.M., & Nagel, M.S. (2009, December 17). Big-time college sport's contested terrain: Jock capitalism, educational values, and social good. *Human Kinetics Sport Management News.* Available at http://www.humankinetics.com/hkarticles/hk-articles/big-time-college-sports-contested-terrain-jock-capitalism-educational-values-and-social-good?associate=5167

Southall, R.M., & Staurowsky, E.J. (2013). Cheering on the collegiate model: Creating, disseminating, and imbedding the NCAA's redefinition of amateurism. *Journal of Sport and Social Issues*, *37*(4), 403–429.

Southall, R.M., Brown, M.T., Nagel, M.S., & Southall, C. (2014). Media March Madness: A comparative content analysis of 2006 and 2011 NCAA Division I Men's National Basketball Tournament broadcasts. *International Journal of Sport Management, 15*(3), 367–383.

Southall, R.M, Nagel, M.S., Amis, J., & Southall, C. (2008). A method to March Madness: Institutional logics and the 2006 National Collegiate Athletic Association Division I men's basketball tournament. *Journal of Sport Management, 22*(6), 677–700.

Southall, R.M., Southall, C., & Dwyer, B. (2009). 2009 Bowl Championship Series telecasts: Expressions of big-time college-sport's commercial institutional logics. *Journal of Issues in Intercollegiate Athletics, 2,* 150–176.

Southall, R.M., Wells, D.E., & Nagel, M.S. (2005). Organizational culture perceptions of intercollegiate athletic department members. *Applied Research in Coaching and Athletics Annual, 20,* 65–93.

Sperber, M. (2001). *Beer and circus: How big-time college sports is crippling undergraduate education.* New York: Henry Holt and Company.

Thornton, P.H. (2002). The rise of the corporation in a craft industry: Conflict and conformity in institutional logics. *Academy of Management Journal, 45,* 81–101.

Washington, M. (2004). Field approaches to institutional change: The evolution of the National Collegiate Athletic Association 1906-1995. *Organization Studies, 25,* 393–414.

Washington, M., & Ventresca, M.J. (2004). How organizations change: The role of institutional support mechanisms in the incorporation of higher education visibility strategies, 1874–1995. *Organization Science, 15,* 82–97.

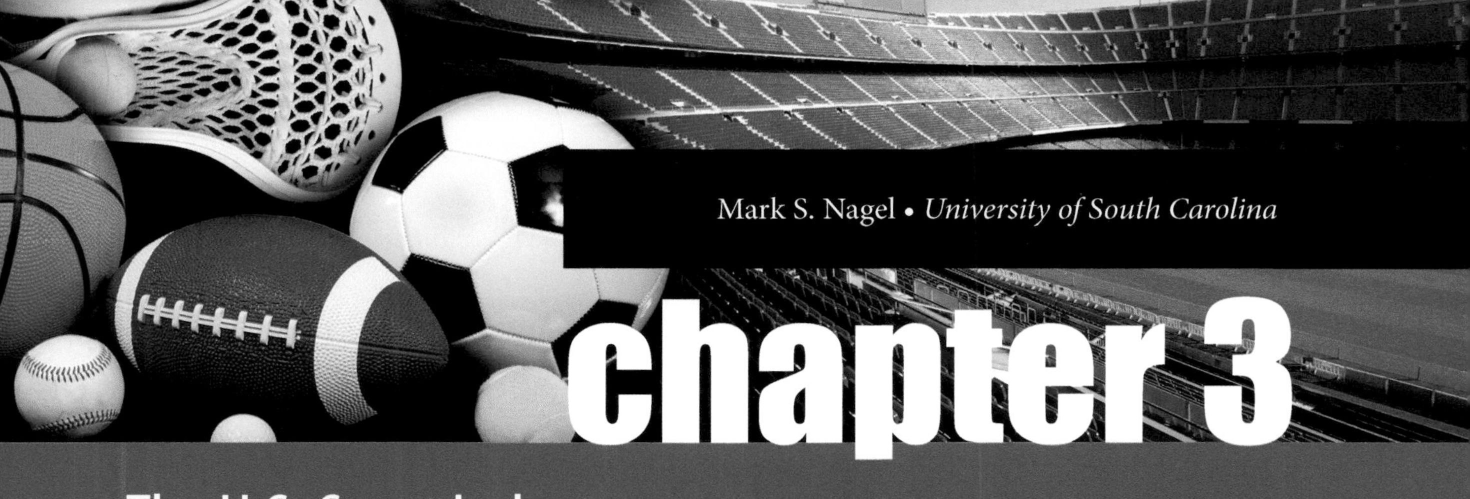

Mark S. Nagel • *University of South Carolina*

chapter 3

The U.S. Sport Industry

CHAPTER OBJECTIVES

After reading this chapter, you will be able to:

- Explain the breadth of the U.S. sport industry.
- Identify and describe selected organizations working within the subindustries of the U.S. sport marketplace.
- Describe potential internship and entry-level employment opportunities in sport management.

KEY TERMS

College Football Playoff

Cost of attendance

Football Bowl Subdivision

Football Championship Subdivision

Independent teams

Licensed merchandise

Power 5 Conference

> *Find a job you love and you will never work another day in your life.*
> —Confucius

Introduction

The vast majority of entry-level sport-management students will answer the question "What do you want to do in your sport-management career" with one of the following responses:

1. "Become a general manager of a franchise in the National Basketball Association (NBA), National Football League (NFL), National Hockey League (NHL), or Major League Baseball (MLB)."
2. "Become an athletic director at a National Collegiate Athletic Association (NCAA) Division-I athletic department, preferably one that is a member of one of the largest conferences (Big 10, Big 12, ACC, SEC, or PAC-12)."
3. "Become a player agent."

While each of these choices is a potential career option, they are certainly not indicative of the breadth of the sport-management industry. The above-listed positions typically generate extensive media attention, so most students, parents, and non-sport-management faculty tend to think sport-management graduates primarily work in these subsectors of the industry. Though positions in these areas do exist, there are usually few such entry-level positions available and higher-ranking positions are especially scarce. For instance, there are only 32 NFL teams, meaning there are only 32 NFL general managers. Mathematically, students have a higher likelihood of becoming a member of the U.S. Congress than of becoming an NFL, NBA, NHL, or MLB general manager.

In addition to there being few opportunities, general managers, athletic directors, or prominent player agents are often people who were high-level athletes. Though certainly not a requirement, being a well-known former athlete can often provide a springboard to eventual success as a general manager, athletic director, or player agent. It is wonderful if a student desires to someday obtain one of these positions, and, while students should not be discouraged from pursuing a career path with these eventual outcomes as the primary goal, they should understand the reality of the situation. Becoming a NCAA Division-I athletic director, general manager, or prominent sport agent requires intellect, determination, countless hours of learning, and years of preparation. Though it is highly unlikely that obtaining one of those positions will occur, by setting an "ultimate" goal, along with smaller goals that serve as steps along the way, either that final goal will be achieved or other career opportunities will present themselves. While this advice may seem "cliché-like," it is actually true.

This chapter discusses various subsectors of the sport industry that may provide internship opportunities and eventual employment. It is designed to provide students with a broader perspective of the industry than a "traditional" view of sport management that consists of only involving college and professional sport employment or becoming an agent. The categories are certainly not exhaustive as the sport industry is constantly evolving, with new subsectors emerging almost daily. Regardless of your career path (Just a note: By enrolling in a sport-management class your career has already begun!), be prepared to work long hours in order to achieve your career goals. Remember, your career will not develop overnight. The adage, "You learn in your 20s and begin to earn in your 30s" is certainly applicable to the sport-management industry. Maintain your focus while working diligently and good things will eventually happen.

Professional Sport

Professional sport franchises have two distinct sets of employees. The "talent" side of the organization deals with preparing the team to achieve on-field success. The general manager, player-personnel director, coaches, full-time scouts (and certainly the players) usually receive salaries considerably higher than those earned by employees on the organization's "business" side. Players, coaches, and general managers also typically receive extensive media attention and are readily identified by fans and many members of the team's local community. The desire to work on the "talent" side of professional sports is what initially attracts many students to sport-management programs. However, in the vast majority of cases, sport-management students will be hired to work in the business side of the organization. It is certainly possible, but extremely rare, for a sport-management student who is not a former college or professional sport player to be hired by a professional sport franchise to work on the "talent" side of the organization. Most sport-management students who work for a professional sport franchise will be employed in one or more of a variety of sport business areas (marketing, finance, game operations, sales, etc.).

When most students think of working in professional sports, they focus upon the NBA, NHL, NFL, and MLB as likely employers. These leagues tend to attract large fan bases and have games that are often televised. Potential internship or employment openings at these organizations usually attract hundreds of applicants and therefore have extremely low salaries. Much of the "compensation" for working for a franchise in one of these leagues is the ability to say that you work for the team. Sport franchises realize there are often hundreds of potential employees who would "love" to work for their organization, so they often keep salaries low and demand long working hours, particularly for those employees who have been with the team for less than five years.

Professional sport franchises from the "Big 4" leagues tend to have distinct compartmentalized divisions in marketing, sales, game operations, finance, media relations, human resources, and law. Interns or entry-level employees hired to work for these teams may find they work almost exclusively in one area and do not get exposed to many facets of the organization. Working exclusively in the marketing department certainly enables an intern or entry-level employee to learn detailed aspects of marketing, but it may not be conducive to understanding how the other departments interact in order for the franchise to operate effectively.

Though not nearly as popular as teams in the "Big 4" sports leagues, there are many other professional-sport franchises. Sports such as soccer, lacrosse, and volleyball have financially viable professional leagues, and the NBA, NHL, and MLB also have extensive minor-league systems where clubs may be owned and operated by the major-league franchise or owned and operated by an independent owner. In baseball, there are also **independent teams** that operate without the direct support (in the form of players) of a major-league affiliate. Most students do not initially consider a career working with franchises other than those in the "Big 4" leagues, but often there are much greater career advancement opportunities in these situations. For instance, though not the norm, it is not uncommon for general managers of minor-league baseball teams to be hired prior to reaching their 35th birthday. It is also not uncommon for talented interns to be promoted quickly after an internship with a "minor league" franchise. There are many prominent sport managers who have achieved great success in (so-called) minor-league sport, who refuse "major-league" job offers because their "minor-league" careers are fulfilling.

Independent teams Baseball teams that operate without a direct affiliation with any Major League Baseball franchise.

Since the team's overall staff is much smaller, minor-league sports franchise employees (including interns) typically have multiple areas of responsibility within the organization. For instance, an NBA team will likely have at least five marketing department staff members. Each employee will likely have a narrowly defined job description. However, an NBA D-League franchise will have a much smaller marketing staff that will, most likely, have daily interaction with members of many different departments. By being thoroughly exposed to the smaller organization's various facets, skills are developed that can be applied to future work activities. Even more prominent minor league sports, such as Triple-A teams in minor-league baseball, will present opportunities for employees to see and understand how the various aspects of the organization function. For instance, it is not uncommon for every member of a minor-league franchise, including the general manager, to help pull the tarp during rain delays.

In addition, the world of professional sports is not limited to "team" sports. There are numerous organizations that operate tournaments for professional athletes in sports such as tennis, golf, fishing, boxing, mixed martial arts, and track and field. Though events such as the U.S. Open Tennis Championship or Professional Golf Association (PGA) Championship garner extensive media attention, there are other internship and employment opportunities in these sports, since tournaments are held most weekends during the year. Sports such as mixed martial arts and lacrosse have only recently launched viable leagues, but they are growing—in both popularity and employment opportunities.

The growth of NASCAR over the past 15 years is an excellent example of an emerging professional sport and the potential for growth. For many years, automobile racing was seen as a niche sport in the United States, with little national interest beyond the Indianapolis 500 each spring. Until the 1990s, NASCAR was perceived primarily as a "southern" sport that did not generate much national media attention. However, as NASCAR racing became more popular, various NASCAR employees were recognized for their expertise in a variety of sport-business areas, particularly sponsorship sales and fulfillment. While NASCAR has recently faced numerous challenges, with a concurrent slowdown in television ratings and revenue, its rise as a "major-league" sport is an indication that "niche" professional sport organizations can provide excellent employment opportunities.

Though working for a team is certainly one of the most popular potential sport-management careers, professional-sport opportunities are not limited to team-sport franchises. Each professional-sport league has a league office. League office employees are charged with creating a fair environment for all league participants, enhancing the league's brand, and developing league revenue sources. Most leagues have a commissioner or league president who oversees the league office. For instance, Major League Baseball has a commissioner who hires a staff that schedules games, hires and supervises umpires, negotiates media contracts, and markets the league. Minor League Baseball (MiLB) has a president responsible for all of the affiliated minor-league baseball teams. In addition, each minor league (Midwest League, Southern League, etc.) has a president who hires and manages a full-time staff, as well as league interns.

Working for a professional sport league does not offer the emotional highs and lows associated with an individual franchise, because team employees have a vested interest in each game's results. The day-to-day excitement of working for an individual franchise can be intense, especially at the end of the season when a team is in the playoffs. Though "business-office" staff members do not directly influence the outcome on the field, they certainly contribute to franchise success by marketing to fans and providing a positive game-day experience. In recognition of their contributions, most professional sport organizations reward all full-time employees, not just the coaches and players, with rings and other awards if the team wins a championship.

To truly understand the professional-sport environment and to determine if it is a good fit, students should seek volunteer and internship opportunities with individual franchises—as well as league offices. It certainly is appropriate to pursue positions with a "major-league" franchise or league, if that is your primary goal, but do not fail to at least consider a "minor-league" position, since many wonderful career opportunities are available.

College Sport

Football Bowl Subdivision
A segment of the National Collegiate Athletic Association that is comprised of schools playing the highest level of football (formerly known as Division IA).

When most people think of intercollegiate athletics, they tend to focus upon **Football Bowl Subdivision** (FBS) football playoffs and bowls and the NCAA Division-I Men's and Women's Basketball Tournaments. Though these are certainly the most-watched college athletic events, they are a small fraction of the total opportunities in college athletics. The NCAA is divided into three divisions (I, II, III). Currently, there are over 1,100 member schools with 351 in Division I, 320 in Division II, and 450 in Division III. The NCAA organizes championships in 23 different sports with schools offering opportunities for men and women to compete.

To be eligible to be a member of Division I, an institution must offer at least seven sports for men and seven for women (or six for men and eight for women) with at least two team sports for each gender. Division-I members may offer athletic scholarships and most schools recruit potential athletes from various regions of the country. Though nearly every Division-I athletic department is part of a regional conference, most teams schedule some competition with schools outside of their immediate geographic area. Division-II institutions must sponsor at least five sports for men and five for women (or four for men and six for women) with two team sports for each gender. Though Division-II institutions may offer athletic scholarships, their recruitment efforts are usually regionally based. In addition, athletic-competition travel tends to be local or regional. Division-III institutions must offer at least five sports for men and five for women. They are not permitted to offer athletic scholarships ("Divisional difference and . . .," n.d.).

Football Championship Subdivision
A segment of the National Collegiate Athletic Association that is comprised of Division-I schools that are not playing at the highest level of football competition (formerly known as Division IAA).

Division I is further separated into three divisions (formerly known as IA, IAA, IAAA). Division-IA institutions that offer "big-time" football compete in the Football Bowl Subdivision (FBS), while D-IAA schools—now **Football Championship Subdivision** (FCS)—do not provide as high a financial commitment to their football programs. Division IAAA members do not field D-I football teams. It is important to remember that all Division-I schools compete for the same championships in all sports besides football. Except for a

Division-I football teams usually compete in large stadiums, whereas Division-II or Division-III programs typically have much smaller facilities.

Courtesy Mark Nagel

Courtesy Mark Nagel

few rare instances, schools must compete at the same level for all of their sports. Such instances are often in Olympic sports (skiing, hockey, wrestling, etc.).

In 2014, the NCAA Bowl Championship Subdivision further split as a new model permitted **Power 5 Conferences** to create some of their own rules. Leaders of many of the athletic departments in the Power 5 Conferences noted that NCAA rules limiting full scholarships below **the cost of attendance** were inappropriate for most of the top athletic programs as they generated sufficient revenue to compensate their profit athletes with additional monies. The decision to permit greater autonomy to Power 5 Conferences coincided with the first ever College Football Playoff after the 2014 season.

The various NCAA divisions roughly approximate varying philosophical perspectives and financial commitments to intercollegiate athletics. Division-I programs tend to provide coaches with greater financial resources for scholarships, personnel, and equipment; upgraded facilities; large travel budgets; and extensive opportunities to compete against other schools across the nation. Most Division-II institutions offer athletic-related scholarships across a variety of sports, but travel and expenses are typically much lower than in Division I. Division-III members, while still committed to intercollegiate athletic competition, in most instances have deemphasized a highly commercialized approach to college sport. According to the division's mission statement, member institutions prohibit athletic-related scholarships and "...place special importance on the impact of athletics on the participants rather than on the spectators. The student-athlete's experience is of paramount concern" ("Divisional differences and...," n.d., para. 3).

Most NCAA members have maintained their current affiliation for many years. However, each year a handful of members attempt to move divisions. In most cases, the movement is prompted by a desire to enhance athletic commitment and "upgrade" to a higher division. Most schools rationalize such a move (from Division III to Division II or from Division II to Division I) as a means to enhance the institution's "marketability" and focus on the potentially drastic increases in athletic revenue. Competing at a high level of intercollegiate athletics is perceived by many to be critical to attracting and retaining students, since competing at the Division I-level offers a greater opportunity to be mentioned on ESPN's *SportsCenter* and in other media outlets. Though examining the specifics regarding the costs and benefits of moving up a division is beyond the scope of this chapter and book, a focus on athletic-department expansion and increased use of college sport as a marketing platform has resulted in concern among many faculty, students, alumni, and administrators regarding institutional priorities. These concerns have resulted in a small number of schools "downgrading" their NCAA status. Recently, Birmingham Southern College realized an increase in overall athletic participation and an increase in campus minority enrollment, university giving, and applicant quality after it moved from Division I to Division III.

Though the importance placed upon winning and academic achievement may differ by sport and NCAA division, regardless of division, athletic directors' and athletic department staff roles are similar. Athletic directors are expected to hire coaches and other staff members, manage an athletic department's budget, generate revenues to ensure the department's financial viability, and interact with various on- and off-campus constituencies. Reflecting the enhanced commitment to the business of intercollegiate athletics, the vast majority of coaches and athletic department personnel who work at Division-I institutions tend to not maintain formal roles in other areas of the university. However, at many Division-II and (especially) D-III institutions, coaches and athletic department staff members often teach classes and assume other campus roles.

Students wishing to eventually work in college athletics should develop and fully understand their personal philosophy of the relationship between athletics and academics before pursuing potential college-sport internships. At Division-I institutions, a primary focus (and some would argue the only focus) is winning. Athletes' education and character development, while still ostensibly important, are often secondary, particularly in revenue-generating sports. At the Division-II and Division-III levels facilities typically are not as lavish, and media attention is often nonexistent. As a result, there is often less commercial intrusion, which may allow athletes to maintain more focus on their academic and social development. At most Division-III institutions, coaches and administrators are evaluated primarily on how well their program contributes to students' education.

The Division-I focus on winning, particularly in revenue sports, is not necessarily a "bad" thing, but sport-management students must attempt to ensure that philosophy and expectations match a university's mission and goals. If a student's personal values are incongruent with those of the athletic department in which they work, frustration often occurs. Having a general idea of expectations and the work environment prior to taking a job in college athletics can alleviate potential philosophical disagreements.

Though most students seeking employment in college athletics will gravitate toward a job at an individual school, there are additional administrative positions available at the NCAA as well as other college-sport-governing bodies. Each Division-I conference maintains a league office and employs a full-time staff. Certainly, conferences such as the Southeastern Conference (SEC) and the Big Ten Conference have many more staff members than the West Coast Conference (WCC) or the Western Athletic Conference (WAC), but all conference employees attempt to market the conferences' brand and enhance athletic-related revenue streams. Much like working for a professional sport league, NCAA and conference administrators will not have the emotional highs and lows of individual school employees.

There are also opportunities outside of the NCAA umbrella. The National Association of Intercollegiate Athletics (NAIA) governs sport activities for member NAIA schools. Though not as large as the NCAA, the NAIA currently has over 260 member institutions, and organizes championships in 13 sports. The NAIA maintains a full-time staff that works to organize championships and market NAIA members. In addition, though their athletic departments will likely be small compared to NCAA Division-I institutions, every NAIA school will have athletic employment opportunities.

Intercollegiate athletics opportunities are also offered at many junior colleges. Junior college athletic department administrators are also often members of the physical education faculty. Since junior colleges typically attract students from the local area, rather than from throughout the country, such athletic department budgets are often much more limited. However, many states organize championships for a variety of sports at the junior college level. These championships can attract local media attention and fans. The National Junior College Athletic Association (NJCAA) works to promote the efforts of junior college athletics.

College-Sport License Holders

The development and expansion of the business of intercollegiate athletics has resulted in the proliferation of numerous college-sport marketing companies. Since many athletic departments do not have adequate personnel with the expertise to evaluate and sell sponsorship inventory, negotiate media rights to athletic department content, and seek advertisers, they often partner with third-party license holders. As these license holders have proliferated, they have provided excellent internship and employment opportunities for sport-management students.

There are a variety of college-sport licensees. One of the most important people in the development of this subindustry is Jim Host. In the 1970s, Host established Jim Host & Associates, which provided assistance to college athletic departments looking to outsource some or all of their marketing activities. After initially working with the University of Kentucky, Host's company became more and more successful. As Host expanded his influence throughout the industry, other competitors entered the marketplace. In the early 2000s, prominent college sport-marketing companies included ISP Sports, Learfield Sports Properties, and Nelligan Sports Marketing, Inc.

In 2007, International Management Group (IMG) purchased Host Communications and combined it with the recently acquired Collegiate Licensing Company (CLC), an entity that had initially been established to assist colleges and universities to create and expand their **licensed merchandise** sales, to form IMG College. The merger established IMG College as the nation's largest provider of marketing services to the college-sport industry. In 2014, JMI Sports acquired the rights to the University of Kentucky athletic department with a

Licensed merchandise
Granting another entity the right to produce products that bear a trademarked logo.

$210 million deal (Rovell, 2014). Despite the dominance of IMG College, it is likely that other entities will continue to enter the college rights holder industry.

Though the aforementioned companies provide a variety of marketing services to college athletic departments, there continues to be new opportunities for college-sport consulting. In 2009, Georgia Tech hired the Aspire Group to organize its ticket sales for football and men's basketball games. It was believed to be the first time an athletic department outsourced its ticketing operations to a third party (Lombardo & Smith, 2009). Since then, it has expanded its client list to include dozens of colleges and professional sports teams, and some sport leagues. It is likely many future employment opportunities in college athletics will involve working for an outside entity, rather than directly for the athletic department.

Youth Sports

Professional and intercollegiate athletics typically generate significantly higher attendance and greater media attention than organized youth sports; however, over the past 10 years high-school athletics has become dramatically more commercialized. At many high schools, since the athletic director is no longer expected to teach classes, his/her energy can be fully devoted to selling tickets, executing fund-raising initiatives, seeking sponsorship agreements, and raising awareness of the high school's athletic exploits in the media. High-school football and basketball games are increasingly being broadcast on local or regional television and radio stations, or sport networks. In addition, ESPN has recently dramatically increased its coverage of selected games. It is not uncommon for prominent high-school athletic teams to travel via airplane to participate in prestigious tournaments. As many high-school athletic departments have begun to model their structure and activities after prominent colleges, athletic directors with advanced sport-business skills are needed.

Other youth sport activities have also recently seen dramatic changes. Little League Baseball and the Amateur Athletic Union (AAU) have long attracted thousands of participants, but the scheduling and marketing of their athletic contests now mimics commercialized sport properties. Not only are Little League World Series games televised live on ESPN, but most regional championships are also covered extensively by the media. AAU tournaments in a variety of sports no longer merely attract parents and close friends of the participants. With much of the college recruiting for some sports (such as basketball and volleyball) occurring during summer AAU tournaments, fans have begun to attend, and media outlets have begun to cover, some of these events in the hopes of seeing the "next" great college players before they have graduated from high school.

With the growing emphasis on commercialized youth sports, parents now often insist that their children's sporting activities be organized and operated like "professional" sport entities. Some affluent parents have also retained "performance" coaches to work with their child—in some cases before their son or daughter has enrolled in junior high school. The increased emphasis that parents have placed upon organized, elite youth-sport activities is of grave concern to many people. During much of the 20th century young kids participated in athletics without direct parental organization or supervision (Coakley, 2009). Sport was as much about "play" as it was about winning. Participants (children) often amended rules to allow for a more competitive and "fun" environment. While some sociologists lament the current state of youth sports, with today's emphasis on adult-organized and-directed youth sports, there are opportunities for sport-management graduates to establish, organize, and promote youth-sport events.

Olympic Sports

In 1896 the first "modern" Olympic Games took place in Athens, Greece. Though the "first" Olympics attracted "only" 14 nations and 241 athletes, the games slowly expanded during the first half of the 20th century. Since it was impractical to hold competitions for many popular sports, such as skiing and ice-skating, during the summer, in 1924 the first Winter Olympic Games were held in Chamonix, France. As the Olympics continued to attract larger contingents of athletes and greater media attention, they became an outlet for countries' nationalism. During the 1936 Summer Olympics in Berlin, the Nazi Party utilized the Games as the focal point to demonstrate the "rebirth" of Germany after World War I. Despite Adolf Hitler's propaganda campaign about the Aryan "master race," U.S. track star Jesse Owens won four gold medals to become the hero of the 1936 Olympics.

Though the popularity of the Olympics grew following World War II, many Olympic Games have been marred by tragedy, financial problems, and political turmoil. During the 1972 Munich Games, members of the Israeli Olympic team were taken hostage and eventually murdered by Black September, a militant group with ties to the Palestinian Fatah organization. By the end of the ordeal, the death toll stood at 17. The terrorists eventually killed eleven Israeli athletes and coaches and one West German police officer. Five of the eight Black September members were killed during a failed rescue attempt. Though certainly not as tragic as the loss of life in Munich, the 1976 Montreal Games were a financial disaster as millions of dollars of facility investments required decades for the citizens of Montreal and the rest of Canada to repay. At the height of the "Cold War," the United States and many of its allies boycotted the 1980 Moscow Games in protest of the Soviet Union's invasion of Afghanistan. By 1984, there was considerable concern about the financial viability of the Los Angeles Games, especially after the Soviet Union and other "Eastern Bloc" countries boycotted the Games in retaliation for the 1980 boycott. Despite

The 1984 Summer Olympics generated a profit and changed the way future Olympic Games would be organized.

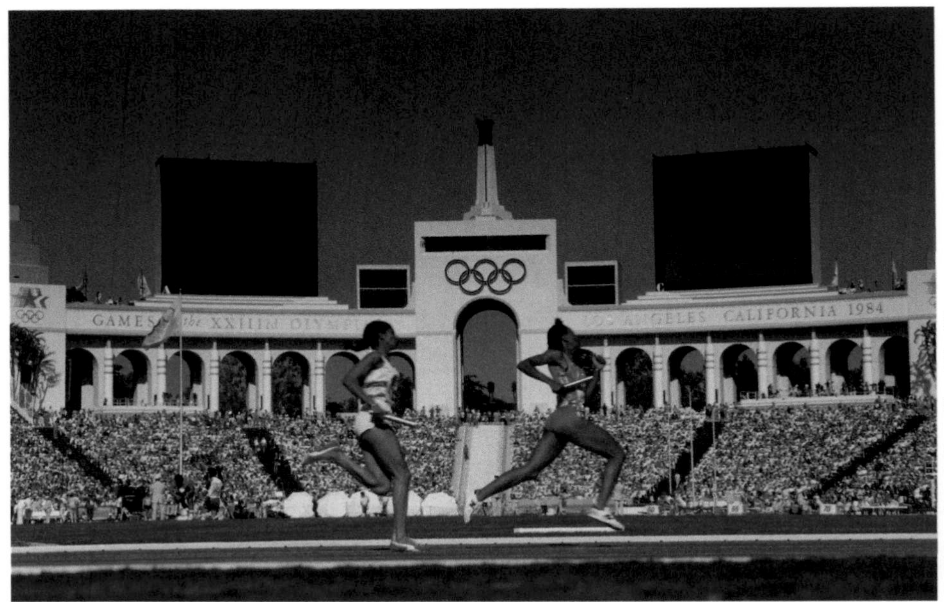

© Gilbert Lundt/TempSport/Corbis

concerns, the financial and marketing success of the 1984 Summer Olympics changed the Olympic movement.

Peter Ueberroth served as the Executive Director of the 1984 Summer Olympics. Where all of the proceeding Olympic Games were primarily financed and operated by government entities, Ueberroth organized the Los Angeles Games as a private entity. Ueberroth managed the Olympics as a separate, stand-alone business and he solicited extensive sponsorship and licensed merchandise sales to generate revenue. The Los Angeles Olympics was such a financial success that Ueberroth was named *Time Magazine's* Man of the Year. Cities and countries that had viewed hosting the Olympics as a financial risk, changed their opinion of hosting future games. The Los Angeles Olympics caused many worldwide sporting events to become "mega-events" requiring extensive and highly-trained staffs in order to solicit bids, develop financial plans, schedule facilities, organize event employees, and maximize revenue opportunities. Today, sport-management students have the opportunity to pursue an Olympics-based career, whether working for the International Olympic Committee (IOC), U.S. Olympic Committee (USOC), one of the USOC's national sport governing bodies (NGO), or for a potential host city.

The Olympic Games are not the only mega-event to attract competitors and spectators from throughout the world. In 1948 Sir Ludwig Guttman organized the first sport competition for injured soldiers from World War II. Guttman's event would grow and eventually be called the Paralympics. Starting in 1988 with the Seoul Olympics, the Paralympics have been held in the Olympic host city shortly after the Olympic Games have concluded. The Paralympics, as well as other sporting events for the disabled, have grown in popularity. Much like the Olympics, the Paralympics must be organized and managed. With thousands of athletes and spectators attending, there are numerous career opportunities in this area.

Sport Facilities

Regardless of the size or scope of a sporting event, facilities will be needed to ensure the event is successful. Even outdoor events, such as cross-country races, require facilities for spectators, members of the media, and race officials. Certainly, major professional sports facilities and Division-I athletic-department facilities receive considerable media attention, but there are also many potential career opportunities associated with smaller venues. As discussed in Chapter 12, sport facilities may include stadiums (both indoor, outdoor, and retractable roofed) for events such as football and soccer games, arenas for events such as basketball and volleyball games and facilities designed specifically for sports such as tennis, swimming, auto racing, horse racing, and dog racing.

Though high-profile "competitive" sport facilities tend to initially attract sport-management students, there are also numerous opportunities to work in recreation and fitness facilities. Most communities have private and publicly-owned recreation centers that offer general recreation opportunities as well as scheduled events such as tournaments. Over the past 10 years, colleges and universities have come to realize on-campus recreation centers can be utilized to recruit and retain students (as well as faculty and staff). Most campuses have at least one recreation center, and offer extensive intramural programs. Military bases, both in the United States and throughout the world, also offer recreation opportunities. Community recreation centers, like other facilities, require professional, part-time, and volunteer staff members to ensure operational efficiency. Employees at all venue types establish budgets, organize programs, ensure the safety of equipment, and attract and retain customers.

Over the last 15 years, as the importance and complexity of managing sport facilities has increased, numerous private management companies have offered sport facility-management services. Though there are numerous private management companies that offer such full-scale management, three organizations currently dominate the marketplace. SMG World is the leading provider of management for arenas, convention centers, stadiums, and theatres throughout the world. It currently manages 10+ stadiums, 60+ theatres, 60+ convention centers, and 65+ arenas, with more than 1.5 million seats. SMG continues to expand its operations and influence in the sport facility marketplace.

Global Spectrum, a division of the Philadelphia-based sports and entertainment company Comcast-Spectacor, has dramatically increased its presence and influence in the industry over the past 15 years. Global Spectrum presently manages over 100 venues throughout the world; and is expanding its global presence, with offices in the United States, Canada, the United Kingdom, and Singapore.

AEG Live has only recently begun soliciting facility-management contracts as it has a long history of presenting live music and other entertainment events. AEG Live has signed contracts with some of the top-grossing facilities in the world. It currently oversees the development of L.A. Live, a 4-million-square-foot, $2.5 billion sport, residential, and entertainment district. AEG has committed to expanding its presence in the sport facility-management field.

Each of these companies offers extensive internship and entry-level employment opportunities. Since SMG, Global Spectrum, and AEG manage multiple facilities around the world, there are tremendous opportunities to advance your career, if you are able and willing to relocate. It is not uncommon for these companies to "fast-track" exceptional students from internships to full-time employment and from entry-level employment to middle management.

In addition to full-service facility-management companies, there are also potential sport-management employment opportunities in firms that offer specific services in subsectors of facility management. Since selling food and beverages is a critical revenue stream for most sporting events, many facilities have outsourced concession-sales responsibilities to private companies. Though there are many food-service companies, a few dominate the marketplace. Aramark is the largest sport concessionaire and it continues to expand its presence in the United States and international markets. Other prominent concessionaires include Centerplate, Delaware North Sportservice, Levy, and Ovations Food Services (owned and operated by Comcast Spectacor). Much like the large full-scale facility management companies, these concessionaires have multiple accounts across the country, providing employees many opportunities for career advancement.

Though crowd safety has always been an important issue, after the terrorist attacks on 9/11 most facilities and events realized they needed to reassess their crowd-management practices. There are many companies that work directly or indirectly with sporting events to create a safe environment. Contemporary Services Corporation (CSC) is the best known. With multiple offices throughout the United States and accounts with many of the top college and professional sport teams, CSC is a leader in providing staffing for sport-event crowd management.

Most live sport events require patrons to purchase tickets to gain entry to the facility. For many years, tickets were sold primarily at a facility's box office. By the 1970s, tickets could be purchased over the phone with a credit card, but the sales process was still inefficient. In 1976, two Arizona State students founded Ticketmaster—a company that designed software that allowed for "remote" ticket sales. In the 1980s, as Ticketmaster developed and enhanced its technology, it quickly became the industry leader. With the proliferation of the Internet in the

1990s, Ticketmaster captured nearly the entire sport and entertainment ticketing industry. In 2010, it merged with Live Nation. Though many students may not have an interest in working for Ticketmaster, it is important to understand how its operations impact nearly every aspect of live sport and entertainment events.

There are a variety of other employment opportunities in sport facility and event management. Sport events cannot function without office equipment, landscaping, trash removal, and a myriad of other services. There are many lesser-known companies that work intimately within the sport industry. In addition, there are companies that have not even been established that will provide future employment opportunities. For instance, in 1981 Sports Team Analysis and Tracking Systems (STATS, Inc.) was established by John Dewan. In the early 1980s, statistical analysis (particularly in sports) was often seen as a "fringe" activity reserved solely for "nerds." Since 1981 the importance of sport statistical analysis (as well as statistical analysis in all aspects of business) has grown tremendously and companies such as STATS, Inc. (now STATS LLC) play an important role in the industry. Many students reading this book will likely have ideas for aspects of the sport industry that have not yet been contemplated. Do not discount emerging ideas or companies as they may become a critical component of the sport industry in the future!

Licensed Merchandise

In the 1950s, New York Yankee's General Manager George Weiss was asked about having a Yankee Cap Day. He supposedly replied, "Do you think I want kids in New York wearing Yankee hats?" Certainly, the use of team or league logos on hats, shirts, jackets, sweaters, and various other articles of clothing and other products has greatly expanded since the 1950s. Today, any sport executive would welcome the opportunity for logoed merchandise to be worn by fans, especially when the fans pay for the "privilege" of being associated with the sport organization.

Most teams, leagues, and athletic department sell licenses that permit third parties to produce various products that display a sport organization's name and logo. The profit margin on sales of licensed merchandise can be quite high. One only has to look at the price of a plain sweatshirt sold at a department store, and compare it to the price of a sweatshirt bearing a college or university logo, to see the profits generated through licensed merchandise sales. The cost of ink is likely pennies, but the addition of a school logo on a plain piece of clothing can double, triple, or even quadruple the product's price!

Licensed merchandise sales are a critical component of most sport organizations' revenue plans. The tremendous profit margins available through the sale of licensed merchandise have led most sport organizations to devote at least one employee to this area. For extremely popular sport teams, an entire franchise division or functional area may work to investigate potential licensing opportunities, negotiate licensing contracts, and ensure that counterfeit merchandise is not sold. In order to maximize profits, sport leagues typically create league-wide licensing agreements. These league agreements typically disburse revenues to each team, which enables every team (though their individual sales may fluctuate each year due to team performance and other factors) to receive a more consistent revenue stream.

Companies that design and sell apparel have been interested in utilizing sport logos for many years. Recently, various nontraditional products and services have sought associations with sport organizations. Some college athletic departments offer their fans the opportunity to purchase licensed products as varied as seat cushions, plates, silverware, glasses, futons, toilet seat covers, DVDs, photographs, and other new-media products. Some schools and professional sport franchises have even begun offering officially licensed urns and coffins for fans who wish to be buried in "their" school or team colors (Jones, 2008).

Sport Media

Sport events typically attract the attention of fans, and therefore are often covered by various media outlets. Certainly, sport organizations seek to maximize media exposure. Most hire employees to work with the media to generate positive publicity. In addition, media-relations departments must also prepare and handle potential crises that develop. An organization that is not prepared for a crisis will likely experience significant negative feedback from fans and other constituents who view the sport entity as unprepared, uncaring, or unprofessional in their dealings with the media.

The media industry has changed dramatically over the past 100 years. The primary mode of information gathering for most sport consumers has progressed from newspapers to radio to television to the Internet. Changes in media platforms have resulted in employment opportunities and in alterations to some established sport norms. In addition to a proliferation of satellite and cable TV networks and delivery options, many professional and college leagues and conferences now have their own cable sports networks. The NFL, NBA, and MLB all have their own networks. The Mountain West Conference (Mtn) and Big Ten Conference (Big Ten Network) led the way in college sport in the early 2000s, with other conferences creating their own networks, including the SEC starting theirs in 2014. Individual franchises (such as the New York Yankees with the YES Network) as well as individual schools (such as the University of Texas) have developed their own cable networks.

The Internet's "viral" nature (through the sharing of files, video-sharing websites, blogs, digital networks, and "old-fashioned" email) has enabled bloggers to wield significant influence in the sport industry. For many years, many sport franchises did not view Internet writers as "real" journalists. Today, most teams have begun to recognize prominent bloggers are an important part of their media constituencies. As technology continues to evolve, the need for sport organizations to tell their "story" through the media will not change, but the platforms by which that story is conveyed will undoubtedly be much different. Students seeking employment in sport media should understand the unique nature of sport media relations, and prepare for continued rapid changes in the future.

Sports Agents

Though being a "player agent" is probably the number-one career non-sport-management people think of when sport management is mentioned, an infinitesimal fraction of sport-management students will ever work as a player agent. Though multimillion-dollar athlete contracts and movies like *Jerry Maguire* make the layperson think there are numerous player agents and many of them are financially successful, in reality only a few player agents make substantial salaries. For every Scott Boras, Drew Rosenhaus, or David Falk, there are thousands of other agents who have considerably more dreams than clients. In many years, the reported number of agents exceeds the number of players in several sports. Leigh Steinberg was once a prominent agent who fell from grace due to alcoholism and other personal problems. He has written a book describing his own career path and the struggles agents face in a cutthroat industry.

Though the player-agent industry now involves millions of dollars, the first athlete-agent agreement began with little more than a handshake. In 1960, Attorney Mark McCormack noticed that golfer Arnold Palmer had established his career as a successful performer. With television rapidly increasing its coverage of golf tournaments, McCormack approached Palmer about managing his endorsement opportunities. McCormack's success with Palmer's career attracted other golfers such as Jack Nicklaus and Gary Player. McCormack's agency, IMG, would eventually sign numerous other golfers and tennis players. Later, IMG expanded its agency to represent athletes from other sports, as well as entertainers, politicians, and models. IMG also began to manage sport and entertainment events.

The success of McCormack and IMG led other individuals to work in the player-agent business. During the 1970s, numerous attorneys expanded their business to include athlete representation. As the value of player contracts escalated in the 1980s, many individuals became full-time agents rather than attorneys who "also" represented athletes. In the 1990s many prominent agents began to expand their client services. Instead of merely negotiating player contracts, most large agencies began to design marketing and sponsorship campaigns; offer financial advice; retain nutritionists, personal trainers, and sport psychologists; and perform statistical analysis of their clients' athletic performance. Currently, most "successful" agents represent many clients and allow their past successes to supplement their recruiting efforts.

Becoming a prominent player agent is one of the most difficult sport-career paths. Competition within the industry is fierce, with some agents notoriously circumventing established rules, laws, and ethical guidelines (see Chapter 5) to attract clients. The actions of players, coaches, parents, and "advisors" can make the life of an agent difficult—particularly since most agents rely on their commission as a primary source of income and are therefore usually not in a position to say "No" to most requests. Few sport-management students realize an agent's long hours, tough working conditions, and stressful lifestyle. Students wishing to become an agent should seek opportunities to work for an established agency. Though most agents are reluctant to share their secrets regarding recruitment and retention of clients—for fear of training someone to eventually become their competition—there are typically opportunities to work for agents doing a variety of tasks such as coordinating athlete appearances and researching marketing opportunities. Students who desire to become an agent should not abandon that dream, but should realize the incredibly tough environment in which player agents operate.

Athlete Foundations

With the large salaries that some professional athletes earn, there is often a pressure to "give back" to the community. Most prominent athletes have either established charitable foundations or work closely with organizations that attempt to enhance the livelihood of various constituents. Athletes can generate positive publicity through their charitable work with schools, hospitals, and other entities that serve the community. There are potential internship and employment opportunities working for athlete foundations. This has become especially important over the past 10 years as many athletes have been publicly chastised and, in some cases prosecuted, for allowing family members and close friends to improperly operate their charitable foundation. With an increased emphasis on operating athlete foundations as a legitimate non-profit organization, many of these organizations have sought sport-management students for internships and entry-level employment.

Sport Tourism

Though tourism is one of the world's oldest industries, many components of organized sport tourism in the United States have only been developed in the past 30 years. In the United States, the 1904 St. Louis (Missouri) World's Fair was organized in concert with the 1904 Olympic Games. Hosting both events was designed to maximize the number of tourists who would visit St. Louis. Despite the success of the 1904 Olympics, most sport events in the first third of the 20th century were primarily viewed as "local" events. However, during the height of the Great Depression, the 1932 Los Angeles Olympics attracted many spectators who spent money in the Los Angeles area. In 1939, the National Baseball Hall of Fame and Museum was opened in Cooperstown, New York. Despite the ongoing economic depression, the induction of the first class of baseball hall of famers generated substantial onsite attendance and national media attention. Other sports and leagues would later establish their own Halls of Fame to attract tourists.

In the United States, the link between sports and tourism has continued to grow. Various companies, particularly those in the restaurant, hotel, and car-rental industries, reap economic benefits when sport events attract tourists from outside the community. Tourists who spend money generate "economic impact," which can spur employment opportunities and enhance tax receipts. Certainly, most cities' convention and visitors bureaus attempt to attract as many sport events, and sport tourists, as possible.

Courtesy David Eadie

The San Jose Sports Authority works to bring events such as the Rock 'n' Roll San Jose Half Marathon, with an estimated economic impact of over $16 million annually, to San Jose.

Attracting sport events to a local community is perceived to be important enough for many municipalities that agencies specifically tasked with attracting such events have been established. The San Jose Sports Authority (SJSA) is an excellent example of an agency established to attract sport events to a community, in order to attract tourists and generate economic activity. Long overshadowed by San Francisco and Oakland to the north, the City of San Jose established the SJSA in 1991. Since its creation, the SJSA has worked to bring sport events such as the NCAA Division-I Women's Final Four, NCAA Division-I Men's Basketball Western Regional Finals, Major League Soccer All-Star Game, Siebel Classic (Senior PGA event), and numerous U.S. Olympic trials to San Jose.

There are numerous opportunities to work in sport tourism and new opportunities are continually being developed. Recently, travel companies have developed sport tourism packages that offer organized tours of stadiums and other sport facilities in a variety of cities. It is likely that sport tourism opportunities will continue to expand in the future, making this an important potential outlet for internships and employment opportunities.

Employment Placement

The growth of the sport industry and the proliferation of sport organizations have resulted in the creation of companies that specialize in helping sport-management students find internships and entry-level employment. In addition, many such organizations link established sport management professionals to sport organizations that need specific skills. For instance, TeamWork Online (through its web-based services) assists sport organizations in finding employees and employees finding open sport-management positions. Six Figure Sports is another company that specializes in helping sport organizations seeking employees, but their focus is typically upon executive-level searches. It is likely that as the sport industry continues to develop, additional organizations that provide employment consulting will be established, creating additional sport-management employment opportunities.

Sport Sponsors

The importance of sport sponsorship has grown over the past 20 years—both for sport entities and for local, regional, national, and international companies. With sports becoming a larger component of many individuals' everyday lives, many organizations have realized that they must actively attempt to understand sport sponsorship and its potential costs and benefits. Many Fortune 500 companies have staff members specifically tasked with evaluating sport-sponsorship opportunities. Sport-management graduates often have a unique understanding of what makes a sport athlete, team, league, or event worthwhile for potential sponsorship. Though working in the corporate world may not seem as "exciting" as working for a team or league, there are some potential benefits. Most Fortune 500 companies offer much higher salaries than those in other sport-industry sectors. In addition, though employees are expected to work diligently, especially during sponsored events, there tends to be a more "reasonable" expectation of working hours and better fringe benefits (excluding the opportunity to be a part of a potential championship team). Even if a company does not have a division devoted specifically to sport-sponsorship, most organizations task their marketing staffs with exploring all possible outlets to enhance their brand. There are many sport-management graduates working in "marketing" for non-sport organizations who maintain a close contact to the industry through marketing and sponsorship opportunities.

Conclusion

Opportunities for internships and entry-level employment in the U.S. sport-management industry are extremely diverse. There are myriad avenues for students to pursue. Certainly, developing a knowledge base by studying the industry is important for future success, but understanding the nuances of various subsectors can only be accomplished by working in that industry area. Students should begin to explore potential opportunities immediately, as no employer will ever tell an applicant that they have "too much experience" for a sport-management position.

chapter 3
Interviews

Interview 3.1

Dr. Tom Regan
Associate Professor &
Graduate Director
Department of Sport
and Entertainment
Management
University of South Carolina

In the nine years that Dr. Regan served as chair of the University of South Carolina Department of Sport and Entertainment Management, the undergraduate program expanded to over 500 students, new faculty were hired, a master's program was created, and plans to start a doctoral program were implemented. Throughout Dr. Regan's tenure as chair, the academic requirements consistently increased and USC's graduates positively impacted numerous areas of sport and entertainment management. Through Dr. Regan's leadership, USC's sport and entertainment management undergraduate program has become one of the best in the country and its graduate program is in position to begin to attract quality students from throughout the world.

Q: Can you briefly describe your background and career path?

A: I was born and raised in Miles City, Montana, one of six children of blue-collar working parents. I attended the University of Wyoming on a baseball scholarship and graduated with undergraduate (1979) and master's (1981) degrees in Accounting. My first job after graduation was as a staff accountant for Fox and Co. CPA's (later Fox/Grant Thorton after a merger). After two years I took a job as the senior accountant at Natural Gas Processing Company. Within six months I became the controller and worked for the next eight years with NGP, Wyoming Gas Co. and other entities we purchased.

I then wanted to do something that involved my passions of sport and business. The University of Northern Colorado had a new sport-management doctoral program. Though I was initially concerned about some aspects of the new program, I enrolled and enjoyed taking courses that conformed to my business background. I finished my degree by writing my dissertation on the Economic Impact of the Denver Broncos. After graduation in May 1991, I took an academic position at the University of South Carolina in the Department of Sport Administration (since renamed) under the tutelage of Dr. Guy Lewis, who started the University of Massachusetts sport-management program many years before. USC's program was attractive because it was business oriented rather than physical education or recreation focused.

I have stayed at the University of South Carolina in the Department of Sport and Entertainment Management since my initial appointment. After being tenured and promoted in 1997, I was named the department chair, a position I held for over nine years. During that time the department grew from 151 students and three full-time tenure track faculty members to over 500 students and 10 full-time faculty members.

Q: What have been the biggest challenges you have encountered during your career?

A: Balancing work and family is always a challenge. I have tried to never let work get in the way of being at my children's games or significant events. I can work later in the day, at home, or on weekends to make sure I keep my priorities in order. Everyone needs to maintain balance in their mental, social, spiritual, and physical lives. Properly juggling home and work lives often takes planning and commitment.

The academic world often reacts slowly to change and accomplishing goals quickly can sometimes be a challenge. Working within a bureaucracy is often difficult and a university has multiple layers of approval for most activities.

Q: What are the most important issues sport-management programs, and specifically sport-management faculty members, currently face?

A: The ongoing struggle is to stay current and relevant to the sport and entertainment industry. Programs should focus on doing practical, applied research that the industry can use to enhance their business activities. Research should impact the financial bottom line not only by enhancing revenue but also by containing costs.

Q: What are the most important skills for sport-management students to develop?

A:
- Interpersonal communication (writing, especially activities outside of Twitter/Texting)
- Entrepreneurship (ability to problem solve and incorporate ideas from various aspects of business)
- Public speaking
- Sales—the ability to sell is critical
- Accounting
- Strategic management—this is often the difference between the manager and the subordinate.

Q: What classes do you recommend students take while an undergraduate (especially electives)?

A:
- Public speaking
- Accounting
- Finance
- Marketing
- Sales
- Graphic design (helps with sporting events—creating brochures, etc.)
- Foreign language—It is a global economy and foreign language skills are invaluable.
- Computer skills—this is essential. At a minimum a comprehensive understanding of MS Office is needed but additional skills are helpful, particularly a comprehensive understanding of MS Excel.

Q: How do you teach students to understand that sport management extends beyond becoming an agent or a general manager of a professional sport franchise?

A:
- There are more neonatal surgeons than general managers of a professional-sport franchise. Considering how difficult it is to become a surgeon, students should consider the likelihood of becoming a GM.
- I tell the students who are interested in being an agent to go to law school and build the agency after they have established a solid practice as an attorney. You have to make a living, and agency work is a dog-eat-dog world where lots of financial resources and contacts are needed. If you do not have a client, you are not an agent!
- I tell them to read biographies of successful sport managers from a variety of fields.

Q: Where are the best places to find jobs in sport management presently? Where do you see the largest areas of growth for sport-management jobs in the future?

A:
- Jobs that are related to facilities (professional, college, and interscholastic sport and entertainment venues of all sizes) are available. The challenge for many facilities is how they will pay for the debt that was accumulated to build the venue. Increasing the number of events is the likely answer and there will be jobs in that area of the business.

- Largest area of growth will be international events in Asia. Many Asian countries have a growing middle class with disposable income and free time, which means they will be looking for opportunities to spend some of that money.

Q: Once students start their first sport-management job, what are the most important things they should consider as they plan their career path?

A: First, listen during meetings and don't speak because you think you can add content. Listen, learn, see who the leaders or power players are in the meetings. Then as you continue to learn and listen, one day you will be asked your thoughts. Be ready and have content to add to the discussion. It is a test – are you ready?

Next, learn corporate structure. You can see it in class in a book and tell stories about management, leadership, and bosses, but experience is the only way you really understand corporate America. It is a great thing to learn and it is a great system that benefits the brightest.

Don't be afraid to relocate. Great careers are not born in your backyard. Relocate and be willing to have a sense of adventure. If you want to be the AD at your alma mater, you better move a couple of times; get the experience and hopefully the break to get back home. It is not an easy journey.

Q: Do you typically advise undergraduate students to pursue graduate school?

A: For students who want to pursue a career in college athletics a master's degree is required. For other fields it is not required, but the skills that can be learned in graduate schools can certainly help. Specific careers (agent—law) do require a specified graduate degree, but there are many successful sport managers who do not have a graduate degree.

Interview 3.2

Dr. Norm O'Reilly
Richard P. and Joan S. Fox
Professor of Management
Professor and Chair,
Department of Sports
Administration, College of
Business
Ohio University

Q: Could you briefly describe your career path from undergraduate student to your current position?

A: Honestly, I never intended to be a professor. I entered my undergraduate in science hoping to learn more about being an athlete (I was a serious triathlete and Nordic skier) and potentially going to medical school or chiropractic college. After spending time volunteering at both a doctor's office and a chiro clinic, I learned quickly the field was not for me. Following my third year at the University of Waterloo, I had a chance to work the summer at Triathlon Canada and I loved it. My first boss—Bill Hallett—was president of Triathlon Canada and really introduced me to business (I had not taken business courses up to that point) and my career path formed. I worked again for Triathlon Canada the next year, then went to graduate school, doing both an MA (Sports Admin) and an MBA. I still had no intention of being a professor. Following my MBA, I did some consulting for a while (we started our own firm in management and biotech consulting), then worked for the 2008 Toronto Olympic bid, finally getting a job at Sport Canada (the Government of Canada's department responsible for sport in Canada), where I stayed for about three years. During that time, I had a chance to teach part time at my alma matter—the University of Ottawa—and loved it. I did this for four years and also started my PhD at Carlton University's Sprott School of Business working with my advisor, Dr. Judith Madill, a marketing and social marketing expert. My thesis built a process model for sponsorship evaluation, something of both academic and practitioner need—which I think is what I aspire to do. This led me into an interest in research in the area, spawning into sport finance, sport marketing, sponsorship, social marketing, and tourism marketing. While at Sport Canada, an opportunity came to interview for a professor job at Laurentian University's School of Sports Administration, Canada's oldest sports administration program (SPAD). I didn't win the competition but when they couldn't sign with the first choice, I got a call just days before the term was to start and made the quick and risky decision to leave the government and try an academic life. After one year in Laurentian, I moved to Ryerson University's Rogers School of Management in Toronto for three years (2003-2006) and then back to Laurentian as Director of the SPAD program for another three years (2006-2009), followed by a year at Syracuse University and a sabbatical as Visiting Professor at Stanford University's Graduate School of Business. In 2010, I returned to the University of Ottawa as a professor in the School of Human Kinetics and have just recently moved to Ohio University's Department of Sports Administration as Chair of the Department and a full Professor. In addition to these roles, I have continued to work professionally as a consultant (Senior advisor at Toronto-based TrojanOne Ltd from 2005 to today), taken on Visiting Professorships (Stanford, Limerick, AUT University, UNSW Canberra), and built research partnerships with colleagues around the world.

Q: What have been the biggest challenges you have encountered during your career?

A: Time management. Keeping research going while doing other things (and having a family) is very challenging and requires sacrificing sleep and balancing work with life.

Q: Are there specific skills sport-management students should look to develop while still in school?

A: Yes! I've been doing a project on this led by Dr. David Finch of Mount Royal University and Dr. John Nadeau of Nipissing University and we're finding there is a disconnect between what managers want and what most schools are providing. This includes both hard and soft skills. So, this is a multilevel answer. Simply put, we need to narrow the gap with practice, in my view.

Q: How does Ohio University work to develop those skills in students?

A: I've only been here for a few months and, wow, the faculty here amaze me, as do the 3,400+ alumni with their focus on students, placements, industry-projects, and applied research. There is a reason they—now we—are ranked as one of the top schools and programs in our field. Tremendous attention is paid to the curriculum and staying up-to-date on what employers/industry wants/needs. An alumni board (one for graduate programs and one for undergraduate) provide input as well. Any changes are vetted through them.

Q: What are the biggest changes you see occurring in the next three to five years in sport-management academic programs?

A: We have lots—it's a growing field.

1. Too many programs/places and not enough jobs for graduates
2. Achieving a global body (The WASM is starting this effort now, which is good.)
3. Low entry-level pay for graduates
4. Making sense of accreditation—AACSB, ASB, COSMA, etc.—and making accreditation matter industry wide
5. Enhancing 'hard skills' in our curriculums (finance, accounting, etc.)

Q: What publications do you regularly read to stay apprised of sport-business events?

A: I am biased as I also write a regular column with Rick Burton, but *SportBusiness Journal* is my number-one source for industry biz info.

Q: Would you recommend students pursue graduate school? If so, when should they pursue a graduate degree and what area of study would you recommend?

A: Yes, but only after a few years of work experience and after achieving a keen understanding of what they want to do. I'd also say that if your career is progressing as you want without it, then keep progressing. When you stall or want to change fields/sports, graduate school is an ideal 'diving board' to move.

Learning Activity

Create a list of 25 sport-management professionals who have achieved success in an area you feel you might have interest. Contact each of those professionals and ask to conduct informational interviews so that you can begin to build not only your knowledge base, but also your professional network.

References

Coakley, J. (2009). *Sports in society* (9th ed.). New York: McGraw-Hill.

Divisional differences and the history of multidivisional classification. (n. d.). Retrieved from http://www.ncaa.org/about/who-we-are/membership/divisional-differences-and-history-multidivision-classification

Jones, A. (2008, February 13). Regents board approves logos on coffins. *The Atlanta Journal-Constitution.* Retrieved March 14, 2010 from http://www.ajc.com/metro/content/metro/stories/2008/02/13/coffin_0214.html

Lombardo, J. & Smith, M. (2009, May 25). Ga. Tech hands ticket sales to Aspire Group *SportsBusiness Journal.* Retrieved March 27, 2010 from http://www.sportsbusinessjournal.com/article/62558

Rovell, D. (2014, June 23). UK sells marketing rights to JMI. Retrieved from http://espn.go.com/college-sports/story/_/id/11122483/kentucky-wildcats-sell-marketing-rights-jmi-sports

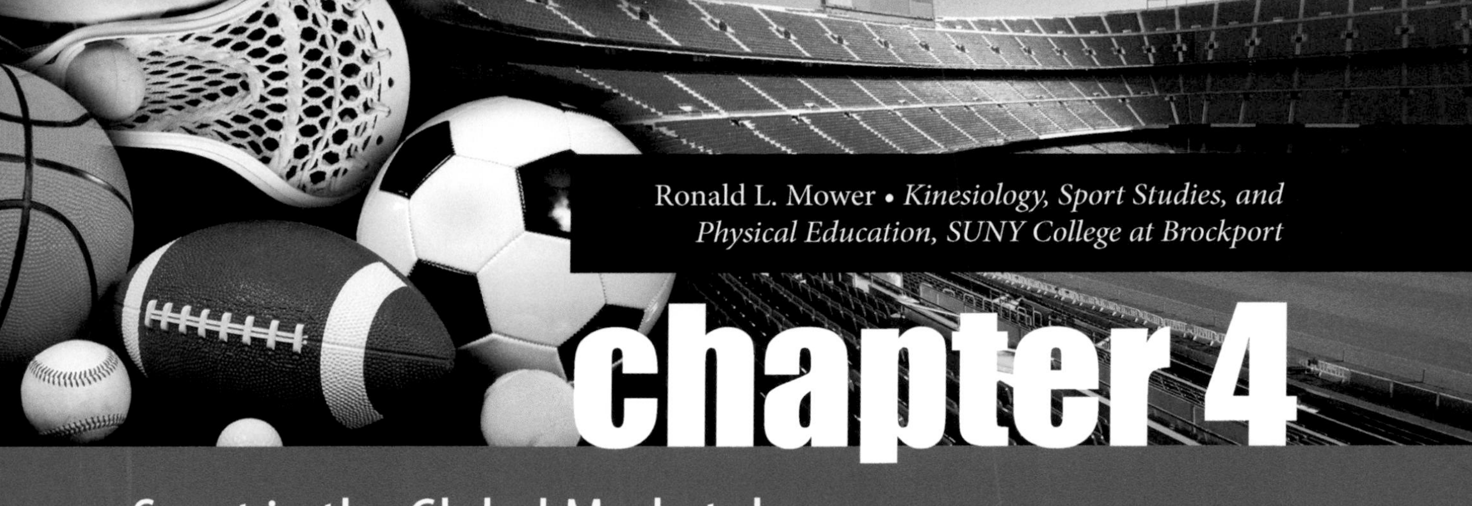

Ronald L. Mower • *Kinesiology, Sport Studies, and Physical Education, SUNY College at Brockport*

Sport in the Global Marketplace

CHAPTER OBJECTIVES

After reading this chapter, you will be able to:

- Understand and analyze some of the key transformations in the global (cultural) economy and the role that sport plays within it.
- Compare and contrast specific examples of how sport constitutes, and is constituted by, intricate processes of global interconnectivity.
- Synthesize an array of basic global theories to interpret and explain the character and influence of sport in diverse global contexts.
- Think critically about issues facing the production and management of sport in nations possessing different politics, cultures, technologies, and economic infrastructures.
- Enter the global sport marketplace with an appreciation for new technologies, cultural differences, and the need for new solutions in a complex global age.

KEY TERMS

Commodification

Complex connectivity

Cultural (symbolic) production

Global heterogenization

Global homogenization

Global hybridity

> *Sport is probably the most universal aspect of popular culture. It crosses languages and countries to captivate spectators and participants, as both a professional business and a pastime.*
>
> —Miller, Lawrence, McKay, & Rowe, 2001, p. 1
>
> *Globalization is like putting together a jigsaw puzzle: it is a matter of inserting a multiplicity of localities into the overall picture of a new global system.*
>
> —Morley & Robins, 1995, p. 116

Introduction

The world has continued to become smaller as technology has enabled communication and travel around the globe to become easier and faster. The world of sport business is not immune to these changes that have occurred. Successful sport managers in the 21st century must not only think local, regional, and national but international in scope. Understanding and appreciating the global sport business environment will continue to grow in importance in the future.

The impact of organized sport can be witnessed throughout the world, just as broader societal forces and processes (culture, technology, politics, and the economy) help constitute the very nature and experience of contemporary sport. Without question, sport has developed in tandem with new technologies and political arrangements that enable sport to surpass national boundaries as it presents itself through media (satellite television, Internet, radio), products (merchandised apparel, sporting goods equipment), and services (live games, ticket sales, concessions). The mass consumption of sport (purchasing sport-related products and services) proliferated dramatically in the latter half of the 20th century with the advent of television, and in the 21st century with the prevalence of the Internet, and new communication technologies. Technologies of instantaneous mass communication not only link disparate peoples across the globe, but also alter the way information is accessed, thereby affecting the influence, presentation, and role of sport in our daily lives. Further, despite economic crises and security threats, modes of global transportation facilitate rapid business and tourist travel, or permanent migration to any location on the planet. Conceivably, one could ride the ferry from Amsterdam to London, fly from London to New York, take a bus from New York to Baltimore, and still get home in time to catch a few late innings of the Orioles on the Mid-Atlantic Sports Network (MASN); all the while surfing the net to catch the latest *SportsCenter* highlights, chatting with family in California, sending text messages to friends in New Zealand, and listening to reggae music on the all-encompassing iPhone. These diverse technologies of travel and communication interact with sport in some important ways. However, in order to begin understanding the nature of these interrelationships, and their potential impact, it is important to try to think relationally about sport within the wider context of societal structures, institutions, and processes. In other words, consider how a particular sport—the way it is played, where, under what circumstances, by whom, and for whose ultimate benefit—is both a product, and producer, of its contextual location, and the social relations that exist there within a globally interconnected society. This idea is extremely important for sport managers seeking to understand how global processes are inherently tied to, and reflective of, sport in its various iterations.

With the steady growth of (inter)national sporting competition, and professional leagues across the globe vying to expand into new markets, tomorrow's sport managers face not only numerous challenges, but also unique opportunities to shape the workings of the global sport marketplace (see Table 4.1 for a glimpse of current global sporting leagues). Within this chapter, some basic theories, and key issues affecting the global sport marketplace will be discussed with the intention of guiding you towards a conceptualization of managing effectively, ethically, and with a respectful understanding of sport's local, national, and global character. As the opening quotes to this chapter might suggest, globalization (and the globalization of sport in particular) is an extremely complex process, with the term itself being quite protean in nature, and frequently debated within academic and professional circles. Given the degree of dispute concerning its meaning and influence, globalization, and its impact, is perhaps an overlooked, or taken for granted, phenomenon amongst most people who are nonetheless affected by it every day, with or without realizing it. However, for those seeking to be successful in an increasingly complex global market, developing a more global perspective, informed through an understanding of interconnectivity, and the interplay of culture and commerce, is a good place to start.

Before discussing the global interconnectivity of sport commerce and culture, it must be noted that both critical and complementary theories from a range of disciplines will be presented throughout this chapter. While there are vast literatures sometimes contradicting the basic values and ideals of one another about the topic—some lauding the pursuit of efficient operations and enhanced profit margins, others criticizing human rights abuses and increasing wealth/health disparities—this chapter will present just a glimpse of the complexities involved in globalization, and particularly that of the globalization of sport. Ultimately, it is hoped that a greater understanding of such issues, and the ability to think critically about them, will translate into more effective problem solving and management in the future. Discussion of various global sport properties, transnational corporations (TNCs), and sport-related businesses will arise throughout the chapter, culminating in some more detailed explanations of careers in global sport-related commerce and in particular, that of a sport practitioner for Visa Europe and one in China.

TABLE 4.1 Major Sporting Leagues and Organizations around the Globe

Australian Rules Football
Australian Football League
Victorian Football League
West Australian Football League
Auto Racing
National Association of Stock Car Auto Racing (NASCAR)
Formula 1
National Hot Rod Association (NHRA)
Baseball
Major League Baseball (MLB)
Nippon Professional Baseball (Japan)
Puerto Rican Professional Baseball League
Korean Baseball Organization
Basketball
National Basketball Association (NBA)
Women's National Basketball Association (WNBA)
Ligue Nationale de Basketball (France)
Baltic Basketball League (BBL; Latvia, Lithuania, Estonia, and Sweden)
Super Basketball League (SBL; Taiwan)
Fédération Internationale de Basketball (FIBA)
Bowling
Professional Bowlers Association (PBA)
Boxing
International Boxing Federation (IBF)
World Boxing Association (WBA)
Cricket
International Cricket Council (ICC)
National Elite League Twenty20 (Kenya)
Women's National Cricket League (Australia)
Indian Premier League (IPL)
Major League Cricket (United States)
National Cricket League of Bangladesh
Curling
Canadian Curling Association

Football
National Football League (NFL)
United Football League (U.S. league in beginning stages of development)
Arena Football League (Canceled 2009 season)
Canadian Football League (CFL)
Golf
Professional Golf Association (PGA)
Ladies Professional Golf Association (LPGA)
European Tour
Hockey
National Hockey League (NHL)
American Hockey League
Kontinental Hockey League (Russia, with teams also in Belarus, Kazakhstan, and Latvia)
Deutsche Eishockey Liga (Germany)
Hurling
Gaelic Athletic Association (GAA)
National Hurling League (Ireland)
Lacrosse
Major League Lacrosse (MLL)
National Lacrosse League (NLL)
Major Series Lacrosse (Canada)
Rugby
Rugby Football League (RFL)
Rugby Union (RU)
Super League (England, Wales, France)
National Rugby League (Australia, New Zealand)
Professional Rugby League (Russia)
Soccer
FA Premier League (England)
Primera División de México (Mexico's Premier Division)
Campeonato Brasileiro (Brazil)
Major League Soccer (MLS; United States)
Professional Football League (Trinidad & Tobago)
Tennis
Association of Tennis Professionals (ATP)
Women's Tennis Association (WTA)

*Note: This list is by no means exhaustive; there are hundreds of sporting leagues and organizations not listed here, including entire sports not mentioned as well. The International Olympic Committee (IOC) alone recognizes over 200 international sport federations and nongovernmental organizations that promote, develop, and organize global sport competitions.

Basic Theories in the Globalization Debate

In order to grasp the place of sport within processes of globalization, we must first understand what globalization is, and take at least a cursory look at some theories of globalization emanating from disciplines as diverse as political science, economics, and sociology. First, as technological capacities and modes of transportation continue to increase, the rate at which "goods, capital, people, knowledge, images, crime, pollutants, drugs, fashions, and beliefs . . . flow across territorial boundaries" has likewise intensified (McGrew, 1992, p. 66). In this sense, our existence in a "global age" (Albrow, 1996) has been described as a compression of time (instantaneous global mass communication) and space (rapid global mass transportation) where, hypothetically speaking, our globe is shrinking (Harvey, 1989). No matter what our country of origin, our ancestors as recently as the early 20th century envisioned the world much differently than we do today. While we send messages instantly to remote locations across the globe using our Droid or iPhone, imagine the time it took to compose a handwritten letter, and have it shipped across the frontier via railroad, or across the ocean by boat. Further, with the time it took to communicate or travel globally, many cultures maintained a degree of autonomy and isolation from people of different cultures in distant regions. The world seemed a much larger place, with many different ideologies, politics, economies, cultural practices (like sport), and social relations that were completely unknown or misunderstood by the majority of the worlds' population outside of any given locality and its immediate reach.

Complex connectivity
Tomlinson's (1999) notion of an ever-densening network of global interconnections and interdependencies that characterize modern life. Rapid increases in technology, modes of communication, travel, and trade have enabled an intensification of global flows—for example, the speed at which intangibles (ideas and information services) and tangibles (products and people) can circle the globe is either instantaneous (Internet, cable television, satellite) or quite swift (plane, train, ship). As a result, cultures and peoples who were once so detached are now incredibly connected and dependent upon each other, especially in realms of politics and economics.

Today, however, the barriers that once separated disparate peoples and cultures have largely dissipated, leading to new connections and dependencies in a global world order in which the spatial organization of social relations is altered through transcontinental or interregional *flows* and *networks* of activity (Held, McGrew, Goldblatt, & Perraton, 1999; Maguire, Jarvie, Mansfield, & Bradley, 2002). As an important conception of the global condition, John Tomlinson stated that globalization is "an empirical condition of the modern world: what I shall call—**complex connectivity**. By this I mean the rapidly developing and ever-densening network of interconnections and interdependencies that characterize modern social life" (1999, p. 2, *emphasis added*). In other words, complex connectivity refers to the development of various *networks* of organizations, governing bodies, and corporations (an idea we will come to shortly) and the connected and dependant nature with which they operate and/or conduct business, resulting in a rapid *flow* of exchange (see also Castells, 1997). With this in mind, the increased connectivity of the global age indicates that no country, region, city, or individual is completely isolated from (or rather, unaffected by) the broader processes, practices, and products of the global marketplace (McLuhan & Powers, 1989). It is important to understand that not only can this intensified *interconnectivity* produce positive outcomes like the ability to communicate widely or to break down cultural barriers, but it also presents the possibility of negative outcomes when irresponsible decisions are made without concern for others. In a more disturbing and sobering aspect, events occurring in country X can have implications and effects for people in country Y, whether by intervention, or the lack thereof, during environmental or natural disasters, economic crises, political strife, or war and acts of terrorism. In many cases, the problems arising from the international relations of countries are due to established hierarchies of power, cultural differences, and disparate ideological values. While not as dramatic, sporting institutions face similar barriers, as sport is intricately tied to the cultural values and political ideals of particular nations and regions. Sports marked as being distinctly American (basketball, football, baseball) or European (soccer, cricket, rugby), for example, have developed over time and represent many years of political ideals, technological innovations, cultural changes, and national identities that resonate with people sharing those common points of reference. As a global sport manager, expanding into foreign markets, or working in a foreign market to begin with, requires a sensitivity and understanding of such differences to make informed decisions that are both profitable for your organization, and ethical toward the consumers and country in which you operate.

Understanding the managerial context of a particular sporting organization, or associated entity, is a vital part of operating efficiently and effectively in any market. This means that in order to be successful, one must have a working knowledge of the conditions and factors that may influence or effect business. For example, since sport is linked to broader political, technological, and cultural forces, it has tremendous power to influence, impose, or alter the lived experiences and identities of people, communities, and nations. Likewise, individuals, communities, and nations have power to influence the production of sport in various ways. Thus, within foreign markets in particular, having knowledge of the cultural differences, political ideologies, and common business practices of the locality will be a valuable asset in making sound decisions. As one potential barrier to foreign expansion, negative perceptions of Western developed nations (the United States and United Kingdom, for example) sometimes hinder the reception of brand names, sport leagues, and products emanating from such countries. Some scholars have described such sentiments as being critical of the unequal power structures (the "west and the rest") and corporate ambitions of Western developed nations (especially the United States) for imposing distinct cultural, economic, and political forms upon poorer developing nations, sport being an important part of this process (see, for example, Hall, 1992). Or, as noted by Kuisel (2003), "the import by non-Americans of products, images, technologies, practices, and behavior that are closely associated with America/Americans" has been defined as *Americanization* (p. 96). Nevertheless, while globalization has often been attributed to various processes of Americanization, the complexities of global relations cannot be reduced to a unidirectional flow. We can see some obvious examples of globalization's multidirectional flow just by looking at the cultural and ethnic diversity of America: the international foods we eat, languages spoken, prevalence of foreign-made products, growing popularity of soccer, and so on. While the outcomes of these processes traverse both the negative aspects of capitalist globalization and the positive aspects of multiculturalism and flow of ideas, they also denote the complex and irreducible nature of globalization as a dispersed phenomenon. It is within this conception that we can see political, economic, cultural, and technological *networks* playing a role in the development of interdependencies and interconnections between and within nations (see Table 4.2). In addition to global events like the Olympics and the World Cup, for example, the World Baseball Classic (WBC) demonstrates the development of global networks through the coming together of nations and the shared technological platforms that each country (in varying degrees) uses to stream media coverage of the event to their home nations. Furthermore, although baseball is widely known as a distinctly American sport, events like the WBC indicate the extent to which the game has been spread through various modes of global travel and communication technologies. As interconnected and interdependent networks continue to intensify the means and ease with which global flows occur, three basic theoretical frameworks or paradigms (ways of viewing and thinking about something) have emerged from the scholarly community to describe our condition in the global age: global homogenization, global heterogenization, and global hybridity.

TABLE 4.2 Various Networks of Global Connectivity

Political Networks
• Global government organizations United Nations (UN) World Bank (WB) World Health Organization (WHO) • Regional political structures European Union (EU) • Regional military alliances NATO • Global non-governmental organizations Red Cross/Red Crescent Greenpeace Amnesty International
Economic Networks
As economies globalize, corporations look beyond national boundaries for raw materials, production, and markets. This was possibly due to changes since 1980: I. Increased deregulation of economic protectionist policies; tariff and quota barriers loosened. II. Opening of financial markets, and establishment of a truly global financial structure. III. Increased foreign investment in national markets. IV. Emergence of truly global corporations.
Technological Networks
• Advances have radically changed the speed and scope of global transport and communications technologies. • Transport technologies With the development of the jetliner we are now in an age of RAPID GLOBAL MASS TRANSPORTATION. • Communications technologies. With the development of satellite television and Internet technologies, we are now in an age of INSTANTANEOUS GLOBAL MASS COMMUNICATION. • TV—people in the United States can watch European soccer and Europeans can watch NFL (satellite).
Cultural Networks
Political, economic, and technological shifts have increased the rate of flow of objects, images, and people across national, regional, and global space. This has led to the emergence of: I. Diasporic populations: New waves of immigration and establishment of ethnically diverse communities. II. A new global multiculturalism: Greater flow of previously indigenous cultural practices and styles. III. A new global monoculturalism: Increased spread and influence of culturally homogenizing global products, practices, and images.

Global homogenization
Theory that countries, nations, corporations, politics, economies, and cultures are becoming increasingly the same. More specifically, it generally cites three main forces responsible for the global diffusion of ideas, information, products, and an accelerated level of cultural convergence/sameness/uniformity: (1) free market liberal economics, (2) global corporate structures and technologies, and (3) a consumer capitalist culture. In relation to sport, the processes and structures of global sporting organizations and events can be said to operate much the same, mainly due to the adoption of principles of American business and corporate structure.

As the term suggests, **global homogenization** refers to a condition in which everything is the same or in the process of becoming uniform and undifferentiated; a convergence of cultures, ideas, politics, and the like. Global corporations like Nike, McDonalds, Coca-Cola, and Walmart are often discussed as being primary proponents of global *homogenization* due to their involvement in scouring the globe for cheaper production costs, new markets, and raw materials. Since their presence is felt and known nearly everywhere in the world, the conditions relative to their overwhelming success often call into question the extent to which they are exploiting or altering the economies, cultures, and politics of foreign nations to make them more like America; thereby simplifying and increasing profitability in the mode of production and consumption in transnational business. With regard to sport, then, we can see definitive relationships between the overzealous expansionism of Western thought, politics, economics, and cultural values and the global diffusion of popular sporting forms as constitutive elements in the flattening of cultural difference. In other words, according to this theory, the fact that you can go practically anywhere in the world and still have access to ESPN, McDonalds, Coke products, Nike, and a range of other distinctly American products and brand images denotes the scale and scope of global *homogenization*. Over 10 years ago, managers in predominantly American sports (basketball and baseball, primarily) realized the need to, or were already actively engaged in, seeking out new markets globally, recognizing that there were:

> fans willing to buy into the excitement of American-style entertainment. . . . Sports leagues are discovering what Coca-Cola., McDonald's Corp., Disney Co. and the makers of Marlboro cigarettes figured out long ago: The trappings of America's consumer culture will sell overseas (Alms, 1994, p. 1D).

McDonalds is an example of a company that has experienced some resistance as it expanded operations throughout the world.

With the aforementioned success of other American corporations overseas, it is perhaps not surprising that former NBA commissioner David Stern famously quoted so long ago: "There are 250 million potential NBA fans in the U.S., and there are 5 billion outside the U.S. . . . We like those numbers" (Comte, 1993, p. 42). Since that time, the NBA has become a leader in establishing overseas networks and tapping new markets to become a "multifaceted marketing and entertainment conglomerate incorporating over 20 divisions, including NBA Properties, NBA Entertainment, NBA International, and NBA Ventures" (Andrews, 2006, p. 95). Stemming from the 1992 Dream Team in particular, the level of international talent has grown immensely, and has thereby produced an increasingly steady stream of foreign-born celebrity athletes who, representing their NBA team, but also the country of their birth, help to popularize the sport, and their local team, within their home nations. Already broadcast in over 215 countries in 41 different languages, the NBA's marketing expansion into China has produced considerable results. In 2007, the NBA's own global website proclaimed that the NBA had recently:

> . . . added 24 TV partners in China and currently has relationships with 51 TV stations that provided NBA programming to 34 million viewers per week and more than 1.2 billion viewers for the 2006–07 season. With 20% of traffic to NBA.com coming from China, basketball is rapidly growing in popularity . . . ('NBA China,' 2007, para. 8).

However, while China represents a highly valued market with millions of potential consumers, the increasing international success of basketball is also reflective of the proliferation of foreign-born players being recruited by NBA teams. In 1992 for example, only 21 international players appeared on NBA rosters (5%), while the 2013 season boasts an increase to 90 international players or 20% of all players on opening night rosters (NFAP Policy Brief, 2014). The recent success of the 2013-2014 NBA Champion San Antonio Spurs also points to what is likely to be a greater emphasis on recruiting foreign talent. With 7 foreign-born players on their roster, the Spurs led the NBA in this category, and having beaten out the defending champion Miami Heat, provide a compelling example of how global interconnectedness has raised the bar of international talent. It is thus likely that more NBA teams will seek out foreign talent, and as a result, we could see even further shifts in the ethnic/national makeup of the NBA in the future. Nevertheless, while this process represents a potential catalyst for change and diversity, one must also consider the governing structures, regulations, and business interests of league and team officials, who control the packaging and promotion of a carefully managed and controlled NBA product.

With regard to its global homogenizing effects then, it is not only that basketball is generally played the same way (at least in terms of basic rules

China built new facilities, such as the Bird's Nest, to host global sport competitions such as the Olympic Games and Paralympic Games.

Courtesy Richard Southall

Global heterogenization Largely in response to the real and/or perceived threat of globally homogenizing forces, this theory asserts that countries, nations, corporations, politics, economies, and cultures are actually becoming more differentiated, not less. In this sense, local difference has intensified by both the reaction to global uniformity by local cultures and through corporations' realization of the value of cultural niches and marketing of local difference. Sport has been argued to play a considerable role in this process, as fans tend to feverishly support place-based teams that reflect a specific locale and its unique cultural nuances.

and tenets of the game) in China or Australia that it is in America, but it is also broadcast across the globe in much the same fashion (albeit in different languages) denoting processes of increasing technological and economic uniformity in the global sport structure. In other words, while the subtleties of cultural communication and performance might differ from one locale to another, the commercial aspects of its production (media broadcasting, merchandising, sponsorship, advertising, management, and marketing) would seem to affirm the homogenization thesis as one potential lens through which to view this phenomenon.

While homogenization suggests a creeping uniformity, what do we make of the deeply held national and local cultural traditions, values, and allegiances so central to sports' ubiquitous global success? Another way of viewing global sport processes is that sport, unlike other institutions, depends upon the appeal of locality, difference, and uniqueness. In this sense, the notion of **global heterogenization** suggests that, in fact, nations, cultures, and peoples are becoming more differentiated, not less; opposed to the idea of global uniformity and holding dearly to the particularities of their own local cultures. As suggested by David Rowe (2003), "the social institution of sport is so deeply dependent on the production of difference that it repudiates the possibility of comprehensive globalization while seeming to foreshadow its inevitable establishment" (p. 282). In other words, the success of sporting teams and leagues is dependent on consumers' affiliations with a particular place, albeit a town, city, or country. More specifically, sport has the capacity to (re)define the unique cultural and national meanings, histories, and ideals of a country and its citizens due to the visceral and emotional attachment fans maintain with their sporting teams, places, and heroes. Just think about your favorite sport team for a moment. How did you fall in love with that particular team? Was it influenced by the country, region, or locality in which you were raised? Or could it be the cultural meanings associated with a particular team, player, or coach that resonated with your own identity? Many fans of the Pittsburgh Steelers will, to varying degrees, cite the hard work mentality, blue-collar tradition, and masculine toughness associated with the historical memory of past Steelers teams, and their geographic and historical location in a once-thriving industrial economy of steel production, as emblematic of their individual identity and collective affiliation despite their current location (McCollester, 2005). Through communication technologies then, fans can feel like they are still part of a local sporting community no matter where they are geographically. The particular values, beliefs, and cultural norms associated with a team and its city reflects the importance of locality in defining a particular social grouping and imagined community (an imagined community being something like Red Sox Nation where disparate peoples across the globe share interests, information, and norms tied together by a common point of reference; see, Anderson, 1991; Hobsbawm, 1990). This example is interesting because it denotes the obvious existence of global forces (ability to access Red Sox media anywhere) while communicating the cultural resonance of a particular locality (Boston) and its attendant racial and class identities, social norms, and lived experiences (see, for example, Klein, 2000).

However, these American examples are somewhat limited in what they can tell us about such forces on a global scale. While technological innovations and global media play an obvious role, much can be said about the cultural meanings and emotive potential of sport to break down international borders and encourage transnational sport-related commerce through an appeal to the nation and national identity. As ideas, products, people, and organizations rapidly navigate the globe, it would seem inevitable that countries would eventually begin to look the same, espouse the same ideas and values, and exist under the same political and economic logics (reflecting the homogenization thesis). While some of these changes have begun to occur (shopping malls, theme parks, and restaurants, for example, can be difficult to distinguish from one developed economy to another), there remains a great deal of cultural diversity that represents both the potential for **commodification** (turning something into a product for sale on the market) and a refutation of the powerful forces of (corporate) globalization.

One could argue that since WWII, baseball in Japan has been played very much the same as it has in the Unites States. However, others might note the particular manner in which the game is played, aspects of performance that are more valued than others, and the differences in food, music, dress, and behavior that accompany the game atmosphere, and reflect the broader social contexts within which the sporting event occurs. Refuting the global homogenization

Commodification
Refers to a process through which a cultural form is turned into a product to be sold on the market. For example sport, in and of itself, is a cultural practice that has developed over time and throughout history, and reflects the people/civilizations that created, played, and modified it according to the social conditions of that moment. Many of us still play sport just for fun, but the meanings we attach to it are heavily influenced by our consumption practices (purchasing related products and services) of the sports we love. In the 20th century, many popular sports became professionalized and pulled into the imperatives of the market. Thus, sport became a means through which to generate capital (profit) in the rapidly developing entertainment economy.

thesis, these differences embody powerful representations of national identity. Thus, in addition to the political and economic structures of nations, sport functions to constitute the nation through, "a cultural formation, a feeling of belonging, and a shared heritage" (Hardt & Negri, 2000, p. 336). The intense emotional bonds and nationalistic expressions of England's Barmy Army (supporters of England's cricket club) or Korea's Red Devils (supporters of the Korea Republic national football team) are just two examples of organized sport fans that closely relate the meanings, success, and identity of sporting teams with that of the nation. In terms of representing the nation and developing individual national identities through sport, Hobsbawm (1990, p. 143) notes that:

> What has made sport so uniquely effective a medium for inculcating national feelings, at all events for males, is the ease with which even the least political or public individuals can identify with the nation as symbolized by young persons excelling at what practically every man wants, or at one time in life has wanted to be good at. The imagined community of millions seems more real as a team of eleven named people. The individual, even the one who only cheers, becomes a symbol of his nation himself.

Of course, this quote must also be applied to female spectators/athletes, as women have increasingly become regular consumers of sport and have long represented nations themselves in sporting competition. In this regard, Brownell (2008) recounts the historical significance of China's female athletes in the Olympics; promoted as representatives of the strength, virility, and progressive ideologies of the nation amidst dominant global perceptions of China as "the sick man of East Asia" (p. 102). Depending on the popularity of a sporting team and its historical legacy within a given nation, people identify and align themselves with it as one of the most important "badges of membership" within the nation and the imagined community in which they exist and find commonalities (Hobsbawm & Ranger, 1983). On a similar level of global significance, soccer also represents a key site where sporting competition facilitates the development of communities of supporters and intense national rivalries.

As the quintessential global game, football (soccer in the United States) matches bring together local (Fulham vs. Liverpool in the FA Premier League, for example), and global (Korea vs. Japan in the World Cup, for example) competition in spaces where cultural values are made salient and can incite passionate fan support, rivalries, and sometimes violence. In perhaps the most deadly and tragic display of football fan violence in recent years, a 2012 Egyptian League match between Al-Masry and Al-Ahly resulted in the deaths of at least 74 people. Amidst broader political and protest movements within the country (including conflict between organized fan groups called 'ultras' and military forces under former President Hosni Mubarak's regime), the melee between sides was, as one commentator put it, "a result of intentional reluctance by the military and the police" to intervene (Associated Press, 2012, para. 36). In another less violent, yet perhaps surprising incident of international fan violence, given its context within the seemingly more virtuous sport of tennis, an Australian open match between Novak Djokovic (Serbian defending champion) and Amer Delic (born in Bosnia but playing for the United States) in January 2009 erupted in violence between Bosnian and Serbian supporters immediately following Djokovic's victory (Tallentire, 2009). Thus, while we often see the excitement and camaraderie of sporting competition between nations, in some cases, the intense emotional ties of fans with sporting figures, and their local roots, can sometimes facilitate negative perceptions and violent consequences. In addition to the obvious and unfortunate acts of violence, the way that local sporting traditions are remembered, and reproduced, sometimes causes controversy.

In this sense, fans' attachment and loyalty to particular teams, cultural meanings, and values, is often leveraged by corporations seeking to increase brand recognition within countries identified as having untapped markets for TNCs. At the same time, due to the passion and allegiances of consumers to particular sporting forms, teams, and players (Giulianotti, 2002; Lewis, 2001)—concomitant with the strong national, regional, or local ties they espouse—it is often assumed that sport acts as a key site of resistance to these global forces (Rowe, 2003). One interesting example was Adidas's entrance into the New Zealand market by appropriating a traditional dance called the "haka" (performed by the New Zealand All-Blacks rugby team before matches) in an advertisement

Soccer is the world's most popular game and nearly every country on earth supports a team that attempts to compete in the World Cup.

depicting rugby, the haka, and stereotypical images of ancient Maori warriors, to authenticate the brand (Jackson & Hokowhitu, 2002). Local leaders and scholars subsequently criticized the company for exploiting part of an ancient cultural heritage purely for capital gain (see also, Scherer & Jackson, 2007). The extent to which local cultural uniqueness is discovered, commodified, and mass produced can sometimes be disheartening to those whose culture appears to have been trivialized to sell products.

Depending on how you conceptualize what is truly local, it has become nearly impossible to find a unique cultural form that has not, in one way or another, been appropriated, commodified, marketed, and/or mass produced for commercial purposes. Given the realities of our presence in the global age, however, perhaps it is not as important to lament and fight against the loss of perceived locality, but rather to ensure responsible and inclusive global processes, especially when matters of commercializing local culture is involved. This is particularly important for sport managers involved in marketing campaigns, sponsorship deals, or advertising that plays upon aspects of culture to legitimize and popularize sport products or services. If done responsibly and with an informed understanding, cultural references can have an extremely powerful emotive commercial purpose while avoiding stereotypical representations or offensive exploitation; of course this also depends on the credibility and reputation of the company. With this in mind, the third concept of **global hybridity** offers another way of viewing processes of globalization and arguably a more positive and fluid outlook concerning the global-local debate.

Global hybridity
Refers to a theoretical mixture of both the homogenization and heterogenization theses. The hybridity thesis acknowledges that the relationship between local and global forces is much too complex to easily categorize. As such, this theory suggests that a better way to understand globalization is to view it as a global-local nexus, characterized by a complex and ever-changing dynamic between change and continuity, difference and sameness, universality and particularity. As such, global sporting events reflect markers of both local elements (nationalities, cultures, style of play) and global prerogatives (media broadcasting, revenue generation, and marketing).

A hybrid is essentially a mixture of two or more component parts that results in a new sum product. Certainly, sport and its accompanying structures, processes, and outcomes cannot be easily categorized as either local or global in nature. As such, they represent a key site for engaging the complex and ever-changing tensions between change and continuity, difference and sameness, universality and particularity, as experienced by diverse people in local settings across the globe (Robertson, 1995; Robins, 1997). Understanding how people receive and engage with cultural forms and products emanating from the global-local nexus is a key issue at hand for anyone working in the global sport marketplace. As such, the local particularities of any sporting form and its ancillary productions must be understood as a "fluid and relational space, constituted only in and through its relation to the global" and vice versa (Robins, 1991, p. 35). In this sense, an English Premier League (EPL) team like Manchester United, represents locally unique aspects of the broader British culture and more specific peculiarities of Manchester city and its social, cultural, and sporting history. However, it also espouses and is regarded as one of the most Americanized EPL teams due to its corporate sport model; negotiating sponsorship contracts with American companies like Nike, Pepsi Co., and Anheuser Busch, mirroring the "American-style, brand-led media business" in areas of advertising, marketing, and sponsorship, and making promotional tours of the United States (Manchester United, 2002; see also, Hill & Vincent, 2006).

Ironically, when Malcolm Glazer (an American businessman and owner of the Tampa Bay Buccaneers and Manchester United until his recent passing in May 2014) purchased a controlling stake in the United in May 2005 (valued at approximately US$1.5 billion), local fans protested the action with explicit anti-American demonstrations against Glazer and the perceived American values he represented (Brown, 2007; Hill & Vincent, 2006).

Despite the already Americanized business model under which the United operated, for local fans, the idea of an American actually owning the team conjured up the unique place-based memories, values, and traditions that continue to shape the collective experience of being a local Manchester fan. Such emotions are germane to nearly all sport teams, in some degree, across the world, and represent the most salient form of opposition to perceived infractions from the corporate-sport model. It is in these common and increasingly complex tensions between global and local forces that Robertson's (1995) notion of *glocalization* theorizes the relationship arising from both cultural and commercial forces, being relational and complimentary to each other. In other words, the *glocal* represents a continuum between these forces, or rather, "the interpenetration of the global and the local, resulting in unique outcomes in different geographic areas" (Andrews & Ritzer, 2007, p. 135; see also, Ram, 2007). Nevertheless, while some scholars envision local forces as having a real impact on the structure and processes of global commerce, it is questioned

Courtesy Mark Nagel.

Emirates Stadium, home of Arsenal of the English Premier League, is an example of American sport facility design and revenue-generating capabilities being exported to another country.

whether the modifications of global companies to meet the cultural tastes and preferences of a local market is truly evidence of the local's power. A simple and common example of this is McDonald's attempts to cater to their customers in foreign markets through themed restaurants or by offering renditions of local fare: "Kosher Mcnuggets" in Tel Aviv, "kiwiburger" in New Zealand, non-beef "Mcpatties" in India, "McSushi" in Japan, and so forth (see, Watson, 1997). While some may see the local impact of these decisions, others note the overarching logics of the corporation and the principles guiding organizational adaptation and change (Ritzer, 1998, 2008; see also, Amis, 2005). In other words, while the organization may adapt to local markets by offering specialized menu items that mimic local cultural cuisine, the management logics and operational processes remain the same globally.

TABLE 4.3 Basic Principles of McDonaldization

Calculability
Emphasizes the quantitative aspects of products (portion size, cost) and services (time it takes to get the product) over their quality. Value is thus measured in things like portion size and quick delivery of the product. For workers in a McDonaldized system, the lack of variation in the product means they are forced to focus on how quickly tasks can be accomplished (i.e., a lot of work, quickly, for low pay).
Predictability
The assurance that products and services will be the same over time and in any location. The lack of significant change means consumers know exactly what to expect when entering a McDonalds, Walmart, or Starbucks, for example.
Control
Both customers and workers are controlled by systems of rational management. For example, uncomfortable seating and drive-through windows encourage customers to eat quickly and leave or buy their food and drive away. Workers are trained to do a limited number of routine tasks in a precise way; technology controlling the bulk of the labor process leaving behind the mundane service tasks, food preparation, and cleaning.
Efficiency
The optimum method for getting from one point to another. In McDonalds or any other institution, this involves a predesigned process to achieve a desired end result (getting fast food, an insurance quote, or paying for groceries, for example) as quickly as possible (instant consumer gratification).

Before relating this to sport, and sticking with the McDonald's theme, a helpful concept is Ritzer's (1998, 2008) notion of *McDonaldization*; the process through which the principles of the fast-food chain are coming to dominate more and more sectors of American society and the world. Important to note here is that it is an overall business philosophy and four key operational principles (see Table 4.3) that Ritzer envisions as central to the McDonaldization thesis, and not the actual product itself (burgers and fries). Further, like many other ideas presented in this chapter, McDonaldization is a theory (a way of interpreting and making sense of something) created by Ritzer that can be applied to other social phenomena, and is not endorsed by or affiliated with the McDonalds Corporation in any way.

Stemming from the rational production processes of *Fordism* (assembly-line manufacturing of Model T Ford cars in the early 20th century), the principles of McDonaldization are reflective of the dominant governing logics of American business and industry, and as a result, have also been deployed by sporting organizations likewise seeking to increase efficiency, both in sporting and business terms. Further, while these processes represent the global forces we have been discussing, the existence of local particularity is embodied by cultural difference; something that has become highly valued for its ability to distinguish product offerings and create emotive meanings to entice consumers (Silk & Andrews, 2001). In practical terms, effectively managing and balancing the cultural production of local difference ethically through the logics of global free market capitalism is not an easy task. Just imagine you are the acting director of marketing and promotions for the NBA in Australia. Following the established business model of the company, how do you capitalize on the essence of the NBA's American authenticity while appealing to the nuances of Australian cultural sensibilities in an accurate and effective manner? As one example of this complexity, a KFC commercial in Australia created a stir in the U.S. media after spreading via the Internet (the advertisement was only intended to be seen in Australia). In it, a white Australian man is surrounded by West Indies supporters in the stands, during a cricket match between the two countries. Appearing somewhat annoyed by the raucous cheering of the West Indies fans, the man offers them fried chicken to quiet them down. While considered somewhat innocuous within an Australian context (the idea being that by generously sharing good food with opposing fans, they can be distracted from supporting their own team), once virally dispersed across international borders, the ad communicated a quite different and problematic meaning within the U.S. context where a tragic history of racial oppression and injustice continues to inform socially constructed ideas and stereotypes about what it means for Black people to eat, specifically, fried chicken (see "KFC accused," 2010). In particular, the comments of Fuzzy Zoeller following Tiger Woods's 1997 Masters Tournament win, for example, reflect the lingering presence of racism, and the use of racial stereotypes like this particular one, to hurt, discredit, undermine, and subjugate people of color. It is thus of critical import to be conscious of the socially constructed meanings that exist within a particular country, and how the commercial representation of race, ethnicity, gender, sexuality, nationality, religion, age, and ability might be perceived within various contexts and locales. However, navigating such complexities begins with an understanding of the political and cultural economies developed in the late

20th century, which gave rise to new media technologies and the possibility of using certain celebrity figures to represent, and thereby sell, particular products and services in the first place. After a brief discussion of this *postindustrial* shift in the mode of production, two case studies (Nike and News Corporation) will be discussed in relation to the contemporary structure and experience of globally interconnected TNCs.

The Global Sporting Goods Trade: Postindustrialism, Transnational Corporations, and the Rise of Global Branding and Sponsorship

Cultural (Symbolic) Production
A related process to commodification that involves the inscribing of meaning to a particular product. During the industrial revolution, in order to differentiate one product from another, proprietors of a company would advertise the positive attributes of their product over their competitors. With increasing technologies, sophistication in advertising and marketing, and a decreasing industrial base after WWII, branded corporations turned to cultural meanings to attach symbolic value to their products. For example, while two athletic shoes may be made in the same overseas factory, the symbol inscribed on it denotes a greater value than just the cost to produce it. The cultural meaning and symbolism established by marketing/advertising initiatives bestows the product with greater perceived value for consumers.

> It is a world of industrialism and its longstanding imagery that we are leaving behind—the modern factories in an urban setting, the heavy machinery and the ever-present noise, along with the massed ranks of workers in overalls. In its place, we are told that we have entered a *postindustrial era;* one that is characterized by information technologies and networked offices rather than by coal or steam power and sprawling workshops (Allen, 1996, p. 534).

After World War II, rising labor costs (due to the increased standard of living in developed economies), increased production costs (due to the OPEC oil crises), and growing global competition caused countries like the United States and United Kingdom to shift from "dirty" (producing tangible goods in factory settings) to "clean" technologies like information, services, and entertainment (Allen, 1996). Within this new digital economy, the production of "things" became outsourced to developing or underdeveloped economies where labor was cheap, labor laws were weak or nonexistent, and free trade agreements favored large corporations. With manufacturing occurring in other countries, TNCs could focus their attention on the intangible aspects of consumer goods (design, marketing, advertising, and branding). In this sense, the postindustrial shift to **cultural (symbolic) production** at the developed economic core, and mass industrial (material) manufacture at the developing economic peripheries, exemplifies the current state of global sport commerce and international trade. As one of the most telling examples of this, Nike was extremely successful shifting from material to symbolic production to become a leader in the athletic footwear and apparel industry (Willigan, 1992). To be sure, CEO Phil Knight once stated:

> For years we thought of ourselves as a production-oriented company, meaning we put all our emphasis on designing and manufacturing the product. But now we understand that the most important thing we do is market the product. We've come around to saying that Nike is a

> marketing-oriented company, and the product is our most important marketing tool (Willigan, 1992, pp. 93–94).

These developments are further reflected in the gradual decreased production of footwear in the United States, concomitant to the ever-ballooning expenditures on media, advertising, and marketing campaigns. The amount spent on developing the product's *cultural capital* (attaching symbolic meaning and brand identity via marketing and branding initiatives) also positively correlates with the overall return in bottom-line sales relative to other market competitors. For convenience, the extent of Nike's global interconnectedness can be divided generally into two categories along the production process: raw materials, manufacturing, and transportation on one side, and design, marketing, and branding on the other. Countries like Indonesia, China, Thailand, and South Korea are among the many developing economies involved in *global commodity chains* in which the production process in various locales is minutely divided, routinized, and highly regulated to maximize profit (Klein, 1999; Korzeniewicz, 1994). Some scholars are critical of companies like Nike, arguing that the conditions of outsourced manufacturing processes represent the "dark side of flexible production" in which low-wage workers are exploited and local governments and contractors are manipulated into accepting contractual terms that, once entered into, maintain economic stagnancy and dependence (Harrison, 1994; Klein, 1999; Korzeniewicz, 1994). Further, once the resources (raw materials and labor) in a particular country become too expensive, corporations often quickly relocate to less-developed economies that will accept lower wages and trade agreements that disproportionately favor the company. Nevertheless, Nike has continued to deflect global criticism and protest about human rights abuses, and unfair labor agreements, with public-relations campaigns, assuring its efforts at improving working conditions and promoting social and environmental justice. In the 2008 annual report, Nike President and CEO Mark Parker stated:

> We're very focused on creating products that reduce their environmental impact and showcase sustainable innovation. We're committed to helping improve working conditions across the industry's supply chain. And we continue to invest in our communities. . . . Every day we see how social and environmental change can promote innovation and growth in our business and in the world (www.nikebiz.com).

The difficulty of operating with a prescient sense of corporate social responsibility (CSR) while remaining competitive in a complex and saturated global market is aptly reflected in the case of Nike. It could be argued that since 99% of total product manufacturing takes place outside the United States, Nike has made good business decisions, benefitting from strategic outsourcing and flexible production (enabling greater focus on promoting the product), but is not responsible for the conditions of production directly affected by foreign contractors. In fiscal 2008 for example, Nike's contracted suppliers manufactured the following percentages of total Nike footwear: China 36%, Vietnam 33%, Indonesia 21%, and Thailand 9% (www.nikebiz.com). Within these primary contractual arrangements, further contracts are negotiated independently in as many as 34 other countries, including, but not limited to: Malaysia, Turkey, Sri Lanka, Honduras, Mexico, Taiwan, Israel, Cambodia, India, and Bangladesh.

While Nike profits from these arrangements, it is hotly contested whether the individual contractors are liable, or whether Nike, and other companies like them, should play a greater role in alleviating poor working conditions likely caused by contractual pressures and unregulated worker zones in individual countries (Frenkel, 2001; Klein, 1999). While the purpose of this chapter is not to delineate where responsibility begins or ends, this example demonstrates the tremendously complex nature of international business and trade when tangible products like sporting goods are involved. In this sense, it could be argued that advanced economies like those of the United States and the United Kingdom are nearly inconducive to the production of goods when faced with the realities of global market competition. The question is, given the current economic and political model in developed nations, as the economy in countries like China and India, for example, continue to mature, catch up to, and surpass Western nations, where will product manufacturing move next, and how long will this process remain sustainable? Further, what can be done in the immediate interim to protect worker rights and encourage a more egalitarian arrangement of production while keeping in mind the need for corporations to remain competitive in the global marketplace?

Despite such uncertainties on the side of material production, Nike has been extremely successful in producing symbolic value through commercial advertisements and marketing campaigns. Realizing that that they could not treat the "entire world as a single, undifferentiated entity, thereby selling the same things in the same way everywhere" (Andrews, 2008a, p. 3) as multinational corporate structures (MNCs) once attempted to do, Nike has adapted to local market specificities and established itself as the prototypical TNC (see Table 4.4).

TABLE 4.4 Global Corporate Structures

Multinational Corporations (MNCs)
Entities that can be identified with a particular country/nation but operate some production processes abroad, seeking to move into external markets.
Transnational Corporations (TNCs)
Entities dissociated from a specific home country/nation. They insert themselves and their products into the local cultures of the markets they seek to penetrate.

The rise of transnational corporations (TNCs) can be attributed generally to this desire to operate globally, in as many foreign markets as possible, and with the capability of being culturally resonant (fitting in with local peculiarities) and horizontally integrated (a flexible chain of command that permits local adaptations). In many ways, sport has played a key part in this process due to the expressions of cultural differentiation that tie a particular sport, team, or athlete to the local histories, values, and shared traditions of the nation, region, or community.

As previously discussed, Rowe's (2003) notion of sport repudiating global forces (part of the global heterogenization thesis) corroborates the driving logic behind TNC's need to adapt and modify their market strategies using local sporting cultures to gain entry. Denoting the commercial viability of sport in the global market, Andrews (2008) notes that:

> Transnational brand strategies use locally resonant sport practices, teams, spectacles, and celebrities as a means of engaging local consumers and markets. This is because the dominant sporting culture of a nation represents a compelling cultural shorthand for the nation itself. Sport clearly exerts considerable influence upon the hearts, minds, and spending habits of the public (pp. 4–5).

It is thus no wonder that brand corporations representing all manner of products and services look to sport as a way to generate visibility, affiliation, and loyalty for their brand from the globally diverse consumer marketplace. Everything from Ford, Visa, and Pepsi, to Home Depot and Gatorade can be immersed within the sporting landscape; their proponents finding different ways to use sport to differentiate themselves from market competitors and establish credibility with consumers.

Global Sport Media: Mega-Events and Mass Entertainment Spectacles

To this degree, this final section will draw together the cultural nuances of sport and commercial sport properties with the modes of mass mediation and corporate branding just alluded to. Encompassing a substantial portion of sport-related commerce, media entities (television, radio, newspaper, Internet) play a vital role as the mediums through which products, people, events, and ideas are disseminated nationally and globally. In the case of Nike or with any other brand corporation, popular media platforms represent the means through which effective communication with target markets is achieved and sustained. Furthermore, media conglomerates have become branded entities in themselves, and represent formidable actors in the global dissemination of sport products and services. One such company, News Corporation, represents one of the most aggressive media properties using sport as a primary source of broadcasting content across the globe. In the United States, big-name media formats like Fox, MySpace, FX, and the *New York Post* are among the most recognizable holdings of the company. However, such entities represent only a fraction in scale and scope of the media giant's global portfolio. News Corporation reaches three quarters of the world's population across six continents, in more than 100 countries and 30 languages, employing 64,000 workers in film, television, cable, satellite, newspapers, magazines, books, and digital media ("News Corporation," 2008). In regard to sport, then, a central philosophy of CEO Rupert Murdoch is that sport generates unparalleled viewer loyalty in all markets across the globe:

> Sport absolutely overpowers film and everything else in the entertainment genre. . . . Football, of all sports, is number one. . . . Sport will remain very important and we will be investing in and acquiring long-term rights. . . . We have the long-term rights in most countries to major sporting events and we will be doing in Asia what we intend to do elsewhere in the world, that is, *use sports as a battering ram* and a lead offering in all our pay television operations (Rupert Murdoch, 1996 speech at News Corporation's annual meeting, Adelaide, Australia, Quoted in Milliken, 1996, p. 28, *emphasis added*).

Thus, some of News Corporation's most viable sport-related networks include Fox Sports, Fox Soccer Channel, Big Ten Network, SPEED, and the FUEL TV in the United States; and Sky Sports, Sky Italia, and Premier AG in Europe; and STAR in Asia. Fox Sports alone holds contracted broadcasting rights for the NFL, MLB, BCS, and NASCAR; this is not to mention the other media formats that regularly feature sport content as a leading source in product offerings.

Given the global scale and scope of News Corporation, it is a useful example to consider the complexities involved in leveraging sport as a commodified and consumable product. As noted by Rowe (2003), "there is no one in the media world who has a greater commitment to the commercial exploitation of sport than Murdoch" (p. 191). With an expressed interest in expanding globally by continually penetrating new markets, sometimes with ruthless tactics of business competition (Grainger & Andrews, 2005), some scholars, critical of capitalist globalization, question the methods and outcomes of News Corporation's insatiable quest to secure a controlling stake in global media platforms. Nevertheless, on the other side of the debate, some see corporations like News Corporation as leaders in a global pursuit of enhanced choices and freedoms for consumers previously cut off from the global flow of media and entertainment. As world economies continue to advance in sophistication to rival the West (most notably China and India as they advance through their own [post]industrial phases), early penetration of such markets by TNCs arguably represent a necessary and unavoidable step to continually increase profits. Such sentiments were expressed by Rupert Murdoch in the 2008 annual report:

> . . . we are seeing the creation of a global middle class of more than two billion people who are well educated, well remunerated and increasingly sophisticated in their choices . . . they will be increasingly hungry for better sources of news and entertainment. And we are in a strong position to provide it (News Corporation, 2008, p. 15).

No matter where one stands as to the ethics of global expansionism, the fact that an American/European-based TNC is aggressively seeking to control the means through which newly developed foreign economies access digital information and entertainment must be considered. Returning to an earlier point about "operating in the language of the local" and catering products and services toward diverse local cultures, News Corporation has been one of the most savvy media conglomerates in this regard (Dirlik, 1996; Silk & Andrews, 2001). Such a sensibility extends from Murdoch's own experiences with global expansion:

> You would be very wrong to forget that what people want to watch in their own country is basically local programming, local language, local culture . . . I learned that many years ago in Australia, when I was loading up . . . with good American programs and we'd get beat with second-rate Australian ones (quoted in Schmidt, 2001, p. 79).

In this sense, Murdoch's expressed proclivity to use sport as a battering ram to infiltrate new markets by first providing greater mediated access to local sports, extends from this logic. Once obtaining all media broadcasting rights and/or purchasing sport franchises/properties to reduce rights fees in a particular market, the introduction of pay-per-view services and cable/satellite fees take the place of basic programming access (Andrews, 2003). Thus, it may be surmised that media conglomerates operating in foreign economies are only tangentially concerned with local economic development because it may eventually affect their bottom line and ROI. As both the Nike and News Corporation examples attest, the global sport marketplace is fraught with complex situations and difficult decisions. The need for culturally aware, and socially conscious, marketers and managers has never been more urgent to develop new solutions for global challenges, and balance the drive for profit with practices of corporate social responsibility (see, Thomas, Schermerhorn, & Dienhart, 2004; Gustafsson, 2003). It is with such sensibilities that the next generation of sport managers and marketers has the opportunity to positively impact the communities in which they labor (see Table 4.5). With rapidly advancing technologies and the uncertainties of global economies and politics, new solutions will be needed to provide equitable access and facilitate local investment, while maintaining a global competitive perspective.

TABLE 4.5 Examples of Global Sport-Related Organizations/Careers

Amateur Athletics/ Governing Bodies	1. **Olympic**—Recognized sport federations/positions in coordination, management, and promotion of Olympic competition and development around the world. For example, the *Ministry of Sports and Physical Education in Cameroon* or the *Korean Olympic Committee and Sports Council.* 2. **Collegiate**—Athletic Directors and Assistants/Compliance Commissioners/Managers of equipment, facilities, fund raising, etc. 3. **Non-Governmental Organizations (NGOs)**—Often closely related to some Olympic organizations. For example, the *European Non-Governmental Sports Organisation (ENGSO).* 4. **Government Sanctioned Sport Commissions**—President Obama recently instituted the "The White House Office of Olympic, Paralympic and Youth Sport" for example. 5. **Convention and Visitor's Bureaus (CVBs)**—Place-based leadership positions in convention sales and marketing, communications/event managers and coordinators/ tourism promotion. For example, the *Paris Convention & Visitor's Bureau.* 6. **Youth Sport Organizations**—High-school sports administration/ *Amateur Athletic Union (AAU).*
Corporate Management/ Marketing	1. **Corporate Sponsorship**—Various positions dealing with partnership marketing, brand management, and development of effective synergies with large corporations and sport. 2. **Advertising and Marketing**—In every country where sport is commercially produced and consumed, there exists ample need for the management of advertising and marketing campaigns for leagues, teams, official sponsors, products, and services. For example, *Tiger Sports Marketing (TSM)* in India, specializing in the development of golf in the country. 3. **Professional Services**—Sport organizations also need support in the form of financial, legal, and information technology services to maintain efficient and profitable operations. For example, IT service managers, accountants, legal counsel, corporate auditors, etc.
Sport Media	1. **Electronic and Digital Media**—Maintenance and development of websites, online communications, and new media to reach target consumers. For example, www.guardian.co.uk is a leading online news source for global sport information in the United Kingdom. 2. **Broadcast & Print**—Broadcasters, journalists, editors, researchers, and others involved in the production and dissemination of sport information products. For example, *FoxSports broadcasting* and *ESPN network* and magazine in the United States, or *SportzBlitz* sports publisher in Australia.

Facilities/ Events	1. **Arena/Stadium Management**—Whether a professional team owns its arena or not, they often outsource the maintenance of the facility and event operations to a professional company. In developed economies, large leisure settings like a pro stadium require significant and complex organizational management in a number of areas including merchandise, concessions, premium services, and housekeeping. 2. **Event/Facility Development**—Creating, managing, and promoting events and leveraging the use of space within a facility to maximize profit and customer satisfaction. Directors, coordinators, and managers of annual events or high profile games like the *Rose Bowl* or *UEFA Champions League Final*, for example.
Sporting Goods/ Consumer Products	1. **Product Promotion & Distribution**—Management positions dealing with contractual sales and point of distribution/coordination and supply chain management on the retail end. 2. **Product Marketing/Advertising**—Positions in marketing and developing advertising campaigns for individual products, brands, or retail outlets.

*Note: This chart is by no means comprehensive and is intended to provide merely a glimpse into the potential fields of global sport commerce. Further, each example represents a general description of organizations and careers that exist in varied iterations across the globe. Outside the United States and Europe in particular, the development of sport organizations, governing bodies, commercial properties, and professional entities will likely continue to proliferate as we continue to experience an intensified global interconnectedness through new technologies. Thus, combining principles of Western style sport management with a heightened perspective of global issues in culture and commerce will enhance one's marketability abroad.

Conclusion

As sport has increasingly become a central feature of everyday lived experience, cultural practice, and communication, it has also morphed into a multibillion-dollar entertainment economy, forging partnerships and driving supply and demand in countless mediums of global commerce from large (major sponsorships and media contracts) to small (merchandise and concessions). As a result, while there are many opportunities to work in a sport organization, there are countless opportunities to work in companies that profit from or do business with sport entities. For example, during major sporting events, large quantities of select merchandise are transported to meet market demands, and someone has to coordinate these activities. Within one particular company, these duties are executed by the managing director for the promotion and distribution of sporting goods merchandise to large retail outlets across the United States and Europe. When big events like the Super Bowl, NBA Finals, or World Cup happen, this individual travels to the host city (or the city of the team favored to win) to coordinate the rapid production and distribution of time-sensitive sporting goods apparel. For example, when it looked like Pittsburgh was going to prevail in Super Bowl XLIII, the managing director was responsible for assessing local demand and predicting quantities of Super Bowl merchandise with Steelers insignia to be sold in select retail outlets. While not working in the conventional sense of sport management, this position requires diverse knowledge of a wide range of sports, consumer behavior, and management of supply and demand.

This example brings up an important point because future sport managers are more likely to labor within the processes of cultural and symbolic production (sales, marketing, advertising, branding, sponsorship, etc.), rather than something like product manufacturing and personnel or facility management. In this regard, it is important when seeking employment within sport organizations to also look beyond sport at companies and positions that deal indirectly with sport as a means to leverage the visibility and power of their brand. In other words, while there are opportunities to work directly with a team or sport organization in management, marketing, sponsorship, or promotion and sales, there are also many prospects in "non-sport" settings that deal with sport properties through various modes of partnership. This broad view of sport-related occupations becomes even more pronounced when considering the increasingly global interconnectedness of sport organizations, MNCs, and TNCs as previously discussed. Thus, a working knowledge of the global, national, and local intricacies of sport culture and commerce will be a valuable asset in successfully navigating a career path within a multitude of global companies.

Without question the global sport marketplace is extremely complex and diverse. This chapter has attempted to provide an introduction to global processes, networks, and flows of activity as they relate to sporting organizations and the promotional armatures of global corporations. We have discussed several theories through which to interpret global sporting phenomena (heterogenization, homogenization, hybridization, for example), and which can be used to explicate the production of sport as a significant motor in the development of global networks, commerce, and trade. With rapidly changing communication technologies and media formats, shifting political and economic priorities within countries, and global financial crises and cultural conflicts, the institutions of sport and sport-related companies face significant challenges, but also unique opportunities. Certainly, the globally ubiquitous popularity of sport has not diminished amidst such commotion, but it is up to the next generation of internationally astute, and culturally aware, sport management professionals to ensure its continued viability in a responsible, effective, and ethical manner.

chapter 4
Interviews

Interview 4.1

Colin Blount—Visa Europe
Vice President
Partnership Marketing

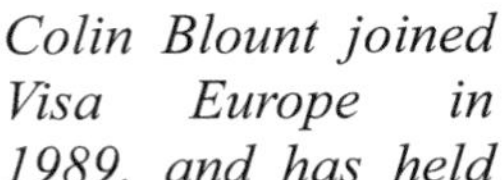

Colin Blount joined Visa Europe in 1989, and has held a variety of posts including Head of Network Infrastructure for Visa Europe and CEMEA regions, Head of Member Connectivity, Head of Office Systems, and Head of Technical Projects. He has also managed a number of important Visa EU and Visa International projects such as IARS, VSAT, and the development of the Operation Centre Basingstoke (OCB).

Until 2001 he held the post of Head of Virtual Visa Programmes where key responsibilities were to develop and maintain technology standards and specifications, program and service management, and new technology MIS. From then, the Management of Visa's activities towards the Athens 2004 and Torino 2006 Olympic and Paralympic Games provided the platform for his current role.

Mr. Blount joined Visa from National Westminster Bank, where for two years he was involved with mainframe systems design, planning, and hardware installation. Previously, he was employed by Shell Expo on the Tern Project from 1984–1987 where he was responsible for Document Control Migration from manual to computerized function.

Mr. Blount is a former Associate of the Institute of Wood Science, and from 1976–1984 was involved in the sales of timber products.

Q: What steps did you take to get into your current position? What was your career path?

A: From timber technology, to the oil industry, to computing, to banking, to Visa! Within Visa, IT, project management, managing Olympic projects, managing sponsorship properties, expanding to partnership marketing!

No planned steps, just things I find interesting/exciting and being in the right place.

Q: What role does knowledge of sport management and/or marketing play in gaining entrance and achieving success in your field?

A: As a generalist, I would describe my field as People and Project Management, which can apply to any discipline. Sports marketing provides a healthy mix of challenge, opportunity, and excitement.

Q: What are you looking for in new hires to your specific organization or similar ones? More specifically, positions in marketing or management that deal with sport entities?

A: As an organization we work to a set of defined competencies, which we seek in all employees:

- Focused on customers
- Focused on results
- Commitment to quality
- Leading and working with others
- Integrity and accountability
- Effective in different markets and cultures

In addition to these I would be seeking flexibility and a fit with the team, alongside any role-specific skill or knowledge sets.

Q: Could you give me a general sense of the global scale and scope of Visa's business operations—basic examples of the global reach of the organization?

A: Visa is owned by 16,400 financial institutions who issue 1.7 billion Visa cards which are accepted at 30 million merchant outlets in 170 countries. These currently generate 55 billion transactions per annum with a value of US$4.3 trillion.

Q: In what ways have rapid changes in the "global age" (evolving technologies in communication, information, and travel, for example) affected your external market environment? How has the company responded to these challenges?

A: As market leader, Visa plays a key role in identifying, responding to, and leading change. In recent years we have moved from offline to online authorizations, chip technology on cards, secure Internet payments, and contactless technology.

Q: What are some of the sport-related business partnerships Visa Europe has, and in what ways have they affected the success and visibility of the organization?

A: Visa has sponsored the Olympic Games since 1986 and this has been the global flagship property. This partnership has been instrumental in establishing strong brand values and adding some interest to a low-interest business sector. We have now added FIFA to the global portfolio, which further strengthens our global positioning. Local markets have exercised other sporting partnerships (e.g., NFL in the United States, Argentine Rugby Team), which have raised the profile in key markets.

Q: It has been said that sports fans have an unparalleled devotion to their nation when it comes to international sporting contests like the Olympics or World Cup. In your branding and promotional efforts, how do you leverage the cultural nuances of national difference to generate appeal and visibility for Visa?

A: I would agree with that statement and it is always challenging to take something so massive and make it relevant to an individual. Use of appropriate imagery can make a national statement and selection of local ambassadorial talent (e.g., Team Visa is effective).

Q: What sports or sporting events are of interest for Visa to become involved with and why? How do you determine what sport-related partnerships will be viable?

A: We have the two global partnerships that provide the foundation for all other sporting partnerships. As a pretty ubiquitous brand we focus less on visibility but more on brand health and the ability to drive a positive return on investment.

Q: What specific strategies do you employ in trying to appeal to the broadest market demographic possible? In what ways has sport facilitated this?

A: Our sporting partnerships provide us with a broad demographic so the main challenge is to ensure they are used effectively—the right message at the right time.

Q: What are the biggest challenges/issues/ trends you face in the near future in general; but more specifically in regard to your sport marketing and promotional initiatives?

A:
- The banking crisis and public perceptions
- Achieving and proving a real ROI on our investments
- Rights holders diluting their assets
- Maintaining a long- as well as a short-term view

Q: In response to the global and local sport partnerships you mentioned, how much autonomy is given to brand directors in local markets to select and pursue sport partnerships within various locales?

A: No autonomy, more working partnerships. We are driven by business needs and if there is a local need that requires an enhancement to an existing property or sourcing something new, then we agree and proceed. Additional funding typically would come from local budgets.

Q: **It seems likely that Visa has found it more effective to maintain brand health through large-scale sport promotions like the Olympics rather than local partnerships such as the Argentine Rugby team, for example. Whether this is accurate or not, could you explain how both global and local partnerships strengthen the position of the brand, how they are different, and how a consistent message and identity is maintained between them?**

A: Again, it depends on local business needs. The Argentina Rugby Team ran alongside our global sponsorship of the Rugby World Cup, and enhanced that partnership locally. It is of course a valuable brand-building partnership for the Argentine market. As a general rule, global partnerships are featured in the brand messaging to reinforce our position as a global brand, but there are occasions when it is necessary to tactically build the brand locally.

Q: **What advice would you give to a burgeoning sport manager/marketer intent on working in a capacity that requires international and global sensitivities?**

A: Be patient, culturally aware, and sensitive to local needs. Do the research so that you can argue your case from a factual rather than emotional position—individuals have strong preferences, which may not reflect market preferences. Don't forget to enjoy it—it's a privilege to work in this environment!

Interview 4.2

Eric Bruzzone
General Manager
Bravium9 Sports
Management

Q: Could you briefly describe your career path from undergraduate student to your current position?

A: I graduated from law school in Ecuador in the year 2000. In Ecuador it is almost mandatory to work at the same time as we study so I began working at a top law firm in 1997. My graduation from law school did not affect much of my work, with the only exception that I could attend court by myself.

After succeeding at many work challenges, I decided to move to Asia in 2005, where I have worked and lived in Taiwan, Singapore, and Shanghai, always practicing law.

The 2008 financial crisis was a big wakeup alarm. With several big clients moving out of China or redefining their business scope, I decided to choose a new career challenge and pursue a master's degree in Sport Management. I chose the IE Business School (in Madrid) because of its top-ranked program and by the year 2012 I completed my studies there. My goal was to get necessary academic and practical tools that would enhance my skill set and network to build my own company. I have achieved initial success and continue to build my company.

I currently still practice law at a Chinese law firm (as a partner) and run a sport-marketing agency, with a strong emphasis on Chinese digital media (all foreign digital media is blocked) towards monetization through sponsors for my clients.

Q: What have been the biggest challenges you have encountered during your career?

A: As a sport-marketing entrepreneur in China, my main source of clients are Western athletes and clubs. In less than two years I have reached agreements to represent football clubs in Argentina, Ecuador, Spain, Italy, and France. So the main challenge has not been getting clients, but being able to maintain a long-distance relationship which can cement the deals and maximize value for all parties.

Q: What attracted you to work on another continent?

A: I wanted to get out of my comfort zone. I thrive for challenges and I usually look for the next one, no matter how impossible it may seem. Many years ago I would not have believed that I would be practicing law in China and would have created my own sport-marketing company. It might be a virtue or defect, but it is on my nature to continue to seek new challenges and opportunities.

Q: Was that a difficult transition? What things did you do to make the transition go as smoothly as possible?

A: It was certainly tough to go to Taiwan without a job, but finding my "place" at a local law firm surely sped the adjustment process. But then I did it again when I moved to Shanghai, and yet I was lucky enough to repeat the experience. I also have pursued an LLM and then a master's degree in Sport Management which have required me to rely on my skills and make adjustments to maximize my opportunities.

Part of soothing the various transitions has been to be humble and admit it was a new culture and I should adapt to the ways of the new place I now call home. Learning the language as fast as I could surely helped since Chinese people typically do not expect foreigners to learn their language (confront this with France or Germany) so they typically appreciate any Westerner taking the effort to speak it.

Q: Are there specific skills sport-management students should look to develop while still in school?

A: Entrepreneurship should definitely be one of the courses students take, even if their career goal is to find a job at a large, established company such as Nike or Adidas. More and more sports companies are basing their strategies on employees forming teams who can "own" projects. Having a strong skill set in entrepreneurship is an important foundation.

I would definitely suggest schools provide a thorough "General Culture" course to their students, where topics as wide as Greek history to rock-and-roll, contemporary art, to opera, literature, comics, sculpture, poetry, etc. could be learned and discussed. If you look at any "cool" advertisement in sports, there is always one of these elements included, so any student who is soon to be part of said market should be able to distinguish among the rest of the population (who often know nothing about the various aspects of our diverse worldwide culture and the unique aspects in specific countries or regions of the world).

Q: What specific classes would you recommend students take to best position themselves for a sport-industry job?

A: Most jobs on the sports industry require thinking outside of the box. This is why I tried to justify on the earlier question why there should be courses on cultural segments that may provide students with skills not so easily found on applicants to a job.
As for more related to sport-management courses I could list:
Sports marketing
Digital marketing
Sports sponsorship

Q: When you talk to potential interns and/ or employees, how important is it for them to understand the "global world"?

A: I am lucky to be working at two different places and I am able to hire different profiles (lawyers and marketing people). Since my clients (at the law firm and my marketing company) are usually foreigners either entering China or already doing business here, my added value is to be able to understand what they want so I can communicate with my team, which in return will reach a local audience (either a judge, a public officer, or football fans). But the irony is that, at least so far, who I need my team to really understand is our audience, and that we should actually remain local while communicating the needs of a foreign client. So yes, it is important that my employees understand the "global" environment, but it is way more important that my clients understand that this is not "Kansas anymore" and individual situations need to be analyzed and understood.

Q: What publications do you regularly read to stay apprised of sport-business events?

A: My main source of information is Twitter, Facebook, and *SportsPro* magazine.

Q: Would you recommend students pursue graduate school? If so, when should they pursue a graduate degree and what area of study would you recommend?

A: I definitely recommend graduate school, but hopefully after a student has traveled to as many countries as possible. I am not saying to just backpack, but to look for as many business opportunities abroad. As a post-graduate teacher I can surely tell when a student has taken such time to get to know other cultures and possibilities before embarking on graduate studies, not to mention, travel increases their language skills. It is truly a change of "vision" instead of "mind."

Study Questions

1. How has advanced technology affected the production and dissemination of sport?
2. Is the homogenization thesis still a relevant way to think about global process of interconnectivity and interdependency? Why or why not?
3. In what ways is sport production considered to be the same globally?
4. How does the heterogenization thesis inform your perspective concerning the role of sport in foregrounding national difference?
5. If working in a sport organization or targeting key markets outside of your home nation, why is an understanding of cultural difference so important?
6. Name three sport-related examples of global hybridity.
7. In what ways are the principles of McDonaldization (calculability, predictability, rational control, and efficiency) evidenced in the production of sporting events, products, or services?
8. Drawing upon the concept of symbolic production, explain why Nike is one of the most successful sporting goods companies in the world.
9. In what ways has sport been so integral to the success of TNCs?
10. Other than Nike and News Corporation, what TNCs have leveraged sport to enter new markets and increase global resonance?
11. Drawing from the three global theories discussed, which one most closely resembles News Corporation's global strategy? Why?
12. In what ways can TNCs invest in the nations in which they operate while simultaneously benefiting from knowledge of local cultural sensibilities and market trends?

Learning Activities

1. As noted in the example of Nike, the production of sporting goods involves a complex system of global commodity chains that link nations and laborers in countries all across the world. In order to enhance profitability, most brand corporations invest more time and money into the intangible processes of symbolic production (marketing, branding, and advertising) while cutting costs in the tangible aspects of production (raw materials, manufacturing, distribution). Imagine you just inherited enough money to launch your own footwear and apparel company and are in the early phases of developing your brand identity and marketing plan, and identifying where production and distribution will occur. *First, decide where to place greater emphasis by assigning a number to each of the five areas below out of 10 total points. Then, justify your decisions by developing a strategic plan for operations in each area, including a description of who, what, where, how, and why for each phase of the process.*

- **A.** Product Design—The ideas and technologies behind the development of new product lines. In order to remain competitive, it is vital to continue creating new, higher quality products to keep consumers wanting more.
- **B.** Branding/Marketing—Knowledge creation. Cutting-edge branding/marketing campaigns are not cheap but in order to compete with the major players, it is impossible to develop a sustainable and profitable global or national market without attaching symbolic value to entice consumers and justify increased cost.
- **C.** Raw Materials—Quality of materials that will compose your product. Cheaper materials will net more short-term profit, but may also deter consumers on account of poor durability/comfort.
- **D.** Labor/Manufacturing—Outsourcing all material labor to poor developing economies is proven to cut costs and increase profitability, but how will this effect brand reputation, visibility, and corporate social responsibility? For example, choose either Sri Lanka (0.5), India (1), China (1.5), Korea (2), Japan (2.5), France (3), the United Kingdom (3.5), or the United States (4).
- **E.** Distribution/Transportation—The development of strong networks and efficient routes to transport raw materials and finished products to their destinations can affect supply and demand.

For example, we could assume that Nike would look something like this:

Product design—3
Branding/Marketing—4
Raw Materials—1.5
Labor/Manufacturing—0.5
Distribution/Transportation—1

2. Stemming from our discussion of TNCs and the importance of sport in media broadcasting, marketing, and branding initiatives for all manner of products, leagues, and teams around the world, the process of attaching symbolic (cultural) meaning cannot be understated. In this regard, many large corporations hire global advertising agencies (Wieden & Kennedy, for example) to develop new marketing campaigns to enhance the visibility, reputation, or strength of their brand. Using the Wieden & Kennedy website (http://www.wk.com/#/) as a source for commercials, identify the ways in which sport is used to engage different national markets for their clients—Nike, Electronic Arts, Coca-Cola, Starbucks, Converse, etc. Focusing on one in particular, how would you approach the development of a similar advertising campaign if you were:

- **A.** The Senior Director of Marketing for the professional soccer club Monaco in the French League?
(http://www.asm-fc.com/uk/)

B. An Assistant Director of Marketing & Communications for the U.S. Olympic Committee (USOC)?
(www.usoc.org)

C. An Assistant Marketing Director for HSBC Private Bank?
(http://www.theworldsprivatebank.com/en/)

References

Albrow, M. (1996). *The global age: State and society beyond modernity.* Stanford: Stanford University Press.

Allen, J. (1996). Post-industrialism/post-Fordism. In S. Hall, D. Held, D. Hubert, & K. Thompson (Eds.), *Modernity: An introduction to modern societies* (pp. 533–563). Oxford: Blackwell.

Alms, R. (1994, November 1). Globe trotters: NBA takes a world view of marketing. *Dallas Morning News,* pp. 1D.

Amis, J. (2003). "Good things come to those who wait": The strategic management of image and reputation at Guinness. *European Sport Management Quarterly, 3,* 189–214.

Amis, J. (2005). Beyond sport: Imaging and re-imaging a global brand. In M. Silk, D. Andrews, & C. Cole (Eds.), *Corporate nationalisms: Sport, cultural identity & transnational marketing* (pp. 143–165). Oxford: Berg.

Amis, J., & Cornwell, T.B. (2005). *Global sport sponsorship.* Oxford: Berg.

Amis, J., & Silk, M. (2005, August). Transnational organization and symbolic production: Creating and managing a global brand strategy. Paper presented at Academy of Management meetings, Honolulu, HI.

Amis, J., Mower, R.L., & Silk, M. (2009). (Michael) Power, gendered subjectivities & filmic representation: Brand strategy and Guinness' critical assignment in Africa. In L. Wenner & S. Jackson (Eds.), *Sport, beer and gender: Promotional culture and contemporary social life* (pp. 97–120). New York: Peter Lang Publishers.

Anderson, B. (1991). *Imagined communities: Reflections on the origins and spread of nationalism.* London: Verso.

Andrews, D.L. (2003). The global sport media economy: News Corporation, entertainment cultures, and vertical integration. In D. Rowe (Ed.), *A reader in sport, culture and the media.* Buckingham, UK: Open University Press.

Andrews, D.L. (2006). Disneyization, Debord, and the integrated NBA spectacle. *Social Semiotics, 16*(1), 89–102.

Andrews, D.L. (2008a, Spring/Summer). Nike nations. *Brown Journal of World Affairs, XIV*(2), 1–13.

Andrews, D.L. (2008b). [Various networks of global connectivity]. Unpublished raw data.

Andrews, D.L., & Ritzer, G. (2007). The grobal in the sporting glocal. *Global Networks, 7*(2), 113–153.

Associated Press. (2012). More than 70 dead after Egypt match. Accessed June 19, 2014 from http://espn.go.com/sports/soccer/story/_/id/7528889/egypt-soccer-match-postgame-more-70-dead-melee-fan-violence

Brown, A. (2007). "Not for sale": The destruction and reformation of football communities in the Glazer takeover of Manchester United. *Soccer & Society, 8*(4), 614–615.

Brownell, S. (2008). *Beijing's games: What the Olympics mean to China.* Lanham, MD: Rowman & Littlefield Publishers.

Caldwell, M.L. (2004). Domesticating the French fry: McDonald's and consumerism in Moscow. *Journal of Consumer Culture, 4*(1), 5–26.

Castells, M. (1997). *The rise of the network society.* Oxford: Blackwell.

Cochrane, A., & Pain, K. (2000). A globalizing society? In D. Held (Ed.), *A globalizing world? Culture, economics, politics* (pp. 5–46). London: Routledge.

Collins, T., & Vamplew, W. (2002). *Mud, sweat and beers: A cultural history of sport and alcohol.* London: Berg Publishers.

Comte, E. (1993, June 7). How high can David Stern jump? *Forbes,* 42.

Dirlik, A. (1996). The global in the local. In R. Wilson & W. Dissanayake (Eds.), *Global local: Cultural production and the transnational imaginary* (pp. 21–45). Durham: Duke University Press.

Dunning, E. (1999). *Sport matters: Sociological studies of sport, violence and civilization.* London: Routledge.

Frenkel, S.J. (2001). Globalization, athletic footwear commodity chains and employment relations in China. *Organization Studies, 22,* 531–562.

Giulianotti, R. (2002). Supporters, followers, fans, and flaneurs: A taxonomy of spectator identities in football. *Journal of Sport & Social Issues, 26*(1), 25–46.

Grainger, A., & Andrews, D.L. (2005). Resisting Rupert through sporting rituals? The transnational media corporation and global-local sport cultures. *International Journal of Sport Management and Marketing, 1*(1-2), 3–16.

Guibernau, M., & Goldblatt, D. (2000). Identity and nation. In K. Woodward (Ed.), *Questioning identity: Gender, class, nation.* London: Routledge/The Open University.

Gustafsson, C. (2003). New values, morality, and strategic ethics. In H. Mintzberg, J. Lampel, J.B. Quinn, & S. Ghoshal (Eds.), *The strategy process: Concepts, contexts, cases* (4th ed.) (pp. 295–299). Upper Saddle River, NJ: Prentice Hall.

Hall, S. (1992). The west and the rest: Discourse and power. In S. Hall & B. Gieben (Eds.), *Formations of modernity* (pp. 275–320). Cambridge: Polity Press.

Hardt, M., & Negri, A. (2000). *Empire.* Cambridge, MA: Harvard University Press.

Harrison, B. (1994, September 22). The dark side of flexible production. *National Productivity Review, 13*(4), 479–501.

Harvey, D. (1989). *The condition of postmodernity: An enquiry into the origins of cultural change.* Oxford: Blackwell.

Held, D., McGrew, A., Goldblatt, D., & Perraton, J. (1999). *Global transformations: Politics, economics and culture.* Stanford, CA: Stanford University Press.

Hill, J.S., & Vincent, J. (2006, May). Globalisation and sports branding: The case of Manchester United. *International Journal of Sports Marketing and Sponsorship,* 213–230.

Hobsbawm, E.J. (1990). *Nations and nationalism since 1870: Programme, myth, reality* (p. 143). Cambridge: Cambridge University Press.

Hobsbawm, E.J., & Ranger, T. (1983). *The invention of tradition.* Cambridge: Cambridge University Press.

Holt, R. J. (1989). *Sport and the British: A modern history.* Oxford: Clarendon Press.

Jackson, S.J., & Hokowhitu, B. (2002). Sport, tribes, and technology: The New Zealand All Blacks Haka and the politics of identity. *Journal of Sport & Social Issues, 26*(2), 125–139.

Jameson, F. (1991). *Postmodernism, or, the cultural logic of late capitalism.* Durham: Duke University Press.

KFC accused of racism over Australian advertisement. (2010, January). *Guardian.co.uk.* Retrieved from http://www. guardian.co.uk/business/2010/jan/06/kfc-advertisement-accused-of-racism

Klein, A. (2000). Latinizing Fenway Park: A cultural critique of the Boston Red Sox, their fans, and the media. *Sociology of Sport Journal, 17,* 403–422.

Klein, N. (1999). *No logo: Taking aim at the brand bullies.* New York: Picador.

Kobe Bryant tops NBA jersey sales in China. (2008, August). *Brandweek.* Retrieved from http://www.brandweek.com/bw/ content_display/news-and-features/retail-restaurants/e3idfed28cc72bd8cb6ac411101179c14e5

Korzeniewicz, M. (1994). Commodity chains and marketing strategies: Nike and the global athletic footwear industry. In G. Gereffi & M. Korzeniewicz (Eds.), *Commodity chains and global capitalism* (pp. 247–265). Westport, CT: Greenwood Press.

Kuisel, R.F. (2003). Debating Americanization: The case of France. In U. Beck, N. Sznaider, and R. Winter (Eds.), *Global America? The cultural consequences of globalization.* Liverpool: Liverpool University Press.

Lee, F.L. (2009, March). Negotiating sporting nationalism: Debating fan behavior in "China vs. Japan" in the 2004 Asian Cup Final in Hong Kong. *Soccer & Society, 10*(2), 192–209.

Lewis, M. (2001). Franchise relocation and fan allegiance. *Journal of Sport & Social Issues, 25*(1), 6–19.

Maguire, J., Jarvie, G., Mansfield, L., & Bradley, J. (2002). *Sport worlds: A sociological perspective.* Champaign, IL: Human Kinetics.

Manchester United expands its global reach. (2002, September). Forbes.com. Retrieved from http://www.forbes.com/ 2002/09/30/0930manchester.html

Mandel, E. (1975). *Late capitalism.* London: NLB, Atlantic Highlands Humanities Press.

McCollester, C. (2005). The glory and the gutting: Steeler nation and the humiliation of Pittsburgh. *Monthly Review,* 57(7), 1–7.

McGrew, A. (1992). A global society? In S. Hall, D. Held, & A. McGrew (Eds.), *Modernity and its futures* (pp. 61–116). Cambridge: Polity Press.

McLuhan, M., & Powers, B.R. (1989). *The global village: Transformations in world life and media in the 21st century.* New York: Oxford University Press.

Miller, T., Lawrence, G., McKay, J., & Rowe, D. (2001). *Globalization and sport.* London: Sage.

Milliken, R. (1996, October 16). Sports is Murdoch's 'battering ram' for pay TV. *The Independent,* p. 28.

Moor, L. (2007). *The rise of brands.* London: Berg Publishers.

Morley, D., & Robins, K. (1995). *Spaces of identity: Global media, electronic landscapes and cultural boundaries.* London: Routledge.

NBA China games to reach 209 countries. (2007, October). NBA.com. Retrieved from http://www.nba.com/news/ china_games_071016.html

News Corporation Annual Report. (2008). Adelaide, Australia. Retrieved from http://www.newscorp.com/AR2008 Flash/NC_AR_Editorial_2008.pdf

NFAP Policy Brief. (2014). Immigrant contributions in the NBA and Major League Baseball. *National Foundation for American Policy*. Accessed June 14, 2014 from http://nfap.com/wp-content/uploads/2014/06/NFAP-Policy-Brief.Immigrants-in-NBA-and-MLB.JUNE-2014.pdf

Pieterse, J.N. (2004). *Globalization and culture: Global mélange.* Lanham: Rowman and Littlefield.

Ram, U. (2007). Liquid identities: Mecca Cola versus Coca-Cola. *European Journal of Cultural Studies, 10*(4), 465–484.

Ritzer, G. (1998). *The McDonaldization thesis: Explorations and extensions.* London: Sage.

Ritzer, G. (2008). *The McDonaldization of society 5.* Los Angeles, CA: Pine Forge Press.

Robertson, R. (1995). Glocalization: Time-space and homogeneity-heterogeneity. In M. Featherstone, S. Lash, & R. Robertson (Eds.), *Global modernities* (pp. 25–44). London: Sage.

Robins, K. (1991). Tradition and translation: National culture in its global context. In J. Corner & S. Harvey (Eds.), *Enterprise and heritage: Crosscurrents of national culture* (pp. 21–44). London: Routledge.

Robins, K. (1997). What in the world's going on? In P. Du Gay (Ed.), *Production of culture/cultures of production* (p. 28). London: The Open University.

Rowe, D. (2003). Sport and the repudiation of the global. *International Review for the Sociology of Sport, 38*(3), 281–294.

Scherer, J., & Jackson, S.J. (2007). Sports advertising, cultural production and corporate nationalism at the global-local nexus: Branding the New Zealand All Blacks. *Sport in Society, 10*(2), 268–284.

Schmidt, R. (2001, June). Murdoch reaches for the sky. *Brill's Content,* pp. 74–79, 126–129.

Silk, M., & Andrews, D. (2001). Beyond a boundary: Sport, transnational advertising, and the reimaging of national culture. *Journal of Sport & Social Issues, 25*, 2.

Tallentire, M. (2009, January 23). Violence erupts between Serbs and Bosnians after Djokovic's win. Retrieved from http://www.guardian.co.uk/sport/2009/jan/23/australian-open-violence-djokovic

Thomas, T., Schermerhorn, J.R., & Dienhart, J.W. (2004). Strategic leadership of ethical behavior in business. *Academy of Management Executive, 18*(2), 56–68.

Tomlinson, J. (1991). *Cultural imperialism: A critical introduction.* Baltimore: Johns Hopkins University Press.

Tomlinson, J. (1999). *Globalization and culture.* Cambridge: Polity Press.

Turner, B.S. (2003). McDonaldization: Linearity and liquidity in consumer cultures. *American Behavioral Scientist, 47*(2), 137–153.

Watson, J.L. (1997). Transnationalism, localization, and fast foods in East Asia. In J.L. Watson (Ed.), *Golden arches east: McDonald's in East Asia* (pp. 1–38). Cambridge, MA: Harvard University Press.

Willigan, G.E. (1992, July/August). High performance marketing: An interview with Nike's Phil Knight. *Harvard Business Review,* 91–101.

Suggested Readings

Appadurai, A. (1996). *Modernity at large: Cultural dimensions of globalization.* Minneapolis: University of Minnesota Press.

Barnier, A. (2001). *Sport, nationalism, and globalization: European and North American perspectives.* Albany, NY: SUNY Press.

Dirlik, A. (1996). The global in the local. In R. Wilson & W. Dissanayake (Eds.), *Global local: Cultural production and the transnational imaginary* (pp. 21–45). Durham: Duke University Press.

Donnelly, P. (1996). The local and the global: Globalization in the sociology of sport. *Journal of Sport & Social Issues, 20*(3), 239–257.

Maguire, J.A. (1999). *Global sport: Identities, societies, civilization.* Cambridge, MA: Polity Press.

Ritzer, G. (2004). *The globalization of nothing.* Thousand Oaks, CA: Pine Forge Press.

Rowe, D. (1996). The global love-match: Sport and television. *Media, Culture & Society, 18*(4), 565–582.

Silk, M. (2002). "Bangsa Malaysia": Global sport, the city and the mediated refurbishment of local identities. *Media, Culture & Society, 24*(6), 775–794.

Silk, M.L., & Andrews, D.L. (2005). The spatial logics of global sponsorship: Corporate capital, cola wars and cricket. In J. Amis & T.B. Cornwell (Eds.), *Global sport sponsorship* (pp. 67–88). Oxford: Berg.

Sklair, L. (2006). Capitalist globalization: Fatal flaws and necessity for alternatives. *The Brown Journal of World Affairs, XIII*(1), 29–37.

Stabile, C.A. (2000). Nike, social responsibility, and the hidden abode of production. *Critical Studies in Media Communication, 17*(2), 186–204.

Tomlinson, A. (1996). Olympic spectacle: Opening ceremonies and some paradoxes of globalization. *Media, Culture & Society, 18*(4), 583–602.

Richard Southall • *The University of South Carolina*

chapter 5

Critical Thinking and Ethical Decision Making

CHAPTER OBJECTIVES

After reading this chapter, you will be able to:

- Differentiate between thinking and reasoning.
- Identify two theories of truth.
- Critically analyze an argument for logical consistency.
- Produce, articulate, and defend reasons for a given position and respond to objections raised to this position.
- Understand various ethical theories and how they apply to the sport-management industry and society.
- Given a specific issue, demonstrate the ability to examine it, identify alternative resolutions, and present specific resolutions consistent with positions on other ethical issues.

KEY TERMS

Categorical imperative
Consequentialism
Critical thinking (reasoning)
Cultural relativism
Deductive reasoning
Deontology
Divine-command theory
Duty
Ethics
Existentialism
Hedonism
Inductive reasoning
Moral relativism
Norms
Values

> *We are discussing no small matter, but how we ought to live.*
> —Socrates
>
> *I think it's not an understatement to say cheating pays presently. If you seek to conspire to certainly bend the rules, you can do it successfully and probably not get caught in most occasions.*
> —Big XII Commissioner, Bob Bowlsby
>
> *Well, then it's not cheating, is it? If nobody finds out? Yeah, it would be like finding a gray area. In motor sports, we work in the gray areas a lot. You're trying to find where the holes are in the rule book.*
> —NASCAR driver, Danica Patrick (who later apologized and said her comments were meant to be a joke)

Introduction

In preparing to be future sport managers, students will probably not be able to resolve every issue they encounter, but gaining a greater understanding of how to critically analyze and reason through alternatives is an important managerial skill. A critically-thinking sport manager may pose the following questions as he or she grapples with a vexing managerial challenge:

- How does this issue affect me personally?
- How does this issue affect my organization and/or society?
- What value, norm, or ethical framework can I utilize to examine this issue?
- How can the issue be resolved in a manner that demonstrates respect for individual differences?

Answering such questions requires not just being able to think, but possessing critical-thinking and reasoning skills.

In this chapter we will discuss these skills, as well as examine several developed ethical frameworks that provide useful structure. Whether you become a coach, athletic director, league administrator, park-district supervisor, fitness-club manager, or professional sport organization marketer, having honed your critical-thinking skills and having a solid understanding of how to think ethically will be useful.

Reasoning and Critical Thinking

At some time during a class period, you may have taken a mental break and "daydreamed" or "thought" about something else you would rather be doing. At another time, you may listen to a song and "think" about the lyrics. Both activities involve a level of "thinking." All rational beings are capable of such thinking.

However, to a large degree, this type of thinking is passive. During such activities, we simply take note of our surroundings: absorbing the "white noise" of life, watching television, or surfing the web. Much of this type of thought is uninformed and subject to bias, distortion, and partiality.

Different from such thinking, **critical thinking** or **reasoning** (note the two terms will be used interchangeably in this chapter) is purposeful, and based upon theoretical perspectives and logical assumptions (i.e., premises). Critical thinking utilizes questions and seeks additional information (e.g., data) to generate solutions. These solutions have implications for future considerations or questions. Critical thinking is often an inferential process, providing a basis for subsequent reasoning. For example, if we infer something about B from A, we do so on the basis that A supports or justifies our inference of B.

Reasoning often involves the use of inferential language to construct a statement or argument. Logical strength is a property of an inference that can be drawn from premises. The "truth" of a statement may be related to its logical strength, but a logically strong inference is not necessarily "true." In addition, when we are discussing an argument's "soundness," we are looking at the totality of the argument.

Critically thinking about an argument involves first determining its precise meaning. This determination may be a difficult process, involving—as we have discussed—different types of statements or arguments and different methods of assessing applicability, truth, falsity, usefulness, and meaning. Such assessment challenges sport managers' interpretive, verification, and critical-thinking skills.

Why is such assessment so important? In a fast-paced sport industry setting, managers must make decisions, often having to choose between several alternatives. A chosen decision may be made without having access to all the data. It may be affected by stakeholder pressure that skews a manager's perception of reality. In addition, a manager needs to possess the necessary critical-thinking skills to be able to recognize when she or he is faced with a difficult decision. Based upon the best available information, being equipped to conduct an ethical analysis of possible alternatives is a valuable skill. Since each of us has to live with our personal and professional decisions, the goal of this chapter is to provide guidance for you to think for yourself. Don't let others make your decisions.

Deductive and Inductive Reasoning

Critical thinking involves analyzing two different types of arguments: **deductive reasoning** and **inductive reasoning**.

First, a deductive argument has three elements:
1. Premise(s)
2. Inference(s)
3. Conclusion

A deductive argument is built upon accepted assumptions. Once the premises have been accepted, then the inferential process takes place. If the inferences are valid, then the conclusion (i.e., the proposition) should also be accepted.

In examining a deductive argument, we seek an affirmative answer to the question: "Does the validity of the premises lead to our accepting the conclusion?" If the answer is "Yes," then the statement is a strict proof or deductively-sound or "strong" argument.

An example of a deductively strong argument is as follows:

If Town A has 5,000 people who live within its city limits, and
If Town B has 4,000 people who live within its city limits
<u>Then</u>, Town A has a larger resident population than Town B.

Note the word "if" in both premises. This type of argument is constructed as part of gathering and clarifying accepted "facts." In many cases, this is the first step in critically thinking about an issue. We gather facts and determine whether our conclusions (and subsequent or preceding beliefs) are consistent with these facts and the inferences we make based on these facts. Often, this sort of deductive argument forms the basis for moving on to making an inductive statement (see Box 5.1).

A weak argument is one in which the premises actually provide little or no support for the conclusion. Two examples of weak arguments are outlined below:

Example 1
- All of these remedies are natural;
- Therefore, you should always choose a natural remedy.

Example 2
- 70% of all Americans support position A;
- Therefore, Position A is morally justified.

BOX 5.1

Assessing Deductive Arguments

Three criteria for "accepting" a deductive argument include:

1. Premises must be **acceptable**.
    - We have "good" reasons to accept the premises.
    - We do not have certainty, but reasonable acceptance.
2. Each individual premise must be **relevant** to the conclusion.
3. Premises must be **adequate** to support the conclusion.

Basic Rules for Assessing Arguments

1. IDENTIFY THE MAIN CONCLUSION
2. IDENTIFY THE PREMISES
3. IDENTIFY THE STRUCTURE OF THE ARGUMENT
4. CHECK THE ACCEPTABILITY OF THE PREMISES
5. CHECK THE RELEVANCE OF THE PREMISES
6. LOOK FOR COUNTER-ARGUMENTS
7. IDENTIFY THE MAIN CONCLUSION
    - What is the main point of the argument?
    - Is there an argument being made at all?
        1. Every argument presents a CLAIM and a REASON to support that claim
        2. IDENTIFY THE PREMISES
    - What information is presented to support the conclusion?
    - Are there missing premises that can be supplied or gleaned from the context?
        3. IDENTIFY THE STRUCTURE OF THE ARGUMENT
    - The structure of the argument may be convoluted or confusing
    - It may be necessary to diagram the structure
    - Keep it simple
    - Identify the CONCLUSION
    - Identify the PREMISES
        4. CHECK THE ACCEPTABILITY OF THE PREMISES
    - If there are two independent premises, the unacceptability of one does not preclude the other from being true
        5. CHECK THE RELEVANCE OF THE PREMISES
    - Relevance is contextual
    - Other premises may contribute to the relevance of any given premise

There are common mistakes or *fallacies* that are sometimes made when constructing deductive arguments. Fallacies may be logical or rhetorical. Using anecdotal evidence as a proof of a universal statement is one easy example.

> "Three people I know like vanilla ice cream. Therefore, vanilla ice cream is the best ice cream flavor!"

Different than in a deductive argument, the posed question in an inductive argument becomes: "Do the data we've gathered provide reasonable support for accepting the conclusion and acting on the basis of that judgment?" Inductive reasoning involves using specific observations to develop reliable generalizations and theories. Inductive reasoning occurs in the real world in which we live. Distinct from a deductive argument, the truth of an inductive argument is not based solely upon the truth of the premises.

The entire scientific method relies on inductive reasoning. In addition, just as do scientists, sport marketers continually gather data to see what generalizable patterns can be detected. If NBA franchise executives want to determine if fans "like" [have a positive emotional response to] the music being played during a game, they may conduct an in-arena study (Southall & Southall, 2014). Almost all sport-market research is inductively based. Inductive arguments are deemed to be "strong" (e.g., useful) to the degree they are reliable and can be replicated. Sport managers rely on inductive reasoning to develop reasonable and workable answers to vexing industry problems.

Importantly, such inductive truth is always subject to subsequent verification and confirmation. It is not TRUTH in the sense of an answer to a religious or spiritual question, which we may believe to be TRUE in spite of evidence to the contrary. Answers to many religious questions deal with the nature of spirituality, and are culturally dependent. Such TRUTHS are often referred to as "articles of faith." There are at least 300 different religious-belief systems.

Critical Thinking versus Truth

Contrary to the concepts of critical thinking and reasoning that have been discussed, many people believe the following:

- IT'S TRUE IF I BELIEVE IT.
- IT'S TRUE IF WE BELIEVE IT.
- IT'S TRUE IF I WANT TO BELIEVE IT.
- IT'S TRUE IF IT SERVES MY VESTED INTEREST TO BELIEVE IT.

As we move forward and examine the application of ethics in the sport and entertainment industry, we need to remember the study of sport ethics is related to and may draw upon personal values, societal norms, or religious belief. However, ethics DOES NOT simply involve personal opinion. Ethics relies upon the use of reasoning and critical thinking to examine and determine a logical rationale for adopting a specific ethical framework to guide personal or organizational action. Ethics provides a lens through which individuals, organizations, and society can examine human action. This will become clearer as we progress through the chapter.

What Is Ethics?

At its core, **ethics** is examining—as impartially and objectively as possible—individual human values. To some observers, ethics also involves exploring societal norms. Ethical analysis allows sport managers to move beyond looking at managerial issues from only their personal or limited-societal contexts, and instead critically examine such issues utilizing broad-based ethical frameworks. Fundamentally, sport-ethicists hope that developed "big picture" constructs can help sport managers answer the question, "What should I do?" when faced with an ethical dilemma in their roles within the sport industry. Developing a "satisfactory" answer is ethics' central function.

Why is the study and use of ethics important within the sport industry? Sport managers' decisions and actions affect everyone with whom they interact. Their decisions and actions affect co-workers, families, other sport organizations, communities, countries, and, ultimately, the world. Ethics is the blueprint for policy development and problem solving in the sport industry.

When we discuss ethics, we are at the end of a continuum that begins with values and ends with an examination of ethics (see Figure 5.1). The study of value, very broadly construed, examines the nature of right v. wrong, good v. bad, and authenticity v. inauthenticity (or hypocrisy). Ethics deals with notions of duty, obligation, freedom, and virtue. Ethics is sometimes referred to as the philosophy of morality, or a prescriptive guide to how people should act. It is an attempt to achieve a systematic understanding of the nature of morality.

FIGURE 5.1 Values, Norms, and Ethics

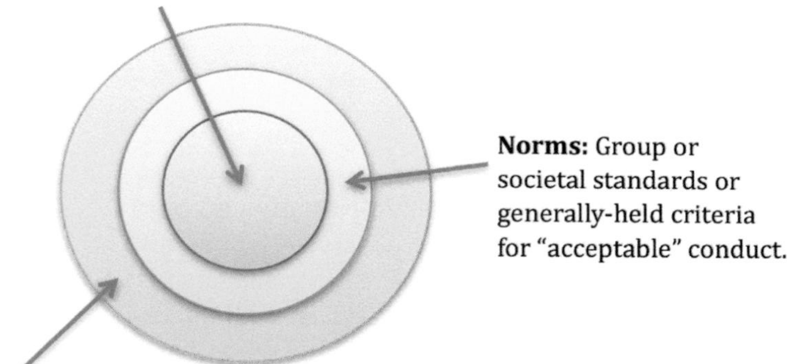
Values: Individual beliefs that motivate and guide behavior.
Norms: Group or societal standards or generally-held criteria for "acceptable" conduct.
Ethics: Objective basis upon which judgments are rendered regarding right or wrong, good or bad, authentic or inauthentic behavior.

Four-Part Ethical-Reasoning Model

Building upon our discussion of critical thinking, ethical reasoning utilizes a similar structure. First and foremost, ethical reasoning involves constructing and evaluating the process of developing value-based decisions. This is typically not easy as there is no simple ethical recipe. While there is not a specific algorithm, in order to practice ethical reasoning it is important to formulate a framework, which provides a context from which to examine specific situations and to evaluate possible courses of action. One such framework is comprised of four interrelated components, which can serve to guide ethical reasoning:

1. Description
2. Analysis
3. Vision
4. Strategy

This ethical decision-making guide provides a structure from which to examine an existing situation and develop new insights.

1. **Description:** "What is reality?" is a basic human question that most often (especially among students enrolled in an introductory sport-management course) elicits the following response: "You have to be kidding!" While answering such a fundamental question may be difficult—if not impossible—gathering facts (i.e., who, what, when, where) about a specific situation, and evaluating and interpreting these

"facts" is something managers do every day. While our individual perspective limits our ability to "objectively" analyze a given situation, we can somewhat mitigate our subjectivity by attempting to openly and transparently compare our gathered facts.

2. **Analysis:** Analysis involves openly examining and asking questions about our facts. It involves scrutinizing such facts' origins and proposed reasons for their existence. While such analysis is crucial, it is often complex, and may not offer a single, satisfactory explanation.
3. **Vision/Goal:** This component looks at a person's ideals, or how one thinks things "ought to be" or should exist. Determining what should exist requires a person to refer to goals and established principles. It involves asking the question, "What is the best way things could turn out?"
4. **Strategies/Means:** Strategies provide a roadmap to get from how things are to how they ought to be. This step also involves asking if proposed strategies can be ethically justified. It also involves determining available tools and potential costs. It is probable that what may be the "right thing to do" may conflict with other identified goals.

Using this four-part model takes into account factual, analytical, existential, or strategic differences. Such ethical reasoning allows us to go beyond simply reacting to a situation. It provides a systematic and analytic ethical decision-making framework. This model recognizes that whenever we "think" critically, our point-of-view is still based on assumptions. In addition, our thinking has implications and consequences. In all reasoning, we use ideas and theories to interpret data, facts, and experiences in order to answer questions, solve problems, and resolve issues. The process of ethical reasoning and ethical decision making must include the idea of impartiality, and assumes that each of us is a conscientious moral agent, which means—as much as possible—an ethical thinker must be impartial and listen, and must gain facts before acting.

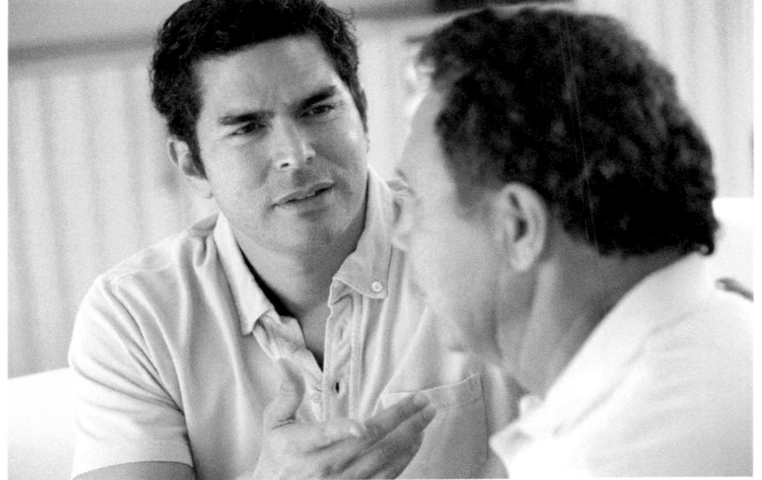

Shutterstock, Inc.

Ethical disagreements can arise based upon factual, analytical, existential, or strategic differences.

Obstacles to Ethical Decision Making

There are at least three main obstacles to ethical decision making:

1. Confusing ethics with religion, culture and the law;
2. Difficulty in gathering facts; and
3. Lack of moral courage.

Confusing Ethics with Religion, Culture, and Law

It is important to differentiate ethics from other modes of thinking or justifications for decisions and actions. Ethics is not religion, culture, or the law. However, all of these "others" also play a role in our day-to-day decision-making process.

- **Religion:** While religion may provide codified values, the answers provided are not subject to deductive and inductive reasoning and critical thinking. Since ethics utilizes such critical-thinking skills, it is not religious morality. Being religious is not a necessary condition for acting in accordance with an ethical framework. While a religious person must "believe" in a specific religion, an ethical sport manager can act "ethically" on her own, without receiving specific religious instruction from "on high," regarding how to act. In addition, deciding whether to follow any religious instruction still requires making an ethical judgment.

According to **divine-command theory**, moral or ethical rules are a "divine" deity's (i.e., god[1]) commands. Consequently, religious people's "moral" actions are those commanded or forbidden by this deity. In addition to the difficulty in determining, which "god" is making the "divine" command, divine-command theory raises the following dilemma:

> (A) Is something right because god commands it, or (B) does god command something because it is right or good? If (A), then morality is based on the deity's arbitrary will. It is conceivable a deity could order a person to do things a person previously viewed as immoral. If morality is based on the deity's will, a person would be morally required to do potentially bad things, if so commanded. Therefore, objective claims about god's divine benevolence or goodness are empty. If (B), while there is an independent standard from which to evaluate if an action is right/wrong, and possibly good/bad, god is reduced from a divine commander or decider, to nothing more than an ethical intermediary (e.g., an ethical umpire, if you will).

1 In philosophical or ethical analyses, a "small g" is utilized when referring to what religious adherents refer to as divine entities or deities.

- **Society and Culture:** Social and cultural questions (e.g., norms) deal with customs, traditions, and taboos of a society, culture, or group. As is evident in a diverse society, norms vary significantly. Sometimes social/cultural/group customs have ethical implications, but they are not themselves the basis for ethical reasoning.
- **The Law:** Legal questions deal with societal rules of behavior that have been codified as "a law" in a particular society. Particular law or laws may or may not have an ethical basis. Laws often emerge out of social conventions, so what is "legal or illegal" may or may not be a matter of ethics.

It is important for sport managers to understand ethical questions involve evaluating human behavior toward people or other creatures. Ethical principles converge across cultures and groups, and give direction for how we "ought" to behave.

Difficulty in Gathering Facts

As everyone—from a crime-scene investigator (CSI) to a sport marketer—knows, gathering facts is often not easy. In addition, uncovered "facts" may turn out to be unreliable, since facts often reflect the complexity of reality. Human prejudice can also interfere in determining facts. Every person operates from a set of assumptions and perspectives, and has different agendas and points of view. Emotions often play a role and can cloud "objectivity." All of these factors affect how facts are viewed.

There are some remedies for these potential obstacles. Responsible moral thinking involves attempting to see things—as much as possible—as they are. While "objectivity" is a fundamental philosophical question, in order to engage in ethical reasoning, we must attempt to adopt (as much as possible) an "objective point of view." This requires not assuming a particular point-of-view is the *only* one, or that it is inherently the "*right*" one. It is crucial to attempt to "see" other perspectives and understand other people's assumptions. Acceptance of diversity is a must. (It should be noted that acceptance of diversity is not the same as **moral relativism**, which will be discussed later.)

Homogeneity (reflective in the extreme by *groupthink* or *cultural myopia*) is an obstacle to gathering objective facts and analyzing reality. People of similar backgrounds, ethnicities, and cultures are unlikely to easily see other perspectives. While groupthinkers may believe they are being "objective," this is often an illusion. Unless people are aware of their limitations and are willing to adjust their perspective and view an alternate reality, such cultural or ethical myopia cannot be overcome.

Many ethicists (especially deontologists) contend every person, regardless of background, culture, or ethnicity, "knows" right from wrong. Sometimes the issue is a person simply lacks the moral courage to follow his or her duty and do the "right thing," and act to prevent or correct a "bad thing" that has happened. Opportunities for ethical action are plentiful, but so are reasons not to act. For example: A part-time concession worker at a Major League Baseball (MLB) park who sees a fellow employee steal a t-shirt from a merchandise kiosk across the concourse may not report the theft if he is worried about being labeled a "snitch."

Lack of Moral Courage

Not demonstrating moral courage in one's actions does not make someone a "bad" person; it means the person failed to act ethically. There are many reasons why people fail to take action based upon their values. The discussion that follows highlights five reasons for people's lack of moral courage:

1. **Discomfort:** Doing the right thing is often uncomfortable. Few like to stand up to a group, whether small or large. Suppose a classmate makes an offensive joke; how many students would say, "That's not funny; I find that offensive." Such uncomfortable events provide opportunities for sport-management students to "practice" for the real-world when acquiescence should not or may not be an option. While it may be uncomfortable, acting ethically (in accordance to one's values) sometimes requires a person to defy social conventions and deal with discomfort.
2. **Futility:** Doing the right thing is often seen as futile. Acting ethically may be viewed as a "no-win" situation. If people believe they cannot make a difference, they may feel there is no justification for doing anything.
3. **Socialization:** In many ways, athletes and sport-managers are socialized to be submissive; they are often instructed to be a "team player." Such socialization may reflect culture, gender, or social class. Although being "happy" may be a worthy outcome (see discussion on ethical hedonism), there may be far better reasons for ethical action than personal happiness. It is likely that socialization played a critical role in Major League Baseball's (MLB) recent steroid era. The lack of moral courage among many baseball players, executives, and fans resulted in what almost everyone believes is a stain on America's pastime.
4. **Bystander effect or diffusion theory:** When confronted with a situation where action is needed, people often hope or expect others will take the initiative. The greater the number of people who witness any event, the less likely any one of them will act. There have been reports of crimes being committed where witnesses heard cries for help from the victim

but they did not call the police since they felt someone else would have made the call. In addition to potentially letting someone else take action, people are often only as ethical as their peers or contemporaries. Diffusion theory (as well as socialization and discomfort) seems to explain why across the country National Football League (NFL) fans participate in and/or tolerate NFL game-day experiences that include not only cheering on one's favorite team, but what also has been described as a "culture of intoxication" (Southall & Sharp, 2006) (see Box 5.2).

5. **Personal cost:** Personal cost involves individuals' ethical inactions based upon a fear of losing their job, their income, or "lifestyle to which they have become accustomed." Such concerns are understandable. However, as will be discussed in Chapter 6, inaction may have severe legal consequences. In addition, as Spike Lee so creatively documented in his classic *Do the Right Thing*, the emotional toll or guilt associated with not doing the "right" think cannot be lightly dismissed.

© Brian Smith/Corbis

José Canseco, named in the Mitchell Report about steroid use in baseball in December 2007, wrote in his autobiography *Juiced* that he used steroids throughout virtually his entire 17-year major league career. Canseco was the first major leaguer in history to hit 40 homeruns and steal 40 bases in a season (1988).

Cultural Relativism

The fact that people from various cultures or societies disagree in a given situation has led some ethicists to contend universal ethical truth is unattainable and that every standard or "right or wrong" is culturally bound. Instead of universal truths there are simply different cultural codes, traditions, or folklores. This position is known as **cultural relativism**.

Faced with claims of cultural relativism, it is important to examine if there are substantive differences among fundamental belief systems or values across cultures or societies. It is important to remember that many times apparent differences arise from different belief systems (such as religions), not from fundamental values. A culinary example might make this distinction clear.

Let's imagine that while you are eating a hamburger at a café near campus, three friends in succession walk up to you and express differing viewpoints on whether it is ethical to eat cow "muscle." Each person's perspective may be based on a number of factors. (Note: If you are a vegetarian, pretend you are a carnivore for the sake of this example! Also, pretend that the way these fictitious friends talk even remotely resembles how your real friends talk!)

BOX 5.2

The Cost of Simply Standing By

Fans' NFL game-day experiences include not only cheering on one's favorite team, but also often being immersed in a "culture of intoxication" prevalent at such contests. Whether it is ritualistic tailgating or consumption of numerous alcoholic beverages during the game itself, the inextricable ties between spectators and alcohol consumption are easily identified.

On October 24, 1999, the parking lots at Giants Stadium, which opened four hours before kickoff, witnessed a Sunday game-day ritual played out at professional football stadiums across the United States: "... pre-game and post-game tailgate parties at which persons consume alcoholic beverages" (Sixth amended complaint and jury demand, *Verni v. Lanzaro*, 2003, p. 7). As the afternoon turned to early evening, the New York Giants had easily beaten the New Orleans Saints 31–3, to run their record to 4-3 on the season (NFL 1999 Season Archives, n.d.). Celebratory Giants fans, among them 30-year-old Daniel R. Lanzaro of Cresskill, New Jersey, poured out of Giants Stadium to begin their journey home or to continue their celebrations at one of the local bars, such as Shakers or The Gallery, in the borough of Hasbrouck Heights in Bergen County (Sixth amended complaint).

Returning home from a family outing to pick up pumpkins for Halloween, Ronald Verni, accompanied by his wife Fazila and their two-year-old daughter Antonia, passed through Hasbrouck Heights, about five minutes from Giants Stadium, via Terrace Avenue (Crusade against DWI, 2002; Cable News Network, 2003). After purchasing and consuming at least 14 beers and an undisclosed amount of marijuana (Sixth amended complaint, 2003) while participating in pre-game tailgating and viewing the day's game at Giants Stadium, Lanzaro lost control of his 1994 Ford pickup, hit one vehicle and then collided, head-on, with the Verni family's 1999 Toyota (Coffey, 2005).

The results of the accident were horrific. Antonia, who was resuscitated by Hasbrouck Heights EMTs (emergency medical technicians), suffered a broken neck and spent the next 11 months in the hospital and in rehabilitation. The accident left the child "... a quadriplegic in need of round-the-clock care. Her mother went into a coma, needed reconstructive surgery on her face and had a rod inserted into her leg" (Coffey, 2005, para. 6). Antonia's father, Ronald, was unhurt in the accident.

According to a newspaper report of the accident, Hasbrouck Heights police officer Corey Lange found Lanzaro and a passenger sitting on the curb near the accident site. Both Lanzaro and the passenger had trouble standing up. When asked how much he had been drinking Lanzaro replied, "Too much" (Gaudiano, 2002, para. 2). A security guard at the hospital reported finding a marijuana "joint" in Lanzaro's pocket (Gaudiano). Lange later said that Lanzaro admitted to drinking before and during the game, and to also smoking some "pot" (Gaudiano). According to police, Lanzaro's blood alcohol level was "...0.266, two times the legal limit of 0.10" (Gaudiano, para. 2). In August 2003, Lanzaro pled guilty to vehicular assault and was sentenced to five years in Riverfront State Prison (Coffey, 2005).

- Friend A says, "Like, eating a cow is wrong, because dead souls inhabit cows. My grandfather is like dead. I do not want to eat my grandfather. Therefore, eating a hamburger is wrong."
- Friend B says, "I know dead souls inhabit cows, but that burger smells like really great, and no one in my family has died yet. I am going to buy one and eat it now, while my grandfather is still alive and well. Eating a hamburger does not bother me if I do not like know the soul I am eating!"
- Friend C says, "There are no such things as dead souls. However, eating red meat is not good for a person's heart, so I think you should not eat that hamburger."

The three friends arrived at their "ethical" position in very different ways and for a variety of reasons. Friend A believes dead souls inhabit cows, so he does not eat cows in order to not eat a dead grandparent. Friend B also believes dead souls inhabit cows, but is not personally offended by eating the souls of people she does not know. Meanwhile, Friend C is not in favor of cannibalism, and also does not believe a dead grandparent's soul inhabits the cow. She simply believes (based on the latest scientific research) eating red meat is unhealthy.

As this vignette highlights, many factors work together to produce societal or cultural norms. Individual values are only one factor. Others include religious beliefs, factual beliefs, and physical circumstances. It does not follow from the mere fact that people disagree or have different beliefs that we should not seek to examine human actions and seek "objective" ethical truth.

While different ethical positions may be based upon different values, they may also arise from different circumstances. In a legal setting, differing circumstances are referred to as a "fact pattern." Differing fact patterns or circumstances may force people to make different and "difficult" choices. Making a different choice than another person does not mean each person's values are different. Two college athletes may both "value" an education, but their individual sport's physical, psychological, and time demands may be different. In addition, their socioeconomic, familial, or cultural circumstances may be markedly different. These differences may allow one student to spend more time and energy studying, or may result in an inability to fully access the educational opportunity afforded. Within the context of differing fact patterns, does each person's class grade "truly" reflect the degree to which each valued the class or their education? Quite the contrary; both may have equally valued the course, but—based on a variety of circumstances—they may have prioritized certain things and therefore made different choices.

Outside of sport, such "values" as caring for children, telling the truth, and refraining from murder are often considered "universal." Some observers have contended that without truthfulness, duty has no meaning. However, it has also been argued there are limitations on lying. Some have argued that lying is universally acceptable only to avoid an innocent person being harmed. The most common formulation justifying lying is the "Anne Frank" dilemma. Simplified, it asks the question: "Would you lie if it meant saving an innocent person's life?" (See the discussion on consequentialism.)

With regard to murder (e.g., taking an innocent life), suppose there was no such prohibition. There would be no security, and society would collapse. Small groups could band together and trust not to murder each other, but in order to survive they would simply be forming smaller societies that did adopt a rule against murder. It seems there are some general moral rules that all societies have in common because such rules are necessary for their existence. Cultures may differ regarding specific exceptions, but these are against a background of general agreement on larger issues. Such ethical agreement can be seen in the following frameworks for ethical reasoning. They are some of the most common ethical constructs in Western thought.

Some Frameworks for Ethical Reasoning

Now that we have discussed the need for thinking critically when engaging in ethical reasoning, let's spend some time dissecting some ethical theories often used to guide ethical decision making: (1) consequentialism, (2) deontology, and (3) existentialism.

Before looking at each theoretical framework in greater detail, here are some highlights of each:

- **Consequentialism** focuses on consequences. A "good" decision is the one that results in beneficial consequences.
- **Deontology** emphasizes moral duty. The right decision is one that intends to fulfill an individual's duties.
- **Existentialism** concentrates on individual responsibility and authenticity of action. An authentic decision is one that is free of hypocrisy.

Consequentialism

When deliberating about what ought to be done, often the first thought involves asking, "What are the possible and likely consequences of my action?" This is a natural starting place when thinking about either moral or practical decisions. From a consequentialism perspective, people do a "good" thing when their actions result in consequences that produce the greatest balance of good over bad.

In Western philosophy, consequentialism (also referred to as utilitarianism—a well-known formulation of consequentialism) is most often associated with three philosophers:

- David Hume (1711–1776),

- Jeremy Bentham (1748–1832), and
- John Stuart Mill (1806–1873).

For a consequentialist, happiness is the only thing people value for its own sake; therefore, happiness is the sole measure of value. Mill contended the principle of utility or greatest happiness principle is the foundation of morals. This principle can be stated as follows:

> *Actions are good in proportion as they tend to promote happiness; bad, as they tend to produce the reverse.*

Happiness (more or less) equals pleasure or the absence of various types of pain (e.g., physical, psychological, emotional, or economic). For example, the following conversation is replete with consequentialist references:

QUESTION:	Why are you going to college?
ANSWER:	To get an education.
QUESTION:	Why do you want an education?
ANSWER:	To get a <u>good</u> job.
QUESTION:	Why do you want a good job?
ANSWER:	Because I want to be <u>happy</u>.

It is important to note this example makes no distinctions about what constitutes or qualifies as "happiness."

Let us look at another example in which a student engages in a form of consequentialist-based reasoning to make a decision on whether or not to go to a party instead of studying:

FRIENDS:	Let's go party!
STUDENT:	I have to study.
FRIENDS:	Partying is much more <u>pleasurable</u> than studying.
STUDENT:	Yes, I agree going out with you will produce much more <u>pleasure</u>.
FRIENDS:	Then you should come out with us; after all, what produces the greater amount of physical pleasure over pain is good. Clearly partying is more pleasurable than studying, so…?
STUDENT:	But I will learn more from studying.
FRIENDS:	Ignorance is bliss. You will have a better time and be more <u>content</u> if you just party.
STUDENT:	Well, if the <u>best</u> thing to do is that which produces the greatest amount of pleasure, I guess I should go to the party. So let's party!!!

The "let's party!" ethos is really more accurately described as simple **hedonism** (a search for short-term physical pleasure). However, in the consequentialist framework short-term physical pleasure is not the only form of pleasure. "Good" should not be confused with instant gratification, or with sensations or simple contentment, although at times a happy person may be content. As a rational human being, short-term physical contentment is not the only "good" that can be desired.

So what kind and whose pleasures are to be considered good? Since even an oyster can experience simple physical pleasure, intellectual pleasures, which are unique to human beings, are deemed superior to short-term physical pleasures. According to this line of thought, intellect, which separates humans from other animals, is a superior pleasure.

The argument is based upon the premise that humans are not static beings on par with non-sentient or unaware creatures. They possess reasoning, intellect, imagination, aestheticism, productivity, and morality. In addition, humans have higher aspirations than animals, so "goodness" cannot simply involve discussions of *quantities* of physical pleasure or sensations. Consequently, some pleasures are more desirable than others. In this way, a pleasure's quality outweighs quantity. While this may be difficult to determine, a pleasure that involves and employs the "higher faculties" (e.g., the intellect) is deemed to be of higher quality and to be given higher preference.

Unfortunately, for students who want to party with their friends at the expense of their intellectual education, Hume, Bentham, and Mill did not believe "ignorance was bliss." Ignorance was not "good." In an intellectually-based consequentialist framework, a longer-term, intellectual pleasure is better than a short-term, physical one.

But since people are all equal, no person's happiness counts more than any other's. Thus the standard is not the agent's own happiness but all concerned. The moral agent must be strictly impartial, a disinterested and benevolent spectator. This requires one to recognize the effects or consequences of decisions. Such recognition becomes crucial for leaders, managers, advisers, and anyone making decisions for others.

Sport managers must make numerous decisions about resource allocation, marketing strategies, alcohol management, security and staffing issues. These decisions are often based upon anticipated consequences. Contingency planning in event management makes use of utilitarianism, since it involves asking the question, "What if?" Sport managers attempt to minimize unwanted (bad) consequences and maximize desirable (good) intended consequences. Therefore, utilitarianism and consequentialism are not only ethical theories, they are also potential management tools. The theories help sport managers develop, plan, and organize their management strategies to meet their consumers' wants, needs and desires.

In summary, for utilitarianism, good actions are those that have the best consequences. A good action produces a greater balance of happiness over unhappiness, in a setting where every person's welfare or happiness is equally important.

While this is a popular theory, it generates some perplexing questions:

- Is happiness the only good?
- How do we define happiness?
- Is "goodness" determined by utility, or do we think that some things are "right" irrespective of consequences?
- Just because something satisfies a greater number of people, does that fact make it right?
- Would a "good" action still be "good" if it contradicts some of our most deeply held beliefs, or if it just seems "wrong" to us?
- Would we be willing to sacrifice someone, or even ourselves, for the "good" of the whole?

In addition to the many questions utilitarianism seems to raise, from a practical standpoint, the theory is somewhat dependent on a person knowing all the facts and being able to calculate all the consequences prior to acting. (Such calculation is known as *hedonistic calculus*.) Although obviously thinking rationally about the possible or likely consequences of one's actions makes a great deal of sense, it may be impossible for a person to know all the facts and determine who will be affected by the actions. Clearly, considering consequences is an important element of ethical decision making, but looking only at consequences may not be enough.

Deontology

While utilitarianism focuses on the consequences of an action, deontological theories focus on the motives, obligations, or duties that lead to actions. These motives must be analyzed independent of anticipated consequences. Deontologists claim an action is morally wrong, not because of its consequences, but because the action *a priori* (i.e., having knowledge or justification independent of experience) involves a moral violation. The philosopher most associated with deontology is Immanuel Kant (1724–1804). Although often difficult to assess, his ethical ideas have greatly contributed to Western ethical thought.

For Kant there are three important concepts: "The Good Will," duty, and reason.

- **The Good Will:** The only thing that is good, without qualification, is a good will. The Good Will is intrinsically good, but not because of what it affects or accomplishes. Its value is wholly self-contained and utterly independent of its external relations.
- **Duty:** Kant distinguishes (1) actions done from the motive of duty and (2) actions done in conformity with duty. An act is praiseworthy not for

self-interested reasons, nor as a result of natural inclinations, but only if done from duty. The moral value of an action can only reside in a formal principle or "maxim," which is the general commitment to act out of reverence for universal moral law. For Kant, acting in this manner is a rational person's duty.

- **Reason:** If there is a universal moral law, it must be the same for all rational agents. The only thing all possible rational agents share is reason. So, universal moral law must be discoverable by practical reason. Therefore, right actions are those that practical reason would will as universal law.

What is the moral law discoverable by reason? Morality can be summarized in an ultimate universal principle of moral law, from which all duties and obligations are derived. This principle is the **categorical imperative**:

> *Act only on that maxim through which you can at the same time* will *it should become a universal law,*

summarizes a procedure for determining whether an act is morally permissible. Though expressed as a simple sentence, the categorical imperative requires further explanation to better understand and apply its principles.

There are several steps in constructing and analyzing the categorical imperative. The process involves a series of statements. As we work through the various sentences, remember to keep the various definitions in mind.

- A *maxim* is a general, but not universal, principle of action.
- An *imperative* is a command usually stated in terms of "ought" statements. Kant distinguishes between two kinds of imperatives: hypothetical and categorical.
  - A *hypothetical imperative* depends on a desire, and contains conditions. If one wants to earn a college degree, then classes must be successfully completed. This imperative depends on the desire to receive a college degree. If there is no such desire, then one is released from this imperative. However, imagine if morality was based only on hypothetical imperatives. A person could easily be released from the imperative if they so desired. But morality imposes a duty to do certain things, which leads to a system of categorical imperatives.
  - A *categorical imperative* is a command without limiting conditions that is discoverable by rational moral agents. Consequently, a rational moral agent has a duty to obey a universal or categorical imperative. Desires, inclinations, preferences, and emotions are irrelevant. The moral duty to follow a categorical imperative is paramount.

What Is Duty?

Duty is an obligation one has to act or refrain from acting in a given manner. Our duty is often related to another person's inherent or universal right.

Kant believed every time people perform an action, they act from a maxim, even though they may not be able to articulate or know that maxim before they choose to act. However, each action can be traced to a prescribed maxim. For example, if people choose to lie (not tell the truth) in a certain situation, the maxim they are following is logically that it was right for them to lie in that situation.

However, since duty cannot be based solely on changing and/or capricious circumstances, the most important element of the categorical imperative is the requirement that any developed maxim must apply universally to everyone. No maxim upon which we act can result in our fact pattern–based exceptions. A maxim that we will to be a universal law must apply to everyone; it cannot lead to contradictory conclusions.

An example Kant discussed is promise-keeping. Suppose after graduation a student lands a job as an inside sales representative for a National Basketball Association (NBA) team. Despite the initial excitement and desire to do a great job, after a few weeks the employee begins having trouble maintaining his outbound call volume (inside sales reps must make a specified number of calls to identified prospects). In a panic he decides to start calling fax-machine numbers he found by searching the Internet. The employee promises himself he will stop making the fake calls when he has collected sufficient referrals. After all, he thinks, "Nobody is being hurt. I'm still doing my job!"

After thinking about this situation, some questions might come to mind:

- What is the action's maxim?
- In this situation, what is the categorical imperative?
- Is it universally permissible to CHEAT? Is it universally permissible to keep a promise?

While the employee might rationalize cheating because it will help him keep his job this month (note, this is a consequentialist formulation), cheating cannot be a universal law. It would lead to a contradiction—the sales manager could never trust the employee.

> *One might think the Golden Rule satisfies the categorical imperative. The Golden Rule is certainly a good principle, but it is not a duty, since it depends on individual preferences.* (Again, the reference to treating others as they wish to be treated is a consequentialist formulation.)

Kant divides the universe into persons and things. Things are nonrational entities of any kind. Persons are autonomous rational agents. In all actions there are ends and means. Kant maintains every rational being exists as an end in him or herself, not merely as a means to an arbitrary end. While ethicists since Kant have attempted to develop more than one categorical imperative, for Kant THE categorical imperative is as follows:

> *The practical imperative that follows from the categorical imperative is: Act so that you always treat humanity—whether in your own person or in that of any other—never simply as a means, but always at the same time as an end in itself.*

This practical imperative (a universal maxim) requires respecting persons as autonomous human beings with rights and dignity, not treating people as things or objects to be "used" to achieve an end. Basically people should not be treated as things; to do so would fail to respect the most important aspects of being a rational being: autonomy and dignity.

According to Kant, we should look at our intentions, not at how much misery and happiness an act is likely to produce. Our intentions are what matter. According to the categorical imperative, we must ensure our contemplated act will not treat anyone as mere means to an end, but will treat all people as ends in themselves.

Treating people as mere means to an end involves using them in a manner that a "rational moral agent" would not consent. Kant noted that while we do use each other in reciprocal or cooperative ways (e.g., NBA ticket-sales representatives sell game-tickets to clients and are paid a commission), treating a person as a mere means might involve the customer not agreeing to buy the ticket, but the sales representative tricking the person into releasing a credit card number and not delivering the tickets. Successful false promising (e.g., not delivering the tickets) depends on deceiving the person to whom the promise has been made, about the real maxim. (It has already been noted that this cannot be universalized.)

> *A person who promises falsely (lies) treats the acceptor of the promise as a prop, or as a thing, not as a person. According to the categorical imperative, this makes lying wrong.*

Standard ways of using others as mere means include deceiving them and/or coercing them. If a person is coerced, there is no consent. According to deontology, acts done following maxims that require deception or coercion of others are wrong and cannot be universalized. In addition to their being wrong, they are also unjust. For Kant, acting in a just manner is the most important of our universal duties. When we fail in these duties, we have used others as mere means. But respecting persons and not treating them as things requires respecting them as rational human beings—as members of the "Kingdom of Ends."

As you can surmise, Kantian (e.g., deontological) ethics differs from consequentialist or utilitarian ethics. Deontological theory looks at the intentions and duties that underlie the action. Consequentialism looks at an action's consequences. With all the facts, information, and knowledge of the ultimate consequences, a consequentialist can—after the fact—access an action's moral worth. But as noted, such "Monday-morning quarterbacking" is a daunting task, unlimited in scope, often imprecise, and leaves out a person's intentions. Kant's ethics are more limited in scope in assessing intentions. However, it must be remembered that deontology does not allow people to simply claim their intentions were "good" and then do whatever they want. It is not enough to say, "I did not intend for anyone to get hurt!" A person's intentions reflect the reasonably anticipated immediate results of an action. Provided we have not intentionally used another person as a mere means, we have done nothing "unjust" or immoral.

Existentialism

Elements of consequentialism and deontology are often used in combination to develop policies or make ethical judgments in real-world settings. However, sometimes these two frameworks may seem to be in conflict. When that occurs, existentialism may be a useful mediating framework.

Existentialism—as the name implies—is a philosophical school of thought that focuses on human "existence." One of its primary tenets is, human beings create meaning and fulfillment without reference to universal laws or rules. Existential meaning is the result of free will, choice, and personal responsibility. Our lives involve searching to find out who and what we are—in other words, to discover our existence. We make choices based on our personal experiences, beliefs, and outlook.

Existentialism expresses the angst generated among philosophers in response to the "problem of evil" (e.g., How can a divine god allow so much evil to exist in the world?"). This most basic of philosophical issues calls into question the existence of a higher moral authority. In Western philosophy, the problem of evil has resulted in the decline of religious authority and the rise of atheism among philosophers. One of the earliest existentialists, who did not rely on universal laws from a "Creator," was Friedrich Nietzsche (1844–1900), who famously said: "God is dead. God remains dead. And we have killed him. How shall we comfort ourselves, the murderers of all murderers?" (Nietzsche, 1887/1974, p. 181).

If God is dead, then what process allows for ethical decisions to be made? Unique human choices must be made without an objective form of truth. An existentialist believes ethical choices must be made without the help of laws, ethnic rules, or traditions. While each person has free will, human nature must also be struggled against. In addition, since all human beings are responsible for their own free choices, their choices are (as is all of life) a struggle, but life is about struggle. Human choice is not always rational and is fraught with stress and irrational consequences. Regardless of whether it is rational or not, personal responsibility and discipline is crucial. Inherent in the death of Nietzsche's God is the belief that society is unnatural and its traditional religious and secular rules are arbitrary.

Many of existentialism's concepts reflect the profound influence on Western thought of three epochal 20th-century events: World War I, the Great Depression, and World War II. By the late 1940s any lingering sense of optimism among intellectuals had been destroyed. This sense of despair, articulated by Jean-Paul Satre (1905–1980) and Albert Camus (1913–1960) has continued to be popularized to this day. The freedom to choose one's preferred moral belief system and lifestyle has increased with the decline in religious moral authority and the questioning of government ethics as well. The arbitrary nature of religious and/or governmental strictures is what existentialism finds most objectionable. The imposition of beliefs, values, or rules that must be followed out of a sense of duty is anathema to existentialist freedom. Existentialists contend those in positions of power tend to dehumanize others and make them into objects or—within a capitalist system—commodities.

While existentialists almost universally agree that suffering and loss preclude human life from ever being considered fully satisfying, the struggle to live as full a life as possible, in spite of the lack of perfection, power, and control one has over life, is what gives life meaning. This search for self-fulfillment and personal meaning in life is the essence of existentialism.

To struggle against this dehumanization, existentialism stresses a person's individual judgment (based on individual life experiences) is the determining factor for what should be believed rather than arbitrary religious or secular world values. As a result, existentialism is often seen as useful as an ancillary ethical framework to help deontologists and/or consequentialists choose between alternatives when several "right/good" or "wrong/bad" choices present themselves (Badaracco, 1997). Existentialism is not just doing what "feels good," it involves acting in a manner consistent with the range of positive human emotions: compassion, justice, integrity, and kindness. As a result, existentialism is not a rational axiological framework, but a nonrational emotive source—a check and balance—to rational ethical analyses. It provides a human face to rational ethical thought, based upon critical thinking. It is the "heart" to the other frameworks' brain.

Conclusion

The process of thinking critically and engaging in ethical decision making is not easy, but can be "learned." After becoming familiar with the various ethical frameworks, applying these frameworks and acting ethically requires being willing to apply ethical decision-making skills in the real world of sport management! Ethical issues arise often when a sport manager least expects them. However, just as athletes practice for an upcoming contest, sport managers can prepare to respond to an ethical dilemma by thinking critically about values, norms, and ethics.

FIGURE 5.2 Ethical Complimentarity

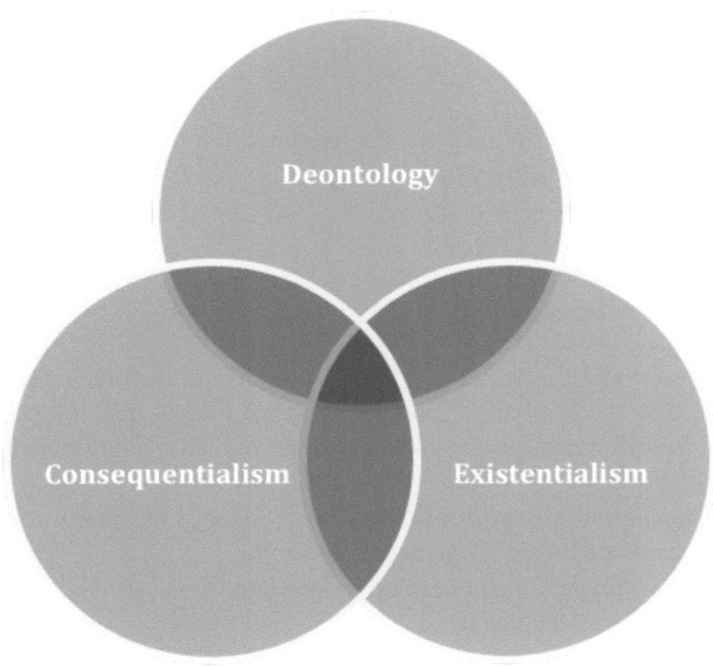

In your career there will be many opportunities for ethical action. There will also be plenty of obstacles or excuses to acting consistent with your values. While there is no single algorithm or recipe to follow, this chapter has highlighted several useful guidelines. It might be that as you contemplate various ethical dilemmas, you are—at one time or another—drawn more to one ethical framework. However, you may also utilize elements from one or all of the delineated frameworks (see Figure 5.2). Such a multifaceted approach is consistent with Heisenberg's uncertainty principle and Bohr's principle of complimentarity. These principles posit that subatomic particles manifest themselves in contradictory forms at different times (e.g., light sometimes exhibits properties of waves and sometimes of particles, a concept discussed as wave-particle duality). Both manifestations are "true" at the same time. This is not "relativism," but duality. This duality is also related to Eastern philosophy's *yin* and *yang*, in which two complimentary forces maintain the universe's harmony.

Ethical reasoning involves contemplation and systematic introspection. It does not provide easy, cut-and-dried or black-white answers, However, if you desire to be a conscientious and ethical sport manager such self-analysis can be of great benefit. If you are—at your core—a "moral" person, it is hoped this chapter's ethical frameworks have provided you with some guidance about how you can make decisions consistent with chosen ethical framework(s).

As was discussed, it is helpful to utilize some interrelated components in ethical decision making:

- **Goal/Vision:** What is the goal you want to achieve? How should things be?
- **Social Reality:** What is the description of how things are? Gather facts, and process information.
- **Analysis:** Why are things the way they are? What assumptions contribute to this reality?
- **Strategies/Means:** How do we get from where we are to our goal: how things ought to be?

There are often obstacles to ethical decision making, which include gathering facts, lack of moral courage, and relativism. This chapter outlined several ethical frameworks and concepts worthy of investigation by future sport managers:

- **Consequentialism/utilitarianism** (Hume, Bentham, and Mill): Focuses on the consequences of an action.
- **Deontology** (Kant): Focus on motives and sense of duty that lead to an action.
- **Categorical imperative:** Always act so that your maxim can become universal law; this requires universalizability.
- **Kingdom of Ends:** Never treat people purely as means, but always as ends in themselves: treat people with dignity and respect.
- **Existentialism:** The struggle to live as full a life as possible, in spite of the lack of perfection, power, and control one has over your existence, is what gives life "true" meaning.

Concluding Thoughts

This chapter has not presented a single ethical prescription, or delineated how you *should* act. Consistent with that perspective, the following thoughts are not intended as rules that must be followed, but simply words for consideration. As a future sport manager you will help write the sport-management ethics manual. Consider the following as entries in that manual:

- Scrutinize your motives.
- Be "careful" and thoughtful in your deliberations about your actions.
- Infallibility is not the goal.
- Respect for diversity is not the same as succumbing to cultural or ethical relativism.
- Examine your perspectives.
- Do not assume your point of view is the correct one.
- Adopt as objective a point of view as possible.
- Take others' perspective into account and respect their interests.
- Try to imagine each proposed policy or procedure as if it were a rule for everyone.
- Listen to others.
- Reflect on actual and hypothetical cases.
- Be impartial. Do not make an exception of yourself.
- Be consistent—apply principles consistently to yourself and others.
- Get the facts straight.
- Listen to your existential conscience.
- Take into consideration virtues, duties, and consequences.
- Develop strength of will.
- Have self-respect.
- Think for yourself.
- Think about what it means to say you have "integrity."
- Have moral courage.
- Recognize that inaction may often be as "bad" as implementing a "wrong" action.

Remember that there are lots of opportunities for ethical action; so, too, there will be many obstacles. Ethical action and ethical decision making are not easy, but can be learned and practiced so they become part of your sport-manager tool box. Finally, in recognition of philosophers, ethicists, and sport managers who have come before, remember that acting ethically is a journey, not a destination.

chapter 5
Interview

Interview 5.1

Dr. Jon Ericson
Professor of Rhetoric and Communications Studies
Drake University

Jon Ericson is an Ellis and Nelle Levitt Professor of Rhetoric and Communications Studies (Emeritus) and former Provost at Drake University. He is the founder of The Drake Group, a national organization working to end the academic corruption in college sport. In 2001 Mr. Ericson was named an Ethics Fellow by the Institute for International Sport.

Our initial discussion with Mr. Ericson began with this exchange:

Q: **What was the catalyst for founding The Drake Group?**

A: I didn't do it because of ethics; I did it because I was angry.

Q: **What caused you to become angry?**

A: I saw the academic records of athletes.

Q: **Why did the academic records make you angry?**

A: Maybe the words of a student who saw the records will capture why I was angry:

The NCAA established a self-examination program for every Division-I institution. Self-study is good. Good for the NCAA. We had one at my university. Drake University's self-study consisted of carefully, very carefully selected members and was pronounced a complete success. During the time of the study, I was preparing a minority report to accompany the report of our Academic Accountability for Intercollegiate Athletics Committee to the Faculty Senate, and I invited Wanda Everage, Assistant to the Provost for Academic Enhancement Programs and a member of the academic integrity committee of the self-study, to take a look at the records. The report focused on race and athletics. Ms. Everage arrived as I was collating the material around a large seminar table. She began with the first record, moved to the second. She made it only one-third of the way down one side of the table before stopping and saying: "This makes me sick." [Co-Editors' Note: The table documented the systematic manner in which the student transcript had been altered. The grades reported on the official transcript were fictitious – false.]

When I took the material to the print shop to be copied, a senior faculty member was in the room, and he studied the material. Several days later in the mail I received a handwritten note:

5/7/97
I have known there is corruption in athletics here and other places, but it was a shock to see it laid out so clearly as in your report to the Senate. Does it all come down to $ and power? And why are we so out of step with the rest of the world?

The work-study student who assisted in preparing the materials had left me a note on my desk:

. . . I hope you are still interested in getting a "student perspective" on all this record stuff . . . perhaps we could talk Friday morning around 8 or 8:15?

He was a reserved, easygoing, laid back, intelligent young man. In three years working with him, I never heard so much as a "damn" or a "hell" from him. He graduated with a GPA of 3.9 with a major in Economics and Mathematics, and he applied to and was accepted at all of the following law schools: University of Minnesota, Washington University in St. Louis, University of

Iowa, University of Colorado, and Northwestern University. He chose Washington University.

He arrived, sat down, said he wanted to talk about the records he had been working on, and he began with sly amusement: *"You know they will say you are a racist."* I nodded. He didn't break stride, *"You know they will say you are out to get Sociology."* I thought to myself, this guy is on a roll. Still not breaking stride he said, *"And, you know that no one cares."* Well, he hit all three I thought, and I assumed he was finished and probably quite pleased with himself. Then his features quickened, and it was clear he did not come to exchange pleasantries. He leaned forward and said: *I guarantee you. I wouldn't have paid $20,000 a year to come here if I had seen this shit first.*

The public received a press release announcing that the NCAA certification self-study found Drake to be fully certified. The president, faculty, staff, and athletics personnel who served on the committee were, no doubt, pleased, happy and proud. The staff person, faculty member, and student who saw my minority report were sickened, shocked, and angry.

So what do I—or any professor—owe this student? To defend the records, to explain them away, to avoid facing what was in front of us? Or to see wrong and try to right it? It's about choice. Choice is about measuring what we are.

Sometimes the choice is downright scary. Take Andre Trocme. In *Lest Innocent Blood Be Shed: The Story of the Village of Le Chambon and How Goodness Happened There,* Philip Hallie paints a picture of what it means to face making a choice:

When Andre Trocme said good-bye to his children, he did not know if he would ever see them again. The Maquis around LeChambon were getting more numerous and more violent, and so were the German troops and the Gestapo. Those days were full of disappearances and sudden death. But he was calm, almost joyous, not only in order to keep his family from knowing terror but because for a long time he had been hoping for a test, a hard test. His warmth, the speed of his intelligence, the vigor of his pain-wracked body that could work efficiently with only a few hours of sleep, and his luck had kept death away from him and his family and had brought admiration and love to them. Moreover, he had been efficient: he had created a rescue machine made of poor people who had enough problems of their own to keep them fully occupied. But he did not know whether he could be helpful under great pain and under the immediate threat of death. Now he would find out. He was like an eager chemist watching the results of one last acid test that would tell him if the substance before him was, indeed, gold. The substance before him was himself.

Thank goodness being a professor doesn't require such a choice. Choices, scary or banal, are tests. The academic corruption in sports is but one of those tests, some seemingly banal—beginning class on time; some with consequences—grade inflation—that professors face every day. Seeing academic records that by the most elastic of measures betrayed my university and my profession provided a good test.

You ask, what is moral courage? In terms of college sports, it takes no great courage to complain about the costs of big-time college athletics. Oh, it would appear that taking on the monster is "David and Goliath" with sticks and stones heading their way—a few nasty emails maybe but little harm done. And some will see such critics as heroes. But those who select money as their cause leave open the charge that they can be bought. Fighting for money means taking on the commercialized college sports industry; fighting for academic integrity requires a faculty member to take on his colleagues. When it comes to courage, it is no contest. A friend, Kevin Braig, wrote "that to inspire others, you have to put yourself at the center of the issue" and to make the point he forwarded Theodore White's comment that "to go against the dominant thinking of your friends, of most of the people you see every day, is perhaps the most difficult act of heroism you can have." This is why public disclosure of fraudulent academic records of college athletes is the most difficult—but necessary—solution for the academic corruption in college sports: It requires a faculty member having the courage to go against colleagues who are collaborators in the corruption.

Why do a few get involved when "the majority merely stay quiet and keep their heads down"? People become professors to be scholars, not warriors. It is a full-time job. Years later now, I am asked whether it (founding The Drake Group and disclosing the fraudulent academic records at Drake University) was worth it. For me, "Oh my, yes!" It was so damned much fun.

You asked what advice I might have for undergraduate sport-management students. I have given it. This is your field of study; other students are just "fans"; you are—and will be—closest to the problems. That gives you a particular and special opportunity to measure yourself. What could be more fun than that?

Veritas.

("Veritas," indeed, Dr. Ericson.—The Co-Editors)

Study Questions

1. Identify the basic elements of each ethical framework discussed in this chapter.
2. Explain the differences between inductive and deductive reasoning.
3. Discuss the fundamental differences between deontology and consequentialism?
4. Highlight how social-contract theories incorporate elements of both deontology and consequentialism.
5. List and discuss the obstacles to moral behavior identified in this chapter. Use these obstacles to analyze the death from an inebriated fan at Giants Stadium. Highlight the obstacles that contributed to the situation.

Learning Activities

1. Go to a sport website or daily online news source (e.g., *Yahoo, USA Today, NY Times*) and find a news item that involves an ethical issue. Utilizing one or more ethical framework from this chapter, analyze the situation and make an ethical judgment.
2. Which ethical framework is most appealing to you as a future sport manager? Which one do you feel will be of most use in making managerial decisions? List the reasons why you made your choice.
3. As a manager, you must deal with the inside sales representative discussed on pages 139–141. What action would you take? What theory or theories would you use to justify your action?

References

Badaracco, J.L. (1997). *Defining moments: When managers must choose between right and right*. Boston: Harvard Business School Press.

Cable News Network. (2003, October 13). *Lawsuit targets NFL.* Retrieved April 27, 2005 from http://cnnstudentnews. cnn.com/TRANSCRIPTS/0310/13/ltm.14.html

Coffey, W. (2005, January 29). Wasted innocence. *nydaily news.com.* Retrieved April 12, 2005 from http://www.ny dailynews.com/sports/

Gaudiano, N. (2002). Crusade against DWI. North Jersey Media Group Inc. Retrieved September 28, 2004 from http://www.hhpd.com/forms/CrusadeagainstDWI.pdf

Hobbes, T. (1651). *Leviathan, the matter, forme and power of a common wealth ecclesiastical and civil* (Chapters 17–31). Retrieved January 22, 2010 from http://www.earlymoderntexts.com/pdf/hobbes2.pdf

Nietzsche, F. (1974/1887). *The gay science: With a prelude in rhymes and an appendix of songs* (W. A. Kaufmann, Trans.). New York: Random House, Inc.

Sixth amended complaint and jury demand, Verni v. Lanzaro, Docket No. BER-L-10488-00 (Superior Ct. N.J. Law Div. Bergen County, Oct. 16, 2003).

Southall, R.M., & Sharp, L.A. (2006). The National Football League and its "culture of intoxication": A negligent marketing analysis of Verni v. Lanzaro. *Journal of Legal Aspects of Sport, 16*(1), 101–127.

Verni v. Lanzaro and Stevens, No. L-10488 (Superior Court of New Jersey, Law Division: Bergen County, January 20, 2005).

Suggested Sources

The following sources are examples of critical thinking, ethical analysis, or just worth reading:

Andersen, H., Barker, P., & Chen, X. (2006). *The cognitive structure of scientific revolutions*. New York: Cambridge University Press.

Badaracco, J.L. (1997). *Defining moments: When managers must choose between right and right*. Boston: Harvard Business School Press.

Blackburn, S. (2009). *Ethics: A very short introduction*. New York: Oxford University Press.

Byers, W. (1995). *Unsportsmanlike conduct: Exploiting college athletes.* Ann Arbor, MI: The University of Michigan Press.

Eitzen, D.S. (1988). Ethical problems in American sport. *Journal of Sport and Social Issues, 12*(1), 17–30.

Funk, G.D. (1992). *Major violations: The unbalanced priorities in athletics and academics*. Champaign, IL: Leisure Press.

Kuhn, T.S. (2012). *The structure of scientific revolutions* (4th ed.). Chicago: The University of Chicago Press.

McInerny, D.Q. (2004). *Being logical: A guide to good thinking*. New York: Random House.

Putler, D.S., & Wolfe, R. A. (1999). Perceptions of intercollegiate athletic programs: Priorities and tradeoffs. *Sociology of Sport Journal, 16,* 301–325.

Sack, A.L., & Staurowsky, E.J. (1998). *College athletes for hire: The evolution and legacy of the NCAA's amateur myth.* Westport, CT: Praeger Publishers.

Southall, C., & Southall, R. M. (2014). Atmospheric music in the NBA servicescape: Fan involvement, team loyalty, consumer attitudes and emotional responses. *Journal of Applied Marketing Theory*, *5*(1), 45-61.

Southall, R.M., & Staurowsky, E.J. (2013). Cheering on the collegiate model: Creating, disseminating, and imbedding the NCAA's redefinition of amateurism. *Journal of Sport and Social Issues*, *37*(4), 403–429.

Linda A. Sharp, J.D.[1] • *University of Northern Colorado*

chapter 6

Legal Aspects of Sport

CHAPTER OBJECTIVES

After reading this chapter, you will be able to:

- Understand the necessity of becoming knowledgeable about legal concepts to be a better sport manager.
- Define and understand the legal theory of negligence, its elements, defenses, and some important applications.
- Define and understand the important elements of a contract.
- Understand how constitutional law applies to sport management.

KEY TERMS

Constitutional law

Contract law

Negligence law

1 Some material in this chapter is compiled and adapted in part from Chapters 1, 4, and 15 in *Sport Law: A Managerial Approach,* Third Edition, by Linda Sharp, Anita Moorman, and Cathryn Claussen. Copyright © 2014. Scottsdale, AZ: Holcomb Hathaway, Publishers. Used with permission.

> *Sports law is an amalgamation of many legal disciplines, ranging from antitrust to tax law. These disciplines are applied to facts arising from sports contexts and are supplemented by case law nuances and a growing body of state and federal statutes specifically applicable to sports. Sports law, with its wide variety of legal aspects, probably encompasses more areas of law than any other discipline. Sports law is also a dynamic field of the law with new issues arising on an almost daily basis due to court decisions, new legislation and regulations.*
>
> —Dean Robert Garberinio (1994)

Introduction

You have recently been hired as your town's youth soccer league administrator. As you begin your first day on the job you are overwhelmed by how many of your responsibilities have legal implications:

- How do you ensure your coaches are competent and "fit" to work with young athletes?
- What emergency medical care is available for participants?
- What state law is applicable regarding concussion protocols that must be used for youth sport participants?
- What policies and procedures do you implement to make sure unruly fans do not pose a danger to game officials, other fans, or players?
- How do you properly maintain equipment and the playing fields?
- What provisions should be included in your contract with the vendor who will provide food and beverages at games?
- What levels of insurance are necessary?

Whether you become a coach, high-school or college athletic director, sport league administrator, park district supervisor, fitness club manager, sport organization marketer, or commissioner of the National Football League (NFL), you will need to understand your job's legal aspects.

As you read your daily newspaper's online website, note how many pages are devoted to issues other than box scores and game stories. Whereas casual sports fans used to be exposed only to on-field results, numerous media outlets now analyze and discuss sport's legal aspects. Numerous stories on Entertainment and Sports Programming Network (ESPN) deal with legal issues. In fact, new sports programs such as ESPN's *Outside the Lines* often detail how the law impacts the sport industry. Popular media's focus on sport law has resulted in fans being more informed regarding legal issues and judicial decisions.

It is imperative that as a future sport manager you recognize not only the U.S. legal system, but also the law's applicability to sport and recreation settings. In addition, all sport management students must understand that our country's "open door" philosophy of hearing disputes may sometimes lead to abuses of the system. Fundamentally, our legal system operates under the premise that all citizens should have nearly unfettered access to formal legal adjudication of disputes. This philosophy is fine when people use the system only to bring meritorious claims. However, as Taylor, Jr. and Thomas (2003) noted, "Americans will sue each other at the slightest provocation" (p. 44). To some observers, our country's judicial system allows seemingly "nonsensical" lawsuits to be filed; however, as long as such claims have an underlying legal theory, such suits can be filed.

For example, a California cheerleading coach was sued by a student who alleged his failure to make the squad resulted from the coach changing his high score. The student's family sought damages and the coach's dismissal, alleging the coach sabotaged the student's cheerleading chances (Taylor, Jr. & Thomas, 2003). Another peculiar lawsuit involved a volunteer youth-league baseball coach who was sued by a player's father after the team's winless season. The suit alleged the coach's incompetence cost the team a trip to an out-of-state tournament. Other frivolous suits have involved innocuous situations in which a coach benched a player during a critical hockey game, two baton twirlers were cut from a high-school majorette program, and an athlete was placed on a junior varsity instead of a varsity team (Asquith, 2002).

What does this mean for prospective sport or recreation managers? In order to avoid lawsuits or adequately address lawsuits—whether meritorious or not—future managers need to learn as much about the law as possible.

Sport facilities and events provide numerous areas of potential litigation.

Shutterstock, Inc.

Shutterstock, Inc.

Lawsuits are time consuming and expensive, regardless of whether a judgment is ever rendered against an individual or organization. Therefore, this chapter will seek to help you understand the law and use it as a tool to help prevent litigation or lessen its consequences.

In preparing for a sport or recreation industry career, students also need to utilize the law as a guide to draft better organizational policies and procedures. Better policies and procedures make such organizations safer and more hospitable environments for internal (employees) and external (clients, customers, athletes) constituencies. The law is, of course, only the starting point for having an ethical organization but we need to use the law well to have a firm foundation in building a well-run and ethical sport organization. (See Chapter 5.)

This chapter is intended to serve as an introduction to legal theory in order for sport managers to function effectively. Because of space limitations, the emphasis will primarily focus upon **negligence law**, contract law, and constitutional law, with a brief mention made of other pertinent topics. Since the law is continually evolving, it is critical sport managers consistently update their sport-law knowledge.

Negligence law
A part of tort law dealing with unintentional conduct that falls below a standard established by law for the protection of others against unreasonable risk of harm.

Overview of Negligence Law

Negligence is conduct that "falls below the standard established by law for the protection of others against unreasonable risk of harm" (Restatement [Second] Torts §282). Negligence is an *unintentional tort* (a civil wrong other than a breach of contract) so it is at the other end of the "intent spectrum" from *intentional torts* such as battery and assault. In a negligence action, the defendant (the party alleged to have committed the wrongdoing) has allegedly acted in an unreasonable fashion, but did not *intend* to commit the act or to cause harm. In most negligence cases, the plaintiff alleges the defendant acted in a careless or inadvertent fashion; however, this conduct is far removed from conduct in which a defendant intended to commit the act and to cause harm. Such intentional acts by a defendant often lead to *punitive damages* being awarded. (An award of punitive damages goes beyond *compensatory* [actual] damages sustained by a party. Punitive damages try to deter such conduct from happening again.)

In order for a plaintiff to successfully proceed with a negligence cause of action, four elements must all coexist. These elements are (1) duty, (2) breach of duty, (3) causation, and (4) damages. Each of these elements will be discussed next.

Duty

The first element necessary for a successful negligence case is *duty*, which means that the defendant must have some obligation, imposed by law, to protect the plaintiff (the party who commences the lawsuit) from unreasonable risk. Duty is a question of law for the court to ascertain and is a foundational issue. The legal concept of duty is based on policy considerations that lead courts to determine a particular plaintiff is entitled to protection. Fundamentally, absent duty, there is no cause of action for negligence.

In most of this chapter's cases, the duty of care is quite evident. Some examples of a duty of care are between K-12 teacher/coach and student-athlete, or facility owner and spectator. In a K-12 setting, the duty arises based on the concept of *in loco parentis* (in the place of the parents). Schools have custodial and tutelary responsibilities for the minors in their care. The duty between facility owner and spectator arises based on the facility owner selling the spectator a ticket.

Breach of Duty

There is a *breach of duty* if the defendant has failed to meet the required *standard of care*. The court ascertains the standard of care by asking this question, "What would a reasonably prudent person have been expected to do in the same or similar circumstances?" The law of negligence is closely tied to factual circumstances. There can be no breach of duty in the abstract; whether a breach of duty exists is always relative to particular circumstances.

To assist in this determination, courts have developed an objective standard, the "reasonably prudent person." This hypothetical person is the legal standard to which an actual defendant is held. If a defendant's actions are consistent with those of the reasonably prudent person, then the defendant has met the duty of care; thus, element number two of the cause of action is not met. However, if the defendant's actions fall below what would have been expected of the reasonably prudent person, then the defendant has breached the duty of care.

If the defendant possesses knowledge that is superior to an ordinary person, then the defendant is accountable for care that would be reasonable in light of such special skills, knowledge, or training. Thus, a coach with a master's degree in physical education, who has coached for 10 years and who has special certifications pertinent to coaching, will be held to a standard of care based on that special skill and knowledge.

Because jury members most likely do not have the expertise to ascertain the standard of care on their own, how do they decide what the reasonably prudent person should have been expected to do in a particular context? In an attempt to convince the jury of the applicable standard of care in a particular circumstance, the parties to a lawsuit use expert witnesses. In many cases, the plaintiff's expert witnesses may disagree with expert witnesses called by the defendant. It is up to the jury to decide which expert(s) to believe, since such belief is a question of fact, which is within the jury's purview.

The presence of wet floors can breach the duty of care owed. If an injury were to occur as a result of the floor, the injured party may sue for damages.

Causation

The third element of a negligence cause of action is *causation*, which involves whether there is a "causal connection" between the breach of duty and the resulting injury. This is known as "proximate cause" as it encompasses the notion of causation in fact and the policy question of whether a court should hold someone accountable for an injury based on the notion of *foreseeability*.

Causation looks at whether a particular outcome would have occurred even if the breach of duty had not occurred. The concept is that if something would have occurred anyway, then the breach of duty cannot be said to have caused the outcome.

In addressing causation, courts also look to the question of proximate causation, which goes to the issue of whether the defendant should be legally responsible for the injury, even if there was causation in fact. This issue is primarily a question of law for a court to address, and often relates to the question of foreseeability. This means that courts often decide that the scope of liability should only extend to those risks that are foreseeable.

Damages

The final element of negligence, *damages*, means that some actual loss or damage must have been sustained as a result of the breach of duty. The threat of future harm is not sufficient damage. In a negligence case, successful plaintiffs typically are awarded compensatory damages, which are designed to compensate the victim for such things as medical bills, lost wages, and pain and suffering. However, as was noted earlier, in cases where the defendant may have acted intentionally, the court may also award punitive damages to punish the defendant and send a message that this type of behavior will not be tolerated.

Defenses against Negligence

The defendant's first strategy is always to argue that one or more of the elements of the cause of action have not been established. Once the elements have been established, the question becomes whether the defendant, in whole or in part, can avoid liability. The most common negligence defenses are statute of limitations, an Act of God, and contributory/comparative negligence.

Statute of Limitations

The defense that a claim has not been filed in a timely fashion is known as the *statute of limitations*. This defense is procedural, not substantive, meaning that, regardless of the merits of the plaintiff's case, the cause of action may be dismissed if the complaint has not been filed in a timely manner. Each state has legislation that provides the time period for bringing a certain cause of action. If the action is not brought within that designated time period, usually the action will be dismissed.

Act of God

An *Act of God* defense means that a person has no liability when an unforeseeable natural disaster resulted in injury to the plaintiff; the defendant's negligence did not cause the injury. There are two aspects to this defense that must coexist. First, there must truly be an Act of God (i.e., some natural disaster like a storm, lightning, earthquake, flood, or hurricane) that caused the injury. Second, this Act of God must be unforeseeable. If it is foreseeable the defendant may still have liability since the defendant did not act reasonably in protecting participants from the disaster.

Contributory and Comparative Negligence

As previously discussed, the hypothetical reasonably prudent person concept sets the standard in determining whether the defendant breached the duty of care. With *contributory negligence*, the question involves whether the plaintiff acted in a manner expected of a reasonably prudent plaintiff. We use the reasonably prudent plaintiff hypothetical to determine what the plaintiff should have done in a particular circumstance to protect his/her own safety. If the plaintiff's conduct falls below the standard of care, then the plaintiff is said to be *contributorily negligent*. If a court uses contributory negligence, ANY unreasonable conduct by the plaintiff precludes the plaintiff from recovering any damages.

The rule of contributory negligence is rather harsh, since any negligence by the plaintiff completely bars recovery. Therefore, most states have adopted the rule of *comparative negligence*. Utilizing this rule, the court compares any negligence by the plaintiff to the degree of negligence by the defendant. The court typically then allocates potential damages based upon the degree to which the plaintiff's negligence contributed to the action.

Assumption of Risk

The defense that is most widely used in terms of physical activity and sport is *assumption of risk*. It is frequently discussed as being either primary or secondary, and these distinctions are important.

Primary

Primary assumption of risk means that a plaintiff understands and voluntarily agrees to accept an activity's *inherent risks*. If a plaintiff is "coerced" into attempting an activity, there is no assumption of risk. The inherent risks of an activity are obvious and necessary to its being conducted. For instance, baseball-game participants expect that baseballs may be thrown or hit at a high velocity, or that players may slide into a base while an opponent is trying to make a play. With primary assumption of risk, the defendant has no duty of care toward the plaintiff, since the plaintiff agrees to assume or accept risks that are common to that activity. The plaintiff is not agreeing, however, to accept risks that are beyond those inherent in the activity. In other words, the plaintiff does not assume the risk of the negligence on the part of a coach or instructor. Let's look at this concept in conjunction with a particular activity—skydiving.

When landing in a field at the end of a jump, a skydiver breaks his ankle. This injury is an inherent risk of skydiving, since some impact with the ground is both obvious and necessary for the activity. There is no way to land without risk; sometimes the force of landing may cause a broken or sprained ankle. Likewise, perhaps the wind came up suddenly after the jump was made and the skydiver was injured because he could not avoid a tree. This is another inherent risk that must be assumed by a skydiver.

However, what if the skydiver is killed because neither of his parachutes opened? Is the parachute's failure an inherent risk? Is this failure an obvious and necessary risk of the activity? The answer to both questions is "No" because

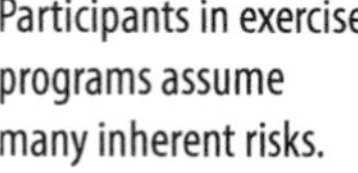
Participants in exercise programs assume many inherent risks.

Shutterstock, Inc.

the parachute not opening was likely caused by the negligence of the person who packed the chute or by the chute's malfunction. In either case, these are not risks assumed by the skydiver; they are risks beyond what the skydiver reasonably anticipated when he began the jump. In this scenario, there is no primary assumption of risk. The concept that the negligence of instructors is not an inherent risk of an activity is an important one.

Secondary

Secondary assumption of risk means a plaintiff deliberately chose to encounter a known risk and in doing so acted unreasonably. In many jurisdictions, the concept of secondary assumption of risk is subsumed within the concept of comparative negligence, as discussed. The underlying notion of secondary assumption of risk is the same as comparative negligence (i.e., the plaintiff acted unreasonably in behaving as he did).

Common Liability Issues Regarding Participants

Lack of Supervision

Many liability concerns relating to participant injuries occur because of supervision failures. Proper supervision means the persons entrusted with this responsibility are competent to oversee the participants (*quality of supervision*) and there are sufficient supervisors to fulfill the duty of care (*quantity of supervision*). The obligation to supervise does not mean there is a duty of instruction, but it does mean supervisors must be able to recognize and prevent or stop dangerous behaviors.

Quality of Supervision

The issue of quality of supervision addresses a supervisor's competence. Even if the supervisor-to-participant ratio is one-to-one, supervision may be inadequate if the supervisor does not have the competence or training to identify, prevent, or intervene when dangerous behavior occurs. Possession of a heart beat and a warm body is not the equivalent of competent supervision; a supervisor must know enough about the activity in question to identify danger.

Quantity of Supervision

Supervision quantity involves determining whether there are sufficient competent supervisors relative to the number of participants—in other words, whether the ratio of supervisors to participants is reasonable.

Whether the ratio is proper is a question that cannot be answered in the abstract. There is no "magic number" for all occasions. The quantity of

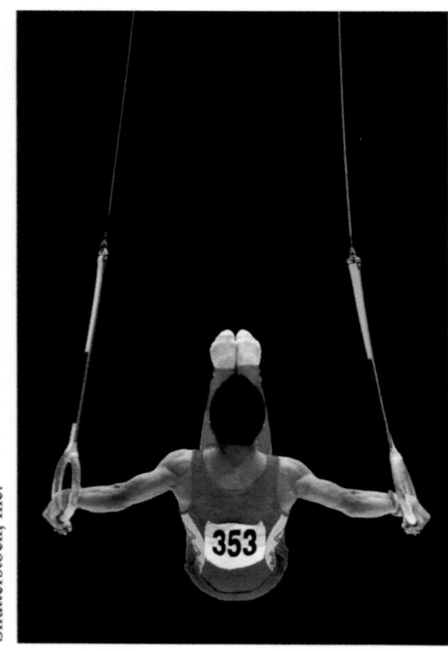
Shutterstock, Inc.

Activities such as gymnastics present greater risks for participants, and therefore require a greater number of supervisors, than many other sports.

supervision is activity specific. Obviously, an activity such as gymnastics presents more risk than table tennis. This would suggest a lower supervisor-to-gymnast ratio than with table tennis players. The age and maturity of the participants must also be considered. Generally, youthful participants require more supervisors. Also, if a particular group has shown a propensity to engage in rowdy behavior, this must be taken into consideration when determining the number of supervisors. If participants have physical or mental disabilities that make them more prone to injury, more supervisors will be necessary. In addition, there may sometimes be concerns with the facility/area in which an activity takes place. For example, more supervisors are necessary if participants are dispersed or because of facility/area configuration supervisors cannot maintain visual contact with all participants.

Supervisory plans should take into account all of the aforementioned principles. Further, supervisory plans should delineate not just the number of supervisors, but also the specific area of supervision. Designating specific supervision areas is necessary because, otherwise, supervisors may tend to cluster and talk with each other, leaving certain areas without supervisory coverage.

All of the abovementioned factors should be considered when making quantity of supervision decisions. Remember, the essential question remains, "What number of competent supervisors is reasonable in that setting, at that time?"

Improper Instruction or Training

The question of proper instruction or training in the context of physical activity/sport has more severe liability concerns than in other educational contexts. If a coach fails to act reasonably when teaching a physical skill, serious consequences may ensue, including severe physical injury or death. The following discussion focuses on a number of critical instruction/training issues.

Adequacy of Instruction

In order for instruction to be deemed adequate, it must be suitable for the intended audience. The language used must be understandable to participants, based on their age and familiarity with the activity. Also, since verbal instruction of physical skills is often accompanied by physical demonstration, these elements must be congruent. If participants are relatively young and immature, important instructional concepts will need to be repeated more frequently than with a more mature audience. Also, minors tend to comprehend presented material very literally, so certain departures from instruction may be foreseeable.

Instructors/coaches should always follow training practices that have been widely accepted by activity experts. Courts will give great deference to the standards developed by persons or organizations that have expert knowledge about the activity. Caution should be utilized when developing drills or methods that vary from widely accepted practices. Even though a certain method may appear to make sense, it should be widely endorsed before being implemented. Coaches and instructors should always attend professional workshops/seminars to ensure they are implementing the most current accepted practices.

Proper Skill Progression

In many cases, a culminating activity should not be attempted unless proper lead-up activities have been presented and practiced. Physical skills are often taught sequentially in order that a participant is properly prepared to engage in the culminating activity.

Dissemination of Safety Rules and Warnings

Part of learning any activity involves "knowing" what aspects are potentially dangerous. During instruction or training, safety rules and procedures should be discussed and reinforced on a frequent basis. The reason for safety rules should also be shared with participants. Every practice session should have some time devoted to safety rules/warnings pertinent to each activity. Participants should be consistently warned about an activity's risks and the adverse consequences of not following safety rules.

Mismatch

Obviously, competitive situations will almost always pit opponents who are not exactly equal in size, strength, or competency. But, in some cases, it is not reasonably prudent to allow competition between those who are so vastly different in size, strength, or competency, because this could foreseeably result in injury beyond what is accepted as inherent to the activity. Often, a league or governing body may adopt formal guidelines to address such disparities. For example, youth-football age and/or weight restrictions are attempts to reasonably even the playing field. In some cases, participants may be equal in terms of size but there is a vast skill differential that makes it imprudent to match up particular opponents.

Safe Use of Equipment

Part of instructing or coaching an activity is providing necessary, proper, and safe equipment. Since the courts do not view lack of funds as a legal defense, if participants cannot afford or be provided such equipment, the activity should not be continued. However, providing "necessary equipment" does not mean the essential equipment supplied must be "state-of-the-art." It means such essential equipment should reasonably meet participants' needs.

Protective equipment must be in good condition and fit properly. For example, a football helmet that is structurally sound but falls over a player's eyes does not meet the criterion of acceptable equipment. In addition, players should be taught how to properly fit equipment and how to inspect equipment prior to each use. Proper instruction in equipment use should also be given. Finally, if equipment is utilized in a nontraditional manner, information about how to use the equipment in that context should be provided.

Emergency Medical Care

Two major issues are associated with the provision of emergency medical care to participants: (1) making sure that qualified personnel are available to render emergency first aid and CPR, and (2) ensuring that there is a protocol to get needed outside medical personnel to the site as quickly as possible.

Transportation

Transportation of participants is a critical function, which when assumed by an organization, must be provided in a reasonably safe manner. There are four primary issues related to transportation: (1) selection of competent drivers, (2) proper training of drivers, (3) selection of a safe mode of travel, and (4) proper maintenance of vehicles.

As has just been discussed, negligence is the failure to exercise the standard of care that a reasonably prudent person would have exercised in a similar situation. It is important for future sport managers to know and understand the elements of negligence and practice appropriate risk management to prevent or mitigate individual or organizational exposure.

Overview of Contract Law

Contract law
A promise or set of promises enforced by courts, which establish a duty to perform between parties.

Knowing and applying **contract law** basics is an excellent vehicle by which organizations can gain managerial and operational benefits. Most contracts of any complexity are negotiated over a lengthy time period and there are usually multiple drafts before the final contract is signed. This provides adequate time for each party to reflect upon the potential agreement and consult with an attorney in order to arrive at a document that will best serve their interests.

Essentially, contract law is concerned with clarifying and enforcing the parties' wills in determining agreements. Courts are concerned with trying to give effect to each party's intent; courts do not try to rewrite contracts to make a better document for the parties or to make sure that each party has negotiated the best deal possible.

Any contract should be drafted from a *worst-case scenario* perspective. Contracts are simply reflections of human relationships and—as with all relationships—sometimes they may deteriorate. Consider the hiring of a college coach. When a coach is hired, everyone is ecstatic about the prospect of new "program" leadership. The last thing most people think about is the partnership's dissolution. However, coaching contracts are frequently breached, either by the college that wants the program to go in a "new direction" or by the coach who seeks the proverbial "greener pastures." Therefore, the coaching contract must be written with this reality in mind. The contract should be drafted to protect the interests of your organization in the event the contract is terminated by either party.

Formation of a Contract

"A contract is a promise or set of promises, for breach of which the law gives a remedy, or the performance of which the law in some way recognizes a duty" (Restatement [Second] Contracts, 1981, §1). There are four fundamental aspects to the formation of a contract: (1) agreement—offer and acceptance, (2) consideration, (3) capacity, and (4) legality.

The formation of a contract begins with an *offer*, which is a conditional promise made to do or to refrain from doing something. For example, a person (*offeror*) may offer to sell a certain piece of fitness equipment for $400. This communicates the terms of the offer; one now knows the price of the equipment.

If a party agrees to the terms as stated, *acceptance* has been given. A promise is provided by the *offeree* to pay $400 when the equipment is delivered. If one does not mirror the offer with acceptance then the offeror is presented with a *counteroffer*. For example, if a potential buyer responded that she is only willing to pay $300 for the equipment, the initial offer has been rejected in favor of a counteroffer at $300.

Consideration involves the exchange of value. Even though there has been an exchange of promises (agreement) there can be no contract until there is an exchange of value (e.g., one party gives up something of value in exchange for the other party's value). Often, consideration takes the form of Y giving X money for a promise to do or provide something. Though there must be an exchange, the exchanged items do not need to be of equal value.

It is important to remember that if one promises to "pay" another person $100, and asks for nothing in exchange, there is no contract. All that has occurred is an unenforceable promise to make a gift of $100. However, if one agrees to pay $100 for a tennis racquet that is barely serviceable, there is consideration. Further, courts do not generally inquire as to whether the consideration was too little or too much. Since, as discussed, a basic premise of contract law is to allow private parties to engage in transactions of their own making, courts will not generally intervene to stop a "bad deal" from taking place. Paying $100 for a much-abused racquet may be a bad choice; however, if the involved parties do so of their own volition and without any misrepresentations about the condition of the racquet, then the contract will be upheld. Sometimes people may make good deals and other times they may make bad deals; it is not the courts' prerogative to be intermediaries in deals, only to ascertain if the law was followed.

Capacity means the parties to the contract are legally competent to enter into a contractual relationship. For example, minors are usually not bound by contracts, since the law makes a presumption that a minor lacks the legal competence (capacity) to enter into contracts. Thus, if a minor signs a contract, it is generally voidable at the option of the minor; that is, a minor can set aside any legal obligations stemming from that contract. There may be other circumstances affecting competence. For example, mental incompetence or intoxication may also result in a lack of capacity.

Legality means that, to be enforceable, the subject matter of the contract must not violate state or federal law. Since a contract that violates the law is—by definition—illegal, it is unenforceable. For example, since in most states it is illegal to bet on college sports, any gambling contract in those states involving college sport betting would not be enforceable.

Contract Remedies

When one party fails to perform essential aspects of a contract, it is termed a *breach of contract*. Sometimes the breach may be remediable, but often the contract is terminated and the nonbreaching party is awarded damages as a result of the breach. In a contract case, a court is not attempting to punish the party that breached the contract; it is simply trying to compensate the nonbreaching party for the loss of the bargain. Essentially, contract damages are designed to put the nonbreaching parties in the position they would have been if the contract had been performed as promised (Restatement [Second] Contracts, 1981, §347).

Compensatory Damages

In most contract cases, the nonbreaching party can be compensated for the loss of the bargain through monetary or compensatory damages. These damages arise directly from the loss of the bargain. For example, let's assume a sporting goods store agrees to sell Person X a football helmet for $125. Person X agrees to buy the helmet for that price, but the store then refuses to sell Person X the promised good. Not only is the store in breach of the contract, but Person X still needs to obtain a helmet. Seeking a helmet, Person X goes to the two other stores in the area that sell that model of helmet and finds that Store A is selling the helmet for $135 and Store B is selling the helmet for $150. In this case Person X can collect damages from the first store. Let's examine what damages Person X can recover.

First, the general rule in a breach of a sales contract is the buyer can recover an amount equal to the difference between the contract and market price. In this case, however, there are two market prices, \$135 and \$150, for the same item. So can Person X recover \$25 (\$150 market price from Store B – \$125 contract price) or only \$10 (\$135 market price from Store A – \$125 contract price)? Assuming the item is identical, Person X's damages are limited to \$10. According to the principle of *mitigation of damages*, a nonbreaching party must act reasonably to lessen the consequences of the breach. In this case, Person X must choose to buy the item for the lesser price of \$135 (\$10 damages). This obligation to reduce the damages, if possible, is not absolute. Person X does not have to get bids on this helmet from every vendor in the United States, just to deal with the vendors usually dealt with regarding this type of equipment.

The principle of mitigation of damages applies to all types of contracts, but may be more difficult to implement than in a sales contract scenario. For example, if a university breaches its employment contract with a coach, the coach is obligated to mitigate damages by accepting a comparable offer of employment if offered by another university. The coach, however, would not have to accept employment that was inferior in compensation, level of competition, geographic location, and so on, just to lessen the damages; that would not be expected as a part of the duty to mitigate.

Specific Performance

In certain rare circumstances, monetary damages will not suffice because the object of the contract is unique. If an item is truly unique no matter what a breaching party pays, money damages will not compensate for the loss of the bargain because the item cannot be purchased on the open market. For example, if the owner of a uniform worn by Babe Ruth in a particular game against the Cleveland Indians agrees to sell the uniform for \$30,000—and then later breaches the contract—*specific performance* is the appropriate remedy. This will force the breaching party to fulfill the terms of the contract (i.e., sell the jersey for \$30,000).

This remedy cannot be used with personal services contracts, however. If Kobe Bryant wanted to breach his employment contract with the Los Angeles Lakers, the franchise could not force Kobe to play by arguing specific performance (his playing) was necessary. Courts will not force someone to compete against his will, though they would likely prevent Bryant from playing for another National Basketball Association (NBA) team. Even if Bryant could be forced to play for the Lakers, it would be difficult to ascertain if his performance was of his highest ability.

Liquidated Damages and Penalty Provisions

Sometimes the amount of damages that should be paid cannot be exactly determined. Although contract damages cannot be mere speculation, sometimes parties have to approximate the anticipated amount of sustained damages. For example, employment contracts often contain such an approximated provision because the parties cannot determine exact damages resulting from the breach. Therefore, when negotiating the contract, parties agree to a *liquidated damages* provision that establishes a reasonable approximation of damages. Care must be taken in drafting the liquidated damages provision because courts do not uphold *penalty provisions* that do not bear a reasonable relationship to damages to be sustained and are simply punishing a party for breaching a contract. Courts will not uphold such provisions, nor will they award *punitive damages*, unless there is some fraudulent behavior.

Constitutional Law

Constitutional law The underlying document of the U.S. government, which sets forth limits on governmental power.

Though negligence and contract law are likely to be applicable in many sport-management settings, **constitutional law** may be applied more often in specific sport-industry segments. Some potential constitutional law issues that may arise include:

- Does a public school district have the right to implement a random drug-testing policy for its athletes?
- Can a public school coach refuse to allow an athlete to miss practice in order to attend religious worship services?
- What are the limits on free speech that a public university may impose upon one of its coaches?
- If a college player at a state university is suspended from some games due to a disciplinary matter, does the player have a right to have an attorney present at the disciplinary hearing?

The United States Constitution sets forth our federal government's basic principles and establishes the limits of governmental power versus individual rights. Essentially, constitutional law provides the framework within which our government can restrict citizens' personal autonomy.

For a plaintiff to make a case that one or more of his/her constitutional rights have been violated, the defendant must be a state actor. A *state actor* is defined as an entity that is directly an arm of the federal, state, or local government, or given authority to act on behalf of the government. Therefore, a constitutional claim cannot be made against a private person or entity (though other areas of law may apply). For example, if a person who owns a private fitness club attempts to fire an employee for negative statements made while on the job, that employee cannot claim the owner violated his First Amendment rights of free speech. The defendant in this case is a private individual—not a state actor—so no constitutional claim can be made.

First Amendment Claims

The First Amendment to the Constitution outlines a number of concepts that are foundational to our society. For example, the First Amendment contains both the Establishment Clause and the Free Exercise Clause. These clauses both deal with religion. The Establishment Clause protects citizens from government's trying to establish a "state" religion; the underlying sentiment is the government should remain neutral on religious matters. The Free Exercise Clause protects our rights to choose and follow our individual religious beliefs.

First Amendment disputes involving the intersection of religion and sport might include the degree to which prayer may be permitted as a prelude to a public school football contest, whether a coach at a public university or school may lead his team in prayer before a game, whether a Jewish student (who attends a public high school) may be prevented from wearing a yarmulke when playing basketball, whether a public school sport team nicknamed "Devils" must be forced to change its name, and whether a person who wore a pentagram pendant honoring her religious beliefs can be forced to take it off in order to attend a public school basketball game.

The First Amendment also has a Freedom of Expression Clause, which protects expressive activity (like wearing a "protest" armband or certain styles of dress) and speech. Relative to sport participants, such disputes center on whether the self-expression was valuable communication under the First Amendment and what interest the state actor (school or university) had in limiting the speech or expressive activity. In employment situations, the courts look at whether the employee is speaking on a matter of public concern, and balance such public concern against whether the employer's business would be adversely affected by the speech. As an examination of case law reveals, courts frequently utilize balancing tests in constitutional law decisions.

Fourth Amendment Claims

The Fourth Amendment, which protects against unreasonable searches and seizures, is often used to assert that drug-testing protocols implemented by public schools or universities to test athletes are unconstitutional. In such cases, a balancing test is also used. Essentially, an individual's privacy expectation and the degree of intrusion posed by the test are balanced against governmental interest in conducting the test. In the case of *Vernonia School District 47J v. Acton* (1995), the United States Supreme Court upheld a random drug-testing policy implemented by a public school district to test its high-school athletes. The Court characterized the degree of intrusion in the test as minimal and found the athletes had diminished privacy expectations. On the other side of the balance, the school district had an important interest in stopping drug use, which had reached epidemic proportions among its high-school athletes.

Fifth and Fourteenth Amendment Claims

The Fifth and Fourteenth Amendments set forth that a state actor must provide fair treatment in any governmental decision that affects a person's life, liberty, or property. This is the concept of *due process*. However, before a due process claim is heard on its merits, the plaintiff has to establish three points: (1) the defendant is a state actor; (2) the plaintiff is a "person"; and (3) the defendant somehow infringed upon a life, liberty, or property interest.

For example, let's look at a situation in which a state university football player has been suspended for a few games for allegedly breaking a team disciplinary rule. The player claims his due process rights were violated because he did not have a fair hearing during which to contest the allegations against him. However, before a court will actually deal with these claims, it will determine whether the plaintiff has established the three points mentioned. In this case there is state action, since the defendant is a state university. However, while the plaintiff is a person, the question is whether the plaintiff has an affected property interest (life or liberty is not at stake here). In such instances, the courts have held sport participation alone is not a property interest. So, unless the university stripped the athlete of a current grant-in-aid (GIA), the plaintiff cannot continue with his case, since he does not have a property interest involved. An interesting Texas Supreme Court case on this point is *NCAA v. Yeo* (2005).

The Raiders have been involved in numerous lawsuits regarding their 1982 move to Los Angeles and their return to the Oakland Alameda County Coliseum in 1995.

Courtesy Mark Nagel

Other Areas of Sport Law

There are many other areas of law relevant to the sport industry and being a sport manager. As you continue your sport-management education you will take courses that focus on specific sport-industry functional areas. Such courses may include concentrated study in sport marketing, facility management, event management, sport finance, sport economics, and sport sales and sponsorship. In addition, you will undoubtedly take a sport-law course, in which you will examine in greater detail a number of legal theories and representative legal issues. See Table 6.1 for a listing of such issues.

TABLE 6.1

Legal Theory	Representative Legal Issue
Antitrust Law	Relocation of a professional sport franchise
Employment Law—Wrongful Discharge	Employee fired without cause
Negligent Misrepresentation	Erroneous information in employment reference
Tortious Interference with Contractual Relations	Recruiting away employee with existing contract
Title VII (a federal statute)	Discrimination in employment on the basis of race or sex Sexual harassment in the workplace
Equal Pay Act (a federal statute)	Unequal compensation of male v. female coaches
Vicarious Liability	Is the employer liable for the negligence of the employee?
Fair Labor Standards Act (a federal statute)	Working conditions issue relating to wages and hours
Workers' Compensation (state statutes)	Employer liability for injuries to employees
National Labor Relations Act (a federal statute)	Collective bargaining and professional teams
Right of Publicity	NCAA student-athletes sue videogame manufacturers based on the use of athletes' likenesses in games
Title IX (a federal statute)	Gender equity issues relating to high school and college athletics
Americans with Disabilities Act	Sport facility accessibility for the disabled (a federal statute)
Products Liability	Liability for defective sports equipment
Waivers	Can a whitewater rafting company excuse itself from its own negligence?
Intentional Tort (assault & battery)	Participant violence
Trademark and Copyright Law	Rights to intellectual property like team logos or products
Tax Law	Should the NCAA be entitled to nonprofit status?

Conclusion

In conclusion, this chapter has been a brief introduction to the wide spectrum of sport law. Sport law is woven into every aspect of managerial practice in the sport industry. While this chapter was only a brief discussion of fundamental issues pertaining to negligence law, contracts, and Constitutional law, it has provided a glimpse into the legal aspects of sport and recreation. As you will learn as you continue your sport-management education, there are many areas of the law relevant to the sport and recreation industries. Hopefully, your future sport-law class will provide essential information for your sport industry managerial career.

chapter 6
Interview

Interview 6.1

Scott Bearby
Associate General Counsel/
Managing Director of Legal Affairs National Collegiate Athletic Association;
Adjunct professor of law at Indiana University School of Law.

Education
Undergraduate degree from the University of Notre Dame; J.D. from Indiana University.

Career
Joining the NCAA as in-house counsel in 1999, Bearby has served as associate general counsel/managing director of legal affairs since December 2001. He serves as primary counsel for the Men's and Women's Division-I Basketball Championships, and also works primarily with NCAA contract and rights issues, including traditional media, new media, marketing, licensing and promotional rights, and championship-related agreements. He also serves as counsel on intellectual property matters and on the NCAA's crisis assessment team. Bearby advises the NCAA on the creation of subsidiary entities and asset acquisitions. He is an officer in the NCAA's limited liability companies that house the NIT tournament assets, eligibility center services, college football officiating, and March Madness intellectual property.

Q: **How did you get into the industry? What was your career path?**

A: After graduation, I worked for a small firm in litigation and then moved over to business litigation and business transactions. At the time partnership was offered to me, I looked at what I wanted to do long term and thought about using my skill set as counsel in higher education and/or as an educator. The NCAA needed a business and intellectual property counsel, so I was attracted to that position. I also have been able to fulfill my desire to teach as an adjunct professor teaching sport law.

Q: **What are you looking for in new hires, beyond a law degree, if you were hiring at the NCAA?**

A: The NCAA has four practicing lawyers, so turnover is infrequent. Our legal staff all had previous legal experience (at least five years). The legal department does have an intern program. In those candidates, we look for their relevant experience within college athletics, either as an athlete or as a volunteer within the athletic department. We also look for their enthusiasm in expressing how they would maximize the unique opportunity to be a law clerk at the NCAA national office.

Within the national office (and college athletics generally), there are many people with law degrees who are using that education and legal experience outside of the practice of law. There are J.D.s in virtually every department, including enforcement/infractions, compliance, and governance. Today, many conference commissioners and athletic directors have J.D.s, and that number continues to increase.

Q: **What are the biggest challenges and issues in college sport, from your role as a lawyer, for the near future and beyond?**

A: In all of our legislation, policy decisions, and business transactions, the NCAA and our membership need to remain consistent in upholding the principle of amateurism as we define it and not as external entities perceive it to be.

More specific to my practice is the need to stay aware of advancements in technology and new media that influence how the competitions are played and consumed. The law struggles to keep pace with these advancements in addressing issues with regard to social media whether it is a podcast, blogs, Twitter, or other forms of communication.

Q: If you had a message to future athletic administrators, from your experience and your expertise as a lawyer, what would it be?

A: Be creative in your job search. Look for the law firms who represent clients that are behind the scenes in the athletic space, including sponsors, stadium vendors, and operators. By gaining experience and connections in that environment, you are going to be much more marketable to a professional sports property, an athletic department, or another sports entity if that is your eventual goal.

Working in sports as a lawyer definitely can create opportunities to attend events and meet interesting people. However, those privileges should not be the primary reason for seeking a career in that space. One has to have a passion for what the client does and to help the client achieve its goals, but counsel must be grounded in reasonable interpretations of the law.

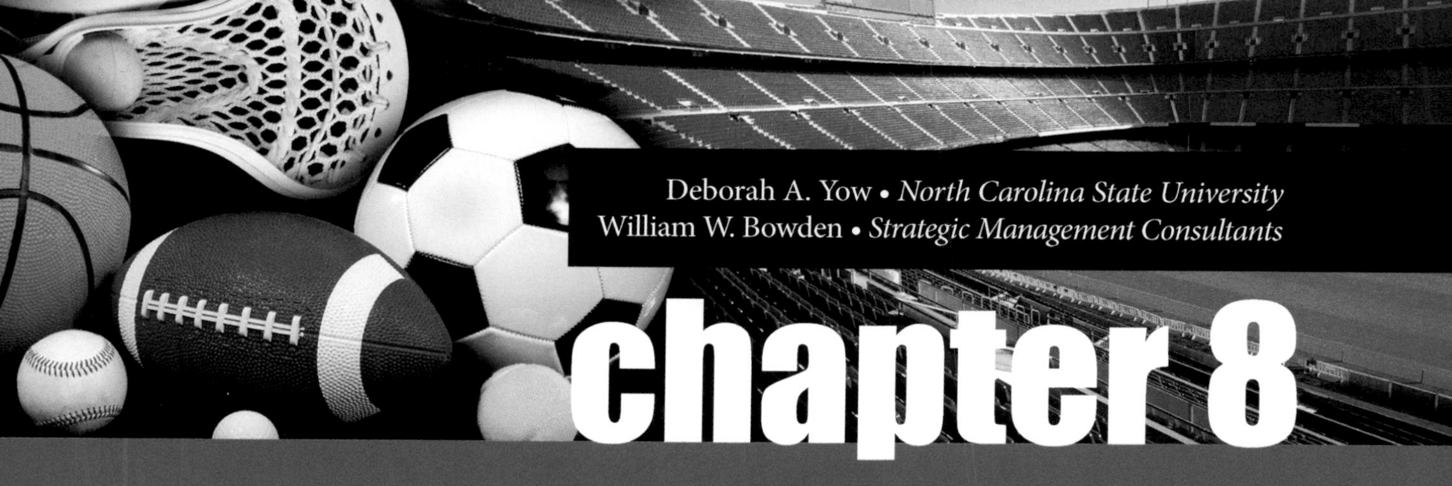

Deborah A. Yow • *North Carolina State University*
William W. Bowden • *Strategic Management Consultants*

chapter 8

Strategic Management

CHAPTER OBJECTIVES

After reading this chapter, you will be able to:

- List and discuss the management functions common to most organizations and enterprises.
- Compare and contrast sport-business enterprises, including intercollegiate athletics departments, to other kinds of business organizations.
- Identify expected positive organizational outcomes from systematic and strategic planning.
- Explain the importance of developing a strategic plan.
- Examine the North Carolina State University (NC State) Strategic Plan case study in order to identify the scope, sequence, and results of strategic planning.
- Identify the role of the North Carolina State University Athletic Department's "Mission Statement and Guiding Principles" document as a resource in developing the department's strategic plan.
- Delineate the use of a performed SWOT analysis as an integral element in the development of a strategic plan.

KEY TERMS

SWOT analysis

The North Carolina State University Athletics Strategic Plan document is available at www.gopack.com then click "Inside Athletics".

> *The future doesn't just happen—it's shaped by decisions.*
>
> —Paul Tagliabue

Introduction

In order to manage a sport enterprise, it is important first to understand a sport enterprise's unique organizational profile. Similar to other businesses, professional sport franchises and college athletic departments involve management functions such as staffing, payroll, purchasing, contracts, planning, budgeting and finance, marketing, and other functions. However, many sport organizations are also uniquely structured enterprises that utilize specialized processes. This is especially true of intercollegiate athletics programs that (1) are departments within an institution of higher education, (2) depend on unique funding formulas, (3) require specialized facilities and support staff, (4) have multidimensional missions, and (5) function within a large and varied stakeholder context. As a result, sport enterprises usually require a specialized management model.

While this chapter examines the strategic-planning process utilizing the structure and operation of a National Collegiate Athletic Association (NCAA) Football Bowl Subdivision (FBS) athletic department, as sport-management students continue their education, they would be well advised to closely examine the unique aspects of a wide variety of sport organizations and various industry segments. Such examination is common practice among today's successful sport managers. While this chapter utilizes a single case-study in order to highlight elements of strategic management, students who wish to work in sport should analyze a variety of professional-sport franchises, sport-marketing firms, hospitality and event-management companies, and so on, to better prepare themselves for a sport-management career. Learning and practicing such strategic analysis on a consistent basis will help students to bridge the gap between theory and real-world practice.

A NCAA FBS athletic-department's organizational chart reflects its specialized management model. Many athletic departments' organizational charts delineate similar functional areas. Figure 8.1 contains the North Carolina State University Athletic Department's basic organizational structure. You will notice each department member has a direct report above the name. This organizational structure is designed to allow information to flow from the bottom of the organization to the top with little crossover between different functional areas. Other organizations may allow more functional-area interaction without the information needing to flow to "higher" organizational levels. For additional information regarding North Carolina State University's intercollegiate athletics program, see Boxes 8.1 and 8.2.

BOX 8.1

North Carolina State University

ICA MISSION STATEMENT AND GUIDING PRINCIPLES

It is the mission of the Department of Intercollegiate Athletics to provide our student athletes excellent opportunities to participate in an intercollegiate athletics experience of the highest quality, with the result that their athletics experience becomes an integral and valued component of their total educational experience at the University.

The mission is further to prepare student athletes to compete at the highest level and to inspire them to be leaders now and for the future by providing the best environment to achieve their athletics, academic, and personal aspirations as well as to provide support for the professional development of our coaches and our staff, all within the role of the greater institutional relationships to the university.

In achieving this mission the Department of Intercollegiate Athletics will embrace these guiding principles:

- To develop and maintain a highly competitive and sound athletic program—reaching a standard of achievement in athletics consistent with our purposes as a University and the excellence of our institution.
- To promote character development, leadership qualities, sportsmanship, and academic excellence in our student athletes.
- To employ coaches and staff members who exhibit high standards of integrity and ethical behavior, including good sportsmanship and a desire to assist student athletes in reaching their academic potential.
- To contribute to the enhancement of institutional morale and esprit de corps among students, faculty, and staff—while providing alumni and friends a means by which they can identify with the University for mutually beneficial purposes.
- To recruit student athletes who are capable of success in the University's academic program and to provide academic support and student development opportunities that will effectively assist student athletes to reach their potential.
- To function responsibly and with accountability in all its initiatives, programs, and operations, which includes providing equal treatment and opportunity for student athletes, coaches, and staff, in employment and in all athletic department programs and activities as required by law and University policy.
- To maintain fiscal and operational integrity by balancing budgets and carrying out sound management practices.
- To provide consistently excellent customer service.
- To comply carefully with institutional, conference, and NCAA regulations.
- To ensure ethnic and gender diversity among its coaches, staff, and student athletes, consistent with the University's educational mission.

BOX 8.2

STRATEGIC PLANNING COMMITTEES AND THE FOCUS AREAS

I. Strategic Planning Steering Committee
- A. Oversight of Process
- B. Guidance in the Review Process

II. Branding, Partnerships, and Outreach
- A. Marketing and Sponsorships
- B. Media Relations
- C. Development
- D. Game Atmosphere
- E. Ticket Services
- F. Video Services

III. Competitive Excellence
- A. Recruiting Expectations
- B. Scheduling Policies
- C. Coaching Standards
- D. Financial and Athletic Aid
- E. Strength and Conditioning
- F. Director's Cup Expectations

IV. Compliance Education and Culture
- A. Title IX Compliance
- B. Representatives of Athletics Interest
- C. Admissions/Eligibility
- D. Drug Testing
- E. Student-Athlete Code of Conduct
- F. NCAA Certification
- G. Agents
- H. Staff Education and Orientation

V. Facility Enhancement
- A. Capital Projects
- B. ICA Facilities Master Plan
- C. Competition Venues
- D. Indoor Training Facilities
- E. Practice Facilities
- F. Facility Scheduling
- G. ICA Offices
- H. Information Technology
- I. Parking
- J. Sustainability
- K. Championship Hosting

VI. Financial Stability
- A. Operational Budgets
- B. Aid Budgets (Wolfpack Club)
- C. Cost Containment
- D. Revenue Growth
- E. Reserve Growth
- F. Personnel Retention

VII. Student-Athlete Well-Being, Academic Performance, and Personal Development
- A. Academic Support/Career Development
- B. Academic Excellence (Graduation Rates, APR, GSR, GPA)
- C. Individual Admits
- D. Student Life (Housing, Campus Safety, Dining Services)
- E. Athletic Training and Sports Medicine
- F. Student Athlete Advisory Committee
- G. CHAMPS/Life Skills

FIGURE 8.1

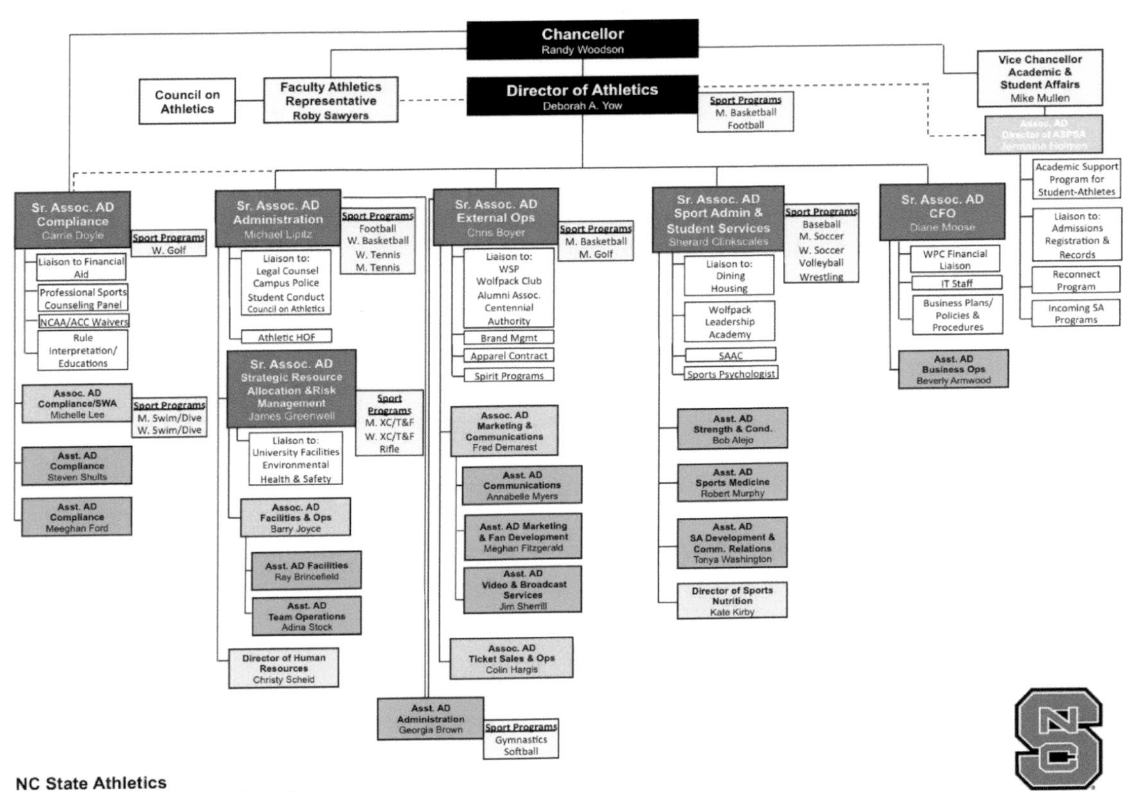

NC State Athletics
Athletics Cabinet Organization Chart

Courtesy Peyton Williams for NC State Athletics.

Carter-Finley Stadium on the campus of North Carolina State University hosts intercollegiate football games and other events.

Courtesy Peyton Williams for NC State Athletics.

Though the chart details the NC State Athletic Department's structure, it does not include its overall reporting structure. In most cases, an athletic director will report to a university vice-president for student affairs, a president, or a chancellor. Despite the athletic department reporting to higher administration, some observers of "big-time" college athletics perceive the athletic department as being a "separate" entity with a distinct mission and operating guidelines from the rest of the academic units on campus. A longstanding and compelling debate continues on many college campuses regarding the scope and purpose of intercollegiate athletic programs within the university community. The fundamental questions typically include:

1. Are athletic departments primarily education programs?
2. Or, are they enterprises unrelated to a university's educational mission?
3. Are athletic departments in the entertainment business?
4. Are the increasing financial and human resources necessary to sustain a major athletic program compatible with a university's educational mission?
5. What exactly are athletic departments and what are their authentic missions?
6. In what ways can an athletic department function as an integral part of the institution and in so doing support the educational mission of the campus?

While each of these questions must be asked and openly discussed by athletic-department members at all NCAA institutions, this is especially true at the NCAA Division-I level. Due to increased economic pressures, the intensity with which these questions are being asked by the media, members of Congress, governing boards, university administrators and faculty, and the general public continues to increase.

Recognizing college sport's disparate nature, throughout this chapter an athletic department will be referred to as an enterprise, a word that—in its generic sense—can embrace any or all of the organizational elements discussed.

The Function of Management

The function of management is continually addressed in myriad articles, books, and online entries. The basic functions are generally understood to be mission-casting, planning, staffing, goal-setting, assessing, controlling, spurring innovation, optimizing productivity, and integrating an organization's goals and operations. Drucker (1994) postulated three essential management tasks, which, by their scope and nature, serve as the foundation for an enterprise's effective functioning:

1. Establishing the specific purpose and mission of the entity,

2. Optimizing employee productivity consistent with the organization's mission and purpose, and
3. Managing the enterprise's social impacts and responsibilities.

These functions are not performed in isolation, but coexist and coalesce into "getting things done through and with people."

Chelladurai (2005) outlined four management functions:

1. Planning,
2. Organizing,
3. Leading, and
4. Evaluating.

Consistent with Drucker and Chelladurai's management descriptions, this chapter will highlight management functions focused on planning, organizing, and evaluating. One step in this management process involves formalizing mission statements, goals, and objectives; determining and ensuring efficiency; minimizing problems; and facilitating employee efficiency.

The North Carolina State University Athletic Department offers a wide array of individual and team sports for men and women.

Photos courtesy of North Carolina State University.

It is critical that all organizational members are aware of and understand the organization's overriding philosophy and mission (see Chapter 10). As part of continuously reviewing and rearticulating the organization's philosophy and mission, members will periodically conduct an organizational analysis. This analysis is often termed a **SWOT** (Strengths, Weaknesses, Opportunities, and Threats) **analysis**. Awareness of an organization's SWOT assists in developing overall long-term goals consistent with the organization's espoused philosophy and mission (see Box 8.3).

SWOT analysis
A strategic-planning tool used to evaluate an organization's strengths, weaknesses, opportunities, and threats (SWOT).

BOX 8.3

What Is a SWOT Analysis?

A SWOT analysis is a strategic-planning tool used to evaluate an organization's strengths, weaknesses, opportunities, and threats (as well as specific objectives an organization wishes to achieve). This process involves identifying favorable and unfavorable internal and external factors specific to the organization and its goals and objectives.

In order to conduct a SWOT analysis, desired goals and objectives must also be identified. A SWOT analysis is utilized in the strategic-planning process and often incorporated into the strategic-planning model.

- **S**trengths: Positive *internal* organizational attributes helpful to the organization in achieving objectives.
- **W**eaknesses: *Internal* organizational attributes detrimental to the organization or objectives.
- **O**pportunities: *External* conditions helpful to the organization achieving objectives.
- **T**hreats: *External* conditions that could damage the organization and prevent achieving objectives.

Identification of SWOTs is an essential first step in the strategic-planning process, because subsequent steps are often derived from uncovered information.

An organization's mission statement should succinctly and articulately express the organization's core beliefs and values. In the best of all possible worlds, it should reflect "the way we do things around here." In other words, the mission statement should reflect the organizational culture (see Chapter 2). If organizational members know and "buy into" the espoused philosophy, values, and mission, then long-term goal development is much more likely to occur. Such goals are broad, qualitative statements designed to provide general direction to an organization.

Measurable benchmarks of performance are often referred to as organizational objectives. Objectives are quantifiable, and are often short term in nature (e.g., each month, season, quarter, or year). Objectives are, however, tied to specific goals. In other words, objectives are methods of measuring the achievement of goals. Quite often goals and objectives are used interchangeably.

However, while the semantics is not crucial, the ability to measure the stated goal or objective is paramount.

Once objectives have been delineated, a manager is responsible for development of specific tactics—how-to steps—that provide a scope and sequence to perform the necessary critical steps to achieve the objectives. Tactical development includes identifying the critical tasks necessary to achieve objectives. In many managerial settings critical-task analysis involves developing checklists and determining in which order tasks must be completed. It does no good to develop tasks if they are not arranged in the proper sequence. In addition to developing specific tasks, explicit identified roles must be assigned. In order to get things done through people, the people must know and accept their roles. Development of organizational units/functional-areas and specific members' roles within these areas/units is critically important. This process is often referred to as the organizing function. Just as objectives must be measurable, so, too, roles must be explicitly outlined and expected observable and measurable behaviors should be outlined.

Finally, management involves an ongoing evaluation of all elements of the strategic management processes outlined earlier. The organization's mission and philosophy must inform all steps in the process. When problems occur, organizational members must understand and refer to the organization's overarching philosophy. A franchise or program's success is measured not only on the playing field or court, but also at the box office, concession stands, and merchandise store. If members of the organization do not know or believe in the organization's overall mission, it becomes much more likely that deviations from the established rules will occur when short-term problems arise. The remainder of this chapter will highlight the strategic-planning process and will outline strategic planning in sport management.

The Importance of the Strategic-Planning Process and an Explicit Strategic Plan in Sport Management

An added consideration in the management of sport enterprises, particularly in intercollegiate athletics, is the elevated stress level that often permeates the organization (Humphrey, Yow, & Bowden, 2000). Such stress may result from the highly competitive nature of college sport and the close public scrutiny that accompanies many decisions in sport management. In addition, it has been contended such stress reflects the existence of competing institutional logics (see Chapter 2) within big-time college sport.

This chapter's essential topic is *strategic* management in a sport-industry setting. Through the use of a case-study approach, this chapter will outline the development of a comprehensive and detailed strategic plan as the basis for the strategic management of a college athletic department.

Just as a thoroughly researched and well-developed game plan is the foundation of a winning athletic team, an appropriate and comprehensive strategic plan is the foundation for effective organizational decision making. While in this chapter we focus primarily on the strategic planning process and the generation of a strategic plan document for an intercollegiate athletic department, the strategic-management principles and perspectives outlined earlier are applicable to any sport business.

A strategic plan is essential for a sport organization's success. Sound strategic planning will result in the following strategic-management outcomes:

1. A multiyear written plan to which most organizational members are committed.
2. A sense of commitment and enthusiasm within the enterprise.
3. A specific set of measurable objectives that provide direction and guidance to the entire organization.
4. Clear job duties and responsibilities.
5. The ability of organizational leaders to pursue management functions essential for organizational success.
6. Clear staff member improvement guidelines.
7. The ability to measure (both annually and at the end of their careers) the growth and contributions of all staff members.
8. An in-place and understood written strategic plan will better ensure leadership continuity and increased institutional memory, and effectively guide the organization's continued growth and development.

Planning and goal setting are fundamental to any successful sport organization. This is especially true for sport organizations in challenging economic times. With competition for resources growing at daunting rates, and pressures to win at all-time highs, the need for strategic planning in sport organizations has increased markedly. A 2002 study by Yow and Bowden that examined the relationship between the use of the planning process and an athletic department's effectiveness found the following:

- Comprehensive, better-funded, and generally respected athletic programs were more frequently engaged in formal planning than other athletic programs.
- Departmental effectiveness was increased by the presence of written annual and long-range plans, when those plans were followed and executed carefully.
- The lack of a written plan (annual and/or long range) hindered the ability of the athletic program to generate consistent support, achieve desired program and service levels, and maintain its image among its numerous publics.

Yow and Bowden (2002) concluded systematic and careful planning contribute to college athletics departments (1) making the most effective use of resources and (2) consistently ranking nationally in such core evaluative criteria as competitive results, academic outcomes, student-athlete welfare, facilities enhancement, fund-raising, and financial stability.

Sport executives and administrators are asked to make many decisions every day. There are, however, decisions that can fundamentally and significantly impact an organization's future culture, direction, and stability. Since previous research indicates planning is an important element in the execution of successful management decisions, it is important to understand the planning process.

What Is Planning?

Planning can be defined as a managerial activity that involves (1) analyzing the environment, (2) setting objectives, (3) deciding on specific actions and timelines needed to reach the objectives, and (4) providing feedback on results. This *process* should be distinguished from the plan itself. The strategic plan is the published document containing the intended results achieved through the planning process. The strategic plan is a guidebook to what has been agreed to and how it will be accomplished. Planning is a continuous process for strategic management. A sport organization benefits from the planning process because this systematic, continuing process allows an organization to regularly perform the following:

- Assess the organization's market position and current state. This involves performing a comprehensive SWOT analysis (see Box 8.3).
- Establish goals, objectives, priorities, and strategies to be completed within specified timeframes; this allows for regular organization assessments and can help motivate staff to work together to achieve specific, measurable, and shared objectives.
- Achieve greater staff commitment and teamwork aimed at meeting challenges presented by the dynamic sport industry.
- Allocate resources, determine priorities, and make appropriate decisions to ensure future stability and success.

When conducting a SWOT analysis, any possible aspect of the organization should be evaluated. In some cases, a detailed SWOT analysis might take considerable time to complete. An example of one aspect of a SWOT analysis for some universities is the consideration for the physical location of the university. For example, imagine a campus located within close proximity to a large (2 million or more metropolitan residents) city's downtown. A campus located in an urban environment can be both a strength and weakness. Certainly, being in a large metropolitan area might be attractive for many potential students, athletes, coaches, and athletic department personnel. However, the presence of a large city nearby campus may be a negative to some potential attendees or employees. Large metropolitan areas often have serious traffic problems and, relative to many other areas of the United States, are often expensive places to live.

The location of the campus within a large metropolitan area offers some unique opportunities for some athletic programs. In these locations there are millions of people and thousands of businesses within driving distance. The opportunity to sell tickets and sponsorships is readily available. In addition, there are multiple media organizations in close proximity to the campus. Competitive athletic department events will likely attract exposure from numerous media outlets. However, the large metropolitan area can also become a threat. Since there are so many "other" things to do in the area, these athletic departments must compete with other entities to attract fans and generate media attention.

A SWOT analysis for an athletic department would not only incorporate location, but would also consider current players, coaches and staff, facilities, past accomplishments and athletic department history, and numerous other factors. Once the SWOT analysis is complete, the athletic department would be in a better position to determine what strategies to implement to achieve success.

Unless planning leads to improved performance, it is not worthwhile. A sport organization that wishes to remain viable and prosperous in a changing environment must continuously and creatively plan. Otherwise, it will blindly react to its immediate environment. For this reason, though a formal written SWOT analysis may be completed once a year or once every two years,

Shutterstock, Inc.

North Carolina State University is located in Raleigh, North Carolina, which presents numerous opportunities and threats.

organizations should have the ability to conduct an "unofficial" SWOT analysis, as the various aspects of an organization and the environment it operates in can change quickly.

The Strategic-Planning Process

While there are many different ways in which a sport enterprise can tackle the strategic-planning process, a *systematic* and *thoughtful* approach is necessary. Indeed, the *process* is as important as the plan itself, because the process is an opportunity for organization-wide input, deliberation, and review. It is crucial that those who will execute the plan are involved in the plan's construction. The strategic-planning process is capable of creating authentic attitudinal change among personnel, as well as increasing productivity (Boyer, 2009; Yow, Migliore, Bowden, Stevens, & Loudon, 2000). The strategic-planning process involves:

1. Defining a department's purpose or reason for being.
2. Analyzing the environment, assessing strengths and weaknesses, and making assumptions.
3. Prescribing written, specific, and measurable objectives that contribute to the organization's purpose.
4. Developing strategies for how to use available resources to meet objectives.
5. Developing operational plans to meet objectives, including plans for all organizational members.
6. Setting up control and evaluation procedures to determine if performance is keeping pace with attainment of objectives consistent with the organization's mission.

The six steps of the strategic-planning process are important because they require a sport organization to consider and respond to essential questions. Each process step requires the people at various organizational levels to discuss, study, deliberate, and negotiate. The process also fosters a planning mentality throughout the organization. Completion of the six steps results in a strategic plan that specifies the following:

- Why the organization exists
- What it is trying to accomplish
- How resources will be utilized to accomplish objectives and fulfill its mission
- How outcome evaluation will be executed

(Note: The application of this planning process to college sport is discussed in Yow et al., 2000.)

Case Study

A Strategic Plan for Advancing NC State Department of Athletics, 2012–2017

Moving from general philosophies, components, and principles in the strategic-planning process and the strategic-plan document, this section presents a case study that demonstrates the strategic-planning process.

In 2011, North Carolina State University completed and adopted a comprehensive, campus-wide, strategic plan entitled, *The Pathway to the Future: NC State's Strategic Plan 2011-2020.* In September 2011, as one of the university's most visible units and activity centers, the Department of Athletics also embarked on a comprehensive strategic-planning process. The intent was to ensure confluence with the university's 10-year strategic plan, while also outlining and prioritizing departmental goals, objectives, and strategies specific to intercollegiate athletics (ICA) for the next five years (2012–2017).

The primary aim of the ICA strategic-planning process was to focus on core evaluative areas including:

1. Branding, Partnerships and Outreach
2. Competitive Excellence
3. Compliance Education and Culture
4. Facility Enhancement
5. Financial Stability
6. Student-Athlete Well-Being, Academic Performance, and Personal Development

In order to study and set the ICA five-year goals and strategies for each core area, strategic-planning committees (comprised of internal and external constituents) were formed. Since effective strategic planning must be an inclusive process, committee representation included athletes, coaches, ICA administrators, donors and ticket holders; University Athletics Council members; as well as students, faculty, staff, and alumni. (Note: Committees and areas of focus are included as an addendum at the end of this chapter.)

The strategic-planning process for ICA included the six distinct steps discussed earlier in this chapter. The first stage also included a comprehensive analysis of the department's current strengths, weaknesses, opportunities, and threats. Each of the 23 intercollegiate athletic teams, and its administrative units (see Organizational Chart), completed a SWOT analysis. The individual analyses were consolidated into a comprehensive ICA SWOT assessment, which was utilized by all strategic-planning committees in developing the department's goals, strategies, and timelines.

The second stage of the ICA strategic-planning process was development of specific, challenging, measurable, attainable, realistic, and timely goal statements by each sport team and administrative unit. These goal statements were consolidated and considered by each strategic-planning committee in developing overarching ICA goals, strategies, and timelines for the next five years.

The third stage of the process was each strategic-planning committee constructing key ICA goals, objectives, strategies, and timelines for the next five years in each core area. These goals, objectives, strategies, and timelines were identified as priority evaluative criteria to measure ICA progress from 2012–2017. (The North Carolina State University Athletics Strategic Plan document is available at www.gopack.com, then click "Inside Athletics.") During this ICA strategic-planning process, each of the seven strategic planning committees, as well as the entire ICA staff, reviewed the department's "Mission Statement and Guiding Principles" that had been drafted by the department. This "Mission Statement and Guiding Principles" document was used to help guide formulation of appropriate departmental goals, objectives, and strategies. This step reflected the department and all stakeholders' recommitment to the department's core mission and principles. (Note: This document can be found in this chapter's addendum.)

The ICA goals and strategies identified in the strategic plan were conveyed to the appropriate coaches and administrative units for implementation and completion. Throughout the strategic plan's lifetime (2012–2017), the department will conduct regular assessments of goal attainment and update the plan, as warranted by changes in the organizational environment.

In addition, developed goals, objectives, strategies, and timelines will be utilized in ICA employees' annual Performance Review and Development (PRD), as appropriate. All ICA personnel are expected to work collaboratively, while basing their respective decision-making, prioritization, and goal-setting toward meeting the departmental goals identified in the North Carolina State University Athletics Strategic Plan (2012–2017). This plenary strategic-plan document can be viewed at the website www.gopack.com, then click "Inside Athletics." This document contains many additional elements of the department's SWOT analysis, including specific strengths developed (e.g., new basketball arena, capable of generating necessary revenue streams), and identified threats (e.g., presence of competitors in the urban location). Students are encouraged to download and critically examine the document and utilize it as a template for future strategic planning.

(Contributing materially and substantially to the development of the ICA Strategic Plan and to the content of this chapter was Mr. Christopher Boyer, Senior Associate Director of Athletics, North Carolina State University; and Mr. Joshua B. Dalton, extern, North Carolina State University Department of Athletics.)

Conclusion

We have established learning objectives for this chapter, reviewed the parameters and components of the function of management, and explored the importance of the strategic-planning process as an integral component of strategic management.

The unique nature of the sport industry requires sport organizations—if they wish to remain competitive—to systematically and strategically plan for their futures. Adopting a strategic-planning culture best positions a sport organization to achieve success.

On an individual level, sport-management students need to engage in the same strategic-planning process. In each of this textbook's chapters there is information that can be used to develop your own strategic plan for a successful sport-management career. Additional, focused coursework in areas such as sport law, marketing, sales, and facility management will provide more opportunities to continually formulate a well-constructed strategic plan. As you contemplate the basic components presented in this chapter, take time to examine and reexamine the addendum items.

chapter 8
Interview

Interview 8.1

Martina K. Ballen
Senior Associate Athletic Director of Athletics for Business and Finance
The University of North Carolina at Chapel Hill

Q: Could you describe your career path from undergraduate student to your current position?

A: I received a Bachelor of Science in Business Administration from UNC–Chapel Hill. I worked a couple of years for the Federal U.S. District Courts as a Deputy Clerk. I then returned to school and earned an MBA from Wake Forest University and was hired by a bank as a credit analyst. After one year, I was assigned to Chapel Hill as a commercial loan officer to manage the main office branch on Franklin Street. I was later hired by the UNC Department of Athletics as Director of Finance. Over the years, my title and levels of responsibility have expanded to my current role of Senior Associate Athletic Director for Business and Finance.

Q: What are the most pressing issues currently facing college athletics?

A: Compensation and facilities are the most important issues we face. Adjusting to the rapid growth in compensation for the coaches of our revenue sports, as well as implementing significant facility upgrades is difficult while at the same time trying to continue to fund a broad-based sports program. Despite allocating major resources to these growing areas, it is becoming increasingly difficult to keep up with demand.

Q: Are there specific job skills sport-management students should look to develop while still in school?

A: I think that a lot of sport-management students tend to shy away from the finance side of the business. Understanding and managing finances in sports is essential to understanding how an athletic department or sport-related business operates. Taking business and finance classes is vitally important.

Q: What publications do you regularly read to stay apprised of sport-business events?

A: *The Sports Business Journal* and *Athletic Business.*

Q: Would you recommend students pursue graduate school? If so, when should they pursue a graduate degree and what area of study would you recommend?

A: Definitely! It is competitive for young people to get into this business. Anything that would give them an advantage is a must! If the focus is finance, marketing, fundraising, or management, then I would definitely recommend a MBA.

Q: Is there a certain business area in college sport you see emerging in importance in the near future?

A: I think that the Internet has emerged as a critical area of importance. Athletic programs are beginning to understand the full range of opportunities available online.

Q: Can you describe or share strategic management or strategic planning situations in which you have participated.

A: Over the years, I have been involved in numerous strategic planning/financial planning processes for the UNC Athletic Department. Through these efforts, we focused on our mission and core values and determined what we would need to do to continue our commitment to meeting Title IX guidelines and funding scholarships for a broad-based athletic program, while maintaining competitive budgets for football and men's and women's basketball. Through our financial planning process, we identified areas where we could generate additional revenue, as well as areas where we could reduce or eliminate costs.

Study Questions

1. What are the functions of management?
2. What are the unique characteristics of the sports/athletics enterprises that set them apart from other organizations?
3. What are the needs and the benefits of strategic planning within sports enterprises?
4. Discuss the scope, content, and expected outcomes of the case study strategic plan. Include the philosophical bases, perceived need, and expected outcomes for the development of such a plan.
5. Using the North Carolina State University Athletics Strategic Plan document, explain how such a document might be helpful in developing a strategic plan within any organization.
6. Explain how an organizational chart for a sport enterprise might indicate the essence of its strategic plan.
7. Are there ways that a SWOT analysis can contribute to the preparation of a strategic plan? How?
8. Outline the organization, processes, and expected outcomes of a strategic plan that you would develop for a sports enterprise, including a flow chart depicting the components of the plan.
9. Evaluate the six-step formula for developing a strategic plan.
10. Critique and make recommended revisions or enhancements to the case study's structure of six committees and the areas of focus of each committee.

References

Boyer, C. (2009). *Strategic planning in intercollegiate athletics.* Chapel Hill, NC: University of North Carolina, Guest lecture, EXSS 740—Administration of Sport.

Chelladurai, P. (2005). *Managing organizations for sport and physical activity: A systems perspective* (2nd ed.). Scottsdale, AZ: Holcomb Hathaway, Publishers.

Drucker, P.F. (1994). *Management.* New York: Harper and Row Publishers.

Humphrey, J.A., Yow, D.A., & Bowden, W.W. (2000). *Stress in college athletics: Causes, consequences, coping.* New York: The Haworth Press.

A strategic plan for advancing NC State Department of Athletics, 2012-2017. (2011). Strategic Plan Document available at gopack.com, click on Inside Athletics. Raleigh, NC.

Yow, D.A., & Bowden, W.W. (2002). A survey of NCAA Division I athletic programs in regard to their planning procedures. Unpublished manuscript.

Yow, D.A., Migliore, R.H., Bowden, W.W., Stevens, R.E., & Loudon, D.L. (2000). *Strategic planning for collegiate athletics.* Binghamton, NY: The Haworth Press.

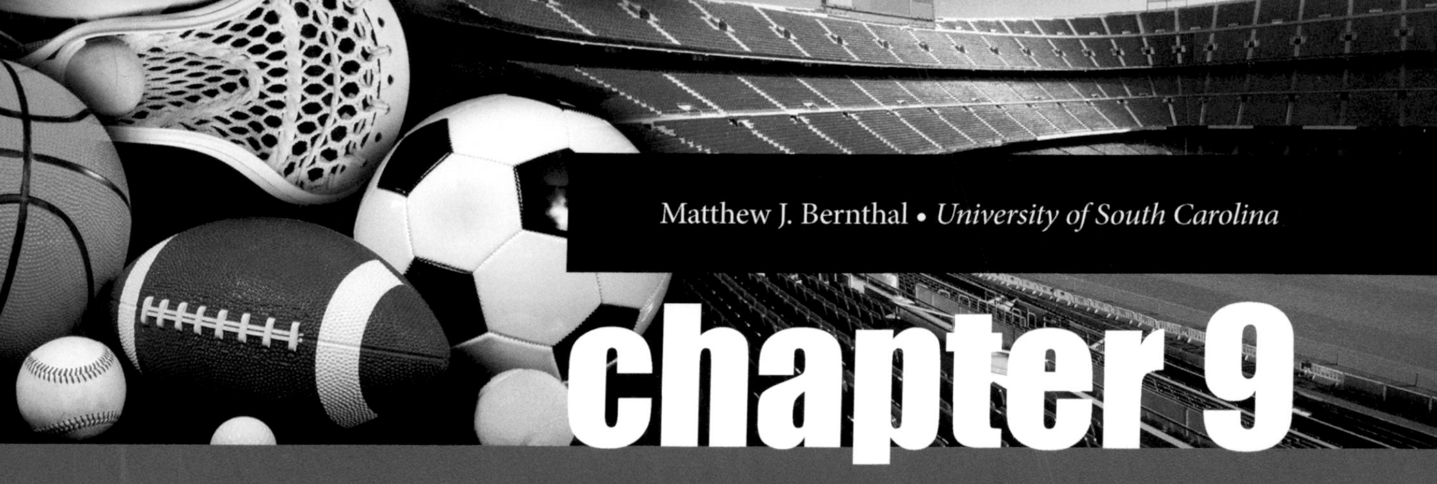

Matthew J. Bernthal • *University of South Carolina*

Sport Marketing

CHAPTER OBJECTIVES

After reading this chapter, you will be able to:

- Properly define marketing and sport marketing.
- Appreciate that successful marketing begins with understanding the customer.
- Recognize the role of marketing in sport.
- Understand segmentation and positioning.
- Appreciate the importance of branding and positioning.
- Identify the key components of a marketing plan.

KEY TERMS

Fan identification

Marketing plan

Market segmentation

Positioning

Relationship marketing

Sport marketing

"To satisfy the customer is the mission and purpose of every business. The question: 'what is our business?' can, therefore, be answered only by looking at the business from the outside, from the point of view of the customer and the market. What the customer sees, thinks, believes, and wants, at any given time, must be accepted by management as an objective fact and must be taken as seriously as the reports of the salesperson, the tests of the engineer, or the figures of the accountant. And management must make a conscious effort to get answers from the customer herself rather than attempt to read her mind." (Drucker, 1973)

—Peter F. Drucker, Management Expert

"Don't find customers for your products, find products for your customers." (Godin, 2009)

—Seth Godin, Author

"Make your customer the hero of your story. In other words, don't make your brand the hero, but really put your customer into the company itself. Talk about everything you do through that customer lens." (Gorgone, 2014)

—Ann Handley, Chief Content Officer, MarketingProfs

Introduction

Sport is big business. In today's marketplace, this statement appears somewhat obvious. Fox, CBS, and NBC will pay the NFL $27.9 billion in broadcast rights fees from 2014 through 2022, with the NFL earning an average of $3.1 billion in these fees per year, an increase from the $1.9 billion per year earned over the 2007 through 2013 time frame (Futterman, Schechner, & Vranica, 2011). Lebron James earns $42 million annually in endorsement revenue from Coca-Cola, Samsung, Nike, and others (Badenhausen, 2014). The Minnesota Vikings are building a new stadium at a cost of $1 billion, partially funded through tax dollars (Olson, 2014). Sport fans spend large amounts of their resources, both money and time, on the "consumption" of their favorite athletes and teams. Average paid attendance was over 30,000 fans for 2013 Major League Baseball games (Brown, 2013), while over 18,000 fans, on average, attended Major League Soccer games in 2013 (Prindiville, 2013). It is not unusual for over 100,000 fans to fill a stadium to watch a college football game. New product offerings, from mixed martial arts events to professional bass fishing events and everything in between, have expanded the options available to sport spectators. It seems that if there is a sport event to be held and/or broadcast, there is a

Courtesy Mark Nagel

One of the goals of sport marketers is to determine the best methods to utilize to attract customers.

market for it. Identifying that market, reaching it, and convincing the consumers that comprise it to spend their money on the sport product is the job of sport marketers.

So, what exactly is sport marketing and what is the main characteristic of successful sport marketers? The answer is surprisingly simple. When most students beginning an introductory sport-marketing class are asked to define sport marketing in their own terms, the two words that are most typically used are *advertising* and *sales*. That is, sport marketing is viewed, rather logically, as the advertising and selling of sport products. This view of marketing is rather typical, yet somewhat narrow. Indeed, good sport marketers must wield many tools successfully, including advertising, personal selling, social media, pricing, and public relations, among other things. However, at its foundation, successful sport marketing is bigger than these instruments that fill the marketer's toolbox. Consider the following questions:

- How does a marketer of a poorly performing baseball team drawing poor attendance design pricing packages and communication strategies that lead more consumers to attend more games?
- How does a marketer of a professional bass fishing event convince consumers to pack a 15,000-seat arena simply to watch fish being weighed?
- What can a golf course do to encourage more play on its course?

- How does a sport team maximize sponsorship sales and sponsor satisfaction?

The answers to these and similar questions must begin with the central component to successful marketing—*understanding the customer.* Successful marketers of any product, including sport, understand that they must think like their customers think, and understand their customers' wants, needs, and dislikes. A marketer of the losing baseball team understands that even losing teams can satisfy a consumer's desire for an affordable family outing, and as a result develop advertisements that appeal to the consumer's desire to spend quality time with family and construct family pricing packages that communicate value to the consumer. Through an understanding of sport consumers, a successful sport marketer would realize that when it comes to attending sport events, females are generally less motivated by winning than are men, leading to an allocation of a higher percentage of the advertising budget to media vehicles that reach women. The marketer of the professional bass fishing tournament will understand that some of the motivations drawing spectators to this event are the desire to view and purchase products and the desire to learn successful techniques used by the professionals. This leads the marketer to develop and market a product exposition along with the weigh-in where consumers can view and purchase the latest and greatest in fishing tackle as well as learn techniques from clinics given by those fishing in the tournament. A marketer for a golf course determines that to increase course play, she would benefit from developing a marketing program that includes rewards for both quantity of play and for consistent play throughout the year (see section on Relationship Marketing later in this chapter for an expanded example of this). The sponsorship marketer knows that in order to maximize sponsorship sales, sponsorship packages must be tailored to meet the specific business needs of various potential sponsors. Through researching and talking with potential sponsors, this marketer will develop sponsorship packages that focus on increasing brand awareness for one, sampling new products to consumers for another, and for yet another, allowing the sponsor to entertain potential clients and reward valuable employees through hospitality at the event(s).

This chapter began with quotes from Peter Drucker, Seth Godin, and Ann Handley, none of whom work in sport marketing. So why do they lead this chapter? For the sole reason that successful marketing in any industry must center on what these three individuals and others like them recognize: understanding and satisfying customer wants and needs. It matters not whether the product is a sport event, a sporting good, a sport franchise, a sanctioning body such as NASCAR, or a sport access facility such as a fitness center or golf course. A focus on the customer, from product development on, is paramount. Chuck Steedman, Fenway Sports Group Executive VP, illustrated this when he commented about determining which concerts to hold in the Boston Red Sox's

Fenway Park: "While I'd like to have Megadeth play Fenway, it doesn't appeal to our season-ticket holders" (Coast to Coast, 2009, p. 29). As sport marketers, it does not necessarily matter how we would like to see our product advertised or how much we might be willing to pay for it. What matters is designing products, brands, marketing communications, and prices that will appeal to our customers. Only by thoroughly understanding our customers will our marketing avoid the pitfall of so many unsuccessful and/or inefficient marketers: throwing ideas (ad campaigns, sales promotions, etc.) against a wall and seeing if they stick. By being in touch with customers, good marketers have a much better understanding of the marketing strategies that are likely to stick, as well as the ones that are likely to fail.

Definitions of Marketing and Sport Marketing

Considering the prior discussion, it should come as no surprise that when definitions of marketing and sport marketing are examined, there is a central component common to each: the customer. The American Marketing Association (AMA) defines *marketing* as "the activity, set of institutions, and processes for creating, communicating, delivering, and exchanging offerings that have value for customers, clients, partners, and society at large" (Dictionary, 2014a). Philip Kotler, one of the foremost experts in marketing, has defined the term as "the science and art of exploring, creating, and delivering value to satisfy the needs of a target market at a profit (Kotler, 2014). While many definitions of sport marketing exist, the vast majority share this focus on the customer either directly or indirectly. Shank defines sport marketing as "the specific application of marketing principles and processes to sport products and to the marketing of non-sport products through association with sports" (Shank, 2009, p. 3). While not directly mentioning the customer, one needs only to look at the AMA definition of marketing itself to see that "applying marketing principles and processes to sport products" means creating, communicating, and delivering value to sport customers and managing sport-customer relationships. Fetchko, Roy, and Clow's (2013, p. 6) definition of sport marketing directly adapts the AMA definition of marketing specifically to sport, in that sport marketing is "the use of marketing for creating, communicating, delivering, and exchanging sports experiences that have value for customers, clients, partners, and society. Fullerton (2007, p. 3) defines **sport marketing** as "the proactive efforts that are designed to influence consumer preferences for a variety of sport products and services." Mullin, Hardy, and Sutton (2007, p. 11) put an even greater focus on the consumer by defining sport marketing as "all activities designed to meet the needs and wants of sport consumers through exchange processes." With its simplicity and its focus on the consumer first and last, this definition is one that students of sport marketing would be wise to adopt.

Sport Marketing
All activities designed to meet the needs and wants of sport consumers through exchange processes.

Market Segmentation

While successful sport marketing centers on meeting the needs and wants of sport consumers, it is clear that not all sport consumers want and need similar things from their sport products. Through market segmentation, sport marketers determine which groups of consumers provide the greatest sales and marketing opportunities (Shank, 2009). **Market segmentation** can be defined as "the process of dividing a large, heterogeneous market into more homogeneous groups of people, who have similar wants, needs, or demographic profiles, to whom a product may be targeted" (Mullin et al., 2007, p. 130). By grouping consumers into relatively similar groups, marketers can increase their efficiency and success through the knowledge that consumers with similar wants and needs will respond similarly to specific marketing efforts. A market is segmented utilizing bases of segmentation. While numerous bases of segmentation exist, common bases include demographics, psychographics, benefits, geographics, and geodemographics.

Demographics include such common variables as gender, age, family size, income, and ethnicity. Since such variables are so easily understood and available (one can obtain the demographic breakdown of a geographic market from any number of sources, including www.census.gov), they tend to be one of the most common ways a market is segmented. As an example of demographics, consider the efforts many sport properties have engaged in to reach females. Many collegiate athletic departments as well as NFL teams offer "classes" designed to teach women the basics of football. At these classes women learn rules and basic strategies, and meet coaches and players. The obvious hope is that the more women learn about the game, the more likely they are to become fans of it and, of course, by extension, consumers of the home team. In attempting to connect with more women, some Major League Baseball (MLB) teams have had wine-tastings at the ballpark. Yet others have featured their players with their own families in team advertisements in the hope that showcasing the players as "good family men" will resonate with women.

As another example, many sport properties have increasingly recognized the importance of attracting the millennial generation (born between 1980 and the early 2000s) in order to strengthen their future fan base, and have engaged in specific strategies that they hope will resonate with them. The Toronto Raptors, for example, have hired Canadian rapper Drake to help develop a new look and logo for the team that will appeal to this generation (Mickle, 2014). Drake has also lent his voice to the Raptors marketing communications. Stadium/arena Wi-Fi connectivity is extremely important for this generation, and sport teams wanting to attract them are increasingly updating facility connectivity. After determining that millennials desire special experiences to a greater degree than do older generations, the Philadelphia 76ers now hold breakfasts for 20 season-ticket holders and the team coaching staff in the locker room every

Friday (Mickle, 2014). Finally, realizing that many millennials are likely to engage in "second-screen viewing" (i.e., engaging with their phone, tablets, often via social media) while watching a sport event, smart sport properties are increasingly leveraging this behavior to better connect with this generation.

Other uses of demographic segmentation can be seen with virtually every sport property. For example, many teams have gameday promotions that target a specific age group (dollar beer night for a minor league team in a college town, autograph night to target families with children, etc.). A fitness center might offer special classes designed specifically to appeal to senior citizens, and free childcare to help attract those consumers with young children.

Another basis of segmentation, *psychographics* can essentially be described as lifestyles or activities, interests, and opinions (*AIO dimensions*) (Wells & Tigert, 1971). Psychographics involves segmenting on activities such as what consumers do for a living, what they do for fun, what types of media they utilize most often, their political opinions, their religious beliefs, the social causes that they support, and the like. If marketers can understand their consumers at this level, they will better be able to predict their product preferences and tailor marketing efforts to appeal to them. For example, the U.S. Open tennis tournament has recently advertised on food websites to attract "foodies" (Kaplan, 2013), those individuals with a strong interest in cooking and/or eating. The ubiquity of "food TV" in today's society has created a strong and growing interest in food for pleasure, and smart sport marketers are leveraging this cultural phenomena. The West Michigan Whitecaps minor league baseball team and their home, Fifth Third Ballpark, were featured on an episode of the

Drake has been utilized by the NBA's Toronto Raptors to help build their brand.

TV show "Man vs. Food" due to their "Fifth Third Burger Challenge" where a fan is challenged to eat a four-pound hamburger between the seventh-inning stretch and the end of the game (winning a t-shirt and their picture on a wall of fame if the challenge is completed). Increasing numbers of teams in many sports are also simply adding more high-end, gourmet concessions to enhance fan experience and appeal to foodies.

As another example of psychographic segmentation, many sport teams are marketing to Christians with Christian-themed events. Third Coast Sports, in fact, is a Nashville company that provides religious themed promotions to sport teams. Such promotions exist in both minor and major leagues and across a spectrum of sports over the entire country. A typical promotion might have a team give away Bibles and religious figure (e.g., Noah, Goliath) bobbleheads to attending fans, entertain the fans pre- and/or post-game with a Christian rock band, and have the players give testimonials about the importance of faith in their lives. These types of psychographic promotions have become extraordinarily successful in attracting large numbers of new consumers to ballgames.

Psychographic segmentation can also be useful in attracting sponsors. For example, Old World Industries (owner of the brand Peak Antifreeze and Peak Motor Oil) recently signed sponsorship deals with Michael Waltrip Racing and the National Hot Rod Association (NHRA). The company's strategy is to increase its market share through attracting more "do-it-yourself" consumers to their Peak brand. Given the large number of "do-it-yourself" consumers who follow NASCAR and NHRA, these sponsorships are an ideal marketing strategy for Old World Industries (Mickle, 2012).

A third common method of segmentation, *benefit segmentation* is based on the realization that different consumers may seek different benefits from the same product. As an example outside of sports, think of the brand Excedrin pain reliever. One might find it surprising that Extra Strength Excedrin has the same exact active ingredients, in the same amount, as Excedrin Migraine. Why would the makers of Excedrin market a brand extension that has the exact same ingredients as one of their existing brands? They understand that there is a segment of consumers that has a specific need from their product: relief from debilitating migraine headaches. They knew that clearly communicating that their product could provide this benefit by creating a brand extension that labeled it as such would increase their overall sales as opposed to if they had continued to market only Extra Strength Excedrin. In other words, consumers see Excedrin Migraine as specifically designed for relief of migraine pain, and not the same as any other pain reliever, not even Extra Strength Excedrin. Successful sport marketers learn from companies like this and recognize that their product can often fulfill a variety of benefits sought by a variety of market segments. For example, through research, suppose a sponsorship salesperson for a spectator arena finds that a potential sponsor is having trouble with high rates of employee turnover. This salesperson might then make the connection that this potential sponsor could benefit from entertaining valuable employees in a luxury suite, and emphasize such a benefit in a sales presentation. On the other hand, this same salesperson discovers that another potential sponsor is seeking more brand awareness in the community, so arena signage is highlighted in a sponsorship presentation pitched to that potential sponsor.

As another example of benefit segmentation, think about the marketing of youth sports. Often, parents and children are seeking very different benefits from participation in youth sports. When communicating with parents, a marketer trying to increase participation in a local youth soccer league, for example, might emphasize the parent-sought benefits that youth soccer provides: it is relatively inexpensive, it emphasizes participation, it is safe, a child does not have to have a great deal of initial skill to begin playing, and it provides great exercise and an "energy-drain" from children participating. On the other hand, imagine the same marketer making a presentation to young children only (i.e., without their parents) in a school assembly. It is highly unlikely that the marketer would focus on benefits such as safety, inexpensiveness, or how soccer can help the children "drain energy" so that they will be easier for their parents to manage. Rather, the marketer would be wise to simply focus on the benefits more likely to be sought by children, such as fun, cool uniforms, more time spent with friends, camaraderie through outside events such as trips for pizza after the game, and the like.

Benefit segmentation is ubiquitous in the sporting good market. Many sporting good product categories base their segmentation primarily on this basis. Running shoes are segmented, in part, based on whether a runner is seeking more stability or more cushioning, more ground feel or less ground feel, comfort over long distances or lightness over short distances. ASICS markets several of their running shoe models and running apparel in "Lite-Show" versions, with enhanced reflective technology designed for runners who run outdoors in the dark and need greater visibility to oncoming vehicles. Tennis racquets are marketed to various specific benefit-seeking segments: players seeking more control, those seeking more power, those seeking a racquet that is particularly suited to net play, etc. Sport apparel is marketed toward consumers seeking clothing that wicks sweat away from the body during athletic participation, those seeking clothing that blocks wind, those seeking clothing that improves aerodynamics, those wanting more "fashionable" sport apparel, and the like.

A fourth basis of segmentation, *geographic segmentation* involves creating market segments that are based on geographic location. Marketing to different geographic segments often necessitates different marketing strategies for each. This could be due to geographic differences in things such as weather, culture, and demographics. For example, sporting good retail outlets such as Golf Warehouse might have several different geographic segments, and treat each differently in relation to marketing strategies such as pricing and promotion. In a northern state, for example, prices for Golf Warehouse's clubs would likely fluctuate much more during the course of a year than they would in a state such as Florida. The reason is that demand for golf clubs in Florida remains relatively consistent throughout the year due to the warm weather, while demand for clubs in northern states drops during the long winter months, simply because consumers are less likely to buy clubs when they know they will not be playing for a while. How can a retailer like Golf Warehouse adjust to this drop in demand in northern states? Through strategies such as price promotions (e.g., sales) and non-price promotions (e.g., buy a set of clubs over a certain price and get a free putter and/or a certain number of free rounds at a local golf course). Strategies such as these help the retailer keep sales much more stable throughout the course of the year than they would be otherwise. The greater demand for golf equipment in general in Florida versus a northern state such as Minnesota would also likely lead to a retailer such as Golf Warehouse investing in more locations in Florida.

A final basis of segmentation that is commonly used in sport marketing is *geodemographic segmentation*, so named because it reflects a synergy of geographic and demographic targeting. It also builds in psychographics, however. It is based on the simple notion that people tend to live around other people that are similar to themselves. What does this mean for marketers? It means that if a marketer can demographically and psychographically identify the type of person that is a likely consumer of their product, they can be located and marketed to with relative efficiency.

One of the most widely known geodemographic segmentation systems is Nielsen's PRIZM system. PRIZM defines every U.S. household in terms of 66 demographically and psychographically distinct segments (Nielsen PRIZM, 2014). Think back to our marketer of youth soccer. It is likely that he or she can envision the typical target segments. Perhaps one segment sounds something like this: "Upper-middle-class, suburban, married couples with children—that's the skinny on Kids & Cul-de-Sacs, an enviable lifestyle of large families in recently built subdivisions. With a high rate of Hispanic and Asian Americans, this segment is a refuge for college-educated, white-collar professionals with administrative jobs and upper-middle-class incomes. Their nexus of education, affluence and children translates into large outlays for child-centered products and services" (Segment Explorer, 2014). Kids & Cul-de-Sacs is one of the 66 PRIZM clusters, and its description certainly sounds like a demographic and psychographic profile of a likely target for youth sports. Once our youth soccer marketer has identified Kid's & Cul-de-Sacs as a likely consumer of his or her product, things become easier. Direct mail pieces, for example, can be targeted to zip codes that have been identified as having high numbers of Kids & Cul-de-Sac households. From the PRIZM data, the marketer can learn which magazines and newspapers these likely consumers read, which television shows they watch, and which websites they frequent. This information can help in placing advertisements for the youth soccer league. PRIZM can also help sport marketers identify which of the 66 segments are the most likely to buy their products. While it is beyond the scope of this chapter to describe exactly how this is accomplished, it is important for the introductory sport-management student to know that such services exist and can greatly enhance the sport marketer's chances of success.

Geodemographic systems such as PRIZM can also assist in new business feasibility or location analysis. For example, if Gold's Gym were scouting several markets in which to locate a new facility, what kind of market segments do you think the company would look for in the various proposed locations? One segment likely to be consumers of Gold's Gym is Young Influentials. This cluster, according to Nielsen, "reflects the fading glow of acquisitive yuppiedom. Today, the segment is a common address for young, middle-class singles and couples who are more preoccupied with balancing work and leisure pursuits. Having recently left college dorms, they now live in apartment complexes surrounded by ball fields, health clubs and casual-dining restaurants" (Segment Explorer, 2014). One consideration for Gold's Gym, then, when deciding among the various proposed locations, would be the relative numbers of likely consumers (e.g., Young Influentials and other PRIZM clusters who are reasonable targets for Gold's Gym) within a reasonable drive time of the various locations.

PRIZM and systems like it are widely used by major sport marketers such as the National Association for Stock Car Auto Racing (NASCAR), and major live entertainment marketers such as Feld Entertainment. Acquiring such data obviously costs money. However, geodemographic systems such as PRIZM help these marketers determine segments that are likely to purchase their products, and locate and reach these segments much more effectively and efficiently.

The Interconnectedness of Segmentation Bases

It is important to realize that while it is expedient to discuss each of the bases of segmentation in isolation, they rarely operate independently from one another. It does little good for a marketer, for example, to target women without understanding and appealing to the psychographics of this segment. The NFL, for example, has engaged in a strategy to increase sales of licensed merchandise to women by utilizing "style lounges" (Lefton, 2012). These lounges are temporary stores at NFL stadiums that include DJs playing music, manicurists, and fitting rooms with mirrors. Understanding that many women are used to shopping at department stores and boutique retailers, the league sought to create more of this environment at their stadiums in order to better appeal to the psychographics of female fans.

As another example of the interconnectedness of segmentation bases, imagine that the United States Tennis Association (USTA) attempts to increase both young adult single and senior citizen participation in its adult leagues across the country through a direct mail promotional piece and a television advertising campaign. Young adult singles and senior citizens are simply two demographic segments. However, should the USTA market the leagues to both segments using the exact same message? Based on their *psychographics,* these two *demographic* segments might be attracted to league play because of very different *benefits.* For example, young adult singles might be convinced to try league play because of the social opportunities it affords, while senior citizens might place more emphasis on the health and psychological benefits that come from staying physically active. Ideally, marketing communications geared toward each segment would then reflect this.

Relationship Marketing

Relationship Marketing
Marketing with the conscious aim to develop and manage long-term and/or trusting relationships with customers, distributors, suppliers, or other parties in the marketing environment.

An increasingly common concept embraced by sport marketers is referred to as **relationship marketing**, defined as marketing with the conscious aim to develop and manage long-term and/or trusting relationships with customers, distributors, suppliers, or other parties in the marketing environment (Dictionary, 2014b). Within the sport industry, marketers have become increasingly aware that to consistently succeed over the long term, satisfactory relationships with consumers must be created and *sustained.* It matters not whether the consumers are fans, sponsors, league participants, retail customers of a sporting goods store, members of a fitness center, or some other type of sport consumer. The bottom line is that sustained, satisfactory relationships with customers are paramount. To illustrate a main reason why, consider the concept of the lifetime value of a customer. *Lifetime customer value* represents the value, in dollars, that one customer is worth to a particular company over his or her lifetime. Let's imagine that you spend an average of $5 per week at McDonald's, and have since the age of 10. That means that since you were 10 years old, you've spent an average of $260 per year at McDonald's. That's probably not a stretch for some of you! If McDonald's can keep this relationship with you as a customer for the remainder of your life expectancy, they will have had you as a customer for 66 years if you are a male, and 71 years if you are a female (the average life expectancy in the United States is 76 years for men, and 81 years for women [Painter, 2014]). This means that you are worth $17,160 (male) or $18,460 (female) to McDonald's in direct revenue over the course of your life. For McDonald's, it certainly pays to keep you as a customer by delivering a satisfactory product and customer service, providing incentive to return, and simply making you feel valued as a customer! Sport marketers should approach their customers with the same mindset. How much is each individual fan, sponsor, fitness center member, and so on worth to the marketers of those products? Not the dollar value of an individual game ticket, a single event sponsorship, or the price of a year's membership at a fitness center. Rather, they are worth what they would have spent on the product over a reasonable lifetime as a customer. Viewing them as such will generally lead to increased efforts at customer satisfaction (e.g., putting on exciting, well-run events) and effective relationship marketing programs.

A relationship-marketing program generally consists of one or both of two primary strategies: financial bonding and social bonding. In general, *bonding* refers to the creation of a unified commitment that holds those in the relationship together (Fullerton, 2007). *Financial bonding* is a type of business practice designed to enhance customer loyalty through pricing incentives (Berry, 1995), while *social bonding* involves creating personal ties to develop buyer-seller relationships through interpersonal interactions, friendships, and identifications (Chiu, Hsieh, Li, & Lee, 2004). Consider a hypothetical local public golf course in Central Florida (a highly competitive market with many public courses) that decides to implement a relationship-marketing program in order to build long-term relationships (and thus revenue!) with players. The course, Baytree, establishes the free Baytree Buff program and collects basic information from those who join. Such information includes contact information, demographics such as gender, age, marital status, presence of children in the household, birthday, anniversary, and other information such as favorite restaurants (from a list of partnering restaurants). This information is used to create a database that serves as a tool to implement the program. A simplified version of the Baytree Buff program might look like that shown in Table 9.1.

TABLE 9.1 Relationship Marketing Program for Baytree Golf Club

Strategy	Goal	Type of Bonding
One round of free golf for every five rounds played	• Encourage more rounds played by each customer than they might have otherwise • Discourage play at competing courses	Financial
Play at least once every month and at least 18 times for the year and receive unlimited play during one week of the following summer	• Encourage consistent play throughout the year • Discourage play at competing courses • Reward increases course usage during the slower summer season, enhancing atmosphere and ancillary revenue (food/beverage, clubhouse merchandise)	Financial
Program members are invited to annual party at clubhouse	• Social gathering for members, thanking them for their patronage	Social

Course partners with local restaurants to provide gift certificates to members on their birthdays. Certificate is mailed to members by the course with a birthday card. In exchange, each participating restaurant receives a hole sponsorship (name on tee box sign).	• Regular reminder to members that Baytree appreciates them • Provides opportunity for creating relationships/partnering with local businesses	Social and Financial
Baytree Buff League: Members form two-person teams for Friday afternoon 9-hole competitions. Teams pay flat yearly fee amounting to a per-9-hole rate heavily discounted from the regular rate.	• Encourage social activity, friendships, and competition among players in the context of Baytree • Encourage regular play at Baytree • Increase ancillary revenue	Social and Financial

With this program, Baytree is well on its way to developing sustained, valued relationships with local players, and gains a competitive advantage over the many competing courses in its market that are not aware of the value of relationship marketing.

Relationship marketing programs can be constructed in any number of ways, limited only by the marketer's creativity and/or resources. They may be based primarily on social bonding, financial bonding, or (as in our Baytree example) both. Many are relatively simple. Dick's Sporting Goods, for instance, has a simple financial bonding program called ScoreCard. Shoppers sign up for the program and receive a barcoded ScoreCard that they present to the cashier every time they purchase something at Dick's (if shopping online, the related ScoreCard number is entered). One point is earned for every dollar spent. Every time the customer accumulates 300 points, they are mailed a $10 gift certificate to Dick's. Dick's regularly mails members added incentives to reach the 300 points, such as a coupon for 100 or even 200 ScoreCard points with the customer's next purchase at Dick's. This encourages members to visit Dick's more often and make more purchases than they otherwise might. Further, it encourages Scorecard members to avoid shopping at Dick's competitors. The regular mailings also simply keep Dick's Sporting Goods top-of-mind with members.

Fan Identification
The personal commitment and emotional involvement customers have with a sport organization.

Sport teams in various leagues regularly employ relationship-marketing programs to help build **fan identification**, defined as the personal commitment and emotional involvement customers have with a sport organization (Sutton, McDonald, Milne, & Cimperman, 1997). Think of a sport team that you are very passionate about. Perhaps you consider yourself a die-hard fan of the Boston Red Sox. You would be considered to have "high identification" with that team. The reasons sport marketers want high fan identification are relatively obvious. Such fans generally attend more games, support the team through good seasons and bad, and buy and wear/display more team merchandise. Through helping fans feel a sense of belonging and staying actively involved with a franchise, relationship-marketing programs strengthen two factors identified by Sutton et al. (1997) as antecedents of fan identification: affiliation and activity. Such programs help fans build a sense of connection with the team and stay actively involved with the team. The San Diego Padres have one program called Compadres Fan Rewards. Members are automatically enrolled in the program when they purchase at least a partial-season ticket. They then earn points for purchasing tickets, attending games, using e-cash (a form of payment for purchases in the ballpark), and the like. Points can be redeemed for rewards such as ticket upgrades, game-used and autographed items, and special fan experiences. Further, they receive 10% off concessions and merchandise, as well as 5% cash back for e-cash use. In addition, members can choose one of four types of membership based on their lifestyle (family, business, fanatics, social), and they then are able to participate in team-sponsored activities that fit into that lifestyle. For example, members choosing the "family" membership type can have their children participate in a postgame Q & A with players, a family trip day on the field at Petco Park, etc. In these ways, the Padres show a clear understanding of how financial and social bonding can be an integral part of team marketing strategy. Such relationship marketing programs, combined with other bonding strategies (e.g., a strong presence on social networking sites such as Facebook) increase the likelihood of teams generating high identification with a core group of fans.

Sport marketers also value the establishment of strong, sustained relationships with sponsors, engaging in strategies to help sponsors feel valued and connected to the sport property (team, event, etc.). In fact, the word "partner" is increasingly used in place of sponsor, as partner suggests a two-way, mutually beneficial relationship between sport property and sponsor. That is, sport properties develop relationships with sponsors through caring about each sponsor's needs, and tailoring sponsorship packages to fit these needs, as briefly described earlier in this chapter. They also develop relationships with sponsors by providing each with *fulfillment audits*, post-sponsorship reports that illustrate and highlight how the sport property fulfilled their corporate needs. For example, a sponsor might sponsor a sport event primarily to entertain valued clients (and prospective clients) in a large, catered, hospitality tent provided as part of their sponsorship package. The sport property that recognizes the value of a sustained relationship with this sponsor would be wise to provide them with a fulfillment audit that contained (among other things) pictures, and perhaps even video, of the clients enjoying themselves in the hospitality area. In short, sport marketers develop sustained relationships with sponsors by *caring about their business needs, developing sponsorship plans to satisfy these needs, and documenting for them how these needs were satisfied.*

Branding and Positioning

Another extremely important aspect of sport marketing is branding and the related concept of positioning. The American Marketing Association dictionary defines a *brand* as a name, term, design, symbol, or any other feature that identifies one seller's good or service as distinct from those of other sellers (Dictionary, 2014c). Having a strong sport brand helps that brand create what is termed *brand equity,* the marketplace value that a brand contributes to a product (Shank, 2009). To illustrate, think of consumers wishing to purchase a few new t-shirts in which to work out. They go to the apparel section in their local department store and find a three pack of generic t-shirts and a three pack of Nike t-shirts. The package of generic shirts costs $12, while the package of Nike t-shirts costs $39.99. Do you think some of these consumers would purchase the more expensive Nike t-shirts? Now add in the information that the shirts are exactly the same, except for a small Nike swoosh in the upper right corner of the Nike t-shirts. Do you still think that many consumers would purchase the more expensive Nike shirts? The answer to each question is an absolute yes! The value of the Nike brand, in the visual representation of the name and the logo and all of the perceptions ("fashionable," "reliable quality," etc.) that go with it, adds significant value to the products on which it is placed. Quite simply, significant value resides in the Nike name and swoosh.

Other powerful brands having strong brand equity exist across the sport product spectrum. Others in the sporting good and apparel arena include brands such as Adidas and Under Armour. Some apparel companies have strong equity within a specific sport (for example, Asics and Brooks in running).The NFL as a league has strong brand equity, as do a number of individual teams within the league (e.g., Dallas Cowboys, Pittsburgh Steelers). University athletic programs can benefit from strong brand equity, as evidenced by brands such as the University of Texas Longhorns, the University of Florida Gators, and the like. In these cases, winning certainly helps, but also important are the strong and valued brand symbols themselves (the Cowboy's star, the University of Florida's popular gator head logo, etc.). Strong brand equity helps these teams generate everything from ticket and sponsorship revenue to significant licensed merchandise revenue. Gold's Gym is a fitness center that benefits from the strong brand equity it has created. Many athletes benefit, in the form of product endorsement revenue, from creating (often with the help of their agents) strong brand equity, with themselves as the brand. The New York Yankees have such extraordinary brand equity that because of the power of their brand, they decided against selling naming rights to their stadium and thus bypassed the revenue that would have resulted. Yankees COO Lonn Trost said "You would not rename the White House and you would not rename Grant's Tomb or the Grand Canyon. We will not rename Yankee Stadium" (Trost, 2008). Such a statement is a powerful testament to the brand equity that team enjoys.

Positioning
Establishing a brand's image in the minds of consumers.

Brands that have high brand equity are usually well-positioned. **Positioning** is essentially establishing a brand's image in the minds of consumers. It may be thought of as establishing a brand's "personality." Many things contribute to a brand's positioning, such as the brand name, logo, colors (e.g., team colors), price, and advertisements, to name but a few. To illustrate positioning, think back to the XFL, a professional football league created by World Wrestling Entertainment (WWE) head Vince McMahon. While the league folded after its inaugural 2001 season, it provides a clear and classic example of the concept of positioning. The WWE was in charge of branding for the league and for each of the league's individual teams, and did many things in an attempt to position the brand as a differentiated alternative to the NFL. First, the name of the league itself, XFL, was part of a positioning attempt. The letter X represents specific meaning to many in our society: extreme, edgy, hardcore, violence, sex. Therefore, its use next to the "FL" communicated to consumers that this meaning was part of the XFL's personality. Second, team names were chosen in an effort to build on this personality. Teams had names such as the Rage, Demons, Hitmen, Outlaws, Maniax, and Xtreme (note the use of the letter X in the spelling of the latter two). Third, team logos were chosen to build on this personality as well. For example, the Orlando Rage's logo represented an enraged, red, Hulk-like figure, while the Los Angeles Xtreme's logo represented what appeared to be a ninja-throwing star. Fourth, the football used by the XFL itself was designed to contribute to the positioning of the league in that its colors were black and red as opposed to the traditional brown. Much like the letter X represents meaning in our culture, so do colors. Dependent upon the context of their use, black and red in combination can communicate meaning such as powerful, fast, violent, and fearsome. Fifth, the league created rules in order to position themselves as a more fun and "extreme" league as compared to the NFL. For example, players were allowed to place nicknames on the back of their jerseys in place of their last names. A game rule allowed no fair catches on punts (potentially leading to violent hits). Another required only one foot in bounds on catches. Halftimes were only 10 minutes long, ostensibly to keep the pace of the entire event experience from lagging. Finally, microphone and camera use during the broadcasts attempted to position the league as more extreme than the NFL. Microphones were placed in a myriad of places (e.g., huddles, locker rooms, coaches) to provide the television viewer with new and unique access to the game that they had not experienced before. Cameras were placed in numerous positions to provide the viewer with new viewing angles. There are numerous reasons postulated as to why the XFL did not survive past its first year of play, and one primary reason relates to positioning. It might be hypothesized that fans saw too much of the WWE (WWF at the time) "sport-entertainment" personality in the XFL, and simply did not desire this personality for their professional football. In other words, it might be contended that while the XFL successfully differentiated its image from that of the NFL, it did a poor job predicting the extent to which fans desired to consume that image within the sport of football.

Fireworks are a popular entertainment activity that is often incorporated into sporting events.

Courtesy Jeff Nycz.

The concept of positioning is important not only for professional leagues and teams, but for many types of sport products, whether they be sport equipment brands, collegiate athletic programs, access facilities such as fitness centers, spectator facilities, or athletes themselves. For example, Brooks Sports, a company that makes running apparel, has effectively utilized positioning to become one of the leading marketers of running shoes. Decades ago, Brooks used to sell shoes and apparel for multiple sports (e.g., running, tennis, basketball, football). In 2001, Brooks repositioned their brand solely as a running brand, and focused on distributing their brand in specialty running stores (Badenhausen, 2013). In doing this, CEO Jim Weber repositioned Brooks as a more specialized running brand when compared to companies that continued to operate across a plethora of sports (e.g., Nike, Adidas). Brooks further positioned its brand in the minds of consumers by communicating an image of a "fun," "happy" running brand. The brand slogan is "Run Happy," and it creates fun and almost whimsical experiences for runners who compete in events that it sponsors. For example, as a sponsor of the popular Rock 'n' Roll Marathon & Half-Marathon series, Brooks has created unique sponsorship activation at the series' health and fitness expos (the product expositions associated with each race where vendors and sponsors market to the racers). The activation involves "Run Happy Island" where racers (and others attending the expo) can watch light-hearted entertainers dancing and singing around a volcano (named Mount Crackatoe-A), ride a large mechanical Brooks shoe (much like riding a mechanical bull), compete with other attendees in a running-in-place contest that moves each person's small mountain climber up the volcano, and the like. Of course, Brooks employees are on hand to educate the consumers about Brooks running shoes. CEO Weber compares Brooks to the Volkswagen automotive brand: both brands have superior engineering yet also convey a sense of fun (Badenhausen, 2013). In consumers' minds, this image helps set the Brooks brand apart not only from goliath brands such as Nike, but from other brands that are perceived, like Brooks, as specialty running brands (such as Asics or Saucony).

When one considers University of Oregon football, they might have the image of "sleek," "modern," and "flashy," while when one considers University of Alabama football, adjectives such as "traditional," "classic," and "no-nonsense" are likely to come to mind. In part, these images are fostered through the branding of the two teams via their respective uniforms (Oregon with bright neon colors and seemingly endless uniform combinations, and Alabama with a relatively plain, "old-school" look). Seeking to target the fitness novice that is relatively self-conscious about his or her body and inexperienced with fitness center use, a fitness center might position its brand as welcoming, "non-judgmental," and "non-intimidating" by having (among other things) no mirrors in the workout room(s), instructors who are skilled and encouraging with beginners, and the majority of its classes and programs predominantly designed for such beginners. An agent marketing Dennis Rodman in the twilight of his NBA career might have found success marketing him to teams struggling in attendance by positioning him as an entertaining, flamboyant, "character" who could provide somewhat of a boost to ticket sales and media attention. In any case, whether it is in relation to leagues, teams, equipment brands, facilities, or athletes, strategic positioning is an extremely important skill for the sport marketer to master.

External Contingencies

It is important to understand that sport marketers do not operate in a vacuum. The environment in which they operate contains many factors beyond their control. These factors, which can be termed *external contingencies*, include the economy, technology, competition, physical environment, cultural and social trends, the political and legal environment, and demographics (Shank, 2009). Such contingencies can present both opportunities and threats to sport marketers as they develop strategies to market their products. To illustrate the necessity of sport marketers' attention to these factors, consider the economy and technology.

The state of the economy affects both the amount of money consumers have to spend on sport products, as well as their willingness to spend the money that they do have. This applies to both individual consumer spending on sport products and corporate spending on sponsorship. As an example of this, the U.S.

economy experienced an economic downturn beginning in late 2008. The stock market plunged, unemployment rose, and wages for those employed stagnated. Further, people were bombarded on a daily basis with media messages reminding them how bad the economy was. This resulted in an economic climate that had individual consumers more hesitant to spend their money on non-necessities, and corporations less willing to allocate tight dollars to sport sponsorship. One obvious way this affected marketing strategy was in pricing. In down economies, sport marketers must pay particular attention to their pricing strategies and must often adjust prices to meet reduced demand. This may mean ticket price reductions, special ticket promotions, or simply avoiding ticket price increases in a down economy. The NFL, for example, introduced a limited number of lower-priced tickets ($500) to the 2009 Super Bowl in response to the poor economy. Further, and perhaps more illustrative, most NFL teams kept ticket prices the same for the 2009 season in response to the down economy. Eighteen NFL teams held prices steady, while three teams reduced prices. Much of this pricing strategy can be attributed to the poor economy (Team Marketing Report, 2009b). For example, the Chicago Bears senior director of sales and marketing said his team's decision to keep ticket prices flat was a "good decision in a tough economic environment" (Team Marketing Report, 2009b). The economy contributed to teams in other leagues following suit. For example, in Major League Baseball, while only six teams held prices steady or increased less than 1% over the 2008 season, a full ten teams actually reduced ticket prices, with several teams also offering cheaper concession options (Team Marketing Report, 2009a). As the economy has slowly rebounded since 2009, the prices charged to attend sporting events has generally increased (see Table 9.2). The FCI is a standard index used to track the price of attending events within the four major U.S. professional leagues, and represents the average price for a family of four to attend one of these events. The index includes four averaged-priced tickets (for two adults and two children), four hot dogs, four small soft drinks, two small beers, two programs, two hats, and parking. The average FCI for the four major U.S. professional leagues is provided in Table 9.2.

TABLE 9.2 2009 and 2014 Fan Cost Index for NFL, MLB, NBA, NHL

League	Average Ticket Price (2009, 2014)	FCI (2009, 2014)
NFL	$74.99, $81.54	$412.64, $459.65
MLB	$26.64, $27.93	$196.99, $212.46
NBA	$49.47, $52.50	$291.93, $326.60
NHL	$49.66, $61.62	$288.23, $359.17

Source: Team Marketing Report, Chicago, IL.

As noted, the economy can also affect sponsors' ability and willingness to sponsor sport events. A major industry survey found that 51% of those companies surveyed said that their sponsorship spending would decrease in 2009, and another 36% said their spending would remain relatively unchanged (Klayman, 2009). In this same survey, 47% of companies even reported that they would be seeking to get out of current sponsorship deals. It is quite clear that in poor economies, sponsors become hesitant to sign new deals because of economic uncertainties, as well as because of fears that consumers will see the spending as wasteful at a time when the sponsors may, for example, be laying off workers. This can affect sport marketers in a number of ways. Realizing that sponsorship revenue might suffer in poor economic times, wise sport marketers pay particular attention to the investigation of new revenue streams. For example, the NBA recently reversed a longstanding (1991) ban on courtside advertising by liquor brands in an attempt to increase revenue during the period following the 2009 economic crash (Lombardo & Lefton, 2009). Poor economic conditions also present a challenge to the sport marketer with regard to sponsorship sales. In economic downturns, sport marketers must increasingly seek to put together sponsorship proposals that directly address the specific needs of each individual potential sponsor and must be particularly cognizant about sponsorship pricing. In addition, they must seek improved leveraging opportunities for their sponsors. *Leveraging* (sometimes referred to as *activation*) refers to the utilization of various marketing strategies to improve sponsor value. For example, in order to leverage a sponsorship of a college football team, a local auto dealer, along with team marketers, might develop a "Youth Captain of the Week" program to leverage the sponsorship. This program might entail having those who test-drive a car during a certain time frame at that dealership enter a child of their choice to win the opportunity to be a "youth captain" of the team for a game during the season, whereby the winning child gets to meet coaches, be on the field for player warmups, enter the stadium with the team, and remain on the sidelines during the game. Through this leveraging/activation program, the sponsor receives customer prospect data through the entry form and directly encourages more test drives among local consumers.

Technology is another external contingency that has had significant recent impact on sport-marketing strategy. Where beneficial, sport marketers look to technology with an eye toward how it can help them better market their product and improve the fan experience. For example, the University of California has adopted marketing automation technology (which has been used in professional leagues for some time) that allows its ticket department to better target ticket offers to potential buyers. The technology tracks where potential customers visit on the athletic department's website (e.g., a specific sport's page), and responds with ticket offers based on this behavior (Smith, 2013). The Dallas Cowboys are utilizing technology to collect fan satisfaction data from fans in real time (i.e., while they are attending Cowboys' games). A program called Express Feedback allows fans to use their mobile phones to select their seating section and rate their event experience across the four dimensions of entertainment, food and beverage, service and staff, and traffic and parking (Muret, 2013). The NFL has recently launched a partnership with a mobile app developer that allows fans to use their mobile phones to upgrade their in-stadium gameday experience. Through a mobile app, fans can purchase things such as upgraded seats, an in-seat visit from a cheerleader or mascot, or the ability to be on the field pre-game or in the post-game press conference (Kaplan 2013). Perhaps ironically, through adoption of this app, the league is combatting improving technology in the home-viewing experience in part through technology that enhances the in-stadium experience, hoping it gives fans one more reason to buy a ticket rather than stay home and watch the games on television.

Advances in video and broadcast technology have allowed sport marketers to offer enhanced products and enjoyment to fans. The Dallas Cowboys installed a $40 million high-definition video board in their new $1.15 billion stadium in Arlington, Texas. The board is four-sided, with a 160-foot wide by 71-foot high screen for fans on both sides of the stadium, and a 50-foot wide by 28-foot high screen for fans in both end zones. Such boards offer fans enhanced views of the action and replays, and offer increased value to sponsors through enhanced messaging opportunities. Sports broadcaster ESPN continues to blaze trails through the use of technology. It recently made a foray into 3D television with ESPN 3D. While ESPN 3D ultimately failed due to lack of consumer adoption, ESPN continues with its technologically forward thinking by advancing on other technologies such as 4K (ultra high definition) TV. ESPN is the first high-profile television content provider to announce a focus on this emerging technology (Pendlebury, 2013). Interestingly, the National Hot Rod Association (NHRA) has partnered with Guitammer Co. to capture sounds and sensations at races, and then transmit these sensations to viewers of NHRA events on ESPN through Guitammer's ButtKicker device. This device is installed under furniture by home viewers and receives signals that shake the furniture, allowing viewers to "feel" part of the event and experience it in a sensory-enhanced way. Guitammer has tested the device at NHL arenas also, and has plans to apply the product to other contact sports as well (Mickle, 2013).

Opportunities for sport marketers made possible through advancing technology are certainly not limited to advances in web tracking, mobile devices, or video and broadcast technology. Yet another strategy increasingly used by sport organizations combines technology with another external contingency—cultural and social trends. Specifically, smart sport marketers are increasingly taking advantage of social media. It is now standard for teams, sporting goods brands, individual athletes, access facilities such as fitness centers and golf courses, and virtually any other type of sport product to create a presence on social networking sites such as Facebook and Twitter. Related specifically to sport teams, these sites allow teams to build fan identification through connecting and involving the fan with the team and other fans. These sites accomplish this in a number of ways. For example, fans can communicate with other fans, find other fans in their geographic location with which to connect, post pictures, and the like. Teams can share information (such as player roster moves, news from training camp, etc.) that keeps the fans informed, and they can involve the fan in community dialogue by asking for responses to posts or tweets (for example, asking which player is likely to have the best upcoming season), among other things. Not only do such sites help teams build fan identification and community, but also through the process of participating in such sites, fans provide the team with information that can be used to target future marketing messages. While it is beyond the scope of this chapter to detail the marketing benefits and strategies associated with social media, it is clear that sport properties that fail to effectively capitalize on this technology in the current environment will fail to realize their full potential.

With regard to all external contingencies and the role that they play in shaping marketing strategy, the key lesson for sport marketers is to always pay close attention to all that is happening in the environment (cultural environment, technological environment, competitive environment, etc.) in which they operate. Such attention will illuminate both marketing threats and opportunities that less attentive sport marketers will, at their own peril, miss. Attention without action, however, does little. Marketers must respond creatively to their external environment. As a brief example, recall the surge of U.S. gasoline prices in 2007-2008. Understanding the "pain at the pump" consumers were

Dallas Cowboys Video Board

experiencing, creative sport marketers took advantage, turning this economic threat into an opportunity. Callaway Golf, for example, gave away gift cards worth $100 in free gas with the purchase of certain drivers (Ramde, 2008). For fans buying 2008-2009 season tickets, the New Jersey Nets offered 10% of the purchase price back in the form of free gas. While not offering a price promotion, the Detroit Pistons utilized the gas price surge as a public-relations tool, having Pistons players pump $20 of free gas per car during a 1.5-hour period at a local gas station. In each case, these organizations attended to a happening in the external environment and utilized it to their advantage.

The Marketing Plan

A **marketing plan** can be defined as the document containing an analysis of the current marketing situation, opportunities and threats analysis, marketing objectives, marketing strategy, action programs, and projected income (and other financial statements [e.g., budget]) (Dictionary, 2014d). Formulating a marketing plan guides the sport marketer in developing a strategic plan that increases the probability that the product will find success in the marketplace. The plan includes items such as a SWOT analysis, intended target markets, and strategies for promotion, pricing, and distribution. A marketing plan will also often include performance objectives, such as goals for a percentage increase in event attendance over the prior year, quarterly sales objectives, brand awareness objectives, and the like.

To illustrate the basics of a marketing plan, consider a plan for a February Philadelphia stop for the event "Monster Jam," a monster truck competition sanctioned by the U.S. Hot Rod Association. A brief summary of selected strategies of the marketing plan for the Monster Jam show is provided in Box 9.1. Not all strategies in the actual plan are presented, nor is every detail provided about the strategies that are presented. The summary is simply intended to give the reader a glimpse of the content of an actual marketing plan.

Marketing plans vary widely in their detail and thoroughness. For example, an expansion of the Monster Jam plan might provide additional demographic and psychographic detail about the target markets, including income levels, areas of geographic concentration, other activities of interest, types of media that they consume, and the like. This can provide insight into how to reach the targets with various marketing messages. It might also include budgetary information such as the amount allocated to each media outlet (e.g., radio station, television station). However, the idea behind each plan is the same. The process of formulating the plan is an exercise that assists marketers in thinking strategically about how to best market their product, and the resultant plan essentially acts as a marketing "recipe" to follow. A marketing plan does not guarantee success, but it certainly increases its probability.

BOX 9.1

Strengths/Opportunities

- Ticket prices remain affordable for a large portion of the overall population at $27, $22, and $5 for children.
- The Philadelphia market is focused on football, but it is unlikely the Eagles will be in the playoffs and thus take focus away from show promotion or consumer's disposable income allocated to entertainment.

Weaknesses/Threats

- The show has been in the market for several years and is thus in need of fresh marketing ideas.
- The marketing budget has not increased over the last two years.
- No big names are part of the show.
- Normally snowy and cold weather hurts the possibilities of doing a PR event outside.

Target Audience

- Primary target market: Males 18–44
- Secondary target market: Children 6–11

Ticket Prices

- Adult: $27, $22
- Child: $5
- Discounts: Group Tickets for 20+ people: $14 per ticket
- Boy Scouts 12 or older: $13
- Early Bird purchases: $22, $17
- Adult coupon: $22, $17

Promotions

Radio

- WWMR (rock), WXTU (country)
  —WWMR sponsors a truck
  —WWMR runs ride to work/school in a monster truck with the morning show promo
  —Fifteen 10-second advertisements
  —Hourly Monster Jam on-air promotions during weekend of event
  —Advertisements on WWMR.com
  —Live mentions by on-air personalities
- For the following stations, seek to provide tickets in exchange for on-air ticket giveaways, on-air mentions, website inclusion, email blasts, and distribution of Monster Jam promotional material at station events: WJSE, WJBR, WMGK, WSTW, WZZO, WTHK, WPST, WRDW, WIOQ

Outdoor Advertising

- Ads on 60 bus backs on suburban bus routes
- 12 billboards

Internet

- Monster Jam logo and web page link on every partnering radio station website
- Email blasts in early December to database lists, including Tony Hawk, Boom Boom, HuckJam, WWE, Motocross, Incubus, Linkin Park, Beastie Boys, prior Monster Jam shows, American Idols Live, Van Morrison, Red Hot Chili Peppers, Barenaked Ladies, Panic at the Disco, Wachovia Complex Cyber Club
- A presence on MySpace, Facebook, and Friendster will be created to help reach the younger crowd
- Sixers, Flyers, Phantoms, and Kixx to send discount email to members promoting Monster Jam

Television

- KYW-TV 3 (CBS)
  —The Early Show (M–F, 5 am–7 am)
- WPVI-TV 6 (ABC)
  —TGIF (Friday during news 5 pm–6:30 pm)
  —Fast Forward (last Saturday of each month)
  —Visions (Saturday at 7:30 pm)
- WCAU-TV 10 (NBC)
  —10! Show (M–F, 10 am–11 am)
- WTXF-TV 29 (FOX)
  —Good Day Philadelphia (Weekdays 5 am–9 am)
- Comcast SportsNet
  —Daily News Live

Partnerships

- Wendy's
  —Tray liners in-store mid-through-late December
- Bally's Total Fitness
  —Prominently displayed promotional information at front desk of all area locations
  —Promotional offer and show information in all Bally print advertising
  —"Bally Total Fitness Discount" to Monster Jam displayed on Ballytotalfitness.com with direct link to purchase tickets
  —Monster Jam information included in Bally's e-blast

Monster Jam marketing plan information provided courtesy of Feld Motor Sports, Inc.

Conclusion

Sport marketing is a fascinating and growing industry. It is impossible to fully describe or even briefly discuss everything that sport marketing entails in one chapter. The purpose of this chapter, rather, has been to highlight and emphasize the foundation upon which sport marketing, and indeed all of marketing, is built: understanding and satisfying customer wants and needs. Through this, you have been introduced to the key related topics of sport marketing, market segmentation, relationship marketing, branding and positioning, external contingencies, and the marketing plan. There are many interesting and important aspects of sport marketing that have not been either directly addressed or addressed in great detail here. For example, there is much more to learn about pricing, sponsorship, public relations, advertising, and marketing research, to name but a few. There are indeed a myriad of tools in the marketer's toolbox, and the person who is an expert at using each has yet to be found. However, if in using each one of the tools of the trade, the marketer keeps the customer front and center, his or her chances for success increase exponentially.

chapter 9

Interviews

Interview 9.1

Mike Boykin
CEO, Bespoke Sports & Entertainment

Q: Describe your career path.

A: My path has not been a direct line. There were times that I felt I was failing or lost. What's next? Why did I choose this career? Why don't I have the income of other friends or family members? But looking back, it was the diverse experiences that prepared me for success. I knew a great deal about a lot of areas that impact sport marketing and brands. It set me up for the past successes with GMR and for the new adventure I am about to launch with my good friend Greg Busch. But like many in the industry, the entry into the sport business was murky.

Like many college students, I came to the University of South Carolina thinking I knew what I wanted to do. Boy was I wrong! I quickly found out that my family aptitude and passion for medicine was not for me. Thankfully, I had a teacher at USC-Aiken, Mrs. Ernestine Law, who cared for me and asked me to lunch to discuss my future career path. She was an incredible person and professor and with her encouragement, I began on a path of finding a career that combined my love of sports with business. The path was not a straight line for sure. Mrs. Law encouraged me to try everything I could. I started writing for the local paper, working events, interning for a radio station sports talk show.... you name it, I tried it and made notes on what I liked and did not like. After that brief stint at USC-Aiken, I returned to Columbia and the main campus of USC.

While there I worked for *The Gamecock* and WIS Radio, paged at the State House, and got introduced to the Athletic Department at the University of South Carolina (USC). I remember going into the Roundhouse (the building housing the USC Athletic Department at the time) on Sundays and helping USC Sports Information Director Julian Gibbons and Mike Nemeth stuff game stats and mailing them to hundreds of media outlets across the southeast. (There was a time before computers!) As time passed I was asked to write for the game program, assist on game-day operations, and eventually travel with various USC athletic teams. The trip to UCLA with the women's basketball team for a holiday tournament was especially memorable. I was the acting business manager. It was really cool and opened my eyes to a lot of potential jobs that might exist in the new world of sport business.

I timed my graduation perfectly. After 4.5 years and George Rogers winning the Heisman Trophy, I departed Columbia and moved to Athens, Ohio, to pursue my master's in Sports Administration at Ohio University (OU). At that time, I believe there were three graduate programs offering that degree. It was during my time in Athens that my career path took a hard turn. I went to Ohio fully expecting to come back to USC and eventually be the Athletic Director. It was during the first quarter at OU that I heard Steve Greenberg from the Spectrum in Philadelphia speak to our class. It shocked me. The creativity and aggressive financial approach employed by the Spectrum and their parent company, Spectacor, blew me away. I could not imagine 225 plus events a year, often with more than one event on a day. There were two internships available and I was fortunate enough to land one of those positions. That was certainly a tipping point in my career.

While in Philly, I learned about marketing and business from some of the brightest people in the sports industry. They were always willing to answer my questions, and I know I brought much comic relief to the staff with my southern accent. From being on site at the Final Four the day President Ronald Reagan was shot, to six nights of Bruce Springsteen concerts in a week, the Spectrum was about big events and optimizing revenue. I was very fortunate to learn from so many great people and departments...marketing, production, public relations, finance, event operations, and more.

Graduation from OU followed. I stayed on the facility management path and landed in St. Louis at the Checkerdome (the nickname for the St. Louis Arena which opened in 1929 and was demolished in 1999). Once again I worked for a dynamic leadership team led by Charlie Mancuso, who was one of the hardest working executives I ever worked for and he was never satisfied. Promotions could always be better. Sponsorship sales could improve. Novelty sales needed a boost. Charlie was always thinking about the business and was the first person who I knew that asked everyone "what's going on in town?" It was going to be a long day or night if Charlie asked the cab driver or the waitress and they did not respond with "well, the Circus is at the Checkerdome" or whatever show happened to be next at the old arena. Working at the Checkerdome was more than a job. It required a fast-paced day of work planning for upcoming events, and then execution of more than 175 events after you finished your day job. It was not unusual for the small management team to log 80 to 100 hours per week. And to be sure. . .don't ever come in late. If Mancuso saw you come strolling in at 9:10 am. . . .let's just say he was passionate and his language colorful.

It was during my days at the Spectrum and Checkerdome that I was exposed to an eclectic group of businesspeople referred to as "Promoters." They were the risk takers. They were the creative geniuses. They were the hard-nosed businesspeople who focused on putting on a good show, and equally as important. . .on making a profit. Think of them as event stock brokers surveying the marketplace for what America wanted to see and what they would pay for. They were in charge of booking the talent or creating the show, buying the advertising, public relations, sponsor sales, building rentals and staffing, production, and at the end of the night. . .taking home the profits.

Over the next eight years I worked for several small promotion companies. I learned a lot about sponsorship sales, researching and marketing events, sponsor services, media buying and promotions, negotiations, public relations, crisis management, and making a profit. One of the more memorable lines I heard often during this part of my career was "events are for fun and profit. . .without a profit there ain't no fun." It was a fast-paced, party type of lifestyle. My wife Kim and I were just starting a family and it was clear I needed to move on and find a different part of the sport and entertainment world. That led me to the media rights business and a brief move to Lexington, Kentucky.

I worked 3+ years for Host Communications/Creative Sports. It was a turbulent time and the two companies split one year after their merger. I was moved to Charlotte to work for Creative Sports. I learned a lot about college and conference media rights. There were good deals that worked for both the company and the institution and there were difficult deals. One of the best negotiations I ever witnessed was when the company was in a bad deal and had to seek relief from the property. I learned a lot about true partnership and that if a deal is not working for both sides, additional options need to be considered. In this particular situation it did not totally reverse the outcome of the business deal but it did forge strong relationships across the two parties. It was never a winning deal for the company but I am confident the two leaders did more deals in the future. A little history lesson, Creative Sports was sold to ESPN and became ESPN Regional. I still consider myself fortunate to have learned from the talented leaders at both Host and Creative Sports, many of whom are still major players in the sport-marketing and broadcasting industry.

I realized that selling media was not my strength. I did OK, but I was not passionate about the job. With a little push from Creative Sports, I became a free agent. As we thought about our next move, my wife and I had decided Charlotte was a great place to live and raise a family. We were committed to exploring all options to remain there. Going through the process, an opportunity developed at a boutique motorsports agency. At this point in my career, I had never worked in motorsports or for an agency. It was a tremendous learning experience and broadened my network to include many of the leaders from NASCAR, IndyCar, and the NHRA. I learned about how agencies work and how they make money. I learned how to manage a very diverse group of people, from creative and client management to finance and business development.

After 18 months I decided to try my hand with a startup agency. Along with two friends and a partner, we launched a sports agency in Charlotte. The agency had a successful start but the partnership was not going to work. There is a lot to learn from a startup and for that I am thankful. The business of running a business can take up a lot of time. I also learned that doing your due diligence on your partners to determine if you can work together is critically important.

The next stop was a brief one with Agency One. I started as a consultant and then moved to full-time after three months. Just as I was getting settled in, I got a call late one

Friday afternoon from a former professor at Ohio University. He outlined a position, and it sounded like a fantastic opportunity but there was one problem, it was in Milwaukee, Wisconsin! He called back early the next week and arranged a couple of calls with OU alumni that worked for GMR, the agency in Milwaukee. I was interested in the opportunity because it was on a big stage. I would be managing the Miller Brewing Sports account, one of the largest sports spenders in the nation. Additionally, we talked about building a major sports practice at GMR, a sports practice that could compete with the best agencies in the business. Kim and I flew to Milwaukee and were impressed with the company and people. It was Kim who convinced me to take the job. While comfortable in Charlotte, Kim shared that she did not want to live with me if I was going to say *what if we had taken the job?* What could have been? Well, we took it, and for close to 16 years we had a great run at GMR. We hired some of the best and brightest talent in the industry, and were fortunate to grow our award-winning sports practice to be among the best in the world.

Now the time has come for a new adventure. To take all the mistakes and key learnings and build something great. Along with my good friend and business partner Greg Busch, we are prepared to build a sports agency that they write books about. The agency will launch in Q3 of 2014. I can't wait to get started!

Q: Describe what you consider to be one of the most valuable learning experiences that you have encountered during your career and how that experience has contributed to your success and/or made you a better sport marketer.

A: The headline here is the learning experiences keep coming. As I have moved through my career I have finally figured out that I know very little. Every day I truly learn something new. It might not be major but it builds on all of the other insights and experiences. As you can see from my career path, many of the key experiences led to my changing or learning about people. I believe my ability and desire to network with a diverse group of people has helped my career. As I have moved through my career I have learned that "doing my homework" and due diligence is a great way to start any project or relationship. As a leader, I believe in servant leadership. I have been managed and led by all types of leaders, I have found that leaders who care for their people have the greatest impact and achieve sustainable success.

Q: In general, what do you see as the two biggest detriments to successful marketing?

A: The basics of fundamentals and communication top my list. Throughout my career I have seen some incredible marketing ideas/campaigns not work due to a lack of integration. I would encourage all sports marketers to think critically. How does the idea or concept affect the different stakeholders, both internal and external? The second detriment is when a brand, team, or media outlet does not truly communicate the campaign to the stakeholders. In this nano-second world, fundamentals still matter and making sure everyone truly understands the mission is time well spent.

Q: What do you believe to be the biggest challenges faced by the sport-marketing industry in the near future?

A: I think we are beginning to see the challenges of balancing technology and the live experience. Younger consumers want it all, and leagues/brands are challenged to deliver both a great game experience and a great digital experience. Mastering the costs of innovation and not overdoing technology will be both a challenge and an opportunity. The other major factor in this equation is the cost of attendance. We all feed off the energy of a sold-out crowd but with higher costs for tickets, gas, food and beverages, parking, etc., more consumers may choose to stay home. Sports marketers want great game experiences and environments, as well as large media audiences. I would also keep an eye on youth participation and their level of interests in the various sports. The pipeline needs to be filled. Are they playing the sport? Are they engaging in other ways? Measurement and the changing demographics will also continue to be crucial for successful sport marketers. Staying relevant and aware of the marketplace will be a must.

Q: What is your advice to students considering a career in sport marketing?

A: Do your homework! If you visit our website for 30 minutes and Google a few executives, you are one of the masses. If you are indeed passionate about a career in sport marketing, you should remember that there are 300 universities offering some type of degree. The competition is tougher than when I broke into the industry. . . by miles. Differentiate yourself. Know everything you can about the business and its leaders...and I don't mean game stats. If you want to impress someone in the industry, ask great questions. It will blow them away. Make it about the organization and their challenges, not about you. Network, network, network! This will never change. People you would never expect can help you with an insight or connection. Also important, you have to do this for others. Sport-marketing agencies are looking for talented, inquisitive, and team-oriented people. Lastly, make sure you know you are doing what you love. If you have not taken some sort of personal assessment, make that a priority. It will help guide you to your personal passions and fuel your success.

Interview 9.2

Eric Nichols
Chief Marketing Officer
University of South Carolina
Gamecock Athletics

Eric Nichols was named director of marketing for the University of South Carolina athletics department in June 2008 and was promoted to associate athletics director/chief marketing officer in the summer of 2013. Nichols oversees all aspects of athletics marketing and serves as the marketing liaison to the athletics ticket office, website, as well as Gamecock Sports Properties, Barnes and Noble merchandising, university licensing and communications, and Global Spectrum. Nichols came to USC following a successful stint at Vanderbilt University, where he served as the athletic department's director of marketing and promotions since January 2004. He has a bachelor's and a master's degree from the University of Tennessee–Martin

Q: **Describe your career path.**

A: I began my athletic administration career as a student assistant women's volleyball coach at the University of Tennessee at Martin (UTM). From there I was offered a graduate assistantship and earned my MBA from UTM. After a brief six-month stint with Nike, I went back to college administration as a facilities assistant at Vanderbilt University in 1998. I was promoted to Director of Game and Event Management in 2000 and later switched gears and became the Director of Online Services with the primary responsibility of managing the official athletics' website. In 2004, I was promoted to Director of Marketing where I served until I took a similar position at the University of South Carolina in 2008.

Q: **Describe what you consider to be one of the most valuable learning experiences that you have encountered during your career and how that experience has contributed to your success and/or made you a better sport marketer.**

A: I did not know at the time how valuable the information would be, but during college I had a professor stress how important it would be to "study your profession." He encouraged me to continue to learn and soak up as much knowledge as possible through trade journals, networking, and professional organizations. I have taken that advice to heart and passionately seek to learn anything that might give me an advantage to doing my job better.

Q: **In general, what do you see as the two most important determinants of successful marketing and why?**

A: Listen and create buzz. The audience is ever-changing and without really listening to your audience customer failure is a certainty. We must always be adaptable. The creation of buzz stems from the method by which consumers communicate now. Word-of-mouth has become more prevalent than ever due to the explosion of social media. Therefore, one must have a great story or product or event with which to gain attention. Also, a good product just so happens to be the most important attribute to retaining a customer.

Q: **What do you believe to be the biggest challenges faced by the sport-marketing industry in the near future?**

A: Easily the most daunting challenge is the battle between television and a live sporting event. While creating an influx of revenue at all levels of sport, the home viewing experience is cannibalizing the live event.

Q: **Given this reality, what are some of the things you and the USC Athletic Department have done to retain current customers and attract new ones to the live experience?**

A: While I have been a staunch supporter of outbound ticket sales for years, the situation here allowed us to contract with a third party for a full-time staff member making outbound sales calls the entire year. Retention is still a battle we are working to improve for the new season ticket holders. Finally, we have invested a significant amount of resources into research to understand our fans and our brand.

Q: As Director of Marketing for Gamecock Athletics, what are the primary things you look for in new hires?

A: I'll credit Rick Pitino for this one—a PHD—Poor, Hungry, and Driven. But in all honesty, the perception of our business is vastly different from the reality, and having the hunger to work long days and nights while also being driven to get better is what I would like to have on my staff. Oh, and you have to be creative, too.

Q: What is your advice to students considering a career in sport marketing?

A: Start now. Whether it is two hours a week or two hundred, students have to begin now. With the stiff competition for these jobs, displaying an understanding of what it takes and having a reference in the business is critical. Finally, when you get your foot in the door, do not blow it! Figure out how you can help the department, and help them better than anyone they have ever had in their office.

Study Questions

1. This chapter has defined good sport marketing as being customer-focused. Explain what this means and provide an example of a sport marketer (can be an individual, franchise, league, etc.) that you believe has a strong customer focus.
2. Give an example of a sport marketer who you believe has a relatively weak customer focus and has suffered because of it.
3. Describe what is meant by fan identification. What are the various reasons that we want highly identified fans?
4. What businesses do you frequent outside of the sport industry that use relationship-marketing strategies? What are the various financial and/or social bonding strategies they use? Do you believe that you have spent more money with some of these businesses and/or have been a customer of theirs for longer than you would have otherwise due to these marketing efforts?
5. Describe the concept of lifetime value.
6. A key to successful sport marketing is staying tuned in to external contingencies (competition, technology, social/cultural trends, etc.). This chapter has very briefly illustrated the external contingencies of the economy and technology. What are some examples of how other external contingencies can affect the strategies of sport marketers?
7. What are the major components of a marketing plan?
8. What are the major bases of market segmentation?
9. What is meant by positioning? What are some sport brands that you believe position themselves well? What are some sport brands that you believe could be positioned better?
10. What is included in the Fan Cost Index (FCI), and what is the average FCI for the NFL, NBA, MLB, and NHL?

Learning Activities

1. You are the marketing director for a minor league hockey team in a city of your choice. Using each of the bases of segmentation discussed in this chapter, identify five distinct market segments that you will target. Develop 10 gameday promotions (autograph night, discount beverage night, etc.), with each segment that you have identified being targeted by at least two of them. Try to be creative with your promotions. Now, develop other marketing strategies that you might use to target each of your five segments. Your strategies should include, but not be limited to, advertising and pricing.
2. Working for the PGA, you have been charged with developing marketing

strategies that will take advantage of the millennial generation's tendency to engage in second-screen viewing while watching television. The goal of these strategies, as a whole, is to make the viewer feel more involved in the PGA event that he or she is watching and more connected to others watching the event. What specific strategies would you suggest?

3. You work in marketing for a Major League Baseball team. You have been charged with developing a relationship-marketing program for the team, a program to increase fans' involvement with the team throughout the year. What might your relationship-marketing program look like? Be sure to include elements of both social bonding and financial bonding.
4. "Like" on Facebook and/or "Follow" on Twitter two sport franchises of your choice, or pick two that you have already Liked/Followed on these sites. Keep a log of how these franchises utilize both sites in their marketing efforts every day over the course of at least two weeks (preferably longer). How does each franchise utilize this medium to build fan community? What does each franchise do to build fan identification? After analyzing your log, which franchise do you think better utilizes social media in its marketing efforts and why? What suggestions for improvement do you have for each franchise?

References

Ad Spotlight. (2004, February 6). *Team Meeting Report.*

Badenhausen, K. (2013, May 20). Brooks running shoes hit their stride. *Forbes.com.* Retrieved June 13, 2014 from http://www.forbes.com/sites/kurtbadenhausen/2013/05/20/brooks-running-shoes-hit-their-stride/

Badenhausen, K. (2014, January 22). Lebron James' endorsements breakdown: By the numbers. *Forbes.com.* Retrieved June 4, 2014 from http://www.forbes.com/sites/kurtbadenhausen/2014/01/22/lebron-james-endorsements-breakdown-by-the-numbers/

Berry, L.L. (1995). Relationship marketing of services: Growing interest, emerging perspectives. *Journal of the Academy of Marketing Science*, *23*(4), 236–245.

Brown, M. (2013, October 3). The good, the bad, and the ugly about MLB's 2013 attendance. *Forbes.com.* Retrieved June 4, 2014 from http://www.forbes.com/sites/maurybrown/2013/10/03/the-good-the-bad-and-the-ugly-of-mlbs-2013-attendance/

Chiu, H., Hsieh, Y., Li, Y., & Lee, M. (2004). Relationship marketing and consumer switching behavior. *Journal of Business Research*, *58*(12), 1681–1689.

Coast to Coast. (2009, December 22–28). Coast to coast. *Street and Smith's SportsBusiness Journal,* 29.

Dictionary. (2014a). Marketing. *ama.org.* Retrieved on June 9, 2014 from https://www.ama.org/resources/Pages/Dictionary.aspx?dLetter=M

Dictionary. (2014b). Relationship marketing. *ama.org.* Retrieved on June 12, 2014 from https://www.ama.org/resources/Pages/Dictionary.aspx?dLetter=R

Dictionary. (2014c). Brand. *ama.org*. Retrieved on June 12, 2014 from https://www.ama.org/resources/Pages/Dictionary.aspx?dLetter=B

Dictionary. (2014d). Marketing plan. *ama.org*. Retrieved on June 13, 2014 from https://www.ama.org/resources/Pages/Dictionary.aspx?dLetter=M

Drucker, P. (1973). *Management: Tasks, responsibilities, practices*. New York: Harper & Row Publishers.

Fetchko, M., Roy, D., & Clow, K. (2013). *Sports marketing*. Upper Saddle River, NJ: Prentice Hall.

FFA. (2008, January 14). FFA fundraiser night at the Blazers. *Business Wire*. Retrieved on January 4, 2009 from http://www.businesswire.com/portal/site/google/index.jsp?ndmViewId=news_view&newsId=20080114006248&newsLang=en

Fullerton, S. (2007). *Sports marketing*. New York: McGraw Hill.

Futterman, M., Schechner, S., & Vranica, S. (2011, December 15). NFL: The league that runs TV. *The Wall Street Journal*. Retrieved on June 4, 2014 from http://online.wsj.com/news/articles/SB10001424052970204026804577098774037075832

Godin, S. (2009). First, organize 1,000. Retrieved on June 4, 2014 from http://sethgodin.typepad.com/seths_blog/2009/12/first-organize-1000.html

Gorgone, K.O. (2014). Battling mediocrity in content: Ann Handley talks to marketing smarts [Podcast]. Retrieved on June 4, 2014 from http://www.marketingprofs.com/podcasts/2014/25029/writing-content-ann-handley-marketing-smarts

Kaplan, D. (2013, September 9-15). DDB helps Open sharpen digital strategy. *Street & Smith's SportsBusiness Journal,* 17.

Kaplan, D. (2014, March 24-30). NFL ups fun factor via technology. *Street & Smith's SportsBusiness Journal,* 1.

Klayman, B. (2009, October 28). Over half of firms to cut sponsorship spend: Study. Retrieved on November 3, 2009 from http://www.reuters.com/article/idUSTRE52969320090310

Kotler, P. (2014). Dr. Philip Kotler answers your questions on marketing. Retrieved on June 9, 2014 from http://www.kotlermarketing.com/phil_questions.shtml#answer3

Lefton, T. (2012, October 1-7). Marathon starts campaign; NFL effort targets women. *Street & Smith's SportsBusiness Journal,* 13.

Lifestyle. (2010). Lifestyle and behavior segmentation: Nielsen PRIZM. Retrieved on January 7, 2010 from http:// enus.nielsen.com/etc/medialib/nielsen_dotcom/en_us/documents/pdf/fact_sheets.Par.69269.File.dat/PRIZM_US_SS_n8006.pdf

Lombardo, J., & Lefton, T. (2009, January 19-25). NBA cans ban on liquor ads. *Street & Smith's SportsBusiness Journal,* 1, 26.

Mickle, T. (2012, September 17-23). New deals for Old World brands. *Street & Smith's SportsBusiness Journal,* 6.

Mickle, T. (2013, September 30-October 7). NHRA broadcasts will rock the sofa. *Street & Smith's SportsBusiness Journal,* 41.

Mickle, T. (2014, March 24-30). Industry looks for right recipe to attract fans among millennials. *Street & Smith's SportsBusiness Journal,* 1.

Mullin, B., Hardy, S., & Sutton, W. (2007). *Sport marketing* (3rd ed.). Champaign, IL: Human Kinetics.

Muret, D. (2013, October 7-13). Cowboys plug feedback tool into app. *Street & Smith's SportsBusiness Journal,* 10.

Nielsen PRIZM. (2014). Nielsen PRIZM: Overview. Retrieved June 11, 2014 from http://www.claritas.com/MyBestSegments/Default.jsp?ID=70&&pageName=Learn%2BMore&menuOption=learnmore

Olson, R. (2014, February 8). Personal seat licenses will raise $100 million for new Vikings stadium. *StarTribune.* Retrieved on June 4, 2014 from http://www.startribune.com/politics/statelocal/244270481.html

Painter, K. (2014, May 15). Life expectancy up worldwide; Japanese women live longest. *USA Today*. Retrieved on June 12, 2014 from http://www.usatoday.com/story/news/world/2014/05/15/world-life-expectancy/9123889/

Pendlebury, T. (2013, June 12). ESPN to drop 3D channel in 2013. *CNET*. Retrieved June 10, 2014 from http://www.cnet.com/news/espn-to-drop-3d-channel-in-2013/

Prindiville, M. (2013, October 29). Seattle Sounders break MLS attendance record, average 44,038 fans per game. *ProSoccerTalk*. Retrieved June 4, 2014 from http://prosoccertalk.nbcsports.com/2013/10/29/seattle-sounders-break-mls-attendance-record-average-44038-fans-per-game/

Ramde, D. (2008, June 8). Companies offering free gas to attract business. *USA Today.* Retrieved on June 8, 2008 from http://www.usatoday.com/money/economy/2008-06-08-2344632439_x.htm

Segment Explorer. (2014). Segment explorer. Retrieved June 11, 2014 from http://www.claritas.com/MyBestSegments/Default.jsp?ID=30&menuOption =segmentexplorer &pageName=Segment%2BExplorer&id1=1027

Shank, M. (2009). *Sports marketing: A strategic perspective* (4th ed.). Upper Saddle River, NJ: Prentice Hall.

Smith, M. (2013, September 16-22). Cal uses tech to track potential ticket buyers. *Street & Smith's SportsBusiness Journal,* 4.

Sutton, W., McDonald, M., Milne, G., & Cimperman, J. (1997). Creating and fostering fan identification in professional sports. *Sport Marketing Quarterly, 6*(1), 15–22.

Team Marketing Report. (2009a, April). Team marketing research. *Team Marketing Report,* 6–7.

Team Marketing Report. (2009b, September). Team marketing research. *Team Marketing Report,* 8–9.

Team Marketing Report. (2013a, September). Are you ready for some FCI: Rising prices in the NFL. *Team Marketing Report.*

Team Marketing Report. (2013b, November). Buck handling: NHL prices increase in 2013-2014. *Team Marketing Report.*

Team Marketing Report. (2013c, December). Alley oop: NBA ticket prices on rise. *Team Marketing Report.*

Team Marketing Report. (2014, March). 2014 MLB fan cost index. *Team Marketing Report.*

Trost, L. (2008, December 22–28). They said it. *Street and Smith's SportsBusiness Journal,* 29.

Wells, W., & Tigert, D. (1971). Activities, interests, and opinions. *Journal of Advertising Research, 11,* 127–135.

Suggested Sources

Street and Smith's SportsBusiness Journal—www.sportsbusinessjournal.com
Team Marketing Report—www.teammarketing.com
American Marketing Association—www.ama.org
Sport Marketing Quarterly, Morgantown, WV: Fitness Information Technology.
Duffy, N., & Hooper, J. (2003). *Passion branding: Harnessing the power of emotions to build strong brands.* West Sussex, England: John Wiley and Sons, Inc.
Martin, A. (2012). *Renegades write the rules: How the digital royalty use social media to INNOVATE.* San Francisco, CA: Jossey-Bass.
Newman, T., Peck, J., Harris, C., & Wilhide, B. (2013). *Social media in sport marketing.* Scottsdale, AZ: Holcomb Hathaway.
Ries, A., & Ries, L. (1998). *The 22 immutable laws of branding: How to build a product or service into a world-class brand.* New York: HarperCollins.
Ries, A., & Trout, J. (1993). *The 22 immutable laws of marketing: Violate them at your own risk.* New York: HarperCollins.

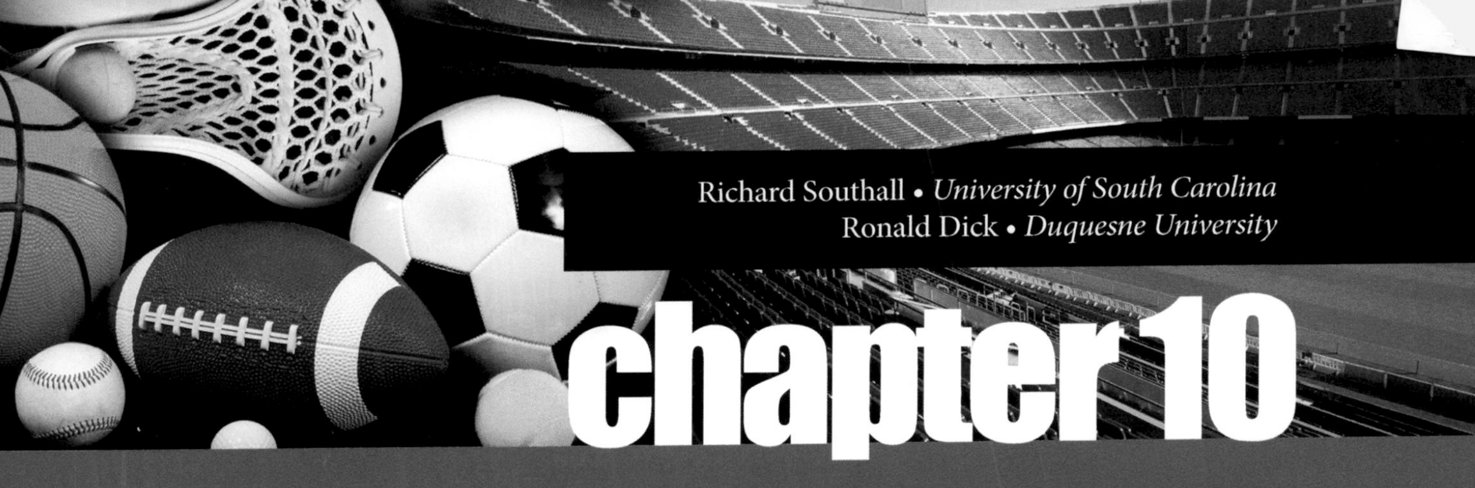

Richard Southall • *University of South Carolina*
Ronald Dick • *Duquesne University*

chapter 10

Sport-Sales and Revenue Generation

CHAPTER OBJECTIVES

After reading this chapter, you will be able to:

- Describe how consultative selling differs from traditional selling.
- Articulate how consultative selling creates an impact.
- Demonstrate how to use the bridging-the-gap sales process.
- Highlight how to keep good relationships and help clients make investment decisions.
- Understand how to establish business credibility.
- List some rules that help influence buying decisions.
- Apply these influence rules to the sport-sales setting.
- Demonstrate the ability to analyze customer needs.
- Outline the process of recommending solutions and gaining commitment.

KEY TERMS

80/20 rule
Base salary plus commission
Closes for the next step
Closing
Commitment and consistency
Liking
Override
Prospecting
Reciprocity
Referral
Relationship marketing
ROI
Social proof
Sport sponsorship
Telemarketing/teleselling

> *What have I done to make money for my company today?*
>
> —Jon Spoelstra

Introduction

The United States is a capitalistic, sales-driven society, and the sport industry is particularly capitalistic (Southall & Nagel, 2009). If you can sell, you have a high likelihood of being able to procure a sport job and position yourself to advance rapidly. Completing an undergraduate sport-management program—even one that requires a sport-industry internship—does not guarantee an entry-level employment position. However, the easiest way to ensure a career in the sport industry, regardless of undergraduate major or advanced graduate studies, is through sales. Many people in sport start off in sales and then transition to other areas, such as public relations, finance, advertising, marketing, promotions, production, research and development, or human resources. Some sport organizations require all of their employees to complete a sale-training program so they better understand the sales process. Since sales is the lifeblood of the sport industry, most sport organizations want all of their employees to "always be selling." Many sport-industry chief executive officers (CEOs) and chief financial officers (CFOs) "sold" at some point in their careers. John Spoelstra, former president of the New Jersey Nets and recognized leader in sport marketing, believes the CEO or president of a sport organization should demonstrate the importance of sport-sales by remaining actively involved with the sales department (Spoelstra, 1997). The ability to sell is especially important in sport marketing, because sales and marketing are interrelated. The transition from sales to marketing is often seamless. If you can sell, you can most likely execute a marketing plan.

What Is Selling?

There is no more accurate business statement than the truism, "Nothing happens until we sell something." If you want to work in sport, you need to recognize and embrace the importance and art of selling. Sport-ticket sales are the lifeblood of the sport industry. All functional areas or departments in a sport organization must work with the sales department because ticket revenue is the bedrock upon which all sport revenue depends. Without ticket sales, the value of sponsorship and media contracts significantly decreases. In addition, revenues from parking, concessions, and licensed merchandise cannot be realized unless customers attend events. Though sales is critical to success, many do not understand what successful selling actually entails. Selling is not simply a transaction where money is exchanged for a product or service. Rather, selling is an artistic endeavor and a scientific process that *satisfies customers' wants, needs, and desires.*

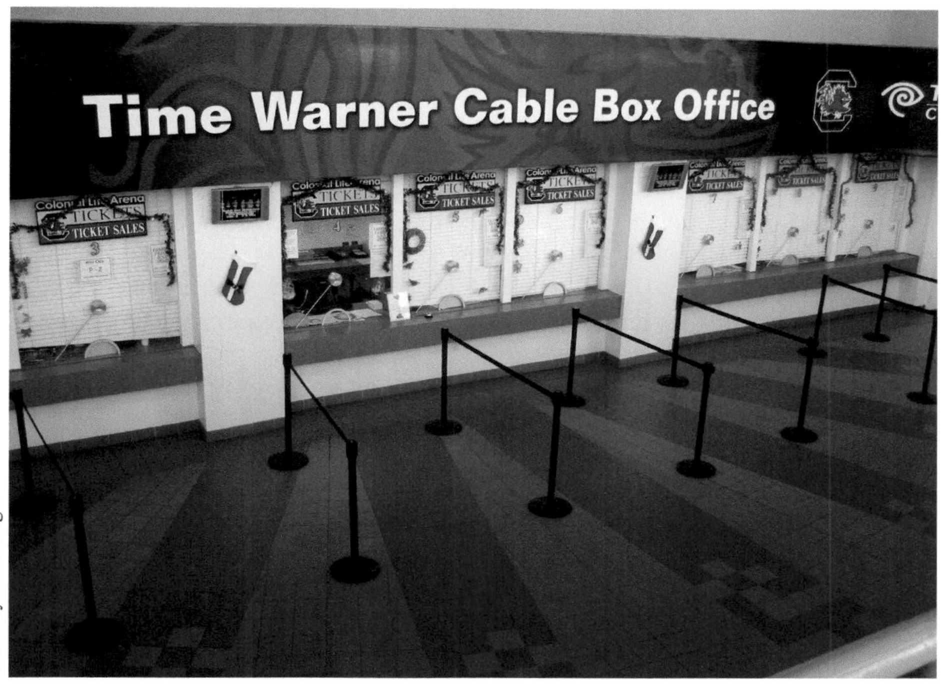

Courtesy Mark Nagel

Though tickets for sport events are sold at the box office, most of the "selling" occurs long before the customer visits a facility.

In the sport industry, revenue generation through sales and associated activities is critically important. Any sport-management student truly interested in a sport career should have an understanding of the revenue-generation (sales) process, and what a salesperson actually does. In sport—or any industry—a salesperson:

- Finds and develops new clients.
- Builds relationships (customer loyalty) by developing goodwill.
- Maintains client contact and continually satisfies current clients' wants, needs, and desires.
- Solves problems and provides service for customers.
- Provides formal and informal marketing-research data.

Students must take sales skills learned in the classroom and apply them in the real world.

Courtesy Mark Nagel

The Sales-Training Process

While today's sport industry makes extensive use of social media (e.g., Twitter, Instagram, Vine, Facebook, Tumblr, email, and whatever new "app" or media platform has burst on the scene since we published this second edition), as is often the case, fundamental processes still apply. Even in a social media–focused landscape, sport-management students who want to become sport-sales consultants must learn sales-process fundamentals and apply these principles in a variety of experiential settings. For the past decade, a number of sport-industry practitioners have criticized sport-management professors and programs for not offering sales as part of their curriculums (Dolich, 2004; Helyar, 2006). In response to such criticism, there has been a sustained effort by several sport-management scholars (Irwin, Southall, & Sutton, 2007; McKelvey & Southall, 2008; Southall, Dick, & Pollack, 2010; Southall, Dick, & Van Stone, 2008) to integrate sport-sales training into sport-management programs based upon the following components:

1. **Philosophy Agreement**—Ensure individual philosophical agreement with an organization's mission and goals.
2. **Product**—Develop fundamental product knowledge. Become an expert on the organization's products and services.
3. **Prospect**—Learn and apply basic prospecting principles in order to develop a consistent prospect database.
4. **Practice**—Begin the process of practicing and refining sales fundamentals under a sales professional's direction and guidance.
5. **Performance**—Bridge the gap between theory and practice by combining real-world selling with ongoing analysis and refinement of sales strategies.

Irwin et al. (2007) coined the phrase "Pentagon of Sport-Sales Training" to describe this process and developed a schematic representation to provide a roadmap to sport-sales success (Figure 10.1).

FIGURE 10.1 Pentagon of Sport-Sales Training

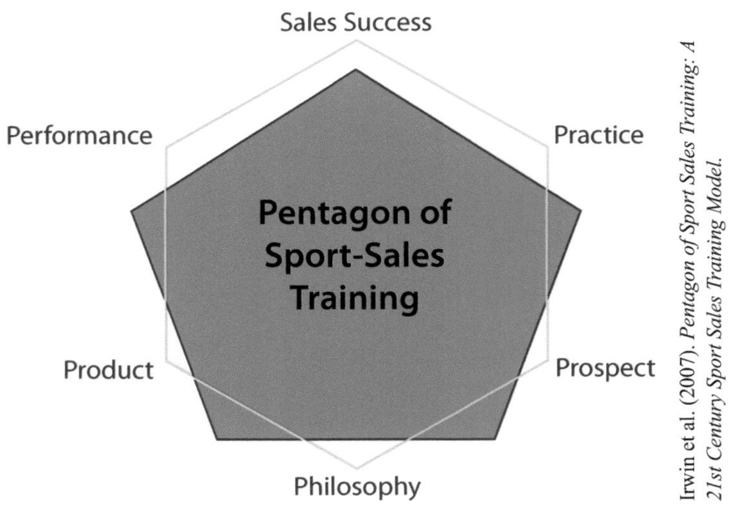

Irwin et al. (2007). *Pentagon of Sport Sales Training: A 21st Century Sport Sales Training Model.*

Aware that the fastest track to a sport-industry job is through sales, Southall, Dick and Pollack (2010) provided empirical evidence that participating in a *metadiscrete experiential* sales-training program can improve sport-management students' chances of landing a job in the highly competitive sport industry. Based on this and other studies highlighting the need for students to have a basic understanding of sales fundamentals, this chapter offers you an introduction to the fundamental components of the sales process and provides an opportunity to gain insight into methods that sport organizations use to generate revenue. You are strongly encouraged to take this information and apply it to real-world settings prior to completing your degree.

As part of your preparation for a sport-management career, you will undoubtedly take concentrated coursework in such areas as sport law, sport marketing, sport finance, and sport facility/event management. In addition, it is a great idea to take a course that focuses on the sales process, even if that course is not offered as part of the standard sport-management curriculum. Check out course offerings in your university's business school. In addition, look for other opportunities to sell!

The Sales Process

While there may be variations, the sales process consists of at least the following components:

1. Ensuring philosophical agreement
2. Developing and organizing prospects
3. Adopting a sales-consultant approach
4. Opening the sale—presenting
5. Conducting the analysis
6. Reaching an agreement
7. Closing—Getting an action commitment
8. Obtaining personal introductions

Step 1—Ensuring Philosophical Agreement

Ensuring philosophical agreement involves learning, understanding, and internalizing an organization's sales culture and sales philosophy. A sales organization's culture reflects its physical, emotional, and developmental environment. Reflecting this environment, a sales philosophy is an organization's strategic approach to selling. A firm's sales philosophy is continually revised and modified based upon consumer feedback and sales-success levels.

An organization's sales philosophy and culture are derived from—and must be consistent with—the organization's organizational culture and philosophy. These elements are reflected in organizations' developed mission statements and goals, as well as its organizational artifacts, rituals, habits, and reality view. All facets of an organization's strategic marketing plan, including such marketing-mix elements as sponsorship partnerships, advertising strategies, and promotional contests should be consistent with the sport organization's overall organizational culture.

For instance, many beer companies would willingly agree to **sport sponsorship** partnerships, develop advertising campaigns, and integrate promotions in conjunction with college-sport events. However, many universities decline to pursue extensive alcohol sponsorships, allow such advertising, or engage in beer-company-sponsored promotions since that would conflict with their core educational philosophy. But, as has become more apparent in the past few years, some athletic departments and universities willingly embrace such activities, since developing such partnerships provides additional revenue-generating opportunities.

These concepts and issues, as well as fundamental elements of ethics, are discussed in Chapters 2 and 5. Before you interview for your first sport-industry job, and throughout your sport-industry career, it is crucial you identify and articulate an individual ethical belief system. Before you interview, analyze the sport organization's organizational culture. Make sure you are in agreement with "the way they do things!"

An organization's sales culture manifests itself in various selling environments, including management, sales room, sales-peer group, and customer service. Examining and evaluating this selling environment involves investigating:

- Staff performance expectations
- Sales managers' experience levels
- Sales training and technologies utilized
- Product or services (including the public's perception and demand) (Irwin et al., 2007)

An organization's sales culture and selling environment may affect and be affected by dramatic ideological, political, and/or organizational shifts, depending upon the organization's success or failure:

- Hiring or laying off sales staff
- Adding or eliminating discounts
- Leveraging or courting behaviors
- Adding or eliminating ticket plan options
- Early payment incentives or payment plans
- Adding or eliminating promotional nights and giveaway items
- Adding to or cutting group-sales inventory
- Implementing or cutting back on sales contests and other performance incentives

For instance, in 1991 the National Basketball Association (NBA) established rules restricting its teams from selling TV-visible hard liquor signage. However, by 2009 changing cultural norms and a slumping economy caused the NBA to rescind those rules. Though franchises were able to sell those previously restricted advertisements, not every team elected to implement hard liquor sales as part of their sponsorship sales philosophy. Today, hard liquor sales are common throughout many aspects of the sport industry. Changing societal norms result in changes to the sales environment. As some states and municipalities change laws related to marijuana use, the sport industry will be faced with potential pressures to utilize this product category to generate revenue. However, just as was the case with the tobacco industry, don't expect change to occur overnight or to be fully embraced by every organization or constituent group.

While you may not have developed a coherent and consistent sales philosophy, studying traditional sales philosophies, best practices, and new segmentation or technological approaches can enhance your understanding of the sales process. Some common sport-industry sales philosophies are listed in Table 10.1. While not an exhaustive list, four of the five philosophies emphasize salespersons' roles prior to and after a sale. In addition, four philosophies stress "customer satisfaction" and the need for sales staff to fulfill customer expectations. It is also no surprise all five sales philosophies highlight the importance of personal interaction in the sales process.

TABLE 10.1 Common Sport-Industry Sales Philosophies

Sales Philosophy	Summary
Sun Tzu–Art of War Adaptation	Relationship selling based upon being prepared and anticipating customer needs and interests—win-win thinking (Michaelson & Michaelson, 2004).
Prize Inside	An upfront approach to benefit-based selling based upon the premise that all consumers want to know their prize—how do they benefit from or what do they get from the sale (Godin, 2004).
The Customer Comes Second	Sales staff needs must be satisfied before those of the customer (Rosenbluth, 1992).
Consumer-Behavior Driven	Sales success involves identifying and understanding potential consumers, and creating personal relationships in order to persuade customers (McCormack, 1996).
Eduselling	Educating and partnering with customers before, during, and after the sale leads to purchase satisfaction and long-term customer retention (Sutton, Lachowetz, & Clark, 2000).

Adapted from Irwin et al. (2007). *Pentagon of Sport Sales Training: A 21st Century Sport Sales Training Model.*

Once a sales consultant understands and is comfortable with an organization's sales philosophy, he/she can more comfortably begin the sales process. The next step involves developing and organizing sales prospects.

Step 2—Developing and Organizing Prospects

Prospecting
Searching for and creating new customers.

Prospecting is the process of finding people (also known as "leads") who have the desire and means to purchase a product or service. It is the first step in customer development and directly affects revenue-generation potential. The goal of prospecting is to efficiently determine if a specific individual is actually a "prospect." If a person truly has neither the desire nor the ability to invest in the product or service being offered, there is really no reason to make a presentation. A "real" prospect has wants, needs, and desires that can be satisfied by a product or service, and the ability to act to satisfy these wants, needs, and desires. A sales consultant's job involves uncovering how her product or service can most effectively satisfy these identified wants, needs, and desires. The prospecting process involves determining how best to uncover, generate, and develop qualified leads.

Effective prospecting involves generating a significant amount of prospect volume. The more qualified prospects to whom you speak, the more sales will eventually result. A general rule of thumb is that each 50 to 100 new contacts will lead to 10 sales presentations, which will lead to 2 to 3 sales. Certainly, this ratio can be improved if the prospects' characteristics identify them as more likely to purchase the product or service the salesperson has to offer. However, while enhancing the likelihood of sales success through better analysis may be possible, it is still important for students to remember: "To make one sale, multiple prospects must be contacted." The high contacted-prospects-to-sales ratio is the most daunting part of sales. It often discourages some students from pursuing a career in sport sales since even a successful sales consultant will experience continual "failure." The best sport analogy that puts the importance of prospecting into its proper perspective is to remember that a major-league baseball player who gets a hit 3 out of 10 times at bat will likely be enshrined in the Hall of Fame. What is sometimes forgotten is that a great hitter also "fails" to get a hit 7 out of 10 at bats. Within this context, it is important sport-management students recognize SALES SUCCESS can be greatly increased through more efficient prospecting, but the process is still time intensive and not foolproof.

Effective prospecting typically involves:

- Gathering all relevant contact information (including best method of contact)
- Developing and maintaining prospect and contact history
- Developing a systematic follow-up system (contact software can help with this)

- Maintaining a high level of professionalism
- Consistently sustaining contact with the prospect, even when a sale is not proposed and even after a sale is executed (A rule of thumb is four to seven contacts are necessary before a sale is finalized.)
- **Always** asking for the sale—ABC (Always Be Closing)

The key to effective revenue generation is consistent, professional contact over time. Keep talking to new, qualified prospects and sales will eventually follow!

Sport-Sales Prospecting Sources

Prospecting Lists Provided by Management

There are different techniques to utilize when speaking with prospects from "management" lists. (Note: These techniques are spelled out in greater depth in steps 3 and 5.) Most prospects will have different reasons why they are looking to invest or why they should potentially invest. It is the sales-consultant's responsibility to uncover these reasons so that appropriate sales proposals can be developed. Some examples of prospecting lists provided by management include:

- Facebook, Groupon, Living Social or Daily Deal leads
- Canceled partial-plan or season-ticket holders
- Single-game ticket purchasers
- Current customers (partial-plan purchasers)
- Direct mail/structured campaign lists
- Ticketmaster lists
- Chamber of Commerce database
- Targeted business lists
- Group sales lists
- School lists
- Church lists

Personal Prospect-Lead Sources

A successful sport-sales consultant utilizes provided leads, but also develops multiple prospecting sources. However, even great leads and solid lists do not guarantee sales success. Success requires you to discover each prospective client's *needs, wants and desires*. To achieve success, it is important on each call to ask appropriate questions to qualify prospects (determine their wants, needs, and desires—for example, are they interested in purchasing season tickets for personal or business use, are they a "fan" or more interested in utilizing the ticket for entertaining clients?), and ask for their business on each call (this is expanded upon in the section "Closing for the Next Step" later in this chapter).

As a future sport-sales consultant you must develop a game plan for generating quality leads, over and above those provided by management. Following are a few suggestions of additional ideas for generating quality prospect leads:

- Association lists (i.e., sales and marketing executives, Rotary and Lions Clubs, labor unions, doctors' associations, financial groups, alumni associations, communication associations)
- Business publications
- Newspapers
- Networking groups (Facebook, MySpace, Twitter, Instagram, etc.) (See Box 10.1.)
- Friends/family
- Contacts from previous jobs
- Word of mouth
- Driving by new buildings/new companies/company relocations
- Customized seminars (in-person or online)

It is important to remember the likelihood of sales success increases as potential prospects generated from these lists are segmented by their propensity to purchase. This involves asking questions in order to gauge the *level and intensity* of their wants, needs, and desires, and their ability to act to satisfy these needs. By engaging in this qualification process and gathering as much information before and during initial contact, you can improve your efficiency and enhance your potential sales success.

> ***Brainstorm Activity:*** *Can you identify additional prospecting sources? Can you list three to five names of actual prospects from the several categories listed above?*

Step 3—Adopting a Sales-Consultant Approach

As discussed, a salesperson must eliminate the fear of failure, since it is a part of the sales process. Sales consultants must always remember that since prospects do not know them well, potential refusals to purchase are not personal rejections. If potential clients do not buy, they are not rejecting a sales-consultant's recommendation; they are simply declining the recommended product or service because it is not perceived to be a good fit for them at that time. The product or service just does not satisfy their wants, needs, and desires. The fear of rejection is the single most important obstacle a sales consultant must overcome.

> ***Sell Like a Medical Doctor:*** *A sales consultant should: Examine, diagnose, and prescribe. The mutual trust and agreement between a sales person and client must be similar to that between a doctor and patient.*

In order to become a successful sales consultant, it helps to study and adopt characteristics of successful salespeople. This may involve examining the way veteran and/or younger, but successful, sales consultants dress, as well as their posture, outward behaviors, and public-speaking habits.

> ***Sales-Consultant's Golden Rule:*** *Sell with a level of honesty, integrity, caring, understanding, empathy, and thoughtfulness that your client expects. Truly "care" about your client, and present information in an organized and logical fashion.*

What Is Consultative Selling?

In transactional (i.e., traditional) selling, products and services are often sold as commodities. When you go into a high-ticket-item store (e.g., automobile, electronics, furniture), you may be exposed to transactional selling. Since each retail outlet sells a product that usually can be bought at a nearby competing location, a salesperson may attempt to use high-pressure selling strategies and/or deception in order to make a sale. The salesperson pushes a certain product and tries not to let a visitor leave without feeling awkward about failing to purchase. For many salespeople, the primary determinant of selling high-ticket is believed to be price; therefore, whoever can come up with the "best" price is the one who will likely make the sale. In such traditional commodity-selling, the emphasis is on price, features, and terms of the sale. Typically, "hard" selling techniques are used.

Such techniques may not only be unethical, but they may be fraudulent. One example of such techniques is called the "bait and switch." It involves advertising a product or service (the bait) at an extremely low "bargain" price in order to attract prospects. Then, after a prospect has had his hopes raised that his wants, needs, and desires will be met, the salesperson reveals that while the advertised product/service is not available, a more expensive, but more valuable, substitute product or service is available (e.g., the switch). The goal of the bait-and-switch is to convince a prospect to purchase the switch in order to mitigate the disappointment over not getting the bait, or as a way to recover sunk costs (transportation, time, money, etc.) expended trying to obtain the bait.

BOX 10.1

Social Networking

Social networking (SN) sites, such as Twitter, Facebook, MySpace, Instagram, and Linkedin, have emerged as powerful tools for organizations to connect with current and prospective customers. They are unique in their ability to allow for an immediate and meaningful connection that provides an opportunity to exchange information between sport organizations and fans. Social networking sites appeal to marketers due to their minimal cost and flexibility. Further, contacting consumers via social networking sites has become socially acceptable and considered a less invasive method of contact by consumers than conventional methods such as personal sales calls or emails. If properly managed, sites can be used to engage fans in conversations about an organization's brand, thereby creating a community that shares common interests.

One example of a professional sport organization effectively using both Facebook and Twitter as an integral part of their sales and marketing programs is the Chicago Blackhawks. The Blackhawks utilize each platform (see Table 10.2) in a unique way to promote the organization and connect with fans. The use of these two social networking sites enables the organization to connect with customers, which leads to increased levels of fan involvement and team loyalty. Though social networking is still being studied, there is no doubt that it has tremendous potential as a brand-building tool.

The Internet and social networking sites' open access format provides positives and potential negatives. Organizations need to control the flow of information on social networking sites in order to protect their brand. One concern that has arisen for every major professional sport franchise as well as numerous Division-I athletic departments is the presence of unofficial "official" Facebook pages. Many sport organizations now employ at least one staff member who researches the location of websites claiming to be "officially" associated with the organization. Sport organizations can lose credibility if unauthorized content and commentary is falsely distributed to customers under a website claiming to belong to the team or athletic department.

Sport organizations should also have a clear policy regarding the proper use of SN sites and the nature of posts via any platform by players, coaches, and other members of the organization. Inappropriate posts should be handled in the same manner as other behavioral issues. Further, it may be appropriate

The essence of consultative selling involves a shift in focus from the product to the people involved. In consultative selling the emphasis is on the process of:

- Building high-trust relationships with prospects
- Developing respect between the prospect and salesperson
- Uncovering prospects' WANTS, NEEDS, and DESIRES
- Discovering the impact of these wants, needs, and desires on prospects
- Positioning the product not as a commodity, but as a solution to these wants, needs, and desires

By understanding and applying these principles, consultative salespeople distinguish themselves from others. While applying these elements will not

BOX 10.1 CONTINUED...

for organizations to begin to write clauses into contracts regarding the proper use of social networking sites by players, coaches, and staff. This is even more important given the newly enacted league policies (e.g., NFL and NBA) forbidding the use of Twitter by coaches and athletes just prior to, during, and immediately following games. Though social networking's future specific use and impact is unknown, every sport organization must recognize it is already an important marketing tool, and its impact will likely continue to grow in the future.

TABLE 10.2

Facebook	Twitter
• Official team content, such as: Blackhawk's blog, photos, and video	• Up-to-date information regarding team including play-by-play of game in progress, injury, trade, and scouting reports
• Link to mobile marketing campaigns, Twitter site, and official team website	• Answers to fan questions and trivia
• Dialogue between fans through posts on the team's wall and fan photos	• Updated team event calendar
• Updates on team events, promotions, and player signings	• Events for fans, such as viewing parties for those who are unable to attend games.
• Updates on other organizations of interest to fans	• Up-to-date information on other organizations or events that may be of interest to fans, such as: USA v. Canada in Men's Hockey, World championships, viewing parties—where to watch and listen to game

guarantee a successful sport-industry career, a salesperson's chance of achieving success is greatly enhanced.

What Makes Consultative Selling Different?

Think of the term "salesperson," and write down five adjectives that come to mind. Are most of them negative? If so, this demonstrates negative experiences with salespeople who had a lack of understanding of consultative selling. As a future sport-sales consultant, it is likely some prospects may initially have these same negative perceptions. This negative stereotype is why there is such a need for the consultative approach in sport sales.

As sport organizations continue to reevaluate their sales strategies, consultative selling continues to be viewed as a more professional and effective approach. Not only do consultative salespeople have a higher success ratio, but consultative selling is also seen as an ethical way of doing business (see Chapter 5). While this introduction to consultative sales will not be sufficient training to "make" you a professional sport-sales consultant, it will provide an overview of the knowledge, skills, and attitude necessary to close more orders and generate more revenue for a sport organization, while earning more money and maintaining your self-respect.

Sport-sales consultants "bridge the gap" between sport organizations and prospective customers, by helping prospects identify their individual wants, needs, and desires and make an informed buying decision. Traditional salespeople typically compete primarily on price and try to charm prospects out of their money for short-term financial gains. Consultative selling creates a systematic and strategic problem-solving process.

While the specific order of these listed steps may vary, and they may sometimes occur simultaneously, some initial steps in the consultative sales process are commonly identified as follows:

- Conducting market and prospect research (e.g., prospecting)
- Planning each call (e.g., writing a script)
- Meeting clients
- Generating interest
- Listening to prospects' wants, needs, and desires
- Establishing credibility

Once these initial steps have occurred, consultative selling involves continually analyzing a prospect's wants, needs, and desires in order to develop and present them with possible solutions. Once these solutions have been presented, it is often necessary to justify associated costs.

The final phase of consultative sales consists of **gaining prospects' agreement** to the presented solutions that meet their expressed and emerging needs, **facilitating the investment** (helping them buy), and following up to **make sure they are satisfied**. While transactional salespeople mistakenly believe the sale is the end of the relationship, a sales consultant recognizes the "transaction or sale" is merely the beginning. Taking care of (e.g., servicing) the client is critical to long-term consultative success. Transactional salespeople fail to interact with existing clients until it is time to seek a new sale. This often creates animosity between clients and the organization, since dissatisfied clients perceive the relationship to be one-sided—the sport organization just wants their money, paying attention to them only when it is time to ask for more money.

It is important to make sure to remember a couple of consultative-selling points:

- **Consultants form partnerships and relationships with prospects**, while traditional salespeople treat prospects only as commodities or consumers.
- **Consultative selling is an art form that is shaped by a person's individual personality**. Many factors, including assertiveness, responsiveness, and human instincts, shape one's consultation style and determine how each consultant relates and reacts to each consulting situation. A consultant's attitude and mindset are directly associated with how she will be perceived and accepted by clients, and affect how successful the process is for all involved.

Consultative Sales Skills

One of the most important skills in consultative selling is listening! Listening to and understanding a prospect's needs, before offering a solution, will tremendously enhance your productivity. The initial step in developing a fruitful relationship is to *establish trust*. In traditional selling, the focus on price often causes a prospect to become tense and distrustful, fearful the salesperson is trying to "get my money." As an example, think of yourself as the customer. How much better would you feel if the person to whom you were speaking made an effort to get to know you as a person, rather than viewing you simply as a nameless, faceless commodity?

In addition to building rapport with clients, sales consultants avoid the following traps that reduce effectiveness and lead to sales "burnout." Transactional salespeople are often ineffective, because they:

- Are driven to get an order at all costs.
- Often resort to deceptive sales tactics.
- Are not empathic to prospects' expressed concerns.
- Create a win/lose environment.
- Believe they must "change people's minds."

Sales consultants are most productive when they:

- Are "driven" to satisfy prospects' needs and assist their buying decisions by conducting an analysis of the prospects' wants, needs, and desires.
- Tell prospects the truth.
- Develop genuine and relaxed relationships.
- Create win/win partnerships.

It is important to remember that in consultative selling if telling the truth results in no sale being consummated, it is "better" to have a reputation in the marketplace for being honest in business relationships than to make a sale no matter how it is accomplished. (Note: This point forms the basis for Chapter 5.) A reputation for being honest can result in prospects proactively contacting you once their situation changes and/or recommending you to other prospects (through personal introductions) who may be more likely to invest in the product or service being offered.

Table 10.3 summarizes key terms that differentiate transactional selling from consultative selling.

TABLE 10.3

Transactional Selling Jargon	Consultative Selling Terms
Sell or Sold	Help, Assist, Acquire
Tickets	Seats, Packages
Authorization Form, Contract	Paperwork, Agreement Form
Cost or Price	Investment, Amount
Deal	Opportunity
Problem	Challenge
Pitch	Presentation, Demonstration
Objection	Area of Concern, Request for Additional Information
Customer	Client
Appointment	Visit
Seat Location	Sightline, View
Buy or Pay	Own, Invest
Referral	Personal Introduction
Cheaper	Economical

Step 4—Opening the Sale—Presenting

The heart of the sale is presenting. Presenting deals with participation, proofing, visual aids, persuasive communication, demonstration, and dramatization.

A sales presentation allows the consultant to show the prospect why a product or service is the best solution or how it satisfies their wants, needs, and desires. The presentation must be planned, practiced, rehearsed, and reviewed constantly.

Opening

To a large extent sales success involves capitalizing on a good first impression. However, it is important to remember a good first impression is not all there is to selling. If a sales consultant has done his/her job (e.g., uncovered the prospect's wants, needs, and desires), at the completion of a consultative-sales presentation, a prospect should logically want to purchase. An easy example of the sales-consultant process involves drawing a large "T" on a piece of paper and listing all the reasons to invest on the left side of the page, and reasons not to invest on the right side. (Note: We know using paper is "old-school." You can also construct a T-Chart on an iPad or tablet. You might even have prospects complete the chart themselves.)

A consultant conducts this cost-benefit analysis with a prospect obtaining verbal input. When the exercise is completed, if there are more reasons listed on the left side, "investing" in the product or service makes logical sense. After conducting such an analysis, clients have "ownership" in their decision, since they "know" they participated in the decision by logically analyzing their available options.

Greeting and Introduction—Building Rapport

The confidence and tone projected in the opening are critically important. The opening is more than just saying hello, it is the opportunity to establish who you are, your agenda, and why your prospect should allow you to present your product or service.

Some fundamental points related to the opening include:

- Be energetic and enthusiastic; you may have only about 30 seconds to convey your initial point.
- A simple good morning or good afternoon is an excellent way to start. If you know the prospect's first name, use it. Saying a person's name personalizes the encounter and indicates to the prospect the salesperson is thinking of the potential client as a person rather than merely a potential sale. Next, say your name, and the name of your organization, and ask them how they are doing today. Wait for an answer. Respond appropriately. This response may involve more than just saying, "That's good."
- Find areas of mutual interest.
- Show empathy—How are they feeling? Ask yourself the following question, "How do I think they want to be treated?"
- Ask questions and allow the prospect to answer while you listen intently.
- Provide feedback (e.g., restating their supplied answers) to show you have listened and heard what they have said.

It is important to remember these fundamental elements set the tone for the entire presentation and develop rapport with the prospect. If you are a confident and friendly person, show it. If you are happy, smile. Smiling is contagious, both in person and over the phone. The cliché, "Smile and the whole world smiles with you" is also true!

Agenda, Objective, and Purpose

After being courteous and friendly and building rapport, it is important to clearly identify the purpose of the presentation. In short, tell prospects what is in it for them. Why should they listen to or set aside some of their valuable time? This portion of the presentation is, literally, a matter of seconds. There is no reason to hide the presentation's purpose from the prospect. If—through proper prospecting—it has been determined a prospect has wants, needs, and desires that can be satisfied by the proposed product or service, the purpose of the call is self-evident.

Presenting the Product

Presenting the product is the part of the presentation that allows knowledgeable and well-prepared sales consultants to "shine." It is the part that displays their expertise and product knowledge and allows them to gain complete control of the conversation. In addition, through the needs analysis or qualifying questions it is also the area that allows consultants to tailor their product benefits to meet the clients' needs.

Consultative selling allows for identification and evaluation of prospects' needs and development of strategies to address both short- and long-term needs, wants, and desires. Based on information collected during the prospecting stage, a consultant should be in a position to deliver a logical presentation with recommendations to the prospect. Choosing the correct presentation to satisfy the prospect's wants, needs, and desires does not happen by accident. The chosen presentation is the culmination of professional preparation. Consultants who have internalized a logical sales philosophy are earnestly interested in helping prospects make decisions that are "right" for them. Being knowledgeable about the available products or plans, the consultant will more likely pick the one appropriate for the situation. Based upon solid market research, including prospects' demographic, psychographic, and socioeconomic information, consultants can contextualize prospects' needs, wants, and desires and offer appropriate products or services.

Step 5—Conducting the Analysis

Handling clients' concerns is challenging because it puts consultants in tough situations that may—because of different viewpoints—involve escalating tensions. For clients to change their minds they often have to agree with the consultant and abandon previously expressed concerns and lower constructed defense mechanisms. Doing so may be perceived as dangerous or put the client in a vulnerable psychological position. If the sales consultant has provided logical reasons for a client to invest in the product or service and satisfy expressed wants, needs, and desires, then a "sale" should follow.

However, prior to or during the sales process, there are several mistakes that can sidetrack the sales process. These mistakes include:

1. Lack of product knowledge.
2. Wasting time—Be polite, but get to the point of the meeting.
3. Poor planning—We do not plan to fail, we fail to plan.
4. Pushiness—Phrases like "How can I help?" or "What can we do?" help clients understand you are concerned for their position. (This concept will be covered in depth in "Rules of Influence").
5. Not dependable—Do what you say you will do.
6. Too optimistic or unrealistic expectations—The customer will see right through unobtainable benefits.
7. Unprofessional conduct—Being critical of competitors, using foul language, or dressing inappropriately can potentially prevent a sale from occurring.

Hearing and Addressing Concerns

Hearing and addressing a prospect's concerns does not mean a consultant must attempt to overcome them. However, it is important to shift the prospect's focus from the negative concern to a positive and collaborative problem-solving approach addresses the concern while also finding a way to still satisfy the prospect's wants, needs, and desires. In addition, this process must be undertaken while still maintaining a respectful and friendly relationship.

The following are five concepts that can assist a sales consultant in addressing clients concerns:

1. **Presence**
    - Maintain your presence and project concern and confidence without appearing rejected.
    - Let client articulate their concern without interrupting, showing hostility, or demonstrating you have taken their concern as a personal rejection.

- Welcome their feedback and encourage them to fully express their opinion.

2. **Empathy** (e.g., identifying with and understanding another's situation, feelings, and motives)
   - Demonstrate and articulate empathy for expressed concerns in order to keep lines of communication open.
   - Let clients know in a proper tone that you understand and are open to their point of view. Empathy does not mean you agree, but it does mean you are willing to listen and explore their concerns.
3. **Questioning**
   - Most concerns are expressed in vague and broad language. Most often they are not specifically articulated.
   - A sales consultant must actively listen and ask clients to repeat or redefine vague concerns.
   - Based upon this focused restatement of concerns, a consultant must ask targeted questions in order to uncover specific and often "real" concerns.
   - Specific questions to uncover clients' real concerns are questions focused on the "why" (e.g., "Is there any particular reason why you would not be interested in a season ticket package right now?").
4. **Position Your Idea or Solution**
   - Once you narrow a concern with a "why" question, address your client's real concerns.
   - Sometimes effective positioning can be accomplished through using testimonials from other clients who had similar concerns and discussing how those concerns were addressed. An example of this may be that a season-ticket prospect expressed a concern that she would not be able to attend all the home games on the schedule. The sales consultant could discuss how these concerns have been addressed for other clients through their investing in specific partial ticket plans and also taking advantage of ticket-resale programs the sport organization offers.
5. **Check**
   - Once you have offered a solution to the concern, you should not assume your effort has satisfied the client. Check to see how your client feels about your response. Conducting this check will help to:
     - Prevent assuming the client's concern has been satisfied;
     - Measure the state of the relationship;
     - Move onto the next point; and
     - Develop a climate conducive to achieving agreement.

This five-step process of openly addressing expressed concerns provides a framework consistent with a consultative sales approach. In addition to these steps, the following rules of influence allow sales consultants to effectively and ethically collaborate with prospects to "get to the yes" and satisfy their expressed wants, needs, and desires.

Techniques to Alleviate and Mitigate Client Concerns

In his books *Influence: Science and Practice* (2008) and *Influence: The Psychology of Persuasion* (2006), Robert Cialdini describes several effective methods for positively influencing people's behaviors. Understanding the methods discussed in Cialdini's books and employing *influence judo*—influencing without appearing to influence—allows sales consultants to decrease the likelihood of client concerns arising, and—if they do—mitigate their intensity.

Cialdini's Rules of Influence include:

1. **Reciprocation.** Potential customers will try to repay, in kind, what you have provided that is of value to them. In other words, provide reasons why the prospect should feel obligated to repay you and your franchise/client by making a buying decision. These reasons may be tangible or intangible benefits. Reciprocation motivators can include a free gift, an exclusive t-shirt, a preferred customer party, a chance to rub elbows with celebrities, public recognition associated with their purchase, something that will develop a sense of belonging, or appealing to their sense of purpose.

   Free give-away items for the first 10,000 fans arriving at a home game is one example of **reciprocity**. Another example is providing an opportunity for suite owners to attend exclusive practice sessions or gain access to hospitality events during which they can meet players and celebrities. Reciprocity is designed to satisfy clients' psychological or emotional wants, needs, and desires they may perceive—as the effective MasterCard advertising campaign has expressed as being "priceless."

2. **Commitment and Consistency.** Once clients have made an investment decision, they will encounter personal and interpersonal pressures to behave in a manner consistent with that commitment. By clearly articulating and summarizing the rationale for their decision, a sales consultant allows this commitment to be made. Once people believe they have made a "correct and wise investment," they will most likely follow through on this decision and are also predisposed toward future similar decisions. In other words, if a fan has made a decision to invest in a season-ticket package and has to put down a nonrefundable

Reciprocity
A mutual exchange, a return in kind. People react positively and feel obligated to repay others for favorable treatments received.

Commitment and Consistency
A person making a decision will experience pressure from others and themselves to behave consistently with that decision. Depending on a person's past actions, he or she will be predisposed to making future decisions consistent with those past actions.

deposit, the client is much more likely to follow through and pay off the outstanding balance.

Social proof
People will do things they see other people are doing. Assuming other people possess more knowledge about the situation, they deem the others' behavior as appropriate or better informed.

Liking
A person's feeling of affect on or preference for another person.

3. **Social Proof.** In a given situation, clients view a behavior as correct to the degree they see others performing it. To ensure prospects see purchasing a ticket as a correct behavior, they need to be shown/told that others have made this choice and it has paid off for them. If their neighbor, friend, or business associate has purchased, they are likely to do the same.
4. **Liking.** People prefer to say yes to the requests of people they know and/or like. It is important to *not* alienate your prospect by being too demanding or pushy. Remember, the choice to purchase is theirs, not yours. Addressing concerns to accelerate the sales process is important, but you should not be too pushy.
5. **Authority.** Purchasers tend to follow the dictates of "genuine authorities" because such individuals usually possess high levels of knowledge, wisdom, and power. (See "Sell Like a Medical Doctor" under Step 3.) Customers recognize and appreciate a professional sales consultant who has developed a high level of product knowledge and possesses confidence in a product or service. It is important for sales consultants to know their product's strengths and weaknesses. When selling, be realistic about the product or service and sell to its strengths, but also openly admit any deficiencies and proceed.
6. **Scarcity.** Any product seems more valuable to prospects when the product is less available. Limited-product availability is useful to a sales consultant, especially if the scarcity is a result of high demand (see "Social Proof"). Make sure prospects feel they will join an elite group by making the investment. Make them feel valued. Scarcity is related to the first rule (reciprocity). If not every fan can obtain access to a certain club lounge, concourse, or seating section, then these items' perceived values often increase. If there are only 100 tickets available to a given game, but there are more than 100 fans waiting to purchase tickets, the demand (and perceived value) of those tickets to the general public will increase. StubHub or other resale entities are a reaction to this basic concept of "supply and demand."

Step 6—Reaching an Agreement

Closing
Reaching a sales agreement with a client.

Every professional sales consultant may have different thoughts regarding how to reach an agreement with a client. Reaching agreement or **closing** is simply getting a client to make an investment decision. The following section addresses some misconceptions about reaching agreement and provides some thoughts regarding how to evaluate sales success.

One of the most common misconceptions is that "closing" only means getting a "Yes." Sometimes, consultants feel that if they do a good job presenting their product or service there is really no need to close; the product should sell itself. The following statements exemplify this mistake:

- If I can get the prospect positive about the presentation, I can close a call without a decision.
- When a customer says "I'm interested," there is no reason to push further.
- I cannot close on the first call; it is simply an information-gathering call.

Close for the Next Step—On Every Call or Presentation

Regardless of the sales-process stage, it is important that a sales consultant always **closes for the next step**. Closing for the next step involves always asking for a client's business. Sales consultants who ask for a client's business are both setting up the next step (gaining agreement) and closing for the next step (getting an investment and obtaining personal introductions).

Closes for the next step
Asking for a client's business or requesting referral information.

In order to close for the next step, a sales consultant must be able to ask effective closing questions during each conversation with a prospective client. When envisioning a "close," it may be helpful to visualize the last few minutes leading up to asking for the business. In addition, by effectively and proactively listening to a prospect, in some circumstances a sales consultant may be able to ask for a client's business shortly after first meeting the prospect.

If a consultant always closes for the next step, clients are conditioned to invest. Taking this step is based upon assuming every prospect is going to invest. Making this assumption makes consultants more confident in their presentation and closing abilities. In today's sport industry, one of the most important habits is to become accustomed to and comfortable asking for a prospect's credit card number. Asking for a client's credit card number allows the client to understand that making the investment will be a simple process, expedites the investment, and allows the client to visualize their owning the product or service. While it is crucial to always close for the next step, not all closes will occur on the first call or at the conclusion of the first presentation. Many closes occur after multiple calls or presentations. Most successful multiple-call closes are the result of effective listening, strong communication skills, and diligent follow-up. If it is inappropriate to immediately ask for a prospect's business, begin to set a timeline during which small closing steps can be completed. (This is called "setting the table.") This will culminate in asking for the client's business.

Shutterstock, Inc.

Successful sales consultants help bring enthusiastic crowds to sport events.

Pre-closing Questions

In order to ask for business at the appropriate time, a sales consultant needs to know exactly what the clients want and how their specific needs, wants, and desires can be met. Specific and pre-planned pre-closing questions prevent useless rambling and long-winded explanations. Furthermore, customers like to feel they have an active part in choosing a seat location, partial package, and so on.

Consider the following pre-closing questions (PQ) that might be asked of a ticket prospect:

- Is it more important to you to be closer to the action or closer to the center section?
- How will you be investing in these seats?
- Is it more important for you to see certain teams or is day-of-the-week more important?
- How many games would you like to come to?
- What is your time frame for getting these tickets?
- If it is up to you, would you purchase these seats?
- If your budget is approved, will you purchase these seats?

In addition to utilizing pre-closing questions, another pre-closing technique is to simply quit talking and allow the prospect to think about the investment. In other words, "Silence Can Be Golden!" Silent moments in a telephone conversation or when the client is sitting in the venue in the actual seat being discussed, seeing his or her name on the stadia scoreboard or Jumbotron, allows the prospect to visualize being at the game. This contemplative time can be positive. Therefore, sales consultants must recognize it is not always necessary to fill every conversation or presentation with verbiage. Sometimes it is most effective to let the game experience speak for itself. (Letting the game experience sell itself is exemplified in the saying, "Let the steak's sizzle [the sound of a steak makes when it is placed on a grill] sell the beef.")

Reaching agreement requires the following:

1. Enthusiasm
2. Planning sales calls and presentations
3. Knowing your prospects' wants, needs, and desires
4. Giving a professional presentation
5. Utilizing a trial close and pre-close questioning
6. Sensing the client's real concern(s)
7. Addressing and solving these concerns
8. Reminding the client of the product or service's benefits
9. Asking for the order and then being silent
10. Never burning a bridge

At the completion of the sales process the customer's logical conclusion should be to buy. A purchase decision allows for potential clients to develop "ownership" in the decision making, because they feel they participated in the decision. If clients truly want, need, or desire the product or service being offered, at the conclusion of the sales process they should invest.

Trial Close

Often, a trial close involves asking a prospect a series of "Yes/No" questions. These answers provide the consultant with client feedback. When asking these questions the consultant must be comfortable with silence, since the prospect may take time to think about the answers. Some examples of trial close questions include:

- Does that sound good to you?
- Is this seat location good for you?
- Does this make sense so far?
- Do you like this ticket package, etc.?

Step 7—Close—Getting an Action Commitment

There are several types of closes or closing techniques available to a sales consultant. All such techniques involve the consultant making sure a new client has agreed to the investment and is ready to take action to put the investment in motion. The list of closing statements below is not exhaustive, but provides a starting point.

Types of Sales Closes

1. **The invite close**
   After pre-close questioning and a trial close to uncover and address clients' concerns, a sales consultant has an obligation to ask new clients to initiate their investment. This step (the close) is the final element of reaching agreement.
   A close is simply asking a simple question:
   - "Why don't you give it a try?"
   - "Why don't you give us a chance?"
2. **Directive or assumptive close**
   - An assumptive close is initiated when a consultant moves on to the next step in the process, as if assuming an investment decision has already been made. If the client agrees to initiate the investment by agreeing to the next step, the assumption has been validated and an investment decision has occurred.
   - The following statement is an example of an assumptive close: "If you do not have any further questions, then here is the season-ticket authorization form to sign. (Form is placed in front of client and pen provided.) I will take the completed form back to the office, and deliver your tickets and your season-ticket owner gift to you tomorrow."
3. **Alternative close**
   - Since everyone wants to have a choice, the alternative close provides prospects with two choices from which to choose. To initiate this close a consultant asks the client a series of choice questions.
     For example, the client's choices may be:
     —Which ticket package—A or B—do you want?
     —Should we mail the tickets to your home or work?
4. **Order-sheet form close**
   - During an order-sheet form close, the consultant takes out a ticket order-form and begins to fill it out. Part of the process of completing the form involves asking the prospect a series of questions: "What

is the correct spelling of your name? What is your address? What is today's date?"

- While asking these questions a consultant should not look up. When a prospect provides the information in order for the form to be completed, he/she has agreed to make the investment.

5. **Authorization close**
   - Initiating an authorization close consists of opening an authorization form (e.g., season-ticket authorization form), making check marks to indicate where to sign, and pushing it in front of the client and saying, "Congratulations, you have made a great investment."
6. **"I want to think it over" close**
   This close occurs when a client says, "I would like to think it over." Clients who say this are actually saying, "No." In this situation, a sales consultant should calmly accept the "No," put their padfolio away, stand, and politely say, "Thank you for your time." While shaking the client's hand, the consultant says, "You have concerns. Can you share them with me?" The consultant then simply waits for a response.

Step 8—Obtaining Personal Introductions

For misguided or uninformed salespeople "asking for a **referral**" is viewed as a needless hassle and of little value. On the other hand, a professional sales consultant understands the value of personal introductions. Personal introductions are instantaneous "warm leads" that are much more likely to become clients. Asking a new or existing client for the names of personal friends or business associates who would like to make the same investment (e.g., enjoy the fun and excitement of a football or basketball game, soccer match, or snowboarding competition) they just made is consistent with many of Cialdini's *rules of influence* discussed earlier.

The art of asking for personal introductions involves an ongoing individual commitment to asking prospects or clients for their assistance during all contacts. Asking for personal introductions should be done on all calls.

Forming a relationship with a potential client is much easier when a friend or colleague has suggested the introduction. How much easier is it to introduce one's self based upon a warm introduction through a friend or colleague?

In the sport sales context, questions that best provide personal introductions often need to include certain qualifiers to stimulate feedback. Instead of simply asking, "Could you provide me with the names of four people I could call?" asking for personal introductions may involve asking some simple qualifying questions. For example, in order to obtain some personal introductions from a season-ticket holder, a sales consultant might ask one of the following questions:

- Who might you want to sit with or near?

Referral
When someone gives a salesperson a sales lead (name, address, phone number, and/or e-mail to contact).

- Who do you know who owns tickets to one of the local sport teams?
- Who at your company is responsible for organizing outings?
- Who in your social group (church, etc.) is responsible for organizing outings?
- Who is the coach of your child's youth sport team?

As has been discussed, personal introductions are "warmer" leads, more amenable to being approached by a sales consultant than "cold" leads (e.g., names out of the telephone book). The success of a personal-introduction lead is based upon the concept of social proofing, which is that people are more inclined to behave in a certain way, in this case purchase a product or service, to the degree they observe others doing so. A personal introduction is, at its most basic, simply someone telling a friend or acquaintance, "You should do what I have done!"

Conclusion

Sport sales is a highly competitive sport-industry segment, with wide-ranging salaries. Typically, sport-sales consultants' compensation is a combination of a small **base salary** and **commission** on sales. (Note: A typical commission rate is between 1% and 5% on **renewed** business and 5% and 20% on a new account.). Even the most experienced sales consultants will have a commission structure built into their compensation agreement. This allows the sales consultant to make a large amount of money or a small amount of money, depending on their performance. In some cases, professional sport franchises will have highly successful sales consultants who make as much, if not more, than many of the vice presidents of the organization.

Some Additional Terms

Base salary plus commission

Combination of a set salary—based on a staff member's experience—and a percent of generated sales (typically between 1% and 5% on renewed business and 5% and 20% on new business).

Telemarketing/teleselling

Marketing/sales approach that features the use of personal selling techniques in a non-face-to-face context and utilizes telecommunications technology as part of a well-planned, organized, and managed marketing program.

However, entry-level sales consultants can be overwhelmed by the small "guaranteed" pay and the tremendous amount of time spent **telemarketing/teleselling** to potential prospects. Often, organizations know within a month or two if a recently hired and trained sales consultant will be able to assist the organization. Successful sales consultants typically receive higher commission packages as they advance within an organization. In addition, promotion to sales manager may enable a sales consultant to be paid an **override** for sales executed by staff members. Most sport organizations do not mind paying large commissions to their sales staff as it means revenue is being generated. A sales consultant that makes a 10% commission on $900,000 of sponsorship sales is earning a high income while providing a good **return on investment (ROI)** for the organization.

Override
Compensation paid to a sales manager for overseeing a sales staff. For example, if a sales manager has five employees that report to him, he may receive a 1% bonus of the total revenue generated by the five sales-staff employees.

Return on investment (ROI)
Marketing success is measured by the following ratio: revenue generated/costs incurred.

80/20 rule
Revenue-generation "rule" that 80% of a sport organization's revenue comes from 20% of its customers.

Relationship marketing
Integrating a business partner's wants, needs, and desires with a company's strategic marketing plan in order to create and sustain a mutually beneficial relationship.

Though researching and targeting new clients is critical to the success of any sales operations, sales consultants should remember the **80/20 rule** of sales. Typically, most organizations sell 80% of their products to 20% of their customer base. The "regular" customers of an organization are critical to the financial viability of the organization. It is much more expensive and time intensive to convince a non-customer to become a one-time buyer than it is to maintain a current customer's buying habits. In addition, current customers are more likely to increase their current rate of product or service consumption than a non-customer is to try the product or service one time. For these reasons, **relationship marketing** is an important aspect of selling. Every successful sales consultant will first ensure, and then work to enhance, the commitment from current customers prior to seeking new sales.

Today sport is both a product and a means for other businesses to sell their non-sport products. Fundamentally, the modern sport industry is predicated upon encouraging sport fans and participants to consume the sport product. This consumption is the end result of the sales process. This chapter outlined a sales-training progression and delineated the fundamental steps of the consultative sales process. As will become apparent to sport-management students, if you can sell, you have a high likelihood of being able to find a job in the sport industry. Simply stated, the easiest way to get into the sport industry is through sales.

As part of their career preparation, all sport-management students should take part in a sales-training program, so they better understand the sales process. In addition, students should recognize that selling is simply satisfying clients' wants, needs, and desires. In addition, no matter what facet of the sport industry in which a sport manager works, every sport organization member must "always be selling."

chapter 10
Interviews

Interview 10.1

Jim Van Stone
Chief Revenue Officer and Senior Vice President
Monumental Sports and Entertainment (Washington Capitals, Washington Wizards, and Washington Mystics)

Q: Could you describe your career path?

A: Like many in the business, I dreamed of being a professional athlete but realized quickly that my best path to sport was on the business side. I have always been competitive by nature and love the opportunity that being a sales executive still continues to provide the thrill of winning and losing deals just as when many of us were younger athletes in youth sports and high school with playing games. I was fortunate that an internship led me to my first job in sport as a sales representative with the Philadelphia 76ers. The rest of my career has been spent in sales positions and sales management roles for a number of professional sport organizations and I have never looked back.

Q: What advice would you give a graduating senior in high school that is looking to enter the sport business industry in four years?

A: You should enter the best university that will accept you as you graduate high school. You should learn and do as well as you can in ALL of your classes, especially your business courses. Get the best internship you can. You should work for your athletic department in some way, as this is an easy way to gain experience and build your network of contacts.

Q: What advice would you give a graduating senior in college who is looking to enter the sport business industry today? Is graduate school a good option? Will that change potential job opportunities?

A: A graduate degree will NOT change the first job you obtain after the completion of undergraduate degree. Your first job will likely be in a sales, service, or operations position with or without a graduate degree. The advantage of going to graduate school after completing an undergraduate degree is that the majority of your "formal" education will be completed early in your life and your career may benefit down the road. The disadvantages are you pay for your graduate degree tuition or accumulate more school debt and you are responsible for your health benefits.

Q: You have hired more than 100 young, recently graduated college seniors. What skills do you require and prefer?

A: The industry of sport is no different than other businesses. I look for the "B and B" which is the best and the brightest. I am looking for smart, mature, responsible, and hard-working employees. I want to hire a sales representative who wants to sell. Many sport executives use sales as a stepping-stone to another department within the sport industry. I am fine with that idea, but while you are in the sales department "be" in the sales department.

Q: How important is cover letter, resume, and references to a graduating senior?

A: It is very important. These three pieces of paper are a brochure of who you are, and must be well written while being free of all spelling errors.

The cover letter has to be personalized to the individual, speak to the fact it is a letter of application, list and explain experiences from the resume, discuss examples of your work ethic, thank the readers for their time, and restate an e-mail address and phone numbers.

The resume should be written in Times Roman, size 12 font, on one page with both school and home addresses, anticipated graduation date, education and experiences listed chronologically from today to past. Be sure to avoid using any "crazy" email addresses or any phone messages that are not professional.

The references should include at least three but no more than five with the name, full address, phone number, and email also included. You should ask the individual to be a reference prior to submitting their name and every reference should be a non-relative. Select individuals who do the following: know you well, will definitely return a call or e-mail of a potential employer, and will provide information about you that will make the potential employer want to interview you!

An important reminder for students is to NEVER display pictures of yourself in compromising positions on your Facebook or other social media websites. If you think you "party" too much, then you probably do. Do not advertise it. There have been situations where a potential employee was rejected because of information gleaned from social-media sites.

Q: How important is an internship and networking?

A: It is important to network. Your network is not who you know, but it is who knows you. It is important to seek and obtain "quality" internships. Students constantly ask me the question, "Should I try for an internship with one of the four major teams or a minor league organization?" I would try for one of the four major league teams, especially if that is where you want to eventually be employed, but both levels can provide great educational experiences. While it is easier to go from the majors to the minors than vice versa, the down side to interning in the majors is that sometimes the intern gets pigeon-holed as the finance intern, marketing intern, or the ticket intern. Regardless of where you intern, you should try to gain experience in all departments to learn what everyone in the organization does. Acquiring this wealth of knowledge will more likely occur at the minor-league level since a minor-league organization has fewer employees.

Q: What are the biggest mistakes you see interns and new employees making in the industry?

A: They think that they've made it. You should look at it as just the start of a long successful career and keep working diligently to make a name for yourself, gain experience, and build your network that will lead you into bigger and better positions in the future.

Q: What skills have serviced you well as your career climbed from sales representative to assistant director of sales to director of sales to vice president of sales?

A: I think the skills that have served me well are as follows: being a people person, being willing to work long hours during the season and to relocate for a promotion, being firm, but fair, to my staff, putting the company first, being open minded to new ideas, and being a problem-solver. In addition, the ability to be a team player, set goals, and retain a competitive desire to succeed, while adapting during good and bad times has assisted my career progression. I also think I am able to judge and cultivate talent.

Q: How important was physically relocating to the growth of your career?

A: I would never have become a vice president of sales if I had not been willing to relocate. It meant everything. By relocating, I have learned from so many different people and organizational cultures, which has enabled me to apply different philosophies to solving problems.

Q: How has the industry changed since you were first employed?

A: The following has occurred: the value of professional sport franchises has dramatically increased, the players and coaches salaries have exploded, new arenas with club boxes and suites have proliferated, sport marketing has gone global, technology has advanced and assisted the capturing of names and fan profiling, ticket prices have increased at a higher rate than inflation, secondary ticketing has become "mainstream," and the recent recession has eroded season ticket bases which has forced improvement in selling individual and group tickets.

Q: How does sales and revenue generation impact the other aspects of the organization? Is it important for sport-management students to understand the sales process even if they want to work in other departments?

A: In our business, everybody sells and it's the responsibility of our entire organization to drive to make the company profitable. Even if sales is not in your title you certainly still ensure that customers are secured, serviced, and retained.

Interview 10.2

Jennifer Hale Holman
Manager of Corporate Partnerships
Atlanta Braves

Q: Could you briefly describe your career path from undergraduate student to your current position?

A: I began working at Turner Field while I was still in school pursuing my sport-management degree. I conducted stadium tours, worked in the Braves Museum & Hall of Fame, and staffed gameday positions including pregame ceremonies and club-level hospitality. I interned within the Ticket Sales Department after graduating and obtained my first full-time sales job in 2004. I was promoted to Senior Account Executive after several years and eventually ended up managing the New Business Department under the Season Ticket Sales umbrella. I transitioned to Corporate Partnerships in the fall of 2013. I'm currently in my fourteenth season with the Atlanta Braves.

Q: What are the biggest challenges in selling tickets for the Braves?

A: Ticket sales is all about finding a perfect fit for prospects and educating them regarding their options. It's important to establish a rapport with potential buyers and ask open-ended questions to get to the bottom of what works best for their needs. Many people aren't familiar with the wide variety of discounted plans and packages the Braves have to offer. During my tenure in Ticket Sales, I have found that half the battle is finding out what kind of experience the person wants to have and then prescribing the perfect fit for their budget, preferences, and schedule. Baseball fans are already buying tickets; the key is selling the amazing overall experience of a game at Turner Field and how it can benefit individuals and businesses.

Q: Are there specific skills sport-management students should look to develop while still in school?

A: All sport-management students should do their very best to obtain any and all possible sport-related experience while they are still in school. I was working four different jobs by my senior year of school and each one gave me the skills and experience I needed to succeed in the future. I did everything I could to make sure that my resume contained plenty of relevant employment (paid or unpaid) by the time I graduated. It is important to network within the industry as much as possible and get to know people who can give you advice and mentor you down the road. I happened to get a chance at my Braves' internship because the hiring manager was also one of the supervisors of my gameday job while I was still in college.

Top skills needed to succeed in sports:

1. Efficiency, planning, and ability to manage time properly
2. Ability to work extremely long hours in the elements
3. Stress-management skills
4. A strong work ethic including drive, determination, patience, and persistence

Q: What specific classes would you recommend students take to best position themselves for a sport-industry job?

A: From a professional sports perspective, the most valuable classes were social and economic influences in sport, legal issues in sport, facility management, sponsorship, and women's roles in sport. For students who are focused on careers within amateur athletic associations, I would suggest focusing on the aforementioned classes plus other courses more applicable to collegiate issues.

Q: What publications do you regularly read to stay apprised of sport-business events?

A: The *Sports Business Journal* and the *Atlanta Business Chronicle* are the most vital publications that I read regularly. I also stay on top of all local and national sports websites to make sure I know what other organizations are doing. I even subscribe to European sponsorship blogs and news sites. Right now I am very focused on all newspapers and websites in Cobb County, the future home of our new ballpark. I rely on daily and weekly Google alerts to keep me up-to-date on certain subjects, prospects, and news stories I am following.

Q: Would you recommend students pursue graduate school? If so, when should they pursue a graduate degree and what area of study would you recommend?

A: Graduate school is always something that I've hoped to do for myself one day. However, I feel that getting valuable real-world experience is a great plan when you are first getting started. If you are able to do both simultaneously, that's a bonus. Master's degrees in sport management or sport administration are both applicable, and an MBA can be a valuable boon to certain sports career paths as well.

Study Questions

1. Explain how consultative selling differs from traditional selling.
2. List several ways in which consultative selling creates an impact.
3. List and describe the eight steps of the sales process described in this chapter.
4. Briefly describe how to keep good relationships and help clients make investment decisions.
5. List and describe the elements of the Pentagon of Sport-Sales Training.
6. Illustrate some steps a sales consultant can take to establish business credibility.
7. List and provide sport-specific examples of the rules of influence discussed in this chapter.
8. Describe some methods a sales consultant can utilize to analyze clients' needs.
9. Briefly explain the process of recommending solutions and gaining commitment.
10. Highlight at least three types of closes outlined in this chapter.
11. Illustrate the process of asking for personal introductions and utilize the appropriate rules of influence in discussing why this is a crucial step in the sales process.

Learning Activities

The following activities are designed to bridge the gap between sales theory and practice. Several of the activities require outside planning and organization and may not be feasible in an introduction to sport management course. However, these activities may be utilized as part of ongoing sport-management club activities.

1. Invite a director of sales or vice president of sales from a local major or minor league sport organization to speak to your class or to a sport-management club on campus.
2. Contact your university's athletic director or associate athletic director for external relations (i.e., marketing) and develop a relationship in which the class develops a sales program for an Olympic-sport competition. This would involve the class selling ticket inventory or developing a promotional campaign for the chosen contest.
3. For this chosen contest, each class member should develop a sales script which addresses the following product elements: who, what, where, and when in the first sentence.
4. For the chosen game or another sport product, develop a funnel of 20 prospects. Prospects may be drawn from the following groups: alumni,

local community members, university student-body, friends, relatives, or former ticket holders who have attended a college/university sport event.

5. Break into groups of three students and role-play the script. There are three roles—consultant, prospect, and active observer. All three students should perform each role. After each presentation, critique the presentation, offering constructive advice and suggestions for improvement.

Culminating Activity

As part of the developed sales campaign, call "real-life" prospects from developed funnel lists, or lists provided by the athletic department. If possible, calls should be made from a location in which students can be observed and possibly videotaped. Student cell phones can be used, if necessary. The time when calls are made should vary, occurring Monday–Thursday 4:30–8:30 P.M. and Saturdays 10 A.M. to 4 P.M. Students should be encouraged to participate in a two- to three-hour selling practicum.

References

Cialdini, R.B. (2006). *Influence: The psychology of persuasion.* New York: Harper Paperbacks.

Cialdini, R.B. (2008). *Influence: Science and practice* (5th ed.). Boston: Allyn and Bacon.

Dolich, A. (2004, November). Speech at the annual meeting of Sport Marketing Association, Memphis, TN.

Godin, S. (2004). *Free prize inside.* New York: Portfolio.

Helyar, J. (2006, September 16). Failing effort: Are universities' sports-management programs a ticket to a great job? Not likely. *Wall Street Journal.*

Irwin, R.L., Southall, R.M., & Sutton, W.A. (2007). Pentagon of sport-sales training: A 21st century sport sales training model. *Sport Management Education Journal, 1*(1), 18–39.

McCormack, M. (1996). *On selling*. West Hollywood, CA: Dove Books.

McKelvey, S., & Southall, R.M. (2008). Teaching sport sponsorship sales through experiential learning. *International Journal of Sport Management and Marketing, 4*(2–3), 225–254.

Michaelson, G.A., & Michaelson, S.W. (2004). *Sun Tzu: Strategies for selling.* New York: McGraw-Hill.

Rosenbluth, H.F. (1992). *The customer comes second.* New York: Quill/William Morrow.

Southall, R.M., & Nagel, M.S. (2009, December 17). Big-time college sport's contested terrain: Jock capitalism, educational values, and social good. *Human Kinetics Sport Management News*. Available at http://www.humankinetics.com/hkarticles/hk-articles/big-time-college-sports-contested-terrain-jock-capitalism-educational-values-and-social-good?associate=5167

Southall, R.M., Dick, R.J., & Pollack, T.A. (2010). Assessing sport-sales training effectiveness: To enhance sales performance of prospective sales employees. *Journal of Applied Marketing Theory*, *1*(2), 45–57.

Southall, R.M., Dick, R.J., & Van Stone, J. (2008). *Bridging the Gap ticket sales-training manual.* Pittsburgh: Bridging the Gap, LLP.

Spoelstra, J. (1997). *Ice to the eskimos: How to market a product nobody wants.* New York: HarperCollins.

Sutton, W.A., Lachowetz, A., & Clark, J. (2000). Eduselling: The role of customer education in selling to corporate clients in the sales industry. *International Journal of Sports Marketing & Sponsorship, 2*(2), 145–158.

Brad Schultz • *University of Mississippi*

Sport Communication

CHAPTER OBJECTIVES

After reading this chapter, you will be able to:

- Describe the relationship between sport, media, and audience as it manifests itself in the communication process.
- Explain how sport organizations struggle to control and manage content from a communications perspective.
- Detail how changes in technology have impacted sport media relations.

KEY TERMS

Access

Agenda-setting

Distribution

Fragmentation

Image

Interactivity

Public relations

> *"You folks (the networks) are paying us a lot of money to put this game on television. If you want us to tee it up at two in the morning, then that's when we'll tee it up."*
>
> —Paul "Bear" Bryant, former Alabama football coach.
>
> As cited in Schultz, B. (2001). *Sports broadcasting* (Woburn, MA: Focal Press), 18.
>
> *"This is a time when consumers want whatever they want wherever they want it on the device they want. It's no longer about just sitting in front of the TV."*
>
> —John Skipper, ESPN President

Introduction

On February 2, 2014, the Seattle Seahawks beat the Denver Broncos, 43-8 in Super Bowl XLVIII. At one point, Seattle led, 36-0, leading many to call the one-sided blowout the worst game in Super Bowl history (Folck, 2014). Yet, the game still attracted the largest audience to ever watch a television show in U.S. history—112.2 million viewers.[1] The live Internet stream of the game attracted an average audience of 528,000 viewers per minute to set another record as the most-viewed live stream of a single event in U.S. history. That so many people would tune into such a bad game tells us a lot about sports media, audiences, and technologies. "Sports makes compelling TV and provides great storytelling for producers in the non-scripted side of the business," said Bob Horowitz, president of Juma Entertainment. "When you have authentic, real competition like the Olympics, it can result in unbelievable numbers. Best of all, sports is TiVo-proof—you can't DVR sports" (Pursell, 2008).

This chapter seeks to more clearly define this relationship from a communications perspective. Sport, media, and audiences have changed drastically in the past hundred years, and will likely continue to change in the future. The changes have affected the nature and methods of the communication process. As technologies continue to be developed, the relationships and methods of communication will likely move in new directions. Certainly students aspiring to eventually work in the sport industry should not only remain abreast of changes in communication, but they should also anticipate future changes and prepare for those eventualities.

Figure 11.1 displays a good way to conceptualize the communications relationship between sports, media, and audiences. In a broad sense, sport athletes and events provide *content* for the media outlets that cover them. Large-scale events, such as the Super Bowl and World Series, as well as small-scale events,

1 By comparison, the Chinese New Year celebration event, broadcast the same weekend by China Central Television, reached a staggering 704 million viewers on television and another 110 million online.

FIGURE 11.1 The Relationship between Sport, Media, and Audiences

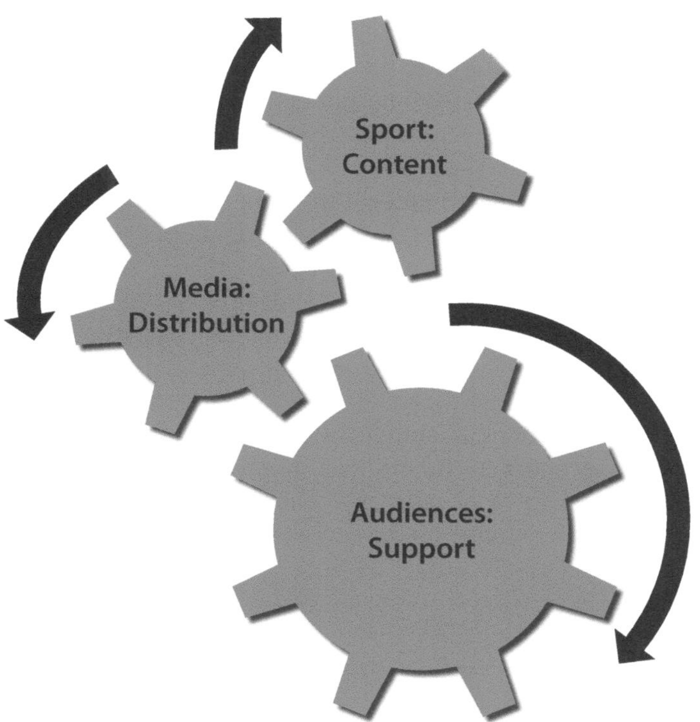

such as a city golf tournament or 5K run, give the sports media content to fill newspaper and magazine pages, and television and radio rundowns. In turn, the media serve as the means of content and information **distribution**; getting those events and the news related to them disseminated to sports audiences. While the means of distribution have greatly changed over the years, with newspapers and other print sources now augmented by various broadcast and Internet outlets, the distribution of sports events to consumers continues to directly *support* sports organizations, teams, and athletes. This support is primarily economic through such things as the purchases of event tickets, merchandise, and ancillary items.

The meshing of gears is a good way to think of sport representation, because sport, media, and audiences are all interrelated and the effect is not simply in one direction. For example, in addition to sports, audiences also support the media through subscriptions, pay-per-view plans, and advertising. In addition to distribution, the media also directly support the sport by paying rights fees to broadcast events. These interrelationships can be examined on a much closer level.

MEDIA

Media and Audience

Media's primary role is to serve as the conduit through which sport content and information passes to the consuming public (Figure 11.2). This has been the media's main function since sports first gained popularity with mass audiences in the late 19th century. The industrialization and urbanization of that time period created audiences large enough to support both sporting organizations and the mass media. The media quickly realized their financial interests were tied to supplying information to a growing sport audience. Fueled by information supplied mainly through newspapers and magazines, interest in sports grew tremendously during this time period. Long-time baseball manager Connie Mack (1950) who was involved in baseball as either a player or manager from 1886 to 1953, saw how much the media meant to the growth of the game. "How did baseball develop from the sandlots to the huge stadiums?" he asked. "From a few hundred spectators to the millions in attendance today? My answer is: through the gigantic force of publicity. The professional sporting world was created and is being kept alive by the services extended the press."

FIGURE 11.2 Information and Image: How Media Affect Audiences

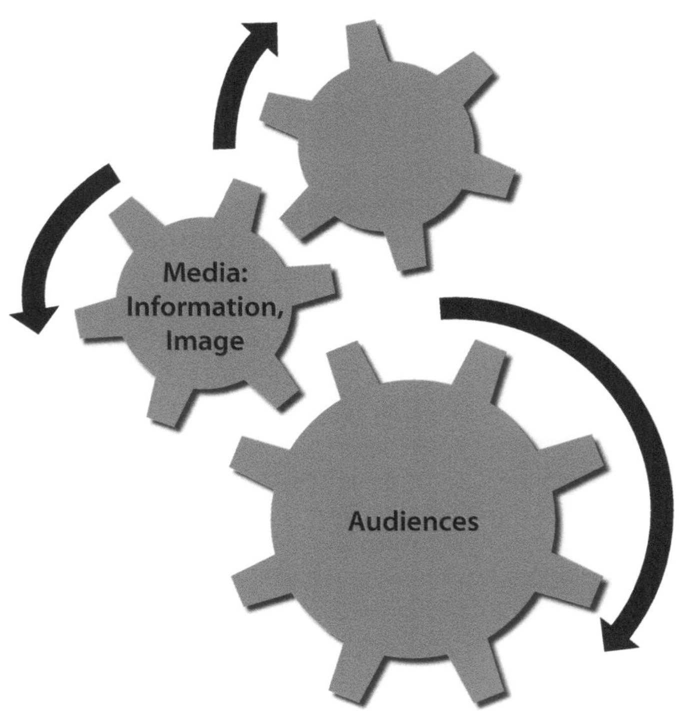

The media role of sports information provider has not changed through the years, although dramatic changes regarding the means of distribution have occurred. Author Mike Sowell (2008) suggested that national sports coverage became possible in 1849 when the telegraph was first used to cover a championship boxing match. Distribution technology has evolved from 19th-century telegraph to 20th-century broadcast (television and radio) and now to more sophisticated 21st-century new media (Internet and digital forms). New distribution methods have created three major changes to the media's information role: (1) There is much more potential information, (2) the information is available instantaneously or nearly instantaneously in most cases, and (3) the information is now accessible almost anywhere. With the advent of the Internet and other broadband technologies, the amount of sport information available to consumers has increased exponentially. The sheer volume of information is almost incalculable, but a look at some of today's most popular sports websites suggests both the size and amount of today's sports audience are growing (Table 11.1).

TABLE 11.1 Growth in Most Popular Sports Media Websites, 2008–2014

Site	2008 Ranking	2014 Ranking	2008 Audience (unique audience in millions)	2014 Audience (unique audience in millions
Yahoo! Sports	1	1	26.0	125.2
ESPN	2	2	22.8	75.5
Fox Sports	3	8*	16	18
CBS Sports	4	5	13.3	28

*BleacherReport moved up to third on the 2014 rankings with 38 million unique visitors.
Sources: Nielsen Online, NetView (September 1, 2008 - September 30, 2008); Alexa Web Traffic Rankings, December 2008; ebizmba, February 2014.

As new media technologies such as mobile television and Google glass continue to grow, so will the amount of sports information available to audiences. Watching a game on mobile television or through live streaming is called second-screen possibilities, and they are becoming much more common. "The standard sports fan move on mobile is, if they're at a child's baseball game or running errands on a weekend, to go their mobile device and check a score," said Clark Pierce of Fox Sports. "What I'm seeing with streaming is that people are doing the same thing, but checking the live game" (Burg, 2014).

These new media technologies have also shrunk the sports-information *news cycle*; that is, the information that is now available to sports audiences is getting to them much more quickly. For the print media the news cycle had typically been about 24 hours, which is how long it took for information to permeate through to most audiences via this distribution channel. The cycle shortened to minutes with the coming of radio and television, and now is only a few seconds due to the availability of the Internet.

This change has had significant consequences for the print media as they have struggled to adapt to the new Internet environment. In the spring of 2013, *Pro Football Weekly*, a magazine that had covered the NFL for 46 years, had assets of $143,000 and liabilities of $8.5 million, and publishers made the difficult decision to cease publication. "We built some truly great stuff that you all seemed to love, but try as we might, we couldn't get enough of you to pay what it cost us to deliver it," said editor Hub Arkush (2013). "There comes a time when there is just no more money to lose, and now we are forced to close the doors." NFL writer Mike Florio (2013) observed, "News and analysis must be delivered in real-time via electronic means, not once per week in a publication that looked and felt more like a newspaper than a magazine."

The sports print media have been quick to transition to the Internet, which given its ability to store large amounts of information and offer consumers the ability to interact with one another is ideally suited for sports coverage. Magazines such as *Sports Illustrated, The Sporting News,* and *ESPN The Magazine* all have an extensive web presence. In 2008, *The Sporting News* debuted a daily digital sports newspaper, what the magazine called "the first step in a reinvention of a title continuously published for 120 years; perhaps the ultimate test of how to take part in the transition to online beyond a website" (Kramer, 2008). As digital subscriptions eventually climbed over 200,000 *TSN* made the difficult decision to go exclusively digital and end its print edition after 126 years. "Having spoken with many of our longtime subscribers, we recognize this is not a popular decision among our most loyal fans," wrote *TSN* President Jeff Price. "Unfortunately, neither our subscriber base nor the current advertising market for print would allow us to operate a profitable print business going forward" (Price & Howard, 2012).

Much of the content is the same as the magazine offers in print, but is provided free on the web. That has raised some concerns about revenue, but the web versions make money from advertising and also offer additional content that requires a subscription. *The Sporting News* originally distributed its digital edition for free, but then began charging a $2.99 subscription price. That's known as building a paywall, and it has met resistance and criticism from audience members accustomed to getting content for free. In some cases, the backlash involves concern for any content being only available for subscription and in other cases, the resistance is to the paywall prices being seen as exorbitant ("Globe and Mail paywall…," 2012).

Though an increase in speed is certainly valuable and appreciated by consumers, it also increases the dangers of publishing rumor, speculation or information that is simply untrue, and in many cases the media has lost credibility. As the news cycle gets shorter there is a tremendous pressure to be "first," and the time to consider whether or not to publish gets shorter. "We're losing the vetting process and a degree of journalistic integrity," said former NFL player and now broadcaster Reggie Rivers. "There's no time to consider or edit anything. A good example is someone who shoots an interview in a locker room. The person behind them may be naked or say something profane, but in the rush to get it posted it may go unnoticed" ("Ahead of the Curve," 2010).

While information is an essential part of the media business, it would be wrong to say that members of the media serve merely as impassive channels of communication. Information does not simply come from the media like water from a faucet; rather, the media also shape the context, form, and tone of that information. Media scholars Maxwell McCombs and Donald Shaw (1972) call this **agenda-setting**—how the media exert a significant influence on public perception through their ability to filter and shape media content. According to McCombs (2002, p. 1), "Not only do people acquire factual information from the news media, readers and viewers also learn how much importance to attach to a topic on the basis of the emphasis placed on it in the news."

In a sports sense, the media present a particular **image** of sporting events and athletes. This image can depend on several factors, including the economic and cultural conditions that exist at the time. For example, the 1920s were a time of great excess and achievement, and athletic heroes such as Babe Ruth, Red Grange, and Jack Dempsey were lauded as heroic figures in the mainstream media. Ruth received perhaps more adulation from the media than any other sports figure, before or since. He was not only the "Babe," but "the Bambino," "the Sultan of Swat," and "the Colossus of Clout." Former teammate Harry Hooper observed of Ruth, "I saw it all from beginning to end, and sometimes I can't believe what I saw: this kid, crude, poorly educated ... gradually transformed into the idol of American youth and a symbol of baseball the world over. I saw a man transformed from a human being into something pretty close to a god" (Connor, 1982, p. 66).

Sportswriters like Grantland Rice, Damon Runyan, and Heywood Broun played key roles in creating the athlete's heroic mystique. "When a sportswriter stops making heroes out of athletes, it's time to get out of the business," Rice once said (Inabinett, 1994, p. ix), and he created plenty of heroes in his 54-year career. He's most often remembered for naming Notre Dame's famous "Four Horsemen" in an article he wrote after the 1924 Notre Dame–Army football game. The story's opening—"Outlined against a blue-gray October sky the Four Horsemen rode again ..."—is one of the most famous lines in sportswriting history.

By contrast, the 1960s was a time of protest and anger that saw the emergence of the "anti-hero"; athletes celebrated for their flaws rather than their heroism. A younger generation of athletes like Joe Namath and Muhammad Ali rejected many of the traditional notions associated with sport, such as morality, clean living, and humility. Author Marty Ralbovsky (1971) noted, "Why, said Ali, can't a black athlete be proud of his blackness and be called what he wishes? Why, said Namath, can't an athlete admit publicly to drinking, smoking (and) making love to beautiful women? Traditionalists answered them by removing them from the mainstream and clouding their accomplishments in controversy" (p. 74).

Sports became a television staple during the 1960s and 1970s, a growth that was further fueled by technological developments. Cable and satellite television dramatically increased the amount of sports content, and also the competition for sports audiences. This ended the dominance of the three major television networks (ABC, NBC, and CBS) in terms of televised sports programming and opened the field to a host of new competitors. Media mogul Ted Turner began broadcasting many of his Atlanta Braves' games on Turner Broadcasting System, which was available to any cable subscriber across the country. Entertainment and Sports Programming Network (ESPN) emerged in the late 1970s and made following sports a 24-hour a day, seven-days-a-week enterprise.

It could be argued that the recent growth of media and competition in the 1990s and 2000s has led to a "celebrity" portrayal of athletes and sports. "This is a tabloid-crazy society," noted longtime CBS sportscaster Jim Nantz. "We love nothing more than a good scandal" (as cited in Schultz, 2005, p. 15). Nowhere was that more evident than the January 2013 story involving Notre Dame football star Manti Te'o. Te'o's story was compelling—he finished second for the Heisman Trophy and led Notre Dame to the national title game, all despite suffering the loss of his grandmother and a girlfriend during the fall. He was portrayed as the shining star of college football on the cover of *Sports Illustrated.*

But shortly after Notre Dame lost in the national championship game in January 2013, the sports website Deadspin published a story claiming that Te'o's deceased girlfriend never existed and the entire story about her was a hoax. The story was further complicated by rumors that Te'o himself may have perpetrated the fraud. Ultimately, a friend of Te'o's named Ronaiah Tuiasosopo admitted to the hoax, but it was Te'o who saw his reputation and his life unravel. Almost overnight he went from football hero to the punch line of a national joke. "I mean, I can't wait till the day I can turn on the TV again or read the sports page without seeing this story about me," Te'o said. "When I went out and around, I could tell people were looking at me. I could hear them whispering and talking about me. And that's when I really started to know how bad this was" (Zeman, 2013). Instead of portraying him as the shining knight of college football, the national media now took a much different view.

The growth of social media demonstrates how the traditional media's ability to exclusively shape and control the nature of sports content has weakened. When long-time Yankees' shortstop Derek Jeter announced his retirement in 2014, he did not take the message through the traditional media. Instead, Jeter announced the news on his personal Facebook page in a 15-paragraph statement that he crafted and controlled. Other media outlets had to report on the announcement secondhand.

Technological developments like personal websites, Twitter accounts, Facebook pages, and blogs have created content outlets for sports athletes, organizations, and even fans. Twitter, while limited in terms of depth, allows athletes and fans to carry on a real-time conversation that bypasses traditional outlets. As can be seen from Table 11.2, both groups are taking advantage of this opportunity.

TABLE 11.2 Athletes with the Most Twitter Followers, 2014

Athlete	Sport	Number of Twitter followers (in millions)	Comment
Cristiano Ronaldo	Soccer	24.3	One of the most recognizable figures in sports, Cristiano Ronaldo, or his PR team, tweets on his page nearly every day, primarily about soccer. Sometimes the Portuguese star announces contests and sweepstakes to win signed memorabilia.
Kaka'	Soccer	17.9	Kaka tweets in Portuguese, English, and Spanish, tweets photos of himself and other soccer stars, and even responds to fans and followers who tweet him.
LeBron James	Basketball	11.6	James has been known to be honest, and at times reckless with his Twitter. His tweets have made news, but recently, James has shown a softer side, posting pictures of his children, whom he is quite proud of.
Ronaldinho Gaucho	Soccer	8.4	If you speak Portuguese, then you should probably follow Ronaldinho on Twitter. If you don't speak the language, you should probably still follow him simply because he is one of the greatest players of his generation.
Shaquille O'Neal	Basketball Announcer	8.0	Now a TNT broadcaster, O'Neal is one of the funniest figures in sports, and even in retirement is capable of saying something hilarious. After all, his bio does read "Very quotatious. I perform random acts of Shaqness."

Source: "Top 10 Twitter Athletes," (2014, February 5). Tweeting-athletes.com. From:http://www.tweeting-athletes.com/TopAthletes.cfm; Comments from: Martin, 2012.

Media and Sports

The media primarily support the sports industry by distributing events and games to large audiences (Figure 11.3). In the early 20th century, sports events and organizations depended mainly on ticket sales for revenue. During that time, newspaper coverage helped increase audience interest, spurring higher ticket sales. When radios became common in the late 1920s and 1930s, baseball owners were worried that broadcasting games live would decrease live attendance by giving away the product for free. Thus, the three Major League Baseball teams in New York agreed to a ban on radio broadcasts until 1938. Later, Major League Baseball, horse racing, and boxing would later make similar ill-fated decisions regarding television in the 1950s.

However, baseball and other sports eventually realized that radio and television broadcasts actually increased interest, ticket sales, and profits as the excitement of the ballpark and arena could quickly be relayed to a large audience. More people became exposed to sports through the mass media and in turn the interest resulted in great attendance. As sports became more popular and more in demand by audiences, sports organizations began charging fees to television and radio stations for the rights to broadcast events. An important legal development was passage of the Sports Broadcasting Act (SBA) of 1961. Until that time, teams

FIGURE 11.3 Rights and Fees: How the Media Affect Sports

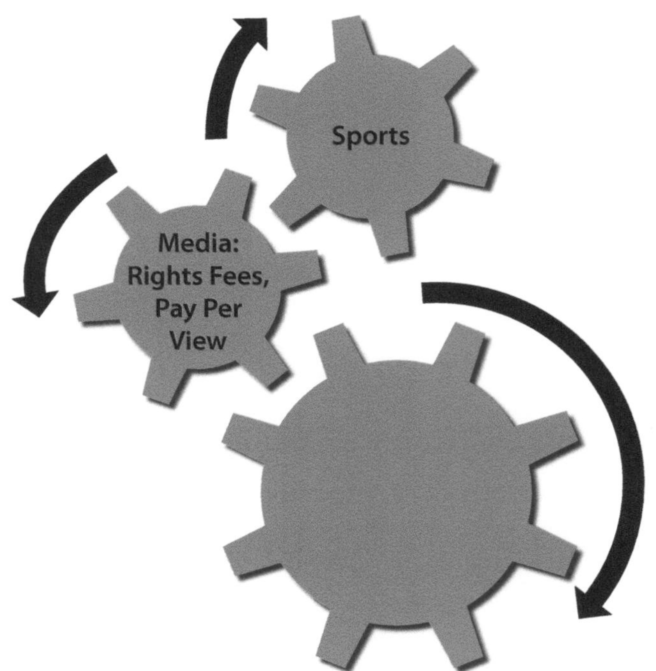

were required by antitrust law to individually negotiate their own television rights deals. The act removed the antitrust restriction and allowed leagues to negotiate as a whole on behalf of their member teams (and distribute the money equally in a revenue-sharing plan). The NFL was the driving force behind passage of the SBA and it immediately saw dramatic increases in television rights fees. Today the NFL has one of the richest rights-fees packages among all sports leagues ($3.7 billion per year). Rights fees for the Olympic Games have also increased dramatically since the 1960s (see Table 11.3).

TABLE 11.3 U.S. Olympic Rights Fees

Games	Site	Network	Rights Fees
1960 Summer	Rome	CBS	$394,000
1984 Summer	Los Angeles	ABC	$225 million
2008 Summer	Beijing	NBC	$894 million
2012 Summer	London	NBC	$1.18 billion
2016 Summer	Rio de Janeiro	NBC	$1.23 billion
2020 Summer	Tokyo	NBC	$1.42 billion
Summer and Winter Games through 2032	TBA	NBC	$7.75 billion

Source: "NBC Retains," 2011; Martzke, 2003.

The media recoup the payment of rights fees via advertising contracts. Larger audiences generate greater interest—and therefore higher payments—from potential advertisers. For example, the Super Bowl typically draws an audience of more than a hundred million viewers (in fact, the five most-watched programs in U.S. television history in terms of total audience are all Super Bowls). The cost of a 30-second Super Bowl commercial has increased from $42,000 in 1967 (Super Bowl I) to around $4 million for the Seattle-Denver Super Bowl in 2014.

But in general, Super Bowls are the exception rather than the rule. Television ratings for sports events have declined sharply in the past 10 years, even for such signature events as the World Series (Sandomir, 2003). Such declines reflect the fact that while televised sports still draws big audiences, television audiences in general have splintered into smaller niche audiences. This **fragmentation** is due largely to new media technologies which give audiences more channels and more consuming options. Thus, the last decade or so has seen the rise of specialized sports channels such as the Golf Channel, Speed TV, and the Tennis Channel (not to mention channels created by the NFL, NBA, NHL, and Major League Baseball), which cater to devoted, but smaller groups of viewers.

The media still pay rights fees to distribute games, but are reluctant to pay enormous sums except for events like the Olympics that can draw massive, diverse audiences. Increasingly, the media are turning to a *pay-per-view* system in which smaller audiences pay directly for the rights to access content. Technologies like digital television, mobile TV, and the Internet make this possible, and the amount of pay-per-view material has increased significantly. NBC's "Triple Cast" Olympic coverage in 1992 was a precursor of today's pay-per-view model. The network offered its usual free coverage of the Barcelona Olympics during prime-time hours, but also gave audiences a chance to purchase additional programming on one of its three sister networks. The plan was largely ridiculed at the time, but today almost all networks and sports leagues offer a similar plan (Payne, 2006). In addition to their free programming offered on television and radio, the NFL ("Sunday Ticket"), NBA ("Full Court), NHL ("Center Ice"), and Major League Baseball ("Extra Innings") all offer pay-per-view content on television and radio. NFL "Sunday Ticket," a program that allows subscribers access to every televised game each Sunday, is probably the most popular of the pay-per-view plans. DirecTV pays the NFL about a billion dollars per year to offer the package, which attracts around 2 million subscribers.

The money DirecTV pays to the NFL is an example of how teams and leagues are creating new revenue opportunities. Several leagues and individual teams are also increasing revenue through the creation of their own networks and Internet sites. When the Big Ten Network began in 2007, many critics wondered how it would fill its ambitious 24/7 programming schedule having to televise only those games the major networks didn't want. Several years later BTN is thriving with a dozen prime-time football games and more than a hundred basketball games scheduled each season. "You can see that the network has become ingrained in the sports television landscape," said Northwestern University's Senior Associate Athletic Director John Mack (Matter, 2010). And other conferences and schools have taken notice. In 2011, the University of Texas, with the largest athletic budget of any school in the country, debuted the Longhorn Network, a joint venture with ESPN that will give Texas $300 million over the course of the 20-year contract. And in 2013, the Southeastern Conference, considered the king of college sports, announced a 20-year partnership with ESPN for creation of an SEC Network that began in August 2014.

SPORTS

Sports and Media

In some instances, the goals of sports organizations and athletes are compatible. Sports and the media are dependent on audiences for revenue; sports provide the content, which the media then distribute. Audiences financially support both

FIGURE 11.4 Control and Access: How Sports Affect the Media

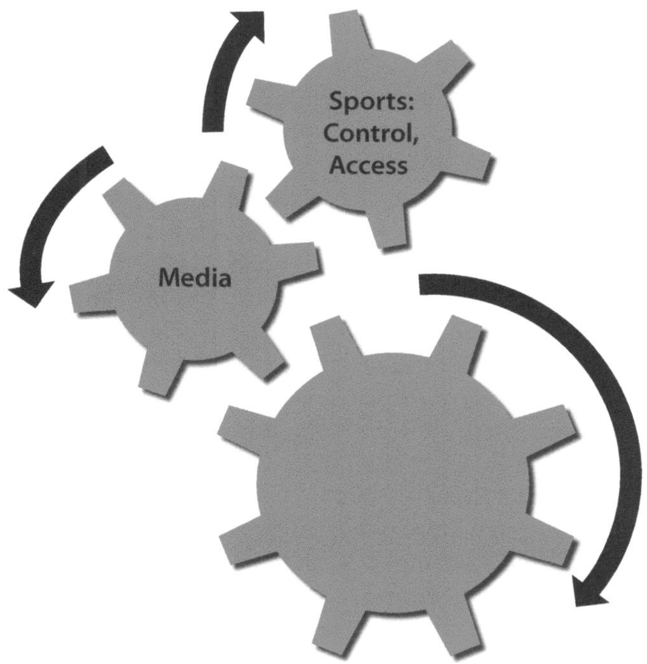

the media and sports entities. But there are times in which the goals of the media clash with the goals of athletes and sports organizations. As noted earlier, today's media often emphasize scandal, investigation, and full disclosure. This is often in direct conflict with athletes and sports organizations, who always want to be portrayed positively. Thus, there is a constant information tug-of-war between sports and the media as both fight to capture the attention of audiences.

Athletes and sports organizations have a major advantage in this struggle: They control the content that the media need. So just as the media try to shape the style and tone of sports content, athletes, teams, and organizations do the same. One of the ways this is accomplished is through **access**, which is the degree to which the sports content providers make themselves available to the media in terms of reporting and coverage (Figure 11.4). Sports figures can usually control and shape the nature of information that gets to the public by determining how much and how often that information is released. Access to practices, games, and interview opportunities is typically controlled by the individual content provider. On the professional level, athletes usually determine for themselves how much access to allow. In some cases, teams or leagues will require access, such as in the case of a Super Bowl or All-Star Game media day. Athletes have been punished for failing to make themselves available for league-mandated media events. But on the whole, athletes determine how much media access they will allow, and some have decided to rarely speak to the media. Duane Thomas, Steve Carlton, and Albert Belle were athletes who refused *all* media access at one point in their careers.

Limited access can create potential problems for the media, which needs content for its audiences. By nature, athletes and coaches are usually suspicious of the media and reluctant to provide any information that might prove to be misinterpreted, damaging, or simply embarrassing. At Super Bowl XLVIII Media Day, Seahawks' running back Marshawn Lynch did not refuse to talk, but his answers were so short as to be almost unusable. For several questions, Lynch simply stared into space and did not respond at all. "I'm just about action," he did say in one of his rare statements. "You say 'hut' and there's action. All the unnecessary talk, it don't do nothing for me" (Myers, 2014). But because the media need content, they keep trying to get coaches and athletes to talk. During Lynch's media appearance, he spoke briefly and then spent the next 50 minutes in bored silence. "Here's the embarrassing part," said one of the reporters covering the event. "The media were lined up five deep in front of Lynch waiting him out" (Myers, 2014).

While Lynch reacted with boredom, other athletes and coaches can react with hostility, as tension can sometimes escalate into open hostility. "Who wouldn't like to yell at a reporter sometimes?" said former NFL quarterback Ryan Leaf (Halverson, 2011). In the course of breaking a story for *Sports Illustrated* in 2009, reporter Selena Roberts flew to Miami to try to get an interview with baseball star Alex Rodriguez about his alleged use of performance-enhancing drugs. After the article was released Rodriguez called Roberts a "stalker" who had tried to break into his home (Koster, 2009). Although Rodriguez later backed off his comments when challenged by Roberts, there have been numerous cases where athletes and the media have clashed, sometimes physically (see Box 11.1). Veteran newspaper and television reporter Bill Plaschke (2000, p. 44) observed, "Athletes are at their most vulnerable when dealing with the media. We're everywhere; and we're not looking to make friends, but front pages. With the proliferation of TV, radio and Internet reporters, pro athletes often need to be rude and pushy just to catch their breaths."

Most sports organizations, and even some athletes, have a system in place to prevent such incidents from happening. On the professional sports level, teams and organizations have a full-time **public relations** staff, which has several responsibilities. One is the production and distribution of information related to the organization and its athletes. This could take the form of a news release (timely or factual information), fact sheet (statistics and related information), quote sheet (direct comments from players, coaches or support personnel), or media guide (a lengthy and detailed compilation of facts, quotes, pictures and historical information). For some staff members their sole responsibility is creating and distributing this information to the media. The

BOX 11.1

Major Meltdowns: Notable Athlete-Media Confrontations

Date	Incident	Result
November 19, 1977	Enraged after his Buckeyes fumbled against arch-rival Michigan, Ohio State coach Woody Hayes punched an ABC sideline cameraman.	The Big 10 put Hayes on probation for this incident, but he was ultimately done in when he physically attacked a Clemson player near the end of the 1978 Gator Bowl. Ohio State fired the volatile coach immediately after the game.
April 26, 1993	Kansas City Royals manager Hal McRae trashed his entire office, throwing things off of his desk including a phone, which cut a reporter, and yelling profanities at reporters. McRae was angry at the questions reporters asked him after a 5-3 loss to Detroit.	McRae was not officially punished, but managed the Royals only one more season.
March 17, 1995	Indiana University basketball coach Bob Knight launched into a lengthy diatribe against an NCAA media liaison at a post-game news conference. The liaison had earlier suggested to the media that Knight would not be attending the session.	It is hard to pick just one incident from Knight's long career of media intimidation. For this one, the NCAA reprimanded Knight and fined the university $30,000.
September 21, 1998	After a particularly bad game against the Chiefs, Chargers' rookie quarterback Ryan Leaf yelled at a photographer for standing too close to his locker. When Jay Posner of the *San Diego Union-Tribune* wrote about the incident, Leaf at first denied it, and then confronted Posner in the locker room the following day, shouting obscenities and threatening a physical confrontation.	If only this were the worst thing to happen to Leaf in his career. The former first-round draft pick spent four undistinguished years with four different teams before leaving the NFL in 2001. He is currently serving a seven-year prison term for a variety of charges, including burglary, theft, and drug possession.
June 30, 2005	As he walked on the field for a practice, Texas Rangers pitcher Kenny Rogers pushed KTVT photographer Larry Rodriguez, threw his camera to the ground and kicked it. Rodriguez was taken to a hospital.	Major League Baseball fined Rogers $50,000 and suspended him for 20 games.
September 22, 2007	Oklahoma State football coach Mike Gundy went on a tirade at a post-game press conference. He verbally attacked newspaper columnist Jenni Carlson for a story she had written about one of Gundy's players.	Gundy was not officially censured, but his comments—including "I'm a man! I'm 40!" –became an instant Internet classic. The YouTube version of the incident has now received more than 3 million views.
March 24, 2010	University of Florida football coach Urban Meyer accosted *Orlando Sentinel* reporter Jeremy Fowler on the practice field, poking a finger at Fowler and threatening to deny him and the newspaper access. Meyer was upset about a quote Fowler printed that was mildly critical of quarterback Tim Tebow. "If that was my son," Meyer lectured Fowler, "we'd be going at it right now."	Meyer personally apologized to Fowler in a 20-minute meeting the two had. The lesson?—don't criticize Tim Tebow, at least among Florida coaches and fans.

Sources: *Sports Illustrated*, NBC, ESPN.

Courtesy of Harrelson Photography.

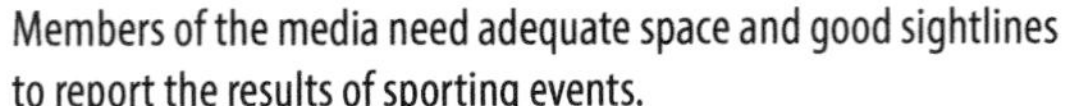

Members of the media need adequate space and good sightlines to report the results of sporting events.

Photo Courtesy Mark Nagel

Sufficient space outside the locker room is often needed for post-game interviews.

other main responsibility of the public relations staff concerns media access and activity. This mainly includes credentialing media members to cover games and scheduling interview access with players and coaches. Although public relations staff members try to accommodate the media as much as possible, access is ultimately decided by the individual athlete.

On the college sports level the public relations functions are usually handled by a sports information department, headed by a *sports information director* (SID). The SID is responsible for all communication with the media and the public, and access is usually much more controlled than at the professional level. Because college athletes have class and outside responsibilities and do not get paid to play, SIDs work with coaches to limit their media access. Most schools have a system in place where access to players and coaches is allowed only through the SID or someone else in the sports information department. In some cases, coaches and SIDs completely prohibit access to certain athletes, most typically for younger players. These restrictions can be frustrating for media members when the story has the potential to put a player or coach in a negative light and in such instances, the media often try to circumvent official channels to get the information they need. A famous example occurred in 2006 and 2007 during coverage of an alleged rape involving members of the Duke University lacrosse team. Duke naturally shut down access to the players and coaches involved, leaving the media to fend for themselves. "We were hampered early on by the unwillingness of the players … to speak with our reporters," said Melanie Sill, at the time the executive editor at the *Raleigh* (NC) *News & Observer*. Responding to charges that media coverage of the case was biased against the players, Sill noted, "Our overall reporting was solid and on point, however ...it intensified as we ran into obstacles. Nonetheless, we should have stated more emphatically that we had not been able to get their side of things" (Ham, 2007, ¶5-7).

The sports information department is organized much like a professional public relations department, with different staff members in charge of different aspects of media relations. For example, in 2008 the University of Texas in Austin listed 25 full-time members in its Communications/Media Relations department. The size of the sports information department depends on the size of the school. A large school like the University of Texas has dozens of staff members, while a smaller Division-II or Division-III school might have only one or two full-time people (Table 11.4).

The size and scope of the sports information department depends on the sizeof the school and its athletic budget. When the first edition of this book came out, it profiled the sizes of the communications specialists at three different schools—the University of Texas, Vanderbilt, and Ohio Northern. We wanted to show you how those schools compare today. Notice how the bigger schools keep adding staff to handle the increasing communications duties. This includes someone to oversee social media, particularly as it regards student-athlete use.

Regardless of size, much of the emphasis in today's sports information departments is shifting from printed to digital material. Traditionally, these departments would send out reams of printed press released each week, and also produce a bulky printed media guide. Now, much of this information is sent by electronic mail or incorporated into the school's athletic web site.

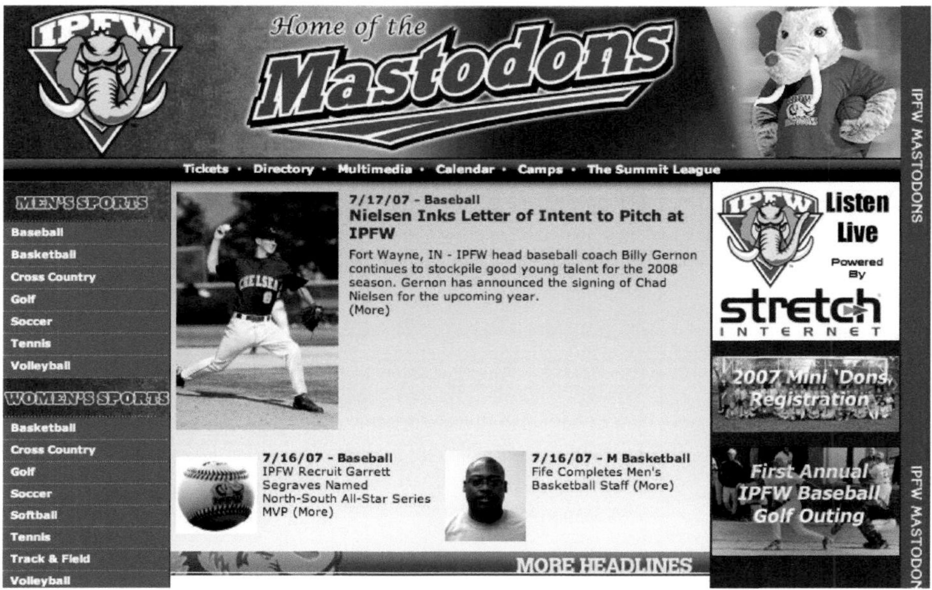

A "typical" college athletic department's web page. Reprinted by permission of IPFW.

TABLE 11.4 University and College Sports Information Departments

School	Enrollment	Full-time Communications Employees—2008	Full-time Communications Employees—2014
University of Texas (Austin)	52,076	22	28 Senior Associate Athletics Director for Communications Publications Supervisor Communications Coordinator Senior Associate Athletics Director for Communications Associate Athletics Director for Media Relations (Football) Assistant Athletics Director for Media Relations (Men's Basketball) Special Assistant to Football Coach for Communications Associate Media Relations Director (Football) Associate Media Relations Director (Volleyball, Men's/Women's Golf) Associate Media Relations Director (Web Video Coordinator) Assistant Media Relations Director (Rowing, Men's/Women's Swimming and Diving, Women's Tennis) Assistant Media Relations Director Assistant Media Relations Director (Women's Basketball, Men's Tennis) Assistant Media Relations Director (Soccer) Assistant Media Relations Director (Baseball, Football) Assistant Media Relations Director (Football/Clyde Littlefield Texas Relays, Track and Field/Cross Country) Assistant Media Relations Director (Director of Creative Services/ Football) Assistant Media Relations Director (Videographer/Editor) Assistant Media Relations Director (Web Video Supervisor) Assistant Media Relations Director (Videographer/Editor) Assistant Communications Manager Senior Administrative Associate Assistant Athletics Director for New Media Senior Web Manager Web Manager Web Manager Photographer Photographer

Vanderbilt University	12,795	8	10 Director of Communications Associate Director (Internal Operations) Associate Director (Digital Strategies) Assistant Director (Football) Assistant Director (Men's Basketball, Golf) Assistant Director (Baseball, Football) Assistant Director (Women's Basketball, Cross Country, Track & Field) Interim Editor, Commodore Nation Social Media Coordinator Administrative Assistant
Ohio Northern University	3,619	2	2 Sports Information Director Assistant Sports Information Director

Sources: University of Texas; Vanderbilt University; Ohio Northern University.

For athletes who are high-school age and younger, there is really no one that controls access other than a coach or parent. Few high schools have anything like a public relations staff or a sports information director, and as a result, media access is often arbitrary. Traditionally, coaches and parents have kept a fairly tight rein on teenage athletes, but technology is changing this dynamic. On the athlete side, many high-school stars now promote themselves through websites, blogs, and social media. They find these tools helpful for self-promotion and as a way of attracting the attention of interested college coaches.

Media members, fans, and college recruiters also use these methods to bypass the high-school coach and administrators and talk directly with the athletes. The most obvious example is the recruiting process, especially for football. "National signing day," the first date at which high-school athletes can officially sign letters of intent to play college football, falls each year on the first Wednesday of February, and it has become a fierce competition not only to sign recruits, but for media members seeking to get the best and latest information. Reporters will monitor the social media of athletes, especially Twitter, for any breaking news about a college decision. College coaches use Twitter as a recruiting tool and send messages right to the athlete, although the NCAA has set a limit on how much social media contact a coach may have. The successful coaches, like Les Miles at LSU, use social media as a fundamental part of the recruiting process. "Coach Miles understands that social media gives him the forum to promote his program to tens of thousands of people at any given time," LSU athletic department spokesman Michael Bonnette said. "He's careful and mindful of the rules when it comes to using social media as a recruiting tool, but he's savvy enough to understand the impact that it can have" (Megargee, 2014).

At any level—high school, college, or professional—access becomes extremely limited and almost nonexistent during a crisis situation. A crisis situation is any type of bad news that could damage the reputation of the athlete, team, or organization. Typically, crisis situations occur away from the playing field. Examples might include a baseball player being accused of using steroids or a football player being arrested for drunk driving. During a crisis situation, media access to the involved athlete, coach, or administration is likely to be next to zero. In many cases, information will be limited to an official statement released by the player or organization or perhaps to a statement from a representative such as a lawyer. Former sports broadcaster and now college educator Charlie Lambert observed, "Journalists who cover top-level sport are facing a real challenge. Teams and organizations are so powerful and so wealthy that they want to control everything that is said or written about them" ("Journalism leaders," 2008, ¶5).

Resistance during a crisis will not mean that the media will give up trying to get access to pertinent involved officials. Certainly, media members will continue to look for access and sources who will adequately help them find and report the needed information. In their attempt to report on the Bay Area Lab Cooperative (BALCO) steroids scandal, newspaper reporters Mark Fainaru-Wada and Lance Williams were stonewalled through official sources. "Going in, we were completely blind," said Fainaru-Wada. "No one had heard of BALCO. It was a matter of chasing as much as you could" ("Mark Fainaru-Wada," 2004, ¶ 4). In their three-year investigation, the reporters eventually turned to anonymous sources to uncover the story. They defied a U.S. district court judge by refusing to identify their sources, and although they were sentenced in September 2006 to 18 months in prison, they never served a day in prison. In his statement before the court, Fainaru-Wada said, "Throughout the BALCO affair, critics have questioned the motives of our reporting, suggesting that it has been little more than a witch hunt or an effort to profit off the big names who have been drawn into the scandal. Supporters have portrayed us as champions in the global fight against performance-enhancing drugs. For us, however, BALCO has always been an earnest and sincere effort to present the truth" ("Fainaru-Wada's statement" 2006, p. A14). In 2004, Fainaru-Wada and Williams won an Investigative Reporters and Editors award and the George Polk Award (Box 11.2).

Given the inherent tension between reporters trying to discover information and athletes and organizations trying to control it, some communications

BOX 11.2

The Bay Area Lab Cooperative (BALCO), under the direction of founder and owner Victor Conte, marketed performance-enhancing drugs to several prominent athletes, most notably in baseball and track and field. Conte eventually pleaded guilty to providing steroids and laundering money in 2005. The work of investigative reporters Mark Fainaru-Wada and Lance Williams was instrumental in developing the BALCO investigation.

BALCO Investigation Timeline

September 3, 2003:	Local and federal authorities raid BALCO offices.
Dec. 2-3, 2004:	The *San Francisco Chronicle* publishes stories containing grand jury testimony given by Jason Giambi and Barry Bonds as part of the BALCO investigation. In it, Giambi admits to steroid use while Bonds says he may have unknowingly taken steroids.
March 23, 2006:	Fainaru-Wada and Williams publish *Game of Shadows*, a best-selling book that highlighted details of their BALCO investigation.
May 5, 2006:	Fainaru-Wada and Williams are subpoenaed to testify before a federal grand jury about how they obtained the testimony of Bonds, Giambi, and other athletes.
Sept. 21, 2006:	Judge Jeffrey White tells *San Francisco Chronicle* reporters Fainaru-Wada and Williams he will order them jailed for up to 18 months if they do not comply with his order to reveal their sources.
February 14, 2007:	The identity of the source of the illegally leaked grand jury testimony is revealed as Troy Ellerman, one of the BALCO defense attorneys. Federal authorities agree to drop their efforts to send Fainaru-Wada and Williams to prison.

Source: Balco investigation timeline, 2007.

strategies have evolved. The oldest and most traditional strategy is to *stonewall*, or simply refuse to give the media any comment or information. When a scandal erupted at the University of North Carolina in 2013—that its athletes were funneled to bogus classes in order to keep them academically eligible—the school's original reaction was along three lines: "1) There's nothing to see here. Everybody move along. 2) This situation was confined to two bad apples in the

African and Afro-American Studies Department who have since departed and 3) Everybody does it. Why are you picking on us?" (Barnett, 2014).

However, it is becoming increasing difficult to control information in the age of digital communication and Internet access. Information can leak from a variety of sources, including blogs, tweets, and Internet bulletin boards. Stonewalling allows others to manipulate and shape public perception since there is no comment from the involved parties. It further suggests that those involved have "something to hide" by not talking to the media. In the North Carolina case, other media picked up the story and made it front page news. The faculty member who originally reported the problem kept the story in the public discussion, even in the face of severe rebuke from her own administration.

That finally convinced UNC officials to change direction and take up the strategy of *full disclosure*. Many believe that freely giving information to the media can prevent the problems associated with stonewalling and bad publicity. In addition, an athlete or coach who is cooperative usually enjoys better media treatment and has a better public image. New UNC chancellor Carol Folt addressed university trustees and said that the school needed to "fully acknowledge and accept lessons of our past" ("Chancellor Folt," 2014). It was a small step that many thought needed to go further. "While it's fine for Folt to want the university to put a multi-year crisis of its own making behind it," editorialized one Carolina newspaper, "that will not happen without candor and full disclosure of pertinent facts, no matter how embarrassing" ("Chancellor Folt," 2014).

Most athletes, coaches, and organizations use a strategy somewhere in between stonewalling and full disclosure. The strategy depends on several factors, including the severity of the incident and the nature of athlete or organization involved. But all those involved are working with one goal in mind—to protect the image and public reputation of those at the center of the controversy.

A more recent communications strategy that has emerged is used by athletes and organizations in both crisis and non-crisis situations. New developments in media technology have given athletes and organizations much more power and control over the messages they send to audiences. Primarily, the ease and **interactivity** of the Internet makes it possible for them to bypass the mainstream media and take their messages directly to sports audiences. While several athletes create their own blogs, many more have turned to Twitter, perhaps because of its ease, compatibility with cell phones, and mobility.

Social media allow the athlete to deliver his or her message without media interference, and thus take much greater control in attempting to shape public opinion. European soccer player Stuart Holden, with more than 400,000 Twitter followers, "uses his Twitter page to present entertaining thoughts on everything from soccer, bros, and even underpants. Of course, he also poses deep philosophical questions to his followers like he did in this June 16 tweet: is it humanly possible to eat a single grape and be done?" (Martin, 2012).

There are obvious drawbacks to teams and athletes getting involved in social media. With so much material available, there is a danger that the message will simply get lost in cyberspace. Studies suggest that most people who use social media do it for personal reasons and create material that is personal and subjective, but not necessarily truthful. As a result, most audiences take blogging and Tweeting for what they are: opinions published to push a certain agenda. To be done well, social media require a lot of time and constant updating, especially for Twitter

The biggest problem may be the unfiltered nature of the medium, and several athletes have run into trouble. Former NBA player Charlie Villanueva was fined for tweeting during halftime of a game. Other athletes have learned that instantly posting material—especially when it's controversial or critical—can force them to apologize and/or delete the offending material. New England Patriots' player Rob Gronkowski found this out in 2011 when he tweeted pictures of himself shirtless with porn star BiBi Jones. He soon apologized, but the pictures are still out there in cyberspace. "If Gronkowski is guilty of anything it's trying to increase his Twitter profile," opined CBS Sports. "And we're pretty sure he did that" (Wilson, 2011).

Sports and Audiences

The relationship between sport and audiences is fairly straightforward and does not require a great deal of elaboration. Across any media platform, the primary benefit sport provides to audiences is attractive and highly popular content (Figure 11.5). One could make it a chicken-and-egg argument: Is there so much sport content in the media because it is popular with audiences or is it popular with audiences because there is so much of it in the media? The likely answer is that sport has a primary place in U.S. culture and its significance is reflected in the high demand for sport content across various media outlets. Author James Michener (1976, p. 355) observed that "one of the happiest relationships in American society is between sports and the media."

Historically, the demand for sports content has been met through a combination of newspapers, magazines, radio, and television. Television is ideally suited because of its ability to present the live drama of sports to large audiences. In fact, the top five television shows in U.S. history, at least in terms of total audience, are now all Super Bowls.[2]

New developments in media technology are creating new distribution systems and dramatically increasing both the total amount of mediated sport content and the demand for it. Broadband technology now allows audiences to access sport content, including video and live game action, directly through a computer via Internet access. The two biggest areas of growth seem to be

2 In terms of television share, which measures how a show does in competition with what's also airing at that time, some shows, including the final episode of *M*A*S*H*, do rank higher.

FIGURE 11.5 Popularity: How Sports Affect Audiences

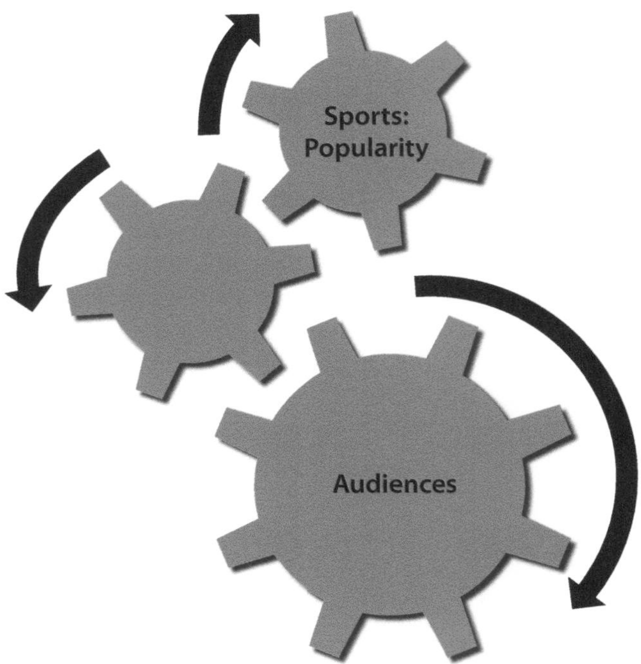

mobile phones and live streaming. A study conducted at the time of the London Olympics in 2012 suggested that online viewing of sports was as popular as traditional television, especially among younger viewers. More than half of consumers (58%) said they planned to watch part of the Olympics online, while another 46% of the 18-26 age group said that "smartphones and tablets have transformed their sport viewing" ("The revolution," 2012).

Sports teams and leagues are taking advantage of these new opportunities by creating their own websites, networks, and pay-per-view packages, all of which potentially increase their revenues. The NFL's Sunday Ticket package enables satellite subscribers to access every televised game each Sunday, and similar services exist for professional baseball, basketball, and hockey. Content providers have learned that audiences are willing to pay hefty subscription fees (in the case of Sunday Ticket, around $250 for the full season of games) for the rights to access this material. "[All of this] builds stronger fan bases among more people who will watch more," says Tennis Channel CEO Ken Solomon. "The more you see, the more you want to see — which is why sports will continue to get stronger and stronger" (Miller, 2008, ¶4).

AUDIENCE

Audience and Media

Traditionally, the audience has been a passive consumer of sport's content. Athletes and sport organizations created the content, the media distributed it, and finally audiences watched, read, or listened to it. Other than niches like sports talk radio, most sport communication was a one-way communication process in which the audience had little or no input other than the decision to consume. This relationship has changed drastically in the past 20 years, due mainly to advances in media technology. This new technology has significantly empowered audiences who now have more consumption options, and have greater input into how the content is presented (Figure 11.6).

Much of this new power comes from developments in broadband technologies, such as the Internet, digital television and radio, and satellite delivery. Sports fans now have access to much more information and can get it almost instantaneously, which puts pressure on the content providers to have more content choices. The number of channel options has increased

FIGURE 11.6 Empowerment: How the Media Affect Audiences

tremendously and much of that space has been used to meet the increasing demand for sports content. Audiences can now customize their consumption habits by picking and choosing from a variety of sports content offerings.

Perhaps the greatest advances are occurring on the Internet, where audiences not only have greater access, but now also have the opportunity to create and distribute their own sports content. Message boards, community fan forums, and blogs allow audiences much greater control over what content they choose to consume and how they consume it. In 2007, four anonymous fans decided they weren't getting the kind of sports coverage they wanted on the Internet, so they decided to start their own company to write and distribute content. Thus, Bleacher Report began as:

- An amplified outlet for writers whose unique voices were routinely drowned out by cookie-cutter analysts and celebrity "experts."
- A localized network for readers whose favorite teams were routinely undercovered by national wire services and mainstream news corporations.
- A civilized community for commenters whose intelligent debates were routinely overrun by message-board blowhards and mean-spirited trolls ("Company overview," 2014).

By reaching out to similar disaffected fans, writers and contributors, Bleacher Report became one of the most popular sports sites on the Internet, and in 2012 was acquired by Turner Broadcasting for a reported $200 million.

It's sometimes tempting to dismiss such efforts as the opinions or ravings of a few rabid fans, but increasingly such audience-generated content is directly competing with and impacting the traditional sports content providers. The website Deadspin has pushed several stories into the mainstream sports discussion, including Brett Favre's alleged sexual misconduct with a journalist, and most famously, the hoax surrounding Notre Dame linebacker Manti Te'o. The story "was further proof that a website, once derided as little more than a repository for juvenile jokes and throwing spitballs at the mainstream press, had become a permanent presence in the sports mediasphere" (Freedlander, 2013).

The Manti Te'o episode and other similar situations have direct consequences on the traditional sports-media-audience relationship, particularly in terms of how the media must now adjust to new competition. "I would watch ESPN and it didn't appeal to me," said Jack Dickey, who wrote the Te'o story as a senior at Columbia Univeristy, "and I didn't understand to whom it would appeal" (Freedlander, 2013). ESPN is still the undisputed leader in providing sports content and commentary, but a new breed of Internet journalists—young, hip, and unafraid—are certainly challenging that authority.

Traditional sports journalists have reacted with a combination of disgust, anger, and derision, but there's no doubt this new breed has changed the landscape. "I go on [the Internet] every day," says Steve Irvine of the *Birmingham News*, "but mainly for the humor. They're clowns, basically, but you get a pulse on what the fans think. Everyone on this beat is looking at them, though" ("Internet allegation," 2003, ¶8). Adds Mike Fish, a senior writer for *Sports Illustrated*'s website, "They make our jobs harder because there's so much stuff out there [and] we have to do a massive amount of screening. There's a lot of vicious, ugly stuff" ("Internet allegation," 2003, ¶6).

More media and more attention also mean that sports athletes, teams and organizations lose some ability to control their content and image. It is extremely difficult for athletes to escape the spotlight; the camera is always on, mainly because since most cell phones now have cameras, aspiring investigative sport reporters can not only blog about their breaking news but also can easily provide digital photos. Just as Manti Te'o was caught in a difficult and unintended situation, other athletes and coaches must now be aware that anything they say or do can be caught on camera and put into the public domain. In 2014, NBA superstar Kevin Durant was embarrassed when a photo of him smoking hookah showed up on his Twitter page. Durant quickly deleted the image and issued a statement saying that his cell phone had been hacked. Exactly who took the photo and how it got to Durant's account remained a mystery, but Durant's clean-cut image took a bit of a blow.

There is a big debate in journalism today about this audience-generated content and whether is qualifies as "real" journalism. In some cases, the people who write and distribute this content ignore many of the traditional journalistic values such as checking facts and citing sources, and do not even consider themselves journalists. However, there is no debate about its impact on today's sports media. Sites like Deadspin and Bleacher Report are both extremely popular and financially successful. Even mom-and-pop sites can carve out their own unique space in sports cyberspace, if they have enough time and dedication. Many of them, especially at the youth and high-school levels, serve niche audiences that otherwise would not get covered by traditional media.

Conclusion

The basic framework that athletes, teams, and organizations provide content and related information for the media to distribute to interested audiences, who financially support both entities, certainly still exists. However, there are important changes taking place within that basic framework that will have consequences for the future of the interrelationship. These changes raise several questions, the answers to which might significantly alter the accepted communication model involving sports, media, and audiences.

**What role will technology play in the future?* Emerging technologies have already influenced the sports-media-audience relationship. As technology gets more sophisticated how will it affect communication? With a few exceptions, the mass audience of yesterday has evolved into the smaller, niche audiences of today. Communication is more targeted and more specific, meaning that audience *demographics* are now just as important as sheer audience size. Will future technological advances make audiences even smaller? In other words, will we soon be seeing such things as an ESPN channel dedicated specifically to 18- to 24-year-old male outdoorsmen who like to hunt deer with a crossbow? The sports information of the future might be tailored to a specific individual and delivered to that person via cell phone or other similar device. Technology also promises to continue increasing the amount of information available and the speed at which it is delivered. Sports organizations and the media will have to make sure they are technologically up to date and able to satisfy the growing demand for sports information.

**Where will audience-created content lead?* The hot trend now is social media message and anything else that lets the audience participate in the sports communication process. Athletes, teams, leagues, and the media have been quick to pick up on the trend and incorporate it into their communication strategies. In fact, it is almost impossible today to find an outlet that does not let the audience participate through such methods as fan contests, message boards, trivia games, and the like. What will be the next new developments in this area? Now that audiences have both the means of creating and distributing content, will that seriously threaten the traditional distribution function of the media? Will the media respond by incorporating more audience content?

**How will economics affect all this?* Obviously, all sports communication takes place within a larger economic context that makes all such communication possible. The media are able to distribute and shape sports content and information only to the extent that they can do so profitably. In a media era where there is increasing emphasis on the bottom line, some sports content and communication could be altered, reduced, or simply eliminated. Several local television stations, including those in Wichita, Pittsburgh, and Albany, have made major changes to the sports segments within their newscasts. WTEN in Albany, New York, did away with the sports anchor and its traditional sports content. "The traditional sportscast features highlights and scoreboards from national teams that most viewers just don't care about, and those who do already know if their team won," said news director Rob Puglisi. "In the days before the Internet, before ESPN, people had to rely on their local TV sportscast for these national scores and highlights. It's just not the case anymore" (McGuire, 2005, ¶13). This might be another reason that tweeting, websites, and audience-generated content are becoming increasingly popular. Such content is relatively inexpensive to produce and distribute, which makes it attractive for media outlets.

The basic economic model of the sport communication system is also changing. Advertising to mass audiences through print and broadcast sources has been the main economic engine for decades, but with the breakup of the mass audience into niche audiences there are questions as to whether advertising can continue to sustain the established system. Increasingly, media outlets and content providers are turning to subscriptions (such as with the NFL's Sunday Ticket) and pay-per-use plans. Advertising on the Internet is also growing and may one day exceed advertisement levels for television and newspapers, especially as technology opens up more opportunities like mobile television. If the economic system of the future changes drastically it will have a corresponding effect on the sports communication process.

* *Will the delicate balance of the sport communication process tip in a certain direction*? This is the big question—will technology, economics, or some other factor cause one group to dominate the other among sports, the media, and audiences? Technology has empowered audience members and taken away a certain degree of power from the media. However, it is highly unlikely that consumer-driven content could one day ever completely replace the distribution function of the traditional media. Although much of today's online content is produced by volunteers, numerous analysts doubt they could fill the information gap that would occur if traditional media organizations disappeared.

It is more likely that the basic communication relationship between sports, media, and audiences will stay intact, but undergo some retooling. After all, athletes, teams, and organizations still own what drives the entire process—content and information. That fact is inescapable, no matter what the media and audiences do. Despite trends toward audience participation, the media are still the most efficient system of distributing that content and the communication related to it. The media and sports are still dependent on audiences for feedback and support. As long as those pillars remain in place, one group or another may become more powerful for a time, but the traditional relationship between sports, media and audiences will continue long into the 21st century.

chapter 11
Interviews

Interview 11.1

Cassandra Zebisch
Senior Manager of
Communications
AEG

Q: Could you briefly describe your career path from undergraduate student to your current position?

A: My first internship when I started at USF was as a communications intern for AEG in 2007, so I could gain experience for a full-time paid internship with the Angels. After a semester with AEG, I was hired as the operations intern for the Angels in 2008. Once the season ended with the Angels, I was hired back full time as a Communications Coordinator at AEG, filling a position that had been vacant for a year. I currently serve as the Senior Manager of Communications for AEG.

Q: What have been the biggest challenges you have encountered during your career?

A: The biggest challenges have been juggling so many different projects at the same time, but this is also my favorite part of my job. At AEG, we are constantly working on new projects, some planned and some unexpected, so we are constantly working in a very high-paced environment, so it is important for me to stay on top of all of my projects at all times to keep everything in order.

Q: In May 2012, the STAPLES Center had the Lakers, Clippers, and Kings in the playoffs at the same time and the Tour de California finishing in front of the building. Over a short period of time, the venue had multiple events on the same day. How did you keep yourself and your staff motivated during such a hectic time? What did you learn from that experience?

A: STAPLES Center hosted six playoff games in four days, while more than 250,000 sports fans descended upon Downtown Los Angeles and L.A. LIVE, on top of L.A. LIVE hosting the final stage of the Amgen Tour of California. While this was the busiest weekend ever for the campus and arena, we wanted to make it fun and enjoyable for all staff and wanted to remind them how much they were appreciated. During the very little down time during event conversions, we filmed a music video with the staff to build camaraderie and give the staff their time to shine. We created a music video for "Call Me Maybe" and it currently has more than 700K views (https://www.youtube.com/watch?v=RLraLnaXEI8).

Q: Are there specific skills sport-management students should look to develop while still in school?

A: I think many skills that are needed to thrive in the sport management business are skills needed to thrive in any business; it's a given that one should be knowledgeable in the sports industry, but students should also research the business side of it as well. Who are the executives that are running these sports teams and management companies? How did they get their start? What types of people do sports teams/companies like to hire? Building contacts, relationships and networking are skills that begin in school, but should continue your entire career.

Q: What specific classes would you recommend students take to best position themselves for a sport-industry job?

A: I think a well-rounded sport management program should provide all of the necessary classes that are needed to succeed in the sports industry. This way, students are able to see what they are interested in and pursue internships or voluntary positions to further gain experience in that area.

Q: What publications do you regularly read to stay apprised of sport-business events?

A: *SportsBusiness Journal, Venues Today Magazine,* and *Los Angeles Business Journal,* but I also read *Pollstar, Billboard, Variety,* and *The Hollywood Reporter* to keep up on the entertainment industry as a whole. It is very important to be knowledgeable across all entertainment platforms and not just sports. It provides an advantage to know what is happening in pop culture as well.

Q: Would you recommend students pursue graduate school? If so, when should they pursue a graduate degree and what area of study would you recommend?

A: I get asked this by many of my interns and I always say that too much education is never a bad thing. As a student athlete in undergrad, I wasn't able to participate in internships programs due to my busy training schedule, so I felt that I still had a lot to learn and still wanted to get my foot in the door with a lot of companies that I wasn't able to during my first four years of college. As a graduate student, I was finally able to explore careers that always intrigued me but I wasn't able to be part of. It gave me time to see what I did and didn't like and further my education while gaining real-work experience. The sports industry is highly competitive, so anything that provides a leg up on the competition and sets you apart from others is always a benefit.

Interview 11.2

Leland Barrow
Associate Sports
Communications Director
University of Georgia
Athletics

Q: Could you briefly describe your career path from undergraduate student to your current position?

A: I received my undergraduate degree in journalism, with a focus on newspapers, from the University of Georgia. With full intentions of becoming a legendary sports writer, I took a sports reporter position with a small newspaper in middle Georgia within a month of graduation in 2001. I wrote a WIDE variety of stories at the newspaper for two years (and mostly had a great time doing it other than getting the minuscule paycheck and spending every Friday night covering high school sports) until deciding I would be more marketable and have a bigger variety of jobs to choose from if I earned a master's degree in sport management. I was accepted into Georgia State University's program and completed my degree. I was then offered an internship in the University of Georgia's Sports Communications Department and after a year, I was hired to fill an open position. My position came about because of a strong network I had developed and because of lucky timing. I am one of the very few in my department who did not work in a Sports Communications department during my undergrad years. There was a steep learning curb at first but I think I have gotten over the hump during my nine years.

Q: What have been the biggest challenges you have encountered during your career?

A: College athletics presents a variety of challenges and most of them I have been able to figure out or overcome by being able to communicate well with other people. The ability to write and speak well is invaluable, especially when much of my job involves multitasking in a high-pressure environment. In sports communications, you have to love, and I mean love, what you do. The time-intensive nature of our jobs sometimes runs head-on with the time you want to spend with your family and free time for yourself. I feel like I get better and better dealing with time management each year, but it helps to have an understanding boss who realizes that there has to be some balance to prevent burnout. In sports, the paycheck can also be a challenge, since most weeks, especially during a team's season, will require 60+ hours of work. Though there is no such thing as "overtime" in this job, it is something that I thoroughly enjoy and I know that being happy and excited about my job each day outweighs the negatives. Now with two kids, I am in a constant state of trying to incorporate the whole family into my "non-traditional" work hours while also doing my job up to the level I expect. I always try to keep my family as my top priority.

Q: Can you identify what you consider to be the "hot topics or issues" in sport, either directly related to your functional area or the sport industry in general?

A: One hot topic issue in my specific line of work is the explosion of social media. This topic affects me directly, our coaches, our student-athletes, our recruiting departments—the list goes on and on. Between NCAA rules, SEC rules, school rules, and general code of conduct, it has become a challenging item on our agenda. Our Sports Communications department has a team of media professionals each year that come in and talk to our teams and one of their subjects is social media—the good, the bad, and the ugly. This kind of reminds me of a line in the movie *Dazed and Confused*, but as we in the industry age year by year, the students in our institutions always stay the same age (although there are new faces) and continue to make the same mistakes (ones I could have easily seen myself make at that age).

Q: Are there specific job skills sport-management students should look to develop while still in school?

A: While in school I continually tried to develop my communication skills, particularly my ability to write. A good writer cannot be easily replaced, and communication skills make working in ANY office situation much easier. Networking has also been instrumental to my career—establishing, maintaining, and expanding your network is paramount. Part of networking is breaking out the old-fashioned stationary and writing thank-you notes and catching up by mailed letters to keep relationships going. Learning to recognize and understand different jobs and problems within your organization is an important skill, as that enables you to better understand the challenges your co-workers and the overall organization are facing.

Q: What specific classes would you recommend students take to best position themselves for a sport-industry job?

A: Media relations, networking, facility management, and sport sociology are all important, no matter which direction someone goes with his or her degree. Although I had to work especially hard in the finance classes since I avoided any and all while pursuing my journalism undergraduate degree, the finance courses are critical and I wish I could retain more of what I learned in graduate school. Those are beneficial in the office and in my personal life. I see more and more general business classes being significant as well since no matter what is said, someone with business sense is going to thrive and move up in college athletics at most institutions.

Q: What publications do you regularly read to stay apprised of sport-business events?

A: I read the local Athens paper, the *Atlanta Journal-Constitution*, and the daily publication by the *Sporting News* almost every day. I also try to keep my *Sports Illustrated* magazines from piling up and I read the *Sports Business Daily* as much as I can. I wish I had time to read more, but working in sports communications and having a family does not leave much time for extensive reading. Lately, I have been trying to do more enjoyment reading that might or might not have to do with sports in the evening. I feel like this sharpens my mind more than my regular TV time.

Q: Would you recommend students pursue graduate school? If so, when should they pursue a graduate degree and what area of study would you recommend?

A: I enjoyed taking a two-year break from my undergraduate degree before starting my master's program. I needed a break from school and got it during my two years in the newspaper industry directly after college. But then I was reminded that who was I kidding, to be back in school was a dream come true because work, especially in my low-paying expertise, will go on for a LONG time to come. I thought it was key to have a glimpse at every puzzle piece there is in the sport business industry, which is why I would definitely go through graduate school again. Working a variety of internships never hurts, since each provides an opportunity give a thumbs-up or thumbs-down to a career path before beginning full time. For sports communications, my graduate degree was not a necessity, but it did give me something else on my resume. More importantly, the curriculum broadened my horizons in other sport-related fields in case I decide to go a different direction in my career at some point.

Study Questions

1. Looking at some of the new communications technologies coming out on the market, which are the ones most likely to impact the sports-media-audience communication process? How do you think these might make an impact and what part of the process would they be most likely to affect?
2. If you could remove one part of the sports-media-audience communication process without harming the overall system, which part would it be and why? Is it even possible to remove one of the parts without rendering the entire system dysfunctional?
3. There has been a recent movement toward more pay-per-use and subscription models in sports content and communication. Assuming all the material currently on the Internet became pay-per-use, which of the following do you think audiences would be most willing to pay for and why?
   a. Live game action of a favorite team or player(s)
   b. Statistics and/or other factual information
   c. Interviews with athletes, players, coaches, and other sports figures
   d. Commentary or stories contributed by sportswriters
   e. Interactive sports material such as fan forums and message boards

Learning Activities

1. Peruse some of the Internet sports sites dedicated to audience-created content (such as Bleacher Report). Why do you think people would want to spend the time and money creating and distributing such content? Is such content merely a fad or perhaps the future of sport communication? Explain your reasoning.
2. Consider the well-publicized steroid scandal in major league baseball (and all of sports, for that matter). How did baseball handle the situation in terms of protecting its image and controlling its message? What, if anything, should baseball executives have done differently?
3. You are the beat reporter for the local college football team. A star player for the team is arrested on drug charges and the school has refused all media access beyond an official statement. What are some ways you could go about getting the information you need to report the story?

References

Ahead of the curve. (2010, August 5). Panel presentation at the national convention for the Association of Education in Journalism and Mass Communication, Denver, CO.

Arkush, H. (2013, May 31). Pro Football Weekly says goodbye. *Pro Football Weekly*. Retrieved June 7, 2013 from: http://www.profootballweekly.com/2013/05/31/pro-football-weekly-says-goodbye

BALCO investigation timeline. (2007, November 27). *USA Today.* From: http://www.usatoday.com/sports/balco-timeline.htm

Barnett, N. (2014, January 11). Time to come clean at UNC-CH. *Charlotte News-Observer*. Retrieved February 6, 2014 from:http://www.newsobserver.com/2014/01/11/3522217/ time-to-come-clean-at-unc-ch.html

Breech, J. (2014, January 9). Colts punter fined for tweeting naked photo of Andrew Luck. *CBS Sports*. Retrieved February 5, 2014 from: http://www.cbssports.com/nfl/eye-on-football/24403939/colts-punter-fined-for-tweeting-naked-photo-of-andrew-luck

Burg, N. (2014, January 31). What is the future of mobile streaming for major sports events? *Adweek*. Retrieved February 5, 2014 from: http://www.adweek.com/brandshare/should-marketers-care-who-live-streaming-big-game-155289

Chancellor Folt must face UNC scandal with candor. (January 23, 2014). *Charlotte News-Observer*. Retrieved February 6, 2014 from: http://www.newsobserver.com/2014/01/23/3558726/chancellor-folt-must-face-unc.html Company overview. (2014). *Bleacher Report*. Retrieved February 6, 2014 from: http://bleacherreport.com/about

Connor, A. (1982). *Voices from Cooperstown: Baseball's Hall of Famers tell it like it was*. New York: Collier Books.

Fainaru-Wada's statement to the court. (2006, September 22). *San Francisco Chronicle*, A14. Florio, M. (2013, May 31). 46-year run ends for Pro Football Weekly. Pro Football Talk. Retrieved June 7, 2013 from: http://profootballtalk.nbcsports.com/2013/05/31/46-year-run-ends-for-pro-football-weekly/

Folck, J. (2014, February 4). Super bowl: Was Denver Broncos-Seattle Seahawks game the worst one in history? *Lehigh Valley (PA) Express-Times*, 4 February 2014. Retrieved February 5, 2014 from: http://www.lehighvalleylive.com/sports/index.ssf/2014/02/ super_bowl_was_denver_broncos-.html

Freedlander, D. (2013, February 5). Deadspin rides Manti Te'o hoax story to renown—and keeps heat on ESPN. *The Daily Beast*. Retrieved February 6, 2014 from: http://www/thedailybeast.com/articles/2013/02/05/deadspin-rides-manti-te-o-hoax-story-to-renown-and-keeps-heat-on-espn.html

Globe and Mail Paywall upsets readers unwilling to shell out $20 a month for news site. (2012, October 15). *The Huffington Post*. Retrieved from http://www.huffingtonpost.ca/2012/10/15/globe-and-mail-paywall-up_n_1967807.html

Halversen, M. (2011, September 21). The redemption of Ryan Leaf will be televised. *Seattle Met*. Retrieved February 5, 2014 from: http://www.seattlemet.com/news-and-profiles/people-and-profiles/articles/redemption-of-ryan-leaf-october-2011/2

Ham, J. (2007, April 16). Media rehab and the Duke lacrosse case. *Carolina Journal Online*. From: http://www.carolinajournal.com/mediamangle/display_story.html?id=4011

Inabinett, M. (1994). *Grantland Rice and his heroes: The sportswriter as mythmaker in the 1920s*. Knoxville, TN: University of Tennessee Press.

Internet allegation comes true for Alabama coach. (2003, May 6). *USC Online Journalism Review*. From: http://www.ojr.org/ojr/glaser/1052193609.php

Journalism leaders forum. (2008, January 16). 8th forum asks to explore the impact of digital on sports journalism. From: http://journalismleadersforum.blogspot.com/2008_01_01_archive.html

Koster, K. (2009, February 9). Alex Rodriguez takes shot at Sports Illustrated writer Selena Roberts. *Chicago Sun-Times*. From: http://blogs.suntimes.com/sportsprose/ 2009/02/alex_rodriguez_takes_shots_at.html

Kramer, S. (2008, July 29). 'Sporting News Today' Publisher: New Digital Daily Has 75,000 Subs, Aims For 200,000 Before Ad Push. *paidConten*t. Retrieved May 14, 2013 from: http://paidcontent.org/2008/07/29/419-first-look-sporting-news-today/

Mack, C. (1950). *My 66 years in the big leagues*. Philadelphia: John C. Winston. Mark Fainaru-Wada on the sports doping probe and protecting sources. (2004, December 17). *Columbia Journalism Review*. From: http://www.ergogenics.org/blc28.html

Martin, P. (2012, June 23). The 50 best athletes to follow on Twitter. *International Business Times*. Retrieved February 6, 2014 from: http://www.ibtimes.com/50-best-athletes-follow-twitter-704050

Martzke, R. (2003, June 6). NBC keeps rights for Olympic broadcasts through 2012. *USA Today*. From: http://www.usatoday.com/sports/olympics2003-06-06-nbc_x.htm

Matter, D. (2010, January 22). Big Ten's behemoth. *Columbia Daily Tribune*. Retrieved May 9, 2013 from: http://www.columbiatribune.com/sports/big-ten-s-behemoth/article_a6b4a2d5-c3df-5588-bce1-e3d1232c7785.html

McCombs, M. (2002). Agenda-setting role of the mass media in the shaping of public opinion. *Suntory and Toyota International Centres for Economics and Related Disciplines*. From: http://sticerd.lse.ac.uk/dps/extra/McCombs.pdf

McCombs, M., & Shaw, D. (1972). The agenda-setting Function of Mass Media. *Public Opinion Quarterly, 36*(Summer), 176–187.

McGuire, M. (2005, March 23). WTEN to alter nightly sports. *Albany Times-Union*. From: http://timesunion.com/aspstories/storyprint.asp?StoryID=344447

Megargee, S. (2014, February 5). College staffs turn to Twitter for recruiting edge. *Highschoolot.com*. Retrieved February 6, 2014 from: http://www.highschoolot.com/college-staffs-turn-to-twitter-for-recruiting-edge/13360720/

Michener, J. (1976). *Sports in America*. New York: Random House.

Miller, S. (2008, November 24). Playing the online field. *Multichannel*. From: http://www.multichannel.com/article/CA6617210.html

Myers, G. (2014, January 28). Seahawks' Marshawn Lynch not doing himself any favors with Super Bowl Media Day silence. *New York Daily News*. Retrieved February 5, 2014 from: http://www.nydailynews.com/sports/football/myers-super-bowl-confidential-silence-golden-lynch-article-1.1594861

NBC retains Olympic TV rights. (2011, June 7). *ESPN*. Retrieved February 5, 2014 from: http://sports.espn.go.com/oly/news/story?id=6634886

Payne, M. (2006). *Olympic turnaround*. New York: Praeger.

Plaschke, B. (2000, January-February). 'That's twice you get me. I'm gonna hit you, right now, right now!' *Columbia Journalism Review*, 42–44.

Price, J., & Howard, G. (2012, December 11). An update on Sporting News for 2013. The *Sporting News*. Retrieved May 14, 2013 from: http://aol.sportingnews.com/sport/story/2012-12-11/sporting-news-magazine-ipad-yearbook-2013-ios-android

Pursell, C. (2008, August 24). Sports: TV's power play. *TV Week*. Retrieved from http://www.tvweek.com/news/2008/08/sports_tvs_power_play.php

Ralbovsky, M. (1971). *Super bowl.* New York: Hawthorn. Sandomir, Richard. (2003, September 10). The decline and fall of sports ratings. *New York Times*. http://www.nytimes.com/2003/09/10/sports/10ratings.html

Schultz, B. (2005). *Sports media: Reporting, planning and producing*. Burlington, MA: Focal Press.

Sowell, M. (2008). The birth of national sports coverage: An examination of the *New York Herald*'s use of the telegraph to report America's first "championship" boxing match in 1849. *Journal of Sports Media 3*(1), 53–75.

The revolution in sport viewing. (2012). *Level 3 Communications*. Retrieved February 6, 2014 from: http://www.iptv-news.com/wp-content/uploads/iptv-news/2012/08/Level3-Sport-Report.pdf

Wilson, R. (2011, October 26). Rob Gronkowski apologizes for pics with porn star. *CBS Sports*. Retrieved February 6, 2014 from: http://www.cbssports.com/mcc/blogs/entry/22475988/32953549

Zeman, N. (2013, June). The boy who cried dead girlfriend. *Vanity Fair*. Retrieved May 10, 2013 from: http://www.vanityfair.com/culture/2013/06/manti-teo-girlfriend-nfl-draft

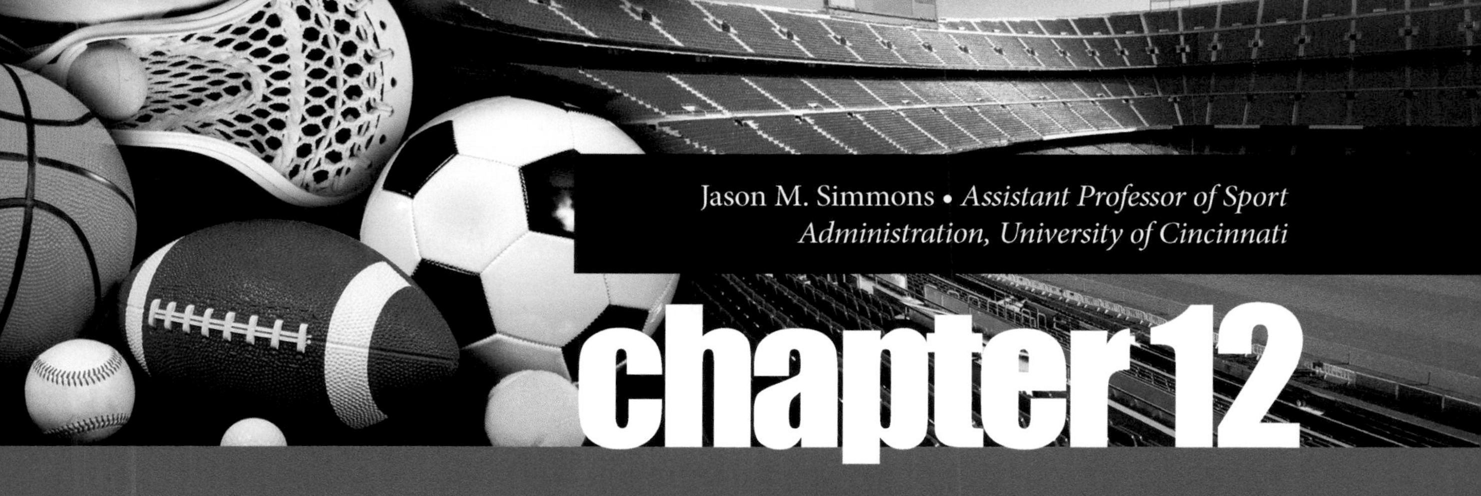

Jason M. Simmons • *Assistant Professor of Sport Administration, University of Cincinnati*

chapter 12

Facility Management

CHAPTER OBJECTIVES

After reading this chapter, you will be able to:

- Understand how technology is affecting the facility management industry.
- Identify key sources of revenue for a sport facility.
- Develop a comprehensive risk management plan.
- Explain various aspects of facility operations including housekeeping, maintenance, and security.
- Describe how legal requirements affect various aspects of facility management.

KEY TERMS

Alcohol management

Americans with Disabilities Act

Arena

Clutter

Crowd management

Festival seating

General admission

Outsourcing

Personal seat license

Qualifying the event

Reserved seating

Risk management

Stadium

> *More than anything, facility management is about communication. There are so many moving parts in a facility, and it doesn't come together without everyone communicating and being on the same page. As much as it takes to plan, build, budget, market, and design; at the end of the day we have to communicate effectively to make this operation run effectively.*
>
> —Rhett Blewett, Director of Facility and Event Services, Tampa Bay Times Forum, Tampa, Florida

Introduction

The successful management and operation of a facility is vital to any sport-related business. The facility is where the sport product is both produced AND consumed. The facility is where customers interact with the sport organization. Perhaps most importantly however, sport organizations are dependent on the revenue generated through the facility to sustain their business. Regardless of the facility's size or specific purpose, facility management encompasses a multitude of functions including:

- Planning, designing, and constructing new and/or renovated facilities
- Scheduling and booking events
- Selling tickets to attending customers
- Developing a risk management plan for attendees
- Managing crowd behavior and movement throughout the facility
- Maintaining facility systems and spaces to ensure a clean and safe environment
- Providing services and amenities to generate revenue
- Remaining aware of emerging trends in advertising and sponsorship sales
- Adhering to legislation regarding accessibility
- Budgeting for revenues and expenses
- Preparing the facility for events

Although many of the concepts discussed in this chapter can be applied to a variety of public assembly facilities such as gyms, convention centers, amphitheatres, and auditoriums, this chapter will focus on stadiums and arenas used primarily for sport.

History of Sport Facilities

The use of public assembly facilities for sport can be traced back thousands of years to the ancient Greek and Roman civilizations. In 776 B.C.E, the first

Olympic Games were hosted in Olympia Stadium, which was built into a hillside providing sloped seating for spectators. One of the most famous landmarks in the world, the Roman Coliseum, was used as a sport facility following its construction in 80 A.D. Circus Maximus, an ancient Roman racetrack which could seat upwards of 300,000 spectators, featured a number of modern amenities including concessions, seat cushions, and luxury boxes (Fried, 2010). In addition, reserved seating formats resembling ticket strategies used in today's stadiums were also featured. Broken pieces of clay pottery, which were dyed to match entrances and seating sections within the facility, were distributed to spectators prior to entry (Russo, Esckilsen, & Stewart, 2009).

The earliest sport facilities in the United States could hardly be considered stadiums in the contemporary context of the word. Ballparks in the 1860s were typically nothing more than a temporary fence designed to keep spectators off the field during a game. Sport facilities were not built with permanence in mind until the turn of the 20th century when Harvard University built the first steel-reinforced concrete stadium for its football team. Major League Baseball (MLB) franchises also built a number of stadiums using concrete and steel designs, including Tiger Stadium in Detroit, Comiskey Park in Chicago, and Fenway Park in Boston (Trumpbour, 2007).

Prior to the 1950s, the majority of sport facilities in the United States were privately financed by individual teams. However, as metropolitan areas on the West Coast and in the Southeast began to grow rapidly and the transportation industry increased its efficiency, established professional sport franchises began to investigate the potential for publicly-funded facilities. The Boston Braves moved to Milwaukee in 1953 primarily to play in a new facility. In 1958, the Brooklyn Dodgers and New York Giants moved to Los Angeles and San Francisco, respectively. The success of these teams in generating revenue in publicly-financed facilities convinced other municipalities that they could attract franchises, and convinced many teams that they needed to potentially move if their home market would not begin to pay a significant portion of their stadium expenses.

As governmental entities began to build new facilities, a sport facility construction boom began in the 1960s and 1970s. Many of the newly constructed facilities were designed to house multiple tenants, and, coinciding with a boom in automobile sales, were built in areas where large parking lots could be built around the facility. A number of publicly funded multiuse sport facilities were constructed during this time to house both baseball and football teams. Examples of these facilities included Veterans Stadium in Philadelphia (Phillies and Eagles), Three Rivers Stadium in Pittsburgh (Pirates and Steelers), and Candlestick Park in San Francisco (Giants and 49ers). Teams leased the facility from local governments, while the revenue from parking and concessions were often split between the two parties (Howard & Crompton, 2005).

In the late 1980s and early 1990s, sport franchises began to realize tremendous profits from luxury suites and club seating. The National Basketball Association's (NBA) Detroit Pistons opened The Palace at Auburn Hills in 1988 and MLB's Baltimore Orioles opened Oriole Park at Camden Yards in 1992. Each of these facilities altered the sport facility financial landscape by offering numerous luxury suites, wider concourses for concession sales, and a more pleasant entertainment experience than many other established facilities. These landmark facilities caused many other sport franchise owners to either seek a new facility or to investigate the feasibility of significantly remodeling their existing facility, often at taxpayer expense.

Franchises also began to sell more advertisements in the facility and naming rights packages became commonplace in the 1990s. Rapid expansion of franchise revenues coincided with an expiration of many of the leases initially signed in the 1960s and 1970s. Many taxpayers and government officials observed the rapid escalation of franchise revenues and player salaries and, consequently, began rejecting large subsidies for new professional sport facility construction. Though some new facilities were built with significant public dollars in the 1990s, by the latter half of the decade the trend away from large subsidies had begun.

Facilities today can cost several hundreds of millions of dollars, with some, such as AT&T Park (Dallas Cowboys) in Arlington, Levi Stadium (San Francisco 49ers) in Santa Clara, and the Atlanta Falcons' new stadium yet to be completed, eclipsing the $1 billion mark. Given these enormous price tags, teams are faced with the challenge of raising the majority of the construction costs privately. Revenue secured from luxury suite sales, personal seat licenses, and naming rights agreements typically are allocated to paying back stadium debt. That is not to say public subsidies are a thing of the past. In Atlanta, the Falcons are funding the majority of the $1.2 billion stadium bill privately; however, the city is contributing $200 million, somewhat controversially, through a citywide hotel tax (Pearson & Beasley, 2014). The Atlanta Braves, meanwhile, are relocating from their downtown Atlanta residence to the Cobb County suburbs just northwest of downtown. Several factors contributed to this decision including site accessibility and the opportunity to develop the land around the stadium into an entertainment destination; something the Braves could not do at Turner Field (Tucker, 2013). Cobb County officials also committed $300 million in public funds towards the stadium construction project (Klepal, 2013). The Braves also recognized their season ticket base was located in the northwestern suburbs in much higher concentrations than anywhere else in the Atlanta Metropolitan Region. Building the new stadium closer to the largest groups of their heaviest consumers was a wise decision, especially given the traffic congestion that often grips Atlanta.

Types of Facilities

The term "public assembly facility" is used to describe "all public and private facilities designed to accommodate people wishing to assemble for a common purpose" (Russo et al., 2009, p. 4). Amphitheatres, convention centers, and auditoriums are different types of public assembly facilities commonly used for a variety of purposes. An auditorium or theatre hosting a touring musical production serves as a gathering place for patrons to watch the performance. An outdoor amphitheatre can hold thousands of congregating spectators for a summer concert. Much like these entertainment facilities, the venues used for sporting events are also considered public assembly facilities.

In sport, the most common public assembly facilities are arenas, stadiums, and special event facilities. An **arena** is an indoor, multipurpose facility capable of hosting an assortment of sport, entertainment, and business events. A defining characteristic of arenas is a portable seating design that allows the floor area to be arranged to accommodate a variety of tenants. Basketball and hockey games are typically associated with arenas; however, a number of other sport and entertainment alternatives can utilize the flexibility an arena provides. Madison Square Garden is an example of an arena. The primary tenants of Madison Square Garden are the New York Knicks of the NBA, the Women's National Basketball Association's (WNBA) New York Liberty, and the New York Rangers of the National Hockey League (NHL). Aside from these three sport entities, the arena also hosts a number of other events, including boxing, college basketball, wrestling, lacrosse, tennis, and concerts.

Arena
Indoor facilities used to host sport, entertainment, and business events; portable seating designs allow the floor area to be arranged to accommodate multiple tenants.

Courtesy Mark Nagel

The Colonial Life Arena at the University of South Carolina is an example of a facility that hosts a variety of sport and entertainment events.

Stadium
Outdoor or domed public assembly facility that hosts sport and entertainment events.

Stadiums are typically larger than arenas and can be either outdoors or domed. An alternative design has been to incorporate a retractable roof, allowing stadiums to capitalize on both open-air and dome elements. Facilities such as Lucas Oil Field in Indianapolis (Colts), University of Phoenix Stadium in Glendale (Cardinals), and Minute Maid Park in Houston (Astros) are examples of stadiums with retractable roof designs. Stadium use is commonly associated with football and baseball, yet a number of other sports such as soccer, tennis, lacrosse, and cricket may stage their events in these large public assembly facilities.

Aside from its primary tenants, stadiums regularly host a variety of alternative events such as concerts, conventions, and trade shows. In 2014, North Texas's AT&T Stadium was the site of the National Collegiate Athletic Association (NCAA) men's basketball Final Four. In 2010 and 2011, Progressive Field in Cleveland was converted into a winter amusement park during the holiday season, complete with a tubing hill and ice skating. The Pensacola Blue Wahoos, a minor league baseball team in Pensacola, Florida, have also converted their facility into a "winter wonderland" in an effort to turn their stadium into a yearround entertainment destination. A primary responsibility for sport facility managers is to develop creative ways in which the facility can be utilized. A college football stadium, for example, is only used by its primary tenant six to eight times a year. Aside from team practices, the facility will sit empty unless the facility manager and the athletic department can develop alternative event

Nationals Park, home of MLB's Washington Nationals, was one of the first professional sport facilities to incorporate "green" technology into its design.

Courtesy Mark Nagel

opportunities. A full discussion on qualifying an event for a public assembly facility will be presented later in this chapter.

Many sports like horse racing, golf, and auto racing require a specialized facility to meet their needs. These single-purpose venues are known as special-event facilities. Indoor soccer fields, ice-skating rinks, bowling alleys, and softball complexes are also considered special-event facilities. Unlike arenas and stadiums, special-event facilities are built with a specific event in mind. Churchill Downs in Louisville, Kentucky, is an example of a special-event facility built uniquely for horse racing. Despite this classification, special-event facilities also branch out to host events outside of their intended purpose. For example, Churchill Downs hosted a Rolling Stones concert in 2006, the first event of its kind at the famed track.

Risk Management

Risk management Process of identifying, assessing, and treating risks in order to reduce facility liability and ensure a safe environment for employees and spectators.

Risk management is the process of identifying potential risks and reducing the likelihood those risks will occur (Fried, 2010). An effective risk-management plan has three goals: (1) minimize liability and financial loss, (2) reduce insurance premiums when risk is transferred to another party, and (3) maintain a safe environment for employees and spectators.

Every activity within a sport facility carries with it the potential for risk. A spectator could trip walking down a flight of stairs or be burned while sipping hot chocolate. A foul ball may hit an unsuspecting spectator in the head at a baseball game. The potential for harm is everywhere in a sport facility. As a facility manager, it is impossible to anticipate or plan for every risk, regardless of the effectiveness of a risk-management plan. It is important to remember that the purpose of a risk-management plan is not to identify every possible risk, but rather to reduce the frequency of risks as well as minimize liability.

What exactly is risk management? Risk management is a three-step process that involves forecasting, assessing, and treating risks (Ammon, Southall, & Nagel, 2010). It is a proactive strategy aimed at reducing risk and liability, as opposed to solely reacting once a risk or crisis has occurred. When forecasting risks, the most important thing to keep in mind is communication. A facility manager is typically not involved in the day-to-day operations of every aspect of the facility. In order to develop the most comprehensive list of potential risks, a facility manager should consult with staff members from concessions, security, maintenance, housekeeping, public relations, and the box office. In addition, it would be prudent to seek advice from managers of other sport facilities to get an idea of any additional risks they may have encountered. Lastly, previous incident reports are a vital tool in identifying risks that are likely to occur in a facility.

The risks one may encounter in a sport facility are contingent on a number of factors. Weather, event type, design flaws, type of facility, and patron demographics all pose the potential for harm (Ammon et al., 2010). For example, the atmosphere at an NBA playoff game is going to be much different than that at a trade show. Potential risks associated with each event are going to vary accordingly. Spectators at an NBA playoff game are more likely to consume alcohol and become disruptive to fans around them. Such a risk is unlikely to be an issue at trade shows, where alcohol may not even be served. Similarly, a football game played at Lambeau Field in January is going to carry different weather-related risks than a game played in Arizona in the winter. However, an outdoor Arizona venue may pose heat-related risks in the summer that would not be present in Wisconsin. Winter storms bring snow and ice, which can lead to a variety of special risks. The parking lots and streets surrounding the stadium will be slick, increasing the likelihood of an accident. Sidewalks and stadium steps will also gather ice, increasing the likelihood of a slip-and-fall incident. Each added variable presents a new set of risks. As a facility manager, one must account for each of these variables when identifying potential risks.

The second step in the risk-management process is assessing the risks identified during step one. A useful tool in assessing risks is a simple risk matrix that accounts for both the frequency and severity of risks (Ammon et al., 2010). Frequency refers to how often a risk is likely to occur: infrequent, moderate, or frequent. Severity refers to the loss attributed to a risk, both physical and financial. Level of severity can be classified as low loss, moderate loss, and high loss. An example of a risk category matrix is presented in Table 12.1. Using the example of a National Association for Stock Car Auto Racing (NASCAR) event, one can see how the risks associated with this event fit into the risk matrix. The use of a risk matrix allows facility managers to make better decisions regarding the treatment of these risks.

TABLE 12.1 Risk Category Matrix

	High Frequency	Moderate Frequency	Low Frequency
High Loss	None	Debris from wreckage flies into stands	Serious injury or death of spectator or driver
Moderate Loss	Excessive alcohol consumption	Spectator accident (i.e., slip and fall)	Physical altercation between spectators
Low Loss	Stadium traffic following the event	Sunburn	Fraudulent tickets

A facility manager has four options when it comes to treating risks: avoidance, assumption, transfer, and reduction. The first option, risk avoidance, should only be used for risks in which the potential for loss is high and the risk has a high frequency of occurrence. Events carrying risks that are likely to often result in physical harm and/or damage to the facility should probably be avoided (Ammon et al., 2010).

The second option for treating risks is risk assumption. A facility will be financially responsible for any risks it assumes. Therefore, a facility will only want to assume a risk if the potential for loss is minimal. For example, sport facilities typically charge for event parking. The potential exists for financial loss associated with the parking operation in the form of employee theft, inaccurate change being given, patrons being permitted to park in the wrong lot, and/or the failure to monitor the actual parking process to maximize the number of cars the lot can hold. These are risks that occur with low to moderate frequency, but result in relatively low loss for the facility. Such a risk should be assumed by the facility, as the loss is not significant enough to avoid offering parking all together or transfer the risk to a third party. Rather, facility managers should take proactive steps to reduce this risk. Risk reduction is described in more detail later in the chapter.

Risk transfer simply means transferring the financial liability of a risk to another party. Ammon (2003) suggests the risk transfer treatment be used for risks which are not severe enough, in terms of loss, to avoid completely, yet are still too great for the facility or sport organization to bear on its own. Types of risk transfer include insurance, waivers, indemnification clauses, and the use of independent contractors. Insurance is the most common form of risk transfer. Most students are probably familiar with insurance as it relates to an automobile. The risk of driving a car is not so great as to warrant avoiding the activity all together, yet the potential risks are probably too large for one to accept financial responsibility if something goes terribly wrong. The medium to utilize then, is insurance. The driving risks are transferred to another party who is willing to assume that risk. Insurance companies require regular payments in exchange for coverage. In the event of an accident, the insurance company will pay damages to the injured party, assuming the deductible has been met. Insurance works in a similar fashion for sport facilities. The types of insurance typically available to facility managers include property, business interruption, general liability, employment practice liability, professional liability, liquor liability, and product liability (Sharp, Moorman, & Claussen, 2007).

The final type of risk treatment, risk reduction, should be used in combination with the treatments outlined above. Risk reduction is the practice of taking preventative measures to minimize risks in a facility. Fewer risks mean lower insurance premiums and a safer environment for spectators and employees. Returning to the parking example, sport facilities have employed a number of reduction strategies to limit the risk of financial loss with parking. Season ticket holders typically pay for parking up front and are given a season parking pass, essentially eliminating the need for a cash exchange on site. Automated payment systems that accept credit cards serve this same purpose. Issuing parking ticket stubs to vehicles upon entry allows the organization to more accurately tally and audit the revenue from the parking operation. Finally, better training and on-site supervision can aid in reducing financial loss.

Another example of risk reduction can be seen in hockey arenas around the country. One of the risks associated with hockey is pucks flying into the stands and injuring guests. A reduction strategy the NHL utilizes to deal with this risk is the use of protective netting behind the goals. The net reduces the frequency of pucks flying into the stands, which reduces injuries associated with this risk, which in turn lowers insurance premiums and makes a safer environment for spectators at hockey games. Remember, risk reduction should not be used as an alternative to avoidance, assumption, and transfer. Instead, risk reduction should be used to complement each of these risk treatment strategies. The risk treatment matrix in Table 12.2 outlines the risk treatment option best suited for each risk category.

TABLE 12.2 Risk Treatment Matrix

	High Frequency	Moderate Frequency	Low Frequency
High Loss	Avoidance	Transfer/Avoidance and Reduction	Transfer and Reduction
Moderate Loss	Transfer and Reduction	Transfer and Reduction	Transfer/Retain and Reduction
Low Loss	Transfer/Retain and Reduction	Retain and Reduction	Retain and Reduction

Source: Ammon, Southall, & Nagel, 2010

Revenue Sources

Increasingly, stadiums and arenas have become tools to generate additional revenue for sport organizations. When one thinks of revenue generated from a sport facility, ticket sales typically first come to mind. However, sport facilities are able to generate revenue from a variety of additional sources as well. Revenue from modern facility features such as luxury seating, naming rights, and personal seat licenses (PSL) often help underwrite new facility construction costs and major renovations. Ancillary services such as concessions, merchandise, and parking also contribute to a facility's potential profits.

Economic generators for a sport facility do not exist in a vacuum. Attending a sport event is about more than just watching a game; it is an experience. Food, beverages, parking, promotions, and facility cleanliness all contribute to the fan experience. A negative experience in the parking lot might affect one's decision to attend events in the future. This decision affects not only facility ticket revenue, but revenue from concessions, merchandise, and parking as well. This section will explore the primary sources of revenue for a sport facility, as well as discuss the role of the facility manager in generating additional revenue.

Outside Events

As noted, stadium and arena construction often comes with an extremely large price tag. Ironically however, the facilities' primary tenants will only use the venue a handful of dates out of the year. National Football League (NFL) teams usually only use their facilities 10 times each season. Even Major League Baseball stadiums, whose teams have more home games (81) than any other professional sports league in the United States, have 284 open dates per year. An additional revenue source for sport facilities comes from leasing/renting the facility to outside events such as concerts, performing arts shows, conferences, trade shows, and conventions. Not only does the facility profit from rental fees, but these events generate revenue for the facility through ancillary services such as concessions, parking, and merchandise sales, each of which will be discussed later in this chapter.

When scheduling an outside event, a facility manager must consider several things. The first involves the schedule itself. In order to maximize attendance, most events should be scheduled at a time that does not conflict with other prominent events or community activities. For example, the facility manager for the Matthew Knight Arena in Eugene, Oregon, will want to avoid scheduling an event on the same day and time as the "Civil War" football game between Oregon and Oregon State, as most of the community will be watching the game. Second, careful consideration must be taken to determine the risks associated with an outside event. For example, the very nature of moshing at heavy metal concerts increases the likelihood of damage to the facility and spectator injury, as seen in the later example of the AC/DC concert. Knowing the risks beforehand will allow the facility manager to develop a more comprehensive risk management plan. Finally, the facility manager must determine if the event is a match for the facility. This is known as **qualifying the event**. During this process, the facility manager must consider each of the following questions:

- What are the values and expectations of the event? Are they similar to the values and expectations of the facility?
- Is there room on the schedule for this event? Does the event conflict with the facility's primary tenant?
- Does the event fit the facility in terms of space requirements and specialized support (ventilation for pyrotechnics or dirt for monster trucks)?
- Does the event have a sound financial plan? Will profits from the event exceed expenses?
- What are the demands of the event (time, staffing, changeover)? Can the facility meet these demands (Russo et al., 2009)?

Qualifying the Event
Process of determining if an event is appropriate for a facility.

The process of qualifying the event should not be overlooked. Each event is unique and will present different challenges for a facility manager. Outside events are significant economic generators for a sport facility; however, issues with scheduling, risks, and event fit must be considered prior to booking an event.

Tickets

Ticket sales not only account for a large portion of a facility's revenue, but a significant portion of a sport organization's overall earnings as well. Manchester United grossed €423.8 million for the 2012-2013 season, 42% of which came from gameday revenues consisting largely of ticket sales (Battle et al., 2014). At the NCAA Division-I FBS level, ticket sales account for an average of 27% of athletic program–generated revenue (NCAA, 2013). Further, according to PricewaterhouseCoopers's (2013) North American Sports Outlook, ticket revenue is expected to remain the largest source of revenue across professional (MLB, MLS, NBA, NFL, NHL) and collegiate (NCAA) sport combined through 2017. This data suggests that despite the dramatic improvements to the at-home viewing experience, ticket sales have been, and will continue to be, a primary revenue driver for sport organizations.

Reserved seating
Ticketing system used for events that require a designated ticket for each seat; reserved tickets indicate the section, row, and seat a patron is assigned for a specific event.

General admission
Tickets are sold on a first-come, first-served basis; each patron pays a fixed price and can sit in any unoccupied seat in the facility.

Festival seating
Form of general admission ticketing in which spectators are not assigned to a specific seat, but rather a standing/seating area within a facility such as in front of the stage at a concert or outfield berm seating at a baseball game.

Tickets are categorized as reserved, general admission, or festival/lawn seating. **Reserved seating** is used for events that require a designated ticket for each seat in the facility. Much like the system used by the Romans more than 2,000 years ago, reserved tickets will indicate the section, row, and seat a patron is assigned for a specific event. Tickets may be sold on a first-come, first-served basis. This is known as **general admission** seating. Each patron pays a fixed price and can sit in any unoccupied seat in the facility. Lawn or hillside seating at an outdoor facility is another form of general admission ticketing known as **festival seating**. Floor seating in front of the stage at a concert is another type of festival seating. By nature, this type of seating carries unique risks not present in alternative ticketing formats. For example, three fans were trampled to death in front of the stage at an AC/DC concert in 1991, resulting in a trend away from festival/floor seating near the front of the stage. However, some college stadiums such as Memorial Stadium at Clemson, as well as many minor league baseball parks with berm seating in the outfield, still use hill-seating formats in designated sections of their stadiums.

Most facilities sell tickets prior to the actual event. Advanced ticket sales allow the facility manager to prepare for an event both in terms of services offered and staff required (Ammon et al., 2010; Russo et al., 2009). For example, larger events will necessitate the use of additional concession stands. Consequently, additional staff will be required to operate concessions services.

The ticket sales industry is in the midst of a seismic transformation as more and more teams turn to demand-based pricing strategies to realize the full market value of their product. Traditionally, tickets purchased on the primary market (i.e., from the team directly) cost the same from game to game. However, not all games/events are created equal. Typically, games featuring prominent opponents, or weekend games, or games with attractive promotions such as post-game concerts, fireworks, or unique giveaways draw a bigger crowd. Games/events can have varying demand. Just like one would expect to pay more money for a plane ticket to Key West during spring break (flights to Key West during this time are in higher demand than other times throughout the year), one can expect to pay more for single-game tickets to higher demand games if the teams are utilizing demand-based pricing strategies.

The Baltimore Orioles, for example, recently switched to a demand-based model, known as variable ticket pricing (VTP), prior to the 2014 season. Games are now segmented into one of five pricing options based on opponent (a variable affecting demand). Elite games (the most expensive tier) include home games against the Yankees, Red Sox, and Cardinals. Prices drop throughout the remaining tiers as the perceived quality of the opponent decrease demand (Orioles, n.d.). Dynamic ticket pricing is another version of demand-based pricing which takes into account additional variables that could affect demand on a day-by-day or even a minute-by-minute basis. Such variables might include weather, player injuries, recent team/opponent performance, playoff races, and ticket availability. Whereas prices under the variable model are set prior to the season, variations in ticket price under the dynamic model coincide with real-time fluctuations in demand.

Naming Rights

Thirty years ago, most stadiums and arenas were usually named after important public figures, geographic regions, or in some cases, even the home team. However, most sport facilities now are named after a corporate sponsor who has paid to attach their moniker to the facility. A brief look at the sport facility landscape reveals only a handful of venues that have resisted the urge to succumb to corporate sponsorship. Facilities such as Lambeau Field in Green Bay, Fenway Park in Boston, and Soldier Field in Chicago have become the exception rather than the rule. Naming rights agreements can generate considerable revenue for sport organizations, which explains why teams are so willing to name their facility after a corporate sponsor.

The New England Patriots were one of the first sport organizations to realize the potential for generating revenue through naming rights agreements. In 1971, the Patriots sold the naming rights to their stadium to Schaffer Brewing Company for $150,000. It was not until the mid-1990s, however, that sport facility naming rights became popular. A distinguishing characteristic of stadium construction during this time was the diminished reliance on public funds to build new

AT&T Park is an example of a corporate-named facility.

Courtesy Mark Nagel

facilities (Howard & Crompton, 2005). Naming rights provided a major source of revenue for team owners looking to finance construction costs. At the end of the 20th century, sport facility naming rights sold for an average of $87 million (Greenberg, 2000). Today, corporations are willing to pay more than four times that amount in certain situations. Citi Field (New York Mets) has the largest naming rights agreements at $400 million over 20 years (Leuty, 2013).

Aside from financing facility construction costs, the revenue generated from naming rights also allows teams to pay higher player contracts and add amenities to their facilities (Greenberg, 2000). The primary benefits sought from corporations in naming rights agreements are exposure and increased sales. Naming rights are a type of corporate sponsorship that allows businesses to break through the clutter of more traditional advertising and signage. A company name on the side of a sport facility is much more noticeable than a billboard next to a highway. Other benefits associated with such agreements include access to premium seating, free tickets, parking passes, and additional signage within the facility (Howard & Crompton, 2005).

Collegiate sport facilities are often named after a booster who contributed a large portion of funds for facility construction. These naming rights are usually permanent and cannot be resold later when the facility requires renovations (Howard & Crompton, 2005). To avoid this potential problem and to maximize revenues, many facilities have opted to sell the naming rights to other areas of the facility such as the playing surface, seating areas, and entryways. For example, the University of Maryland football team plays at Capital One Field at Byrd Stadium. This strategy is also used at the professional level. MetLife Stadium, home to the New York Giants and New York Jets, features "cornerstone partners," who have essentially purchased naming rights to the four quadrants for the facility. Each corner of the facility is not only named after one of the corporate partners (Verizon, Pepsi, Bud Light, and EMC/SAP), but has been designed to incorporate each company's brand into the fan experience within that quadrant (Metlife Stadium, n.d.). The Verizon quadrant, for example, is themed to feel as though one is walking through a massive Verizon store. Not only are the Verizon name, logo, and colors prominently featured throughout, an actual Verizon studio has been built into the concourse providing fans the opportunity to receive real-time updates from around the league, play games for prizes, and even sample the latest Verizon products and services just as one would in a local Verizon store at the mall (Cohen, 2012).

Advertising and Promotions

Naming rights are just one form of advertising available in a public-assembly facility. Additional sponsorship within the facility can generate millions of dollars in annual revenue for a sport organization. A facility manager has the responsibility to create space for sponsor integration and activation throughout the stadium. Signage, for example, should be strategically placed throughout the venue in locations that draw the attention of spectators. Most commonly these locations include the scoreboard, the scorer's table for basketball games, along the outfield wall and behind home plate for baseball, either directly on the ice or along the dasher boards in hockey, along the sidelines and behind the goals in soccer, and even on cup-holders and the backs of restroom stall doors.

Improvements in technology have paved the way for advancements in facility advertisement/sponsorship. Digital video boards, such as the main scoreboard/video board, ribbon boards spanning the length of the upper-level seating bowl, Dorna boards along the sidelines in basketball and/or soccer, or even digital displays within the concourse allow for more engaging signage that might include videos, animations, creative graphics, and bright colors to catch fans' eyes. Further, digital signage eliminates the need to pay for traditional static signage manufacturing/printing and installation costs. Teams are also able to sell this advertising space multiple times over, as the digital boards can rotate through a series of displays at different times throughout the event.

Technology can drive advertising revenue within sport facilities beyond just signage. Bright House Networks (a communications provider in the Tampa Bay area) is a sponsor of the Tampa Bay Lightning. As part of their sponsorship activation, Bright House offers free Wi-Fi access throughout the Tampa Bay

Times Forum to all Bright House customers in attendance. Two facilities in Sydney, Australia, The Sydney Cricket Ground and Allianz Stadium, have incorporated a digital component, Fan360, into live event attendance in an effort to enhance the fan experience. Fans in attendance can now watch live video directly from their phone/tablet, purchase concessions from their seat, and interact with various social media platforms, all through the Fan360 application on their mobile devices. It terms of revenue, however, unique in-venue promotional offers can be sent directly to fans based on data collected about an individual's experience, interest, and past behaviors via the Fan360 application. Teams are also able to incorporate sponsors into the app's interface (Belzer, 2013; Muret, 2014; Sporting Innovations, n.d.). Similar applications have made their way into North American sporting venues, aimed at both increasing revenue and improving the fan experience at events. This topic is discussed in more detail later in this chapter.

Printed materials are another source of advertising in a sport facility. Businesses may purchase space in media guides, game programs, ticket backs, seating charts, and team schedules to advertise goods and services. Other businesses will sponsor fan giveaways such as water bottles, posters, tee-shirts, and noise-makers with the team and company logos on them. Announcements and in-game promotions are additional opportunities for businesses to partner with the sport facility.

The opportunities for generating revenue through advertising are seemingly endless; however, too much signage and sponsor integration can be a bad thing. Not only does signage tarnish a facility's aesthetic appeal, it can also cause **clutter**. Advertisers seek recall and recognition when purchasing sponsorship opportunities in a sport facility. Clutter decreases the likelihood of advertiser recall, thus reducing the value of facility advertising (Russo et al., 2009).

Clutter
Product of too much signage and sponsor integration within a facility; decreases the likelihood of advertiser recall, thus diminishing the value of facility advertising.

Personal Seat Licenses

Personal seat licenses or permanent seat licenses (PSLs) are widely used in sport facilities, particularly the NFL, as a primary source of revenue for stadium construction. The San Francisco 49ers generated more than $400 million in PSL revenue to help fund construction costs at Levi's Stadium (Rosenburg, 2013). PSLs do not provide annual operating income like many of the sources previously discussed in this chapter. Instead, personal seat licenses require individuals to pay in advance for the right to purchase tickets to an event in the future. The revenue generated from PSLs can greatly reduce the amount of money a team owner or athletic department has to raise to build a new facility. The New York Giants sold personal seat licenses for as much as $20,000 to help offset the $1.6 billion construction costs of their new stadium (Sandomir, 2008).

Personal seat license
Source of facility revenue that requires guests to pay a one-time fee for the right to purchase tickets for a specific seat.

Aside from the upfront revenue, PSLs also represent a financial commitment from the fans. The one-time costs to own a seat means fans only own the right to buy tickets for that specific seat. They still have to purchase tickets to each game. In fact, most personal seat license agreements require fans to purchase tickets to all home games over the life of the contract (Howard & Crompton, 2005). By requiring PSL owners to purchase tickets, facility managers can estimate attendance figures with greater accuracy. For example, if a facility has sold 70,000 personal seat licenses, the facility manager can expect at least 70,000 tickets will be sold to the events. This information will allow the facility manager to better prepare in terms of proper staffing and budget projections.

PSLs are not without their disadvantages, however. In most cases PSLs are permanent, but in some cases a personal seat license may expire. The Oakland Raiders encountered difficulties selling their PSLs in 1995 because they were only valid for 10 years. Facilities also run the risk of disenchanting a portion of their fan base by asking customers to essentially pay twice to attend a game. For this reason, among others, the Cleveland Browns discontinued their personal seat license program in 2013. Some fans may have been season-ticket holders in the past and are now being asked to purchase a PSL for the continued right to purchase season tickets. Additionally, purchasing expensive PSLs may restrict a large portion of a team's fan base from attending games. For example, PSLs at Levi's Stadium range from $2,000 to $80,000 for a single seat (Rosenberg, 2013)!

Though a PSL may allow the customer to purchase seats into perpetuity, it may not be convertible to another patron. Some facilities limit the transfer of PSLs to certain family members, or may only allow a PSL to be sold one time.

Premium Seating

Premium seating is one of the most significant sources of revenue sport organizations realize from the operation of their facility. Traditionally, premium seating referred to suites or boxes. These luxury suites were primarily marketed to corporations with large amounts of money to spend entertaining clients and employees. The sizes of suites varied from facility to facility, but typically could accommodate anywhere from 12 to 25 patrons. Premium seating has evolved from the one-size-fits-all approach that traditional suites offered, to an array of options to accommodate the unique needs/wants of attendees.

Luxury suites, club seats, and loge seats are the most common forms of premium seating available at modern stadiums and arenas. Luxury suites typically offer premium sightlines and are designed to include personal comfort amenities such as carpet, hi-definition televisions, wait service, wet bar, air-temperature control, and private restrooms. Access to the facility's club level is another common amenity offered to suite holders. Clubs, such as the Chase Club at the Tampa Bay Times Forum, offer an exclusive atmosphere for patrons to socialize, mingle, and network. These hospitality areas commonly feature gourmet food offerings, craft beers, and wait/concierge service; and are outfitted with high-end furniture, fixtures, and equipment. Suite sizes/layouts vary and can be sold on an individual game/event basis, all the way up to a full season commitment. Much like PSLs and naming rights, team owners are often dependent on the revenue from luxury seating to fund new stadiums. Not surprisingly, access to these premium seats come with a high price tag. United Club Suites at Dodger Stadium cost $235,000 for a full season. Individual game rentals start at $4,000 (Dodgers, n.d).

Club seats are not as luxurious as a suite, but feature many of the same amenities at a lower price, while usually offering closer proximity to the on-field action. The price of club-level seats can vary dramatically depending on the seat location and services offered. Club seats may cost anywhere from a few hundred dollars per season to several thousand dollars for a single premium event. Amenities typically reserved for club seating include padded seats, premium parking/valet parking service, wait service, gourmet food and drink items, and access to club-level bar or lounge.

Loge seats are a hybrid option of sorts, combining the privacy elements of a suite, with the in-bowl comfort amenities of club seating. Loge seats can be thought of as seating pods separated by a partition. Each pod consists of a group of seats (typically four to six), counter space, and room to stand, stretch, or even let the kids play on the floor. These seats are ideal for corporate clients who do not need or want the space and costs associated with a suite, or fans coming to an event in small groups who want an upscale, exclusive experience.

The revenue generated from premium seating will vary based on amenities, location, and contract length. Suites located on the 50-yard line or behind home plate are going to be considerably more expensive than suites located in the end zone or down the right field line. Amway Center (Orlando Magic) is a prime example of the variations in premium seating available at sporting and entertainment events. The suites available at Amway Center include many of the amenities previously described, but range in size from the 16- to 20-person Presidents Suite, to the 45-person capacity Silver Suites, to the IOA Hospitality Rooms, which can accommodate up to 185 people. In terms of club seats, Amway Center has a plethora of options including courtside (first two to three rows) and "ultimate seats" (first six to seven rows behind courtside seats) offering access to the Fields Ultimate Lounge and Icon Suite. These seats are sold for $150 to $1,500 per game, and include food and nonalcoholic drinks available in the Fields Ultimate Lounge. The Icon Suite is the ultimate in exclusivity at a sporting event. The suite is located underneath the seating bowl along the hallway Magic players take to access the court from their locker room. Adorned with posh furniture and chic interior design elements, members of the Icon Suite pay up to $80,000 a year for access (Amway Center, n.d.). This does not include the cost of the per-game ticket noted above (Muret, 2013). Loge seats are also plentiful in Amway Center, and include a $1,500 to $2,500 food and beverage credit for a full-season commitment (Amway Center, n.d.)

Ancillary Services

In addition to the revenue generators discussed, facility revenue can come from a number of other sources. Ancillary services such as concessions, novelties, and parking are usually reliable sources of revenue for a sport facility during an event.

Concessions

Food and beverage services are critical to a facility's success because sporting events often overlap mealtimes. Fans expect concessions to be available at sport events. If operated correctly, concession services can be a significant source of revenue for a sport facility.

The most popular traditional concession items have typically been hotdogs, hamburgers, nachos, peanuts, cotton candy, popcorn, ice cream, and soft drinks. Alcohol sales also typically contribute significantly to the revenue generated from concessions. A trend in newer facilities has been to offer specialized or gourmet food and beverage options. For $10.50, Kansas City Royals fans

Courtesy Mark Nagel

Concessions are an important revenue source for sport facilities.

at Kauffman Stadium can purchase a grilled sausage piled high with pulled pork, macaroni and cheese, crumbled bacon, and scallions (Schupmann, 2013). Fans of the Milwaukee Brewers can enjoy meatballs stuffed with spaghetti and cheese, and topped with marinara sauce at Miller Park (Deptolla, 2014). In addition to specialty items, research has shown customers are more likely to purchase products with familiar brand names such as Pizza Hut or Dunkin Donuts (Russo et al., 2009). Some facilities are now offering "all you can eat" sections to attract customers. Tickets to those sections usually allow patrons to consume as much food and drink as they want. Some facilities have included alcohol in the all-you-can-eat offer while others have elected to require fans in those sections to pay for alcohol. Certainly, any alcohol consumption should be monitored by the facility but it is particularly important in situations where adults can consume as much as they want as part of their ticket.

Outsourcing
Hiring an outside organization or private contractor to operate facility services such as concessions, security, and maintenance.

A facility manager can either operate concession services in-house, or hire a private contractor, which is known as **outsourcing**. Like any choice, there are advantages and disadvantages for each. Running the food and beverage service in-house allows the facility manager to directly control the staff and the products being sold. The facility will also retain all of the revenue generated from concession sales. The disadvantage is that the facility manager must assume all the risks and responsibilities of operating concession services including training staff, monitoring alcohol sales, keeping product inventory, and adhering to health and labor laws. Conversely, when outsourcing food and beverage services, such responsibilities are shifted to a private contractor. In addition, a private contractor may have more experience and expertise in the industry, and likely has greater leverage with food and beverage suppliers. The downside of contracting out is that the facility must split the revenue from concessions with the concessionaire (Russo et al., 2009).

Regardless of whether food and beverage services are operated in-house or contracted out, the facility manager has the responsibility to ensure the concessions experience is positive for guests. This means making efforts to reduce the amount of time customers spend in line. Menu boards should clearly indicate products, sizes, and prices to limit questions and confusion at the counter. Simple price increments will reduce the complexity of monetary transactions for both customers and employees (Ammon et al., 2010). Customers will also expect supplementary items such as napkins, plastic ware, and condiments to be available.

Merchandise

Another source of revenue for a sport facility is selling merchandise products such as programs, tee-shirts, hats, jerseys, pennants, foam fingers, and posters. When determining which novelty products to sell, a facility manager needs to consider the audience demographics, the past purchase history of that audience, and the potential profits garnered from each item (Russo et al., 2009).

Much like concessions, facility managers can either choose to operate merchandise services in-house, or contract the service to an outside party. Facility managers can sometimes maximize revenue by operating merchandise in-house; however, the risks associated with this operating arrangement must be assumed by the facility as well. Revenue from merchandise sales is directly linked to the risk and responsibilities assumed by each party. Usually, the most profitable method for the facility is the percentage-of-sales contract in which the facility staff takes a more active role in novelty operations, and pays the vendor a percentage of the total merchandise sales (Russo et al., 2009).

Parking

According to Gorman (2003), sport facility parking revenue is derived from three different sources: event parking, lot rentals, and alternative forms of parking-related revenue such as sponsorship or games. Fans have few alternatives when it comes to parking for an event; therefore, sport facilities are typically able to charge for this service. The Miami Dolphins, for example, charge a flat fee of $25 per vehicle for on-site parking at Sun Life Stadium on game day (Sun Life Stadium, n.d.). Seasonal parking passes may also be available for purchase by frequent visitors such as season-ticket holders or luxury-seating tenants.

Lot rentals may take several forms depending on the size and location of the parking lot. Facilities located in or around a city's downtown business district are often able to open their lots, for a daily fee, to other companies' employees who work during the day, as games/events primarily occur in the evenings or on weekends. Papa John's Cardinal Stadium in Louisville, Kentucky, annually opens their lot for Kentucky Derby overflow parking from neighboring Churchill Downs, generating parking revenue from an event at a different facility. Other times, outside organizations will rent the parking lot space to host an event of their own. In 2012, Cirque Du Soleil rented one of the parking lots at Tropicana Field (Tampa Bay Rays) for their touring production held under a tent that could seat thousands of spectators.

Beyond event parking and rentals, the ability of a facility to generate alternative forms of parking revenue hinges on the creativity of the sport organization's marketing and sales staff. Tiered or dynamically priced parking for amenities (i.e. distance from facility, valet service, covered parking, tailgating space) or higher demand events can lead to an increase in parking revenue. As part of their sponsorship agreement with the Atlanta Braves, both Hyundai and Delta have designated lots at Turner Field for their customers. The Delta Medallion lot at Turner Field is among the closest lots to the facility's entrance, and is open, free of charge, to Delta SkyMiles Medallion members (Braves, n.d.). The Chicago Rush has utilized sponsor giveaways, such as an ice scraper or car air freshener, upon entry to their parking lot, as opposed to giveaways when fans enter the facility (Migala, 2007). This way, the giveaway has a greater chance of being used as it is already in the car, as opposed to being thrown out or left at the facility, thus creating more impactful activation for the sponsor.

Not only is parking a source of revenue for a sport facility, it is also a service. Parking lots are the first and last point of contact fans have at an event, and play a large role in a fan's overall experience at the facility. Parking lots should be designed with convenience and accessibility in mind to minimize traffic congestion. Facility managers should also utilize parking staff and law enforcement officials to direct traffic flow before and after an event. Another parking issue facility managers need to be aware of is safety/security. Parking lots/garages should have adequate lighting and the parking surface should be well maintained. The visible presence of law enforcement officials in and around the parking area will also deter criminal activity such as theft, vandalism, and the sale of pirated merchandise (Russo et al., 2009).

Operations

A facility's ability to generate revenue is largely dependent on the operations services it provides. The purpose of operations is to provide not only a clean environment for spectators, but a safe and comfortable one as well. The operations department has many responsibilities in a facility. These responsibilities typically include developing policies and procedures, booking and scheduling events at the facility, box office management, concessions management, purchasing, and equipment inventory. Additionally, a facility's operations department is also responsible for housekeeping, maintenance, and security. While these services are not a direct source of revenue for a public assembly facility, they may affect a customer's decision to visit a facility again in the future. This is especially true if these functions are managed poorly.

Housekeeping

It is easy to overlook housekeeping services when attending a sporting event. Housekeeping is responsible for keeping the public assembly facility clean. This includes the seating area, restrooms, suites, concourse areas, concession stands, stairways, and ramps. Patrons expect the seating area to be free from trash from the previous night's event. Any beverage spills in the concourse should be cleaned and an ample supply of toilet paper and paper towels should be available in the restrooms.

An additional housekeeping crew will be required for facility clean-up following an event, as such an endeavor requires significantly more labor than everyday housekeeping duties such as vacuuming and emptying trash cans (Russo et al., 2009). This is especially true in large public assembly facilities such as stadiums and arenas. As is the case with concessions and novelties, a facility manager usually has the option to operate custodial services in-house or outsource housekeeping responsibilities to a private contractor.

Custodial efforts will be aided by the strategic placement of janitorial closets throughout the facility. Housekeeping staff need space to store equipment and cleaning supplies, as well as access to a water source. At a minimum, there should be one janitorial closet on each floor of the facility. It is also recommended that each restroom contain a janitorial closet to store common restroom supplies like toilet paper, soap, and paper towels (Stotlar, 1997).

Maintenance

Car owners are all too familiar with the concept of maintenance. Vehicles require oil changes, engine tune-ups, new brakes, and replacement tires. While these minor maintenance functions are a nuisance, they serve the purpose of preventing costly repairs later.

A sport facility is no different. A facility's ability to generate revenue and provide services to its guests can be attributed to how well it is maintained. A facility maintenance staff is responsible for preventative/routine maintenance, keeping inventory of supplies and ordering new parts, maintaining repair records, minor repair work, and serving in an advisory role for major projects such as facility renovations or large equipment replacement (Fried, 2010).

Courtesy Mark Nagel

Opened in 1913, Croke Park in Ireland is an example of an older facility that requires extensive maintenance.

An effective maintenance plan is critical to extending the life of a sport facility and its equipment/mechanical devices. Preventative maintenance should be scheduled on a daily, weekly, monthly, and yearly basis. Cyclical repairs on the other hand, such as replacing carpet every five years in a heavily trafficked area, should be planned for on a recurring basis. Breakdown maintenance is appropriate when equipment eventually stops working (Fried, 2010). As equipment breakdowns are inevitable, facility managers should have funds set aside to aid in overcoming the financial burden associated with large equipment replacement.

Security

A facility manager has a responsibility to make sure all guests are safe while attending a sporting event. The primary resource for ensuring the safety and comfort of facility patrons is security. In addition to venue guests, security serves the purpose of protecting the facility itself.

The most common security practices used to protect the public at sport facilities include bag checks upon entry, metal detectors or handheld wands, security cameras, and turnstiles to manage crowd ingress to the facility. In addition, the labor required to effectively secure a facility has increased significantly since September 11, 2001. Ancillary systems such as fire alarms, sprinklers, and emergency power are also utilized to protect the facility and its patrons. Emergency power is the most important element of a security plan during a facility evacuation. Should the facility's power fail, a generator can provide power for emergency lighting and sound systems, allowing updates and evacuation instructions to be relayed to facility guests (Sedlak & Traugott, 2002).

Security is another service that may be operated either in-house or contracted out. Contracting some or all of the security responsibilities offers a number of benefits to facility managers. First, the cost of hiring, training, and maintaining a security staff will be deferred to the private contractor. It may be cost prohibitive for a facility to employ an in-house security staff that is only needed on a limited basis. Second, inconsistencies in work availability for security personnel at sport facilities may result in high turnover rates. Having to hire and train new staff members on a regular basis will be both expensive and time-consuming for facility managers. Third, security needs will vary based on the type of event. Contractors are usually able to provide appropriate levels of security, tailored uniquely for individual events. Another benefit of contracted security is expertise. Contracted security personnel will be expertly trained and will be knowledgeable of potential risks within a sport facility. Finally, using a private contractor lessens the liability the facility must retain related to security risks (Price, 2007).

Facility security during an event often deals extensively with crowd management and alcohol management. Crowd management is a necessary security component and should be part of a facility's risk-management plan. Once a crowd mobilizes or becomes violent, it is difficult, and often dangerous, to attempt to control its behavior. Crowd management, therefore, is designed primarily to supervise the crowd before it gets out of control (Fried, 2010).

An effective crowd-management plan should include four components: a well-trained staff, an ejection policy, effective communication, and signage throughout the facility (Ammon et al., 2010). Directional signs are designed to guide patrons to various locations within the facility such as emergency exits, ticket windows, restrooms, concession stands, and first aid stations. Signage is also a useful crowd-management tool in guiding spectators to their seats. An ejection policy will help protect guests from violent and disruptive fans. Many times these behaviors are amplified through the consumption of alcohol. Naturally, an ejection policy will be a vital component of an alcohol management plan as well.

Crowd management
Strategy designed to prevent crowd from getting out of control; security, signage, and communication all serve to effectively maintain crowd control.

Alcohol management
Limits the risks associated with alcohol consumption, as well as reduces facility liability regarding alcohol-related incidents.

Alcohol is a difficult issue for facility managers. Alcohol sales at sport events are usually a significant revenue generator. But alcohol sales often enhance disruptive behavior during the event and increase the likelihood of drunk driving once the event has concluded. An alcohol management plan will limit these risks, as well as reduce facility liability regarding alcohol-related incidents. Alcohol policies vary from facility to facility, however, recommended alcohol management practices include:

- Denying admittance to guests who visibly appear impaired;
- Prohibiting guests from bringing outside beverages or beverage containers into the facility;
- Prohibiting guests from leaving the facility with alcoholic beverages;
- Requiring a valid government ID for all alcohol purchases;
- Prohibiting the passing of alcohol to minors;
- Reserving the right to refuse service to guests who visibly appear impaired;
- Designating a cutoff point for alcohol sales (e.g., the end of the third quarter in football or basketball games); and
- Limiting alcohol sales to two beers per purchase with a 20 oz. maximum container size (Hambrick, Simmons, Greenhalgh, & Brownlee, 2009).

Americans with Disabilities Act

Signed into law by President George Bush in 1990, the Americans with Disabilities Act (ADA) prohibits discrimination based on disability in four areas: employment, state and local government activities, places of public accommodation, and telecommunications (Department of Justice, 2009). Public

Americans with Disabilities Act
A law signed in 1990 prohibiting discrimination based on disability in employment, state and local government activities, places of public accommodation, and telecommunications; sport facilities are considered places of public accommodation and therefore must be accessible to persons with disabilities.

Accommodation (Title III) is of particular importance to facility managers. Places of public accommodation include hotels, restaurants, movie theaters, grocery stores, gas stations, airports, parks, day care centers, and even sport and recreation facilities such as stadiums, arenas, and gyms (Sharp et al., 2007). Sport facilities are required by law to be ADA-compliant. It is the responsibility of the facility manager to ensure the facility is accessible to patrons with disabilities.

The ADA defines an individual with a disability as "a person who has a physical or mental impairment that substantially limits one or more major life activities, a person who has a history or record of such an impairment, or a person who is perceived by others as having such an impairment" (Department of Justice, 2009, p. 1). Major life activities include walking, speaking, seeing, hearing, breathing, learning, working, and the ability to care for one's self (Greenberg, 2000).

Facilities built for occupancy after January 26, 1993, must be fully compliant under the ADA (Ammon et al., 2010). The Department of Justice outlined a number of facility features that must meet ADA standards. One such feature is the seating area. At least 1% of a facility's seating area must be wheelchair accessible and provide companion seating. Accessible seating must be available throughout the venue, including the club level and luxury suites, and should be elevated to provide unobstructed sightlines over standing spectators (Department of Justice, 1997).

Beyond the seating area, persons with disabilities should have access to the same amenities and features of the facility as able-bodied patrons. Such amenities include concession and merchandise stands, parking, and restrooms. Concession stands should have lowered counters to provide service to individuals in a wheelchair. Parking for guests with disabilities should be made available near accessible facility entrances, and restrooms should be equipped with lowered mirrors and larger stalls (Department of Justice, 1997).

Facilities occupied prior to the ADA's enactment have different regulations from newer facilities. Architectural barriers that restrict access to existing facilities must be removed if such a renovation is "readily achievable." The term "readily achievable" refers to alterations that are relatively simple and inexpensive, such as the addition of wheelchair ramps and the replacement of thick carpets, which are not suitable for wheelchairs (Ammon et al., 2010).

It may not be readily achievable to remove all barriers that restrict access to a facility. In such instances, a demonstration of "good faith" in achieving accessibility is sufficient to meet ADA standards. Mingus (2005) suggests four steps by which a facility manager can demonstrate "good faith" towards ADA compliance. The first step is a self-evaluation of the facility. A facility manager should identify areas where the facility meets or falls short of ADA compliance. The second step is the formation of an advisory council, which should include individuals with a disability, to help plan for future facility alterations. Next, a plan and timeline for improvements should be developed. The final step in "good faith" compliance is the adoption of a facility philosophy regarding ADA that welcomes people of all walks of life, including those with a disability, into the facility. What is most important is that all guests, including those with disabilities, have access to the facility and can enjoy the experience.

While the ADA establishes a legal requirement which facilities must meet to provide access for persons with disabilities, sport organizations would be wise to consider the unique needs of various demographic groups beyond just those with disabilities with respect to facility design and the programs/services offered. Families with small children, for example, require space to change dirty diapers; a clean, quiet space for nursing or bottle feeding; a family-friendly section free of rowdy fans, and an extra bag/stroller to carry baby supplies such as snacks, a change of clothes, bottles, and diapers. Facility managers should review their policies regarding bag size limitations, outside food/drink permissions, and alcohol-free seating sections to ensure the needs of families with small children are being met. Family bathrooms and/or nursing stations should also be considered. Otherwise, a sport facility may run the risk of disenchanting the "family" demographic, potentially leading to non-attendance at events. Other groups with unique needs may include the elderly, special interest groups, and school teachers/administrators chaperoning a large group of kids on a field trip during an afternoon event.

Conclusion

Facility management is a critical segment of the sport industry. Public assembly facilities, such as stadiums and arenas, provide significant sources of revenue for sport organizations through modern features such as luxury seating, naming rights, and personal seat licenses. Ancillary services such as concessions, merchandise, and parking are also important economic generators for a sport facility. A facility's ability to generate revenue is directly linked to the services and operational functions it provides. Housekeeping, maintenance, and security services contribute to the overall fan experience at sport and entertainment events.

Facilities pose a number of additional challenges for facility managers, including risk management and complying with the Americans with Disabilities Act. Sport facilities offer many potential dangers. A comprehensive risk management plan will help facility managers minimize the risks associated with a sport event. In addition, the amenities and services offered in a sport facility should be fully accessible to all patrons, including those with disabilities.

Finally, live gate attendance at sporting events is being threatened by the ever improving at-home-viewing experience. From one's couch, a fan can literally have "the best seat in the house" without having to deal with traffic, big crowds, and the rising costs of attendance. Sport organizations must work harder than ever to provide a unique experience at the facility that cannot be found at home. Currently, this is being done in several ways. Aside from the variety of seating options and amenities associated with those seating options described previously, modern facilities are being designed with socialization in mind. Concourses are wider than ever and open so as not to keep attendees from missing the action while they're in line for concessions or meeting with friends. Gathering places, like "The Porch" behind the centerfield wall at Tropicana Field, promote socialization in a sports bar–like atmosphere.

As noted, technology can also aid in enhancing the fan experience. Examples such as more interactive promotions or games displayed on the video boards during stoppages in play to actual bolts of lightning thundering above the crowd at Tampa Bay Lightning games in the Tampa Bay Times Forum are becoming common. More and more teams, such as the New England Patriots and Atlanta Falcons, are introducing mobile applications into their fans' gameday experience. From their phones, fans can purchase seat upgrades, order concessions, watch NFL RedZone, check the current bathroom waiting times, and even purchase what the Falcons call "experience memories," essentially creating a customized experience for each fan with options such as in-seat mascot visits to personal messages on the video board (Florio, 2013; Kaplan, 2014). The Lehigh Valley Iron Pigs can perhaps stake claim to the most outrageous example of technology-aided fan experience enhancements. Prior to the 2013 season, the Iron Pigs installed a urinal gaming system into the men's restrooms which allows male attendees to "compete" against others in digital games controlled by aiming one's stream as instructed by the interactive video display above the urinal. Talk about an experience you can't get at home!

The key takeaway for facility managers is that the televised sport product will continue to improve. High-definition televisions are bigger and better now than they were only a year ago. On-screen graphics, commentaries, and animations, such as the first-down line in football, have become part of the viewing experience that cannot be easily replicated in the facility. Fantasy sports and second-screen content also entice fans to watch from their couch. Sport organizations must not only be aware of these challenges, but also continually strive to provide a unique experience fans cannot realize at home. At all times, facility managers must provide superior facility operations functions and excellent customer service.

chapter 12

Interviews

Interview 12.1

Craig Lovett – Partner/Principal
Paul Lovett – Partner/Principal

Craig and Paul Lovett are among the most experienced professionals in the area of event management, cleaning, waste management, and sustainable strategies for venues and global events. They have organized activities that have supported dozens of mega-events including the Olympic Games, U.S. Open Tennis Championships, Australian Open Tennis Championships, Wimbledon Tennis Championships, ICC World Cup Cricket, Manchester Commonwealth Games, Australian Motorcycle Grand Prix, and many others. Both Craig and Paul are invited to speak all over the world on issues such as venue design, construction, international event project mobilization, labor management, and environmental integrity at public assembly and retail facilities.

Q: What have been the biggest challenges you have encountered during your career?

CL: Learning to respect the true value of relationships, and to make sure I always give more than I take in order to maintain that value recognition.

Q: How do you identify potential events/facilities to approach with your services?

PL: It's about brand alliance and working with companies and individuals that truly value our involvement rather than simply trying to purchase a service that they are prepared to undervalue and expect a discount.

Q: What are the most important issues facing your company now?

CL: Balancing workload with life balance; maintaining a focus on "family first" not only for myself and Brother Paul, but also for the people that work within Incognitus.

Q: What issues do you see evolving in the future?

CL: The journey through the "experience economy" whereby people are valuing the involvement within events by the personal experience they take away from them. There are so many options for the spend of recreational investment, value for money will not cut it alone through the next decade

Q: Are there specific skills sport-management students should look to develop while still in school?

PL: People skills are critical. Learning to acknowledge that we are all of a different makeup, different composition etc., and that "that's ok." To respect diversity in opinion is important in this industry.

Q: How do you identify people skills among your new hires and then develop those people skills among your staff members?

CL: Paul and I have always adopted a "hire-for-cultural-fit-and-teach-the-skills-if-required" approach to our new crew members. And whilst this has on occasions let us down, in the overwhelming majority of times it has served us well over the journey.

Q: When you hire recent graduates at your company, what are the biggest mistakes that you have seen them make?

PL: Many feel that they are "owed a living" and do not have to work to achieve. Over and over again new crew members, especially among the younger generations feel that they simply have to get a job, and the career pathway is assured. Getting a job is just the first step. One has to then continue to develop their skills and demonstrate their commitment.

Q: What specific classes would you recommend students take to best position themselves for a sport-industry job?

CL: Certainly business-related coursework is important! Each campus will have different unique course offerings. Students should use their time on campus to learn about things that will help their career and personal development.

Interview 12.2

Katie White
Associate Director
Campus Recreation
Towson University

Q: Can you describe your career path?

A: I recently took a job as associate director of campus recreation at Towson University where I oversee various programs including outdoor adventures and fitness as well as departmental assessment. Prior to that, I was at the University of Tampa for seven years after completing my master's degree in exercise science at Cleveland State University. Throughout my graduate program, I held a graduate assistant position in campus recreation. In this role, I was responsible for writing policies, procedures, and risk management protocol for the new on-campus recreation facility, as well as working in sales with member services. My undergraduate degree was in leisure studies with a concentration in recreation management from Kent State University. It was during this time where I was first exposed to campus recreation as I worked at our campus recreation facility for two-and-a-half years. I was also fortunate to secure an internship my senior year with the United States Navy as part of their Military Welfare program. I was charged with running the fitness and recreation programs for military spouses and children living at a naval base in Italy.

Q: What were your primary duties at the University of Tampa?

A: One of my primary roles at UT is being the facility manager for our on-campus recreation facility, McNiff Fitness Center. Running a fitness center like McNiff involves a diverse set of tasks dictated by factors such as weather, patron demographics, facility design, and budget. In general, I am responsible for risk management and crowd control, staffing, assisting in class setup, troubleshooting problems as they arose, and equipment purchasing, repairs, and maintenance.

Unlike private gyms or YMCAs that typically deal with the same members on a regular basis, one of the biggest challenges of managing an on-campus recreation facility was trying to keep up with the needs, wants, and interests of a constantly evolving body of people. The student body turns over every four years, and each year, a new group of students from all over the world were introduced to our facility. With that came a wide range of fitness interests and workouts. We were limited in terms of size and space at McNiff, so trying to provide space for these alternative workouts, such as CrossFit, became a challenge. Beyond just space, different workouts (i.e., CrossFit and Yoga) have different requirements with respect to equipment, flooring, sound, and even air temperature. This created scheduling problems when trying to utilize the same functional area space for different activities throughout the day.

Q: How do campus recreation facilities generate revenue and what are the main expenses?

A: Like any facility, the budget dictates a lot of what we're able to do. Unlike private gyms, however, our primary focus is not on generating revenue for the university, but rather providing recreation and fitness options for the entire campus community. Our operating revenue comes primarily from university subsidies. The university's facilities department funds structural related expenditures, while student government funds student salaries and the programs and services offered throughout the facility. We also have a capital line budget for capital replacements. Staffing is by far the biggest expenditure in most campus recreation facilities. When you're open seven days a week from morning until night, you're going to need a lot of workers. Other expenses include general facility and equipment maintenance, housekeeping, and student programing—which includes purchasing equipment for student rentals and putting on campus recreation-related events.

Q: Are there any general trends you see emerging in the industry?

A: Budgeting is always going to be an issue in campus recreation facility management, especially at state-funded public schools. School budgets are decreasing, and that trickles down to campus recreation. Figuring out how to adjust with less money is critical. Keeping track of what's working, what's not, and what's working for your peers at other institutions is paramount.

Aside from budgeting, risk management is another challenge facing the industry moving forward. Right now, two of the hot button issues in risk management are concussion protocol and active shooter policies. Being prepared in these situations is vital, as one may have limited time to respond/plan once a situation or emergency occurs.

Q: What advice would you give to students starting their career?

A: Industry experience is a must for any student aspiring to work in campus recreation, let alone facility management. Most entry-level coordinator positions in campus recreation require a master's degree AND one to two years of experience in a campus recreation environment. The graduate degree requirement has the potential to be burdensome, as oftentimes, low starting salaries make it difficult to pay off additional student loan debt. Qualified applicants should also be CPR/AED certified, preferably as an instructor, and if the facility has a pool, CPO (certified pool operator) certification is a must.

Study Questions

1. Identify and define the four treatment options of a risk-management plan.
2. Why is it important for a sport facility to comply with the Americans with Disabilities Act (ADA)? Which areas of the facility must be accessible to persons with disabilities?
3. Define demand-based pricing. Why has this ticket pricing strategy become more commonplace in the sport industry?
4. What are the advantages and disadvantages of operating concessions in-house? What about through a private contractor?
5. What is a personal seat license? How does a PSL generate revenue for a sport facility?
6. How do housekeeping and maintenance operations contribute to the fan experience?
7. Discuss the versatility of the parking lot in terms of generating revenue for a facility.

Learning Activities

1. Attend a sport event at your college. Rather than experiencing the game solely as a fan, pay attention to the different ways the athletic department is generating revenue through the facility. Bring a notebook and record the various revenue sources. What types of ancillary services are offered? Is corporate sponsorship or advertising present in the facility? Does the public address announcer mention athletic department sponsors during stoppages in play? Identify two areas where the facility could generate additional revenue for the athletic department.
2. While you're at the game, also take note of what is being done to compete with the at-home experience (particularly for football and men's basketball games). What elements of the event cannot be replicated at home? How is the facility incorporating technology into the fan experience?
3. Conduct an interview with a facility manager. Discuss the potential risks associated with an event at the facility. Using the information in this chapter as a reference, complete the following risk category matrix with the risks you identified with the facility manager. After completing the matrix, discuss how you would treat each of the risk categories. Identify strategies you would use to reduce the frequency and/or severity of those risks.

	High Frequency	Moderate Frequency	Low Frequency
High Loss			
Moderate Loss			
Low Loss			

References

Ammon, R. (2003). Risk management process. In D.J. Cotton, and J.T. Wolohan (Eds.), *Law for recreation and sport managers* (3rd ed., pp. 296–307). Dubuque, IA: Kendall/Hunt Publishing Company.

Ammon, R., Southall, R.M., & Nagel, M.S. (2010). *Sport facility management: Organizing events and mitigating risks* (2nd ed.). Morgantown, WV: Fitness Information Technology, Inc.

Amway Center. (n.d.). *Premium seating.* Retrieved from http://www.amwaycenter.com/tickets-and-seating/premium-seating

Battle, R., Bosshardt, A., Bridge, T., Hanson, C., Savage, J., Shaffer, A.,…Thorpe, A. (2014). *All to play for: Football money league.* Manchester, UK: Sports Business Group at Deloitte.

Belzer, J. (2013, November 21). *Barclays Center teams up with Cisco to revolutionize In-Venue Fan Engagement.* Retrieved from http://www.forbes.com/sites/jasonbelzer/2013/11/21/barclays-center-teams-up-with-cisco-to-revolutionize-in-venue-fan-engagement/

Braves. (n.d.). *Parking options.* Retrieved from http://atlanta.braves.mlb.com/atl/ballpark/directions/index.jsp?content=parking

Cohen, A. (2012). Building sponsors into the design of spectator facilities. *Athletic Business.* Retrieved from http://www.athleticbusiness.com/Fundraising/building-sponsors-into-the-design-of-spectator-facilities.html

Department of Justice, Civil Rights Division, Disability Rights Section. (1997). Accessible stadiums. Retrieved on from http://www.ada.gov/stadium.pdf

Department of Justice, Civil Rights Division, Disability Rights Section. (2009). A guide to disability rights. Retrieved from http://www.ada.gov/cguide.pdf

Deptolla, C. (2014, April 25). Miller Park food offerings go way beyond the brat. *Journal Sentinel.* Retrieved from http://www.jsonline.com/entertainment/dining/miller-park-food-offerings-go-way-beyond-the-brat-b99251306z1-256547361.html

Dodgers. (n.d.). *United Club suites.* Retrieved from http://losangeles.dodgers.mlb.com/la/ticketing/suites.jsp#pricing

Florio, M. (2013, August 29). *Pats try to upgrade in-stadium experience with WiFi improvements, app.* Retrieved from http://profootballtalk.nbcsports.com/2013/08/29/pats-try-to-upgrade-in-stadium-experience-with-wifi-upgrades-app/

Fried, G. (2010). *Managing sport facilities* (2nd ed.). Champaign, IL: Human Kinetics.

Gorman, W. (2003). That asphalt jungle in not just for cars: Making money from your parking lot. *Facility Manager.* Retrieved from http://www.iaam.org/facility_manager/pages/2003_jan_feb/Feature_1.htm

Greenberg, M.J. (2000). *The stadium game* (2nd ed.). Milwaukee, WI: Marquette University Press.

Hambrick, M., Simmons, J., Greenhalgh, G., & Brownlee, E. (2009, March). *Grading the alcohol policies of professional sports leagues: A practical application of dram shop statues.* Paper presented at the Sport and Recreation Law Association Conference, San Antonio, TX.

Howard, D.R., & Crompton, J.L. (2005). *Financing sport* (2nd ed.). Morgantown, WV: Fitness Information Technology.

Kaplan, D. (2014, March 24). NFL ups fun factor via technology: Team apps could offer experiences. *SportsBusiness Journal.* Retrieved from http://www.sportsbusinessdaily.com/Journal/Issues/2014/03/24/Leagues-and-Governing-Bodies/NFL-tech.aspx

Klepal, D. (2013, November 14). Cobb County paying $300 million toward Braves new stadium. *The Atlanta Journal-Constitution.* Retrieved from http://www.ajc.com/news/news/local-govt-politics/cobb-county-paying-302-million-toward-braves-new-s/nbr4m/

Leuty, R. (2013, May 8). Top 10 stadium, arena naming rights deals. *San Francisco Business Times.* Retrieved from http://www.bizjournals.com/sanfrancisco/blog/2013/05/stadium-naming-rights-deals-49ers-levis.html

MetLife Stadium. (n.d.). *About us.* Retrieved from http://www.metlifestadium.com/stadium/about-us

Migala, D. (2007, June 3). Parking lot drives revenue growth: A look into parking space business opportunities. *The Migala Report.* Retrieved from http://migalareport.com/node/239

Mingus, M. (2005). The ADA: Does your facility demonstrate "good faith progress" towards compliance? *Facility Manager.* Retrieved from http://www.iaam.org/facility_manager/pages/2005_Apr_May/LEGAL.HTM

Muret , D. (2013, September 30). Deal triples value for Magic clubs. *SportsBusiness Journal.* Retrieved from http://www.sportsbusinessdaily.com/Journal/Issues/2013/09/30/Facilities/Magic.aspx

Muret, D. (2014, April 14). Australian deal is a first for Sporting Innovations, its Fan360. *SportsBusiness Journal.* Retrieved from http://www.sportsbusinessdaily.com/Journal/Issues/2014/04/14/Facilities/Fan360.aspx?hl

NCAA. (2013). *Revenues & expenses 2004-2012: NCAA Division I intercollegiate athletics programs report.* Indianapolis, IN: National Collegiate Athletic Association.

Orioles. (n.d.). *Individual game seating and pricing.* Retrieved from http://baltimore.orioles.mlb.com/bal/ticketing/seating_pricing.jsp

Pearson, S., & Beasley, D. (2014, April 11). *Atlanta stadium for Falcons prompts bond fight.* Retrieved from http://www.bloomberg.com/news/2014-04-10/atlanta-stadium-for-billionaire-s-falcons-prompts-bond-fight.html

Price, C.L. (2007). Choosing and using contract security: Learn how to make the most of your venue's investment in "ambassadors for hire." *Venue Safety and Security.* Retrieved from http://www.www.ifea.com/pdf/VSSVol1Issue1Summer2007.pdf

PricewaterhouseCoopers. (2013). *At the gate and beyond: Outlook for the sports market in North America through 2017.* Retrieved from http://www.pwc.com/en_US/us/industry/entertainment-media/publications/assets/pwc-sports-outlook-north-america.pdf

Rosenburg, M. (2013, May 9). 49ers stadium revenue tops $1 billion after Santa Clara leaders approve Levi's Stadium name deal. *San Jose Mercury News.* Retrieved from http://www.mercurynews.com/ci_23211519/49ers-stadium-revenue-tops-1-billion-after-santa

Russo, F.E., Escklisen, L.A., & Stewart, R.J. (2009). *Public assembly facility management: Principles and practices* (2nd ed.). Coppell, TX: International Association of Assembly Managers, Inc.

Sandomir, R. (2008, July 18). Giants seat licenses priced from $1,000 to $20,000. *New York Times.* Retrieved from http://www.nytimes.com/2008/07/18/sports/football/18seats.html?_r=0

Schupmann, M. (2013, June 20). Food offerings at Kauffman Stadium hit a culinary home run. *The Kansas City Star.* Retrieved from http://www.kansascity.com/entertainment/restaurants/article318941/Food-offerings-at-Kauffman-Stadium-hit-a-culinary-home-run.html

Sedlak, R., & Traugott, A. (2002). Is your venue ready for an incident? *Facility Manager Magazine.* Retrieved from http://www.iaam.org/facility_manager/pages/2002_Jan_feb/Feature_7.htm

Sharp, L.A., Moorman, A.M., & Claussen, C.L. (2007). *Sport law: A managerial approach.* Scottsdale, AZ: Holcomb Hathaway, Publishers.

Sporting Innovations. (n.d.). *Fan 360.* Retrieved from http://www.sportinginnovations.com/fan360/

Stotlar, D.K. (1997). Operations and maintenance. In M.L. Walker, and D.K. Stotlar (Eds.), *Sport facility management* (pp. 31–42). Sudbury, MA: Jones and Bartlett Publishers, Inc.

Sun Life Stadium. (n.d.) *Parking.* Retrieved from http://www.sunlifestadium.com/parking

Trumpbour, R.C. (2007). *The new cathedrals: Politics and media in the history of stadium construction.* Syracuse, NY: Syracuse University Press.

Tucker, T. (2013, November 12). Braves plan to build new stadium in Cobb. *The Atlanta Journal-Constitution.* Retrieved from http://www.ajc.com/news/sports/baseball/braves-plan-to-build-new-stadium-in-cobb/nbpNQ/

Matthew T. Brown • *University of South Carolina*

Sport Finance

CHAPTER OBJECTIVES

After reading this chapter, you will be able to:

- Properly define basic terminology common to finance and accounting.
- Understand the importance of sound financial management practices in sport management.
- Identify and interpret basic financial statements.
- Have the ability to perform a basic analysis of an organization's financial performance.
- Properly identify five forms of financing a sport organization.

KEY TERMS

Debt

Expenses

Finance

Financial management

Revenues

Wealth maximization

> *Professional baseball is on the wane. Salaries must come down or the interest of the public must be increased in some way. If one or the other does not happen, bankruptcy stares every team in the face.*
>
> —Chicago White Stockings owner Albert Spalding, 1881

> *Anyone who quotes profits of a baseball club is missing the point. Under generally accepted accounting principles, I can turn a $4 million profit into a $2 million loss and I could get every national accounting firm to agree with me.*
>
> —Paul Beeston, then a Toronto Blue Jays vice president, formerly president and COO of MLB, now president and CEO of the Blue Jays and Rogers Centre, 1979

> *You go through The Sporting News for the last 100 years, and you will find two things are always true. You never have enough pitching, and nobody ever made money.*
>
> —Former MLB players' association head Donald Fehr, 1995

Introduction

Successful sport managers have many things in common. For one, they pay attention to the current activities of their organization and monitor environmental factors that might impact operations. For example, the Great Recession, lasting from December 2007 to June 2009, followed a period of rapid economic expansion starting in the 1990s. As the economy expanded, the sport industry grew. New venues were built, leagues formed, and teams were added. Corporate America funded much of the sport industry's expansion through advertising, sponsorship, ticket purchases, and luxury suite consumption. The impact of the Great Recession on the sport industry was therefore significant. Advertising spending in sport decreased 3.2% in 2009, while sponsorship spending grew at its smallest rate ever, 2.2%. No other recession in the 20 years prior to the Great Recession had a similar negative impact on sport spending (IEG, 2009).

Post-recession, sport sponsorship revenues once again grew. While $11.6 billion was spent on sport sponsorship in 2009, $14.35 billion is forecasted to be spent in 2014 (IEG, 2014). While the economy is not growing as it did prior to the Great Recession, growth has been slow and stable.

Today, rather than economic conditions impacting sponsorship revenues, a change in corporate priorities is slowing revenue growth in this area. The greatest threat to traditional sponsorship revenues is the shift of advertising spending away from sponsorship to digital platforms, which includes social media and mobile advertising. Smaller sport organizations are expected to be particularly hurt by this shift and will be at a financial disadvantage as a result (IEG, 2014). Figure 13.1 illustrates the disparity in sponsorship revenues for kits (player uniform advertising) in the Barclays Premier League.

FIGURE 13.1 Annual Value of Premier League Kits: 2014-2015

Team	Sponsor	Manufacturer	Value
Manchester United	Chevrolet	Nike	$ 108.9
Arsenal	Fly Emirates	Puma	$ 100.0
Chelsea	Samsung	Adidas	$ 80.0
Liverpool	Standard Chartered	Warrior	$ 75.0
Manchester City	Etihad	Nike	$ 53.4
Tottenham Hotspur	AIA	Under Armour	$ 43.4
Queens Park Rangers	Air Asia	Nike	$ 19.1
Aston Villa	Dafabet	Macron	$ 14.5
Everton	Chang Beer	Ubmro	$ 10.9
Newcastle United	Wonga	Puma	$ 10.0
Sunderland	Bidvest	Adidas	$ 8.3
Hull City	12Bet	Ubmro	$ 7.6
Swansea City	Goldenway/GWFX	Adidas	$ 6.7
Crystal Palace	Neteller	Macron	$ 5.5
Stoke City	Bet365	Warrior	$ 5.0
West Ham United	Alpari	Adidas	$ 5.0
West Bromwich Albion	Intuit QuickBooks	Adidas	$ 4.5
Burnley	Fun88	Puma	$ 3.3
Leicester City	King Power	Puma	$ 1.7
Southampton	Veho	Southampton	$ 1.7

Source: More than a shirt. (ESPN FC, 2014).

At the start of the 2014-2015 Premier League Season, Manchester United had a $107.2 million sponsorship advantage from the sale of rights, both sponsorship and manufacturing, from *only* its kit deal as compared to Southampton ("More than a shirt," 2014). Further, the top six clubs generate at least $40 million each while the bottom 14 bring in less than $20 million each. For the bottom 10 clubs, less than $10 million is generated through kit sponsorships during the year. There clearly is a differentiation between the wealthiest Premier League clubs and the poorest, making it even more difficult for some clubs to compete financially. Manchester United's kit deal with Nike ends after the season. It will be replaced by Adidas, doubling in value to $1.3 billion over 13 years. This is the most lucrative kit manufacturing deal in soccer history.

While there is great disparity between the top clubs and the bottom clubs in the Premier League, change in sponsor priorities can cause a top team to lose significant sponsorship revenue. In 2014, Dale Earnhardt, Jr. learned his sponsor, the National Guard, was ending its $32 million sponsorship of his car despite Earnhardt having his best seasons on the track since 2004. In addition, the National Guard was ending its $12 million sponsorship of Graham Rahal's IndyCar team.

To be successful, sport managers also must pay attention to the future operations of their organization. In professional sport, labor relations often impact the operation of teams and leagues as new collective bargaining agreements (CBAs) are negotiated. The National Football League (NFL) once again restructured its revenue-sharing system between team owners and players when it signed its last CBA in 2011. The change in revenue-sharing should make it easier for a few small-market teams to remain financially viable while enabling large market teams to use their facilities to generate and keep a majority of locally produced revenues. The Dallas Cowboys sold naming rights to their new stadium to AT&T for $500 million in a 25-year deal. The team charges up to $75 to park at a game, $10 for a program, and $8.50 for a beer. The stadium has hosted a Kentucky basketball game, an LSU football game, and the NCAA Final Four, and is the site for the first College Football Championship game. The Cowboys keep all revenue from each event held in their stadium. The National Hockey League (NHL), the most international of the North American leagues, faces financial challenges as the exchange rate between the U.S. dollar and the Canadian dollar (Loonie) fluctuates. All sport organizations faced some uncertainty, though, after the collapse of the financial markets in 2008 and through the Great Recession.

Dale Earnhardt's loss of the National Guard sponsorship discussed earlier came after a long debate in Congress related to the use of taxpayer dollars to fund sporting events (Gluck, 2014). Early in 2009, then Massachusetts Senator John Kerry proposed the TARP Taxpayer Protection Corporate Responsibility Act after celebrity website TMZ posted a story questioning the use of taxpayer funds at the Professional Golf Association's (PGA) Northern Trust Open (Newport, 2009). The act would prevent any TARP recipient from hosting, sponsoring, or paying for entertainment events unless the company received a waiver from the Treasury Secretary ("Secretary of Golf," 2009). The TMZ story stated that Northern Trust, recipient of $1.6 billion from the Troubled

Asset Relief Program (TARP), held lavish parties, fancy dinners, and concerts with famous singers. After learning of the sponsorship, Representative Barney Frank sent a letter to Northern Trust, co-signed by 17 additional congressmen, demanding that it return the $1.6 billion. Columnists from across the political spectrum joined in the criticism, including Maureen Dowd and Bill O'Reilly (Newport). Ignored in the criticism were the potential business benefits the sponsorship brought to Northern Trust, such as providing access to decision makers in business, reaching potential new customers, and increasing the firm's visibility.

At the time TARP was proposed, the banking industry spent $900 million on sport sponsorship rights fees and $122.3 million on sport advertising. Of the top 10 stadium naming rights holders, four were companies operating in the financial sector.

While legislation restricting sponsorship spending did not pass in Congress, the impact of the earlier government outcry was damaging. In 2009, Morgan Stanley, recipient of $10 billion in TARP funds, and Wells Fargo, recipient of $25 billion, announced changes to their golf sponsorships. Morgan Stanley decided to remain a sponsor of the Memorial Tournament, but company executives did not entertain clients at the event. Wells Fargo, owner of Wachovia, cut its presence at the Wachovia Championships held outside Charlotte, North Carolina (Newport, 2009). Congress also began to watch its sport sponsorship spending closely. Missouri Senator Claire McCaskill held hearings on the military's recruitment programs and began to criticize sponsorship spending as an ineffective way to recruit soldiers. The debate in the Senate over whether the use of taxpayer dollars was warranted revolved around the value of the exposure created through the sponsorship of its NASCAR and IndyCar teams versus the number of recruiting prospects gained through the sponsorship program. For McCaskill and others in the Senate, exposure alone was not enough. The sponsorship needed to lead to prospects and new recruits so these taxpayer-funded sponsorships were ended (Vanden Brook, 2014).

There are many environmental factors that affect the current and future operations of sport organizations. These pressures shape the way the sport industry has evolved and influence how it will continue to evolve. Successful sport managers understand the impact of various forces. However, the most successful sport managers also must have an understanding of the *goal of the firm*. The goal of most firms is **wealth maximization**, the maximization of the overall value of the firm or organization. To truly understand wealth maximization, sport managers must have a solid understanding of finance.

Wealth maximization
The goal or outcome of financial management for most organizations; increasing the overall value of the firm.

Finance

Finance
The science of fund management that incorporates concepts from accounting, statistics, and economics.

Financial management
Financial decision-making within a firm with wealth maximization being the goal for most organizations.

Finance is the science of fund management that incorporates concepts from accounting, statistics, and economics. Within finance, there are three distinct sectors. One has been discussed already, **financial management**, which focuses upon financial decision making with the outcome for most organizations being wealth maximization. The *money and capital markets* sector includes securities markets like the New York Stock Exchange (NYSE) and the Chicago Mercantile Exchange. Investment banking, insurance, and mutual fund management are also in this sector. The **investments** sector includes firms like Merrill Lynch and Edward Jones. The focus of the investments sector is portfolio management. Companies help individuals and institutions invest in securities and select investment choices based upon risk and the risk tolerance of the investor.

Most working in the sport industry will not be involved with the investments sector or the money and capital markets sector. However, everyone working in sport will either be directly or indirectly impacted by the financial management of their organization. As the goal of financial management is wealth maximization, those working within financial management of a sport organization are concerned with the acquisition and use of funds to meet this goal.

For wealth maximization to occur, the finance department forecasts future revenues and plans for future costs and expenses. In sport, this may include calculating cash flow increases resulting from higher television rights fees, and determining how much the organization can enhance player payroll as a result of the forecast. The finance department also fills one portion of the control

The Wall Street Bull is a well-known symbol of stock market and financial optimism

Shutterstock, Inc.

function of management. Through coordination with other departments in the organization, efficiency of operation and resource utilization can be achieved. The finance department makes investment and financing decisions while working with financial markets and investment firms when necessary. The type of debt financing used when constructing a new arena is but one example.

Although firms in the sport industry may be structured as a for-profit, not-for-profit, or governmental entity, in terms of for-profit enterprises, sport has many commonalities with other types of business. Therefore, much that applies to the financial management of a sport organization is similar to the financial management of an organization in any other industry. These commonalities include value creation, or increasing the value of a firm over time, and revenue growth. However, there are areas of difference.

One major difference is the wide variety of ownership objectives within sport (Foster, Greyser, & Walsh, 2006). Typically, companies within an industry compete for wealth maximization. Owners in professional sport, however, might not be primarily interested in this goal. Rather, they may be more interested in winning championships. Or, they might be seeking celebrity status by being one of a select few professional sport-franchise owners nationwide. Another goal may be to protect a community asset. Particularly relating to winning championships, differing objectives of owners can harm the competitive balance in a league. Extremely wealthy owners with a willingness to incur financial losses over several seasons can create an imbalance in competition. As a result, at the beginning of a season, only a few teams may have a realistic chance of winning a championship. Leagues have reacted by implementing salary

Jerry Jones has worked tirelessly to enhance the Dallas Cowboys brand and spent extensively to win championships.

constraints, revenue sharing, and other similar mechanisms that create both competition between franchises on the field and cooperation regarding financial management of it.

Basic Finance and Accounting Concepts

To truly understand financial management and the financial operations of an organization, a sport manager needs a basic knowledge of accounting. Accounting data provides information that can be used to make decisions regarding the use of limited resources. For example, if transportation costs are expected to increase by 15% during the season due to a sudden increase in fuel prices, an organization needs to determine if it can absorb the increased costs within its budget. If not, the organization must determine whether alternate, cheaper forms of transportation are available or if expenses can be cut elsewhere.

Accounting data also helps an organization effectively control human and material resources. Data from sales revenues can be used to determine which intern is generating the most revenue for the organization and which intern will be hired for a full-time job at the end of a season. Finally, accounting data can be used to ensure that ownership of resources is maintained. Inventory can be tracked and equipment replacement cycles can be developed using accounting data.

Importantly for financial management, accounting data includes information regarding an organization's revenues, expenses, and debt. **Revenues** include money coming into an organization. Selling tickets is a common revenue-generating activity in sport. **Expenses** are costs incurred by the organization. Common costs in sport include wages, utilities, equipment, and transportation. **Debt** is the owing of money to others.

Revenues
Money coming into an organization. Selling tickets is one common example of generating revenue in sport.

Expenses
Costs incurred by the organization. Common costs in sport include wages, utilities, equipment, and transportation.

Debt
The owing of money to others.

Accountants prepare many financial statements, but four are particularly important for use in financial management. These include budgets, income statements (or profit and loss statements), balance sheets, and statements of cash flow. Each financial statement is important and each is used in slightly different ways. They are the primary source of information used to assess the financial health and performance of an organization.

Budget

Simply stated, a *budget* outlines where a business intends to spend its money and where it plans to receive revenue. It is a tool for financial planning. A budget is created based upon projections made about the future financial performance of the organization. For example, Figure 13.2 shows the 2014-2015 operating budget of the "State University's" athletic department. The department estimates that revenues will be $90.4 million over the fiscal year. The State University estimates a $10.3-million net operating surplus over fiscal year 2014-2015. After transfers to cover the costs of building, renovating, and maintaining facilities, the department is left with almost a $2.6-million increase in its current fund balance. State University has been using its surplus to fund the department's capital needs (i.e., facility renovations and improvements).

From a planning standpoint, a financial manager can use several budgets types to track his or her organization's revenues, expenses, cash, and capital expenditures. These budgets-within-budgets depict the impact of the budgeting process on overall organizational revenues, expenses, cash flows, and capital expenditures. For example, the State University's athletic department has three budgets-within-budgets. The department prepares an operating budget (see Figure 13.2) revenue budget and a capital expenditure budget. During the 2014-2015 fiscal year, the department plans to transfer $7.7 million from its operating budget to its capital expenditure budget. It does not anticipate a transfer to or from its revenue (endowment and other funds) budget however. The department denotes transfers to its other budgets under the *Transfers and capital expenditures* section.

Income Statement

An *income statement* is also known also as a profit and loss (P & L) statement. The income statement measures an organization's expenditures and receipts between two specific points in time. It consists of three sections: operating, nonoperating, and net income. The operating section contains the operating revenues and expenses of an organization. Operating revenues typically include proceeds from sales. In sport, this may include ticket sales, sponsorship sales, advertising income, parking revenue, concessions revenue, and merchandise revenues. Operating expenses may include salaries, selling expenses, and general and administrative expenses. Stepwise, expenses are subtracted from revenues, leaving operating income, also referred to as earnings before interest, taxes, depreciation, and amortization (EBITDA). Or,

Revenues
– Expenses
Operating Income (EBITDA)

The nonoperating section includes noncash expenses like depreciation and amortization expenses. Also included are interest and tax expenses. Stepwise, depreciation and amortization expenses are subtracted from operating income to leave earnings before interest and taxes (EBIT). Interest expenses are subtracted from EBIT to leave earnings before taxes (EBT). Corporate income taxes are calculated based upon the firm's EBT. Or,

FIGURE 13.2 State University Athletic Department Budget

Fiscal Year 2014-2015 Operating Budget (in thousands)

Revenues	Budgeted Amount	% of Total
Spectator Admissions		
Football	$31,570	35%
Basketball	1,895	2%
Hockey	1,857	2%
Other	229	0%
Conference Distributions		
Television (Football and Basketball)	12,660	14%
Football Bowl Games	1,747	2%
NCAA Basketball	2,612	3%
Other	400	0%
Priority Seating and other Annual Gifts	13,600	15%
Corporate Sponsorship	9,880	11%
Licensing Royalties	3,800	4%
Radio	2,100	2%
Facilities	1,870	2%
Concessions/Parking	1,860	2%
Other	937	1%
Investment Income	3,444	4%
Current Revenues	$90,461	100%
Expenses		
Salaries	$30,860	38%
Student Financial Aid	15,129	19%
Team and Game Expense	15,005	19%
Facilities	7,093	9%
Deferred Maintenance Fund Transfer	4,500	6%
Other Operating and Administrative Expenses	6,575	8%
Debt Service Transfer to Plant Fund	1,029	1%
Current Expenses	$80,191	100%
Net Operating Surplus	$10,270	
Transfers and Capital Expenditures		
Capital Expenditures from Current Funds		
And Transfers to Plant Fund	$(7,700)	
Transfers to Endowment Fund	—	
Net Transfers and Capital Expenditures	$(7,700)	
Increase (Decrease) in Current Fund Balances	$ 2,570	

Operating Income (EBITDA)
− Depreciation
− Amortization
EBIT
− Interest
EBT
− Income Taxes

The third section is net income. Here, income taxes are subtracted from EBT to leave the increase or decrease in the organization's income over two points in time. Or,

EBT
− Income Taxes
Net Income

Combined, the income statement framework is:

Revenues
− Expenses
Operating Income (EBITDA)
− Depreciation
− Amortization
EBIT
− Interest
EBT
− Income Taxes
Net Income

Figure 13.3 shows a sample income statement of the Wisconsin Ham Fighters, a professional sport franchise. From the income statement it can be seen that approximately 38% of the team's income comes from television and radio revenue, or $95.9 million. An additional $37 million (14.7% of overall income) is transferred to the team from the league's properties' division and $16.4 million is transferred from the league to the team for the Ham Fighters' share of road game revenues. Revenue from league properties comes from the sale of licensed merchandise. Combined, approximately $149.3 million comes from the league to the Ham Fighters. This is 59.3% of their overall revenue in 2014.

Most of the operating expenses of the team go to player costs. During the 2014 fiscal year, player costs were $140.7 million. This was 60.9% of overall operating expenses.

FIGURE 13.3 2014 Wisconsin Ham Fighters Income Statement

Wisconsin Ham Fighters Statements of Income
Year ended March 31, 2014

OPERATING INCOME	
Ticket & Media Income	
Home games (net)	$ 31,097,266
Road games	16,175,953
Television and radio	95,901,900
TOTAL TICKET AND MEDIA INCOME	$ 143,884,218
Other Operating Income	
Luxury site income	$ 13,020,027
Properties income (Other League Revenue)	37,005,636
Marketing/Retail Operations (net)	44,373,516
Other—Local Media, Concessions and parking (net)	13,365,493
TOTAL OTHER OPERATING INCOME	$ 107,764,672
TOTAL OPERATING INCOME	$ 251,648,890
OPERATING EXPENSE	
Player costs	$ 140,777,731
Game expenses (Operations/Maintenance (net))	7,816,059
General and Administrative	32,169,400
Team expenses	26,790,015
Sales and Marketing expenses	23,684,410
TOTAL OPERATING EXPENSES	$ 231,237,615
PROFIT (LOSS) FROM OPERATIONS	$ 20,411,275
OTHER INCOME (EXPENSE)	$(11,355,506)
Income before expansion revenue and provision for income taxes	9,055,769
Provision for income taxes	$ 4,973,500
NET INCOME before expansion revenue	$ 4,082,269

Balance Sheet

The *balance sheet* measures the financial condition of an organization at a specific point in time. The balance sheet reflects an organization's stock, or a rough estimate of its wealth. There are three sections of a balance sheet. *Assets* indicate ownership and include items like cash, inventory, accounts receivable, land, equipment, and buildings. *Liabilities* are financial obligations and debts owed to others. Accounts payable, accrued expenses, and long-term debt are examples of liabilities. *Owners' equity* reflects the owners' investment in the company and includes retained earnings, paid-in capital, and stock held by the organization. At all times, the value of an organization's assets must equal the value of its liabilities plus owners' equity. This equation is:

Assets = Liabilities + Owners' Equity.

On the balance sheet, assets and liabilities are listed in order of *liquidity* and are divided into short-term and long-term accounts.

The Ham Fighters' Balance Sheet can be seen in Figure 13.4. Assets were \$302.8 million at the end of the 2014 fiscal year. Current assets, those assets that can quickly be converted into cash, totaled \$44.5 million. This was 14.7% of total assets. The majority of the Ham Fighters' assets were investments. In total, the Ham Fighters hold \$168.5 million in investments. This amounts to over half of the assets owned by the franchise (55.7%).

The total liabilities (current + long term) of the team were \$66.2 million (see Figure 13.4). Within the next year, the Ham Fighters will pay \$5 million in deferred compensation. This is a current liability. Deferred compensation owed after the current year is a long-term liability. The Ham Fighters owe players an additional \$11.5 million in long-term deferred compensation. Equity was \$236.6 million with a majority being retained earnings (99.7%).

Statement of Cash Flows

A *statement of cash flows* measures cash moving into and out of an organization. For publicly traded firms, preparing a statement of cash flows is a relatively new requirement. The Financial Accounting and Standards Board (FASB) required companies to present a statement of cash flows in published financial statements beginning in 1987.

In sport especially, statements of cash flows are extremely important as they provide the best picture on the overall financial health of the organization. A statement of cash flows differs from income statements. This is due to the difference between a firm's cash flows and accounting activities. For example, on an income statement there are several recorded expenses, like depreciation and amortization expenses, that are noncash expenses. While counted as expenses on the income statement they do not negatively impact cash.

Sport leagues have received several favorable rulings from the Internal Revenue Service (IRS) that have enabled team owners to create tax shelters through their franchise purchase. Additionally, the U.S. Congress has enacted laws that enable the sport franchise owner to amortize the value of the franchise when purchased over the first 15 years of ownership. Therefore, franchise owners may have large depreciation and amortization expenses entered on the income

FIGURE 13.4 2014 Wisconsin Ham Fighters Balance Sheet

Wisconsin Ham Fighters Balance Sheet Year ended March 31, 2014	
ASSETS	
Current Assets	
Cash	$ 3,686,648
Inventories	4,227,311
Unamortized signing bonuses	15,167,782
Accounts Receivable	9,856,132
Deferred income taxes	7,536,534
Other current assets	4,033,842
TOTAL CURRENT ASSETS	$ 44,508,250
INVESTMENTS	$168,526,011
Property & Equipment (net)	51,492,416
Other Assets	
Unamortized signing bonuses	15,495,649
Deferred income taxes	—
Other noncurrent assets	22,784,489
TOTAL OTHER ASSETS	$ 38,280,137
TOTAL ASSETS	$302,806,815
LIABILITIES AND STOCKHOLDERS' EQUITY	
Current Liabilities	
Current maturities of long-term liabilities (Deferred Compensation)	$ 5,022,429
Notes payable	1,016,187
Accounts payable	2,826,248
Accrued expenses	12,502,389
Accrued income taxes	—
Deferred revenues	10,251,042
TOTAL CURRENT LIABILITIES	$ 31,618,295
Long-Term Liabilities	
Note payable	$ 8,594,002
Deferred compensation	11,516,509
Other	14,456,667
TOTAL LONG-TERM LIABILITIES	$ 34,567,178
Stockholders' Equity	
Common stock and additional paid in capital	$ 22,670,747
Retained earnings	235,904,954
Accumulated other comprehensive income	(21,954,360)
TOTAL STOCKHOLDERS' EQUITY	$236,621,341
TOTAL LIABILITIES AND STOCKHOLDERS' EQUITY	$302,806,815

statement. As stated in the chapter's opening quote, this could turn an actual $4 million profit into a $2 million "book" loss. However, while the club has an accounting loss of $2 million, it likely will see an increase in cash flows over the same period.[1] Most sport teams can follow Generally Accepted Accounting Procedures (GAAP) and use depreciation and amortization expenses to make the income statement look like the team is losing money when actually the team has increased its cash position from the previous year. This in part explains why throughout history owners have claimed that they are not making money.

Cash flow is the sum of net income plus noncash expenses minus noncash revenues, or

$$\text{Cash Flow} = \text{Net Income} + \text{Noncash expenses} - \text{Noncash revenues}$$

Noncash expenses include the amortization of intangibles, depreciation, and accounts payable. Noncash revenues are items like accounts receivable and accrued revenues not yet collected.

To calculate cash flows over a period of time, several adjustments to net income are made. First, sources of cash, or cash inflows, are added to net income. Cash inflows occur when noncash assets decrease, liabilities increase, or owners' equity increases. Next, uses of cash, or cash outflows, are deducted from net income. Cash outflows occur when noncash assets increase, liabilities decrease, or owners' equity decreases.

Statements of cash flows are divided into three areas. The first is cash flow from operating activities. Here adjustments to net income are made which result from positive and negative cash flows related to the firm's basic operating activities. Figure 13.5 is a statement of cash flows for Under Armour®. The adjustments made related to operating activities include the addition of the organization's noncash items (depreciation and amortization expenses). Further changes to accounts receivable, inventories, accounts payable, and current liabilities are recorded in this section.

The second section of the statement of cash flows is cash flow from investing activities. Here, adjustments are made to cash that are related to the purchase and sale of property, plant, equipment, and other noncurrent assets. Through the second quarter of 2014, Under Armour® had purchased over $68 million in property and equipment (see Figure 13.5).

The final section is cash flow from financing activities. The effects of financing transactions like issuance and repayment of debt, issuance and repayment of stock, and payments of dividends are recorded in this section. Under Armour® received $150 million from a long-term loan during the second quarter of 2014 while paying off $106.3 million of long-term debt (see Figure 13.5).

1 This explains why the values of sport franchises typically increase over time. Without positive cash flows, there would be no increase in franchise value.

FIGURE 13.5 Under Armour Statement of Cash Flows

Under Armour, Inc., and Subsidiaries Consolidated Statements of Cash Flows (Thousands)	
Cash flows from operating activities	
Net income	$ 31,228
Adjustments to reconcile net income to net cash used in operating activities	
Depreciation and amortization	$ 34,347
Unrealized foreign currency exchange rate (gains) losses	$ (100)
Loss on disposal of property and equipment	$ 73
Stock-based compensation	$ 23,860
Deferred income taxes	$ (7,388)
Changes in reserves and allowances	$ 1
Changes in operating assets and liabilities, net of effects of acquisitions:	
Accounts receivable	$ (53,090)
Inventories	$(195,406)
Prepaid expenses and other assets	$ (16,514)
Accounts payable	$ 175,674
Accrued expenses and other liabilities	$ (14,286)
Income taxes payable and receivable	$ (24,065)
Net cash used in operating activities	$ (45,666)
Cash flows from investing activities	
Purchases of property and equipment	$ (68,901)
Purchase of business	$ (10,924)
Purchases of other assets	$(260)
Change in loans receivable	$ -
Net cash used in investing activities	$ (80,085)
Cash flows from financing activities	
Payments on revolving credit facility	$(100,000)
Proceeds from long-term loan	$ 150,000
Payments on long-term debt	$ (6,286)
Excess tax benefits from stock-based compensation arrangements	$ 26,301
Proceeds from exercise of stock options and other stock issuances	$ 10,196
Payments of debt financing costs	$ (1,714)
Net cash provided by financing activities	$ 78,497
Effect of exchange rate changes on cash and cash equivalents	$ 199
Net decrease in cash and cash equivalents	$ (47,055)
Cash and cash equivalents	
Beginning of period	$ 347,489
End of period	$ 300,434

Changes to cash in each section are then summed. So,

Changes in cash in 2014 = Net cash provided by operating activities + Net cash used in investing activities + Net cash provided by (used in) financing activities
Changes in cash in 2014 = ($45,666) + ($80,085) + $78,497
Changes in cash in 2014 = ($47,254)

As Under Armour® operates in several nations, cash is affected by changes in the exchange rates between countries. During the second quarter of 2014, the effect of the exchange rate differences increased cash by $199,000. The net increase (decrease) in cash for the period is:

Net increase (decrease) in cash = Changes in cash in 2014 + Effect of exchange rate differences
Net increase (decrease) in cash = (47,254) + $199
Net increase (decrease) in cash = ($47,055)

T-accounts

To track revenues and expenses and create accounts to be entered on balance sheets and income statements, accountants historically have used the *T-system.* Today, organizations often rely on computer software like QuickBooks to create accounts that are used to automatically generate financials. Though computerized software is available and has simplified the accounting process for many firms, an understanding of the T-system will help with the understanding of balance sheets, income statements, and statements of cash flows.

A *T-account* is created using a ledger. *Credits* are entries made on the right hand side of the ledger, or "T." *Debits* are entries made on the left hand side of the "T." For accounting purposes, credits and debits just refer to each side of the "T." Following is a basic T-account:

T-account	
Debits	*Credits*

The balance sheet provides the best example of the application of the T-system. Assets are listed on the left side, or debits side, of the T while liabilities and owners' equity are listed on the right side, or credits side, of the T.

Balance Sheet	
Assets	*Liabilities* *Owners' Equity*

Example of the T-System

To fully understand how the T-system and T-accounts work, the transactions of two members of a fitness center can be monitored. Each customer, Customer A and Customer B, is sent a monthly membership charge from the club. The monthly fee is $100. This transaction affects the T-accounts of the two members and the *accounts receivable* account of the fitness center. The accounts receivable account includes money owed to the club by its customers for services or products provided on credit. Here, membership is provided to each customer on credit.

Customer A

Debits	*Credits*
(A) $100	

Customer B

Debits	*Credits*
(B) $100	

Accounts Receivable

Debits	*Credits*
(A) $100	
(B) $100	

Three T-accounts are used for this transaction. The customers each have their own T-accounts and the accounts receivable T-account is used as well. The amount each customer owes is entered on the debits side of the account. The information also is entered on the left side of the fitness center's accounts receivables T-account.

The club also has a cash account (or bank account). Here is the cash T-account:

Cash

Debits	*Credits*
$10,000	

Based upon the cash account, the fitness center currently has $10,000 cash in the bank. If Customer B pays her $100 membership, changes will be made to several T-accounts.

Customer B

Debits	*Credits*
(B) $100	(C) $100

Accounts Receivable

Debits	*Credits*
(A) $100	(C) $100
(B) $100	

Cash

Debits	*Credits*
$10,000	
(C) $100	

First, Customer B's T-account is credited with the $100 payment. Next, the fitness center's accounts-receivable account is credited with $100 as Customer B has now paid her bill and she no longer owes that amount to the fitness center. Finally, the fitness center's cash account is debited $100 as the amount Customer B paid is deposited in the center's bank. At the end of the month, the T-account entries are finalized and financial reports are prepared using each account's end-of-month total.

Customer A

Debits	*Credits*
$100	

Customer B

Debits	*Credits*
$0	

Accounts Receivable

Debits	*Credits*
$100	

Cash

Debits	*Credits*
$10,100	

The T-accounts show that Customer A still owes $100. This amount remains in both the customer's account and the accounts receivable account. Customer B no longer owes the club money and her account balance is zero. Finally, the cash account for the fitness center grows to $10,100.

As depicted in this example, it can be seen that asset accounts record increases on the lefthand, or debit, side of the T-account. For liability and owner's equity accounts, increases are recorded on the righthand, or credit, side. Also, this example demonstrates how *double-entry bookkeeping* is used. Generally Accepted Accounting Principles require the use of double-entry bookkeeping.

Using this method of bookkeeping, multiple accounts are charged and each transaction has two effects. One requires a righthanded credit entry (either an increase or decrease), and one requires a lefthanded debit entry (reflecting the opposite).

The method of accounting utilized also impacts T-accounts and the creation of financials. Under GAAPs, an organization can operate on an *accrual basis* or a *cash basis*. The preferred method is the accrual basis of accounting. Using this method of accounting, revenues are recognized when they are earned and expenses are recorded when they are incurred. For example, a group sales representative has just sold 500 tickets at $10 per ticket to the Boy Scouts for an upcoming game. The group sales representative creates an invoice for payment and mails it to the Boy Scouts leader. The invoice is for $5,000 and no cash has been exchanged between the two parties. Using accrual-based accounting, the $5,000 is recorded as ticket revenue even though the Boy Scouts have not yet paid for their tickets. Here, the $5,000 is earned and recorded at the time of the transaction. Under a cash basis, transactions are recorded when cash is actually paid or received. Going back to the previous example, if the organization was using cash-based accounting, the $5,000 sale would not be recorded as revenue until the team receives the payment from the Boy Scouts. Here, the transaction would be recorded when the payment was received. Organizations, when formed, can select to use either method of accounting; however, an organization cannot switch between the two methods during the year.

Financing the Operation of a Sport Organization

Understanding how to read and interpret changes in financial statements is just one part of the financial management equation. For all in sport, whether you work for a team where the owner's objective is wealth maximization or winning or whether the sport organization is for profit, not-for-profit, or government owned, a manager in the sport industry will encounter five methods used to finance the organization. These include, debt, equity, reinvesting retained earnings, government, and gift financing.

Debt Financing

When an organization borrows money that must be repaid over a period of time, usually with interest, *debt financing* is being utilized. Typically in sport, teams issue bonds or borrow from lending institutions, or even in some instances their league, to finance operations through debt. The New York Yankees financed the new Yankee Stadium by borrowing $105 million from a group of banks including Goldman Sachs to pay for cost overruns. Also, the team borrowed more than $1.2 billion through the tax-exempt and taxable bond market (Kaplan, 2009). Debt financing can be either short term or long term, with short-term debt obligations being repaid in less than one year and long-term obligations being repaid in more than one year. A key to financing operations via debt is that the lender does not gain an ownership interest in the organization. The sport organization's obligation is limited to the repayment of the debt.

Bonds

A *bond* is a promise by a borrower to pay back to the lender a specified amount of money, with interest, within a specified period of time. Private-placement bonds and asset-backed securitizations are two ways sport organizations finance operations through debt. Private-placement bonds have been used to finance the construction of the Wells Fargo Center, Moda Center, and TD Garden (among many others). Here, all revenues from the arena are pledged to repay the amount of money borrowed from the bond holders plus interest. Asset-backed securitizations have been used to finance the construction of venues such as the Pepsi Center in Denver and Staples Center in Los Angeles. Using asset-backed securitizations, specific revenue streams are pledged to repay the bond holders. For both private-placement bonds and asset-backed securitizations, revenue used to repay the debt obligations typically comes from luxury seating sales, naming rights agreements, and the sale of personal seat licenses.

Equity

In contrast to debt financing, in *equity financing* a share or portion of ownership is exchanged for money. Funds for operations, therefore, can be obtained without incurring debt and without having to repay a specific amount of money at a given time. A drawback, however, is that ownership interest will be diluted and there could be a loss of control as additional investors are added. Stephen M. Ross used equity financing to raise capital after purchasing the Miami Dolphins in 2009. He sold minority interests in the team to several partners, including singers Marc Anthony and Gloria Estefan (Talalay, 2009). Few sport organizations issue stock, a common form of equity financing used outside the industry. One of the few, the Green Bay Packers, has been publicly owned since 1923. In total, there have been five stock sales to help finance the team and 352,427 individuals own over 4.7 million shares of the team. Revenue generated through the most recent stock offering, December 6, 2011 to February 29, 2012, helped support the expansion of Lambeau Field ("Shareholders," 2014). Professional sport organizations typically do not sell stock to the public to raise equity capital. One reason for this is that little remains hidden when a company is publicly traded. To comply with Security and Exchange Commission (SEC) regulations, annual reports must be made detailing the accounting activities of the organization. Teams often claiming financial hardship while seeking a new publicly funded stadium may have difficulty convincing the municipality of the need if there is significant positive cash flow. Teams also have to answer to shareholders when issuing stock. Stockholder demands for profitability might be counter to winning on the field (i.e., not acquiring a player at the trading deadline because of a near-term financial loss resulting from the acquisition). Concern over public ownership in leagues is so great that since 1960 the NFL has banned public ownership of its teams (Kaplan, 1999).

As mentioned, the Green Bay Packers are an exception to the private norm and the NFL rule. To keep the franchise from leaving Green Bay, Wisconsin, the team went public in 1923. Today, the Packers continue to be exempt from the NFL's prohibition on issuing shares, but the shares they have issued do not appreciate in value and are not traded on a stock exchange. Further, they pay no dividends and no person can own more than 200,000 shares of Packer stock. The prohibition on the number of shares one can own protects the team against someone coming in and buying a majority of shares and gaining control of the franchise ("Shareholders," 2014).

Despite the reluctance to use equity financing, teams in other leagues have raised significant amounts of capital when doing so. The Cleveland Indians raised $60 million through the team's Initial Public Offering (IPO). The Florida Panthers, Boston Celtics, Vancouver Canucks, and Colorado Avalanche all used equity financing at one time. Today, however, each team is privately held (Kaplan, 1999).

Retained Earnings

In addition to financing through debt and equity, organizations can finance operations or the acquisition of assets through the reinvestment of prior earnings. This reinvestment is a part of the firm's *retained earnings*. The reinvestment of retained earnings is considered a part of equity financing as money not reinvested will typically be sent to the shareholders of publicly traded firms as dividends. However, in sport, financing through the reinvestment of retained earnings should be examined separately from equity financing as the industry, with the exception of sporting goods manufacturers and retail stores, is mostly privately held. Although earnings can be distributed to team owners, in sport they are often used to finance the acquisition of players, improve operations, or make other investments.

The Green Bay Packers have reinvested retained earnings to provide a competitive and successful football operation and to preserve the franchise and its traditions ("President's Annual Report," 2005). As the franchise is owned by its shareholders and not a single, wealthy individual, the organization is at a financial disadvantage when reacting to foreseen or unforeseen business challenges. A wealthy individual is able to use personal funds to infuse cash into a sport franchise. The Packers, to increase liquidity, stockpile their retained earnings.

Government

In the sport industry, it is common for private organizations, like professional sports teams, to receive funding from governmental sources. Further, public high schools and universities typically receive a portion of financing through direct or indirect government funding. For all sport organizations, *government financing* may include land use, tax abatements, direct stadium financing, state/municipal appropriations, and infrastructure improvements. Figure 13.6 provides examples of direct stadium financing.

FIGURE 13.6 Select Tax-Backed Stadium/Arena Bond Issues

Stadium/Arena	Issuer	Funding
AT&T Stadium	City of Arlington	Admission Tax Revenue
Banker Life Field House	Marion County Convention and Recreation Facilities Authority	Ticket Tax, Hotel Tax
Comerica Park	Detroit/Wayne County Stadium Authority	Tourist Tax
Gila River Arena	City of Glendale	Concession Taxes, Parking and Ticket Surcharges, Excise Tax Revenue
Great American Ballpark	Hamilton County, OH	Sales Tax Revenue
Lucas Oil Stadium	Indiana Finance Authority	Excise Tax, Innkeepers Tax, Food and Beverage Tax, Admissions Tax, Auto Rental Tax
Marlins Park	Miami Dade County	Hotel Tax, Tourist Tax, Non Ad Valorem Tax Revenue
Miller Park	Southeast Wisconsin Professional Baseball Park District	Sales and Use Tax
Target Field	Hennepin County	Sales Tax
Yankee Stadium	NYC Industrial Development Authority	Payments-in-lieu-of-taxes (PILOT)

Source: UBS Wealth Management Research (2012).

Most stadium and arena projects funded by a governmental agency use either short-term or long-term debt because this debt places less of an immediate financial burden on taxpayers. Bonds are the traditional source of capital improvement revenue for governmental entities. In order to issue bonds, the municipality or district has to receive approval to borrow money from either the voters or the appropriate legislative entity. The process will vary depending on state and local laws in each jurisdiction. Once legal authority to issue bonds is given, the bonds are usually issued on the municipality's behalf by an underwriter—typically a national or regional investment bank.

One of two types of municipal bonds will typically be issued (Bynum, 2003). These will either be revenue bonds or general obligation bonds. Revenue bonds are secured by future revenues generated by the project being funded whereas general obligation bonds are secured by tax revenues and the issuing entity's ability to impose new taxes. General obligation bonds must get voter approval prior to their issue.

Gift

Gift financing includes charitable donations, either cash or in-kind, made to an organization and is a primary source of operating and investing income for major collegiate sports programs. It is also a supplemental source for minor college programs and non-profit sport organizations.

College athletic programs use revenue from gifts to offset the rising costs of collegiate sport, build or renovate facilities, and grow endowments (Figure 13.7). Duke University, for example, hopes to raise $250 million for its athletics department during its Duke Forward campaign. Other institutions use gift financing to offset losses in institutional (government) financing resulting from state governments cutting funds to state colleges and universities. Most institutions are also seeking to grow their athletic department endowments. Duke University hopes to grow its endowment by $50 million during this capital campaign. Stanford University's athletic endowment is between $450 and $500 million and pays out 5.5% each year (Cohen, 2013).

Sources of Revenue

For most industries, financial management focuses solely on analysis of financial performance and the financing of company growth. In sport, there tends to be an added emphasis on revenue acquisition. As discussed throughout this text, there are many forms of revenue generated by sport organizations. Most spectator sport organizations derive the majority of their revenues either from ticket sales or broadcasting rights. Minor leagues and the National Hockey League

FIGURE 13.7 2013 Southeastern Conference Athletic Donations

School	Total
Florida	$48,407,105
Alabama	$34,233,035
Louisiana State	$32,089,896
Georgia	$28,645,025
South Carolina	$25,887,641
Tennessee	$24,258,597
Arkansas	$19,426,047
Kentucky	$19,070,356
Mississippi	$18,454,960
Mississippi State	$16,868,035
Missouri	$15,885,863
Texas A&M	$15,291,423
Vanderbilt	NA

Source: USA Today (2014)

(NHL) are highly dependent on ticket sales. NASCAR, the National Basketball Association (NBA), Major League Baseball (MLB), and the NFL are primarily dependent on broadcasting rights.

The NFL receives the highest percentage of revenues from its variety of national rights fees. On an annual basis, the league receives $4.0 billion per season from network, cable, and satellite operators (Figure 13.8). The NBA receives a combined $930 million per year from ABC, ESPN, and TNT. Of the major professional leagues, the NHL receives a “paltry” $77.5 million as an upfront rights fee from Versus per season. As a comparison, the Southeastern Conference (SEC) receives $68.4 million annually from its television rights deals with ABC, ESPN, and CBS. For further discussion of other revenue streams, see Chapters 9, 10, and 12.

FIGURE 13.8 Seasonal Media Rights Fees of Select Professional Leagues

	Network TV	Cable	Satellite/ Digital	Total
NBA				$ 930,000,000
MLB	$ 500,000,000	$1,000,000,000		$1,500,000,000
NASCAR				$ 820,000,000
NFL	$3,307,000,000	$1,900,000,000	$1,000,000,000	$6,207,000,000

Conclusion

The sport industry is large and diverse with many factors affecting financial management within the industry. Financial managers strive to maximize wealth while forecasting revenues and planning for expenses. They primarily rely on four financial documents to aid decision making: budgets, income statements, balance sheets, and statements of cash flows. A budget provides an outline of where money will be spent and where revenue will be generated. The income statement measures flow, or the organization's expenditures and receipts between two periods of time, while the balance sheet measures the financial condition of the organization at a specific point in time.

A statement of cash flows measures cash moving into and out of an organization. For sport organizations, statements of cash flows provide the best picture of the organization's total financial health. Using GAAP, most team owners can use depreciation and amortization expenses to make the income statement look like the team is losing money while the team actually is increasing its cash position.

In addition to reading and interpreting financial statements, financial managers are concerned with the financing of the operation of sport organizations. Debt and equity financing are commonly used across all industries. Sport organizations also rely on retained earnings, government financing, and gift financing. These forms of financing will be used to varying degrees based upon the subsector of the industry. Also, the ownership structure of a team and the structure of a league will impact financing decisions.

Finally, financial managers in sport often are tasked to focus on revenue generation. Common forms of revenue generated in sport include ticket sales revenues, revenues from the sale of television broadcasting rights, advertising revenues, and sponsorship revenues.

chapter 13
Interviews

Interview 13.1

Daniel S. Barrett
Principal and Founder
Barrett Sports Group, LLC

Q: Could you briefly describe your career path?

A: I graduated from UCLA with degrees in economics and international studies. During my senior year, I prepared a feasibility study for a new arena in Orange County, California (before the Arrowhead Pond [now Honda Center] was developed) for one of my classes. I was always passionate about sports and was determined to find a job in the industry. When I graduated, I had an opportunity to work in the marketing department for an NBA team and I also had an opportunity to work for a boutique economic and real estate consulting firm (NLW). I decided to work for the consulting firm because I believed I would develop a strong foundation in finance, real estate, and other important disciplines. I was fortunate to work on several sports and recreation projects while I learned many of the skills I use to this day.

I decided to get my MBA from the University of Southern California (USC) after working at NLW. My focus was real estate and finance. After graduating from USC, I took a job working at Deloitte & Touche, in their Solutions Consulting Group. While at Deloitte & Touche, I led the Sports and Entertainment consulting practice for the Western Region for a number of years and then went to work for A.G. Edwards investment bank (now Wells Fargo). I was the managing director of their sports finance practice for the Western Region.

In early 2000, I founded Barrett Sports Group, a boutique sports management consulting firm. We specialize in the sports industry and focus on several areas including:

- Sports Facility Planning, Feasibility, Leases, Financing and Operations
- Sports Team and Facility Valuation
- Sports Team and Facility Acquisition/Disposition

I have more than 24 years of experience and have personally worked on well over 1,000 sports industry projects. I have authored sports industry articles and been quoted in numerous publications. In addition, I have been a speaker at sports industry conferences and conventions and a guest lecturer at the University of Southern California, California State University, Long Beach, and the University of San Francisco. I am also an adjunct professor having taught The Business of Sport at the University of San Francisco graduate program in Sport Management.

Q: What have been the biggest challenges you have encountered during your career?

A: Early in my career, the biggest challenge I faced was finding the right opportunity to pursue my goal of working in the sports industry. I knew that I wanted to work in sports, but I also wanted to be able to use the finance skills that I developed in college and business school.

After firmly establishing myself in the sports industry, my next biggest challenge was figuring out how to continue to focus exclusively on sports projects while I was working for large firms like Deloitte & Touche and A.G. Edwards. The sports industry is a niche market within large organizations like those and it was a challenge to grow in that environment.

Q: What prompted you to found your own company?

A: I decided to start my own firm so that I could continue to focus exclusively on sports business and not have to worry about the challenges of working for a large firm in a non-core area. I also preferred working on projects rather than just managing them. In larger firms, I found I was spending a significant portion of my time on administrative issues and other non-project-oriented issues.

Q: What are the most important issues facing your company now?

A: Managing the workload is always a challenge—a good challenge. Also, trying to be in two places at once can be a challenge! Finding the right staffing balance and work-life balance is always a challenge in a small firm.

Q: What major issues do you see evolving in sport finance in the next 5 to 10 years?

A: Team values continue to escalate to unprecedented levels. Leagues will face the challenge of identifying individual buyers who can afford the escalating prices while still maintaining debt limitations and other restrictions.

Increased costs associated with the development or renovation of sports facilities and the increased resistance to spend public money on these facilities make the viability of these projects challenging.

Broadcast rights are likely to continue to escalate given that sports provides one of the few programming options that must be watched live. The ongoing battles between content providers and distributors will continue to be a challenge. The rising costs of programming to the consumer will also continue to be an issue.

The in-stadium fan experience as compared to watching the game at home is another significant issue. As tickets, concessions, parking, etc., continue to increase in price and home television options continue to improve, teams and leagues will be forced to make adjustments to continue to attract fans.

Globalization is a major topic in the sports industry and one that could have a material impact on the team valuations and financials. Leagues and teams are aggressively pursuing opportunities throughout the world.

Q: Are there specific skills sport-management students should look to develop while still in school?

A: Writing skills are critical in virtually every business. Students need to make sure to focus on developing their writing skills during college.

Students also need to understand the financial side of the business. Many students want to work in sports marketing, but do not really understand the financial side. It is important to understand how decisions impact the overall profitability and viability of the business. You cannot simply focus on one aspect of the company and ignore the impacts it may have on other aspects of the company.

Q: What specific classes would you recommend students take to best position themselves for a sport-industry job?

A: It is important to develop a strong foundation that will allow you to understand business from a broad perspective. Although you may be focused on one area (e.g., sports marketing, sports law), it is important to understand how that one area fits within the overall operation of the business. Key classes would include courses in finance, economics, accounting, marketing, and even law.

Some schools offer classes where the students complete a project or case study for a sports team or sports company. These projects provide excellent experience and contacts.

Q: What publications do you regularly read to stay apprised of sport-business events?

A: *SportsBusiness Daily* is the best source for timely information about the industry. It is a must read for anyone who is serious about sports business.

SportsBusiness Journal is also a good source of information and is worth reading on a weekly basis. The *SportsBusiness Journal* provides a more in-depth examination of key issues and trends in the industry.

Q: Would you recommend students pursue graduate school? If so, when should they pursue a graduate degree and what area of study would you recommend?

A: I would recommend that students consider graduate school, particularly if you have the time and resources. Many top executives in the industry have attended law school or business school. Graduate school allows you to continue your education and develop key skills that will help you grow and learn how to add value to an organization.

It is important to get two to three years of work experience before going back to school. You will get more out of your graduate program if you have some real-world experiences.

Interview 13.2

Gina Rosser Bradley
Assistant Director of Athletics/Business Operations
Duke University Athletic Department

Gina Rosser Bradley became the Assistant Director of Athletics for Business Operations at Duke University in July 2011. In her role, she supervises daily operation of the business office while also working closely with the Associate Athletic Director of Business on budgetary issues within the department.

Rosser Bradley received her master's in business administration (2004) and master's in sport administration (2005) from Ohio University in Athens, Ohio. She worked in Ohio University's Athletic Ticket Office as a graduate assistant while pursuing her sport administration degree. As an undergraduate, Rosser attended High Point University and was a four-year member of the women's basketball team. She received degrees in business administration and sport management from High Point. While a student, Gina worked in various offices within High Point's Athletic Department.

Q: Can you briefly describe your career path?

A: Only after participating as a student-athlete at High Point did I realize that I could have a career in college athletics. During my time there I was able to work in various offices within the department such as Sports Information, Marketing, and Development. Those experiences led me to pursue a graduate degree in Sports Administration. While at Ohio University I was a graduate assistant in the Ticket Office which was a great learning experience. My objective up to that point was to get a taste of as many areas within college athletics to find my true interest and passion. After graduate school I was hired as the Assistant Business Manager at Duke University Athletics which seemed to be a perfect fit. In addition to my business office responsibilities, I also worked with Game Operations.

After two years at Duke I knew I wanted to concentrate on the business side of college athletics, but my opportunity to advance was limited. I accepted a position at Temple University to serve as their Athletic Business Manager. After six months at Temple my former boss at Duke unexpectedly left. I then returned to Duke as the Director of Business Operations. This move was good for me in that I got a promotion with a raise, but also it brought me back to my home state of North Carolina and to an athletic department with more prominence. After being promoted to Assistant Athletic Director for Business Operations I have since taken on sport supervision responsibilities.

Q: What was one of the most valuable learning experiences you encountered during your career and how has that experience contributed to your success?

A: I am not sure if there was one specific instance, but overall it has been learning how to relate to people. I really think that intrapersonal skills and recognizing how best to get through to different personalities is important in any sport management job, even one focused upon finance.

Q: What do you see as the most important determinants of a successful financial/ business manager? Why?

A: A strong understanding of the department's financial needs, as well as the flexibility of the university, are big factors in succeeding in this position. Maintaining good relationships with campus offices such as Accounts Payable, Procurement, HR, Payroll, and Employee Travel is also important. On the departmental level, it is imperative to be able to communicate effectively with coaches and staff so they can have a good understanding of what is expected of them in the budgeting process and the purchasing limitations they will encounter.

On a personal level, attention to detail, timeliness, and being able to prioritize effectively are essential factors in success. Being approachable and open to answering even the most mundane and repetitive questions definitely helps build trust among coaches and staff.

Q: How have the recent changes to conference affiliations impacted business operations in college athletics?

A: Some of the changes have been positive for many schools in terms of the increased distribution of TV revenue and also opportunity for increased ticket sales. On the flip side, conference distribution of other revenues (such as bowl revenue) are being split in more pieces, which could result in a decrease per institution. Further, with the creation of conference-specific TV channels, having a larger footprint has increased viewership and as a result the channels have seen success and higher profits than expected. The negatives associated with realignment have come with added team travel costs. The ACC for example, now extends all the way from Syracuse, New York, down to Miami, Florida. The distance traveled now requires more flights than bus trips. With large teams, this is a huge financial burden.

Q: What are the biggest financial challenges facing college athletics in the near future?

A: Ever increasing scholarship costs, reliance on annual gifts and major gifts to support operations, and the large expense of facility improvements are big issues that we are facing now and will likely face in the near future. Also, now with the NCAA loosening regulations on meals and other student-athlete benefits, there is a huge burden on athletic department budgets to provide as much as is allowed so that each team can stay competitive on the recruiting front.

Q: In college athletics, what are the primary things looked for in new hires?

A: The primary things would be strong, reliable references, a master's degree, and work experience at a reputable institution. During the interview process good communication skills along with confidence is important. I also want to know that applicants have done homework about the position and institution. If others will be working directly for me I want to know for sure that their personality will mesh well with mine and that they will be a good fit in our office.

Q: What is your advice to students considering a career in sport business operations and/or sport finance?

A: Prepare with a solid business education and once you get in the field, do everything you can to understand all aspects of finance within your department and university. You want to be able to understand your job completely, as well as what your boss does on a daily basis. Even if you cannot work on the "big picture" items immediately, having a good understanding of the planning and decision-making processes will be key as you advance in your career.

Study Questions

1. What must a sport manager due to be successful in his or her job? Why?
2. What is finance?
3. Of the three sectors of finance, why is financial management the most important sector for the sport industry?
4. What is wealth maximization and why is it an important concept to understand?
5. Of the four commonly used financial statements, which is most important to understand firms in the sport industry? Why?
6. T-accounts are commonly used to track revenues and expenses. What are debits and credits?
7. Either cash- or accrual-based accounting can be used according to GAAP. What is the difference between the two methods of accounting? Which is the preferred method of accounting? Why?
8. Debt and equity financing are often used in sport. Define debt financing and equity financing and discuss the differences between the two methods of financing an organization.
9. Why are retained earnings, gift, and governmental financing common methods of financing activities in the sport industry? Provide examples of each method of financing when answering this question.
10. There are many sources of revenue in the sport industry. In professional sport, two are most prevalent. What are the two sources of revenue and how do they impact the financial operations of professional teams and leagues?

Learning Activities

You just purchased an Arena Football 2 team (af2), the Columbia Destroyers. The team is located in South Carolina and requires an infusion of capital. Your previous chief financial officer (CFO) has just left your organization and unfortunately was not good at his job. The financials are a mess. You need to create last year's financial statements for the team's board of directors meeting. The information is not altogether good, but you know how to create financial statements for the club. The facts you do know regarding the financial operation of the club are as follows:

a. No balance sheet, income statement, or ledger/T-accounts exist.
b. The club was purchased for $1 million and uses the accrual basis of accounting.
c. The club was capitalized as follows:

- Borrowed $1,000,000 at 7% interest for seven years (PMT = $185,553; i = $70,000)
- Investor provided $1,500,000 to fund the new venture

d. The team paid certain costs and expenditures in 2008:
- Purchased
  —Equipment: $250,000
- Cash Expenses
  —Player compensation: $195,000
  —Football operations: $459,700
  —Business operations: $497,000
  —Rent: $64,155

e. The team generated cash receipts in 2008 as follows:
- Ticket sales: 40,000 fans at $16.25 per ticket
- Concessions: 40,000 fans at $3.50 per fan
- Parking: $50,000 per year
- Advertising/Sponsorship: $456,000
- Merchandise: 40,000 fans at $2.00 per fan

f. Depreciation:
- All short-term fixed assets depreciated over a 5-year life using the straight line method

g. Other information:
- The football team paid the city 10% for each ticket sold. This is an expense.
- The accounts receivable for ticket sales is $8,000
- The accounts payable for business operations is $100,000
- Don't forget the depreciation, amortization, and interest expenses
- Franchise value amortized over 15-year period
- Tax rate: 40%

1. Based upon this information, create an income statement for the organization.
2. Based upon the information provided and the income statement completed for Learning Activity 1, create the organization's balance sheet.
3. After examining the income statement and balance sheet completed for the previous learning activities, analyze the financial performance of the club.
   a. How is the team performing currently?
   b. What must it do to improve its financial performance next year?

References

Bynum, M. (2003, August). Bonds. Municipal bonds. *Athletic Business,* 90–98.

Cohen, B. (2013, November 8). The odd economics of Stanford football. *The Wall Street Journal.* Retrieved from http://online.wsj.com/news/articles/SB10001424052702304672404579181803355000052

Foster, G., Greyser, S.A., & Walsh, B. (2006). *The business of sports.* New York: South-Western College Publishers.

Gluck, J. (2014, August 8). Dale Jr. hopes to keep working with National Guard. *USA Today.* Retrieved from http://www.usatoday.com/story/sports/nascar/2014/08/08/dale-earnhardt-jr-national-guard-hendrick-motorsports-nascar/13776847/

IEG. (2009, December). Forecast: Recession slams break on sponsorship spending. *IEG Sponsorship Report.* Retrieved from www.sponsorship.com/iegsr/2009

IEG. (2014, January). Sponsorship spending growth slows in North America as marketers eye newer media and marketing options. *IEG Sponsorship Report.* Retrieved from http://www.sponsorship.com/IEGSR/2014/01/07/Sponsorship-Spending-Growth-Slows-In-North-America.aspx

Kaplan, D. (1999, June 7). Going public makes company an open book. *SportsBusiness Journal.* Retrieved on September 14, 2005 from http://www.sportsbusinessjournal.com/article/16928

Kaplan, D. (2009, March 16). Yanks get new loan for ballpark. *SportsBusiness Journal.* Retrieved March 17, 2009 from http://www.sportsbusinessjournal.com/article/61849

More than a shirt. (2014, August 15). *Espn.com.* Retrieved from http://espn.go.com/espn/feature/story/_/id/11354724/kit-deal-more-important-ever-premier-league#

Newport, J.P. (2009, February 28). No entertaining, please—It's golf. *The Wall Street Journal,* W4.

President's annual report: 2004–2005. (2005). Green Bay, WI: Green Bay Packers, Inc

Secretary of golf. (2009, February 25). *The Wall Street Journal,* A14.

Shareholders. (2014, July 24). Retrieved from http://www.packers.com/community/shareholders.html

Talalay, S. (2009, July 21). Marc Anthony buys stake in Miami Dolphins. *South Florida Sun-Sentinel.* Retrieved on July 21, 2009 from http://www.sun-sentinel.com/sports/miami-dolphins/sfl-marc-anthony-dolphins-s072009,0,3720783.story

Vanden Brook, T. (2014, May 8). National Guard's NASCAR deal leads to virtually no recruits. *USA Today.* Retrieved from http://www.usatoday.com/story/news/nation/2014/05/07/national-guard-recruiting-scandal/8813891/

Suggested Sources

Brown, M., Rascher, D., Nagel, M., & McEvoy, D. (2015). *Financial management in the sport industry* (2nd ed.). Scottsdale, AZ: Holcomb Hathaway.

Howard, D.R., & Crompton, J.L. (2014). *Financing sport* (3rd ed.). Morgantown, WV: Fitness Information Technology.

International Journal of Sport Finance Blog (http://ijsf.wordpress.com/)
Lewis, M. (2004). *Moneyball: The art of winning an unfair game.* New York: WW Norton & Company.
SportsBusiness Daily (http://www.sportsbusinessdaily.com/)
SportsBusiness Journal (http://www.sportsbusinessjournal.com/)
SportsMoney—Forbes.com (http://www.forbes.com/business/sportsmoney/)

Interviews

The best way to develop an understanding of the various segments of the sport industry is to read a variety of sources each week and to interact with as many industry professionals as possible. This chapter provides interviews with numerous sport management professionals from a wide variety of segments of the industry. Certainly, attempting to interview someone from every sport industry segment would be impossible, but this chapter is designed to not only cover executives from the most popular sports such as football and baseball, but to also expose the reader to the breadth that the sport industry offers. As you will see, there is not any one "right" career path. However, there are some commonalities you should note: Each interviewee stresses the importance of working hard and networking to launch and build a successful career. While this is not earth-shattering news, if everyone says the same thing, it might be good advice!

Hopefully, one day you will be interviewed for a sport-management textbook. If so, what advice will you offer to the next generation of sport managers?

Bruce Popko

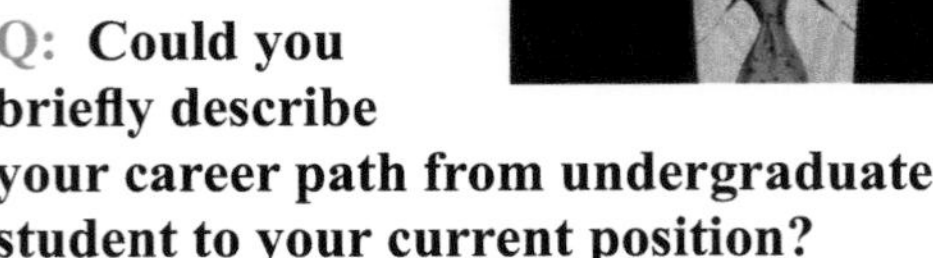

Senior Vice President of Business Development
Buffalo Bills—National Football League

Q: Could you briefly describe your career path from undergraduate student to your current position?

A: I was an undergraduate at the University of Pennsylvania but had worked summers for the New York Jets starting at the age of 15. I was hired full time by the Jets after graduation. I then went to NFL Headquarters for three years to work on the launch of NFL Sunday Ticket and then later I worked on the NFL's retail marketing. I was then recruited to the 49ers from the NFL office and spent three years with the team; I then moved to Cleveland and spent seven years with the Browns, handling all revenue generating functions. I spent four years at IMG heading sales for the golf division. I just started with the Bills in May 2009 and I handle all business development activities.

Q: What have been the biggest challenges you have encountered during your career?

A: The biggest challenges are definitely on the people side of the business—managing a staff, keeping them motivated when the team is not playing their best, and trying to get maximum yield out of (normally) an understaffed situation.

Q: What are some of the biggest issues facing the Bills and the NFL?

A: I think the dynamic of premium seating/hospitality will continue to change. Most teams/stadiums have their seating configured with too many premium seats that are out of the price range of the consumer. The market will go through a natural self-correction, but it will take some time to get demand/supply intersecting in the right spot once again.

Q: Are there specific skills sport-management students should look to develop while still in school?

A: Managing people is a critical skill for success in the sport business. For the sales side, negotiating skills are also a premium.

Q: What specific classes would you recommend students take to best position themselves for a sport-industry job?

A: Sales management, psychology, accounting, and international business.

Developing language skills, whether through specific coursework or through other opportunities, will grow in importance in the future (specifically for Spanish and Chinese).

Q: What publications do you regularly read to stay apprised of sport-business events?

A: *SportsBusiness Journal, Brandweek, Ad Age, BusinessWeek,* and *The Wall Street Journal*

Q: Would you recommend students pursue graduate school? If so, when should they pursue a graduate degree and what area of study would you recommend?

A: It is "great to have," but not absolutely necessary. A graduate degree certainly helps justify a potential wage scale, but it is not a prerequisite to get hired.

Q: Is there any additional advice or insights you would provide to students pursuing a future career in sport management?

A: I am not a firm believer in the "take any job to get your foot in the door" mentality. I think you can, more times than not, end up in a situation that is not to your liking and/or takes you down a path that is tough to change. Instead, spend considerable time researching opportunities for what you really want to do and then fight with everything you have in you to pursue those potential opportunities in those areas of interest.

Jason Breiter

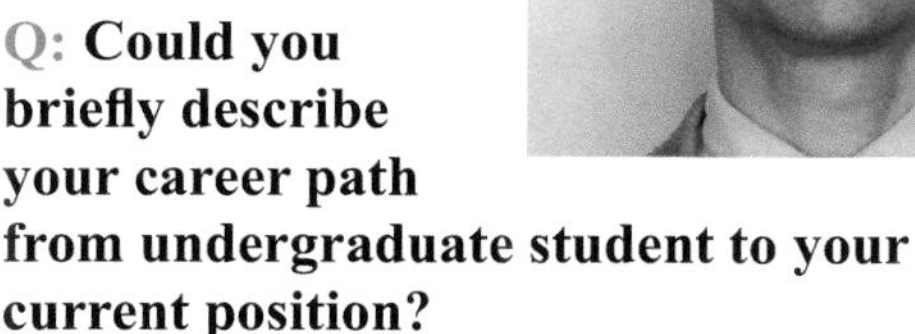

Account Executive
University of California,
Berkeley Athletics

Q: Could you briefly describe your career path from undergraduate student to your current position?

A: My career path into the sport industry was definitely not typical or direct. I studied environmental science and anthropology at a small, liberal arts college in Upstate New York at the foot of the Adirondack Mountains. I loved being outdoors, so a career in field biology and forestry seemed logical and intriguing.

When I graduated in 2003, I accepted a position as a wildlife biologist with the Bureau of Land Management in a small town called Ridgecrest in the middle of the Mojave Desert. This was obviously not the ideal landing spot for a 23-year-old kid right out of college, but the job was in my field of study and it got me to California, where I always wanted to be. Although I really enjoyed the fieldwork and having the wilderness as my office, being isolated in the middle of the desert really took its toll. One year into my two-year contract, I decided to move to Los Angeles and stay at a college friend's house while I looked for environmental consulting jobs in more urban locales.

During this process, my cousin, who also lived in Los Angeles, offered me a position doing real estate appraisals for a new firm he just started. I viewed this as a good opportunity to earn some income while I was searching for new environmental jobs, but at that point, I had no intention of making a career out of real estate. One thing led to another, and I ended up getting promoted into a management role and stayed with them for almost four years. At that point, I decided to make the switch from appraisal to the brokerage side of real estate, an area where I could better use my relationship building and sales skills. I got a job as the marketing director for a commercial real estate firm specializing in restaurants, bars, and nightclubs, which was pretty exciting and profitable in a market like Los Angeles. During my four years there, I pursued my real estate license and was an integral part of some very big and complex transactions.

At a certain point in 2011, I felt my professional career was really at a crossroads. I knew real estate was not my passion, and I always had an interest in working in sports but it never seemed like a "realistic" career option. Like many, I had wanted to work in sports for all the wrong reasons, mainly the fact that I loved sports, both on a participation and spectator level. My girlfriend of six years who knew me better than anyone urged me to look into this option because she believed my passion for sports, coupled with my professional background and diverse skill set, would be an ideal fit for the sport industry. I did some research on sport-management master's programs and started to build my network of sport industry professionals through an aggressive email introductory campaign and informational interviews.

I applied and was accepted into the University of San Francisco Sport Management m' Program, but was not prepared to uproot my life and move to Northern California unless I had a job in sports. During the informational interview and job search process, I developed two extremely important mentor relationships with Andy Dolich and Andy Dallin, who both built their careers in the San Francisco Bay Area and currently lived there. Through extensive networking and persistence, I obtained a position as a Senior Account Executive with the San Francisco Bulls, the brand new minor league professional hockey team in the Bay Area. Two weeks later, I was living in San Francisco and finally working in sports.

Selling tickets for a minor league sports team that few had ever heard of was difficult, but I learned quickly and was very successful. After seven months with the Bulls, I was promoted to Ticket Sales Manager and put in charge of hiring, training, and managing a sales team of nine Account Executives. I stayed in that position with the San Francisco Bulls through the remainder of the team's inaugural season in 2012 and about half of the second season before I started to explore new opportunities. The Bulls' financial struggles had become apparent and I didn't feel there was anything left for me to accomplish there. The opportunity to start my sports career on the ground floor with a new minor league franchise was an invaluable learning experience and I was able to wear many hats there, which helped me diversify my skill set and ultimately made me more marketable as a candidate for future jobs.

By that point, I had built a very strong network of industry professionals and began to tap that network for new people to speak with about possible career opportunities. In January 2014, I left the San Francisco Bulls and accepted a position as an Account Executive in the Department of Intercollegiate Athletics at the University of California, Berkeley, where I have been since. My primary role at Cal Athletics is to sell season, partial season, and group ticket packages for football, men's and women's basketball, baseball, softball, and volleyball to business professionals, Cal alumni and alumni groups, YSOs, non-profits, schools, youth groups, and individuals throughout the Bay aArea.

In May 2014, I graduated from the University of San Francisco with a master's degree in sport management.

Q: What have been the biggest challenges you have encountered during your career?

A: On a macro level, the biggest challenge I've faced thus far was finding an industry and trajectory that I was passionate about. It took me four tries over 10 years to discover the business of sports was my true love.

Since I have been in sports, the greatest difficulty has been finding a balance between my career and personal life. Working in sports is very demanding and usually requires working long hours, including many nights, weekends, and holidays. Hard work and dedication is essential when you are trying to build your own personal brand and move up within an organization, but it is equally important to make time for yourself and your family.

Another significant aspect of working in sports that I have had to adjust to has been dealing with the frequent change and turnover within the front offices I have been a part of. Many times when you choose to work for a certain team or organization, you are also choosing the people and the culture there, so it is tough when you witness so many colleagues and managers coming and going.

Q: What were the biggest issues you faced while working for the San Francisco Bulls?

A: By far the biggest issue I faced at the Bulls was selling the product. When I was hired, virtually nobody knew who the San Francisco Bulls were. We were a minor league sports team in a major league sports town. Within the San Francisco Bay aArea, there are two NFL teams (49ers and Raiders), two MLB clubs (Giants and As), an NBA team (Warriors), an NHL franchise (Sharks), two powerhouse collegiate athletic programs (Stanford and Cal), and a year-round motorsports complex (Sonoma Raceway). In addition, the Bulls had to compete with all the entertainment options outside of sports that also existed in the Bay aArea, whether it was fine dining, the theater and the arts, shopping in Union Square, winetasting in Napa Valley, a boat trip to Alcatraz, Fisherman's Wharf, or enjoying the many national and state parks in the area. Consumers have a limited amount of time and money to spend on entertainment, and convincing them that there was room in their lives, personally or professionally, for the San Francisco Bulls was a tall task.

Q: How did you sell in that type of environment? How did you keep your staff motivated?

A: From a selling standpoint, I think what made me successful was my belief in and passion for the product I was selling. I knew that the fan experience at Bulls games was amazing and I had no doubt that once fans gave us a chance, they would see it that way, too. People invest in people, and I think my passion and enthusiasm for the San Francisco Bulls shined through on every sales call I went on.

As a manager of a staff that had to sell such a difficult product, I think the key was leading by example. Because I was out there on the ground selling every day, I was able to connect with my reps because I knew the challenges they were facing firsthand. I also was able to show them that if they worked hard and dedicated themselves to the organization and the product they were selling, they would be able to persevere. Lastly, I always had an open door policy. Whenever one of my account executives needed guidance, I was there for them. I had weekly meetings with each one of them, went on sales calls, helped them design sales and marketing collateral, and regularly let each one know how important they were to the organization as a whole. I also had the benefit of having a truly great group of people on my sales team, which made it a lot easier.

Q: What are the most important issues facing Cal Athletics?

A: Currently, the University of California, Berkeley Athletic Department is facing some pretty significant issues, especially from a ticket sales standpoint. The football team is coming off its worst season in over 50 years (1-11) and the coaching staff is almost all new, and in the eyes of Cal fans, unproven. The Men's Basketball team completely collapsed last season after beating #1 Arizona, and missed out on the NCAA Tournament. In addition, future Hall of Fame coach Mike Montgomery retired at the end of the season, which left a lot of uncertainty in the eyes of men's Bbasketball supporters. Lastly, the Cal fan base represents a much older demographic than the average sports fan base, which also makes accessibility, convenience, and game times at Cal sporting events all major issues facing Cal Athletics.

Q: Are there specific skills sport-management students should look to develop while still in school?

A: The bottom line is hard work pays off. In order to succeed in the sport industry, you have to not only be able to put in the time and dedication to succeed, you have to be hungry. Therefore, I would urge sport-management students to always go the extra mile. In sports, you often have to wear many hats and juggle multiple jobs or tasks simultaneously. While in college, I would recommend to sport-management students to do as many internships as possible to get practice managing their time and balancing their daily lives.

Secondly, I think personality is very important to success in the sport industry. Having strong interpersonal skills and a sense of humor will get you a long way. As I said before, people invest in people, so it is important for students to be social, have fun, and interact with people from all cultures and walks of life.

Q: What specific classes would you recommend students take to best position themselves for a sport-industry job?

A: I think the most important thing students can do is select courses that they are interested in and passionate about. If you are not excited about what you are reading or studying, you are not going to want to do the work. That being said, there are certainly specific classes that could benefit undergraduates trying to build a career in sports, and I would say the classes you should take would really depend on which avenue you want to pursue. On a general level, undergraduate business and management courses would be beneficial, and I would also recommend any classes that emphasize working collaboratively in groups.

Q: What publications do you regularly read to stay apprised of sport-business events?

A: I read *SportsBusiness Journal* and *SportsBusiness Daily* every day. I also regularly read *Sports Illustrated* and Mark Cuban's blog, "blog maverick." Lately, I have also been getting a lot of my sport-business news on Twitter. Although I would say I am behind the curve when it comes to social media, I am trying to adapt more, and acknowledge how powerful of a source Twitter is for industry news.

Q: Would you recommend students pursue graduate school? If so, when should they pursue a graduate degree and what area of study would you recommend?

A: I found graduate school to be extremely beneficial, but it's not for everyone. For me, it was a little different. I already had a job in the industry I wanted to be in, so my motivations to pursue graduate school were based more on the education and networking aspects. The business of sports is vast, so my master's program helped me narrow down the direction I wanted to go. I also made some great contacts in the industry.

I do not think there is a right or wrong time to pursue higher education. I waited nine years before I decided to go back to school and I was sitting in classes with a lot of 22-year-olds right out of college. I think it only makes sense to go back to school if you are mentally ready. Graduate school is not one of those things you do just to do. You need to have a focused area of study and then find the university and program that is the best fit for you and the path you want to take your career.

Chrissy Baines

Director of Box Office and Retail Operations
Albuquerque Isotopes

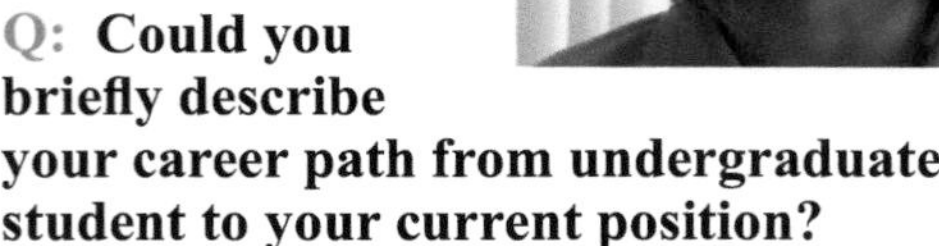

Q: Could you briefly describe your career path from undergraduate student to your current position?

A: While pursuing my undergraduate degree in sport management at the University of West Georgia, I completed my practicum with West Georgia Sports Marketing. I was able to conduct market research, which provided me much-needed knowledge and experience in the different areas of the business of sport. After graduating, I completed an internship with the Savannah Sand Gnats, a Single-A Minor League Baseball Team, and was then hired full time as the Director of Merchandise. After working for the Sand Gnats for two years, I was then hired by the Albuquerque Isotopes, a Triple-A Team in the Pacific Coast League, for a similar position. I have been with the Isotopes for six seasons and currently oversee the Box Office and Retail Operations.

Q: What important skills are needed to work in merchandising?

A: Merchandising involves identifying new trends in products, setting prices, and keeping appraised of licensing guidelines. While other aspects of a sport organization can sometimes be regimented, directing a merchandise operation requires a tremendous amount of creativity. Developing new designs, adjusting logo colors to match garment patterns, or developing store displays requires an ability to visualize and create the future. Since sales can be easily tracked on a daily, weekly, monthly, and seasonal basis, merchandising also involves conducting research to predict what will sell and then analyzing what has been selling, so that adjustments can be made.

Q: Are there specific job skills sport-management students should look to develop before they graduate?

A: Communication skills are critical. Students should become well versed in professional etiquette. Understanding how to interact and communicate with customers, co-workers, and the public is crucial to being a successful leader in any industry, but particularly in sports where everything we do is noted by the public.

Q: What specific classes would you recommend students take to best position themselves for a sport-industry job?

A: Any type of sport marketing or business management class is always helpful. Internet-based classes (web design, Internet marketing, etc.) should augment a strong understanding of basic computer programs (Microsoft Office) as well as graphic design programs (Photoshop). An event management class where the students plan and implement an event is particularly helpful as event management requires the use of every class in the sport management curriculum.

Q: What publications do you regularly read to stay apprised of sport-business events?

A: I read the *SportsBusiness Journal* regularly for information about the industry. I am also a news junkie, so I am always reading online at cnn.com and foxnews.com. I also make sure to read my daily local paper to stay appraised of current events in Albuquerque.

Q: Is there a certain sport-business area you see emerging in importance in the near future?

A: Using different social media outlets to market sports will be incredibly important over the next few years. Learning how to market your business or sport through Facebook, Twitter, online blogs, et cetera, is already important but it will likely continue to expand its influence.

Q: Is there any additional advice or insights you would provide to students pursuing a future career in sport management?

A: The industry is competitive, so prepare yourself for what you want to do after graduation. While in school, volunteer or try to obtain a part-time job within the field. Job experience, as well as a strong academic background, are essential to achieve success.

Charles Waddell

Associate Athletic Director
University of South
Carolina Athletics

Q: Could you briefly describe your career path from undergraduate student to associate athletic director?

A: After a four-year NFL career I returned to UNC-Chapel Hill in 1978 and took an entry-level job with the Athletic Department as an Assistant Academic Advisor and Strength Coach. I worked there for three years prior to returning to school to pursue an MBA. I then spent seven years with NCNB (currently Bank of America) as an investment banker before joining the Big Ten Conference as an Assistant Commissioner in 1990. I then joined the Carolina Panthers in 1994 and spent nine years with the franchise before going to Fayetteville State University as a Vice Chancellor for Advancement for two years. In 2006, I came to the University of South Carolina as an Associate Athletic Director, which is the position I currently hold.

Q: What have been the biggest challenges you have encountered during your career?

A: My biggest challenge was maintaining some consistency with the direction of my career path. I have been fortunate to be able to access different sectors of the sport industry, but the lack of consistency has resulted in not being able to achieve some of my career goals as quickly as I had hoped.

Q: What are the biggest issues facing sport managers today?

A: The most pressing issue is how the unstable economy is affecting various aspects of the sport industry. The economy has caused major adjustments to be made by administrators throughout the industry, from local recreation departments to professional leagues.

Q: Are there specific job skills sport-management students should look to develop while still in school?

A: Get used to working long hours and being able to multitask.

Q: What specific classes would you recommend students take to best position themselves for a sport-industry job?

A: I would recommend a case-study class, a business-of-sport class, and marketing.

Q: What publications do you regularly read to stay apprised of sport-business events?

A: The *SportsBusiness Journal*

Q: Would you recommend students pursue graduate school? If so, when should they pursue a graduate degree and what area of study would you recommend?

A: In an industry that is hypercompetitive, it is always good to have skills that separate one from the pack. Having an advanced degree can help do that. However, I believe if you have a good job that provides good experiences and opportunity for professional growth, it may not be necessary to go back to get a graduate degree.

Q: Is there a certain sport-business area you see emerging in importance in the near future?

A: The fund-raising sector of college athletics is growing rapidly. Facility improvements are critical to an institution's overall success, and the revenue streams from other sources (gate receipts, rights fees from media, etc.) are not growing at the same rate as in the past. Therefore, fund-raising efforts are even more important than they once were.

Q: Is there any additional advice or insights you would provide to students pursuing a future career in sport management?

A: Be patient and persistent.

Alex Berberian

Manager Sales & Operations - Circus
Feld Entertainment

Q: Could you briefly describe your career path from undergraduate student to your current position?

A: In 2006 as a sophomore in college, I interned with the New York Red Bulls soccer team in Box Office Operations. In 2008 upon graduating, I worked with the New York Red Bulls as an Inside Sales Representative. I then briefly moved to the New Jersey Nets basketball (now the Brooklyn Nets) team in sales. In August 2008, I accepted a position with Feld Entertainment as Project Coordinator in Feld Consumer Products – Disney Domestic Sales & Operations. While working with Feld, I received my master's degree in Sports Management – Business & Operations from Georgetown University in May 2013. In December 2013, I moved into my current position as Manager of Feld Consumer Products – Circus Sales & Operations.

Q: What have been the biggest challenges you have encountered during your career?

A: One of the biggest career challenges has been creating and building my "name" to potential employers and industry professionals. Obtaining real-world experience, whether through internships or job positions, can be difficult but is also extremely important. Building your professional brand and image, gaining industry contacts, and getting your foot into doors is challenging. One needs to be proactive and diligent about taking advantage of opportunities and expanding a network of contacts through students, faculty, and industry professionals.

Q: Could you explain how Feld Entertainment is involved in the business of sport and entertainment?

A: Feld is the worldwide leader in producing and presenting live family entertainment. Feld productions include Ringling Bros. and Barnum & Bailey, Monster Jam, Marvel Universe LIVE!, Disney on Ice, and Disney Live! Feld performs in arenas, stadiums, and theatres to over 30 million people in attendance each year. Productions have appeared in more than 70 U.S. cities, over 75 countries, and on six continents. Feld is involved in promoting and marketing shows, ticket and consumer product sales, event and operations management, sponsorship, and many more areas.

Q: Can you discuss your team's role in the overall operation of Feld?

A: Feld Consumer Products (FCP) is the official concessions/merchandising department for Feld Entertainment. We are responsible for the sales and operations aspects of consumer products. FCP develops, manufactures, and imports our own products for every show produced by the company. We sell high-quality toys that enhance the customer's entertainment experience at all our shows.

Q: What are the major challenges you and your company are currently facing?

A: As of 2014, the company is facing challenges of economies that have not yet returned to a 2008 pre-recession level. These include economies not only domestically, but internationally as well. In turn, economic strength affects consumer spending and a family's disposable income. As a global company, many regions and cities we play in have significantly improved, but many unfortunately have not.

Q: What do you think will be the biggest challenges in the next 5 to 10 years?

A: The biggest challenges in the future will be competing with technology in the home. The increased appeal and ease of watching television on cable/satellite, streaming videos over the Internet, and playing computer/video games will further compete with getting people out of the house. The challenge of maintaining the creation of unique family shows and experiences will be crucial.

Q: Are there specific skills sport-management students should look to develop while still in school?

A: Students should look to develop communication and teamwork skills. Being able to interact effectively with fellow students and faculty in any group assignment is advantageous. These are important factors that revolve around any business or organization and will help any student succeed.

Q: What are the biggest mistakes you have seen students or young alums make in this industry?

A: Some students have had the impression that they want to become a general manager (GM) of a sports organization. While a GM position is attractive, it is extremely difficult to obtain. Also, many students hurt their chances of obtaining internships or employment by their social media profiles. Having exposed information for employers to view is typically a disadvantage for job candidates.

Q: What publications do you regularly read to stay apprised of sport-business events?

A: I read *Venues Today* and *SportsBusiness Journal* to stay current of sport business. I also enjoy reading any good articles that are posted on LinkedIn through sports groups or other connections.

Q: Would you recommend students pursue graduate school? If so, when should they pursue a graduate degree and what area of study would you recommend?

A: I would recommend students pursue graduate school if it makes financial sense and is best for one's career. If possible, I would suggest obtaining a few years of work experience before pursing graduate school. In doing so, one can apply what is learned at a company to school and vice versa. In addition, I would suggest studying in areas involving business or management. These areas of study can be utilized in numerous industries and companies.

Q: Is there any additional advice or insights you would provide to students pursuing a future career in sport management?

A: I would advise students to take advantage of as much real-world experience or opportunities that they can. It is important to show potential employers that you're active in things outside of the classroom. I would also advise students to take a sales course if provided. If not, try to gain an understanding of sales another way by research. A sales course was not offered to me while I was in college, but I wish it was. Sales are a crucial component to any sports company or organization.

Malcolm M. Bordelon

Sport Management Consultant

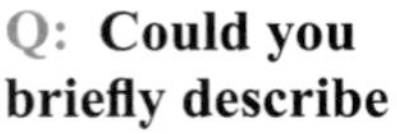

Q: Could you briefly describe your career path from undergraduate student to your current position?

A: I attended Texas Tech University where I graduated in the summer of 1981 with a BS in Advertising/Minor in English. I worked my way through college employed as an advertising sales rep for the school's paper – *The University Daily*. I also served as president of the Advertising Club and director of PR for the Student Body Government my senior year.

My first job after I graduated was with Ogilvy & Mather Advertising (Houston, Texas office). I was hired as Assistant Account Executive and was later promoted to Account Executive. I worked on the Shell Oil account – primarily on Shell Fire & Ice Motor Oil.

I left Ogilvy after about two years and moved to Dallas to work for Cunningham & Walsh Advertising (C&W) as Account Executive on *The Dallas Morning News*, La Quinta Motor Inns, and Lennox Heath & Air Conditioning.

After about 2 1/2 years with C&W I went to work for Carlisle Outdoor Advertising (billboard sales) in Dallas as Director of Sales & Marketing. I worked for Carlisle for about three years and won several local awards and one national award for self-promotion advertising campaigns I created for Carlisle.

The Director of Marketing for the Dallas Mavericks of the NBA (one of my key clients), Greg Jamison, took a job with the Indiana Pacers and asked me to join him with the organization as Director of Sponsorship Sales. I worked in that capacity for the Pacers for six years.

Greg Jamison later took a key role with the San Jose Sharks (NHL) and a year later asked me to join him in San Jose as Vice President/Broadcast & Media Marketing. After two years Jamison was promoted to President and I was promoted to Executive Vice President Business Operations where I eventually oversaw all areas of the business:

Marketing & Fan Development
Ticket Sales and Service
Sponsorship Sales and Service
Suite Sales and Service
Event Presentation
Internet/Digital Services
Broadcasting
Media and Public Relations

In addition, I managed business operations for other Sharks Sports & Entertainment properties including: SAP Open (ATP) and the Worcester Sharks (AHL Affiliate), and SVS&E Merchandise.

I left the Sharks after nearly 20 years (a lengthy term in this business – in many businesses actually) and am currently handling a few consulting projects and investigating potential new opportunities.

Q: What have been the biggest challenges you have encountered during your career?

A: In the professional sports realm, navigating the uncertainty of work stoppages/lockouts has been difficult. Trying to formulate strategy in an uncertain environment is difficult. In the NHL, we had some significant work stoppages (half-season 1994-95, full season in 2004-05, half-season 2012-13). During these times we had to consider the following:

- Not knowing when the work stoppage will end (or if)
- Convincing ownership to go to the expense of retaining key staff (while there were no revenues)
- Managing staff morale challenges in such times of angst and uncertainty
- Maintaining visibility and relevance when there is no primary product available for your customers
- Being constantly prepared to re-launch with very short notice
- Retaining the various customer bases (ticket holders, suite holders, sponsors and other partners)
- Regaining momentum and market stature once back in operation

Even in times of NHL stability, while with the Sharks, building employee morale and retaining key employees in a very expensive part of the country (Silicon Valley) was difficult. Not only is there a very high cost of living, you are also unable to provide the excessive comp and benefit's packages so prominent among much of the working population in the Bay aArea—specifically in the technology sector, which makes up much of the workforce here (and all of the news).

During my time with the Sharks, we had to manage and navigate times of significant change in the organization when business units were restructured. This unfortunately often required layoffs.

Q: As those labor stoppages have been settled, what have been the residual effects?

A: Escalating player salaries could be an entire chapter of discussion. It is a real problem in the sports business. Certainly, every employee wants to earn as much money as possible, and as revenues in sports have increased, so have the player's salaries. The problem is far too often owners spend more than their revenues can sustain and then they try to figure out "what's wrong with the business?" So owners venture into other side/related businesses, not to grow their enterprise and increase its value, but rather to find other revenue streams to feed the beast that is player compensation and related costs to operate the team.

Though this reality is not necessarily ideal, it does create new opportunities for sport-management professionals. Sport businesses are venturing into a variety of areas that will require employees with specific skill sets such as real estate development, broadcasting (since teams and conferences are now running their own TV networks), facilities management, and more.

Q: Can you discuss some of the activities that you undertook while with the Sharks to develop ancillary hockey revenues as well as the various non-hockey activities the Sharks pursued?

A: In an effort to capitalize upon our core competencies we pursued other business ventures that either involved a sport's franchise, facility management, or other related businesses. We operated other sports franchises and ventures (in some cases we were paid a management fee, in others we were owners or involved in a partnership) such as:

- San Jose Earthquakes (MLS)—we operated the Bay aArea's primary professional soccer team for two years on behalf of MLS as they pursued new ownership (we were not in position to purchase)
- Seibel Classic—Senior PGA golf tournament. We operated this event for two years in partnership with the City of San Jose. The event date was not beneficial (the second event rained out) and the events of 9/11 had a negative effect on corporate spending. This event was financially "fragile" already, and reductions in spending on marketing and entertainment made it too difficult to sustain.
- SVS&E Publishing—we had the opportunity to take our publishing needs in-house and hired two people from the company we had previously contracted to manage our publishing needs. We witnessed an overall savings in our related expenses and were able to secure other sports franchise publishing business (49ers, Golden Baseball League, some area colleges). This business was sustained for some time, but eventually self-publishing and competition from large-scale publishers rendered this business too difficult to maintain on a profitable basis.
- SVS&E Merchandise—we purchased a small merchandise company and brought them in-house to handle the Sharks, San Jose Arena, and related properties merchandise needs. We witnessed cost savings and better product controls by handling those responsibilities ourselves. We also pursued merchandise needs of other arena tenants (such as the Arena Football League San Jose Sabercats) and secured outside "non-sports" corporate business —for some of our clients and others—such as Cisco and SAP. We helped produce and distribute company merchandise, golf shirts, mugs, gifts, etc.
- San Jose Champ Car Race—During one NHL work stoppage we provided our services to the San Jose

Champ Car Race (for its inaugural year) and we handled everything from marketing and ticket sales/service to merchandise, hospitality sales/service, as well as some portions of security and operations.

- San Jose Stealth (Indoor Lacrosse)—we had a three-year partnership with the San Jose Stealth (who played at the HP Pavilion) managing all aspects of sales and operations including ticket sales, sponsorship sales, marketing, event presentation, etc.

Q: How do you manage employee performance and attitude in the up-and-down world of professional sports, especially when the business side of the business does not directly impact the wins and losses fans see on the ice?

A: It is important to develop a thick skin. Employees need to focus on the business and that they will be evaluated on how well they do their specific jobs, not on how well the team performs. That's true inside the organization. However, quite often outside the organization many will judge their performance on how the team performs (even though employees in the business side have nothing to do with that). Winning cures all ills. When the team wins you're a genius and fans / the press will often overlook poor customer service and errors in execution. But when the team is losing then everything else is wrong: the drinks have no ice, the hot dogs are cold, the bathrooms are dirty, the music is bad or too loud, the seat is broken, the organization does not know what it is doing, everything is overpriced, sponsor promotions aren't executed properly, etc. The microscope is harsh.

I try to remind employees often of a few key things:

- Don't get cocky when the team wins (enjoy it like the fans do—but you had nothing to do with it).
- Don't feel inferior at your job when your team loses (again, you had nothing to do with it).
- Keep focused on consistently executing—win or lose. Over time fans and clients will actually notice that consistency and appreciate it.

Q: Are there specific skills sport-management students should look to develop while still in school?

A: I think students should focus on the specific area of business that interests them the most. The respective sport they might work in (whatever sport it might be) is the *product*. Unless they are going to be a player, coach, general manager, scout, equipment manager, etc., they will not actually be "working in the specific sport." Their skills will be (and need to be) transferable from sport to sport and business to business. I've worked in basketball, hockey, tennis, golf, car racing, and lacrosse ... all involve similar business operations fundamentals. So if students like sales and marketing they should focus on opportunities to enhance those skills. If they like Broadcasting or Media Relations or Digital Media management they should ensure they do all they can to learn and be the best they can in those areas of interest. Certainly, they will want to try to gain those experiences in relation to a given sports team, league, etc. if possible. But that won't always be possible, so experience in the specific area of interest will be of importance.

When I would interview people and they would tell me "I'm just the biggest hockey fan / basketball fan, ... etc." I would think – that's great, I want them to like the product ... but if that's their main selling point I should just sell them season tickets. They're just telling me they're a fan, and are not differentiating themselves from other candidates or giving me a sound reason to hire them. What I need as a business manager is not a fan, but someone who loves sales, customer service, and putting on a great game presentation or a superior broadcast. I need people who have a passion for community development, executing a great marketing campaign, and developing cutting-edge digital media activities, etc ... Students should strive to be great at *what they do*, and display passion for what they do and are most interested in. Everyone should constantly work at their craft. Sports *Business* requires a focuses on the *Business*: Sales, Marketing, Operations, Revenue generation ... not on the team's Xs and Os. I completely understand the attraction and fun of being associated with a sports team, league, university, governing body, etc ... Sports is a great and fun product to represent. However, your performance will be judged on how well you do your job, not how well the team performs. I can recall working games/events where I saw only a few minutes of the respective competition – because I was talking with clients, dealing with an issue in or outside the arena, handling a problem with broadcast crew ... any number of issues involved with assuring we were handling the business at hand. My job was not to watch the game. It was to ensure everything else went as planned and fans had an enjoyable evening whether the team won or lost. ... Within Sports Business there are many different career paths. Broadcasting, community outreach, sales, marketing, public relations, etc. All of these paths exist in many other businesses as well. Students should pursue the area of business that interests them the most so they can display their passion.

Q: What specific classes would you recommend students take to best position themselves for a sport-industry job?

A: A few subject areas that come to mind include:

- Sales and Marketing
- Sport Sponsorships
- Broadcast and Digital Media
- Market Research
- Some sort of fundamentals in law (intellectual property, entertainment, sports law)
- Management / Leadership
- PR / Media Relations

There are also two key areas that cut across a variety of courses and apply to just about any job in this industry:

- English
  I don't care what line of work you go in to—*Learn to write well*. Businesses repeatedly cite "communication skills" as one of the most desirable traits in new employees. It is apparent that this key communication skill is too often being ignored or lost. Your writing skills provide a reflection of your intelligence and on the organization you represent. Such skills are absolutely necessary to communicate succinctly, motivate, persuade, clearly inform others, and manage well. Presentation, clarity, and professionalism in writing skills can help distinguish you from the pack. The flip side of this is that you don't want others trying to figure out how to "work around you" because you can't write well.
- Finance
  Be sure to get at least a fundamental understanding of finance. I do believe most majors include some classes in this area—if not, make sure you take some finance courses and see if there are additional electives that might be beneficial. My major had no finance-related classes and I received little exposure to finance matters during my first several jobs (other than just managing project expense). What I learned I learned on the job or through separate seminars/classes (after college). The higher you go in an organization, the more you will delve into financial matters and the more you know/are adept at the fundamentals (or more) the better it will be—and the more valuable you will be to your organization.

Q: What publications do you regularly read to stay apprised of sport-business events?

A:

~ *SportsBusiness Daily* and *SportsBusiness Journal*

~ I also follow a variety of people on Twitter and LinkedIn who are in the industry and write, reference or forward various sports business-related news and articles from any number of publications.

Q: Would you recommend students pursue graduate school? If so, when should they pursue a graduate degree and what area of study would you recommend?

A: I do believe an MBA and/or Law degree can be of benefit – depending upon the student's area of interest.

After two years at Ogilvy & Mather I was asked by Texas Tech to come back to join their MBA program. I chose not to, feeling at the time that I learned so much more "on the job" (and I did not want to go back to school). Part of that is my personal learning style. I don't know if it would have helped me or not. I get mixed reviews from those who do and don't have an MBA. Some say it was very important and they "use what they learned in their MBA program every day." Others say it was "just two more years to mature." I can't say I have hired or not hired someone because they have an MBA (or not). I know some place a higher value on an MBA than others, but I don't recall any conversation in which candidates were being discussed in which someone said "he/she has an MBA, so we should hire him/her over the other candidate."

In the end – if one can afford the expense and the time (forgoing income for a few years – or can manage night school), then I actually would be in favor of pursuing an MBA. Not just for your marketability (by the way - you may not end up in sports and may end up in a business that favors an MBA on a resume), but also for the added value the further education should provide you. I believe most "use what they learn" in the process of obtaining their MBA. My experiences speaking to most MBA classes have been enjoyable as the students tend to know more and don't take an answer to questions as gospel. MBA students tend to challenge your thinking, ask hard questions, and create a more dynamic discussion. I do think an MBA has value in enhancing knowledge and improving employee marketability, if the student approaches it with the correct mindset. I believe graduate school should be pursued after about 2 to 3 years of employment so that the student can relate actual work experiences to their learning process in the program.

I also mention Law degree because it seems more and more that leagues and other sport businesses hire more lawyers than ever. While one would not have to go specifically into sport law, a law degree would be of benefit in handling negotiations with cities, broadcast partners, sponsors, and numerous other partners the teams may deal with on the business side. It would be something of value in marketability of the employee and in real value on the job (and many other jobs outside of sports). Like an MBA, if it can be afforded from a time and expense perspective it's worth considering.

Dawn Ridley

Founder and President
Ridley & Associates LLC

Q: Can you briefly describe your career path?

A: I was in graduate school working on my MBA and began seeking internships in sport and entertainment. I had two entertainment internships, but felt that the sport side would be a better fit, so when an opportunity presented itself with the Atlanta Braves, I joined the organization as an intern and eventually an employee.

My full-time position with the Braves was seasonal and I thought I should seek something more permanent, so I secured a great sales position with a leading flooring manufacturer. It was fantastic experience, but my heart was in the sport industry, so I left and quickly secured a sales and marketing position with the Atlanta Committee for the Olympic Games (ACOG). It was a great experience that allowed me to utilize the sales skills I had gained from my previous position in a dynamic, evolving environment.

I unexpectedly came across an amazing opportunity with the NFL Players Association while still at ACOG. Though I had no intention of leaving ACOG or Atlanta, the position was too good to pass up. I was named the Assistant Vice President for Trading Cards and Collectibles for PLAYERS INC (NFL Players Incorporated, now known as NFLPI), the newly launched for-profit subsidiary of the NFL Players Association. It was a position that changed the trajectory of my career. I learned a great deal about all aspects of business and developed strong licensing, athlete representation, business development, and marketing skills.

After about seven years, I was named the Vice President of Corporate Marketing and Business Development. I worked with all NFL sponsors to integrate and promote NFL players and the PLAYERS INC brand within sponsor programs. I also worked very closely with the NFL on related policy and CBA concerns.

I was eventually promoted to Senior Vice President and oversaw the licensing and sponsorship businesses. The 12 years I spent with the organization were very significant in my career. I left to teach at the Carey Business School at Johns Hopkins University and to launch my own consulting firm, which provides marketing, strategy, licensing, and business development services to various organizations.

I have also had the opportunity to work in business development for National Geographic Society and D.C. United and teach at George Washington University and Georgetown University. I also developed a platform to assist recent graduates and those seeking a career transition secure their first job in the sport industry. FirstSportsJob.com launched in 2014 and features targeted content, online courses, and coaching services to help those seeking to enter into the industry.

Q: What have been some of the biggest challenges you have faced during your career?

A: One of the biggest challenges I had was learning how to gain support for strategies that were consistent with current best practices into business environments that had traditionally operated within the framework of an event-focused or sport operations environment. I learned a lot through those processes.

Another challenge was learning new industries and companies quickly, but it was my favorite challenge!

Q: Can you explain how important the retail licensing business is to the sport management industry and to the NFL in particular?

A: Retail licensing is a significant business within the sport industry and one that is often overlooked by those interested in the industry. Licensed products account for a large percentage of revenue for most sport leagues, teams, and players associations. In 2013, the sports category earned $698 million in revenue on $12.8 billion in retail sales. Collegiate licensing earned $209 million in royalties on $3.88 billion in sales. Intellectual property is a one of the most valuable assets for any sport organization, but it is especially valuable for the most prominent leagues. The NFL and NFL Players

Incorporated both rely heavily upon licensing revenue, with apparel and multimedia representing a significant portion of royalty revenue.

Q: What prompted you to start your own business?

A: I was seeking an opportunity to utilize my experience, expertise, and relationships to support businesses that don't have exposure to the sport industry or non-traditional business development. I have been fortunate to have many of my "dream jobs" and the next logical step was to develop a business that enabled me to leverage my background to support others. I have had the opportunity to support businesses through Ridley & Associates and I am excited about helping individuals with FirstSportsJob.com.

Q: What are the most important skills you think students should work to develop while still in school?

A: Critical thinking and analytic skills are very important and are often not considered while in school. I believe an understanding of revenue streams and the importance of the sales function is important as well, even for those who don't intend to go into sales.

Q: What are the biggest mistakes that you see interns and entry-level employees making in this business?

A: Expecting to quickly scale the ladder to their dream job within a short period of time. An internship or entry level position is an opportunity to learn and to prove yourself through hard work, a positive, can-do attitude and consistency. It can also be a time to develop important relationships that can last throughout their career.

Q: Are there specific publications that you read regularly?

A: *SportsBusiness Journal* and *SportsBusiness Daily*. Publications related to specific areas of business (e.g., IEG's newsletters, *License* Magazine, relevant blogs).

Q: Do you advise students to potentially pursue a graduate degree?

A: I think a graduate degree can be valuable for anyone seeking a career in business, and especially those interested in a career in sport. Students should carefully consider their career goals and have a clear vision of how they think the graduate degree will further those goals.

Steve Fanelli

Executive Director of Ticket Sales and Operations
Oakland Athletics

Q: Could you briefly describe your career path from undergraduate student to your current position?

A: I graduated from the University of Kansas with a business communications degree and returned to the Bay aArea to work for the Oakland Football Marketing Association (OFMA). I started as a Customer Service Representative, and was promoted to Customer Service Manager after a few months on the job. After two years at OFMA, I was hired by the Oakland A's to be their Box Office Manager. I came to the A's during an organizational transition period with new ownership and after two seasons was promoted to Director of Ticket Operations. Today, I am the Executive Director of Tickets Sales and Operations and oversee the sales, service, operations, retention, and database efforts. I also oversee our Spring Training sales and operations in Arizona and am responsible for five budgets and over 40 full-time employees.

Q: What have been the biggest changes you have seen in ticketing industry?

A: The ticketing industry has evolved as quickly as any part of the business over the last 17 years. When I started, we were primarily a paper and cash business. Internet commerce was in the early stages and the consumer purchase experience was very similar to how teams operated for decades. The consumer mindset has changed to keep pace with 21st-century technology and today we're seeing a shift for the complete purchase and delivery model to digital.

Q: What changes do you anticipate in the next four to five years?

A: The A's were the first team in North America to accept a mobile ticket for entry into an event in 2006, and within the next four to five years I anticipate mobile being the primary method for purchase, delivery, ticket management, and payment. Personal mobile devices will play a large role in the overall gameday experience and will drive consumer behavior and overall growth. We installed iBeacons this year to auto-check in iPhone users and deliver a special offer. As this technology matures, we'll see the stadium interacting with the individual fan through their mobile device to deliver experiences and offers that are valuable to the individual consumer. It's really an exciting time to be in ticketing and the speed of growth and adoption of these technologies is evolving daily.

Q: What specific classes would you recommend students take to best position themselves for a job in the future, whether that be in the sport industry or some other career path?

A: Sales has always been a great way to break into sports. If you can refine your interpersonal skills and learn to speak to an audience, you'll be able to sell and share ideas in order to grow. There is a very specific area of need right now in sports and that's in the area of Customer Relationship Management (CRM), Database Management, and predictive analytics. More and more teams are relying on the wealth of data that is available to build customer profiles and prospect effectively. I would highly recommend this as an alternative to sales if you're more analytical in nature.

Q: You have been able to stay in one place for some time. That is unusual for some in this industry. Would you offer any advice regarding career progression to students thinking not only about their first job, but how to position themselves to be successful and advance?

A: My career means a lot to me and I've been fortunate to work with a great group of people and in an environment that allows me and my team to be creative without a lot of resistance. We are at the top of our industry in a lot of progressive areas and have provided guidance to the league and our counterparts in the industry regarding best practices. Ultimately, if you land in an environment that challenges you to grow and supports your decisions, there's no real need to search for change.

Q: **What publications do you regularly read and conferences do you regularly attend to stay apprised of sport-business events?**

A: *SportsBusiness Daily* is mandatory to keep up with industry happenings. I typically attend the SportsBusiness Journal conference, INTIX, Tickets.com's Ticketing Summit, and a number of league-sponsored conferences annually. Getting out of the office to collaborate and network with other industry professionals is imperative for growth.

Scott Pederson

President/CEO
Positive Athlete Georgia

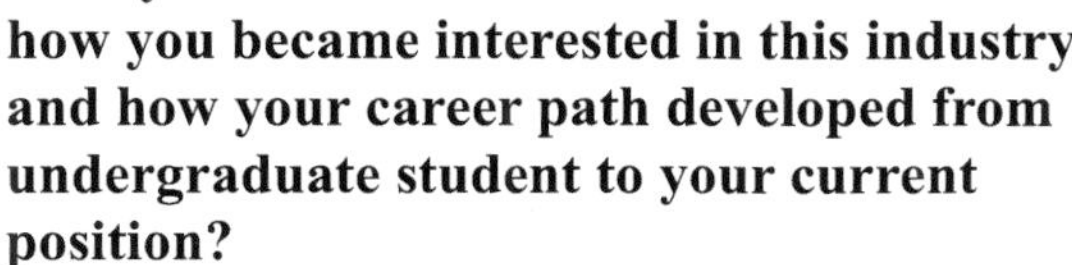

Q: Could you briefly describe how you became interested in this industry and how your career path developed from undergraduate student to your current position?

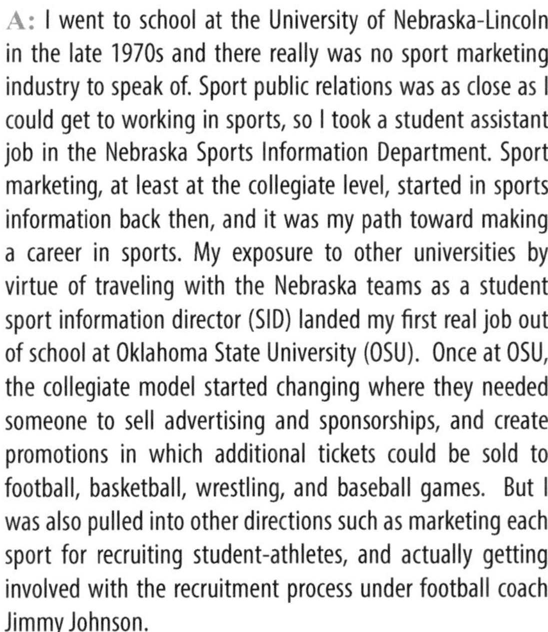

A: I went to school at the University of Nebraska-Lincoln in the late 1970s and there really was no sport marketing industry to speak of. Sport public relations was as close as I could get to working in sports, so I took a student assistant job in the Nebraska Sports Information Department. Sport marketing, at least at the collegiate level, started in sports information back then, and it was my path toward making a career in sports. My exposure to other universities by virtue of traveling with the Nebraska teams as a student sport information director (SID) landed my first real job out of school at Oklahoma State University (OSU). Once at OSU, the collegiate model started changing where they needed someone to sell advertising and sponsorships, and create promotions in which additional tickets could be sold to football, basketball, wrestling, and baseball games. But I was also pulled into other directions such as marketing each sport for recruiting student-athletes, and actually getting involved with the recruitment process under football coach Jimmy Johnson.

When Jimmy Johnson and his staff left for the University of Miami, I had an opportunity to interview with the Kansas City Royals for a marketing director position which I eventually accepted. To show you how far professional sport marketing departments have come, there were only three of us in the department. And I was in charge of sponsorships, group sales, in-stadium atmosphere (scoreboard, PA, organ, etc.), and on-field ceremonies. There are literally 25 to 30 people doing those jobs with an average major league professional team now.

From the Royals I worked for Miller Brewing Company Sports Marketing handling all of their professional and motor sports marketing properties on the East Coast from Atlanta. After Miller, I opened my own sports marketing agency called Universal Marketing Associates which developed marketing properties for the NFL, MLB, NBA, Goodwill Games, and other professional sports organizations, as well as major corporations such as Gatorade and General Mills. I merged my company with the company that lost its chairman and CEO on the tragic flight that killed golfer Payne Stewart. After the merger with Leader Enterprises, the company developed the marketing and PR plan around Nike's LiveStrong campaign, and served companies such as DirecTV, Motorola, and TaylorMade.

In 2009, I decided to sell my interest in Leader Enterprises to develop a brand called Positive Athlete with the help of Super Bowl XL MVP Hines Ward. The program is now in Pittsburgh and Georgia, and will eventually become a national program in 50 markets.

Q: What have been the biggest challenges you have encountered during your career?

A: If you have been in the workplace over the past 30+ years, trying to grow your business while technology is literally exploding has been a challenge. When you grow up with typewriters, long-distance phone, and the U.S. Postal Service as your primary tools, trying to keep up with new technology doing business the way you have for many years is a major challenge. The other main challenge while owning a business has been balancing the difference between working "on" the business, and working "in" the business. I am wired to be creative and engaging with clients which is why all of my businesses flourished in the first place. The challenge is learning how to relinquish some of that because someone needs to run the company and deal with employees and other operational matters. One of my companies grew to 75 employees at one point, and I spent all my time dealing with employee issues instead of growing the business. This was the chief reason for selling my interest in that company and starting over. I missed being creative and engaging with clients.

Q: Could you explain what your current job entails?

A: Positive Athlete is still in its infant stages (less than six years old), so with the exception of having agencies and college interns working on various aspects of the company, I have literally been doing everything else by myself to get it off the ground. This includes recruiting professional athletes and teams to endorse the program, promoting nomination submissions from high schools, selling sponsorships to local companies, and engaging media partners to help promote the program. The accounting aspect has been relatively easy at this point because we're just getting started, but I wear that hat as well.

Q: What are the major challenges you and your company are currently facing?

A: Positive Athlete is a rocket ship right now and growing at a pace that is hard to keep up with. The biggest challenge is to keep focused on the current opportunities in front of me, and not chase several opportunities that have materialized because of the success we're having. My other challenge is helping companies understand that we are a marketing property, not a non-profit organization. Positive Athlete's mission is very much a cause-related endeavor, but we are organized as a for-profit venture because we want Positive Athlete to be a brand and marketing property. The main issue tied to this challenge is which department the company you are pitching sends you to. I want to be sent to marketing and sponsorship folks (more dollars to spend) versus the foundation/community folks (less dollars to spend).

Q: What do you think will be the biggest challenges in the next 5 to 10 years?

A: I believe that controlling our growth and protecting our program from knock offs will be major challenges. Positive Athlete could be done in every market/state in the United States, as well as worldwide. While we have trademarked Positive Athlete, is doesn't keep companies from developing something similar in a market we haven't developed yet. At the same time, I don't want to expand so quickly that we lose the focus that has brought us success to date.

Q: Are there specific skills sport-management students should look to develop while still in school?

A: I believe one of the biggest issues young people in general have these days is learning how to engage people and build relationships. Most of the students today have grown up in an age where everything is communicated via technology, and in 140-character segments. I meet so many smart kids who still can't look you in the eye when they are speaking to you. Good ideas don't go very far if you haven't built relationships with people to listen to them. Sport-management and the industry in general is still a very relational place. The reason Positive Athlete has grown as quickly as is has can be traced back to relationships I had to help me open doors. So building relationships while you are still in school is a great way to set you up for future success. You never know who you are sitting next to in class. They could be someone who will be a great asset to you in the future.

Q: What are the biggest mistakes you have seen students or young alums make in this industry?

A: As much as you try to tell them in advance of entering the market, young people still don't understand that sports is still a dues-paying industry. You do not start as the director of marketing for a professional or college sports team coming out of college making good money. It is a grind and it doesn't pay well to start. And to make it more challenging, too often young college alums see friends getting higher-paying jobs after graduation. You just have to accept the economic reality of the industry coming out of school.

The other mistake I see is the limited focus aspiring sports executives have towards available opportunities. There are lots of ways to be involved in sports that aren't working for a pro team, becoming a sports agent, or becoming an athletic director. Broaden your horizons because there are organizations like Positive Athlete out there with potential opportunities.

Q: What publications do you regularly read to stay apprised of sport-business events?

A: To be completely honest, I don't have time to read sport-business publications. I wish I did. I love the *SportsBusiness Journal*, but don't have time to read it anymore.

Q: Would you recommend students pursue graduate school? If so, when should they pursue a graduate degree and what area of study would you recommend?

A: More and more I see teams, corporations, and sports-marketing agencies using the lack of a master's degree as a weeding out component of their employment process. That alone is a great reason for having the graduate degree. The other reason I like to see students pursue a graduate degree is that extra seasoning they get by doing so. A prime example is that I encouraged my own son to get a graduate degree from the University of South Carolina even though I knew I wanted to bring him on board at Positive Athlete whenever he completed college. I am convinced that the additional time he is spending earning that degree has created seasoning with him that will help him, and Positive Athlete, in the future. I would encourage students to get this degree immediately. It will be much more difficult to find the time once your career is off and running.

Patrick Byrne

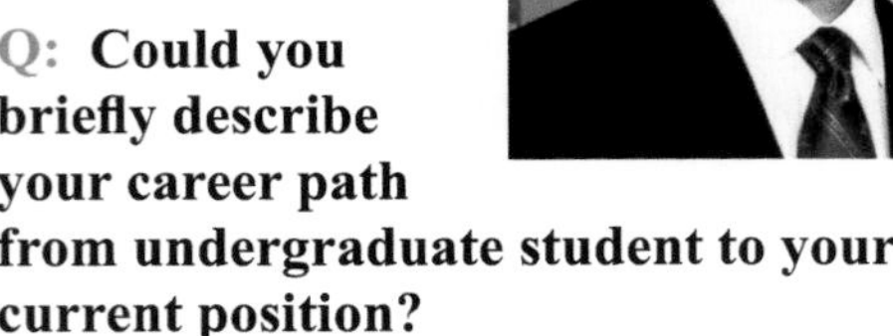

Director of Sales & Marketing
AutoZone Liberty Bowl

Q: Could you briefly describe your career path from undergraduate student to your current position?

A: During the summer before I finished my undergraduate degrees at the University of Memphis, I was afforded the opportunity to work as an intern in the sport marketing department at St. Jude Children's Research Hospital. The experience was eye-opening to say the least. Not only did it provide the opportunity to meet several prominent sport personalities and learn about the various careers in sports but it also convinced me to pursue a graduate degree in sports business. So the summer following graduation, I began working toward a master's degree in sport and leisure commerce. During the spring semester, I was able to reconnect with the executive director of the AutoZone Liberty Bowl (whom I had met during my time interning at St. Jude) through a class project. A few weeks later, he called and offered me a position with the AutoZone Liberty Bowl.

Q: What have been the biggest challenges you have encountered during your career?

A: The biggest challenge I face each year is staying on top of everything that has to be done during our peak season. From late November until gameday we work for about 12 to 14 hours per day, seven days a week. We have a small staff, so we all have to work very closely together to execute first-class events and take care of all the players, coaches, administrators, alumni, and fans. We are very fortunate to have a good internship program and strong base of dedicated volunteers who help put everything together. Early in my career, I found it difficult to find the energy and focus to work long hours at such a quick pace day-in and day-out. Since then, I have learned that surrounding yourself with good people, staying organized, being a good communicator, and asking for help are vital to being productive and staying fresh during bowl season.

Q: What are the biggest issues facing the college bowls?

A: Up until 2013, the biggest issue was whether there should be a playoff in FBS college football and how that would affect bowl games. But now that we have the College Football Playoff system in place beginning in 2014, I feel there is a nice marriage between the playoff system and bowl system for at least the next 12 years. Therefore, I think the biggest issue now facing bowl games is the slight decline in bowl game attendance over the past two- to- three seasons. In my opinion, the prevalence of large-screen HDTVs, smartphones/ social media, and the rising costs of attendance are the major factors in the decline in bowl game attendance. To reverse this trend, the college bowl industry has to find ways to make the in-stadium experience so compelling, entertaining, and affordable that it's better than the watching the game from home. In my opinion, the way college bowl games can shift attendance in a positive direction is by providing fans with services inside the stadium that they are accustomed to having while watching games at home. This means providing in-stadium Wifi (for social media, streaming live telecasts, scores, news, etc...), large-screen videoboards/state-of-the-art sound systems, score updates/highlights from other games, and maybe even power outlets at each seat to charge smartphones/tablets. I think the obvious benefit of adding these types of services is that fans will feel like they are not missing anything by attending the game. Additionally, I think because fans will be getting more for their money, they will place a higher value on attending games which in some cases could justify the cost of attendance.

Q: Are there specific job skills sport-management students should look to develop while still in school?

A: I believe that every college student should try to develop a close relationship with a professor and/or peer who can help them identify their strengths and weaknesses relative to their particular field of study. For sport-management students, a good work ethic, strong interpersonal skills, and a sound understanding of the sport world are important job skills. Having someone to help you recognize your weaknesses and improve those areas is invaluable . . . and much easier than trying to do it all on your own.

Q: What specific classes would you recommend students take to best position themselves for a sport-industry job?

A: Sales training classes and event management classes are critical. A thorough understanding of the sport industry is important but having the knowledge and experience to know what it takes to plan, sell, and execute an event is vital.

Q: What publications do you regularly read to stay apprised of sport-business events?

A: Well, I don't read many print publications anymore. I mostly read online articles from individuals/organizations that I follow on my Twitter feed.

Q: Would you recommend students pursue graduate school? If so, when should they pursue a graduate degree and what area of study would you recommend?

A: I would definitely recommend that students pursue a graduate degree. Attending graduate school was a very enriching educational experience for me. My classmates and professors created a learning environment that made every class and project highly engaging. It was hard work but very enjoyable and rewarding.

While a master's degree in sport management is a great area of study, I would recommend that students first consider pursuing a law degree. It amazes me the multitude of careers one can pursue with a JD. Many highly successful people in the sport world began their careers as lawyers.

I would recommend that students interested in pursuing a graduate degree enroll upon completion of their undergraduate coursework. However, someone who has a few years of real-world experience could also benefit greatly from earning a graduate degree.

Q: Is there a certain sport business area you see emerging in importance in the near future?

A: I think that high school athletics, especially football and basketball, will continue to grow as an important area in sport business. The number of televised games, games streamed online, recruiting services, websites, publications, all-star games, showcase games, camps, etc., has grown tremendously over the past decade. As the profile and importance of these entities grow, I believe fan support and corporate investment will grow as well.

Q: Is there any additional advice or insights you would provide to students pursuing a future career in sport management?

A: Work hard and learn how to sell. The quickest way to get your foot in the door in the sport industry is to have a tireless work ethic coupled with the skills and confidence to sell.

Rebecca M. Nicholson

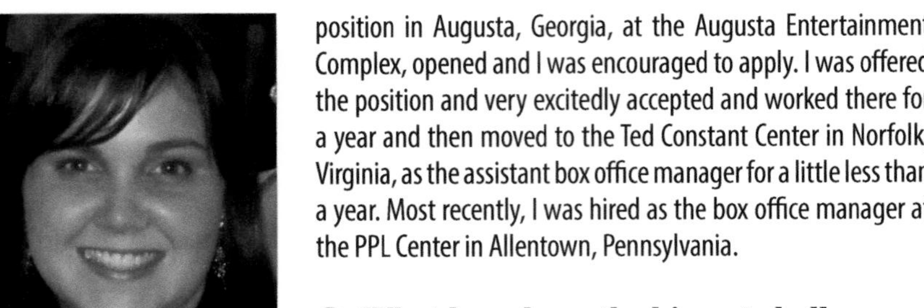

Box Office Manager
PPL Center

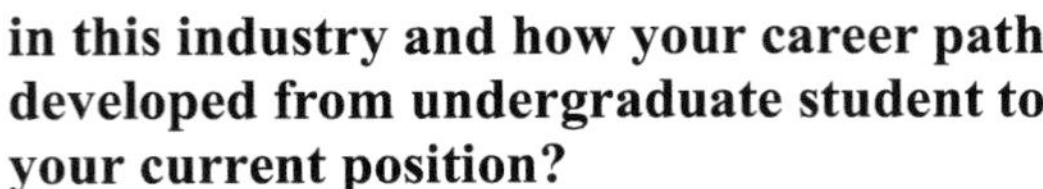

Q: Could you describe how you became interested in this industry and how your career path developed from undergraduate student to your current position?

A: My original career path was music based. I double majored in vocal performance and business management at Salve Regina University and had hoped to somehow combine them to work the "behind-the-scenes" management roles in the music industry. My mind changed a bunch of times from working for a record company to working some sort of event management or production management for an entertainment venue. However, with my main focus in college being on my vocal performance, I did not have the business connections in the industry that others may have had. I lived at home for two years after college while I worked part time at The State Theatre of New Jersey, Roadworks Entertainment, and Papyrus. My time at the State Theatre began as an internship and then turned into part-time work for the programming and production departments. Roadworks Entertainment is a company that one of my directors from the theatre started as a promoter for various traveling Broadway and family shows. Papyrus is an up-scale stationary and greeting cards store. After two years of working three jobs and eventually going full time into retail, I was fed up and decided to look into graduate school for entertainment management programs. This led to me to the Sport and Entertainment Management Program at the University of South Carolina (USC)! This was the best decision I ever made. Going to USC opened the doors to opportunities I had no access to before. I first completed an internship in the box office at Colonial Life Arena. That internship led to a summer internship at the (then) Verizon Wireless Amphitheatre. After my summer internship, I returned to Columbia and began working part time at the Colonial Life Arena box office as a supervisor and aiding the Assistant Box Office Manager as if I were the coordinator. The assistant box office manager position in Augusta, Georgia, at the Augusta Entertainment Complex, opened and I was encouraged to apply. I was offered the position and very excitedly accepted and worked there for a year and then moved to the Ted Constant Center in Norfolk, Virginia, as the assistant box office manager for a little less than a year. Most recently, I was hired as the box office manager at the PPL Center in Allentown, Pennsylvania.

Q: What have been the biggest challenges you have encountered during your career?

A: A big challenge has certainly been the "catch-up" I had to play. Most of my coworkers and fellow graduate students had either studied sport and entertainment management or had been involved and interested in the sport industry prior to graduate school. I knew nothing about sports. Growing up my main focus was always music and I participated in numerous choirs, small vocal ensembles, and theatre programs. So, coming into the USC Sport and Entertainment Management program was daunting. I didn't know a lot of the industry lingo or even much about it at all from the business perspective. I had three semesters worth of learning things many students already knew at a basic level. Another challenge is certainly being a woman in the industry. Now, that is not to say that my gender has held me back, but the sport and entertainment industry is still very much a man's world. I feel sometimes I have to work extra diligently to prove myself against the industry professionals who are male. A third challenge is always pushing to go beyond my comfort zone. This entire experience, from graduate school and entering the industry to even in my current position, required me and still requires me to push myself to learn more and grow. This means sometimes looking like a novice and not always knowing everything about every detail in the facility. I am a control freak so I don't like the feeling of being helpless when you don't know something right away. But, the industry is constantly changing and everyone has to continually adapt. In my job, the tiniest details are extremely important. If I get them wrong, I am in trouble. So, I always have to be focused and on top of every detail.

Q: What are the major challenges you and your company are currently facing?

A: The economy is certainly a challenge. That is pretty much across the board but for our industry it is unique. People will always want to go watch their favorite team take on a rival or go see their favorite band play live. But, we shouldn't think that our industry is completely recession proof. Nor can we assume that people will just come without our marketing. Not only do Global Spectrum buildings compete with each other and other venue management companies, we are competing with budgets and what families and individuals are willing to spend on entertainment.

Q: What do you think will be the biggest challenges in the next 5 to 10 years?

A: Keeping up with technology and what people expect to get out of their experience. Entertainment and sport events cost money that people are willing to use towards a unique experience. As technology continues to change and we have more of a "at-your- finger-tips" culture, our industry will need to adjust. And people will want to make sure their money is being put to good use. For example, there are so many doors opening in terms of ticketing and what we can include with a patron's purchase. Whether it's food and beverage packages or certain exclusive "VIP" additions where the customer actually gets more for less in the bigger picture. People want those types of unique experiences and packaging that makes their visit enjoyable.

Q: Are there specific skills sport-management students should look to develop while still in school?

A: Details, details, details are critical. Listening and responding are skills that are sometimes difficult for younger people to develop. It's one thing to "hear" what someone says and another to actually "listen" to what is being said and respond by doing what is expected. You also have to be detail oriented in this industry. One mistake can cause a lot of problems, even if the public does not immediately notice.

Q: What are the biggest mistakes you have seen students or young alums make in this industry?

A: A lot of young graduates and college students take their opportunities for granted. Our industry has limited supply but extremely high employment demand. I never thought I would work in ticketing nor was it what I thought I wanted to do. But an opportunity came to me and instead of letting it pass by, I took it. And I am very happy I did, because if I didn't I would not have the career I have now.

Q: What publications do you regularly read to stay apprised of sport-business events?

A: I had a *SportsBusiness Journal* and *SportsBusiness Daily* subscription but have not renewed lately. However, I follow them on Twitter and LinkedIn. Global Spectrum also mails out a monthly "magazine" called *The Globe* that keeps everyone up to date on the company and what's going on with our venues.

Q: Would you recommend students pursue graduate school? If so, when should they pursue a graduate degree and what area of study would you recommend?

A: That's a tough question. Honestly, I don't think the industry really requires a graduate degree. Most jobs will not pay you more just because of a master's degree. It doesn't matter how many classes you take or how many books you read in the eyes of many members of upper-level management, though getting an education is certainly helpful in performing better on the job. Students need to focus on learning on the job, making an impression and expanding their network. It sounds harsh to hear, especially if someone is in graduate school, but it is true. I believe my decision to go to graduate school was worth it though. It was my participation in the program and the connections the program had that helped me get my foot in the door. So, I don't think it is a waste of time either. Plus, it means you get to meet more people and learn from them. You can grow your network by attending graduate school.

Q: Is there any additional advice or insights you would provide to students pursuing a future career in sport management?

A: Be willing to adapt and take on new challenges. Don't pigeon hole yourself into one idea or one ideal job/position. This industry has so much to offer and you will need to be open to different things but those things will still teach you a lot and give you great experience.

Andrew Muscato

Managing Member
Makuhari Media

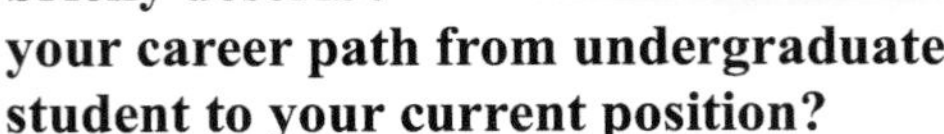

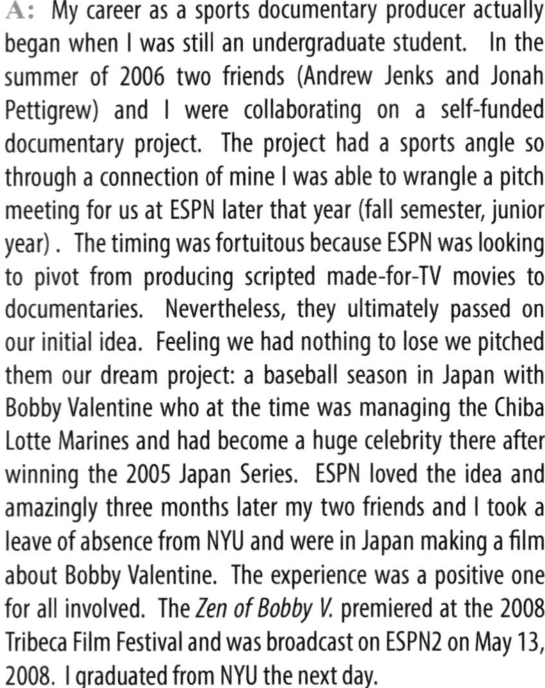

Q: Could you briefly describe your career path from undergraduate student to your current position?

A: My career as a sports documentary producer actually began when I was still an undergraduate student. In the summer of 2006 two friends (Andrew Jenks and Jonah Pettigrew) and I were collaborating on a self-funded documentary project. The project had a sports angle so through a connection of mine I was able to wrangle a pitch meeting for us at ESPN later that year (fall semester, junior year) . The timing was fortuitous because ESPN was looking to pivot from producing scripted made-for-TV movies to documentaries. Nevertheless, they ultimately passed on our initial idea. Feeling we had nothing to lose we pitched them our dream project: a baseball season in Japan with Bobby Valentine who at the time was managing the Chiba Lotte Marines and had become a huge celebrity there after winning the 2005 Japan Series. ESPN loved the idea and amazingly three months later my two friends and I took a leave of absence from NYU and were in Japan making a film about Bobby Valentine. The experience was a positive one for all involved. The *Zen of Bobby V.* premiered at the 2008 Tribeca Film Festival and was broadcast on ESPN2 on May 13, 2008. I graduated from NYU the next day.

I maintained my relationship with Bobby Valentine and when his managing career in Japan ended in 2010 he and I started a production company, Makuhari Media (named after the Japanese town we lived in) to continue making sports documentaries.

Q: What have been the biggest challenges you have encountered during your career?

A: My biggest challenge was realizing that my career path was in producing sports documentaries. It took me two years from finishing *The Zen of Bobby V.* and graduating from NYU to come to that conclusion. Like most college graduates I didn't know what career path I really wanted to follow and although *The Zen* was a success it left me feeling burnt out. In less than a year Andrew, Jonah, and I shot over 500 hours of footage and edited it into a 90-minute movie (all while finishing NYU). After the release of *The Zen of Bobby V.* I signed with agents at CAA and I expected them to offer more career guidance than they ultimately did. For two years I was aimlessly pitching reality TV shows and writing screenplays. Out of all this I learned an important lesson: You have to take charge of your own career because no one is going to care more about your career than you do.

Q: What have you learned about the sport business industry during your last couple of sport-related projects?

A: The sports industry is growing like never before. Youth sports have turned into a highly lucrative industry, college teams and professional franchises are more valuable than ever, U.S. professional sports leagues all have eyes on expanding their international footprint, and TV networks and sports radio are fighting over the rights to broadcast live sporting events which are viewed as "DVR-proof."

Q: Are there things that you have learned or noticed from sport-management professionals that would be important for students to know?

A: One thing I have noticed is that sport management is still an industry where time and energy is rewarded. You're not going to be a GM straight out of college but you can work your way there by starting at an entry-level position. Work hard and be a nice person because your reputation and the professional relationships you cultivate are paramount to success. So far in my career I have found the old adage, "It's not what you know, it's who you know," is 100% true.

Q: What specific classes would you recommend students take to best position themselves for a job in the future, whether

that be in the sport industry or some other career path?

A: I would recommend any courses that put an emphasis on writing and public speaking. Those are two necessary life-skills that students should constantly be honing.

Q: **What publications do you regularly read to stay apprised of sport-business events?**

A: My business partner Bobby Valentine, who is also Athletic Director at Sacred Heart University, shares with me his copies of *SportsBusiness Journal*. I also stay up to date on the sport entertainment industry by reading *The Hollywood Reporter*.

Q: **Would you recommend students pursue graduate school? If so, when should they pursue a graduate degree and what area of study would you recommend?**

A: I think the decision to pursue a postgraduate degree is a personal one (especially with the growing cost of higher education). Although there is a trend of MLB GMs with MBAs I do think there are many important lessons that can only be learned in the real-world by putting yourself out there and getting to work.

Rhett Blewett

Director of Facility and Event Services
Tampa Bay Times Forum

Q: Can you discuss your career path?

A: As Director of Facility and Event Services at the Tampa Bay Times Forum, I oversee the housekeeping, conversion, and event operations components of the facility. This is actually my second stint at the Forum. In 2005, I was an event operations intern as part of the sport-management program at Georgia Southern University. Upon graduation, I worked in minor league baseball with the Asheville Tourists for 10 months, before being offered a position back at this facility. I've been at the Forum for seven years now, moving up through the ranks from guest services manager, to event coordinator, to event manager, and now to my current position.

Q: What are some of your key responsibilities and duties?

A: More than anything, facility management is about communication. There are so many moving parts in a facility, and it doesn't come together without everyone communicating and being on the same page. As much as it takes to plan, build, budget, market, and design, at the end of the day we have to communicate effectively to make this operation run effectively.

On the day of an event, we have a staff briefing in the morning with our group leaders to make sure everyone is on the same page as far as their responsibilities and expectations go. Our event setup sheet provides a rundown of everything our staff needs to know in preparation for the event. We're also cognizant of media requirements. Typically, we host two television affiliates per game. Not only do they need media space and studio space within the facility, they also bring roughly 40 to 50 crewmembers to assist in game production. Finding a balance between spaces for the media so they can capture the shots they need, and not letting the media intrude on the guest experience is a constant challenge for televised events. This can be even more of a challenge during the playoffs when additional television affiliates may be on hand.

We take pride in each point of contact with our guests from when they first purchase a ticket to when they're walking in the parking lot back to their car after the game. Everything we do before, during, and after an event serves to enhance the fan experience in our facility. For example, before games, fans can enjoy live music, food trucks, and sponsor activation on the plaza outside The Forum. During the event, we're focused on customer service and troubleshooting problems as they arise so as not to detract from a guest's experience at our venue. Once the event has concluded, our overnight staff gets to work on conversion and housecleaning.

Q: What are the key revenue generators that you are developing?

A: The key to generating revenue is to provide a menu of entertainment options for all potential customers in our target markets. A primary source of revenue in The Forum is premium seating. We offer a wide range of suite alternatives from the exclusive suites on our promenade level to our Chase Club, which can accommodate up to 400 patrons. Each suite option comes with different amenities. In the traditional suite, for example, guests enjoy a private restroom, their own suite attendant, televisions, gourmet food and beverage options, and access to our club level. Our Chase Club is an all-inclusive environment offering a wide-range of food and entertainment options. The simplicity of this space, in terms of the all-inclusive environment, is what makes it so special. Our Chase Club attracts single game buyers, avid Lightning fans, and corporate clientele who use this area for employee incentives or to entertain clients. Whether a guest is looking for an affordable night of entertainment or a $5,000 seat along the glass, we strive to offer something for everyone and a variety of price points.

Aside from premium seating, food and beverage is another significant revenue generator. The revenue potential from food and beverage sales hinges on the amount of time guests have to wait in line. We recognize this challenge and work to utilize our concepts and spaces efficiently to minimize the amount of time it takes to make a transaction.

We outsource food and beverage services at The Forum. Food is such an important part of the customer experience, whether it is a hot dog or something unique our specialty chefs create, we can't afford to have shortcomings in this area. The concessionaire specializes not only in the service offered, but also preparation, space management, and the equipment necessary to run an effective food service operation. In recent years, we've also incorporated more of a local flavor into our food offerings. Not only do fans recognize these brands, but also it contributes to a sense of ownership fans take in the facility. When fans take ownership in the building, they want to take care of it and they don't second-guess their decision to attend. We're trying to develop a connection between our guests and the facility so they want to come back.

Sponsorship, of course, is another avenue from which we generate revenue. We actively seek sponsors that harbor the same vision and culture we strive for in the facility. Our focus in the sponsorship realm has really turned to the service side of these relationships. It is vital that sponsors feel as though there is a value in our partnership and that their dollar is working for them throughout the facility. Technology aids in our ability to generate revenue as well. Seating bowl signage is completely digital, allowing us to create more engaging sponsor messages, as well as promote upcoming events at tThe Forum which ultimately drives traffic back to our ticket office.

Q: What aspects of the facility are operated by third parties?

A: In addition to food and beverage service, we also outsource post-event housecleaning, valet parking, and many of our back-of-house mechanical engineering services related to maintenance and repair of facility systems such as HVAC, the videoboard, and our chiller plant. We do retain in-house control of security and guest services, as well as our changeover crew. Security and guest services are our front-line employees. We see value in being able to control and supervise the level of service these employees provide to our guests. At the end of the day, we're in the business of dealing with people. We want to provide the best service quality we can to every guest in our building.

Q: What do you see happening in the future in this industry?

A: Looking into my crystal ball, I see two important trends affecting the facility management industry over the course of the next 5 to 10 years: sustainability and technology. Sustainability is an avenue for your organization to save money by driving down costs. Everything helps—from recycling, to reusing products, to using more sustainable products. At The Forum, we recycle everything. We're even able to make a little bit of money from recycling certain materials. All of our light bulbs are energy-efficient bulbs. We use as little lighting as possible on non-event days. When the Lighting are on the road, we cover the ice to reduce the strain on the chiller plan. Finding ways to drive down energy costs keeps our executive team happy.

The endless ceiling of technology will continue to alter what we do in terms of running a facility. We're already using electronic chips sewn into fan jerseys to identify and track buying trends. We also use palm pilots and magnetic wands to expedite the ingress process. Even social media will have an effect on facility management, as it allows us to directly connect with each customer to form a more personal relationship. Staying on top of the latest technological trends and hiring the right people to manage new technologies will be important moving forward.

Q: What advice would you give to aspiring sport-management students?

A: For those of you looking to get into sport facility and event management, I cannot stress enough the importance of internships. Learn as much as you can in a variety of different settings. You can learn so much from seeing how different organizations approach similar issues/problems. A degree in sport management is also beneficial, as you'll learn so much in the classroom that is specific to the job you want. Beyond just the core curriculum though, you'll want to make sure you refine your social skills and familiarize yourself with the budgeting process. This is a service industry and you'll be interacting with people on a regular basis. Being comfortable approaching people, talking with people, taking criticism, and accepting compliments will go a long way in determining whether you are successful. Also, learning how to better manage your money and get the most out of your money is critical. No business will have an endless budget. You must be able to understand how to spend your money wisely, and get creative with your budget to stretch your dollar further.

Mike Nutter

President
Fort Wayne TinCaps
Baseball

Q: Could you briefly describe your career path from undergraduate student to your current position?

A: I graduated from Bowling Green State University in 1995. By graduation I had four summers' worth of experience with the Kane County Cougars where I learned many aspects of the operation of a very successful minor-league franchise. After graduation, I went to work for the Brevard County Manatees for an internship that turned into full-time employment. We had a successful season in 1996 in Brevard County by hosting Florida Marlins Spring Training games as well as the Florida State League's Brevard County Manatees. We also hosted the 1996 Florida State League All-Star Game. Following my experience in Brevard County, I went to work for the Nashville Sounds (AAA) in 1997. This was a tremendous experience. In Nashville, I was a corporate sales representative and Director of Baseball Operations. Following the 1999 season, I relocated to Fort Wayne, Indiana, where I was the Assistant GM during the 2000 season. Following the 2000 campaign, I was named general manager of the Fort Wayne Wizards. I have been the General Manager, and now Team President, for Fort Wayne Professional Baseball for the past 14 seasons. Entering the 2009 season, we moved into one of the best minor-league stadiums in the country (Parkview Field). At the same time, we changed our name from the Wizards to TinCaps (honoring local resident Johnny "Appleseed" Chapman). The 2009 campaign was one of the most successful any team in the minor leagues has ever had at any level. We finished the season with the most wins in the minor leagues, and attracted over 400,000 fans during the season. In the years since the opening of Parkview Field, the operation, attendance, and revenues have continued to grow. In fact, our largest attendance year ever was in 2013. A major reason is a growing trend in Minor League Baseball (MILB) where teams are doing many non-baseball events. This non-traditional revenue can include concerts, weddings, receptions, trade shows, food shows, etc. In 2013, the Fort Wayne TinCaps hosted over 612 non- TinCaps events.

Q: What have been the biggest challenges you have encountered in Minor League Baseball?

A: I believe that sometimes the biggest issue we face is ourselves. We talk about complacency frequently in our office and environment. There is a major effort to challenge ourselves on a daily basis. Sports are a major part of the fabric of our society and there will always be a place for sports teams, but with changes in culture we need to make sure we adapt frequently. We must not accept what we did last year as good enough for this year. We cannot assume that what has worked in the past will work in the future. There are a lot of great teams, ballparks, operations, etc., in MILB across the country. The ones that do it the best continue to challenge themselves, are their own toughest critics, and are not willing to accept anything less than a total effort to give the best fan experience. Our staff is more motivated than ever to come up with the next big thing in promotions, game operations, etc. One of the changes I have seen in my 18-plus seasons in baseball is that there is not as much staff turnover from year to year. In the past it seemed as if the business fostered an environment where one had to often move from team to team for promotion or other career advancement. With teams' business operations beginning to dramatically improve, and franchise values continuing to increase, I believe owners and general managers can pay their people better and retain high-performing employees. It is certainly better to be able to develop and pay great people what they are worth, rather than to have to replace and retrain staff members every couple of years. Though staff turnover is still a potential issue, many in the industry have recognized this inefficiency, and work to change the "move often" mentality.

Q: Can you discuss what you consider the most pressing issues facing Minor League Baseball and the overall sport industry?

A: I think the economy is always an issue for professional sports. The current economic times will dictate success levels for many teams in professional sports. In Minor League Baseball, we are less impacted by the economy, since we have one of the most family-friendly affordable sport products. Fans are able to see future major league talent in over 150 cities across the country for as little as a few dollars. This affordability, combined with promotions, giveaways, and other in-venue entertainment, should keep Minor League Baseball flourishing in tough economic times.

I think the laws of the land and current initiatives in local, state, and federal governments should be considered pressing issues. The Affordable Health Care Act is a work in progress that will have some impact on teams—what exactly that means for teams, fans, operations, etc., remains to be seen. Likewise, I believe there are other issues including labor topics involving payment of interns, hours worked, overtime pay, etc., that are still being deliberated in various legal venues. Over time this, too, will have an impact on teams, operations, and fans.

Q: You mentioned the need to book non-baseball activities at Parkview Field and the need to seek out non-traditional revenue sources. How do you make sure that you maintain a balance with your "primary" baseball activities while also trying to book new events?

A: Great question as it is one facing the entire sport industry. In Fort Wayne playing in full–season Low A, we have 70 home games. The baseball is, and probably always will be, the biggest revenue generator, but there are a lot of other events that can really move the needle as well. This year alone we are hosting three major concerts, 10 to 15 wedding receptions, and hundreds of other events, parties, rentals, etc. Last year we hosted 612 non-TinCaps events. This can be anything small from a sales luncheon for 15 folks for a company to a concert of 12,500 folks. In our case, the biggest challenge is staffing. We have a separate special events division that works these events, but does not have baseball duties.

Q: How do you utilize technology in your game presentation and other marketing activities? Are there concerns that technology is creating a "stay-at-home" competitor for the TinCaps and other live sporting events?

A: Our main focus is to ensure that the production doesn't get stale. We are one of three full season minor league teams to broadcast all 70 home games on television. We were questioned by many when we first started this, but we view it as a great opportunity to showcase the fun and excitement at our ballpark while people are at home. It is similar to a three-hour commercial. That being said, we need to be committed to the fun and overall stadium experience. Because if seeing the event live is not fulfilling fans can stay home and watch. In this immediate gratification society the thought of a three-hour baseball game isn't initially appealing to some folks. We need to make sure the music, promotions, customer service, etc., is better than anywhere else they can go—so they can't stay away. I think with technology folks still get out and about, but there are a percentage of fans that are at events, but focused elsewhere. We try to drive contests, promotions, etc., via Twitter, Facebook, Instagram, and other social media platforms during games to keep folks engaged.

Q: Are there specific job skills sport-management students should look to develop while still in school?

A: Sales! The majority of Minor League Baseball teams have a sales component for front-office employees. I have been with teams where everyone in the front office sold. I think sport-management students should focus on taking sales classes and getting some "real world" sales experience. Additionally, there is a tremendous demand for employment in minor league sports so I encourage students to get internships/summer jobs/experience in your field PRIOR to graduation. In many instances, one can make more money working outside of minor league sports internships, but the experience one receives by working in minor league sports is invaluable and is readily transferable to any other aspect of the sport industry. Regardless of future goals, students should spend considerable time working in the industry prior to graduation so that they have experiences that distinguish themselves from other potential applicants. I truly believe the time has never been better for minorities and women to excel in sports careers as well. There is a great opportunity out there for students at this time.

Q: What specific classes would you recommend students take to best position themselves for a sport-industry job?

A: Sales courses are a great opportunity to learn the basics of the sales process and to get experience. Sales are vital in most organizations, and the more one understands the process and embraces the opportunity, the greater the chance for career success. I think that along with sales, general marketing classes and communications classes are beneficial as well. Many days are spent with our staff members out in the region speaking with clients and other groups, so the more public speaking experience one has the better they will be able to work in the industry. Additionally, marketing classes are crucial as well. Getting comfortable talking with and to people in person and on the phone will go a long way towards the student's success. Many schools have a required public speaking course, but students should look to take additional speech classes if offered.

Q: What publications do you regularly read to stay apprised of sport-business events?

A: The *SportsBusiness Journal* is read regularly by our staff. It provides a good national perspective on the sport industry. It gives a great snapshot of national industry trends that can be used locally as well. I believe there are many other great online resources to get pertinent information. Following the right folks on Twitter can provide a lot of great information for teams. Finally, I think there is a lot of great LOCAL publications that must be read. You have to be an expert on your home town and region first. Local or regional business publications are a must.

Q: Would you recommend students pursue graduate school? If so, when should they pursue a graduate degree and what area of study would you recommend?

A: I believe it depends on the students' long-term goals. First off, I believe it would be beneficial for students to have an MBA or M.S.-Sport Management degree. The question is what are they doing and is it needed for their specific role within the organization? We have hired many students with graduate degrees in the past and I would say that they were all extremely successful with us and within our industry. In some cases, the person is being hired for an entry-level position and they can feel like the graduate degree places them above that sort of position, but in our case, it does not. I can only speak on Minor League Baseball and I would say it would be great to have, but not required. I believe there are many instances in other fields that it would not only be encouraged, but would be required. The majority of our employees that we have hired over the years have had the M.S.-Sport Management and not an MBA. We have also tried to encourage employees over the years to continue their education while a member of our staff. We have one current employee studying for his MBA and another member of management back at school now taking accounting classes. We allow employees to miss some work time and events to allow them to continue to develop and learn, and to hopefully make us a better organization.

Q: Is there a certain sport-business area you see emerging in importance in the near future?

A: I believe social media will continue to be an emerging part of our industry. Even though we have come so far the past 10 years, I believe it will continue to evolve and develop and the teams that do it right and stay current will be set up to succeed. When I wrote my first introduction for this great book nobody had ever heard of Twitter, Instagram, Pintrest, etc. Those are now major components of a team's marketing strategy. What will the next 10 years have in store? The reality is that many folks running teams may not be as capable or knowledgeable regarding social media as some of the students in college today. That could be a great niche for future job opportunities and growth in sport management in the near future.

I believe that marketing in Minor League Baseball will continue to grow on the national level. There is no greater customer value. In Minor League Baseball we have a franchise in most of the largest 175 metropolitan markets in the country. For example, I believe that companies will soon consider advertising in 150 minor league baseball stadiums for the same price as purchasing a 30-second Super Bowl advertisement. The Super Bowl will always be where the money is in terms of advertising, as nobody can compete with the exposure, but I honestly believe that some companies will continue to look at the realized benefits in the tougher economic climate and realize they can do signage and other elements with every team in the country and get a season-long presence for the same price as 30 seconds during the Super Bowl. The reality is that Super Bowl advertisements are impactful and continue to sell out every year, so Super Bowl broadcasters are not going to be hurting for clients, but some established clients will consider season-long opportunities with minor league baseball and other professional leagues.

Sports have always been extremely popular in our society, and I believe that will continue to be the case. I believe that the value of the product (ticket, experience, exposure, etc.) will continue to hold a lot of weight—perhaps much more during these economic times—than ever before. Many options are extremely difficult for a family to afford, but Minor League Baseball is usually an exception.

Q: Is there any additional advice or insights you would provide to students pursuing a future career in sport management?

A: Invest in yourself and stick with it! There is a great demand to get into this field and it can sometimes be difficult to make the kind of money one could make in other industries right out of college. I have found that for students who want to get into sport management who have done their work in terms of sales training, internships, or experience prior to and immediately following graduation, the sky is the limit. It might be a couple of years right out of school making less money than your friends or what you expected, but over time you can make a great income and have a tremendous career in this awesome field. Sports are an incredible part of our society and sport management is a great field to be a part of, but it is hard work—just like any job. If you invest in yourself with attending a great school and get experience along the way, you can be extremely successful in sport management.

Sally Roach

Consultant

Q: Could you briefly describe your career path from undergraduate student to your current position?

A: I have a degree in broadcasting and cinema! I worked for two radio stations in their marketing department (and on air!) then spent four years with Ice Capades (a touring ice show) as their Marketing Director for cities in Canada and the United States. After four years of traveling I was looking for a more "normal" life and thought I might find it with an arena. I spent 15 months as the Marketing Director of the Five Seasons Center in Cedar Rapids, Iowa. Though marketing was my main responsibility, my boss allowed me to work at different jobs including event management, box office, booking, and contract negotiations. From Cedar Rapids I went to New Haven, Connecticut, to work at Veterans Memorial Coliseum as Marketing Director. While there I also assisted with booking, event management, and contract negotiations. I ran my own group sales business in the Washington, D.C., area and I then moved to Los Angeles where I was an event manager at the LA Coliseum and Sports Arena, working with the NBA Clippers, University of Southern California football team, and international soccer matches. After a brief stay at the Rose Bowl in Pasadena, California, I moved to Oakland, and was the general manager of the Oakland Arena (now Oracle Arena), home of the NBA Warriors and the Oakland Coliseum, home of the Oakland Athletics of MLB and the NFL's Oakland Raiders. After moving to Houston, Texas, I was a regional vice president for SMG, a private management company, where I had responsibility for nine venues in Texas, Oklahoma, and California. For eight years I was the executive director of the TOWNSHIP AUDITORIUM in Columbia, South Carolina, a 3,000-seat, 80-year-old auditorium that underwent a $12 million renovation in 2010.

Q: What have been the biggest challenges you have encountered during your career?

A: Working in Oakland was a big challenge because there were two venues and three major league teams, each with their own needs and beliefs regarding how the facilities should be operated. In addition, there were numerous lawsuits involving the teams and the city and county that owned the facilities, which often put the facility staff in awkward situations. Staffing the facilities also presented challenges because there was a strong union presence, which made it difficult to reward top-performing employees, and discipline or remove poorly performing employees.

Q: What did you do to address the various political and employment challenges that you encountered in Oakland?

A: We had a labor attorney on retainer and I consulted with her frequently to make sure that any decisions I was making regarding union employees were within the confines of the contract. I tried to maintain a good working relationship with the business manager of the various unions which helped when dealing with issues that might arise. On the political side, we had a liaison that worked for the city and county but whose office was at the Arena; she was helpful in dealing with the various politicians. Again, having a good working relationship with the key players helped me navigate the various issues that I had to deal with.

Q: Has working in a male-dominated field been difficult?

A: The hardest thing a woman has to deal with is usually not other people in the industry accepting who we are or what job we do. I have almost always found that I could count on support from both men and women in this business. The hard part is people outside the industry who often have a perception that a woman could not operate a 65,000-seat stadium or a soccer game with 92,000 people. Some of the non-industry people are the ones who often seemed amazed at the success of females in the industry. I do not want to give the impression that there are not any problems, as it was only a few years ago that I had to sue a former employer for wage discrimination, but for the most part this industry evaluates women and men for their abilities. Women should look upon a career in sport and entertainment as challenging for everyone, not just for women.

Q: What are the biggest issues facing sport franchises and facilities?

A: The biggest issue facing sport franchises is retaining season-ticket holders. Attracting and retaining customers is critical for ANY facility whether it primarily hosts sport or entertainment events. The economy has certainly hurt many customers, and it is a struggle to market our events to people who have multiple choices for their discretionary dollars. Any venue has to provide high-quality customer service, and training our guest-services staff has always been important, but with the economy it has become paramount.

Q: What do you see happening to address the importance of retaining and attracting new season ticket holders? Will there be fundamental changes in the way tickets are packaged in the near future?

A: What is happening with regards to season ticket holders is that there are more "perks" added to their packages. Just having tickets to the event is not enough anymore; they may get early access to tickets to other events (special pre-sale), upgraded parking access, and discounts at the team store or at concession stands. So the season ticket holder is getting more VIP access. With sporting seasons getting longer and often more expensive, more season ticket packages are shared; you might just purchase a half season, or specific games in the season, so there is more flexibility in each package.

Q: Are there specific job skills sport-management students should look to develop while still in school?

A: Students should observe as many different types of events as they can—even if they "think" they have no interest in pursuing a career in that sport or venue. Understanding how various sporting events operate, or how different venues work with live entertainment shows that attract diverse audiences, is key in this industry. If I only booked shows I personally enjoyed, my facilities would have had a lot of dark days. While completing an internships or practicum, students should take the time to visit with all the employees and ask about what they do. Knowing how various departments function to make an organization a success is key to being able to be promoted. As students advance their career, they need to learn how to interact with employees, especially those who work "underneath" them. As a manager I have always felt it was important to get to know as many people as possible. Whether they work for me full time or part time, they are integral to the facility.

Q: What specific classes would you recommend students take to best position themselves for a sport-industry job?

A: Sport and entertainment management is a business, so it is vitally important students have an understanding of accounting, reading profit and loss statements, and setting budgets. Taking a business law class will enable students to better understand how the law interacts with various aspects of the industry. (I took a great law class when I was in college.) Retaining a good lawyer is still critical, but having a basic understanding of the law enables one to know how to interact with their attorney and how to train others to recognize how the law might influence facility operations.

Q: What publications do you regularly read to stay apprised of important developments?

A: I read the local paper for information about our community. New legislation affects the potential events we can do (for instance, mixed martial arts was not permitted in South Carolina until 2009), so it is important to pay attention to what is happening in our local city and state. It is also important to stay abreast of what is happening within the industry so publications like *Venues Today* and *Pollstar* are also "must reads."

Q: Would you recommend students pursue graduate school? If so, when should they pursue a graduate degree and what area of study would you recommend?

A: If their undergraduate degree is in sport management then an MBA would be beneficial; I would not necessarily recommend pursuing an undergraduate and graduate degree in sport management, particularly from the same institution.

Q: Is there a certain sport-business area you see emerging in importance in the near future?

A: The growth and influence of mixed martial arts has been interesting to track. Much of what they have done in marketing and promotions has benefited the entire sport and entertainment industry. How mixed martial arts and other emerging sports compete in a tough economy will be interesting to watch.

Q: Is there any additional advice or insights you would provide to students pursuing a future career in sport management?

A: Being a fan is not enough of a reason to go into this field. The long hours and low pay early in your career means one must have a passion for being involved in events of all types. If you want to be home nights, weekends, and holidays, sport and entertainment management is not a wise career choice. Be ready to move, as better jobs almost always dictate a move out of your current geographical area. Get your foot in the door and start on the path to what you ultimately want to do. Your dream job will not be your first but each job you take should lead toward your eventual goals. Be careful what you wish for, as being in upper management (in my case being the general manager of a building or team) means dealing with politics, budgets, and staff members who often do not get along or fulfill their responsibilities. Those in management also have the responsibility to hire and fire people, which can be an unpleasant experience. Being in this industry is not just about getting your picture taken with a prominent player, performer, or team owner. Try to work for and with people who have something to teach you and be wary of people who throw around a lot of clichés without having a lot of substance!

Dan Carpenter

Director, Corporate Partnerships
Homestead Miami Speedway

Q: Can you discuss how your career has developed?

A: Armed with a communications degree from the State University of New York at Geneseo and aspirations of breaking into sportscasting in 1992, my first full-time job was in advertising sales and as on-air talent at WDNY Radio. My first job in professional sport came two years later with the Binghamton Mets in sales, operations, and radio broadcasting. In 1995, I transitioned to a job as a corporate ticket sales representative and public address announcer for the New Jersey Devils. Realizing the need to polish my broadcasting skills in the minors, I left New Jersey in 1997 to work for the Rochester Sports Group (which controlled franchises in AHL Hockey, A League Soccer, and NLL Lacrosse) as a radio broadcaster and the director of sales for three franchises. Four years later, I came to a professional crossroads when I was offered a full-time minor league broadcasting job in the AHL and simultaneously an opportunity to become senior vice president of sales and marketing for Scheer Sports, Inc., a company that operated franchises in the ECHL, arena2 football, and the NBDL. I chose the latter and stopped broadcasting altogether. Scheer Sports was sold in 2003, but I was fortunate to earn the opportunity to work in corporate sales and hospitality for Super Bowl XXXIX in Jacksonville, Florida, under the joint supervision of the Jacksonville Jaguars and NFL league office. In 2005, I transitioned into motorsports as the director of business development for Memphis Motorsports Park. Four years later, I accepted my current position as director of corporate partnerships for Homestead-Miami Speedway, host of the NASCAR and IndyCar Championships each year.

Q: What have been the biggest challenges you have encountered during your career?

A: Employee retention. Many young successful people leave organizations for immediate gratification rather than staying put to ascend from within their current organization. Sport industry employers can do a better job of retaining their employees, but many employees also need to exercise a bit more patience, especially early in their careers.

Q: What are the biggest issues currently facing the industry?

A: League television deals and labor issues are always at the forefront. The NFL, NASCAR, and many other sport leagues have had important media contract negotiations with dramatic changes occurring regarding how fans consume sport through the various media platforms.

Another more pressing issue is the lackluster economy's effect on sponsors. Many companies are not willing to spend money to continue their sponsorship activities. Most sponsorships' values have not necessarily decreased; there are just fewer "players" in the market, which can drive down the price even when the asking price is justified given the benefits offered.

Q: Are there specific job skills sport management students should look to develop while still in school?

A: This is a "who you know" as much as "what you know" industry. Students should pursue internships and volunteer opportunities to build their network of contacts while enhancing their various business skills.

Q: What specific classes would you recommend students take to best position themselves for a sport-industry job?

A: Classes that develop public speaking, writing, and sales skills are critical. The future of our business will involve social media marketing, so classes that build skills in that area will be beneficial. Taking a sport law course is also helpful. And a "wildcard" class that I would recommend is an acting course. I took some entry-level acting courses during my undergraduate years, which I still refer to 20 years later. I learned to role-play and think through "scenes" and oftentimes, I apply that process to thinking through how I want to achieve my objectives in business meetings by "acting the part."

Q: What publications do you regularly read to stay apprised of sport-business events?

A: *IEG*, Street and Smith *SportsBusiness Journal*, Jayski.com, partnershipactivation.com, *The National Sports Forum*.

Q: Would you recommend students pursue graduate school? If so, when should they pursue a graduate degree and what area of study would you recommend?

A: My perception is that an MBA is still more valued than a master's degree in sport management, but I feel that will eventually change. Having this opinion will probably not make me popular among educators, but I believe pursuing an advanced degree in sport management right after securing an undergraduate degree is not advisable. I know of no industry peer that has financially benefited from an advanced degree without a large degree of practical experience as well. That being, said, I do know of some people in the sports field who, after three years or so, or maybe even after a decade of work experience, went back to get an advanced degree, and it did benefit them in the workplace immediately afterwards.

Q: Is there a certain sport-business area you see emerging in importance in the near future?

A: I foresee non-marquee teams in the "Big 4" selling uniform sponsorships. Soccer, Lacrosse, NASCAR, and a few other leagues already do this, and when current television deals expire and are renegotiated, the revenue is likely to be lower. Many organizations will then likely seek new revenue sources. I think it is likely the NHL does this first, followed by the NBA, and then maybe the NFL down the road. I am not sure if Major League Baseball ever will pursue this option in the immediate future.

On a broader scale, the role of fantasy sports and social media content is still exploding and has a limitless ceiling to connecting fans with other fans and the athletes themselves.

As for a particular sport, MMA, indoor lacrosse, and extreme sports continue to emerge as long-lasting events for athletes and fans alike.

Damon Zumwalt

Founder/Chief Executive Officer
Contemporary Services Corporation

Q: Could you briefly describe your career path to your current position?

A: It was a case of being in the right place at the right time. I was attending UCLA on a football and wrestling scholarship and returned home to San Diego the summer following my freshman year. That summer I attended a dance where many fights erupted. The promoter of the dance approached me and said, "I hear you can stop these fights," and although I had no formal background in security, I told him that I probably could! I then coordinated a team to provide security for local dances and concerts and thus, my security career was born at the age of 18.

Q: What made you want to start your own security company?

A: I wasn't necessarily seeking to start my own security company but was provided an opportunity of which I thankfully took full advantage. I also didn't intend to continue doing this past college, but by the time of graduation, I had several thousand employees and the company was growing rapidly. I also realized the necessity of our unique approach to security service within the rock-and-roll industry. I had selected individuals from several different ethnic backgrounds and areas of interest who were well known for their athletic abilities and respected within their communities. These individuals were also around the same age as the patrons attending the concerts and other events in which we were working. Our "Peer Security" approach was the foundation for a new security era, one of a cooperative nature rather than brute force.

Q: What has been the biggest challenge you have encountered during your career?

A: The biggest challenge for me has also been the biggest achievement: being the largest and most successful event security and crowd management firm in the United States. While this has its obvious benefits, the challenge is that we find it difficult to compete with smaller companies who may not be under the same scrutiny as Contemporary Services Corporation (CSC) and therefore, are able to underbid us by working outside the scope of the law. CSC prides itself on integrity and providing clients with the best possible service through a variety of avenues: targeted recruiting, training, and ongoing improvement methods. However, maintaining such rigorous standards means higher costs and as a result, we sometimes cannot compete with other companies who don't uphold the same standards. We abide by the laws of each state, even if those laws aren't enforced due to budgetary restraints or other reasons. For example, the State of California requires that all security personnel must undergo a background check and obtain a security license, which requires 40 hours of training. There are approximately 500,000 security personnel in California and it is commonly known that over 400,000 of these individuals are not in compliance with state law. It is a great failure of the states to not enforce their own security laws, especially in an unpredictable and ever-evolving post 9-11 world.

Q: Given that some competitors do not provide the level of service mandated by law, how do you demonstrate to your clients and potential clients that your company will provide a great level of service that the facility/event should insist upon?

A: We provide our clients with documentation detailing our procedures for recruiting and training, as well as our state-of-the art workforce management program. We have also implemented rigorous analysis and self-improvement techniques within our operations. In 2013, the United States Department of Homeland Security awarded CSC with SAFETY Act Designation; making us the only company to hold this designation for both crowd management and event security services. The SAFETY (Support Anti-terrorism by Fostering Effective Technologies) Act was implemented post 9-11 and encourages the development and deployment of new and innovative anti-terrorism products and services by providing liability protections to both the sellers and the users. Users of SAFETY Act approved services receive automatic immunity from lawsuits arising from failure of that service during a terrorist attack. Therefore, CSC's SAEFTY Act Designation provides a great benefit to all of our clients, and it sets CSC apart from its competitors.

Q: What do you think will be the biggest issue facing live event security in the next 5 to 10 years?

A: The biggest issue facing live events will continue to be the threat of terrorist exposure. It remains critical to not allow apathy or complacency, but to consciously follow proper procedures and uphold the highest standards. It will also be critical for state governments to uphold and enforce their security personnel requirements so that event patrons can remain confident that their safety is in the hands of trained event professionals.

Q: What are the most important things that future sport managers should understand about live event security, even if that is not an area of future employment?

A: They simply must understand the importance of security relative to the overall success of the event. The key is to consciously facilitate patrons' enjoyment of each event while still maintaining a safe and secure event environment.

Q: What publications do you regularly read to stay informed of sports-business events?

A: I read various news and industry publications. Also, I generally remain well informed of sports-business news due to CSC's large footprint of more than 50 branch offices across the nation.

Q: Would you recommend that students pursue graduate school? If so, when should they pursue a graduate degree and what area of study would you recommend?

A: This really depends on the individual and the area of sport management desired. The higher the level of executive position one is pursuing, the more beneficial and necessary graduate school might become. However, hands-on field experience is invaluable and may be more attractive to an employer than additional classroom education. It truly depends on the individual and his or her drive to succeed. I firmly believe that the will and ability to succeed comes from possessing that champion mentality in which only the absolute best is acceptable. That's what will guide each individual's success, regardless of the particular career and chosen path.

Brent Koonce

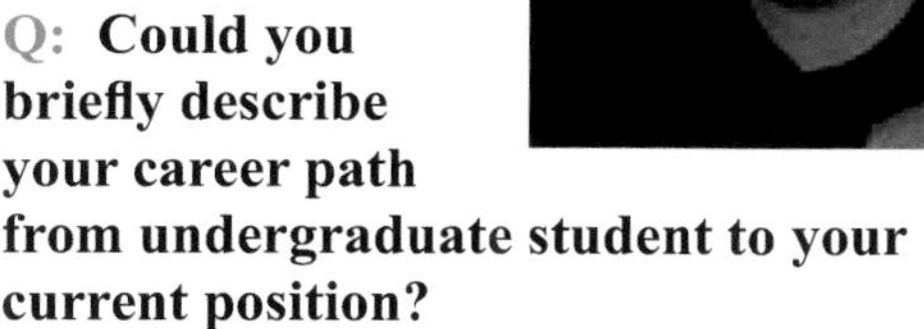

Vice President of Basketball Operations
US Sports Camps

Q: Could you briefly describe your career path from undergraduate student to your current position?

A: During my last year of my undergraduate work at the University of San Francisco, I had three different part-time jobs and no guarantees about full-time employment at any of them. I applied to graduate school, hoping that if no options came through, I could continue to work part time and pursue my graduate degree in sport management.

I knew I wanted to work in the sport and fitness industry, but did not know yet in what specific capacity. I had worked in professional sports with the Oakland Athletics in their Community Affairs Department, at the University of San Francisco's Koret Health & Recreation Center as a Building Supervisor, and had just begun at a small company, US Sports Camps. Looking back it was a unique opportunity to have access and work experience in three distinctly different sport industry jobs.

I did enroll in graduate school and US Sports Camps offered a full-time work opportunity. I have stayed with the company since I was first hired and I am now the Vice President of Basketball Operations. I oversee all basketball operations, which include the Nike Basketball Camps, Snow Valley Basketball Schools, and McCracken Camps.

Q: What does US Sports Camps provide its customers?

A: US Sports Camps is the official licensed operator of the Nike Sports Camps. We offer camps in a variety of sports such as basketball, volleyball, golf, et cetera. We strive to provide an opportunity for campers to have fun, to improve their skills, and to meet new friends. The camp industry is different from most in sports and it certainly does not usually attract as much attention as big-time college athletics or professional sports. However, we have thousands of kids who participate in our camps, and there are certainly thousands more playing sports at other camps across the country.

In 2014, we will host approximately 75,000 campers nationwide across 17 different sports.

Q: What have been the biggest challenges you have encountered during your career?

A: Initially, the biggest challenge was to figure out which career path to pursue. Working in professional sport is a rare and unique opportunity. However, professional sport also presents the most competition, a difficult path to advance, and low initial salaries. Though it was initially attractive to dream of working full time for a professional team, I realized that my personality fit well at an organization like US Sports Camps.

Currently, my biggest challenge is determining which opportunities to pursue and which to let pass. As the leaders in the camp industry, particularly in basketball, many opportunities arise to start new camps or to expand existing ones. It can be difficult to break through the clutter of the marketplace and determine where to assign resources to maximize our chance to succeed. I attempt to look at potential opportunities with a long-term view that will lead to the greatest potential for future success.

Another related challenge is managing our growth while maintaining our high standards at the camp level, but also with our customer service within the office.

Q: Can you identify what you consider to be the "hot topics or issues" in sport, either directly related to your functional area or the sport industry in general?

A: The continued growth and influence of the Internet on the sport industry is fascinating to observe. Our camps are no exception to the expansion of the Internet. For the camp industry, standing out amongst a crowded seasonal business is the biggest obstacle we face. Last year, approximately 95% of our signups came via the Web, and that number will continue to grow. Part of the reason for that is convenience and having an information-rich product. We are selling an experience and the Web allows parents to gather information (dates/prices/locations), and ultimately make decisions for their kids that work best for their summer needs and budgets.

For our camps, it is imperative that we continue to upgrade our website and Web presence. Videos and social networking can help drive traffic to our website, but it must also fit our overall goals. Posting videos and embedding them in our website also increases our relevance on the search engines (i.e., Google). I am very interested in studying the continued growth of Twitter and Facebook, and how it will provide marketing opportunities, drive traffic, and ultimately produce revenues.

Q: Are there specific job skills sport-management students should look to develop while still in school?

A: Every job is different, so some specific skills will be needed more in different departments or organizations. However, work experience and relationship building are critical in all areas of sport management. Opportunities to network often come through working for "free" as an unpaid intern or as a volunteer. There are no shortcuts in this highly competitive industry and working for free weeds out many before they even get a full-time job (that is usually low paying). The greater one's knowledge of an organization and the overall industry, the better one has to understand how to help the organization achieve success.

When I look at a prospective employee, I will not hire someone with no internship or work experience straight out of college. I believe strongly that we all need to start at the bottom and advance our careers. Highly effective leaders are ones who have experienced what occurs at different levels of an organization. Advancing "from the bottom" shows an individual what various levels of an organization do, and it better prepares that person to interact with various employees.

Q: What specific classes would you recommend students take to best position themselves for a sport-industry job?

A: I would always recommend finance classes to anyone who one day would like to be in a managerial role. Regardless of industry or organization, every manager has financial obligations and reporting responsibilities. Being able to manage those expectations can help immensely. Secondly, many of the sport-management classes that examine trends and help students learn to analyze information to make predictions and decisions about the future are especially helpful.

Q: What are the biggest errors you see interns and entry level employees making?

A: The biggest mistake I have seen recently is that they are scared to make mistakes. So much so, that it paralyzes them to do anything without asking first, which in turn takes time away from whatever that person is doing. As a small business, there can be many different ways to solve problems. I'm always more impressed when presented with a new angle from the old way of doing things. Just because, that's always the way it has been done doesn't mean it is right. Don't be afraid to make a mistake.

Q: What publications do you regularly read to stay apprised of sport-business events?

A: I have moved to Twitter for the bulk of my daily information. I used to read the print version of the *SportsBusiness Journal* every week, online blogs, etc., but I found that much of that information is available via Twitter. The brilliance of Twitter is you can find whatever niche you choose. I still subscribe to the traditional mediums of *Sports Illustrated* and *ESPN the Magazine*, but that content is easily accessible everywhere.

Some other blogs that are outside of the traditional mediums like Deadspin.com can also provide content about sport business that the traditional outlets will not cover.

Q: Would you recommend students pursue graduate school? If so, when should they pursue a graduate degree and what area of study would you recommend?

A: I always recommend going to graduate school with some full-time work experience. Ideally, students would come to any graduate program with practical business experience, regardless of the industry. An MBA is invaluable in any industry and provides flexibility if a student later want to leave the sport industry. My master's in sport management was a professional executive program, so it allowed me the flexibility to work and go to school at the same time. That was invaluable.

Q: Is there a certain sport-business area you see emerging in importance in the near future?

A: Compliance and oversight on all levels will increase in importance, especially with the push for college athletes to receive payments or stipends and for there to be more accountability in professional sport. The examples of football coaches Mike Leach (who was fired for abusing his players at Texas Tech University) and Mark Mangino (who accepted a settlement to sever his ties to the University of Kansas after numerous complaints were filed regarding his behavior) are examples where managers not only behaved poorly, but the managers of the managers were unaware of the incidents and could have taken earlier steps to prevent the eventual outcome. In the NFL and NBA, there have been recent incidents where owners and general managers have made statements that were quite offensive to various demographic groups. The great access that consumers have to comments and actions of sport managers means that everyone involved must not only understand the implications of their actions but the actions of their colleagues and subordinates.

Damon Dukakis

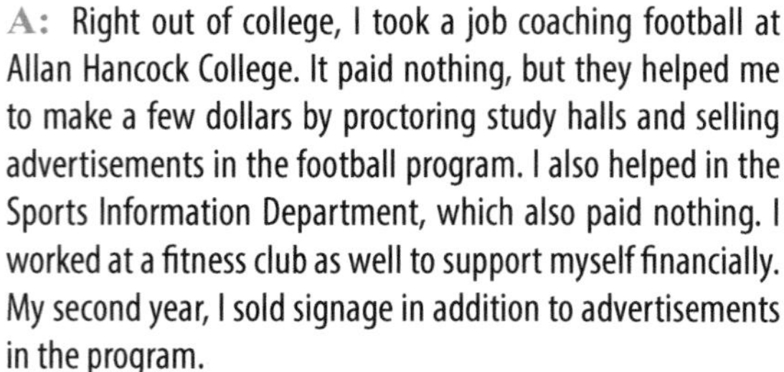

General Sales Manager
UCLA/Rose Bowl

Q: Could you briefly describe your career path from undergraduate student to your current position?

A: Right out of college, I took a job coaching football at Allan Hancock College. It paid nothing, but they helped me to make a few dollars by proctoring study halls and selling advertisements in the football program. I also helped in the Sports Information Department, which also paid nothing. I worked at a fitness club as well to support myself financially. My second year, I sold signage in addition to advertisements in the program.

After two years, one of the local high school athletic directors left his position and he suggested I apply to replace him. I was only 24 years old, but I applied. I had worked as an assistant to the Athletic Director at one of the other local high schools as an undergraduate student, so I knew a lot about the job and the people in the area. I got the job (which also involved teaching classes) and stayed for two years. I enjoyed the experience, but the overinvolvement of parents at this private high school, [a] challenging principal, and low pay led to my decision to move away from high school athletics.

I moved to Sacramento and applied for a position as Marketing Director for Athletics at Sacramento State. There was a huge applicant pool of 75 people, but I was fortunate to possess the skills and experience to get the job. Apparently, selling advertisements and signs at a junior college had more in common with the Sacramento State job than the experience many others had at other institutions. I stayed for three years and then went to fellow Big Sky Conference member Portland State as Associate Athletic Director for External Affairs.

After only a year and a half at Portland State, I was contacted by my old boss from Sacramento State, who had since moved to the University of California–Berkeley. He asked if I was interested in coming back to Northern California and with ISP, the Golden Bears' media rights holder. After much deliberation, and learning that my Athletic Director at Portland State had just accepted a job at his Alma Mater, the University of Wyoming, I decided to head to Berkeley. I was at Cal for seven years as the General Manager. Two years ago, I accepted a position at UCLA Athletics and the Rose Bowl.

Q: Could you briefly explain how IMG College is involved with intercollegiate athletics and then briefly explain what you do in your current position.

A: In the early 1990s, many college athletic departments began to outsource their sponsorship sales. Third-party rights holders would pay a flat fee and, in some cases, a portion of their generated sponsorship sales, to the athletic department. The arrangement enabled the third-party rights holder to—in theory—provide a higher level of expertise than the athletic department could do in house. The third-party rights holder could also potentially broker regional or national deals that an individual athletic department could not execute on their own. There are a variety of areas including ticket sales that have since been outsourced by some athletic departments. It is an interesting decision that athletic departments need to make when evaluating the positives and negatives of selling to an outside agency for any aspect of the athletic department operation.

When I was at Cal, IMG had bought out ISP and created a new agency called IMG College. The job I have at Los Angeles is somewhat unique in that IMG owns the rights to both UCLA Athletics and The Rose Bowl. There is certainly some synergy between those two properties as UCLA plays its football games in The Rose Bowl so we are able to sell some overlapping assets. I work to maximize the revenue and build the brand of each property.

Q: What have been the biggest challenges you have encountered during your career?

A: All of my positions (except high school Athletic Director) have involved generating revenue from the corporate community. The financial challenges at Allan Hancock College, Portland State, Cal, UCLA, and The Rose Bowl are similar—you never have enough revenue. You need to convince people to spend their business dollars in your athletic department. Although UCLA often draws over 80,000 attendees per football game and Allan Hancock drew "only" 2,500, it is still just as challenging to prospect, make cold calls, set meetings, present proposals, and try to close sales at the larger school as it is at the smaller one.

Q: How have selling sponsorships and building brands changed over the past 5 to 10 years?

A: Today, the digital space is enormous. As social media has expanded its reach and impact, its presence as a "component" of sponsorship plans and brand building activities has increased. Even a few years ago, I would not have built an entire sponsorship plan around social media, while today that happens often. Measuring the impact or all sponsorships, but particularly ones built with a significant component of social media is a key in our industry. We constantly look for ways to measure the benefits of various activities such as through open rate of emails and click throughs on advertisements.

Q: Can you identify what you consider to be the main issues facing college athletics and third-party rights holders?

A: With the amount of money changing hands in college sports there are many critics who question the "amateur" status of college athletics. This is an important question that underlies everything we do, especially since there have been a variety of lawsuits which have begun to make their way through the court system.

Q: Are there specific job skills sport-management students should look to develop while still in school?

A: Ironically, the only sport-management-specific class I ever took was Mark Nagel's administration class at Saint Mary's College. Within that class I learned some of the basics of sport marketing. With only one academic class, I did not learn as much as many within my field who have gone through sport-management undergraduate and graduate programs. It certainly would have helped to have a "stronger" academic sport-management background, but this industry is much more about experience and networking than taking specific academic courses before graduation. The most important skill to develop is a strong knowledge of how all the pieces of an organization fit together and affect one another. Knowledge gained through on-the-job training is critical to future success.

Q: What are the biggest mistakes you see interns and entry-level employees making?

A: Social media is important to how we do our business, but it can also be distracting for employees in the workplace. Far too often, interns do not understand that they cannot constantly check their various social media sources during the workday. Also, too many young people have not learned how to communicate through methods other than social media. Much of this business, and most businesses, involves extensive face-to-face communication. Being confident and personable with people in the workplace and with clients is a key to any business. Talking on the phone and writing effectively are other things that set good employees apart from their peers.

Q: What publications do you regularly read to stay apprised of sport-business events?

A: *SportBusiness Journal*

Q: Would you recommend students pursue graduate school? If so, when should they pursue a graduate degree and what area of study would you recommend?

A: I know a lot of people that did not go through a graduate program who are doing fine in the sport-management industry. Pursuing an MBA certainly cannot hurt, as the knowledge and information you learn within an MBA program can do nothing but make an individual stronger (as a candidate and in real-world performance). It is certainly important to have a degree on your resume, but it is even more important to be "educated" about the industry you wish to pursue and to have a strong work ethic.

Q: Is there a certain sport-business area you see emerging in importance in the near future?

A: New technology and media have become critical and they will only grow in importance in the future. More and more content is going to be available online, and a shift away from traditional TV, cable TV, and satellite will continue to occur. The financial model associated with events, both large and small, will greatly evolve over the next to 10 years due to new technology.

Q: Is there any additional advice or insights you would provide to students pursuing a future career in sport management?

A: Revenue is the backbone of our industry. The proven ability to generate revenue will open a lot of doors. Effective salespeople give clients a reason to spend money and buy from them. Whether through ticket or suite sales, sponsorship sales, signing rights, and broadcast contracts, bringing in private donations through annual gifts or major gifts, "rain makers" in the industry will always be marketable for advancement.

Shawni Sullivan

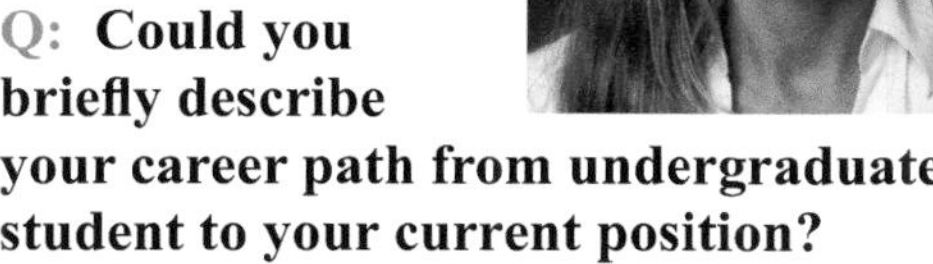

Director of Events
Rose Quarter

Q: Could you briefly describe your career path from undergraduate student to your current position?

A: I attended St. Martin's College (Lacey, Washington) and double majored in accounting and business management. I then went to Ohio University in the Sports Administration and Facility Management Program and earned my MSA in 2001. Following graduate school, I did a one-year internship in Event Management at Disney Sports in Orlando. Following the internship, I was hired as the Director of Game Operations for Tulane University Athletics. While at Tulane, I oversaw the event management of all sports, with my primary focus being football (at the Superdome), basketball, baseball, soccer, and volleyball. In December 2003, I took a position as an Event Manager at the Rose Quarter (Rose Garden Arena and Memorial Coliseum) in Portland, Oregon. In December 2006, I was promoted to Director of Events at the Rose Quarter.

Q: What have been the biggest challenges you have encountered during your career?

A: In regards to my career path, I have been extremely fortunate and had the right opportunities at the right time. I was realistic and flexible from the beginning, though. I knew I would have to work from the bottom up and I was realistic with salary expectations. I was willing to go to different areas of the country to pursue the best position for my career path. In regards to my event-management career, it is one that deals with a multitude of personalities: tour managers, coaches, artists/athletes, guests, media, co-workers, promoters, et cetera. One of the biggest challenges is learning to communicate effectively with this diverse group of individuals in a fast-paced, high-stress environment. Being able to remain calm and confident at all times as well as flexible to the changing needs/requests and then to make sure to deliver desired results and provide a fun atmosphere at the same time . . . it's an exciting challenge!

Q: Can you identify what you consider to be the most important issues currently facing the facility management industry?

A: Sustainability is a huge initiative on our campus. We strive to be the leader of sustainability in our community and the sport and entertainment industry, so we dedicate a lot of time and focus to this initiative; it's an important part of our everyday operation. Also, keeping up with technology is always a challenge. Everything from how we market ourselves (i.e., social networking) and our ticketing systems to how we manage our venues and handle the growing size and complexity of shows (the need for tours to continuously "one-up" what the last show/tour did) involves technology that is constantly changing. Also, as new arenas are built, the bar is set a little higher for the rest of us. We continue to get creative to make sure we still stand out as a leader in our industry. We are currently in the process of numerous renovations ($16 million worth this summer alone). The ever-changing world of promoters, ticketing companies, etc. (i.e., paperless ticketing, mobile ticketing, buy-outs, mergers) and how it potentially impacts how we book and manage shows at our venue is also important. Safety and security are always important; keeping guests and staff safe on our campus is a primary focus for us. We are also involved on a larger scale (city/stage) in regards to mass care and shelter planning.

Q: Are there specific job skills sport-management students should look to develop while still in school?

A: Solid communication and multitasking skills are important in this business. Also, being flexible is critical in this industry. Students should try to develop their skills as much as possible through hands-on experience in internships, volunteer positions, et cetera. The more actual work experience/exposure one can get, the better. Not only is the experience great but the network of contacts they build during this time is just as valuable.

Q: What specific classes would you recommend students take to best position themselves for a sport-industry job?

A: Always look to challenge yourself, and look for opportunities to learn. In event management, we work with every area/department, so the more exposure we have to each area, the better. In graduate school, I took a wide variety of classes so I could get a diverse understanding of how each area works (marketing, facilities, sport law, finance, et cetera). I also participated in several volunteer and internship opportunities in order to gain more hands-on knowledge. Once I was out of school and on the job, I asked lots of questions and shadowed other departments to learn their roles and how they fit into the big picture. The more I understand the other departments/areas, the more I have a better understanding of how my decisions affect everyone else. As far as specific classes to recommend, it all depends on a student's interests and long-term career goals. If students have the flexibility to branch out and take a wide variety of classes, then I highly recommend it.

Q: What publications do you regularly read to stay apprised of sport-business events?

A: I read a mix of sports/entertainment/facility management publications—*Pollstar*, *SportsBusiness Journal*, *Facility Manager*, et cetera. Also, I receive several online articles forwarded through various committees on which I serve and associations where I am a member.

Q: Would you recommend students pursue graduate school? If so, when should they pursue a graduate degree and what area of study would you recommend?

A: I believe education is invaluable. However, I have worked with several peers in this industry who do not have a graduate degree but instead have several years of experience and they are definitely leaders in the industry. If somebody has hands-on experience in their profession, that can be just as valuable as a graduate degree. Graduate school was a good fit for me; it exposed me to an industry that I did not know much about and allowed me to become part of a close-knit Ohio University Sport Administration and Facility Management community. What degree somebody should pursue depends on their specific interests. I received an MSA but I also had a double major from my undergrad in accounting and business management so I felt I had a strong business background already. I could have stayed another year and earned my MBA but I felt the best decision was to do an internship. I am a hands-on learner, so that is the direction I went after I earned my MSA. I think education is one aspect, but what you do to gain experience and exposure to the area you want to pursue is just as important: internships, job shadowing, volunteer opportunities, working in the athletic department, et cetera. Also, getting out and making contacts/relationships is important, because this industry is a small, close-knit community and those relationships will prove to be rewarding in the future.

Ricky Lefft

Sports Attorney
Principal, Lefft Law Group
Lecturer, University of South Carolina

Q: Could you describe how you became an agent?

A: I graduated from high school in 1977 from Orangeburg-Wilkinson High School in Orangeburg, South Carolina. I spent my high school years in Orangeburg, which is the home of South Carolina State University, then known as SC State College. My parents were both double alumni of South Carolina State and throughout my life they told me stories about the extraordinary experience they had enjoyed at the college while matriculating there. I was fortunate that when we arrived in Orangeburg, the college's music and performing arts programs were amongst the best in the country. Additionally, the SC State Football Program was on the rise under Coach Willie Jeffries's leadership; and a number of professional athletes such as Barney Chavous, Donnie Shell, and Harry Carson played on those teams. I played basketball until my sophomore year and marched for the high school band for three years. I also played in a local band that performed in night clubs during my high school years. As a result of my experiences, I developed a passion for sport and entertainment. When I entered the University of South Carolina as a freshman I knew that I wanted to eventually attend law school and to specialize in the representation of entertainers and professional athletes.

While in law school, I took courses such as labor law, intellectual property, business corporations, and mass communications and media law as a part of my preparation to practice sport and entertainment law. Under the tutelage of two of my law professors, I wrote 12 hours of independent-study papers covering specific research topics germane to these areas of practice.

Prior to entering law school, I was commissioned as a United States Air Force Officer and received a deferment to attend law school. I opted for a career path in systems procurement at Wright Patterson Air Force Base in Dayton, Ohio, as an Officer in Aeronautical Systems Division, which was the largest military procurement organization in the world. During my four-year tenure in the Air Force, I was able to negotiate approximately $1 billion worth of contracts for research and development projects and for the purchase of weapon systems such as the F-15E Aircraft system and the Advanced Tactical Fighter, now known as the Stealth fighter. My experience allowed me to interface and interact with executives at the highest levels within companies such as McDonald Douglas Aircraft Company, Raytheon, Northrop, and General Electric. Additionally, I was responsible for overseeing a team of approximately seven other negotiators my last couple of years, and approved and signed approximately another $400 million in contracts.

After I completed my military commitment, I relocated to Northern Virginia where I accepted a position with a startup company as Vice President and General Counsel. I was responsible for negotiating lease agreements and employment contracts with the executives and other professionals who were hired by the company to lead the new enterprise. I was actively involved in, and led efforts to draft, both the business and strategic plans. I was also responsible for interfacing with potential vendors and venture capital firms.

I then returned to South Carolina to accept a position as Special Counsel with the law firm of Nexsen, Pruet, Jacobs, & Pollard. My initial areas of practice were workman's compensation defense and premise liability defense. I represented companies such as UPS, Food Lion, Shoney's, and B.F. Goodrich. I was subsequently moved to the business division where I represented financial institutions such as NationsBank, First Union Bank, Wachovia Bank, Carolina Capital Investment Corporation, and the Jobs Economic Development Authority (JEDA), where I was responsible for closing commercial transactions and real estate deals. Additionally, I represented a number of privately held companies as outside counsel.

In 1992, I formed the firm's Sport Law practice to represent professional athletes and college coaches. Tubby Smith was my first college coaching client and Tyrone Legette was my first NFL player client. After building the firm's practice, I founded Synergy Sports International with two other principals in 1997. At our peak we represented approximately 40 professional athletes in football and baseball. In 2003, I sold the firm and joined the University of South Carolina as a faculty member in the Department of Sport and Entertainment Management. I also maintain a separate law practice in which I represent my coaching clients who were not part of the sale.

Q: What have been the biggest challenges you have encountered during your career as an agent?

A: The biggest initial challenges were finding an entry into the business, recruiting quality clients, financing the business to keep it competitive, and retaining the clients once they were signed to contracts. Entry into the marketplace is a major challenge, because agents by nature are not trusting people. The marketplace is very competitive and oversaturated. Agents typically are not willing to train younger agents, because they are fearful that the younger agent will steal their clients. Most financial institutions do not understand the sport agency business and are not willing to finance such companies.

Q: Can you identify what you consider to be the "hot topics or issues" in sport?

A: Obviously the hottest topic in intercollegiate sports is the Ed O'Bannon class action suit against the NCAA regarding the rights of athletes at the intercollegiate level and their right to be remunerated in some form other than their scholarships. Another case at the intercollegiate level which also has far-reaching implications is the ruling by a regional office of the National Labor Relations Board that "profit" athletes at the intercollegiate level are employees and should have the right to form unions to collectively bargain on their behalf. It will be fascinating to see how these cases are ultimately resolved and the long-term implications.

Q: Are there specific classes sport-management students should take to develop necessary job skills while still in school?

A: If the sport-management program has a business-oriented curriculum, most of the main areas should be covered. However, developing research and writing skills is critically important to future success. Pursuing an MBA is certainly important for long-term success, especially since an MBA should develop marketing and research skills. Law school can hone legal analysis skills. For undergraduates, courses in the following areas can help anyone wishing to become an agent or a member of an executive management team:

a. Legal training
b. Business and strategic planning skills
c. Contract negotiation skills
d. Sales and marketing
e. Critical thinking and analysis

Q: What publications do you regularly read to stay apprised of sport-business events?

A: *SportsBusiness Journal*, various news publications, *Sports Lawyers Journal*, *Marquette Law Review*, various NCAA publications, and biographies of personalities in the industry. Knowledge of current events is critical to achieving ongoing success in this area of the sport industry.

Q: Would you recommend students pursue graduate school? If so, when should they pursue a graduate degree, and what area of study would you recommend?

A: I would strongly recommend that students who are interested in sport representation pursue a joint degree program with a Juris Doctorate and MBA.

Q: What changes are currently occurring in the sport agent industry?

A: Search firms have certainly changed the dynamics in both the intercollegiate and professional coaches' representation industry. Hiring a coach at a Division-I institution has changed from what it was even 10 to 15 years ago. There is a greater need for coaches to engage attorneys specializing in sports law or agents, many of whom have legal educations, to represent and "promote" their interests to more effectively navigate a more complex search process. There is a legitimate argument that agents who engage in the representation of coaches in negotiating, interpreting, and drafting contracts are engaged in the unauthorized practice of law. Often, these agents will have counsel engaged by their firm to review documents which they have negotiated on the behalf of a client, in an effort to insulate themselves from liability for malpractice and (arguably) shield themselves from the claim of unauthorized practice of law. Bar associations have generally not addressed these specific issues because of the unique nature of sports' representation. However, the current trend appears to be that as firms such as Creative Artists Agency (also known as "CAA") and the Wasserman Media Group expand their areas of representation, more attorneys who have previously represented coaches and other sports professionals through traditional law practices are joining these agency firms because of the disproportionate economies of scale and the competitive advantage created by the sheer size and comprehensive nature of the service offerings of these firms. The line between what constitutes the authorized practice of law and pure sports agency will become even murkier as licensed practitioners join these firms in greater numbers as sports agents.

Q: Is there any additional advice or insights you would provide to students pursuing a future career in sport management?

A: Get more experience in the industry from an institutional standpoint. I suggest students try to find positions working for a sport franchise and/or a league before seeking to represent players.

Clara Ríos Grisi

Brand Manager, Strategy and Brand Management – Marketing Division Fédération Internationale de Football Association (FIFA)

Q: Can you describe your career path?

A: After finishing high school in Bolivia, I knew I wanted to have a career in communications with a strong business focus. I decided to move to neighboring Argentina, well known in the region for producing creative advertising campaigns, and finished a bachelor in advertising with an emphasis in creative strategy at the Universidad de Palermo in Buenos Aires. During the last year of school my class collaborated with a local advertising agency and during my last holiday I did a short internship at Draft FCB in Bolivia. After graduation I went back home and entered a Junior Creative program from J. Walter Thompson aimed to train and develop young graduates. After a few months I moved to Spain; it felt like starting all over again but without a local network. I probably went to about 20 or more job interviews—and while doing so I learned a lot about myself! The most extreme recruitment process was with L'Oréal; after a full-day group interview developing a business model and three more individual interviews later on, I started working for one of the company's PR and communications teams.

Similar to my previous work experience, I was really enjoying the job as I was learning a lot, but had to move once again, this time to Switzerland. The move was necessary as my husband was following a wonderful career opportunity. I remind students that it is fine to follow your partner when there are exciting opportunities somewhere else, but to be sure you can find your own professional project there and be ready to work on your determination skills.

It was mid-2009 and the financial decline had also reached companies in wealthy Switzerland and most marketing positions were being downsized. I'm not sure if it was good or bad advice, but given the circumstances a recruiter suggested I use my language skills to get a job, in other words, to be prepared to give up on a position in marketing. Companies based in Switzerland normally require English, German, and French at a high proficiency level for employees, so my chances in the communications area were limited despite knowing the first two languages. I ended up responding to an advertisement that promised a dynamic international environment, great team spirit, and used the word "players" more than anywhere else I had seen. I knew it was FIFA, but it was not in the marketing or communications areas; I actually applied for a position in one of the legal departments. Almost simultaneously I had a job offer from a local publishing company which involved editorial content and sales. The good thing about making a decision between two wonderful opportunities is that since you will never know for sure the "what if," there is no such thing as a wrong decision. I always believe you choose your path and work hard without looking back. I took the job at FIFA and have been working there ever since.

After almost three years overseeing the legal process of the international transfers of football players between clubs and the compliance for the protection of players under 18 years of age, and despite having a fantastic team, I was simply aching to go back to marketing and communications. I spent a third year there while doing the online master's in sport management at the IE Business School in Madrid, which helped me refresh some concepts and get a stronger understanding of the sport industry from different angles. The long hours of work and study were worth the sacrifice; in the process of finalizing the weekly reports for the graduate program I had no option but to sometimes seek information from colleagues within FIFA and that allowed me to expand my network and definitely confirmed I had to switch to marketing. I was lucky and it didn't take too long for that to happen. It's now been two years working in Strategy and Brand Management Department in the marketing division.

Q: What have been some of the biggest challenges you have faced during your career?

A: A great challenge has obviously been arriving in countries where I had no local professional network and adjusting to the overall cultural changes. Keeping a long-term perspective helped me overcome the difficult moments and appreciate the opportunities that came along with being exposed to new experiences. Part of the challenge was to observe, learn, and adapt, while keeping in mind my own nature and reasons to be in every new place. This is noticeable in my rather jumpy career path; I kept trying to find my professional passion, whenever I was close to it I had to move countries—but I finally made it to a position that is a great fit!

In terms of challenges within the companies I have worked for, I have found it difficult to have people come out of their comfort zone when proposing new work processes and trying different solutions to old problems. It is not necessarily a matter of revolutionizing things that have worked for years, but rather finding room for improvement. Some companies are more open to this, especially if you are expected to generate ideas, e.g. in advertising agencies where thinking outside the box is essential to stay relevant in the market.

Q: What are the biggest challenges facing FIFA currently? What challenges do you see emerging in the future?

A: From my point of view, there are a few challenges—and therefore opportunities—facing the sport industry. Three in particular apply to FIFA given its position as the world football governing body. These are *Innovation*, *Competitiveness*, and *Perception* in equal relevance and in a consecutive, cyclical path from one to the next. Working out these three shall lead to overcoming the ultimate challenge that every company and organization has, in sports and beyond, which is *Credibility*. This last one is a perpetual challenge, present and future, whether the goal is to build or sustain credibility. In the past, football was seen as the main, if not the only, power of attraction needed to sustain the business model. Apart from that, there are several factors to account for in order to sustain the success of the game, its professionalization worldwide, its extension to other spheres such as social inclusion and development, and the revenue generating models required to run such programmes.

Innovation

Innovation comes in many forms and applies to all fields, sometimes involving new technologies and platforms, but others simply by reviewing processes. Within FIFA, I see the need to innovate work processes (which is currently an existing project), improve communication channels with internal and external stakeholders, as well as systematically identify risk factors to be assessed. Seen from a marketing perspective, all these correspond to a way of understanding FIFA's stakeholders—that is, football fans, member associations, and media and host countries—not merely from a consumer point of view, but as participating entities that together with FIFA construct the concept of football as a unifying force. Organizations need to innovate and adjust to survive. To do so, gathering and assessing matters in a structured manner, taking the lessons from the past to the next opportunity, strengthening the capacity to compete and have a differentiated position in a saturated market is critical. A concrete example in terms of innovation dedicated to fans is to find the optimal business model to make the best of TV and digital content together, the *second screen* challenge of providing valuable information in the right amount and with the ideal interactivity to generate a worthy experience.

Competitiveness

Part of the challenge in staying competitive, especially for non-profit sport organizations such as FIFA, is to be able to find the right balance between innovative and traditionally efficient processes. In terms of administration, for example, the competitive challenge is to retain talent and keep them motivated, while ensuring an established, solid process of knowledge transfer for the professional know-how to remain in the organization. As in most industries, the specialized knowledge obtained by experience is hard to be replaced, and despite having the chance of engaging with professionals coming from parallel sectors, FIFA has one-of-a-kind deliverables that go from the organization of the biggest football event, to numerous football and social development programmes around the world, including football governance. In other words, losing talent can be more costly to FIFA than to any other company in the industry.

Externally, the competitive challenge focuses on the use of new communication and consumption platforms to reach out to football fans and treat them not as mere consumers of information, but as an engaged and participating figure driving the market. There is an increasing need to be responsive to their feedback in an open, transparent manner, staying loyal to the principles and goals of the organization, while gaining credibility and staying relevant.

Perception
The challenge of perception derives from the effort of being responsive to the internal and external client; building a strong and trustworthy position can only result in a positive perception of the organization by all stakeholders, driving up the value of sponsorship and media rights, retaining talent, and skipping communication intermediates to "talk" to the fans. This will strengthen the organization's model, allowing it to be flexible and continue innovating as required.

Q: How important are language skills and cultural understanding to FIFA and/or the business of sport currently? How do you see those skills changing in importance in the future?

A: They are very important and it shall remain so in the future. FIFA is the governing body to 209 member associations, providing them with logistical, administrative, and financial support to develop the game and other social projects in their respective countries. Therefore, the cultural and linguistic flexibility of the employees is vital to deal with challenges associated with different views and working cultures, where naturally language skills are well valued. The organization works in four official languages: English, German, Spanish, and French; and additionally publishes in Arabic and Portuguese. Generally, at least two of the four main languages are a job requirement, but most importantly the cultural understanding is necessary to work with all of FIFA's international stakeholders.

Furthermore, the cyclical organization of tournaments is becoming more robust with the professionalization of the methodology behind it. The flexibility to assimilate the differences that arise from every new hosting nation becomes a key factor for the delivery of a high-quality product. The same principle applies to all services provided to the member associations directly or through their confederations.

Q: What are the most important (other) skills you think students should work to develop while still in school?

A: Creative skills, parallel thinking, or outside the box, whatever you choose to call it; school is the best moment to try out new ideas and have no fear of letting creativity flow. There are no bad ideas; students should take the time to talk to their teachers, lecturers, and classmates and discuss projects even if these do not seem feasible at the time. You will find it rewarding to have some ideas validated, while also learning to cope with criticism and refine your ideas with solutions.

Another skill to develop is the capacity to interact effectively at all levels of an organization. You may think that some people, be it a lecturer, your boss, or teacher, will have no interest in discussing a topic with you. A good piece of advice I received at business school is that everyone has to eat or have a coffee break, so you can approach people in light spirit to discuss during those necessary breaks and people will usually find those five minutes in their agenda for you. Make sure you make the best out of the time available.

Q: Are there specific publications that you read regularly?

A: I like to keep up with the sport world, mainly football, and the advertising world. Some publications I refer to regularly are *SportBusiness, Advertising Age*, and *LatinSpots*, as I don't want to miss out on my region. And it is equally relevant to stay informed about the organization where I work, so I follow social media accounts that are relevant to FIFA such as sponsors' and competitors' Twitter accounts, and FIFA's own news outlets such as FIFA.com and The FIFA Weekly. It is a lot of information so obviously you would just scan through headlines and get into the details of what seems relevant or of particular interest.

Q: Do you advise students to potentially pursue a graduate degree? If so, in what area/field?

A: I don't think it's possible to provide a generic suggestion in that sense. It very much depends on what you want to focus on and how the market develops by the time you are done with your undergraduate studies. If you can, do a summer internship to have an early look into the business world; if you are lucky you will identify some areas of interest that will help you shape your career in the early stages. It is quite common in some countries to do a graduate degree immediately after the undergraduate studies; if that is a feasible option and you are sure of what you want you should go for it, especially if it will mean a competitive advantage when you enter the labour market.

The main advice I can give in that sense is that you focus on what you are good at and what you love doing, whether at work or school. That is where you will have the best results and no regrets about the time and effort spent. That principle is the same for pursuing a graduate degree: make sure you do it because you enjoy it and it allows you to stay up-to-date in your career. The money spent in education does not lose value, however, it needs to be wisely spent.

Kevin York

Account Executive,
Premium Sales
HORNETS Sports &
Entertainment

Q: Can you describe your career path?

A: My career path has been difficult. I started in inside sales with the Bobcats during the lockout season in which we finished with a historically poor 7-59 record. I was able to stick it out during this season and move up to season sales where I spent two seasons. Each season I have separated myself from others with my work ethic which shows in the numbers by being the top producer in my department each season. Now I am in premium sales with a historical season approaching with the Hornets. All of the work and training over the last three seasons have set me up to have a fantastic year. Now I have so many reasons to sell, be it the Hornets' name, team performance, or the in-game experience.

Q: What were the most important things you learned during your undergraduate education?

A: I learned how important it is to build relationships. Being able to meet with people who know about the sport industry and pick their minds and get advice was the best thing to do. Learning how to interact with people and being able to converse really helped get me to where I am today.

Q: What are skills have you utilized the most in your various positions with the Hornets?

A: My work ethic and conversation skills have helped tremendously. Coming in early and staying later helped set me apart from other members of the sale's team and it shows in sale's numbers. The harder I work the luckier I get. Since I work primarily through the phones it is very important to be able to hold a conversation with people. People want to buy; they don't want to be sold. Opening up and being able to connect and hold a conversation has allowed me to keep a large book of business because my clients like working with me.

Q: What advice would you give to a student interested in a career in sport ticket sales?

A: Be ready to put in the work. Sales are the back bone of any sport team. I have been told that there are two jobs within a sport organization. You are either in sales or you are in support. In sales be ready to come in before and leave after other departments, especially during the off-season.

Q: What was the hardest adjustment you had to make in transitioning into your career?

A: The hardest thing was to learn the sales process. I had to learn that it is more about the experience and not so much about team performance (a good team does help the process). Once I was able to understand this I had to be able to convey this professionally to my clients on the phone, in person, and via email.

Q: What do you enjoy the most about your work?

A: I enjoy being able to see the effect I have in the organization. Knowing that I helped the thousands of cheering fans night in and night out at the games get their tickets is amazing.

Q: What career goals do you have?

A: My goal is to work hard and be the best at what I do, meet and surpass goals, and as I move forward I will evaluate opportunities that I am presented.

Q: Do you see sport sales in general and/ or ticketing sales specifically undergoing significant changes over the next five years? In what ways?

A: I do not see any significant changes in the near future. I can see teams adding more value to being a season ticket member. As for the sales process I could see social media playing a larger part in the communication between the team and the customer. Phone usage does not have the same importance as it used to, but is still important. Despite any future changes in technology, the best way to sell will still be face-to-face interaction.

Deana Itow

Client Partner
Paciolan

Q: Could you briefly describe your career path from undergraduate student to your current position?

A: I graduated with a business administration degree with an emphasis in accounting. I started interviewing for jobs before I even graduated and secured a staff accountant role for the GAP Corporate Office beginning two weeks after my graduation. After a couple years in Northern California I decided I wanted to move back home to Southern California so I started a search for a lateral move down south. I took a job with Pacific Bell Wireless (cell phones were a hot new item at the time) and moved into their Finance Office in Tustin, California. Once I got to Southern California I took advantage of the tuition reimbursement program at my company and completed my MBA. I graduated in three years and was armed with all the credentials I needed to start looking for career growth opportunity.

I have always said and will say it again, networking is key to opening your options for a long-term career path. Get out and meet as many people in the business as you can and never burn bridges. You will be stunned by how small the industry is and one bad encounter can definitely block an opportunity later on. During my tenure at Pacific Bell Wireless I was at an social event and met a CFO for a smaller software company. We kept in touch and very shortly after he was offering me a job to not only assist him with some financial projects but also work on some larger business development initiatives. That company was Paciolan.

At Paciolan, I started stepping outside of finance and working with clients and business partners. I realized that while I liked the numbers, I really loved working with people and solving problems. Lucky for me, we had a client partner leave the company which opened a position for me to fill. I did not have a ton of experience in account management, but I had acquired the basic skills to manage strategy. I also had a personal background in college athletics as a former Division-I basketball player and a "will not lose" attitude. I got that job and I am still here over 10 years later.

Q: What have been the biggest challenges you have encountered during your career?

A: By far my biggest challenge was not understanding where my passion was. I have worked hard to acquire a strong skill set but it took me some time and some good mentoring from others to get an understanding regarding what I wanted to "do." I never wanted to work just to have a job. I wanted to work to make a difference. Knowing what motivates you and understanding how to get to that place is challenging if you don't recognize that it is essential. If you want to enjoy getting up every day to come to your job, you have to have some level of passion for what you do.

Q: Could you explain how Paciolan is involved in the business of sport?

A: Paciolan is a software company that powers ticketing, fundraising, marketing, and sales automation. We have a very large client base in college athletics because we enable the schools to operate under their own brand and set their own rules. Our very first client over 35 years ago was the University of Southern California and the ticketing "system" was literally built in a garage. Today, we power over 100 universities across the country and have the highest market share for the major Division-I schools. We have built relationships with the athletic directors and senior associate athletic directors down to the graduate assistants.

Paciolan also services clients in pro sports, arenas, and performing arts.

Q: Can you discuss your team's role in the overall operation of Paciolan?

A: The Client Partner role is what we call the "secret sauce" at Paciolan because it sets us apart from our competitors. The Client Partner is responsible for driving strategy and best practices with our clients to ensure their success with the tools that Paciolan provides. We have direct relationships with the Senior Executives and high-level decision makers at each of our clients and we dive down into their business to help them drive revenues. We also act as an internal advocate for our clients making sure that key decisions at Paciolan have the best interest of our clients in mind. We meet frequently with our Product Management Team, Sales Team, and Customer Support Department to educate them regarding what is being requested by our customers.

From a sales perspective, the relationships that we develop with our customers make us a key driver in the renewal process. We also sell ancillary products directly to grow the overall footprint at each client.

Q: What are the major challenges you and your company are currently facing?

A: The market is always changing and technology is always keeping us on our toes. We have to be nimble enough to evolve as the world chases new and upcoming technology and we have to have the intellect to understand what is going to stick and what could be just a short trend. Being the first to market isn't always a good thing but you don't want to be last either. The biggest challenge is keeping our roadmap stable and adaptable as needs change for our clients. This is not as easy as it sounds.

Q: Are there specific skills sport-management students should look to develop while still in school?

A: I think that finance and business analytics is underrated. I know that numbers are not something that a lot of people have a passion for but to get a good understanding regarding how to break down a profit and loss statement (P&L) or understand other financial statements is important. This industry is about deals and deals are based on revenue and numbers. Make sure you can understand what those numbers mean and you will have an edge.

Q: What are the biggest mistakes you have seen students or young alums make in this industry?

A: Don't get involved just to be around the sports or the hype. While there are definitely perks, it's not instantly glamorous. Any entry-level job in this industry is going to be hard and demand long hours and little pay. You will have a hard time making your way to the top without understanding how the bottom works. In college athletics, it's long hours during the week and then managing events during the evenings and weekends. There are so many ins and outs, whether it's ticketing, sports marketing, or even fundraising. Each has a foundation that can only be expertly learned by experience and the people who I have seen have the most success are those who were willing to roll up their sleeves and do the work.

Also don't be shy. One of the best things about young alumni breaking into this industry is how fresh they are. Don't be afraid to dive in and get your hands on as much as you can. Internships are definitely a plus while you are in school to get initial experience. A lot of people who are working in college athletics, for example, have been doing it for a very long time and may not have updated expertise on technology or modernism. I have seen some young entry-level people make a fast and significant impact on an organization simply because they have the freshest view on technology and are not afraid to speak up with ideas when appropriate. Those are the people that move up fast and quickly make a name for themselves.

Q: What publications do you regularly read to stay apprised of sport-business events?

A: *SportsBusiness Journal* and *Venues Today* are very popular in our office. I also subscribe to the NCAA and NACDA email serve. NACDA will send an email daily with all the major press release announcements.

Q: Would you recommend students pursue graduate school? If so, when should they pursue a graduate degree and what area of study would you recommend?

A: Absolutely! That being said, I am a firm believer that you need to gain some real-life experience before you try to bury yourself further in textbooks. Waiting for a few years before pursuing a graduate degree allows you to actually apply what you are learning in school to your real-life scenario. You will learn a lot about teamwork and strategy and project management in graduate school and all of those things are key in a real-life career. I don't think you can go wrong with an MBA. It's so well rounded and can push you in so many directions. Like I mentioned before, finance and analytics are very important in sport management. You also will focus on strategic management and business law with an MBA.

Bill Shanahan

Owner
Columbia Blowfish

Q: Could you briefly describe your career path from undergraduate student to your current position?

A: I actually started in radio. I wanted to be on air in sports, so I worked at a college radio station and went on career interviews and landed a spot with a local station in Wichita, Kansas. The sports director said there were no jobs currently open but he wanted to introduce me to the sales manager who said if I could sell I would be able to work all facets in radio. It was the best sales training—having to sell air! It was a great training ground for nearly five years and I ended up managing sales, marketing, promotions, and production.

A Triple A baseball team owner was looking for an injection of enthusiasm and new promotions and needed to boost ticket and advertising sales. I got the call—that was 1984. I have worked in a variety of minor league baseball operations since.

Q: What have been the biggest challenges you have encountered during your career?

A: People do not come to root for their favorite players in minor league baseball and in most cases having an average of 70 events in a short time span means we are always looking to create new ways to get people excited to come to the ballpark consistently. Exploring new ways to continually engage the fans is critical.

Q: What are some of the "best" promotions you have implemented?

A: The best activity we had was relocating Mobile, Alabama–born Hank Aaron's childhood home to the Hank Aaron Stadium grounds in Mobile. We restored, renovated, and transformed it into the Hank Aaron Childhood Home & Museum. We had a variety of baseball dignitaries including Hank and members of his family, MLB Commissioner Bud Selig, Jeff Idelson, President of the National Baseball Hall of Fame, and Hall of Famer players such as Reggie Jackson, Willie Mays, Ozzie Smith, Bob Feller, and Rickey Henderson. That was not just a promotion but something that honored one of the most important baseball players—and a great human being—and provided a lasting legacy that future generations can visit to learn about the history of the game and about one of its greatest players.

We did a variety of other wonderful promotions in the past. We gave away a brand new $125,000 home to a lucky fan. (We actually did this promotion three years in a row with a local home builder tied in with television and radio advertising). We built a BayBears Snow Park at Hank Aaron Stadium in the offseason by partnering with a company, SnowMagic, that utilized a machine that produced snow. We gave Southerners—many of whom had never seen a true winter—a snow park from after Thanksgiving until New Years.

Back in the late 1980s when I was in San Bernardino, California, we had a team named the Spirit (Class A California League/Seattle Mariners) and we tried a number of successful promotions such as Ken Griffey Jr. Appreciation Night (Junior was 18 years old at the time). We gave away the first 1,000 fans the first-ever poster of a Minor A League Player! Griffey played only 2 1/2 months for us but that was how big a star he had become—greatest minor league player I ever experienced in my 30-year career.

We also once had all 51 Miss Teen USA contestants out for a ballgame where they threw out 51 first pitches at one time. Funny thing was most of the girls threw the first pitches all over the place hitting other players than their own designate. We also did the first ever mascot racing with the Spirit "Bug" racing children.

The key with any promotion is to have fun and be willing to be creative. Not everything works out perfectly but if you have a goal to entertain the fans, you will usually find a way to make people have a wonderful experience.

Q: Are there specific skills sport-management students should look to develop while still in school?

A: Selling. Learn how to sell yourself, how to build relationships which build trust with whoever you are working with. Learn about the art of networking.

Q: What specific classes would you recommend students take to best position themselves for a sport-industry job?

A: I am very excited to see the development in sales training that has occurred in some college programs.

Q: What publications do you regularly read to stay apprised of sport-business events?

A: Being in the world of minor league baseball for the last 30 years staying informed has changed dramatically as it's now all online 24 hours a day. I follow numerous sports and marketing social media professional and amateur websites and sports news outlets.

Q: Would you recommend students pursue graduate school? If so, when should they pursue a graduate degree and what area of study would you recommend?

A: An example I can give is our current General Manager of the Blowfish Kelly Evans waited a year after her undergraduate degree before pursuing her graduate degree. She has had an opportunity to get the hands-on experience overseeing the day-to-day club operations and I believe she went in to the graduate program with some experiences that not only is helping her but other graduate students as well. She was able to share what she has learned out in the "Real World." I like the idea of maybe at least a year in between degrees.

Joe Dolan

General Manager
Mullins Center – University of Massachusetts

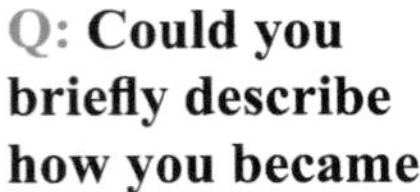
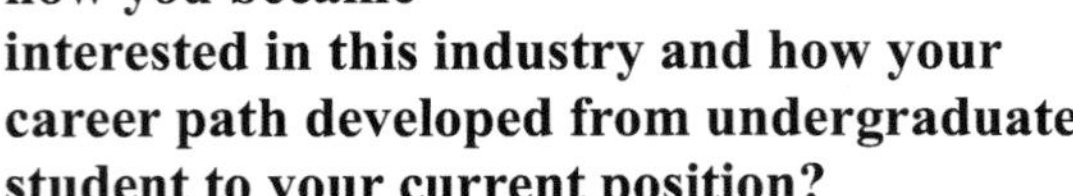

Q: Could you briefly describe how you became interested in this industry and how your career path developed from undergraduate student to your current position?

A: Growing up in Downingtown, Pennsylvania, I used to be as fascinated with the inner workings of running a team as I was with what was happening on the ice or field. The NHL trade deadline was like Christmas to me. My younger brother ended up playing on a hockey team with Peter Luukko's oldest son while I was in high school, and I had the fortune of talking to Mr. Luukko about my interests. He suggested that the best way to advance within the Sport and Entertainment industry was to start on the facility side. I maintained my relationship with Peter as I looked into colleges based on the best programs available. My first internship in college was with the Event Production Department at the Wells Fargo Center in Philadelphia during the summer after my sophomore year. I was very lucky to be hired, in lieu of my second internship, as an Event Manager at the Wells Fargo Center in June 2009 after completing my course work at the University of South Carolina. There is no question that my initial relationship with Peter and my willingness to devote time and energy to the tasks at hand played huge roles in that opportunity. After two years at the Wells Fargo Center, I was promoted to the Global Spectrum–managed Roanoke Civic Center. Within 2 ½ years of graduating college, I was serving as the Assistant General Manager of a multipurpose facility that hosts nearly 300 events a year. After spending three years in Roanoke, I was recently promoted to General Manager of the Mullins Center on the campus of the University of Massachusetts.

Q: What have been the biggest challenges you have encountered during your career?

A: There are two major challenges that I've encountered thus far. The initial challenge was immediately adjusting to the commitment required to work in our industry. I spent four years hearing every professor tell their classes that the hours are long, the pay is minimal, and you need to be prepared to make sacrifices to advance. They were right. I was privileged to start my career at a building like the Wells Fargo Center, but that type of venue isn't going to slow down so you can catch up. I learned a lot of valuable lessons about organizational and time management skills. I can specifically remember having to miss a South Carolina football weekend that all my friends were going back to Columbia for, because I had to manage a weekend event. You quickly determine whether or not this field is right for you. The second challenge, at times, has been my age. I've been fortunate to advance within Global Spectrum, but there have been times when my age has been met with hesitation. I've enjoyed working hard to earn respect from those who had apprehensions about whether my inexperience would correlate to being unqualified.

Q: What are the major challenges you and your company are currently facing?

A: The challenge is always identifying new streams of revenue. Whether it is finding additional methods to increase ancillary revenue or developing new and exciting events that are nontraditional, the focus is always on bringing in more revenue while increasing the customer experience. Our company has a wide variety of events that support our facility, extending well beyond concerts, sporting events, and family shows. My job is to continue looking at creative ways to utilize the space we have and support it with our excellent marketing and operational staff.

Q: Can you provide some examples of creative revenue sources you have developed that did not exist 10 years ago?

A: There are several examples of ancillary revenue that exist today that weren't common a couple years ago. The "loaded ticket" concept that features a certain amount of preloaded money on your ticket for use at concession and merchandise stands is a great example. This is a feature that essentially guarantees ancillary revenue when a customer purchases a ticket. More often than not, customers end up leaving excess money on the ticket or they end up spending more than they originally allotted. Capitalizing on Internet ticket sales has been another major source of revenue. Tagging the seat you bought via Facebook at the checkout window is essentially free event marketing. Another major focus has been creating supplemental events within an event. Hosting VIP pre-show events, outdoor block parties, or a catered meal or buffet prior to the start of a show are inexpensive ways to generate supplemental revenue that might have been spent elsewhere. While I was in Roanoke, we held a "Broadway Buffet" during our Broadway in Roanoke series at the Performing Arts Theatre. These were already high-scale events, so why not offer a great meal at a reasonable price prior to doors opening? Over the course of a six-show season, that's thousands of dollars being spent at your building rather than a local restaurant.

Q: As the General Manager of a venue that hosts university teams and other affiliated events, how do you juggle the need to keep the primary tenants happy with the responsibility to book other outside events? Are there often times when conflict occurs?

A: When it comes to facility management companies, the most important thing to understand is the objective of your client (whether it's a university or municipality). At the University of Massachusetts, the primary function of the Mullins Center is to serve as the home venue for men's and women's basketball, and men's hockey. From there, the objective is to add to the quality of student life, and then supplement additional bookings to generate revenue and positive exposure for the university. I always need to keep that in perspective when I approach bookings. The UMass Athletic Department has been a true partner when I am in need of a date to secure a high-profile artist or event. Once the respective sports schedules are finalized, the objective is to find creative ways to utilize the available dates.

Q: What do you think will be the biggest challenges in the next 5 to 10 years?

A: I think our business has evolved a great deal in the last 5 to 10 years, and so much of that was technology driven. There is always the challenge of enticing customers to attend events at your facility as opposed to another activity, but we will always be an experience driven industry. The biggest challenge (and in many ways, opportunity) will be adapting to the next technological advances and trying to capitalize on new opportunities. I think it's important to make sure you're always evaluating ways to do things more efficiently or successfully.

Q: Are there specific skills sport-management students should look to develop while still in school?

A: Most graduates will land a job similar to my first job. Like I mentioned before, you'll be working hard, and you'll be working a lot. The more you can prepare for a fast pace, the better. I can't stress enough the importance of organizational and time management skills. With that being said, you need a job before those skills will help you in your career. Nothing was more important to me than networking. I met everyone I could at every chance I had. I would encourage students to get involved and separate themselves from everyone else that will be hitting the job market at the exact same time.

Q: What are the biggest mistakes you have seen students or young alums make in this industry?

A: Getting a job shouldn't be the accomplishment that you hang your hat on. I've seen people get hired and lose any sense of urgency or motivation. In my opinion, every day you should be working towards the next promotion or goal you have your sights set on. You should certainly enjoy the here and now that comes with your hard work to this point, but you should always be working towards something. I couldn't work 50+ hour weeks if I wasn't focused on getting better at my job.

Q: What publications do you regularly read to stay apprised of sport-business events?

A: I regularly use *Venues Today* and *Pollstar.*

Q: Would you recommend students pursue graduate school? If so, when should they pursue a graduate degree and what area of study would you recommend?

A: I firmly believe you should never stop learning. Whether you decide to do that via grad school or on the job is a personal choice. I don't think there is anything that can match "real life" training that exists via practicums or internships. As long as you put a value on that experience, I think furthering your education is a tremendous decision.

Lisa Elson

Coordinator, Paralympic Games
United States Olympic Committee (USOC)

Q: Can you briefly describe your career path?

A: Sport has always played a big role in my life. I played volleyball, basketball, and track & field in high school and was a member of the University of Nebraska–Kearney (UNK) Track & Field team. During my first two years in school I was undecided and once I learned about sport administration I knew that was the major to pursue. I had been very involved in communications as well and one of my professors convinced me to double major in public relations. The combination of the two degrees has been very useful.

I completed my undergraduate degree in 2008 and then completed a Master of Science in Sport and Exercise Science, Sport Administration Emphasis from the University of Northern Colorado in 2010. I interned at the Rocky Mountain Athletic Conference (RMAC) in Colorado Springs in Media Relations from August 2008 to May 2009. I started at the USOC in August 2009 as an Executive Administrative Assistant in International Games. In June 2011, I moved into my current role with the Paralympic Games.

Q: What are some of your specific job duties?

A: The USOC is the National Olympic Committee (NOC) and National Paralympic Committee (NPC) for the USA. The USOC is one of four countries where the NOC/NPCs operate under the same roof. We serve as the main liaison between National Governing Bodies (NGBs—every sport has one) and the Organizing Committees (OCOG) for all major international games. The department I work in, International Games, does all of the logistical planning for Team USA for the Olympic, Paralympic, Pan American, Parapan American, and Youth Olympic Games. This includes things like air travel, ground transportation, housing, sport entry, event tickets, etc. Basically we get Team USA to and from the Games and take care of everything in order to positively impact sport performance. I am primarily responsible for planning the Paralympic and Parapan American Games. I help the athletes and team staff register for the Games, enter the athletes in all of their events, determine how many staff each sport can bring and accredit (an accreditation has different access levels and we determine who needs what type of accreditation based on their role). We receive a quota of accreditations from the Organizing Committee and must prioritize how we allocate the accreditations to maximize sport performance. We work with each sport to identify their needs/wants and develop a plan to meet those needs/wants within our budget and communicate Team USA's plans/requests to the Organizing Committee. For Sochi, I was also responsible for entering our Olympic Winter team in addition to the Paralympic Winter team in all of their events (this is referred to as sport entry). I assisted in developing our Games Registration site used for both Games. This is how we collect information (passport numbers, photos, contact information etc.) from all the individuals who have a remote chance of attending the Games (referred to as a long list), then I take that information and enter it into the Organizing Committee's system. We have official meetings to review all of this information called a pre-Delegation Registration Meeting and a Delegation Registration Meeting (DRM—this meeting happens right before we move into the Athlete Village). After the DRM, our team is officially entered for the Games.

Q: What specific challenges does the Paralympic Games face currently?

A: In the United States, the Paralympic Games are still struggling to become a household name. The USOC recently made it a requirement for all sponsors to sponsor both the Olympics and Paralympics. Coverage on NBC has drastically improved, but it is still not equal to the coverage of the Olympic Games. There will be more hours televised for the Games in Rio then in previous Games, which will help our organization immensely.

I think as publicity grows the Paralympics will increase its popularity which is important in a crowded marketplace.

In the recent past, Amy Purdy competed on *Dancing With the Stars* and there have been numerous commercials featuring Paralympians.

Q: What have been the biggest challenges you have encountered during your career?

A: Work/life balance is the biggest challenge. The job is very demanding and I'm gone for long periods of time.

Q: What advice would you give to current undergraduate sport-management students in regards to their career development?

A: The sport industry is very competitive. It is true that much of success is about who you know. However, I am proof that there are exceptions. I was hired at the USOC without anyone knowing who I was. Every other position that has been hired in our department since I started someone knew them and recommended them. I was able to wow them with my solid resume/cover letter interview skills, and past experiences.

Building relationships and a strong network is key to being successful. Internships are the perfect time to get to know how the "real world" works. There's a reason most top sport management programs require them as part of the degree.

Students need to learn from your professors, and not just the stuff that will be "on the test." They know a lot and have been through a variety of experiences. Take the time to hear their story beyond the classroom and of course interact with guest speakers and with professionals you meet on field trips.

Q: Are there specific publications or other resources you read regularly?

A: *SportsBusiness Journal*

Q: Would you recommend students pursue graduate school?

A: I think pursuing graduate school is still somewhat of a personal choice in the sport industry. A lot of the individuals who work at the USOC do not have a master's degree, and the ones who do obtained one for various reasons that aren't really dependent on their career. Some of the service providers like sport psychologists, sport dieticians, etc. have master's degrees, but in those area it's more of a requirement.

I do think event management is useful in all areas of the industry. If you're doing something that involves international business, taking some classes that focus on that would be useful.

Since the USOC is both the NOC (National Olympic Committee) and NPC (National Paralympic Committee) most jobs with the Paralympic Movement are at the USOC. There are some National Governing Bodies that are solely Paralympic like National Wheelchair Basketball is separate from USA Basketball.

Sundeep Kapur

President
Digital Credence

Q: Can you briefly describe your career path?

A: A progressive journey and hindsight makes it all look so perfect. Here are the steps—I started as a teaching assistant, moved to technology solution selling, then brought many "dot com's" to life as web commerce started, started specializing in digital marketing, eventually leading to what I do now—OMNI-channel enablement for brands.

Some of my client work involved brands like AAA, Ann Taylor, Anthropologie, Overstock.com, Dillard's, Equifax, Travel Unie, Meijer Stores, HDFC Bank, Sun Trust Bank, Atlanta Hawks, LA Clippers, Kroenke Entertainment, & AEG Live. These are all different businesses but the focus of every brand is to seek and satisfy a consumer.

I have had an opportunity to learn a lot, have a lot of fun (I absolutely love what I do), and even come to a realization that three things drive a brands' success—sales, transactional commerce (omni-channel / multi-channel), and teaching (being a mentor / solution leader for brands).

The biggest lesson for brands is to realize that the consumer we seek is the same consumer that does business with multiple brands. If only we could focus outside our industry—we would learn so much more.

Q: What prompted you to start your own business? Obviously, you could have stayed with some of the companies you worked for without taking the entrepreneurial risk.

A: The world of digital gives businesses an opportunity to serve their consumers with personalization, efficiency, and speed. What started off as an online only store has now turned into something that "should" be integrated into all consumer touchpoints.

Even if a fan / consumer walks into a store, his or her smartphone can be leveraged to do so much more. The digital world involves search, social media, email marketing, cloud-based Customer Relationship Management (CRM), responsive design, mobile, and so much more.

I always enjoyed teaching and mentoring brands so I decided to focus on helping brands drive "digital credence." I do this through education where I help businesses leverage all channels in the pursuit of the consumer they seek.

I have a passionate desire to teach and mentor—this is what keeps me going and I absolutely love it. Running my own business allows me the freedom to work across a variety of industries.

Q: What have been some of the biggest challenges you have faced during your career?

A: Walking away from so many successful businesses. I could have stayed with any one of my clients but I saw my calling as an opportunity to mentor multiple brands with their own consumer engagement strategies.

When Michael Jackson announced he was coming back, we could not cope with the interest. Multiple millions wanted to purchase a few tickets and it was tough to manage the online traffic. When he passed before the shows could even start—I wrote the shortest marketing message that took the longest amount of time. It wasn't easy.

On and after 9/11/2001 a few financial institutions had to keep running to not cause any further panic. I was fortunate to be part of a team that worked hard to make sure these financial institutions were up and running—it was one of the toughest jobs we had.

Q: Can you explain digital strategies and why they are important in the sport industry now and how they will be incorporated in the industry in the future?

A: Digital is not a separate channel; brands need to integrate digital into their existing channels. Smart devices like mobile phones are creating consumers who are empowered—social media is on 24/7—brands need to learn how to leverage these opportunities.

A sports team's brand, their channels, including their website, is a conduit that connects the consumer with the powerful smartphone to the entire social web. Brands need to personalize interactions by managing preferences, they need to create consumer journeys, and they need to ensure security.

Here are two examples at different ends of the personalized spectrum. I love my Amazon account! I log in, my preferences are stored, I enjoy one click shopping, and all the messaging is completely personalized. By contrast, my financial institution still doesn't know that I speak English and that I always withdraw $60 at an ATM. They have served me for 30 years and yet without this basic level of personalization they always push "personalized offers" to me. Imagine the audacity!

Consumers are expecting smart commerce from brands. Start by keeping track of consumer preferences, train your channels to communicate with Amazon-like finesse, and most importantly, respect your consumers' time. Think about knowledge-based marketing, real-time service, personalization, systematic up selling, and soliciting feedback.

All these are key drivers of digital strategies!

Q: What are the most important skills you think students should work to develop while still in school?

A: Learning how to prioritize, understanding return on investment, and problem solving are three very important skills. What's even more important? Consumer / fan / peer interaction!

Interact with your peers while you are at school, get their different perspectives—when you work for a business you are going to have to pursue different types of consumers. Your connections, your friends, and all these interactions will be invaluable when you have to design a segmentation / marketing strategy for your sport team or business.

Q: What are the biggest mistakes that you see interns and entry-level employees making in this business?

A: Sport and entertainment is a glamorous business; it is very exciting and so much of our focus is on how things work under the lights. We tend to focus on the fans inside the stadium. I would offer two suggestions—work to engage the consumer outside the event and use these skills to help any business turn their customers into fans!

I used to serve three industries as a teacher / consultant: sport & entertainment, financial services, and the catalog industry. My first invoice to a major sport team was for $4,800 but when I received my check it was for $3,100. Confused, I called up the client to learn that they paid me the balance via season tickets. This is a common problem in sport because so many people are willing to work for little compensation or take a portion of their compensation in non-cash forms that many teams do not pay what they should for work by employees or consultants. Because of this, I decided to focus my consulting career primarily on financial services with an occasional sport gig.

I tell this story to inform sport-marketing students to not be disappointed if you do not get your dream job in the sport business (or if you do not get the reward you desire). Your education is vital; any business would love to convert their prospects and customers into fans. What you are learning is coveted and will get you places.

Q: Are there specific publications that you read regularly?

A: *The Wall Street Journal* and *The Economist* educate, provide trends, and provide ideas to converse with people. I also respect what my peers are reading and spend a fair amount of time reading their suggestions via LinkedIn.

Q: Do you advise students to potentially pursue a graduate degree?

A: A graduate degree can be very valuable but only after two to five years of work experience. Think of your time in graduate school as a way to sharpen the saw—like hiring a personal coach to guide you even further.

Q: If there is one thing you want students to remember, what is it?

A: Find your passion and pursue it; you will be surprised how you do not worry about the hours it takes or the money you earn (money will come, trust me ☺).

My passion lies in teaching but the teaching also leads to solving problems which then leads to writing for business publications which often leads to further teaching opportunities. My professional life is filled with great opportunities because I enjoy what I do so I work hard to achieve things not just for money but for the satisfaction it brings. Students need to figure out what their passion is and life will be much more rewarding.

Chris May

Director of Athletics
Saint Louis University

Q: Can you briefly describe your career path?

A: I was a track and field athlete at Iowa State University. After graduation, I moved to the University of Colorado (CU) where I worked in a variety of capacities in the athletic department and completed my MBA. I was at CU for 23 years and held a variety of positions within the athletic department, ranging from ticket seller, to sport administrator, to major event manager. I came to Saint Louis University in 2008 and have worked with great people to move our athletic department forward in a variety of areas.

Q: Working more than 20 consecutive years in the same athletic department is rare in this industry. How did you evaluate opportunities to leave Colorado and why did you make the change to Saint Louis?

A: Certainly, students who desire to work in this industry should understand that moving is something that can and will occur. Students really should know that there is not one exact "blueprint" for career advancement in this field. Each person takes his or her own path. I stayed at Colorado not only because it was a great place to live and work, but because I was given opportunities to grow my skill set and enhance my career. It was nice to be continually presented with new challenges while in the same athletic department. I certainly did not have the same job for all the years I was there, so even though I was not moving to a new athletic department my job titles and responsibilities consistently advanced during my tenure. It does not always work out that way for others.

I took the job at Saint Louis University because of the great opportunity to work with excellent colleagues at a wonderful university in one of the best cities in the United States. In your career, sometimes wonderful opportunities present themselves and one key to success is being able to identify those opportunities and then take action. I am certainly proud of the things we have accomplished since my arrival and we have plans to make things even better.

I think students should plan in terms of one-, three-, and five-year goals. You have to have a plan to know what you want to specifically accomplish. Sometimes achieving those goals may involve moving and sometimes you can accomplish what you have planned in one place. It is much more important to recognize opportunities and to work with supportive colleagues than to be thinking you have to move or you have to stay.

Q: What are the biggest challenges for college sports?

A: Like any other component of the sport industry, athletic departments are always trying to provide great experiences, even in challenging economic times. We need to have clearly established strategic objectives so that we have a roadmap for success. The sport industry is continually changing so it is important that professionals in college sports or any other aspect of the business are being proactive in their approach, particularly when it comes to generating revenue.

At Saint Louis University Athletics, we focus on the following three things at all times:

1) Educating
2) Competing
3) Building community

Every member of our staff knows how important those three focal areas are to our pursuit of success.

Q: What do you regularly read to stay appraised of the sport business?

A: Certainly, *SportsBusiness Journal* and *SportsBusiness Daily* are vitally important to read. Both of those publications track what is happening in all facets of the business of sports. ESPN.com is also a great cite to read as they not only provide great sport coverage, but they also report on many of the sport business topics that are changing. It is the responsibility of professionals to know and follow the subareas of their industry so they are informed.

Q: What classes would you recommend students take in college?

A: There is a growing concern in our industry that college graduates are not able to effectively communicate, particularly through their writing. Students need to continually hone their communication skills and should pursue classes and life experiences where those skills are practiced. We have far too many interns and entry-level employees who cannot write effectively or speak in public with confidence. Those skills are transferable to nearly every industry and students must develop them to advance in their careers.

Q: Are there typical mistakes you see interns making?

A: Too many people have expectations that when they start in this business that they will make a lot of money and will not have to work long hours. Sport is a great and exciting industry, but it is also a lot of work. Students should keep their eyes open as to what the various jobs will entail. It is paramount that interns attack the opportunity with a "how much can I learn" attitude. Interns who show a willingness to work without complaint and who show a curiosity that leads to continual learning are the ones who achieve short and long-term success in this field.

Q: Would you recommend students pursue graduate school? If so, in what area?

A: Absolutely. Graduate school is an opportunity to not only learn new things from faculty but also from other students. It should also provide an opportunity to apply what you have learned in the real world. I highly recommend an MBA, which will provide a great foundation in business that is applicable to sport and many other industries.

Q: Is there any other advice you would give to students beginning their career?

A: Everyone needs to learn from the bottom up. Be prepared to learn and always be available to work, even if it is not in your direct department or area of expertise. Employees who volunteer to go above and beyond the call of duty are eventually recognized and rewarded. Students should always believe that there are no jobs "beneath me." Everyone in this industry has to complete tasks that are stressful and often come with little immediate public acknowledgement. Staying focused and positive even when the hours are long are key to launching and sustaining a successful sport management career. I always tell graduates to embrace their opportunities the way great athletes embrace sports. Go "all-in" and you will enjoy lifetime success. The athletic industry is a wonderful place to work for a career when people have their goals ad expectations in line.

Greg Turner

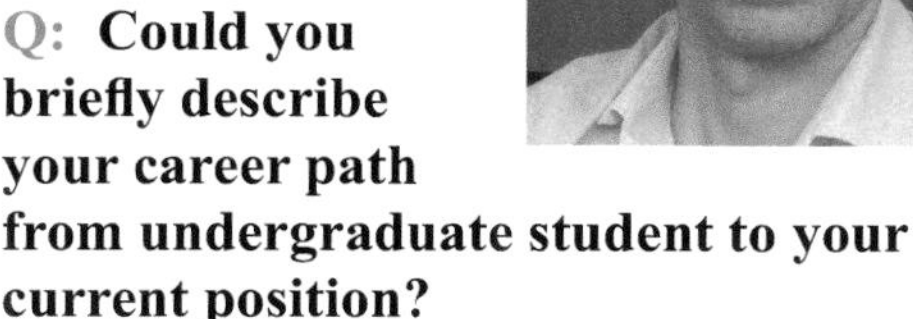

General Manager
Shantou University Sports Park

Q: Could you briefly describe your career path from undergraduate student to your current position?

A: I came to China in 2000 straight out of my undergraduate degree and spent the first few years trying a few different jobs. At one point I set up the Shanghai Hockey Club in my spare time and from that my name got out to a few people in the sport industry and soon I found myself employed by an agency. From there I did some agency work on brand activation for companies like Coke and Adidas helping them do promotions through branded sport-related events. After that I took on a role as the head of a team leading the reopening of the 80-year-old Jiangwan Sports Center. Next I took on a role developing a set of international sports events with responsibilities ranging from negotiating with International Sporting Bodies, to recruiting and negotiating with sponsors, to working with the local sports bureaus and governing bodies on setting up these events.

Most recently, I've been running an ice hockey arena in Shanghai, helping to establish a footprint for ice sports in a city with no history of the sport at all. It's been challenging but it is fun working with kids and seeing them improve. We've also had some opportunities to organize some larger scale events and recently had 2,000 people at our venue to watch a hockey game. Quite an accomplishment! I've recently accepted a position that will require me to move out of Shanghai for the first time in 12 years. I'll be taking a role as General Manager at the David Manica designed Shantou University Sports Park with investment coming from the Li Kashing Foundation. My role will be to develop and execute the vision for the sports park which in and of itself is very exciting. In addition, this will be the first privately funded, commercially operated major sports facility built on a university campus in China. All in all a very exciting project!

Q: What have been the biggest challenges you have encountered during your career?

A: As my career has been based in China for the most part, the obvious challenges have been language and culture. Language issues are pretty self explanatory, but culturally it has taken me some time to adjust my thinking from a western perspective on sport development, participation and business to something that fits better with the Chinese attitudes towards sport.

Q: What advice would you give to other students who may wish to pursue an internship or a potential career in a foreign country?

A: Go for it! It can add a lot of texture and colour to the early part of a career and can offer more challenges and rewards for ambitious people looking to achieve more than what's expected of them. Working overseas isn't for everyone though so my best advice would be to jump in with both feet from the beginning and as long as you're there. Remember, this is an experience in your life that few others will achieve so make the best of it!

Q: As you manage and work with people in a diverse environment, how do you make sure you are connecting with people who may have vastly different experiences and cultural expectations than yours?

A: By listening and asking direct questions. In China, just because someone says yes doesn't mean that they agree or even understand what you're talking about. It's important to push for more comprehensive feedback that shows they understand what you want and have a plan for accomplishing what needs to be done. Also, for those I manage, I put a priority on visibly supporting the decisions they make to help them build confidence in their work so next time they will be more vocal with their thoughts from the beginning. On the flip side though, you need to maintain accountability so when things go off the rails, it's important to review what happened, make sure they understand what could have been done and build them up to achieve greater success next time.

Q: Are there specific skills sport-management students should look to develop while still in school?

A: In the end, sport management is a business just like any other. It contains elements of law, finance, marketing, IT, and administration—all the basic business functions that make any industry tick. Students should get general knowledge on all these topics, which should involve something much greater than "Sports Marketing 101."

Q: What specific classes would you recommend students take to best position themselves for a sport-industry job?

A: That's a tough question because the industry can be so diverse. Getting into specifics when you are just starting to explore the options available can result in missing some great opportunities. I'd suggest instead that students consider two things. First, what are you interested in? Most of us want to get into the industry because we are passionate about sports. What drives that passion for each person is a critical question. Second is what are you better at than anyone else? If you can find classes that address either of these questions, or better yet, both, that's where you'll find both success and enjoyment.

Q: What publications do you regularly read to stay apprised of sport-business events?

A: I'm subscribed to *SportsPro*, *Sports Business International*, and *Pan-Stadia* daily email newsletters. I also follow a couple different podcasts: the Tao of Sports really gets into the nitty gritty details of what makes the sport industry work. Howard Bloom also has a good podcast. Finally, I've also utilized the stadia app on my iPad for their free e-magazine.

Q: Would you recommend students pursue graduate school? If so, when should they pursue a graduate degree and what area of study would you recommend?

A: Yes definitely, when they are ready for it. It does not make a lot of sense to jump from your undergraduate to graduate degree without first gaining some job experience. A graduate degree should be done to help reinforce what you've already experienced and help fill in the gaps and allow you to take the next step in your career. Without spending a couple years working, you might not even know what your own strengths are in the workplace and which direction you want to take your career.

Bob Sivik

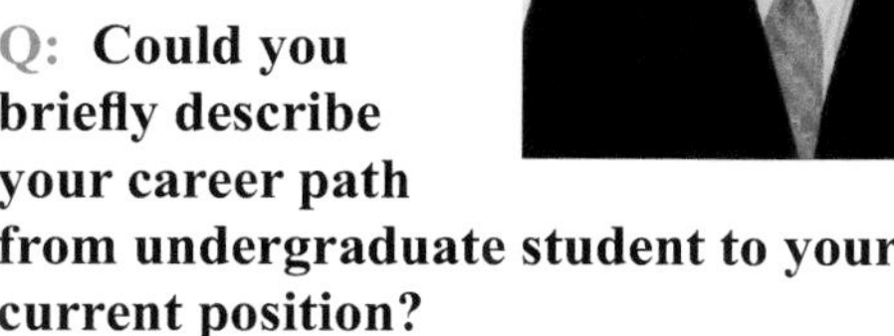

Director of Season & Group Sales
Cleveland Browns

Q: Could you briefly describe your career path from undergraduate student to your current position?

A: I started at Youngstown State University in 1997. After a great career as a student-athlete, I was fortunate to start a career in the sport industry as an Account Executive with the Cleveland Cavaliers. Within eight months, I was promoted to a Sales Consultant. I spent two years selling and servicing accounts until I was promoted to Manager of Inside Sales. I later became Manager of Business Development and then Director of Inside and Organizational Sales for the Cavaliers. I was the Vice President of Ticket Sales & Service with the Columbus Blue Jackets in March of 2010. I recently took the Director of Season and Group Sales for the Cleveland Browns in February of 2013.

Q: You spent a long time with the Cavaliers and had many offers to leave. How did you evaluate the opportunity with the Browns when you obviously have a great affinity for the Cavs?

A: I spent some great years with the Cleveland Cavaliers and learned from some great people. I recently accepted my role with the Cleveland Browns because I believe in the world-class culture we are building. Our leadership team is very strong and I can see this organization moving fast towards being successful very soon.

Q: What are the biggest challenges you face in your work with the Browns?

A: In general, my biggest challenges are always trying to find a better way to operate. Sometimes it is an obsession, but it will always keep our team motivated to be the best it can be.

We have to make sure we manage success with the Browns on the floor to ensure our team members are still receiving top-notch training and leadership.

We are working to create the best culture in professional sports. As most know, the Browns have experienced sales success over the past few years and we would like to continue to grow our fan base. As part of this development, we are rapidly integrating new technology to make our fans have a more enjoyable experience.

Q: Are there specific job skills sport-management students should look to develop while still in school?

A: Being in sales, I would always recommend learning the art of sales. This is a tool that can be transferable for any position you would take in sports. However, I would not recommend starting in sales unless that is your likely career path.

Q: What specific classes would you recommend students take to best position themselves for a sport-industry job?

A: I would strongly recommend Marketing, Sales, Economics, or other business classes. Professional sport may be a fun and entertaining product to consume, but it is still a business.

Q: What publications do you regularly read to stay apprised of sport-business events?

A: *SportsBusiness Journal*

Q: Would you recommend students pursue graduate school? If so, when should they pursue a graduate degree and what area of study would you recommend (e.g., MBA, M.S.–Sport Management, other)?

A: I recommend any chance to learn and to pursue higher education. Education will definitely help throughout your career. Just make sure you are still prepared to take an entry-level position upon graduation, regardless of your degree.

In addition to formal education, I would recommend studying the career histories of people in your ideal future position. The road you start on will help direct your career path.

Q: What trends are emerging in sport management?

A: Sport teams are looking for more information about industry and team trends, so analytics are becoming more important. Also, technology has been growing in importance throughout the industry. The ability to sell continues to remain one of the most important trends individuals and organizations.

Terumi Kaibara

Director, Strategic Properitties
Special Olympics International

Q: Could you explain how sport has helped shape your personality and work ethic?

A: I was born in Singapore and lived in the United States and Japan in the early years of my life. In each country I had to adapt to different cultures and languages. At the age of eight, I returned to Japan to find my gregarious personality posed a challenge in the Japanese culture. However, my love of sports enabled me to break down barriers and assimilate into Japanese culture. Playing basketball helped me learn and share important moments with my friends, as I was always part of a team. I had great success playing basketball as I was a good player on championship teams in junior high, high school, and college.

Participating in basketball and other sports has taught me numerous lessons that are applicable to multiple life situations. For instance, sport taught me an appreciation of team building and creating a common direction for the entire group. Much like business or other aspects of life, playing sports at a high level is important but not just because of winning potential championships. Sport has enabled me to learn about myself and my teammates and to establish common goals. Sport also gave me the opportunity to find common ground when I was experiencing new cultures. My sport experiences extend into everything I do, and my life would be totally different if I had not had my formal and informal sport experiences.

Q: How did your professional sport-management career develop after you finished your undergraduate degree?

A: I lived in four different countries in four different stages of my life, and these multinational experiences shaped my dream since I was a little girl—to be a liaison among different countries and people. When I graduated from Waseda University in Japan, I initially worked as a flight attendant at Cathay Pacific Airways based in Hong Kong. The job enabled me to travel, but I knew that I was missing something—a direct involvement in sports.

After my international work experience in Hong Kong, I followed my passion and determination to work in sport management and decided to pursue my master's degree in Sport Administration at Georgia State University in Atlanta. While at Georgia State, I did an internship at the Professional Golf Association (PGA) TOUR in the New Media department which entailed working extensively on the PGATOUR.com website. After earning my master's degree in 2004, I worked for the Ladies Professional Golf Associations (LPGA), where I started as the New Media Coordinator working for the LPGA.COM website, and eventually became the Manager of Emerging Media and International Television.

While I have always had an interest in a sport-management career, I realized that I needed to enhance my global leadership skills to achieve my long-term goals. I recently joined Green Stamp to enhance my business skills. My current position provides an opportunity to develop and implement international strategic plans. I work directly with the Chief Executive Officer and the Vice President, which enables me to see and influence the company's overall operation. These experiences have broadened my perspective regarding how to approach different global problems. Although I left the sport industry temporarily, my passion and heart are still in sport.

My long-term interest in a sport-management career is based upon a desire to use sport as a basis to break down cultural barriers and solve problems. Sport gave me the opportunity to adjust to different countries, and I chose to initially pursue a career in international sport management because I wanted to create more opportunities for others to have similar experiences. My long-term career ambition is to open my own international organization to support and help children in underdeveloped countries. An important component of that dream is to help children fall in love with sport and to learn about life through their sport experiences.

Q: What are the biggest differences in the work environment in Japan and the United States? How did you adjust to those differences?

A: Japanese and American cultures are different, and in business that is reflected in the "typical" communication style and decision-making process. A typical Japanese company will have distinctly different supervisory styles, management controls, and interdepartment relations. In many ways, the "typical" Japanese employee behaves much like a samurai, having formal duties and loyalties to other members of the organization. In contrast, "typical" American companies have management structures where employees act like a cowboy. An American employee is far more independent in most situations than an employee in Japan. The Japanese emphasis on interdependence and harmony within work groups usually leads to an extensive consultation with pre-meetings, meetings, and after meetings whenever a decision must be contemplated and implemented. American companies are far more likely to have their employees take individual initiative.

Q: As an American-based company, what issues does the LPGA have as it expands it international focus?

A: My experience with the LPGA brought tremendous opportunities to see the existence and advancement of women's sport, and how the LPGA can continue to play a key role creating more opportunities internationally.

During the 2006 Women's World Cup of Golf in South Africa, I observed how golf created opportunities for young girls. The role that the Women's World Cup of Golf had played in the development of the game was evidenced by the 43% increase in the number of South African women playing golf from 2000 to 2005. While I was in South Africa helping to operate a junior golf clinic with LPGA professional golfers, girls at first were hesitant to pick up golf clubs for the first time. Eventually, the significance of language barriers, citizenship, and religion slowly melted away, and their energy transferred to developing their self-esteem and self-confidence through golf.

In 2010, the LPGA has 129 international players from 28 different countries. The LPGA has worked to support international players and worked to immerse international players in American culture, customs, and language. Each year the LPGA is also expanding the number of tournaments played outside of the United States, which will give tremendous opportunities to grow their fan base internationally. Working in a variety of countries with players from varied backgrounds presents marketing opportunities, but also cultural challenges. Some of the challenges facing the LPGA are similar to other sport leagues as well as businesses in other industry sectors.

Q: What advice would you give to students beginning to study sport management?

A: I highly recommend doing an internship, and while working being aggressive to coordinate lunch with your supervisor and any staff members in other departments. I also think it is crucial to outperform and prove you are different from other interns during the internship program, even in a short period of time. If you perform only as well as the other interns, you will likely not advance in your career at a rapid pace. In order to create an excellent impression, you need to make an effort to do extra and be unique. My internship experience with the PGA TOUR changed my whole life, because it not only opened the door with the LPGA, but it continues to open other doors outside of the sport industry.

Q: What advice would you give to students who know they want to have an international focus to their career?

A: Reading a textbook and talking with others is important, but there is no substitute for living and experiencing a different culture. Obviously, studying or working in a foreign country will enhance your understanding. If you cannot visit or live in different countries while in college, there are still opportunities to dive into international initiatives while on campus. International students who are studying in the United States usually are happy to provide information and contacts from their home country. The global economy has spurred nearly every company to think (and recruit) internationally and on many campuses international activities are regularly occurring. Building an international network while still on campus is important and once a network is developed, it is critical that contacts are maintained. Every sport organization now realizes that the Internet has made the world a smaller place, so the opportunities are limitless if one takes the initiative to develop their international focus.

Q: What publications should students be reading on a regular basis?

A: *SportsBusiness Journal* and *The Wall Street Journal.*

Dan Hazlett

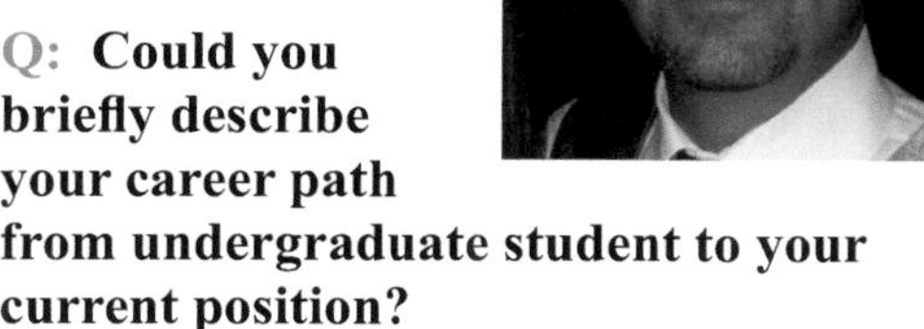

Assistant Director—
Campus Recreation
Georgia Tech

Q: Could you briefly describe your career path from undergraduate student to your current position?

A: My career path was somewhat uncommon for the sport industry. I graduated with an undergraduate degree in psychology and decided to pursue a graduate degree in sport administration. During my last year of school, I secured a graduate assistant position at the Georgia Tech Athletic Association, but the position was not challenging or fulfilling, so I took a position in the recreation department. I was initially hired on a temporary basis to run the new summer camp program. This led to being hired full time to oversee the sport club program. Over time I was promoted to my current position. For most people who want to get involved in campus recreation, the typical path is to pursue an undergraduate degree in sport administration or recreation. While in school that person would likely work in the recreation department as a student assistant and then hope to secure a graduate assistant position that pays for a graduate degree.

Q: What have been the biggest challenges you have encountered during your campus recreation career?

A: My biggest challenge has been change. I am not referring to changes in budgets or personnel. Those changes certainly happen and need to be integrated into operations and professional philosophy. The recreation profession has undergone a complete shift within the last 10 years. Campus Recreation used to be a place to have fun and simply recreate; it is now a place to enhance not only the student experience, but also the student learning. Learning outcomes and formal assessment have become the way of life for a campus recreation professional, so the biggest challenge I have faced is shifting alongside the new landscape that our profession has moved to.

Q: What are the most pressing issues in campus recreation?

A: The budget situation used to be the pressing issue, and it remains a big one. But, the biggest issue now is the ability to remain relevant on campus. How we impact students and how we show that impact are critical to remaining relevant. With relevance, budgets are sure to follow.

Q: Are there specific job skills sport-management students should look to develop while still in school?

A: I would first have all students continually practice their communication skills, both written and oral. Being able to effectively and succinctly communicate to various levels of the organization is critical. A skill now critically important is assessment, in all forms. Developing and enhancing your ability to create an assessment plan is a skill that will set you apart from others coming out of college.

Q: What specific classes would you recommend students take to best position themselves for a sport-industry job?

A: Financial management and budgeting (all levels) is critical since eventually employees (who wish to advance in their careers) will be placed in a position where they will manage a budget and need to develop revenue sources. Again, assessment is in our world now, so any class that provides the fundamentals in assessing is important. Much of what we do focuses on leadership. During the entry level position, your leadership skills apply mostly to students and graduate assistants. Later on in your career, those same traits will apply to the staff you supervise. Take as many leadership development classes as your schedule allows. It applies to all professions. And don't take it only for the grade. Take it to learn and apply.

Q: What are the biggest mistakes you see interns and entry-level employees making when they enter the work environment?

A: This is an easy one. The intern and entry level employee typically have blinders on. It's not something they intend, but due to the newness and perhaps being in a new city, etc. they tend to focus only on the specific tasks they are "required" to complete. It is important they realize they are part of something much bigger. There are reasons for how or why things are operating as they are. It would benefit them to begin learning to view their position and specific job with a much wider perspective. Learn how their role fits in with the rest of the department. Once that becomes clear, learn how their role fits in with the rest of the division and the university as a whole. Each college/university has a strategic plan; determine how your role (even as an intern or entry level employee), can impact that plan. By widening their view, it will become easier to determine how they can be relevant to the mission of the department and university.

Q: What publications do you regularly read to stay apprised of sport-business events?

A: I regularly read all National Intramural and Recreation Sports Association (NIRSA) publications. *Referee* magazine and *Athletic Business* are also helpful. I read a plethora of leadership development authors (e.g. John Maxwell, Mark Miller). I have found those two authors' books to be extremely helpful. There are many others (Lencioni) but Maxwell and Miller also support their books with other educational opportunities.

Q: Would you recommend students pursue graduate school? If so, when should they pursue a graduate degree and what area of study would you recommend?

A: For management positions in campus recreation, it is required to have a graduate degree. I know of only one person who has an undergraduate degree who is in a position at my level, and that was a unique situation. An MBA would be good to have, but typically the graduate assistants for campus recreation are linked with sport management programs or recreation programs in the College of Education. It might be difficult to work as a graduate assistant and have that funding cover an MBA.

Q: Are there any additional advice or insights you would provide to students pursuing a future career in campus recreation or another area of sport management?

A: I would look at a future career like I would look at life (although work should not be viewed at the same level of importance as life). Things change. People change, technologies change, organizations change, situations change. One of the main constants in work and in life is change. Some changes you can directly control or influence, while many other things will remain out of your direct control. Being in a position where you are prepared to take advantage of an opening or opportunity (that may not be in your current geographic area) may significantly influence overall satisfaction and happiness with your career. One should never assume things will always be the same, and, equally, one should never assume everything about their job or their life is determined. As soon as you think your life or your job is set, something or someone will take it another direction. When changes occur, you need to be flexible enough to take advantage of the opportunity. Many of the most successful people in campus recreation and sport management achieved success in their careers in jobs or locations they did not anticipate when they began their career.

Kenneth C. Scull

Colonel U.S. Army Retired
Stadium Manager/
Assistant Athletic Director
University of Louisville—
Papa John's Cardinal
Stadium Retired

Q: Can you describe your career path?

A: I first came to Louisville in 1997 to assist in the completion and the opening of Papa John's Cardinal Stadium. Prior to that I was Deputy Athletic Director at the United States Military Academy at West Point, New York, where I supervised the athletic department from top to bottom, including facilities. I graduated from the United States Military Academy in 1969 with a degree in engineering, and served in the Infantry branch of the United States Army. I also hold master's degrees in public administration and business administration. Currently, I am the stadium manager for Papa John's Cardinal Stadium (PJCS) at the University of Louisville. PJCS is a 55,000-seat facility used primarily for the university's football team.

Q: What are the primary duties you undertake the day of an event?

A: On the day of an event, the first thing I do is make sure the parking lots are open and security is in place. I also make sure everyone in the facility is on time and doing what they are supposed to be doing. If they are not, I need to make adjustments. Prepping the facility on game day is time-consuming, and involves numerous mundane tasks like putting the flags up appropriately. The sound and video board need to be working properly. During the event, my primary function is reacting to situations that are exceptional. I also like to make sure everyone is in the right place and the employees are being courteous to our guests.

Q: What are the main revenue sources at the facility?

A: As a football facility, our primary sources of revenue are ticket sales, luxury seating, parking, and concessions. The ticketing structure is based on a donation level that creates an additional revenue stream for the athletic department. When we are not hosting a game, we create revenue by renting the facility and parking lot to events such as large high school football games, semi-professional games, and concerts. Parking from other big events such as the Kentucky Derby at Churchill Downs creates revenue as well. We also rent locations within the stadium such as the Brown and Williamson Club and the press lounge. Aside from rent, these events also generate revenue from our catering service.

Q: What criteria do you utilize when renting the facility?

A: The most important considerations when renting a facility are the event's promoter and the schedule. The promoter must have a financial structure that makes sense to ensure the event is profitable. If the promoter lacks a good scheme, then most likely the event will not be worth the time, effort, or risk that go into putting on an event. As far as the schedule is concerned, sequencing is critical. It usually takes a week to get ready for a concert, so events need to be sequenced accordingly. Typically, a concert cannot be held the day after a football game. Also, one needs to consider the staff required to put on an event. Large events require large numbers of people to work. If the facility is trying to do something big when another prominent event in town is occurring, there is a good chance that finding staff to work will be challenging, especially for part-time workers.

Q: Do you outscore any of the facility operations?

A: At PJCS, concessions are operated through a private contractor. The primary advantage of outsourcing concessions is that the concessionaire is the license holder for alcohol sales. The state looks to the license holder on the premises for all things related to alcohol law enforcement and dram shop laws. In addition, we do not have to hire and manage employees with a specific set of skills for a one-time event. The concessionaire has staff that works 12 months out of the year at a variety of facilities throughout the region, and is able to provide sufficient qualified personnel for our selective events. Finally, the concessionaires are experts at what they do. Their core competency is food. Ours are facilities and athletics. We do not try to be something we are not.

Security is another service we outsource, for many of the same reasons. During an event, the primary responsibilities of security are crowd management, behavior, and safety. Many of the risks in our facility are associated with alcohol consumption. We assume much of the risk for behavior related to alcohol, which sometimes becomes an issue. The event experience should be fun for everybody. Unruly fans should not be permitted to disrupt other patrons and this can become an issue with alcohol consumption. A lot of drinking goes on in the parking lot before and after an event. Any time a mixture of people who are driving and people who are drinking and not paying a lot of attention is present, risks are increased. Security also needs to be prepared to deal with emergency situations such as bad weather, bomb scares, or a variety of other threats.

Q: What are the biggest challenges the industry is facing now and in the future?

A: The biggest challenge in the field for the near future is money. It is expensive to operate a facility. If it does not look nice, revenue opportunities decrease. Generating revenue to maintain a facility is an ongoing challenge. Another trend for the future of facility management is technology. The industry has benefited, and will continue to benefit, from advancements in technology. Technology has helped tremendously in the areas of crowd management and security. The use of computers saves time previously spent writing everything down. Tickets can be counted faster and the number of patrons in a facility can be more easily tracked now than in the past. In addition, all the systems inside the facility are computer-based so it takes fewer people to operate the facility.

Q: Are there particular things you look for when hiring staff members?

A: One of the things I am looking for in new hires is a sense of mission that exceeds the job description. In addition, a candidate needs a variety of skills and skill sets to be successful in this field. These skills include:

- The initiative and ability to act with minimal supervision;
- Attention to detail;
- Interpersonal skills;
- Business skills including knowledge of the law as it pertains to contracts.

I would advise any student thinking about working in facility management to intern in a sport facility. Students really need to get out from behind a desk to see the scope of what it takes for a facility to function well, from taking out the trash to providing optimal customer service. Internships are the best way to gain practical experience and get a foot in the door. The value of real-life work experience should not be underestimated.

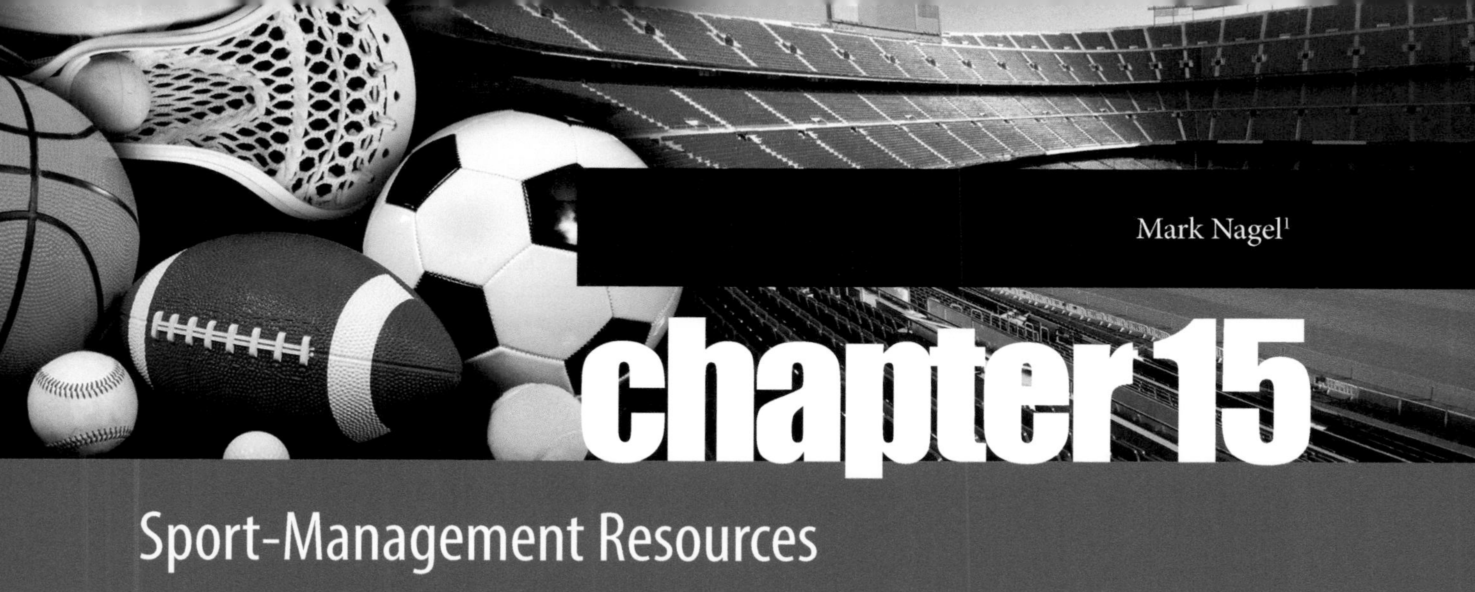

Sport-Management Resources

I don't think much of a man who is not wiser today than he was yesterday.

—Abraham Lincoln

The library is the temple of learning, and learning has liberated more people than all the wars in history.

—Carl T. Rowan

Introduction

The sport business and its various subindustries are continually evolving. True sport-industry professionals consistently examine the industry's history, in order to contextualize current changes and trends in standards and best practices, and attempt to identify future areas of opportunity. The best ways to stay abreast of issues in sport management are to continually read related periodicals, maintain membership in appropriate organizations, attend pertinent seminars and conferences, and make use of the nearly limitless body of available information. Since knowledge is power, students should seek to obtain as much information as possible, going beyond that provided in the classroom.

Students interested in a sport-management career should also seek out opportunities to interact with established professionals. Though some professionals have busy schedules that prevent them from conversing with students, many sport managers appreciate the opportunity to return letters or electronic mail from students seeking information or guidance. In some cases, sport-management professionals find time to meet with a "pleasantly persistent"

1 Evan Keith, Luke Reasor, and Mike Zachrich provided assistance assembling and editing this chapter.

student who seeks to learn more about their past experiences. Nearly everyone who works in the industry began their career "at the bottom" and is willing to give back to the "next generation" if a request is appropriately conveyed. Students should remember that even some of the most powerful sport-business executives, such as National Football League Commissioner Roger Goodell began their careers as interns.

This chapter is designed to provide materials and resources to help sport-management students begin their pursuit of a sport business career. It is certainly not an "exhaustive" reference list, since the number and type of potential resources change as rapidly as the overall industry. This chapter hopefully will expand students' perspective by highlighting resources relevant to possible careers beyond just the "major" North American sport leagues and Division-I college sport. Although those U.S. and Canadian leagues and sport organizations will likely continue to be the focus of many students' career aspirations, other sport entities offer exciting and rewarding opportunities. Since the sport industry is constantly evolving, in 10 years new sport organizations (or ones that currently do not even exist) may provide employment opportunities. In 1990 the idea that a national television audience would tune in to freestyle BMX, snow-cross, or snowboarding half-pipe competitions would likely have been considered crazy, but today these and other extreme sports attract large onsite, as well as television and Internet, viewing audiences during the X-Games and DewSport Tour. In addition, several of these sports are now Winter Olympics mainstays.

One of the best resources for students wishing to research organizations and individuals who operate within the sports industry is the *Sports Marketplace Directory*. Most sport management programs will have a copy available for students to examine. Nearly every sport organization has contact information in the 2,200-page *Sports Marketplace Directory,* which makes it a valuable resource.

In addition to "sport" resources, this chapter also provides "general" resources that will guide and inspire students beginning a career in sport management (or another field). The listed resources will hopefully spur students to continue to search for greater knowledge of the industry and the potential roles someone may have during their career. In addition, one section of the chapter provides some personal finance materials that students may find helpful as they transition from college to their professional careers.

Academic Organizations and Conferences

There are currently over 250 sport-management academic programs. Most sport-management programs offer specific courses in some or all of the chapter topics covered in this book. Students have an opportunity to enhance their on-campus education by attending academic conferences related specifically to sport management. There are a variety of academic conferences specifically designed to introduce students to the sport industry and provide networking opportunities. Some of the more prominent conferences that focus on providing undergraduate students with sport-industry information include:

Sport and Entertainment Venues Tomorrow Conference
http://www.sevt.org/
Florida State Sport Management Conference
http://www.coe.fsu.edu/Current-Students/Departments/Sport-Management/SM-Conferences-and-Events/Annual-Conference
Georgia Southern University Sport Management Conference
http://ceps.georgiasouthern.edu/conted/sportconference.html
Southern Sport Management Conference at Troy University
http://ssmassociation.wordpress.com/
Sport Industry Networking and Career Conference at George Washington University
http://www.sinc-conference.com/
Sport Management Student Conference hosted by Robert Morris University
http://sbus.rmu.edu/sport-management/sport-mgmt-conf
Sports Events Marketing Experience Conference hosted by Georgetown University
http://www.seme-now.com/

In addition to conferences developed with undergraduate sport-management students in mind, there also are numerous academic organizations that host conferences intended for graduate students to learn about research being conducted in various areas of sport management. Some of the more well-known organizations that host annual conferences include:

North American Society for Sport Management
http://www.nassm.com/
College Sport Research Institute: Scholarly Conference on College Sport
http://csri-sc.org/
Sport Marketing Association
http://www.sportmarketingassociation.com/
Sport and Recreation Law Association
http://www.srlawebsite.com/
Sport Management in Australia and New Zealand
http://www.smaanz.org/
European Association for Sport Management
http://www.easm.net/
Asian Association for Sport Management
http://aasm.ntsu.edu.tw/

World Association for Sport Management
http://www.worldsportmanagement.org/
African Sport Management Association
http://www.asma-online.org/
American Alliance for Health, Physical Education, Recreation, and Dance
http://www.aahperd.org/

Professional Organizations

Industry organizations also provide excellent opportunities to network with industry professionals and begin to understand the challenges facing the sport-management industry. Most "practitioner" organizations host a national conference every year and may sponsor local or regional conferences as well. Most industry professionals will attend at least one of their industry conferences and students can often attend at a reduced rate. Students should investigate the many ways professional organizations provide career-development opportunities. Compiling a "complete" list of professional sport-management organizations and conferences is certainly difficult, but here are some prominent sport-industry organizations and conferences:

Sport and Entertainment Venues Tomorrow Conference
http://www.sevt.org/
Athletic Business Conference
http://athleticbusinessconference.com/
National Collegiate Athletic Association
http://www.ncaa.org/
National Sports Forum
http://www.sports-forum.com/
Stadium Managers Association
http://www.stadiummanagers.org/
International Association of Venue Managers
http://www.iavm.org/
IMG World Congress of Sports
http://www.sportsbusinessdaily.com/Conferences-Events/2014/2014-IMG-World-Congress-Of-Sports.aspx
Travel, Events and Management in Sports
http://www.teamsconference.com/
Sport Lawyers Association Conference
http://www.sportslaw.org/index.cfm
National Association of Collegiate Women Athletic Administrators
https://www.nacwaa.org/
1A Athletic Directors' Association
http://www.d-1a.com

National Association of Collegiate Directors of Athletics
http://www.nacda.com/
(NOTE: NACDA coordinates and administers a variety of sub-organizations related to different athletic departments and athletic-department functional areas)
Collegiate Athletic Business Management Association
http://www.nacda.com/cabma/nacda-cabma.html
Collegiate Event and Facility Management Association
http://www.nacda.com/cefma/nacda-cefma.html
Division I-AAA Athletic Directors Association
http://www.nacda.com/div1aaaada/nacda-div1aaaada.html
Division II Athletic Directors Association
http://www.nacda.com/div2ada/nacda-div2ada.html
Football Championship Subdivision Athletic Directors Association
http://www.nacda.com/div1aaada/nacda-div1aaada.html
International Collegiate Licensing Association
http://www.nacda.com/icla/nacda-icla.html
Minority Opportunities Athletic Association
http://www.nacda.com/moaa/nacda-moaa.html
National Association for Athletics Compliance
http://www.nacda.com/naacc/nacda-naacc.html
National Association of Athletic Development Directors
http://www.nacda.com/naadd/nacda-naadd.html
National Association of Collegiate Marketing Administrators
http://www.nacda.com/nacma/nacda-nacma-main.html
National Alliance of Two-Year College Athletic Administrators
http://www.nacda.com/natycaa/nacda-natycaa.html

Professional Periodicals and Blogs

Although magazines such as *Sports Illustrated* and *The Sporting News* have been prominent sport publications for many years, they have traditionally focused solely on the "action on the field." Recently these publications, as well as daily newspapers such as the *Wall Street Journal* and the *USA Today*, have begun to more extensively cover sport business. Students are strongly encouraged to regularly check these periodicals for information regarding important sport business issues. In addition, it is important to remain abreast of local sport-business activities. Certainly, students should regularly read their local newspaper as well as their local Business Journal (if there is one) for information concerning the business of sport.

Since 1997, Street & Smith's has published the *SportsBusiness Journal*. Since its inception, the *SportsBusiness Journal* has been the "Bible" for weekly sport business information and in-depth coverage of events. The *SportsBusiness Daily* also provides daily online information regarding sport business news. In addition to its afternoon publication, the *Daily* also provides a "Morning Buzz" and "Closing Bell" which enable readers to remain appraised of any breaking news in the industry. The Closing Bell provides links to newspaper and magazine stories concerning sport business from around the United States and Canada. Most sport-management professionals read the *Journal* and the *Daily* and students should make reading them a regular part of their professional activities. In addition to publishing the *Journal* and the *Daily,* Street & Smith's SportsBusiness Group also publishes a *SportBusiness Resource Guide and Fact Book,* which contains extensive information regarding the sport industry.

There are a variety of publications that cover subareas of the sport-management industry. Though the number of periodicals continues to expand each month, some of the established publications include the following:

Athletic Business Magazine
Online access: http://www.athleticbusiness.com
Athletic Management
Online access: http://www.athleticmanagement.com/
Facility Manager Magazine.
Online access: http://www.iavm.org/facility-manager
PanStadia International
Online Access: http://www.psam.uk.com/
Sport Travel Magazine
Online access: http://www.sportstravelmagazine.com/
Stadia Magazine
Online Access: http://www.stadia-magazine.com
Venues Today Magazine
Online access: http://www.venuestoday.com (subscription required)

The proliferation of Internet blogs and news clips services has created a nearly limitless amount of available content and information. There are now hundreds of sport and sport-business blogs. Though it would be nearly impossible to list every website that may contain pertinent information some of the most well-known sport-business sites include:

CollegeAthleticsClips
http://collegeathleticsclips.com/
SportsBiz
http://thesportsbizblog.blogspot.com/
Sports Law Blog
http://sports-law.blogspot.com/

Sports Media Watch
http://www.sportsmediawatch.com/
The Big Lead
http://thebiglead.com/
The Sports Economist
http://www.thesportseconomist.com/

Academic Journals

The following is a list of academic journals that publish research specifically related to certain aspects of the sport industry. These journals typically are designed for "academic" rather than "professional" audiences, though some offer specific articles, book reviews, or commentaries that are written for practitioners. Most of the journals are tailored to a specific sport-management subarea.

Applied Research in Coaching and Athletics Annual
Australian and New Zealand Sports Law Journal
Chronicle of Kinesiology and Physical Education in Higher Education
Coach and Athletic Director
DePaul Journal of Sports Law & Contemporary Problems
Entertainment and Sports Law Journal
Entertainment and Sports Lawyer
European Journal for Sport and Society
European Journal of Sport Management (now *ESPQ*)
European Sport Management Quarterly
Florida Entertainment, Art & Sport Law Journal
Global Sport Management
ICHPER-SD Journal of Research (International Council for Health, Physical Education, Recreation, Sport, & Dance)
International Journal of Applied Sports Science
International Journal of Sport
International Journal of Sport and Exercise Psychology
International Journal of Sport Communication
International Journal of Sport Management
International Journal of Sport Management and Marketing
International Journal of Sport Policy
International Journal of Sports Finance
International Journal of Sports Marketing & Sponsorship
International Journal of the History of Sport
International Review for the Sociology of Sport
International Sports Law Journal

International Sports Studies
Journal for the Study of Sports and Athletics in Education
Journal of Contemporary Athletics
Journal of Hospitality, Leisure, Sport and Tourism Education (JoHLSTE)
Journal of Intercollegiate Sport
Journal of Issues in Intercollegiate Athletics
Journal of Legal Aspects of Sport
Journal of Physical Education, Recreation, & Dance (JOPERD)
Journal of Quantitative Analysis in Sports
Journal of Sponsorship
Journal of Sport & Tourism
Journal of Sport Administration & Supervision
Journal of Sport and Social Issues
Journal of Sport History
Journal of Sport Management
Journal of Sports Economics
Journal of Sports Law & Contemporary Problems
Journal of Sports Media
Journal of Sports Sciences
Journal of the Philosophy of Sport
Journal of Venue & Event Management
Korean Journal of Sport Management
Legal Issues in College Athletics
Marquette Sports Law Review
Michigan State University College of Law Entertainment and Sports Law Journal
National Intramural-Recreational Sports Association Journal (NIRSA Journal)
NISR Journal of Sport Reform
Quest
Recreational Sports Journal
Research Quarterly for Exercise and Sport
Seton Hall Journal of Sport Law
Sport, Business and Management: An International Journal
Sport Management and Related Topics (SMART) Online Journal
Sociology of Sport Journal
Sport History Review
Sport in History
Sport in Society
Sport Journal
Sport Management Education Journal
Sport Management Review
Sport Marketing Quarterly

Sport, Education, & Society
Sporting Traditions, the journal of the Australian Society for Sports History
Sports and Entertainment Litigation Reporter
Sports Lawyers Journal
Sports, Park and Recreation Law Reporter
Texas Review of Entertainment & Sports Law
The Sports Law Forum at Fordham University School of Law
University of Miami Entertainment and Sports Law Review
Villanova Sports & Entertainment Law Journal
Virginia Sports and Entertainment Law Journal
Willamette Sports Law Journal
Women in Sport and Physical Activity Journal

Sport-Management Topics

The following sections of this chapter provide resources for various topics directly or indirectly related to pursuing a career in sport management. For each area, the potential list of resources could be nearly limitless as excellent resources are published each day. Each of the subareas contains selected works that may help a person (1) find a sport-management job, (2) advance in his or her career, (3) understand the history or current operations in a specific area of sport management, and (4) better handle the rigors of being a professional in an ever-changing environment. Some of the resources are from the "popular press" while others are written for an "academic" audience. The listing of both types of resources is consistent with the book's overriding goal to link theory and practice in the sport-management industry.

Personal Finance

As a student, personal finance may not seem like an important topic and it may seem odd to have a list of books covering finance before the sections discussion finding a full-time position. For many of you reading this book, earning a full-time salary may not occur until a few years into the future. For most students, saving, investing, and retirement are not typically discussed on college campuses. However, it is important to begin planning for your financial future IMMEDIATELY—even if you do not currently have a full-time job or any savings. One of the best ways for students to prepare for their financial future (and their eventual retirement) is to start thinking about spending habits—particularly if most purchases are currently made on credit. Digging a financial hole through excessive spending for "unnecessary" items will eventually cause potential problems.

The following books provide some guidance regarding personal finance:

Chatzky, J.S. (2001). *Talking Money: Everything You Need to Know About Your Finances and Your Future.* New York: Warner Books, Inc.

Kiyosaki, R.T., & Lechter, S.L. (2000). *Rich Dad, Poor Dad: What the Rich Teach Their Kids About Money—That the Poor and Middle Class Do Not!* Paradise Valley, AZ: Techpress, Inc.

Levitt, A. (2003). *Take on the Street: How to Fight for Your Financial Future.* New York: Knopf Publishing Group.

Orman, S. (2005). *The Money Book for the Young, Fabulous, & Broke.* New York: The Penguin Group.

Ramsey, D. (2003). *The Total Money Makeover: A Proven Plan for Financial Fitness.* Nashville, TN: Thomas Nelson, Inc.

Stanley, T.J., & Danko, W.D. (1996). *The Millionaire Next Door.* New York: Pocket Books.

Starting Your Career

As you begin to think about securing an internship and a job in the sport industry, it is important to know where you will be applying. One of the most important aspects of seeking a position is to research the industry and the organization you would like to pursue. After researching potential organizations, you should better understand the organization and be able to provide the organization with information about your history, skills, and abilities. In most cases, a potential employer will expect to receive a cover letter and resume before deciding to interview an applicant. In the sport industry, hundreds of people are often applying for each internship or job with a specific organization. In such a competitive marketplace, having a strong, yet concise, cover letter and a well-designed resume are critical.

There are hundreds of how-to books on resume writing. Certainly, a resume should be tailored for the desired position. In most cases, a resume's style or format is not as important as making sure it is well organized, is free from spelling and grammar errors, and utilizes action verbs to demonstrate your responsibilities in previous positions. The website *quintcareers.com* offers a variety of resume instructions. Their site that details action verbs is especially informative: *http://www.quintcareers.com/action_verbs.html.*

The following resume and cover letter books may also be helpful:

Bennett, S. (2005). *The Elements of Resume Style: Essential Rules and Eye-Opening Advice for Writing Resumes and Cover Letters that Work.* New York: AMACOM.

Hizer, D., & Rosenberg, A. (2007). *The Resume Handbook: How to Write Outstanding Resumes and Cover Letters for Every Situation.* Avon, MA: Adams Media Corporation.

Ireland, S. (2006). *The Complete Idiot's Guide to the Perfect Resume* (4th ed.). New York: The Penguin Group.

Karsh, B., & Pike, C. (2009). *How to Say It on Your Resume: A Top Recruiting Director's Guide to Writing the Perfect Resume for Every Job.* New York: The Penguin Group.

Whitcomb, S.B. (2006). *Resume Magic: Trade Secrets of a Professional Resume Writer.* Indianapolis, IN: JIST Works

Securing the First Sport Management Opportunity

Of course, writing the "perfect" cover letter and resume is only one part of securing an internship or a job. Other crucial components to launching a successful career include preparing for an interview and researching what to ask for if an offer is made. The following books provide tips on identifying jobs, preparing for interviews, and negotiating salaries:

Dell, D. (2009). *Never Make the First Offer (except When You Should).* New York: Penguin Books.

DeLuca, M.J. (1996). *Best Answers to the 201 Most Frequently Asked Interview Questions.* New York: McGraw-Hill Publishing Company.

Fisher, R., & Ury, W. (1991). *Getting to Yes* (2nd ed.). New York: Penguin Books.

Investor's Business Daily. (2004). *Sports Leaders & Success: 55 Top Sports Leaders & How They Achieved Greatness.* New York: McGraw-Hill Publishing Company.

Krantman, S. (2007). *The Resume Writers Workbook, 3E: Marketing Yourself Throughout the Job Search Process.* Cincinnati, OH: South-Western Educational Publishing.

Levinson, J.C., & Perry, D. (2005). *Guerrilla Marketing for Job Hunters: 400 Unconventional Tips, Tricks, and Tactics for Landing Your Dream Job.* Hoboken, NJ: Wiley Publishing Company.

Mackay, H. (1999). *Dig Your Well Before You're Thirsty: The Only Networking Book You'll Ever Need.* New York: Doubleday.

Oliver, V. (2005). *301 Smart Answers to Tough Interview Questions.* Naperville, IL: Sourcebooks, Inc.

Powers, P. (2004). *Winning Job Interviews: Reduce Interview Anxiety/Outprepare the Other Candidates/Land the Job You Love.* Franklin Lakes, NJ: The Career Press, Inc.

Robinson, M.J., Hums, M.A., Crow, B., & Phillips, D.R. (2000). *Profiles of Sport Industry Professionals: The People Who Make the Games Happen.* Gaithersburg, MD: Aspen Publishers, Inc.

Shropshire, K.L. (2008). *Negotiate Like the Pros: A Master Sports Negotiator's Lessons for Making Deals, Building Relationships, and Getting What You Want.* New York: McGraw-Hill Publishing Company.

Wong, G.M. (2008). *The Comprehensive Guide to Careers in Sports.* Sudbury, MA: Jones and Bartlett Publishers.

Jobs in Sports Links

The following websites provide information regarding internships and jobs in sports. Many of them charge a fee for access to their listings.

http://www.allsportsdirectory.net/
http://www.athleticlink.com/
http://www.internships-usa.com/
http://www.jobsinsports.com/
http://ncaamarket.ncaa.org/jobs/
http://www.onlinesports.com/pages/CareerCenter.html
http://www.sportscareers.com/
http://www.sportscareerconsulting.com
http://www.teamworkonline.com
http://www.womensportsjobs.com/
http://www.workinsports.com/

Career Advancement Tips

Once you have been able to secure an initial internship or job, it is important to continue to learn and to stay motivated. There are a nearly limitless number of books designed to help with career advancement. The following books are some of the ones that may be helpful:

Chandler, S. (2001). *100 Ways to Motivate Yourself: Change Your Life Forever.* Franklin Lakes, NJ: The Career Press, Inc.

Cuban, M. (2011). *How to Win at the Sport of Business.* New York: Diversion Books.

Johnson, S. (1998). *Who Moved My Cheese?: An Amazing Way to Deal with Change in Your Work and in Your Life.* New York: Penguin Putnam, Inc.

Johnson, S. (2003). *The Present: The Secret to Enjoying Your Work and Life, Now!* New York: Doubleday.

Miller, D. (2004). *48 Days to the Work You Love.* Nashville, TN: Broadman & Holman Publishers.

Miller, D. (2008). *No More Dreaded Mondays: Ignite Your Passion and Other Revolutionary Ways to Discover Your True Calling at Work.* New York: The Doubleday Broadway Publishing Group.

Pink, D.H. (2009). *Drive: The Surprising Truth about What Motivates Us.* New York: The Penguin Group.

Management

Motivating yourself is certainly an important step in career development. However, superior sport managers will be attracted to organizations that are moving in a positive direction and they will work to move their organization forward rather than remaining stagnant. Thousands of books have been written about managing, leading, and motivating. Though certainly not an exhaustive list, the following books provide some "general" insights on these topics:

Bolman, L.G., & Deal, T.E. (1997). *Reframing Organizations: Artistry, Choice, and Leadership* (2nd ed.). San Francisco, CA: Jossey-Bass Publishers.

Brown, W.S. (1987). *13 Fatal Errors Managers Make and How You Can Avoid Them.* New York: The Berkley Publishing Group.

Buckingham, M., & Coffman, C. (1999). *First, Break All the Rules: What the World's Greatest Managers Do Differently.* New York: Simon & Schuster, Inc.

Carnegie, D. (1998). *How to Win Friends & Influence People.* New York: Pocket Books.

Collins, J. (2001). *Good to Great: Why Some Companies Make the Leap . . . and Others Don't.* New York: HarperCollins Publishers, Inc.

Collins, J., & Hansen, M.T. (2011). *Great by Choice: Uncertainty, Chaos, and Luck—Why Some Thrive Despite Them All.* New York: HarperCollins Publishers, Inc.

Collins, J., & Porras, J.I. (2002). *Built to Last: Successful Habits of Visionary Companies.* New York: HarperCollins Publishers, Inc.

Covey, S.R. (2004). *The 7 Habits of Highly Effective People.* New York: Free Press.

Deal, T.E., & Kennedy, A.A. (1982). *Corporate Cultures.* Reading, MA: Addison-Wesley Publishing Company.

Martin, J. (1992). *Cultures in Organizations: Three Perspectives.* New York: Oxford University Press.

Maxwell, J. C. (2007). *The 21 Irrefutable Laws of Leadership: Follow Them and People Will Follow You.* Nashville, TN: Thomas Nelson, Inc.

Russell, B. (2001). *Russell Rules: 11 Lessons on Leadership from the Twentieth Century's Greatest Winner.* New York: Putnam.

Schein, E.H. (1992). *Organizational Culture and Leadership* (2nd ed.). San Francisco: Jossey-Bass Publishers.

Silver, N. (2012). *The Signal and the Noise: Why So Many Predictions Fail—But Some Don't.* New York: Penguin.

Sinek, S. (2011). *Start with Why: How Great Leaders Inspire Everyone to Take Action.* New York: Penguin.

Sinek, S. (2014). *Leaders Eat Last: Why Some Teams Pull Together and Others Don't.* New York: Penguin.

Welch, J. (2003). *Jack: Straight from the Gut.* New York: Warner Books, Inc.

Welch, J. (2005). *Winning.* New York: HarperCollins Publishers, Inc.

Williams, P. (2006). *How to Be Like Coach Wooden: Life Lessons from Basketball's Greatest Leader.* Deerfield Beach, FL: Health Communications, Inc.

Ethics

For many sport-industry professionals a key component of effective management is managing ethically. The following books address ethical dilemmas and provide insights regarding how to be an ethical manager and person:

Badaracco, J.L. (1997). *Defining Moments: When Managers Must Choose Between Right and Right.* Boston: Harvard Business School Press.

Blanchard, K., & O'Connor, M. (1997). *Managing By Values.* San Francisco: Berrett-Koehler Publishers.

Dali Lama, H.H., & Cutler, H.C. (1998). *The Art of Happiness.* New York: Riverhead Books.

Kabat-Zinn, J. (1994). *Wherever You Go There You Are.* New York: Hyperion.

Rachels, J. (1999). *The Elements of Moral Philosophy* (3rd ed.). Boston: McGraw-Hill College.

Rachels, J. (2003). *The Right Thing to Do: Basic Readings in Moral Philosophy* (3rd ed.). Boston: McGraw-Hill College.

Finance

Sport finance is an important area of sport management, but many students are intimidated by the "numbers." Having an understanding of accounting, budgeting, and economics will position a sport-management professional to not only secure an entry-level job, but also more rapidly advance within the organization.

Brown, M.T., Rascher, D.A., Nagel, M.S., & McEvoy, C.D. (2010). *Financial Management in the Sport Industry.* Scottsdale, AZ: Holcomb Hathaway.

Downward, P., & Dawson, A. (2000). *The Economics of Professional Team Sports.* New York: Routledge.

Fizel, J. (2005). *Handbook of Sports Economics Research.* Armonk, NY: M.E. Sharpe, Inc.

Foster, G., Greyser, S.A., & Walsh, B. (2005). *The Business of Sports: Cases and Text on Strategy and Management.* Cincinnati, OH: South-Western College Publishing.

Humphreys, B.R., & Howard, D.R. (2008). *The Business of Sports [Three Volumes]: Volume 1, Perspectives on the Sport Industry; Volume 2, Economic Perspectives on Sport; Volume 3, Bridging Research and Practice (Praeger Perspectives).* New York: Praeger Publishing.

Lewis, M. (2004). *Moneyball: The Art of Winning an Unfair Game.* New York: Norton.

Noll, R.G. (1997). *Sports, Jobs, and Taxes: The Economic Impact of Sports Teams and Stadiums.* Washington, DC: Brookings Institution Press.

Quirk, J., & Fort, R.D. (1997). *Pay Dirt: The Business of Professional Team Sports.* Princeton, NJ: Princeton University Press.

Staudohar, P.D. (1996). *Playing for Dollars: Labor Relations and the Sports Business.* Ithaca, NY: Cornell University Press.

Staudohar, P.D., & Mangan, J.A. (1991). *The Business of Professional Sports.* Champaign, IL: University of Illinois Press.

Weiner, J. (2000). *Stadium Games: Fifty Years of Big League Greed and Bush League Boondoggles.* Minneapolis, MN: University of Minnesota Press.

Zimbalist, A. (2004). *May the Best Team Win: Baseball Economics and Public Policy.* Washington, DC: Brookings

Marketing and Sales

Marketing and sales are the lifeblood of any sport organization. Generating interest and creating customers is critical for the sport industry. The following books discuss marketing and sales in general and, in some cases, apply marketing and sales principles to the sport industry:

Carter, D. (2011). *Money Games: Profiting from the Convergence of Sports and Entertainment*. Palo Alto, CA: Stanford Press.

Cialdini, R.B. (2006). *Influence: The Psychology of Persuasion (Collins Business Essentials).* New York: Harper Paperbacks.

Gitomer, J. (2004). *Little Red Book of Selling: 12.5 Principles of Sales Greatness.* Austin, TX: Bard Press

Gitomer, J. (2008). *The Sales Bible: The Ultimate Sales Resource, New Edition.* New York: HarperCollins Publishers, Inc.

Johnson, S. (2002). *One Minute Sales Person: The Quickest Way to Sell People on Yourself, Your Services, Products, or Ideas—at Work and in Life.* New York: HarperCollins Publishers, Inc.

Levison, J., & Godin, S. (1994). *The Guerilla Marketing Handbook.* Boston: Houghton Mifflin.

Rein, I., Kotler, P., & Shields, B. (2006). *The Elusive Fan: Reinventing Sports in a Crowded Marketplace.* New York: McGraw-Hill Publishing.

Schiffman, S. (1997). *The 25 Most Common Sales Mistakes . . . and How to Avoid Them.* Avon, MA: Adams Media.

Schiffman, S. (2008). *The 25 Sales Habits of Highly Successful Salespeople.* Avon, MA: Adams Media.

Singer, B., & Kiyosaki, R.T. (2001). *Sales Dogs: You Do Not Have to Be an Attack Dog to Be Successful in Sales (Rich Dad's Advisors series).* New York: Warner Business Books.

Spoelstra, J. (1997). *Ice to the Eskimos: How to Market a Product Nobody Wants.* New York: HarperCollins Publishers, Inc.

Spoelstra, J. (2010). *Marketing Outrageously Redux: How to Increase Your Revenue by Staggering Amounts!* Austin, TX: Bard Press.

Veeck, B. (2001). *Veeck as In Wreck: The Audiobiography of Bill Veeck.* Chicago: University of Chicago Press.

Veeck, B. (2009). *The Hustler's Handbook.* Chicago: Ivan R. Dee, Publisher.

Veeck, M., & Williams, P. (2005). *Fun Is Good: How to Create Joy and Passion in Your Workplace & Career.* Rodale.

Ziglar, Z. (2003). *Selling 101: What Every Successful Sales Professional Needs to Know.* Nashville, TN: Thomas Nelson, Inc.

Law

This book has introduced some important legal aspects of sport. A sport-management academic career will likely include additional coursework in sport and business law. As the law continues to play an increasing role in business and the sport industry, it is important to remain aware of important legal concepts. The following books are excellent legal resources:

Clement, A., & Grady, J. (2012). *Law in Sport: Concepts and Xases* (4th ed.). Morgantown, WV: FIT.

Cozzillio, M., & Hayman, J. (2005). *Sports and Inequality.* Durham, NC: Carolina Academic Press.

Day, F.J. (2004). *Clubhouse Lawyer: Law in the World of Sports.* Lincoln, NE: iUniverse, Inc.

Sharp, L.A., Moorman, A.M., & Claussen, C.L. (2010). *Sport Law: A Managerial Approach—Achieving a Competitive Advantage* (2nd ed.). Scottsdale, AZ: Holcomb Hathaway Publishers.

Standen, J. (2008). *Taking Sports Seriously: Law and Sports in Contemporary American Culture.* Durham, NC: Carolina Academic Press.

Weiler, P.C. (2000). *Leveling the Playing Field: How the Law Can Make Sports Better for Fans.* Cambridge, MA: Harvard University Press.

Weiler, P.C., & Roberts, G.R. (2004). *Sports and the Law: Text, Cases and Problems.* Eagan, MN: West Publishing.

Wong, G. (2010). *Essentials of Sports Law* (4th ed.). Santa Barbara, CA: Praeger.

Title IX

When Title IX of the Education Amendments Act was passed into law in 1972 it was not designed to specifically address interscholastic and intercollegiate athletics. However, since sport is a component of most U.S. educational institutions, Title IX has applied to numerous aspects of educational sport. The following books investigate Title IX and its impact upon sport management:

Blumenthal, K. (2005). *Let Me Play: The Story of Title IX: The Law That Changed the Future of Girls in America.* New York: Atheneum Publishers.

Carpenter, L.J., & Acosta, R.V. (2004). *Title IX.* Champaign, IL: Human Kinetics.

Hogshead-Makar, N., & Zimbalist, A. (2007). *Equal Play: Title IX and Social Change.* Philadelphia, PA: Temple University Press.

Suggs, W. (2006). *A Place on the Team: The Triumph and Tragedy of Title IX.* Princeton, NJ: Princeton University Press.

Agents

Though most sport-management programs are not designed to prepare students to become agents, many students desire to enter that field. Attending law school is certainly an important step in understanding contract law and developing the negotiation skills needed to be successful in this highly competitive business. The following resources provide some information about agents, their roles, and the legal environment in which they work:

Argovitz, J., & Miller, J.D. (2013). *Super Agent: The One Book the NFL and NCAA Don't Want You to Read.* New York: Sports Publishing.

Crasnick, J. (2005). *Licensed to Deal.* New York: Holtzbrinck Publishers.

Falk, D. (2009). *The Bald Truth.* New York: Pocket Books.
Luchs, J., & Dale, J. (2012). *Illegal Procedure: A Sports Agent Comes Clean on the Dirty Business of College Football.* New York: Bloomsbury USA.
Rosenhaus, D. (1997). *A Shark Never Sleeps.* New York: Pocket Books.
Rosenhaus, D., & Rosenhaus, J. (2008). *Next Question.* New York: Berkley Publishing.
Ruxin, R.H. (2009). *An Athlete's Guide to Agents* (5th ed.). New York: Jones and Bartlett.
Shropshire, K.L., & Davis, T. (2008). *The Business of Sports Agents* (2nd ed.). Philadelphia, PA: University of Pennsylvania Press.
Stein, M. (2008). *How to Be a Sports Agent.* New York: High Stakes.
Steinberg, L., & Arkush, M. (2014). *The Agent: My 40-Year Career Making Deals and Changing the Game*. New York: St. Martin's Press.

Sociology of Sport

The sociology of sport involves examining sport in the context of social interactions and sport as a social construction of the people, organizations, and groups involved in sport. Examining sport as a social construction usually occurs from one of three basic paradigms: functionalism, critical theory, and conflict theory.

Adler, P.A. (1991). *Blackboards and Blackboards.* New York: Columbia University Press.
Anderson, E. (2005). *In the Game: Gay Athletes and the Cult of Masculinity.* Albany, NY: State University of New York Press.
Benedict, J., & Yaeger, D. (1998). *Pros and Cons: The criminals who play in the NFL.* New York: Warner Books.
Bissinger, H.G. (2000). *Friday Night Lights: A Town, a Team, and a Dream.* New York: Da Capo Press.
Coakley, J. (2008). *Sports in Society: Issues and Controversies* (10th ed.). New York: McGraw-Hill Humanities
Crawford, G. (2004). *Consuming Sport: Fans, Sport and Culture*. New York: Taylor and Francis.
Echikson, W. (2009). *Shooting for Tiger: How Golf's Obsessed New Generation Is Transforming a Country Club Sport.* New York: Nation Books.
Eitzen, D.S. & Sage, G.H. (2008). *Sociology of North American Sport* (8th ed.). Boulder, CO: Paradigm Publishers
Entine, J. (2001). *Taboo: Why Black Athletes Dominate Sports and Why We're Afraid to Talk About It.* New York: PublicAffairs.

Gems, G.R. (2006). *The Athletic Crusade: Sport and American Cultural Imperialism.* Lincoln, NE: University of Nebraska Press.

Guttmann, A. (2004). *From Ritual to Record: The Nature of Modern Sports.* New York: Columbia University Press.

Hawkins, B. (2010). *The New Plantation: Black Athletes, College Sports, and Predominately White NCAA Institutions.* New York: Palgrave Macmillan.

Higgs, R.J. (1998). *God in the Stadium: Sports and Religion in America.* Lexington, KY: The University Press of Kentucky.

Hubbard, S. (1998). *Faith in Sports: Athletes and Their Religion On and Off the Field.* New York: Doubleday.

Hyman, M. (2010). *Until It Hurts: America's Obsession with Youth Sports and How It Harms Our Kids*. Boston: Beacon Press.

Kopay, D., & Young, P.D. (2001). *David Kopay Story: An Extraordinarily Self-Revelation.* New York: Alyson Publications.

Messner, M.A., & Sabo, D.F. (1994). *Sex, Violence & Power in Sports: Rethinking Masculinity.* Freedom, CA: The Crossing Press.

Miracle, A.W., & Rees, R.C. (1994). *Lessons of the Locker Room: The Myth of School Sports.* New York: Prometheus Books

Nixon, H.L., & Frey, J.H. (1996). *Sociology of Sport.* Beverly, MA: Wadsworth Publishing.

Powell, S. (2007). *Souled Out? How Blacks Are Winning and Losing in Sports.* Champaign, IL: Human Kinetics.

Rhoden, W.C. (2006). *Forty Million Dollar Slaves: The Rise, Fall, and Redemption of the Black Athlete.* New York: Crown Publishers.

Ruck, R. (2012). *Raceball: How the Major Leagues Colonized the Black and Latin Game*. Boston: Beacon Press.

Ryan, J. (1995). *Little Girls in Pretty Boxes.* New York: Warner Books.

Sage, G.H. (1998). *Power and Ideology in American Sport.* Champaign, IL: Human Kinetics.

Smith, E. (2007). *Race, Sport and the American Dream.* Durham, NC: Carolina Academic Press.

Spindel, C. (2002). *Dancing at Halftime: Sports and the Controversy over Native American Mascots.* New York: New York University Press.

Wetzel, D., & Yaeger, D. (2000). *Sole Influence: Basketball, Corporate Greed, and the Corruption of America's Youth.* New York: Grand Central Publishing.

Wiggins, D.K. (1997). *Glory Bound: Black Athletes in a White America.* Syracuse, NY: Syracuse University Press.

Wolfe, T. (2004). *I Am Charlotte Simmons.* New York: Picador.

Yaeger, D. (2007). *It's Not about the Truth: The Untold Story of the Duke Lacrosse Case and the Lives It Shattered.* New York: Simon & Schuster.

Globalization and Sport

Sport is a global phenomenon that extends beyond national boundaries. Students should be well versed in the structures, institutions, and processes that constitute sport in the global marketplace. The way sport is constructed, by whom, and for what purpose, reflects the economic, technological, and cultural forces at work in any given country. Students should not limit their sport-industry aspirations to just their local environment, but should be open to exploring opportunities around the globe. With international sporting organizations and professional leagues in numerous sports from all over world vying to expand into foreign markets, tomorrow's sport managers will have numerous opportunities to excel in the global sport marketplace.

Friedman, T.L. (2000). *The Lexus and the Olive Tree: Understanding Globalization.* New York: Anchor Books.

Friedman, T.L. (2007). *The World Is Flat: A Brief History of the Twenty-first Century.* New York: Picador.

Foer, F. (2005). *How Soccer Explains the World: An Unlikely Theory of Globalization.* New York: HarperCollins Publishers, Inc.

Gems, G.R., Borish, L.J., & Pfister, G. (2008). *Sports in American History: From Colonization to Globalization.* Champaign, IL: Human Kinetics.

Horne, J., & Manzenreiter, W. (2006). *Sports Mega-events: Social Scientific Analyses of a Global Phenomenon*. Hoboken, NJ: Wiley.

Kuper, S., & Szymanski, S. (2014). *Soccernomics: Why England Loses, Why Spain, Germany, and Brazil Win, and Why the U.S., Japan, Australia—and Even Iraq—Are Destined to Become the Kings of the World's Most Popular Sport*. New York: Nation Books.

Maguire, J., & Falcous, M. (2010). *Sport and Migration: Borders, Boundaries and Crossings*. New York: Taylor and Francis.

Markovits, A.S., & Rensman, L. (2010). *Gaming the World: How Sports Are Reshaping Global Politics and Culture*. Princeton, NJ: Princeton University Press.

Sage, G. H. (2011). *Globalizing Sport: How Organizations, Corporations, Media, and Politics Are Changing Sports*. Boulder, CO: Paradigm Publishers.

Szymanski, S., & Zimbalist, A. (2006). *National Pastime: How Americans Play Baseball and the Rest of the World Plays Soccer.* Washington, DC: Brookings Institution Press.

Whiting, R. (2009). *You Gotta Have Wa.* New York: Vintage Books.

Whiting, R. (2004). *The Meaning of Ichiro: The New Wave from Japan and the Transformation of Our National Pastime.* New York: Time Warner Book Group.

Zirin, D. (2014). *Brazil's Dance with the Devil: The World Cup, the Olympics, and the Fight for Democracy*. Chicago: Haymarket Books.

Sport History

Sport-management students should seek to understand sport in relation to the social lives of the people who created, defined, played, and integrated it into their everyday experiences. A historical examination of sport focuses on what sport can tell us about relationships among various groups of people at particular times and places. However, when students engage in historical review, it is important to remember that history is most often written by the "winners," and sport history publications have often been gender-biased. Therefore, it may be appropriate for students to investigate alternative and non-mainstream historical accounts in order to broaden their historical perspectives.

Davies, R.O. (2007). *Sports in American Life: A History.* Hoboken, NJ: Wiley-Blackwell Publishing.

Fainaru-Wada, M., & Fainaru, S. (2013). *League of Denial: The NFL, Concussions, and the Battle for Truth.* New York: Penguin.

Fainaru-Wada, M., & Williams, L. (2007). *Game of Shadows: Barry Bonds, BALCO, and the Steroids Scandal That Rocked Professional Sports.* New York: Penguin.

Fitzpatrick, F. (1999). *And the Walls Came Tumbling Down: Kentucky, Texas Western, and the Game That Changed American Sports.* New York: Simon & Schuster.

Gorn, E.J. (2004). *A Brief History of American Sports.* Champaign, IL: University of Illinois Press.

Guttmann, A. (1992). *Women's Sports: A History.* New York: Columbia University Press.

Guttmann, A. (1996). *Games and Empires: Modern Sports and Cultural Imperialism.* New York: Columbia University Press.

Guttmann, A. (2004). *From Ritual to Record: The Nature of Modern Sports.* New York: Columbia University Press.

Jacobs, T., & Roberts, R. (2003). *100 Athletes Who Shaped Sports History.* San Mateo, CA: Bluewood Books.

Martin, C. (2010). *Benching Jim Crow: The Rise and Fall of the Color Line in Southern College Sports, 1890-1980.* Champaign, IL: University of Illinois Press.

Rosen, D.M. (2008). *Dope: A History of Performance Enhancement in Sports from the Nineteenth Century to Today.* Westport, CT: Praeger Publishers.

Ross, C.K. (2001). *Outside the Lines: African Americans and the Integration of the National Football League.* New York: New York University Press.

Sports Illustrated. (2004). *Fifty Years of Great Writing: 50th Anniversary 1954–2004.* New York: Sports Illustrated Publishing.

Travers, S.L. (2007). *One Night, Two Teams: Alabama vs. USC and the Game That Changed a Nation.* Lanham, MD: Taylor Trade Publishing.

Zirin, D. (2007). *Welcome to the Terrordome: The Pain, Politics and Promise of Sports.* Chicago: Haymarket Books.

Zirin, D., & Zinn, H. (2008). *A People's History of Sports in the United States: From Bull-Baiting to Barry Bonds . . . 250 Years of Politics, Protest, People, and Play.* New York: The New Press.

Resources and Literature Specific to Certain Sports

The following sections provide helpful links and other resources specific to certain sports and/or organizations. Since the "Big Four" professional leagues are extremely popular in the United States there are many resources devoted to the history and business operation in the MLB, NBA, NHL, and NFL. However, as "emerging" sports continue to grow, more authors are devoting time and attention to the development and marketing of those sports. The authors strongly encourage feedback from readers regarding "missing" pertinent sport management resources. Though this chapter's list of resources is extensive, there are likely valuable resources that have been omitted.

Baseball

baseballamerica.com
mlb.mlb.com/home
collegiatebaseball.com
http://www.milb.com/index.jsp
PBEO.com
http://www.baseball-links.com/

Asinof, E. (2000). *Eight Men Out: The Black Sox and the 1919 World Series.* New York: Holt Paperbacks.

Blahnick, J. (1995). *Mud Hens and Mavericks.* New York: Viking Studio Books.

Feinstein, J. (1993). *Play Ball: The Life and Troubled Times of Major League Baseball.* New York: Random House, Inc.

Halberstam, D. (1989). *Summer of '49.* New York: HarperCollins Publishers, Inc.

Halberstam, D. (1995). *October 1964.* New York: Fawcett Books.

Halberstam, D., & Richmond, P. (1992). *Baseball: The Perfect Game.* New York: Rizzoli Publications.

Helyar, J. (1995). *Lords of the Realm.* New York: Random House.

James, B. (1995). *Whatever Happened to the Hall of Fame?* New York: Free Press.

James, B. (1997). *The Bill James Guide to Baseball Managers: From 1870 to Today.* New York: Scribner Publishing.

James, B. (2003). *The New Bill James Historical Baseball Abstract.* New York: The Free Press.

Kahn, R. (2006). *The Boys of Summer.* New York: Harper Perennial Modern Classics.

Keri, J. (2007). *Baseball Between the Numbers: Why Everything We Know about the Game Is Wrong.* New York: Basic Books.

Keri, J. (2011). *The Extra 2%: How Wall Street Strategies Took a Major League Baseball Team from Worst to First.* New York: Random House.

Lamster, M. (2007). *Spalding's World Tour: The Epic Adventure that Took Baseball around the Globe—And Made It America's Game.* New York: PublicAffairs.

Marshall, W. (1999). *Baseball's Pivotal Era, 1945–1951.* Lexington, KY: The University Press of Kentucky.

Miller, M. (1991). *A Whole Different Ballgame.* New York: Carol Publishing Group.

Neyer, R. (2003). *Rob Neyer's Big Book of Baseball Lineups: A Complete Guide to the Best, Worst, and Most Memorable Players to Ever Grace the Major Leagues.* New York: Fireside.

Neyer, R., & James, B. (2004). *The Neyer/James Guide to Pitchers: An Historical Compendium of Pitching, Pitchers, and Pitches.* New York: Fireside.

Neyer, R., & Epstein, E. (2000). *Baseball Dynasties: The Greatest Teams of All Time.* New York: W. W. Norton & Company, Inc.

Neyer, R., & Schwarz, A. (2007). *How Bill James Changed Our View of the Game of Baseball.* Skokie, IL: ACTA Sports.

Peterson, R. (1992). *Only the Ball Was White: A History of Legendary Black Players and All-Black Professional Teams.* New York: Oxford University Press.

Schwarz, A., & Gammons, P. (2005). *The Numbers Game: Baseball's Lifelong Fascination with Statistics.* New York: St. Martin's Press.

Seymour, H. (1989). *Baseball: The Early Years.* New York: Oxford University Press.

Seymour, H. (1989). *Baseball: The Golden Age.* New York: Oxford University Press.

Seymour, H. (1991). *Baseball: The People's Game.* New York: Oxford University Press.

Snyder. B. (2006). *A Well-Paid Slave: Curt Flood's Fight for Free Agency in Professional Baseball.* New York: Plume Books.

Sowell, M. (2004). *The Pitch That Killed.* Chicago: Ivan R. Dee, Publisher.

Will, G. F. (1991). *Men at Work: The Craft of Baseball.* New York: HarperCollins Publishing.

Football

Nfl.com
http://www.football-links.com/
Afca.com

Benedict, J., & Keteyian, A. (2013). *The System: The Glory and Scancal of Big-time College Football*. New York: Random House.

Davis, J. (2007). *Rozelle: Czar of the NFL*. New York: McGraw-Hill Publishing Company.

Dunnavant, K. (2004). *The Fifty-year Seduction: How Television Manipulated College Football, from Birth of the Modern NCAA to the Creation of the BCS*. New York: St. Martin's Press.

Easterbrook, G. (2013). *The King of Sports: Football's Impact on America*. New York: St. Martin's Press.

Felser, L. (2008). *The Birth of the New NFL: How the 1966 NFL/AFL Merger Transformed Pro Football*. Guilford, CT: The Lyons Press.

Harris, D. (1986). *The League: The Rise and Decline of the NFL*. New York: Bantam Books.

Maraniss, D. (2000). *When Pride Still Mattered: A Life of Vince Lombardi*. New York: Simon & Schuster.

Meggyesy, D. (1971). *Out of Their League*. New York: Paperback Library.

Mortensen, C. (1991). *Playing for Keeps: How One Man Kept the Mob from Sinking Its Hooks into Pro Football*. New York: Simon & Schuster.

Oriard, M. (2007). *Brand NFL: Making and Selling America's Favorite Sport*. Chapel Hill, NC: The University of North Carolina Press.

Oriard, M. (2007). *King Football: Sport and Spectacle in the Golden Age of Radio and Newsreels, Movies and Magazines, the Weekly and the Daily Press*. Chapel Hill, NC: The University of North Carolina Press.

Oriard, M. (2009). *Bowled Over: Big-Time College Football from the Sixties to the BCS Era*. Chapel Hill, NC: The University of North Carolina Press.

Oriard, M. (2009). *The End of Autumn: Reflections on My Life in Football*. Champaign, IL: University of Illinois Press.

Yost, M. (2006). *Tailgating, Sacks, and Salary Caps: How the NFL Became the Most Successful Sports League in History*. Chicago: Kaplan Publishing.

Basketball

nba.com
fiba.com
http://www.infosportinc.com/h-links.html

Axthelm, P. (1999). *The City Game: From the Garden to the Playgrounds*. New York: Buccaneer Books.

Boyd, T. (2003). *Young, Black, Rich & Famous: The Rise of the NBA, the Hip Hop Culture Invasion, and the Transformation of American Culture.* Lincoln, NE: University of Nebraska Press.
Halberstam, D. (2000). *Playing for Keeps: Michael Jordan and the World He Made.* New York: Broadway Books.
Halberstam, D. (2009). *The Breaks of the Game.* New York: Hyperion.
Ham, E.L. (2000). *The Playmasters: From Sellouts to Lockouts—An Unauthorized History of the NBA.* Chicago: Contemporary Books.
Lane, J. (2007). *Under the Boards: The Cultural Revolution in Basketball.* Lincoln, NE: University of Nebraska Press.
Mallozzi, V.M. (2003). *Asphalt Gods: An Oral History of the Rucker Tournament.* New York: Doubleday.
McCallum, J. (2012). *Dream Team: How Michael, Magic, Charles, and the Greatest Team of All Time Conquered the World and the Game of Basketball.* New York: Random House.
Pluto, T. (1991). *Loose Balls: The Short, Wild Life of the American Basketball Association.* New York: Simon & Schuster.
Pluto, T. (2000). *Tall Tales: The Glory Years of the NBA.* Lincoln, NE: Bison Books.
Pomerantz, G.M. (2006). *Wilt 1962: The Night of 100 Points and the Dawn of a New Era.* New York: Three River Press.
Rosen, C. (2003). *The Wizard of Odds: How Jack Molinas Almost Destroyed the Game of Basketball.* New York: Seven Stories Press.
Rosen, C. (2008). *The First Tip-Off: The Incredible Story of the Birth of the NBA.* New York: McGraw-Hill Publishing Company.
Simmons, B. (2009). *The Big Book of Basketball: The NBA According to the Sports Guy.* New York: ESPN Books.
Smith, S. (1993). *The Jordan Rules.* New York: Pocket Books.

Hockey

nhl.com
TheAHL.com
http://www.kuklaskorner.com/index.php/hockey/hockey_links/
Conway, R. (1997). *Game Misconduct: Alan Eagleson and the Corruption of Hockey.* Toronto, ON: Macfarlane Walter & Ross.
Cruise, D., & Griffiths, A. (1992). *Net Worth—Exploding the Myths of Pro Hockey.* New York: The Penguin Press.
Dowbiggin, B. (2003). *Money Players: How Hockey's Greatest Stars Beat the NHL at Its Own Game.* Toronto, ON: Macfarlane Walter & Ross.
Dowbiggin, B. (2007). *Money Players: The Amazing Rise and Fall of Bob Goodenow and the NHL Players Association.* Toronto, ON: Key Porter Books.

Fischler, S. (1995). *Cracked Ice: An Insider's Look at the NHL in Turmoil.* Darby, PA: Diane Publishing Company.

Jenish, D. (2013). *The NHL: 100 Years of On-ice Action and Boardroom Battles*. Toronto: Doubleday Canada.

Stein, G. (1997). *Power Plays: An Inside Look at the Big Business of the National Hockey League.* New York: Birch Lane Press.

Willes, E. (2005). *The Rebel League: The Short and Unruly Life of the World Hockey Association.* Toronto, ON: McClelland & Stewart.

NASCAR

NASCAR.com

Clarke, L. (2008). *One Helluva Ride: How NASCAR Swept the Nation.* New York: Villard Publishing.

Fielden, G. (2007). *NASCAR: The Complete History.* Lincolnwood, IL: Publications International, Ltd.

Golenbock, P. (1994). *American Zoom: Stock Car Racing—From the Dirt Tracks to Daytona.* New York: Macmillan Publishing Company.

Golenbock, P. (2001). *The Last Lap: The Life and Times of NASCAR's Legendary Heroes, Updated Edition.* New York: Hungry Minds, Inc.

Golenbock, P. (2004). *NASCAR Confidential: Stories of the Men and Women Who Made Stock Car Racing Great.* St. Paul, MN: Motorbooks International.

Hagstrom, R. G. (2001). *The NASCAR Way: The Business That Drives the Sport.* Hoboken, NJ: Wiley Publishing.

Menzer, J. (2002). *The Wildest Ride: A History of NASCAR (or, How a Bunch of Good Ol' Boys Built a Billion-Dollar Industry out of Wrecking Cars).* New York: Touchstone.

Miller, G. W. (2009). *Men and Speed. A Wild Ride Through NASCAR's Breakout Season*. New York: Nation Books.

Thompson, N. (2007). *Driving with the Devil: Southern Moonshine, Detroit Wheels, and the Birth of NASCAR.* New York: Three Rivers Press.

Yost, M., & Williams, B. (2007). *The 200-MPH Billboard: The Inside Story of How Big Money Changed NASCAR.* St. Paul, MN: Motorbooks International.

Soccer

http://www.fifa.com/
http://www.ussoccer.com/
http://www.ayso.org/
http://www.womensoccer.com/

http://www.socceramerica.com/

Chadwick, S., & Hamil, S. (2010). *Managing Football: An International Perspective.* Oxford: Elsevier.

Desbordes, M. (2006). *Marketing and Football: An International Perspective.* Burlington, MA: Butterworth-Heinemann.

Dobson, S., & Goddard, J. (2001). *The Economics of Football.* New York: Cambridge University Press.

Galeano, E. (2013). *Soccer in Light and Shadow.* New York: Nation Books.

Goldblatt, D. (2008). *The Ball Is Round: A Global History of Soccer.* New York: Riverhead Books.

Goldblatt, D. (2014). *Futebol Nation: The Story of Brazil through Soccer.* New York: Nation Books.

Kuper, S., & Szymanski, S. (2009). *Soccernomics: Why England Loses, Why Germany and Brazil Win, and Why the U.S., Japan, Australia, Turkey—and Even Iraq—Are Destined to Become the Kings of the World's Most Popular Sport.* New York: Nation Books.

Markovits, A.S., & Hellerman, S.L. (2001). *Offside: Soccer and American Exceptionalism.* Princeton, NJ: Princeton University Press.

College Sport

NCAA.com

NCAA.org

NAIA.org

NJCAA.org

Rivals.com

Byers, W., & Hammer, C. (1995). *Unsportsmanlike Conduct: Exploiting College Athletes.* Ann Arbor, MI: University of Michigan Press.

Clotfelter, C.T. (2011). *Big-time Sports in American Universities.* New York: Cambridge University Press.

Duderstadt, J.J. (2003). *Intercollegiate Athletics and the American University: A University President's Perspective.* Ann Arbor, MI: The University of Michigan Press.

Einhorn, E., & Rapoport, R. (2006). *How March Became Madness: How the NCAA Tournament Became the Greatest Sporting Event in America.* Chicago: Triumph Books.

Gerdy, J.R. (2006). *Air Ball: American Education's Failed Experiment with Elite Athletics.* Jackson, MS: The University Press of Mississippi.

Mandel, S. (2008). *Bowls, Polls, and Tattered Souls: Tackling the Chaos and Controversy That Reign over College Football.* Hoboken, NJ: Wiley Publishing

Sack, A. (2008). *Counterfeit Amateurs: An Athlete's Journey through the Sixties to the Age of Academic Capitalism.* University Park, PA: The Pennsylvania State University Press.

Sack, A.L., & Staurowsky, E.J. (1998). *College Athletes for Hire: The Evolution and Legacy of the NCAA's Amateur Myth.* Westport, CT: Praeger Publishers.

Shulman, J.L., & Bowen, W.G. (2002). *The Game of Life: College Sports and Educational Values.* Princeton, NJ: Princeton University Press.

Sperber, M.A. (1991). *College Sports, Inc.: The Athletic Department Vs. the University.* New York: Henry Holt & Company.

Sperber, M.A. (2000). *Beer and Circus: How Big-Time College Sports Is Crippling Undergraduate Education.* Darby, PA: Diane Publishing Company.

Sperber, M.A. (2002). *Shake Down the Thunder: The Creation of Notre Dame Football.* Bloomington, IN: Indiana University Press.

Tarkanian, J. (2006). *Runnin' Rebel: Shark Tales of "Extra Benefits", Frank Sinatra and Winning It All.* Champaign, IL: Sports Publishing, LLC.

Thelin, J.R. (1996). *Games Colleges Play: Scandal and Reform in Intercollegiate Athletics.* Baltimore, MD: The Johns Hopkins University Press.

Yaeger, D. (1991). *Undue Process: The NCAA's Injustice for All.* Champaign, IL: Sagamore Publishing.

Yaeger, D., & Tarkanian, J. (1993). *Shark Attack: Jerry Tarkanian and His Battle with the NCAA and UNLV.* New York: HarperCollins Publishers, Inc.

Yost, M. (2010). *Varsity Green: A Behind the Scenes Look at Culture and Corruption in College Athletics.* Palo Alto, CA: Stanford Economics and Finance.

Zimbalist, A. (2001). *Unpaid Professionals: Commercialism and Conflict in Big-Time College Sports.* Princeton, NJ: Princeton University Press.

Golf

http://www.golf.com/golf/

http://www.pga.com/home/

http://www.golfdigest.com/

http://www.usga.org/

http://www.lpga.com/

http://www.ajga.org/

http://www.ewga.com/

Callahan, T. (2004). *In Search of Tiger: A Journey through Golf with Tiger Woods.* New York: Crown Publishing.

Clavin, T. (2005). *Sir Walter.* New York: Simon & Schuster, Inc.

Reilly, R. (1997). *Missing Links.* New York: Broadway Books.
Rotella, B. (1995). *Golf Is Not a Game of Perfect.* New York: Simon and Schuster.
Sampson, C. (1999). *The Masters.* New York: Villard Books.
Sounes, H. (2004). *The Wicked Game: Arnold Palmer, Jack Nicklaus, Tiger Woods, and the Business of Modern Golf.* New York: HarperCollins.

Boxing

http://www.eastsideboxing.com/
http://www.wbaonline.com/
http://www.teamusa.org/USA-Boxing.aspx
http://www.womenboxing.com/
http://www.aiba.org/
Boddy, K. (2008). *Boxing: A Cultural History.* London: Reaktion Books.
Newfield, J. (1995). *Only in America: The Life and Crimes of Don King.* New York: HarperCollins.
Remnick, D. (1998). *King of the World.* New York: Vintage Books.
Sugar, B.R. (2006). *Boxing's Greatest Fighters.* Guilford, CT: The Lyons Press.
Ward, G.C. (2004). *Unforgivable Blackness: The Rise and Fall of Jack Johnson.* New York: Random House.

Olympic Games

http://www.olympic.org/
http://www.teamusa.org/
Hoffer, R. (2009). *Something in the Air: American Passion and Defiance in the 1968 Mexico City Olympics.* New York: Free Press.
Lenskyj, H.J. (1999). *Inside the Olympic Industry.* New York: State University of New York Press.
Maraniss, D. (2008). *Rome 1960.* New York: Simon & Schuster.
Pound, D. (2004). *Inside the Olympics.* Toronto: Wiley.
Senn, A.E. (1999). *Power, Politics and the Olympic Games.* Champaign, IL: Human Kinetics
Ungerleider, S. (2001). *Faust's Gold: Inside the East German Doping Machine.* New York: St. Martin's Press.
Wenn, S., Barney, R., & Martyn, S. (2011). *Tarnished Rings: The International Olympic Committee and the Salt Lake City Bid Scandal.* Syracuse, NY: Syracuse University Press.
Young, D.C. (2004). *A Brief History of the Olympic Games.* Carlton, Victoria: Blackwell Publishing

X Games and Winter X Games

http://www.abc-of-snowboarding.com/
http://www.ussnowboarding.com/
http://www.uscsa.com/
http://www.usasa.org/
http://www.ussa.org/
http://www.usskiing.com/
http://www.fis-ski.com/
http://www.isocracing.com/
http://www.usccracing.com/
http://www.sitski.com/pg3.htm

Friedman, G.E. (2000). *Dogtown—the Legend of the Z-Boys.* New York: Burning Flag Press.

Youngblut, S. (1998). *Way Inside ESPN's X Games.* Bristol, CT: ESPN Publishing.

Skateboarding

http://www.thrashermagazine.com/
http://usaskateboarding.org/

Hawk, T. (2002). *Tony Hawk: Professional Skateboarder.* New York: Harper Collins.

Brooke, M. (1999). *Concrete Wave: The History of Skateboarding.* Toronto: Warwick Publishing.

Track and Field

http://www.usatf.org/
http://www.ustfccca.com/
http://www.uscaa.org/index.cfm

Gotaas, R. (2009). *Running: A Global History.* London: Reaktion Books.

Moore, R. (2013). *The Dirtiest Race in History: Ben Johnson, Carl Lewis and the 1988 Olympic 100m Final.* London: Bloomsbury Publishing.

Turrini, J.M. (2010). *The End of Amateurism in American Track and Field.* Champaign, IL: University of Illinois.

Figure Skating

http://www.usfsa.org/
http://www.isu.org/

http://www.sk8stuff.com/
Brennan, C. (1996). *Inside Edge.* New York: Doubleday.
Jackson, J. (2005). *On Edge.* New York: Thunder Mouth Press.

Tennis

http://www.tennis.com/
http://www.atpworldtour.com/
http://www.usta.com/
http://www.itftennis.com/
http://www.tennisw.com/
http://uspta.com/
Agassi, A. (2010). *Open*. New York: Knopf Books.
Ashe, A., & Rampersad, A. (1994). *Days of Grace.* New York: Ballantine Books.
Collins, B. (2008). *Bud Collins History of Tennis: An Authoritative Encyclopedia and Record Book.* Washington, DC: New Chapter Press.
Marks, B.L. (2006). *Taking Your Tennis on Tour.* Vista, CA: Usrsa
McEnroe, J. (2002). *You Cannot Be Serious.* New York: Berkley Publishing.

Fishing

http://www.asafishing.org/
http://www.igfa.org/
http://www.takemefishing.org/
http://www.trails.com/activities.aspx?area=14824
http://www.iwfa.org/
http://fishingclub.com
Andrews, D.S. (2009). *An Impossible Cast: Glen Andrews and the Birth of Professional Bass Fishing.*
Schultz, K. (2006). *Bass Madness.* Hoboken, NJ: John Wiley & Sons.

Lacrosse

http://www.uslacrosse.org/
http://www.laxpower.com/
http://filacrosse.com/
http://forums.insidelacrosse.com/forum.php
Fisher, D.M. (2002). *Lacrosse: A History of the Game.* Baltimore, MD: The John Hopkins University Press.
Vennum, T. (2007). *Lacrosse Legends of the First Americans.* Baltimore, MD: The John Hopkins University Press.

Volleyball

http://www.teamusa.org/USA-Volleyball.aspx
http://www.volleyball.org/
http://www.avp.com/
Dearing, J.B. (2007). *The Untold Story of William G. Morgan, Inventor of Volleyball.* Livermore, CA: WingSpan Press.
Strickland, B. (2009). *Inside the Players' Tent: A Year of Professional Beach Volleyball.* BookSurge.
Wurtz, T.J. (2007). *The Score's Wrong.* Bloomington, IN: AuthorHouse.

Other Helpful Links

The following links provide access to important sport management organizations. In many cases, the best opportunity to work in sports is to work for a sport-marketing firm or a sport sponsor rather than for an individual franchise or league.

Sport Marketing Firms

AMG Sports	http://www.amgsports.com/
Envision Global Marketing	http://www.envisionglobal.com/
The Gazelle Group	http://www.gazellegroup.com/
General Sports and Entertainment	http://generalsports.com/
GMR Marketing	http://www.gmrmarketing.com/
IMG	http://img.com/home.aspx
IMG College	http://www.imgcollege.com/
Integrated Sports Marketing	http://www.ismsports.net/
Keystone Marketing	http://www.keystonemarketing.net/
Knox Sports Marketing	http://www.knoxsports.com/
National Media Sports	http://www.nmgsports.com/
Nelligan Sports Marketing	http://www.nelligansports.com/
Octagon	http://www.octagon.com/
Premier Sports Management	http://www.premiersportsonline.com/
Sports and Sponsorships	http://www.sportsandsponsorships.com/
Sports Loop	http://www.sportsloop.com/
Team Services LLC	http://www.teamservicesllc.com/
Velocity Sports and Entertainment	http://www.teamvelocitymarketing.com/
Wasserman Media Group	http://www.wmgllc.com/

Sport Sponsorship and Research Firms

IEG Sponsorship	http://www.sponsorship.com/
Joyce Julius and Associates	http://www.joycejulius.com/
Performance Research	http://www.performanceresearch.com/
Scarborough Research	http://www.scarborough.com/
Shugoll Research	http://www.shugollresearch.com/
Sponsorship Intelligence	http://www.sponsorshipintelligence.com/
Sponsorship Research International	http://www.teamsri.com/
SportsEconomics	http://www.sportseconomics.com/index.html
Team Marketing Report	http://www.teammarketing.com/
TURNKEY Sports and Entertainment	http://www.turnkeyse.com/

Sport Branding Firms

Strategic Agency	http://www.strategicagency.com/index.html
Studio Simon Sports Design	http://www.studiosimon.net/

80/20 Rule—Revenue-generation "rule" that 80% of a sport organization's revenue comes from 20% of its customers.

A Duty—An obligation one has to act or refrain from acting. A duty often occurs in response to another person's right.

A Right—The basis upon which someone can make a claim; an entitlement one is due. There are various kinds of rights—legal, human, natural, and moral rights.

Acceptance—An agreement to the terms of an offer as stated.

Access—The extent to which sports organizations, leagues, teams, and athletes make themselves available to the media in terms of coverage and reporting.

Act of God—A defense to negligence in which a person has no liability if an unforeseeable natural disaster causes injury to the plaintiff.

Agenda Setting—A theory of mass communication which suggests the media exert a significant influence on public perception through their ability to filter and shape media content.

AIO Dimensions—Activities, interests, and opinions of consumers, commonly used for market segmentation.

Alcohol Management—Limits the risks associated with alcohol consumption, as well as reduces facility liability regarding alcohol-related incidents.

Americanization—Implies America's role in processes of globalization. As noted by Kuisel, "Americanization is the import by non-Americans of products, images, technologies, practices, and behavior that are closely associated with America/Americans" (2003, p. 96).

Americans with Disabilities Act—A law signed in 1990 prohibiting discrimination based on disability in employment, state and local government activities, places of public accommodation, and telecommunications; sport facilities are considered places of public accommodation and therefore must be accessible to persons with disabilities.

Antitrust Laws—The Sherman Antitrust Act (1890) is designed to protect consumer welfare by prohibiting illegal, anticompetitive business activities including monopolies (where one entity controls a high concentration of production and/or distribution of a product). The Sherman Act and subsequent antitrust laws have included provisions banning bid rigging, price fixing, and other practices that harm the consumer by interfering with the normal, competitive marketplace.

Arena—Indoor facilities used to host sporting, entertainment, and business events; portable seating designs allow the floor area to be arranged to accommodate multiple tenants.

Base Salary Plus Commission—Combination of a set salary—based on a staff member's experience—and a percent of generated sales (typically between 1% and 5% on renewed business, and 5% and 20% on new business).

Blog/Blogging—A form of content posted directly to the Internet that is usually subjective and personal in nature. Blogs can be created and maintained by individuals as well as the mainstream media, which opens up the communication process. Blogs also allow for interactivity and direct communication between author and audience.

Bonding—The creation of a unified commitment that holds those in the relationship (marketer and customer or other stakeholder) together.

Bowl Championship Series (BCS)—Created to match the top two Division-I football teams in the National Championship Game and to assign conference champions and other at-large teams to the other top bowl games. The BCS was replaced by the College Football Playoff after the 2014 season.

Brand Equity—The marketplace value that a brand contributes to a product.

Brand—A name, term, design, symbol, or feature that identifies one sport product as being different from another; the mixture of attributes can be tangible or intangible, are usually symbolized in a trademark, and if managed properly, creates value and influence.

Breach of Contract—One party fails to perform essential promises in a contract.

Breach of Duty—The failure to meet the required standard of care in a negligence action.

Capacity—A party must be legally competent to enter into a contract.

Causation—The tie between the breach of duty and the damages in a negligence action.

Chain—A complex network of contractors in disparate global locations involved in manufacturing (often broken down into minute steps) and shipping a tangible product. For example, raw materials may be extracted and shipped from Guatemala, assembled in steps in Sri Lanka, Vietnam, and China, and finally shipped to the United States and Great Britain for promotion and point of sale.

Closes for the Next Step—Asking for a client's business or requesting referral information.

Closing—Reaching a sales agreement with a client.

Clutter—Product of too much signage in a facility; decreases the likelihood of advertiser recall, thus diminishing the value of facility advertising.

College Football Playoff—Competed for the first time after the 2014 season, the College Football Playoff invites the top four teams in Division I to compete for the National Championship.

Commitment and Consistency—A person making a decision will experience pressure from others and themselves to behave consistently with that decision. Depending on a person's past actions, they will be predisposed to making future decisions consistent with those past actions.

Commodification—In a sociological context, commodification occurs when economic value is assigned to something not previously considered in economic terms—that is, gender, race, sexual orientation. In other words, commodification is treating people, ideas, or things as if they were tradable commodities.

Comparative Negligence—A system that allows a plaintiff in a negligence action to recover some damages even though the plaintiff was also partially responsible for causing the injury.

Compensatory Damages—Damages that are awarded to make up for the actual loss sustained by a party.

Complex Connectivity—Tomlinson's (1999) notion of an ever-densening network of global interconnections and interdependencies that characterize modern life. Rapid increases in technology, modes of communication, travel, and trade have enabled an intensification of global flows. For example, the speed at which intangibles (ideas and information services) and tangibles (products and people) can circle the globe is either instantaneous (Internet, cable TV, satellite) or quite swift (plane, train, ship). As a result, cultures and peoples that were once so detached are now incredibly connected and dependant upon each other, especially in realms of politics and economics.

Conflict Theory—Sociological theory emphasizing social and political inequalities and the resulting economic and power differentials; a conflict theory analysis focuses on the inherent and endemic conflicts that arise from economic disparities.

Consideration—Something of value that is exchanged in a contract.

Constitution—A government's foundational document setting forth the operating principles of the government and the limitations on governmental power.

Constitutional Law—The underlying document of the U.S. government, which sets forth limits on governmental power.

Contract Law—A promise or set of promises enforced by courts, which establish a duty to perform between parties.

Contract—A promise or set of promises, the breach of which the law gives a remedy, or the performance of which the law in some way recognizes a duty.

Contributory Negligence—A plaintiff is completely barred from recovery if the plaintiff in any way contributed to his/her own injury.

Cost of Attendance—The estimated amount of money required to complete a full year as a full-time student at colleges and universities in the United States. Every college and university is mandated to compute this each year. It is computed for each individual school and takes into account costs such as transportation and other personal costs. Though the NCAA had previously defined a full scholarship as tuition, room, board, and books, NCAA legislation in 2014 permitted schools to compensate athletes up to the full cost of attendance.

Crowd Management—Strategy designed to prevent crowd from getting out of control; security, signage, and communication all serve to effectively maintain crowd control.

Cultural (Symbolic) Production—A related process to commodification that involves the inscribing of meaning to a particular product. During the industrial revolution, in order to differentiate one product from another, proprietors of a company would advertise the positive attributes of their product over their competitors. With increasing technologies, sophistication in advertising and marketing, and a decreasing industrial base after World War II, branded corporations turned to cultural meanings to attach symbolic value to their products. For example, while two athletic shoes may be made in the same overseas factory, the symbol inscribed on it denotes a greater value than just the cost to produce it. The cultural meaning and symbolism established by marketing/advertising initiatives bestows the product with greater value for consumers.

Cultural Hegemony—A concept that a culturally diverse society can be ruled or dominated by one of its social classes. Cultural hegemony may also be seen as the dominance of one social, political, or economic group over another group.

Damages—The final element in a negligence action, which involves personal injury or property damage to the plaintiff.

Debt—The owing of money to others.

Demographics—Measurable characteristics of the sports audience such as age, gender, income, ethnicity, etc.

Distribution—How sports content reaches the sports audience. The audience itself is taking more of a role in distributing today's content.

Distributive—Retributive justice is concerned with correcting societal imbalances; distributive justice is concerned with the fair allocation of societal benefits and burdens.

Due Process—A constitutional provision that mandates fair treatment for a person who has been deprived of life, liberty, or property by a governmental decision.

Duty—The defendant has an obligation imposed by law to protect the plaintiff from unreasonable risk.

Establishment Clause—A First Amendment provision that protects citizens from the government establishing a state religion or giving preferential treatment to one religion over another.

Ethics—The study of value, very broadly construed. Ethics examines the nature of right and wrong, duty, obligation, freedom, and virtue. It is sometimes referred to as the philosophy of morality, or how people should act. Moral philosophy then is the attempt to achieve a systematic understanding of the nature of morality.

Expenses—Costs incurred by the organization. Common costs in sport include wages, utilities, equipment, and transportation.

External Contingencies—Factors beyond the marketers control that influence marketing strategy.

Fan Cost Index—An index that represents the average cost for a family of four to attend a sport event.

Fan Identification—The personal commitment and emotional involvement customers have with a sport organization.

Fantasy sports—Game in which participants draft real players and receive points for those player's statistics that are produced during the season. Some fantasy leagues are played for large amounts of money. Recently, daily fantasy leagues have become more popular, leading some to speculate that daily fantasy games are more akin to sport gambling than their seasonal counterparts.

Festival Seating—Form of general admission ticketing in which spectators are not assigned to a specific seat, but rather a standing/seating area within a facility such as in front of the stage at a concert or outfield berm seating at a baseball game.

Finance—The science of fund management that incorporates concepts from accounting, statistics, and economics.

Financial Bonding—The provision of financial incentives to your customers in order to encourage a continuing customer relationship.

Financial Management—Financial decision making within a firm with wealth maximization being the goal for most organizations.

Flows—Term used to describe the extent/rate at which people, products, images, information, etc., spread globally. For example, the instantaneous global flow of information via the Internet means that people can learn of current events in distant geographic locations in real time.

Football Bowl Subdivision—A segment of the National Collegiate Athletic Association that is comprised of schools playing the highest level of football (formerly known as Division IA).

Football Championship Subdivision—A segment of the National Collegiate Athletic Association that is comprised of Division-I schools that are not playing at the highest level of football competition (formerly known as Division IAA)

Fordism—Concept stemming from Henry Ford's assembly line production of Model-T Ford automobiles. The principles of scientific management pioneered by Frederick Taylor were used to ensure workers performed routinized tasks quickly and effectively without unnecessary steps.

Fragmentation—The splintering of large, mass sports audiences into smaller, niche audiences due primarily to the growth of media channels and options.

Free Exercise Clause—A First Amendment provision that protects individual rights to worship as one wishes.

Freedom of Expression Clause—A First Amendment provision protecting individual rights for verbal and nonverbal expression.

Fulfillment Audit—A post-event report provided to a sponsor that illustrates and highlights what the sponsor received as part of the sponsorship and how the sport property fulfilled the sponsor's corporate needs.

Full Disclosure—A media strategy in which those involved in controversy or crisis try to manage the situation by being as open as possible with the media and proving a free flow of information.

Functionalist Theory, or Functionalism—A sociological theory in which society is viewed as an organized system of interrelated parts held together by shared values and social processes that minimize differences and promote consensus among people (Coakley, 2008).

General Admission—Ticketing system in which seating is available on a first-come, first-served basis; each patron pays a fixed price and can sit in any unoccupied seat in the facility.

Geodemographic Segmentation—Segmenting a market using a combination of geographics, demographics, and psychographics.

Global Heterogenization—Largely in response to the real and/or perceived threat of globally homogenizing forces, this theory asserts that countries, nations, corporations, politics, economies, and cultures are actually becoming more differentiated, not less. In this sense, local difference has intensified by both the reaction to global uniformity by local cultures and through corporations' realization of the value of cultural niches and marketing of local difference. Sport has been argued to play a considerable role in this process, as fans tend to feverishly support place-based teams that reflect a specific locale and its unique cultural nuances.

Global Homogenization—Theory that countries, nations, corporations, politics, economies, and cultures are becoming increasingly the same. More specifically, it generally cites three main forces responsible for the global diffusion of ideas, information, products, and so on, and an accelerated level of cultural convergence/sameness/uniformity: (1) free market liberal economics, (2) global corporate structures and technologies, and (3) a consumer capitalist culture. In relation to sport, the processes and structures of global sporting organizations and events can be said to operate much the same, mainly due to the adoption of principles of American business and corporate structure.

Global Hybridity—Essentially a mixture of both homogenization and heterogenization. The hybridity thesis acknowledges that the relationship between local and global forces is much too complex to easily categorize. As such, this theory suggests that a better way to understand globalization is to view it as a global-local nexus, characterized by a complex and ever-changing dynamic between change and continuity, difference and sameness, universality and particularity. As such, global sporting events reflect markers of both local elements (nationalities, cultures, style of play) and global prerogatives (media broadcasting, revenue generation, and marketing).

Glocality—Integral to the global hybridization thesis. Glocalization asserts that global and local forces interpenetrate each other, resulting in unique outcomes in different locations.

Good/Bad—Value terms for things, people, or states of affairs. Saying an action is good/bad is most often associated with a judgment based upon the action's consequences.

Image—How sports athletes, organizations, and events, and the information related to them, are portrayed in the media and presented to sports audiences.

Independent Teams—Professional baseball teams that operate without a direct affiliation with any Major League Baseball franchise.

Institutional Logics—A set of material practices and symbolic construction, which constitutes an institution's organizing principles. Such institutional logics (a) determine what are considered acceptable or unacceptable operational means, (b) establish routines, (c) guide the evaluation and implementation of developed strategies, and (d) create precedent for further innovation.

Interactivity—Two-way communication that allows the audience to provide feedback and take part in the communication process. Interactivity has increased with the advent of new media such as the Internet and blogging.

Internet gambling—Gambling that occurs on the Internet rather than in a casino. Internet gambling has received scrutiny from U.S. law enforcement officials who often target these sites for attempting to circumvent U.S. law.

Invitee—A person who is invited by the owner to an establishment with the purpose of conducting business.

Justice—Often seen as synonymous with fairness, is the application of ethics to the structure of society. Justice is commonly divided into two areas: retributive and distributive.

Legality—The subject matter of a contract must not violate the law or it will not be enforceable.

Leveraging (also termed **Activation**)—The utilization of various marketing strategies to improve sponsor value.

Licensed Merchandise—Granting another entity the right to produce products that bear a trademarked logo.

Lifetime Customer Value—The worth of a particular customer to a company over the course of that customer's lifetime.

Liking—A person's feeling of affection or preference for another person.

March Madness—The NCAA Division-I Men's Basketball Tournament is often referred to as March Madness since most of the games occur in March and the numerous games played over three weeks often yield upsets.

Market Segmentation—The process of dividing large, unlike groups of consumers into smaller, more defined groups of people who share similar characteristics.

Marketing—The activity, set of institutions, and processes for creating, communicating, delivering, and exchanging offerings that have value for customers, clients, partners, and society at large.

Marketing Plan—The formal blueprint that marketers follow in the execution of their marketing strategy; the plan includes a SWOT analysis, intended target markets, performance objectives, and resulting strategies for promotion, pricing, and distribution.

McDonaldization—Notion that the four key operating principles of the fast food chain are coming to dominate more and more sectors of American society and the rest of the world.

Metadiscrete Experiential Learning—A learning model, in which staff from partnering sport businesses serve as instructional leaders and facilitators alongside sport-management faculty, that ". . . enhances student understanding of entrepreneurship, sales, sponsorship, event management, and marketing research within the context of the university's sport management program" (Southall, Nagel, LeGrande, & Han, 2003, p. 23). Greater knowledge gain is possible because in a metadiscrete experience, the role of teacher and practitioner are not separate and distinct, but are dual aspects of the same function.

Morality—Concerned with how people act and what they believe to be right or wrong. In practice it is often synonymous with ethics, but morality is also the portion of ethics concerned with interpersonal behavior.

Negligence Law—A part of tort law dealing with unintentional conduct that falls below a standard established by law for the protection of others against unreasonable risk of harm.

Networks—Due to advanced technologies, means of rapid communication, and sophisticated business/management practices, networks have been formed between people, businesses, organizations, and institutions to allow for greater efficiency, accuracy, profitability, and security.

News Cycle—The amount of time it takes for news to reach the general public. The development of new technologies has shrunk the current news-cycle down to just minutes.

Organizational Culture—Pattern of basic assumptions that a given group has invented, discovered, or developed in learning to cope with its problems of external adaptation and internal integration, and that have worked well enough to be considered valid, and therefore, to be taught to new members as the correct way to perceive, think, and feel in relation to those problems (Schein, 1984).

Outsourcing—Hiring an outside organization or private contractor to operate facility services such as concessions, security, and maintenance.

Override—Compensation paid to a sales manager for overseeing a sales staff. For example, if a sales manager has five employees that report to him he may receive a 1% bonus of the total revenue generated by the five sales-staff employees.

Pay-Per-View—Consumers paying directly for sports content, usually through specialized radio, television, or Internet outlets.

Personal Seat License—Source of facility revenue that requires guests to pay a one-time fee for the right to purchase tickets for a specific seat.

Players Union—The formal group that represents employed players in collective bargaining (such as the Major League Baseball Players Union [MLBPA]).

Positioning—Establishing a brand's image in the minds of consumers.

Postindustrialism—Coming after the industrial age of mass manufacturing, smokestacked factories, and large physical labor workforces (making stuff or things), new technologies, increased global flows, and a changing political and economic climate precipitated deindustrialization and the new postindustrial economy of information services, technology, and the symbolic production of goods and services (selling ideas, meanings).

Power 5 Conference—The ACC, Big 10, Big 12, Pac 12, and SEC are the most powerful and popular college football conferences. Though other Division-I football conferences compete for the same championship, they are often at a significant competitive and financial disadvantage compared to the Power 5 Conferences

Prospecting—Searching for and creating new customers.

Psychographics—Variables related to the lifestyle and personality of consumers.

Public Relations—Methods by which sports teams, athletes, and organizations control and manipulate their access and information in regards to the media.

Qualifying the Event—Process of determining if an event is appropriate for a facility.

Reciprocity—A mutual exchange, a return in kind. People react positively and feel obligated to repay others for favorable treatments received.

Referral—When someone gives a salesperson a sales lead (name, address, phone number, and/or e-mail to contact).

Relationship Marketing—Marketing with the conscious aim to develop and manage long-term and/or trusting relationships with customers, distributors, suppliers, or other parties in the marketing environment.

Reserved Seating—Ticketing system used for events that require a designated ticket for each seat; reserved tickets indicate the section, row, and seat a patron is assigned for a specific event.

Revenues—Money coming into an organization. Selling tickets is one common example of generating revenue in sport.

Right/Wrong—Value terms for the permissibility/impermissibility of an action. A judgment regarding an action's being right/wrong is made independent of a decision's anticipated consequences.

Risk Management—Process of identifying, assessing, and treating risks in order to reduce facility liability and ensure a safe environment for employees and spectators.

ROI—Return on investment. Marketing success is measured by the following ratio: revenue generated/costs incurred.

Social Bonding—Providing social or psychological incentives that encourage a continuing customer relationship.

Social Proof—People will do things they see other people are doing. Assuming other people possess more knowledge about the situation, they deem the others' behavior as appropriate or better informed.

Special-Event Facility—Specialized, single-purpose facilities designed to meet the unique needs of a specific tenant or event.

Sport Marketing—All activities designed to meet the needs and wants of sport consumers through exchange processes.

Sport Sponsorship—An opportunity for a sport organization and business partner to utilize two or more marketing mix elements in order to achieve marketing objectives by providing product association, value, and exposure.

Sports Broadcasting Act of 1961—Legislation that permitted professional sport leagues a limited antitrust exemption to pool their media rights to be sold in one package. The Sports Broadcasting Act led to rapidly increasing media rights deals for the NFL and other professional sport leagues.

Sports Information Director (SID)—Person, usually at the college level, in charge of all media relations between the athletic department and media members. The SID is primarily responsible for dissemination of information to the media and regulating media access to players and coaches.

Stadium—Outdoor or domed public assembly facility that hosts sporting and entertainment events.

State of the Union Address—The President of the United States is mandated by the U.S. Constitution to provide Congress with an update on the "state of the union." Though for many years the pPresident submitted a written report to Congress, now the pPresident delivers a State-of-the-Union Address, typically in January.

Stonewall—A media strategy in which those involved in controversy or crisis try to manage the situation by cutting off the flow of information and/or refusing media access.

SWOT Analysis—A strategic-planning tool used to evaluate an organization's **S**trengths, **W**eaknesses, **O**pportunities, and **T**hreats.

Tax-exempt bonds—Promissory notes that are exempt from federal taxation.

Tax-exempt status—Certain business entities are classified by the government as tax exempt, typically because they are non-profit organizations and/or they provide a public good.

Telemarketing/Teleselling—Marketing/sales approach that features the use of personal selling techniques in a non-face-to-face context and utilizes telecommunications technology as part of a well-planned, organized, and managed marketing program.

Television carriage disputes—Television stations (such as the NFL Network or the Big 10 Network) that are unable to agree with cable and satellite distributors (such as Time Warner Cable, Comcast, etc.) because of price or perceived customer interest are often said to be in dispute.

Transnational Corporatism—Associated with the ability of corporations to easily bypass national borders and boundaries to promote and sell products and services in various geographic areas; involves a process of marketing toward the sensibilities of local cultural difference.

Virtue—A trait that contributes to something's being good in some way. Virtue may be referred to as "righteous conduct." As a plural, "**virtues**" refers to character traits such as courage, wisdom, self-control, justice, loyalty, and compassion.

Wealth Maximization—The goal or outcome of financial management for most organizations; increasing the overall value of the firm.

NOTE: Page references in *italics* refer to boxes, figures, and tables.

A

B

C

H

I

J

K

L

M

Q

R

S

T

U

V

W

X

Y

Z